LEGO® Collector

Collector's Guide
Sammler Katalog

Die Deutsche Bibliothek - CIP-Einheitsaufnahme
LEGO® Collector
Verantwortlich für den Inhalt:
Fantasia Verlag GmbH
Internationale Version DIN A5
Fantasia Verlag GmbH, Dreieich 2008

Fantasia Verlag GmbH
Postfach 20 11 88 · D-63272 Dreieich
Info-Line: ++49 (0) 61 03 - 69 95 03 · Fax: ++49 (0) 61 03 - 69 70 72
Email: info@fantasiaverlag.de – Internet: www.fantasiaverlag.de

---

Printed in Germany 2008

Produced by Fantasia Verlag GmbH under license from the LEGO Group.

Thank you / Danke

At this point we would like to thank all collectors and the employees from the LEGO Group and all other people who supported and helped us with their knowledge and provided material, to generate the LEGO® Collector. Without their help, this catalogues wouldn't have become that extensive and of that high quality. In alphabetical order:

Wir möchten uns an dieser Stelle bei den Sammlern, den Mitarbeitern der LEGO Gruppe und allen Anderen bedanken, die uns mit ihrem Wissen und dem zur Verfügung gestellten Material unterstützt haben, und ohne deren Hilfe dieser Katalog nicht so umfangreich und hochwertig geworden wäre. In alphabetischer Reihenfolge:

Frank Abel, Werner Aulbach, Heiko Baum, Jan Beyer, Andrea Courir Ryder, Stefan Ginthum, Torsten Fresemann, Corinna Hoffmann, René Hoffmeister, Christina Horvarth, Gary Istok, Jan Katanek, Joachim „Der Joe" Klang, Johannes Koehler, Christian Köhler, Niels Otto Nielsen, Erik Nobert, Jette Orduna, Michael Peters, Enrico Sauda, Roland Smrsch, Elsebeth Søgaard, Randi Kirsten Sørensen, Oliver Zirkel.

Publisher:	Fantasia Verlag GmbH
Managing Director:	Michael Steiner
Editorial:	Sebastian Eggers, Christian Horstkötter, Tobias Kaminsky
Marketing:	Steffen Maschke
Layout & Design:	Alexander Pitz
Advisory:	Frank Abel, Werner Aulbach, Heiko Baum, Torsten Fresemann, Jan Katanek, Johannes Koehler, Roland Smrsch

Content / Inhalt

Dear reader

The LEGO® brick is 50 years old this year and we want to celebrate it. We, the Fantasia Verlag, wish to dedicate this comprehensive and extensive catalogue to the play material, that conquered the world from the Danish town of Billund.

After intensive research in Billund and thanks to the permanent and generous exchange with collectors and experts, it is possible for us to gather more than 6.000 colored illustrations of almost all sets, produced by the LEGO Group since 1958 in this book. A special thanks to the LEGO Group, who made it possible for us to visit the LEGO Idea House archives in Billund.

A complete and comprehensive catalogue is not our only priority. A rating system makes it possible to judge the rareness of the sets. The system rates the condition and completeness of the sets, including building plans and boxes, as well as all extras and is based on a permanent and accurate monitoring of offers and development on the markets and on the Internet. It is important, that the rating does not reflect on a monetary value.

The catalogue offers information on the number of components the sets consists of, production year and on which continent, the sets were sold. This book is the first reference book of its kind in the LEGO history, which lists almost all LEGO products in chronological order. Please note, that we in spite of thorough research cannot be held responsible for the accuracy of the information.

For further information on our product range and collectors catalogues, please visit our homepage www.fantasiaverlag.de.

We are open for new ideas, information and suggestions.
Please send an email to: LEGO@fantasiaverlag.de or

a letter to: Fantasia Verlag GmbH
Keyword: LEGO Collector
Eisenbahnstraße 102
63303 Dreieich

Enjoy the first edition of the LEGO Collectors catalogue.

Your Fantasia Verlag-Team

Liebe Leserin und lieber Leser,

der LEGO® Stein wird in diesem Jahr 50 Jahre alt. Das gilt es zu feiern. Wir, der Fantasia Verlag, widmen diesem Spielzeug, das vom dänischen Billund aus die Welt eroberte, einen umfassenden und ausführlichen Katalog.

Nach intensiven Recherchen vor Ort und dank des permanenten und ausgiebigen Austauschs mit führenden Sammlern und Fachleuten ist es uns gelungen, in diesem Buch mehr als 6.000 farbige Abbildungen nahezu aller Sets zusammenzufassen, die seit 1958 die LEGO Produktion verlassen haben. Ein besonderer Dank gilt hier der LEGO Gruppe, die uns den Zugang zum umfangreichen LEGO Idea House Archiv in Billund ermöglichte.

Doch wir haben nicht nur auf eine weitestgehend vollständige Zusammenfassung Wert gelegt. Ein Rating versucht, soweit möglich, die Seltenheit des jeweils abgebildeten Sets wiederzugeben. Es bezieht sich auf gut erhaltene und vollständige Sets inklusive Bauanleitung und Karton sowie aller Zusätze und basiert auf einer ständigen und genauen Beobachtung der Angebote und Entwicklungen auf Märkten sowie im Internet. Wichtig ist, dass die Einschätzung des Sets nicht seinen monetären Wert widerspiegelt.

Aus dem Katalog erfahren Sie des Weiteren wie viele Einzelteile ein Set enthält, in welchem Jahr es erstmals erschienen ist und auf welchem Kontinent es verkauft wurde. Zum ersten Mal in der fünf Jahrzehnte währenden LEGO Geschichte gibt es ein solches Nachschlagewerk, das chronologisch geordnet die Produkte kapitelweise nach Erscheinungsjahren aufzeigt. Bleibt noch anzumerken, dass wir trotz sorgfältiger Nachforschungen keinen Anspruch auf die Richtigkeit der Angaben erheben können.

Weitere Sammlerkataloge sowie unser komplettes Verlagsprogramm finden Sie auf unserer Homepage www.fantasiaverlag.de.

Übrigens: Über Vorschläge und Anregungen freuen wir uns.
Senden Sie einfach eine E-Mail an: LEGO@fantasiaverlag.de oder

einen Brief an:

Fantasia Verlag GmbH
Stichwort: LEGO Collector
Eisenbahnstraße 102
63303 Dreieich

Wir wünschen Ihnen viel Spaß mit der ersten Auflage des LEGO Sammlerkatalogs.

Ihr Fantasia Verlag-Team

How to use this book?
Wie funktioniert das Buch?

Image of the product
Abbildung des Produktes

Item number
Setnummer

(i) 1572		EU NA AU AS
Super Tow Truck		
Schwerer Abschleppwagen		
Pcs: 72	1986–1987	Special

Pieces count
Anzahl der Teile

English description of the product
Englische Beschreibung des Produktes

German description of the product
Deutsche Beschreibung des Produktes

Timeframe: Release year until end of production year
Zeitspanne: Veröffentlichungsjahr bis zum Produktionsstop

Special means this set is a campaign or promotional product
Special bedeutet, dass es sich hierbei um ein Kampagnen- oder Promoset handelt

Rating-System:
The more yellow bricks are coloured in, the more rare the set is
Seltenheitsrating:
Je mehr Steine gelb sind, desto seltener ist das Set

On continents marked yellow the set was/is published:
Auf den gelb eingeblendeten Kontinenten ist das Set erschienen:

EU: Europe	Europa
NA: North-America	Nordamerika
AU: Australia	Australien
AS: Asia	Asien

Info-Box: An activated symbol means there is a footnote with further information
Info-Feld: Wenn dieses Symbol eingeblendet ist, gibt es zu diesem Set eine Besonderheit, die am Seitenende aufgeführt wird

(i) 1572	Included in: 1506 (1986)	Enthalten in: 1506 (1986)

The brick with unlimited possibilities

When Ole Kirk Kristiansen founded his carpentry in Billund in 1916, he would not have dreamed of the triumphant development towards establishing one of the most popular toy manufacturers world wide more than 90 years later. Carpenter Kristiansen was during the early years of his enterprise haunted by bad luck since his carpentry and home burnt down in 1924. He made the best of the situation, and eight years later he re-opened a factory for wooden toys, which he produced himself and named LEGO, by putting together the two Danish words "leg" and "godt", which means "play well". These two words transformed into one emphasize what millions of children and adults alike have been doing around the world ever since. Not only with wooden toys, but also with plastic bricks – and sets. In 1947, the Kristiansen family bought a plastic injection-moulding machine, which became the basis for the new generation at the company.

This year Kristiansen's product is celebrating its 50 years anniversary, but the year of its birth was 1949. Back then, the first 2x2 and 2x4 LEGO bricks of cellulose acetate were produced. In 1958, Godtfred Kirk Christiansen, who took over from his father in 1950 was granted the patent for the special interlocking system, we know from the LEGO brick. A genius idea, that is still valid. There are no limits when it comes to imagining building with LEGO bricks - real and fantasy worlds can be built by thousands of different bricks.

When Ole Kirk Kristiansen's grandson, Kjeld Kirk Kristiansen took over as CEO of the LEGO Group in 1979 his grandfather's family business had changed into a company with 2.500 employees and the LEGO patent was also valid abroad. The company flourished further, reaching another milestone in 2000: The LEGO brick became „Toy of the Century".

A moving history for the Danish company. Within the company, four era's are pointed out: The first era does not begin with the foundation in 1916, but in 1955 with the presentation of "LEGO system of Play" (play and learning). This phase was about building and the satisfaction, children and adults felt when building.

The era emphasizes on the mobility of the products. The LEGO Group re-invented the wheel as well as smaller engines and gear systems. In 1969, LEGO® DUPLO® was presented under the motto "a large brick for tiny hands", a special brick for pre-school children. A co-operation with Media Lab at the Massachusetts Institute of Technology was the beginning of a new era that has shown to be the future. Physical and virtual worlds melting together meant whole new perspectives. One of the first results of the co-operation was the LEGO Technic Computer Control Set.

The 1990s proved to be another decade with big changes. In 1992 PARADISA was launched especially for girls. In 1994 the LEGO Technic Supercar was a thrill for many young car fans. That same year LEGO® BELVILLE™ was introduced, another theme for girls. The first computer game was launched by the LEGO Group in 1997. New LEGOLAND® Parks were opened outside Denmark. The launch in 1996 of LEGOLAND Windsor was followed by LEGOLAND California three years later. In 2002, LEGOLAND Deutschland in Günzburg opened.

During the last decade of the last century, the fourth era in the corporate history began; behavior became essential parts of the LEGO product range. In 1998, integration of robot technology was introduced and LEGO® MINDSTORMS™ made it possible to create and programme "intelligent" LEGO models. In the same year, the LEGO Group started yet a new venture by announcing an exclusive and long term licensing agreement with Lucasfilm Ltd. This enabled the Group to start manufacturing and marketing a new series of LEGO sets in relation to themes from the *Star Wars™* trilogy as well as the three new *Star Wars™* movies. Further agreements with Walt Disney, Hit Entertainment and Warner Bros. were in 2000 followed by a partnership with producer Steven Spielberg to bring the LEGO Studios on the market. This instrument makes it possible for players to direct and make their own movies. At the beginning of the new century, storytelling and physical adventure were brought to life, when the LEGO Group introduced the BIONICLE® universe. With this product, the Danes had created a complete story from the beginning. Children and adults were encouraged to tell how they see the story and the action developing.

Production is ongoing and every year new, fascinating products leave Billund. The fact, that there are more than 900 million different ways of combining six eight-stud bricks, makes it impossible to see any limits of what to build.

Der Stein der unbegrenzten Möglichkeiten

Als Ole Kirk Kristiansen 1916 in Billund eine Maschinentischlerei gründete, hätte er sich nicht träumen lassen, dass sein Unternehmen mehr als 90 Jahre später zu den populärsten Spielzeugherstellern der Welt gehören würde. Dabei schien der gelernte Tischler Kristiansen in den ersten Jahren seines Unternehmertums wie vom Pech verfolgt, denn 1924 brannten Werkstatt und Wohnung ab. Doch er machte aus der Not eine Tugend und eröffnete acht Jahre später einen Betrieb für Holzspielsachen, die er selbst produzierte und taufte ihn LEGO, eine Kreation aus den zwei dänischen Worten „Leg" und „godt", was soviel wie „spiel gut" bedeutet.

Genau das taten in den nächsten Jahrzehnten Millionen von Kindern und Erwachsenen. Aber nicht nur mit dem Holzspielzeug aus dem Hause LEGO, sondern auch mit den Plastikbausteinen und –bausätzen. Den „Grundstein" dafür legte Kristiansen 1947, als er die erste Spritzgussmaschine zur Herstellung von Spielzeug kaufte.

Dieses Jahr feiert das Vorzeigeprodukt Kristiansens zwar seinen 50. Geburtstag, doch seine Geburtsstunde fällt auf das Jahr 1949: Damals entstanden die ersten 2x2 und 2x4 LEGO Bausteine aus Celluloseacetat. 1958 ließ sich Godtfred Kirk Christiansen, der 1950 von seinem Vater die Leitung der Firma übernommen hatte, die spezielle Klemmverbindung für Steine aus Noppen und Röhren patentieren. Eine geniale Idee, die bis heute nichts von ihrer Attraktivität eingebüßt hat. Der Vorstellungskraft sind keine Grenzen gesetzt – reale und Fantasiewelten lassen sich mit den vielen Tausend verschiedenen Bauteilen zusammensetzen.

Als Ole Kirk Kristiansens Enkel, Kjeld Kirk Kristiansen 1979 die LEGO Leitung übernahm, erinnerte nichts mehr an das einstige Familienunternehmen: Für ihn arbeiteten rund 2.500 Angestellte und das Patent galt auch im Ausland. Doch damit nicht genug, denn der Konzern florierte weiter und erlebte 2000 einen weiteren Höhepunkt: Der LEGO Stein wurde Spielzeug des Jahrhunderts.

Eine bewegte Geschichte, auf die das dänische Unternehmen zurückblickt. Firmenintern spricht man von vier Epochen: Dabei beginnt die Erste nicht mit der Gründung 1916, sondern erst 1955 mit Einführung von „LEGO System im Spiel" (spielen und lernen). Diese Phase stand im Zeichen des Bauens und der Erfolgserlebnisse, die Kinder und Erwachsene dabei hatten.

Der Abschnitt ist durch die Beweglichkeit der Produkte geprägt. Das Rad wurde von der Firma LEGO neu erfunden sowie kleine Motoren und Getriebe ergänzt. 1969 wurde LEGO® DUPLO® unter dem Motto „ein großer Stein für kleine Hände" speziell für Kinder im Vorschulalter eingeführt.

Die Zusammenarbeit mit dem Media Lab des Massachussets Institute of Technology kennzeichnet den Beginn einer neuen Ära, die sich als zukunftsweisend erweisen sollte. Schuf doch die Verschmelzung realer und virtueller Welten komplett neue Perspektiven. Eines der ersten Resultate der Kooperation war das LEGO Technic Computer Control Set.

Die 90er Jahre kamen mit weit reichenden Veränderungen daher. 1992 kam speziell für Mädchen PARADISA auf den Markt. 1994 begeisterte das LEGO Technic Supercar junge Autofans. Im selben Jahr erschien auch LEGO® BELVILLE™ wiederum für Mädchen. Das erste Computerspiel lieferte die LEGO Gruppe 1997 aus. Neue LEGOLAND® Parks wurden außerhalb Dänemarks eröffnet, zuerst 1996 LEGOLAND Windsor, drei Jahre später LEGOLAND California und 2002 folgte LEGOLAND Deutschland in Günzburg.

Im letzten Jahrzehnt des vergangenen Jahrhunderts begann für das Unternehmen auch das vierte Zeitalter der Firmengeschichte. Intelligenz und bestimmte Verhaltensmuster kennzeichneten zunehmend die Produkte. 1998 gelang es, die Robotertechnik ins Bausystem zu integrieren und LEGO® MINDSTORMS™ ermöglichte es, „intelligente“ Modelle zu bauen und zu programmieren. Im selben Jahr ergab sich Bahnbrechendes als der dänische Konzern eine exklusive, weltweite und langfristige Lizenzvereinbarung mit Lucasfilm Ltd. abschloss. Damit erhielt er das Recht auf Entwicklung, Produktion und Vermarktung einer neuen Serie von Sets, die Themen der *Star Wars™* Trilogie und der drei neuen *Star Wars™* Filmen aufgriffen. Später schlossen die Billunder weitere Verträge mit anderen Lizenzgebern wie Walt Disney, Hit Entertainment und Warner Bros. ab. 2000 kam eine Partnerschaft mit dem Filmproduzenten und Starregisseur Steven Spielberg zustande, um so die LEGO Studios auf den Markt zu bringen. Dieses Instrumentarium erlaubt es Spielern, im Regiestuhl Platz zu nehmen und Filme nach eigenen Vorstellungen zu drehen.

Zu Beginn des Jahrtausends rückten Geschichten und Erlebnisse weiter in den Vordergrund und die Firma präsentierte das BIONICLE® Universum. Damit schufen die Dänen zum ersten Mal einen durchgehenden Handlungsablauf als Grundlage für eine Produktgruppe, die Erwachsene und Kinder ermuntert, selbst in die Handlung einzutauchen.

Die Produktion steht nicht still und jährlich kommen aus Billund neue, faszinierende Produkte auf den Markt. Wenn man die Tatsache bedenkt, dass es mehr als 900 Millionen Möglichkeiten gibt, sechs Steine mit acht Knöpfen miteinander zu verbinden, sind der Vorstellungskraft wahrlich keine Grenzen gesetzt.

The evolution of the LEGO® logo
Die Entwicklung des LEGO® Logos

1934	LEGO
1936	FABRIKEN LEGO BILLUND — FABRIK FOR TRÆVARER OG LEGETØJ — ; LEGO BILLUND ★ DENMARK
1946	LEGO Klodser
1953	LEGO; 
1954	LEGO BILLUND · DENMARK

1955	LEGO MURSTEN; system i leg... LEGO MURSTEN
1956	LEGO SYSTEM; LEGO System; LEGO BAUSTEINE; LEGO SYSTEM
1959	LEGO® System
1964	LEGO® System; LEGO® System
1973	LEGO®
1998	LEGO®

LEGO® Products 1958 – 2008

1958

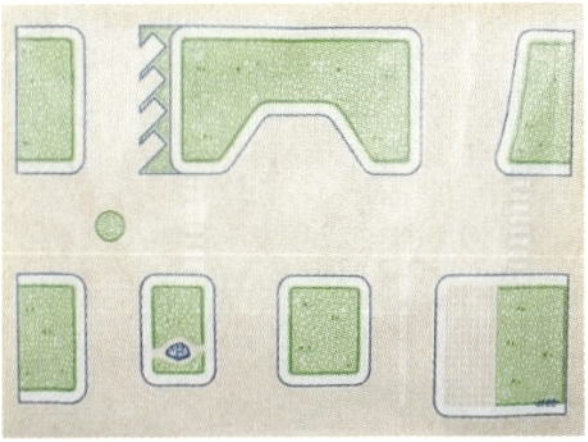

ⓘ 200/200B	EU NA AU AS
Plastic Town Plan Board	
Stadtplan aus Kunststoff	
Pcs: 1	1958–1959

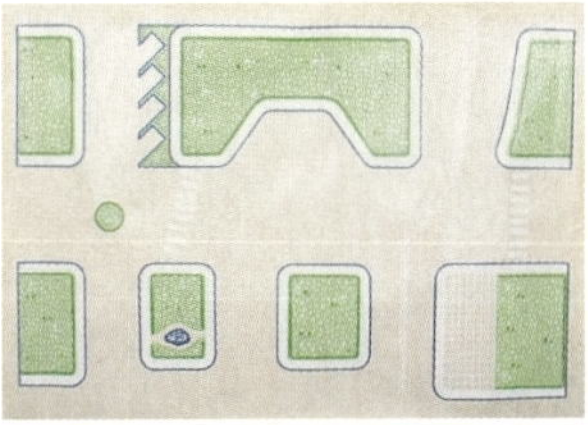

ⓘ 200A	EU NA AU AS
Hard Masonite Town Plan Board	
Stadtplan aus Hartfaser	
Pcs: 1	1958–1968

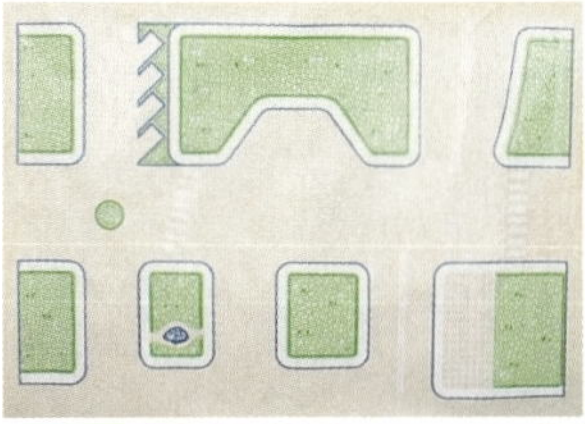

ⓘ 200M	EU NA AU AS
Masonite Town Plan	
Stadtplan aus Holzfaser	
Pcs: 1	1958–1964

ⓘ 210	EU NA AU AS
Small Store Set	
Kleines Geschäft	
Pcs: 30	1958–1962

ⓘ 211	EU NA AU AS
Small House	
Kleines Haus	
Pcs: 20	1958–1962

ⓘ 212	EU NA AU AS
Small House - Right	
Kleines Haus - rechts	
Pcs: 17	1958–1962

ⓘ	Set	English	Deutsch
ⓘ	200	Independent of right/left hand traffic	Verkehrsneutral
ⓘ	200A	6 different covers, 3 different street layouts	6 versch. Titelbilder, 3 versch. Straßenlayouts
ⓘ	200M	Was also released as 200A	Auch als 200A erschienen

i 213	EU
Small House - Left	
Kleines Haus - links	
Pcs: 21	1958–1965

i 214	EU NA
Windows and Doors	
Fenster und Türen	
Pcs: 10	1958–1965

i 215	EU NA AU
2x8 Bricks	
Balken mit 16 Knöpfen	
Pcs: 6	1958–1965

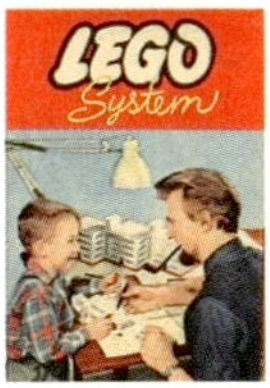

i 216	EU NA AU
2x10 Bricks	
Balken mit 20 Knöpfen	
Pcs: 5	1958–1965

i 217	EU NA AU
4x4 "L" Bricks	
4x4 Winkelsteine	
Pcs: 5	1958–1965

i 218	EU NA
2x4 Bricks	
Bausteine mit 8 Knöpfen	
Pcs: 13	1958–1965

i 219	EU NA AU
2x3 Bricks	
Bausteine mit 6 Knöpfen	
Pcs: 15	1958–1965

i 220	EU NA AU
2x2 Bricks	
Bausteine mit 4 Knöpfen	
Pcs: 20	1958–1965

i 221	EU NA AU
1x2 Bricks	
Bausteine mit 2 Knöpfen	
Pcs: 26	1958–1965

i			
i	214	Available in: red, white; also sold separately	Verfügbar in: weiß, rot; auch einzeln verkauft
i	215-217	Available in: red, blue, white, yellow	Verfügbar in: rot, blau, weiß, gelb
i	218-219	Available in: red, blue, white, yellow, clear	Verfügbar in: rot, blau, weiß, gelb, klar
i	220	Available in: red, blue, white, yellow, black, clear	Verfügbar in: rot, blau, weiß, gelb, schwarz, klar
i	221	Available in: red, blue, white, yellow, black, clear	Verfügbar in: rot, blau, weiß, gelb, schwarz, klar

222	EU NA AU AS
1x1 Bricks	
Bausteine mit 1 Knopf	
Pcs: 40	1958–1965

223	EU NA AU AS
1x1 Round Bricks	
Runde Bausteine mit 1 Knopf	
Pcs: 44	1958–1965

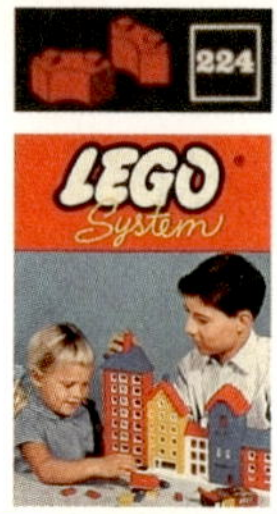

224	EU NA AU AS
Curved Bricks - Half Circle	
Gebogene Bausteine - Halbkreis	
Pcs: 20	1958–1965

225	EU NA AU AS
1x6 and 1x8 Bricks	
Balken mit 6 und 8 Knöpfen	
Pcs: 9	1958–1965

226	EU NA AU AS
Bricks with Names	
Balken mit Namen	
Pcs: 7	1958–1965

227	EU NA AU AS
4 Curved and 1 Rectangular Plate	
4 gebogene + 1 rechteckige Platte	
Pcs: 5	1958–1965

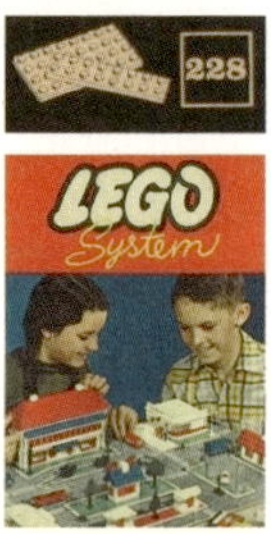

228	EU NA AU AS
Plates	
Bauplatten	
Pcs: 5	1958–1965

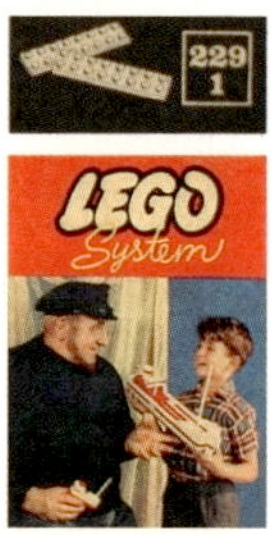

229	EU NA AU AS
Assorted Plates	
Gemischte Bauplatten	
Pcs: 8	1958–1965

230	EU NA AU AS
Trees and Bushes	
Bäume und Büsche	
Pcs: 6	1958–1965

i	222	Available in: red/white, clear, yellow/blue	Verfügbar in: rot/weiß, klar, gelb/blau
i	223	Available in: red/white, clear, yellow/blue	Verfügbar in: rot/weiß, klar, gelb/blau
i	224	Available in: red/white, clear, yellow/blue	Verfügbar in: rot/weiß, klar, gelb/blau
i	225	Available in: red, white, yellow, clear	Verfügbar in: rot, weiss, gelb, blau, klar

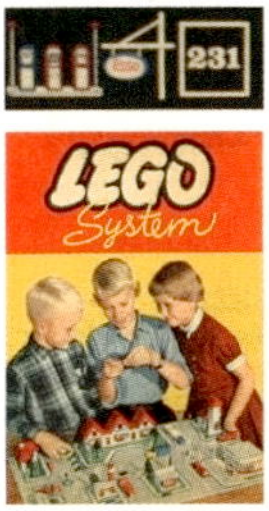

231	EU NA AU
Esso Tank and Esso Sign	
Esso Tank und Esso Schild	
Pcs: 2	1958–1965

232	EU NA
Street Signs for the Town Plan	
Verkehrszeichen für den Stadtplan	
Pcs: 16	1958–1965

233	EU NA AU
Light Masts	
Lichtmasten	
Pcs: 4	1958–1965

234	EU NA AU
Letter Bricks	
Buchstabensteine	
Pcs: 50	1958–1969

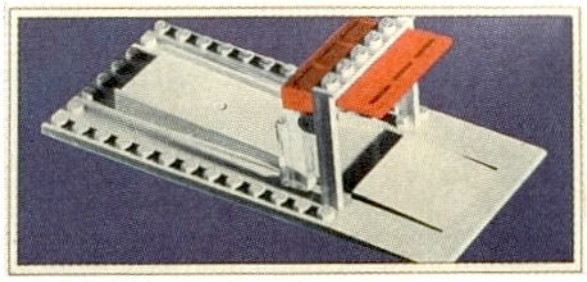

235	EU NA
Garage Plate and Door	
Garagenplatte mit autom. Tür	
Pcs: 3	1958–1966

236	EU NA
Garage with automatic Door	
Garage mit automatischer Tür	
Pcs: 65	1958–1960

242	EU
Danish Flags	
Dänische Flaggen	
Pcs: 5	1958–1965

245	EU NA
Lighting Device Pack	
Leuchtsteine	
Pcs: 8	1958–1964

250	EU
Esso Fuel Tanker Truck	
Esso Tankfahrzeug	
Pcs: 1	1958–1964

ⓘ 245	Similar to: 050 (1969), 456 (1966), 485 (1966)	Ähnlich zu: 050 (1969), 456 (1966), 485 (1966)

251	EU NA AU AS	
Esso Flatbed Truck		
Esso Lastfahrzeug		
Pcs: 1	1958–1964	

252	EU NA AU AS	
Esso Trailer		
Esso Anhänger		
Pcs: 1	1958–1964	

253	EU NA AU AS	
Bedford Flatbed Truck with Dumper		
Bedford Lastauto mit Kipper		
Pcs: 1	1958–1964	

254	EU NA AU AS	
Trailer		
Anhänger		
Pcs: 1	1958–1964	

255	EU NA AU AS	
Bedford Firetruck with Ladder		
Bedford Feuerwehrauto mit Leiter		
Pcs: 2	1958–1964	

256	EU NA AU AS	
Bedford Towtruck		
Bedford Abschleppauto		
Pcs: 2	1958–1964	

257	EU NA AU AS	
Bedford Delivery Truck		
Bedford Möbelauto		
Pcs: 2	1958–1964	

258	EU NA AU AS	
VW Bus		
VW Kleinbus		
Pcs: 1	1958–1964	

259	EU NA AU AS	
VW Pickup Truck		
VW Pritschenwagen		
Pcs: 1	1958–1964	

i	258	Similar to: 658 (1965)	Ähnlich zu: 658 (1965)
i	259	Similar to: 659 (1965)	Ähnlich zu: 659 (1965)

ⓘ 260	EU NA AU AS	
VW Beetle		
VW Käfer		
Pcs: 1	1958–1964	

ⓘ 261	EU NA AU AS	
VW Beetle in Showcase Packaging		
VW Käfer in Schaufensterpackung		
Pcs: 4	1958–1963	

ⓘ 270	EU NA AU AS	
5 Cyclists/Motorcyclists		
5 Rad- und Motorradfahrer		
Pcs: 5	1958–1965	

ⓘ 271	EU NA AU AS	
Traffic Police Set		
Verkehrspolizisten		
Pcs: 6	1958–1964	

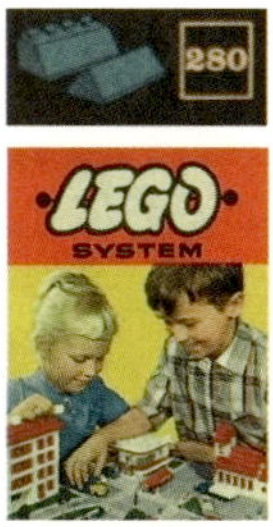

ⓘ 280	EU NA AU AS	
Sloping Roof Bricks		
Schrägsteine		
Pcs: 14	1958–1965	

ⓘ 282	EU NA AU AS	
Sloping Roof Bricks		
Schrägsteine		
Pcs: 22	1958–1965	

ⓘ 306	EU NA AU AS	
VW Garage		
VW Garage		
Pcs: 45	1958–1962	

ⓘ 307	EU NA AU AS	
VW Car Showroom		
VW Verkaufs-Pavillon		
Pcs: 47	1958–1962	

ⓘ 308	EU NA AU AS	
Fire Station		
Feuerwehr		
Pcs: 109	1958–1962	

ⓘ			
ⓘ	280	Available in: red, blue	Verfügbar in: rot, blau
ⓘ	282	Available in: red, blue	Verfügbar in: rot, blau

309	EU NA AU AS
Church	
Kirche	
Pcs: 153	1958–1964

310	EU NA AU AS
Esso Filling Station	
Esso Tankstelle	
Pcs: 96	1958–1965

700	EU NA AU AS
Storage Box	
Sortierkasten	
Pcs: 491	1958–1959

700/0	EU NA AU AS
Giftbox	
Geschenkkasten	
Pcs: -	1955–1961

700/1	EU NA AU AS
Giftbox	
Geschenkkasten	
Pcs: -	1955–1961

700/2	EU NA AU AS
Giftbox	
Geschenkkasten	
Pcs: -	1958-1959

700/3	EU NA AU AS
Giftbox	
Geschenkkasten	
Pcs: -	1955–1961

700/3a	EU NA AU AS
Giftbox	
Geschenkkasten	
Pcs: -	1955–1961

700/4	EU NA AU AS
Giftbox	
Geschenkkasten	
Pcs: -	1955–1961

i	200-310	Sets were released in Denmark since 1955, with four-digit article numbers, starting with "1". These sets were released for international markets, without the leading "1", besides, the number was retained.	Sets sind 1955 schon in Dänemark erschienen, mit vierstelliger Artikelnr., beginnend mit einer „1". Diese Sets wurden dann international ohne die „1" veröffentlicht, ansonsten wurde Nummer zumeist beibehalten.

700/5	EU NA AU AS
Giftbox	
Geschenkkasten	
Pcs: -	1955–1961

700/6	EU NA AU AS
Giftbox	
Geschenkkasten	
Pcs: -	1955–1961

1959

i 200	EU NA AU AS	
Town Plan Cardboard		
Stadtplan aus Pappe		
Pcs: 1	1959–1966	

i 281	EU NA AU AS	
1x2 and 3x2 Sloping Bricks		
1x2 und 3x2 schräge Steine		
Pcs: 21	1959–1965	

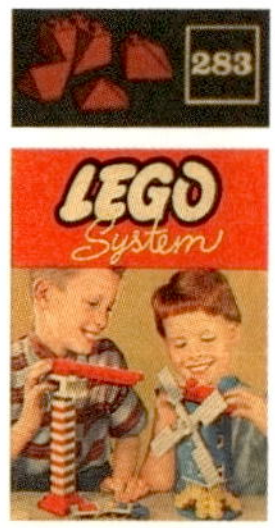

i 283	EU NA AU AS	
Sloping Ridge and Valley Bricks		
Schräge Eck- und Winkelsteine		
Pcs: 20	1959–1965	

i	Set	English	Deutsch
i	281	Similar to: 481 (1966); available in: red, blue	Ähnlich zu: 481 (1966); verfügbar in: rot, blau
i	283	Similar to: 483 (1966); available in: red, blue	Ähnlich zu: 483 (1966); verfügbar in: rot, blau

1960

(i) 237	EU NA AU AS	
Number Bricks		
Zahlensteine		
Pcs: 50	1960–1965	

(i) 238	EU NA AU AS	
Idea Book		
Baubuch		
Pcs: 1	1960–1963	

(i) 237	Similar to: 437 (1966)	Ähnlich zu: 437 (1966)

1961

ⓘ 242A	EU NA AU AS
International Flags	
Internationale Flaggen	
Pcs: 5	1961–1965

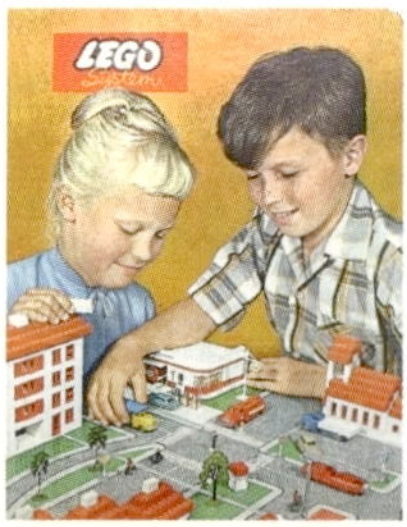

ⓘ 246	EU NA AU AS
Town Plan Board	
Stadtplan	
Pcs: 1	1961

ⓘ 262	EU NA AU AS
Opel Rekord with Garage	
Opel Rekord mit Garage	
Pcs: 3	1961–1964

ⓘ 263	EU NA AU AS
Ford Taunus with Garage	
Ford Taunus mit Garage	
Pcs: 3	1961–1963

ⓘ 264	EU NA AU AS
Mercedes 220 with Garage	
Mercedes 220 mit Garage	
Pcs: 3	1961–1964

ⓘ 265	EU NA AU AS
Karmann Ghia with Garage	
Karmann Ghia mit Garage	
Pcs: 3	1961–1964

ⓘ	242A	DK, SF, IS, N, S or D, CH, F, B, I or A, D, NL, GB, LEGO	DK, SF, IS, N, S o. D, CH, F, B, I o. A, D, NL, GB, LEGO
ⓘ	246	Similar to: 200 (1959)	Ähnlich zu: 200 (1959)

311	EU NA AU AS
Airplanes	
Flugzeuge	
Pcs: 79	1961–1962

312	EU NA AU AS
Ships	
Schiffe	
Pcs: 105	1961–1962

700/0	EU NA AU AS
Giftbox	
Geschenkkasten	
Pcs: -	1961–1965

700/1	EU NA AU AS
Giftbox	
Geschenkkasten	
Pcs: 169	1961–1965

700/3	EU NA AU AS
Giftbox	
Geschenkkasten	
Pcs: -	1961–1965

700/3a	EU NA AU AS
Giftbox	
Geschenkkasten	
Pcs: -	1961–1965

700/4	EU NA AU AS
Giftbox	
Geschenkkasten	
Pcs: -	1961–1965

700/5	EU NA AU AS
Giftbox	
Geschenkkasten	
Pcs: -	1961–1965

700/6	EU NA AU AS
Giftbox	
Geschenkkasten	
Pcs: -	1961–1965

702 — EU **NA** AU AS

Basic Set		
Grundbaukasten		
Pcs: 151	1961	

703 — EU **NA** AU AS

Basic Set		
Grundbaukasten		
Pcs: 126	1961	

705 — EU **NA** AU AS

Medium Basic Set		
Mittlerer Grundbaukasten		
Pcs: 196	1961	

708 — EU **NA** AU AS

Basic Set		
Grundbaukasten		
Pcs: 244	1961	

711 — EU **NA** AU AS

Basic Set		
Grundbaukasten		
Pcs: 374	1961	

717 — EU **NA** AU AS

Junior Constructor		
Junior-Baumeister		
Pcs: 520	1961–1965	

725 — EU **NA** AU AS

Town-Plan Set		
Stadtplan		
Pcs: 712	1961	

810 — **EU** NA AU AS

Big Town Set		
Komplettes Stadt-Set		
Pcs: -	1961–1965	

i	705	Was re-released in 1963, then sold in tin boxes	Erschien 1963 erneut, dann in Metalldose verkauft
i	717	Released: USA (1961), Canada (1962)	Veröffentlicht: USA (1961), Kanada (1962)

1962

ⓘ 400	EU NA AU AS	
Small Wheels with Axles		
Räder und Lagersteine		
Pcs: 11	1962–1972	

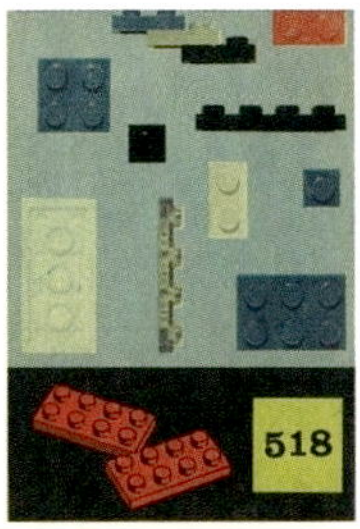

ⓘ 518	EU NA AU AS	
2x4 Plates		
Flachsteine mit 8 Knöpfen		
Pcs: 26	1962–1965	

ⓘ 519	EU NA AU AS	
2x3 Plates		
Flachsteine mit 6 Knöpfen		
Pcs: 30	1962–1965	

ⓘ 520	EU NA AU AS	
2x2 Plates		
Flachsteine mit 4 Knöpfen		
Pcs: 41	1962–1965	

ⓘ 521	EU NA AU AS	
1x1 and 1x2 Plates		
Flachsteine mit 1 und 2 Knöpfen		
Pcs: 70	1962–1965	

ⓘ 704	EU NA AU AS	
Small Basic Set (Canister)		
Kleiner Grundbaukasten, Dose		
Pcs: 165	1962	Special

ⓘ			
ⓘ	400	Similar to: 900 (1969)	Ähnlich zu: 900 (1969)
ⓘ	518-521	Available in: red, white, blue, clear, black, grey, yellow	Verfügbar in: rot, weiß, blau, klar, schwarz, grau, gelb

1962

706	EU **NA** AU AS	
Medium Basic Set (Canister)		
Mittlerer Grundbaukasten, Dose		
Pcs: 233	1962	Special

710	EU **NA** AU AS	
Large Basic Set (Canister)		
Großer Grundbaukasten, Dose		
Pcs: -	1962	

710	**EU** NA AU AS	
Wooden Storage Box with Content		
Holzsortierkasten mit Inhalt		
Pcs: -	1962	Special

i	706	FAO Schwarz toy stores	FAO Schwarz Spielwaren

1963

ⓘ 001	EU NA AU AS	
Gears		
Zahnräder		
Pcs: 43	1963	

ⓘ 002	EU NA AU AS	
4.5V Gears Motor Set		
4,5V Zahnräder- und Motorset		
Pcs: 4	1963	

ⓘ 003	EU NA AU AS	
Master Mechanic Set		
Mechanikset		
Pcs: 403	1963	

ⓘ 004	EU NA AU AS	
Master Builder Set		
Grundbaukasten		
Pcs: 670	1963	

ⓘ 021	EU NA AU AS	
Wheel Set		
Räderset		
Pcs: 183	1963	

ⓘ 042	EU NA AU AS	
Jumbo Brick Pull Toy		
Spielzug zum Ziehen		
Pcs: 9	1963	

ⓘ	001	Included in: 005 (1967)	Enthalten in: 005 (1967)
ⓘ	004	Master Builder Set; similar to: 704 (1966)	Grundbaukasten; ähnlich zu: 704 (1966)

120	Region: NA
Beginners Set	
Anfängerset	
Pcs: 120	1963
Rating: 3/6	

205	Region: NA
Starter Set	
Starterset	
Pcs: 205	1963
Rating: 3/6	

236	Region: EU, NA
Garage & Van	
Garage & Van	
Pcs: 70	1963
Rating: 4/6	

261	Region: EU
VW 1200 Limousine with Garage	
VW 1200 Limousine mit Garage	
Pcs: 3	1963–1964
Rating: 5/6	

266	Region: EU
Mercedes 190 SL with Garage	
Mercedes 190 SL mit Garage	
Pcs: 3	1963–1964
Rating: 5/6	

267	Region: EU
VW 1500 Limousine with Garage	
VW 1500 Limousine mit Garage	
Pcs: 3	1963–1964
Rating: 5/6	

268	Region: EU
Ford 17M with Garage	
Ford 17M mit Garage	
Pcs: 3	1963–1964
Rating: 5/6	

285	Region: NA
Basic Set	
Grundbaukasten	
Pcs: 285	1963
Rating: 3/6	

313	Region: EU
London Bus	
London-Bus	
Pcs: 141	1963–1972
Rating: 4/6	

ⓘ 205	Re-released in 1970 with new layout	Ab 1970 neu aufgelegt, mit geändertem Layout

314	EU NA AU AS
Large & Small Wheels & Turn-Table	
Geschenkkarton Drehelemente	
Pcs: 35	1963–1965

315	EU NA AU AS
European Taxi	
Kleines Auto	
Pcs: 48	1963–1970

316	EU NA AU AS
Farm Tractor	
Traktor	
Pcs: 52	1963–1965

317	EU NA AU AS
Truck	
Lastwagen	
Pcs: 128	1963–1965

318	EU NA AU AS
Warehouse and Mill	
Windmühle mit Lagerhaus	
Pcs: 153	1963–1969

375	EU NA AU AS
Deluxe Basic Set	
Luxus-Grundbaukasten	
Pcs: 375	1963

450	EU NA AU AS
Deluxe Building Set	
Luxus-Baukasten	
Pcs: 450	1963

600/1	EU NA AU AS
Basic Set	
Grundbaukasten	
Pcs: -	1963

605	EU NA AU AS
Wheel Toy	
Rad-Spielzeug	
Pcs: 183	1963

i	450	Similar to: 502 (1968); without Case	Ähnlich zu: 502 (1968); ohne Koffer
i	600/1	With blue and yellow bricks	Mit blauen und gelben Steinen

605	EU NA AU AS	
Pre-School Beginners Set		
Vorschul-Anfängerset		
Pcs: 24	1963	

615	EU NA AU AS	
Samsonite Gift Set		
Samsonite Geschenkset		
Pcs: 615	1963	

700K	EU NA AU AS	
Wooden Box		
Holzsortierkasten		
Pcs: -	1963	

705	EU NA AU AS	
Basic Set		
Grundbaukasten		
Pcs: 196	1963	

1605	EU NA AU AS	
Wheel Toy Set		
Räderset		
Pcs: -	1963	

1964

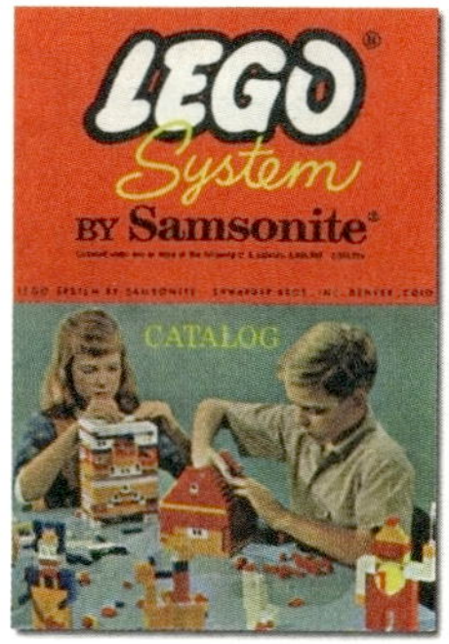

040 — **EU** NA AU AS
Basic Building Set in Cardboard
Geschenkkarton
Pcs: - | 1964–1968

041 — EU **NA** AU AS
Pre-School Beginners Set
Vorschul-Anfängerset
Pcs: - | 1964

050 — **EU** NA AU AS
Basic Building Set in Cardboard
Geschenkkarton
Pcs: - | 1964–1968

105 — EU **NA** AU AS
Pre-School Beginners Set
Vorschul-Anfängerset
Pcs: 24 | 1964

238 — **EU** **NA** **AU** AS
Idea Book
Baubuch
Pcs: 1 | 1964–1970

303 — **EU** NA **AU** AS
Aeroplane
Flugzeug
Pcs: 47 | 1964

i	041	Was released only in USA	Nur in den USA veröffentlicht
i	238	Available in different layouts and languages	Erhältlich in verschiedenen Layouts und Sprachen
i	303	Was released only in UK and Australia	Nur in UK und Australien veröffentlicht

304 — **EU** NA **AU** AS

Tractor & Trailer		
Traktor mit Anhänger		
Pcs: -	1964	

305 — **EU** NA **AU** AS

Fire-Engine		
Feuerwehr		
Pcs: 168	1964	

322 — **EU** NA AU AS

House		
Haus		
Pcs: 163	1964–1966	

323 — **EU** NA AU AS

Train		
Zug		
Pcs: 251	1964–1965	

324 — **EU** NA AU AS

House with Garage		
Haus mit Garage		
Pcs: 174	1964–1969	

395 — EU **NA** AU AS

New York World Fair Promo		
New York World Fair Promo		
Pcs: -	1964	Special

396 — EU **NA** AU AS

New York World Fair Promo		
New York World Fair Promo		
Pcs: -	1964	Special

401 — **EU** NA **AU** AS

Large Wheels with Axles		
Drehelemente		
Pcs: 7	1964–1972	

402 — **EU** NA **AU** AS

White Turntables		
Drehscheiben und Platten, weiß		
Pcs: 5	1964–1972	

i	304	Was released only in UK and Australia	Nur in UK und Australien veröffentlicht
i	305	Was released only in UK and Australia	Nur in UK und Australien veröffentlicht
i	401	Similar to: 901 (1969)	Ähnlich zu: 901 (1969)
i	402	Similar to: 902 (1969)	Ähnlich zu: 902 (1969)

650	EU NA AU AS
Mercedes Esso Road Tanker	
Mercedes Esso Tanklastwagen	
Pcs: 1	1964–1965

651	EU NA AU AS
Mercedes Delivery Truck	
Mercedes Möbelauto	
Pcs: 1	1964–1967

652	EU NA AU AS
Mercedes Truck with Trailer	
Mercedes Möbelwagen m. Anhänger	
Pcs: 2	1964–1967

653	EU NA AU AS
Mercedes Flatbed Truck	
Mercedes Pritschenwagen	
Pcs: 1	1964–1967

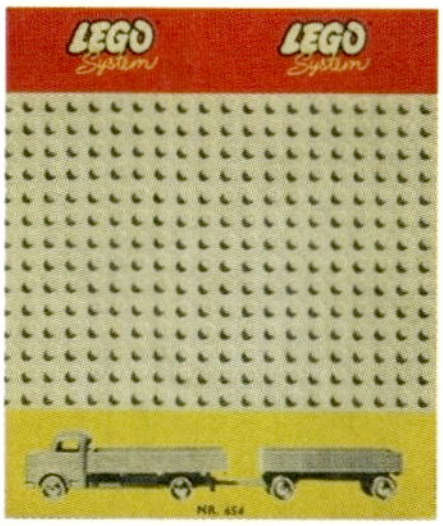

654	EU NA AU AS
Flatbed Truck with Trailer	
Pritschenwagen mit Anhänger	
Pcs: 2	1964–1967

655	EU NA AU AS
Mercedes Firetruck	
Mercedes Feuerwehrfahrzeug	
Pcs: 1	1964–1967

656	EU NA AU AS
Mercedes Tow-Truck	
Mercedes Abschleppwagen	
Pcs: 1	1964–1967

657	EU NA AU AS
Mercedes Long Covered Van	
Mercedes Sattelschlepper	
Pcs: 2	1964–1967

658	EU NA AU AS
VW Van	
VW Bus	
Pcs: 1	1964–1967

i	658	Similar to: 258 (1958)	Ähnlich zu: 258 (1958)

1964

659 EU NA AU AS

VW Pick-up	
VW Pritschenwagen	
Pcs: 1	1964–1967

661 EU NA AU AS

VW Beetle	
VW Käfer	
Pcs: 1	1964–1967

662 EU NA AU AS

Opel Rekord	
Opel Rekord	
Pcs: 1	1964–1967

664 EU NA AU AS

Mercedes 220 S	
Mercedes 220 S	
Pcs: 1	1964–1967

665 EU NA AU AS

Karmann Ghia	
Karmann Ghia	
Pcs: 1	1964–1967

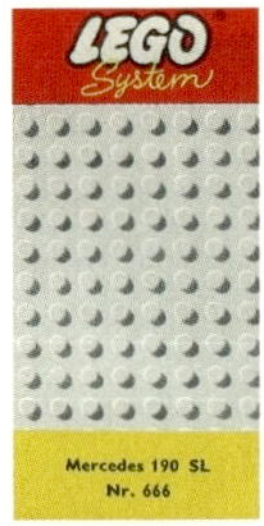

666 EU NA AU AS

Mercedes Sport 190 SL	
Mercedes Sport 190 SL	
Pcs: 1	1964–1967

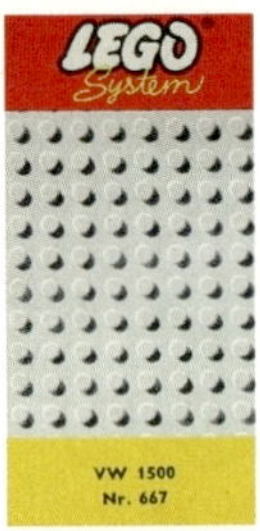

667 EU NA AU AS

VW 1500 Limousine	
VW 1500 Limousine	
Pcs: 1	1964–1967

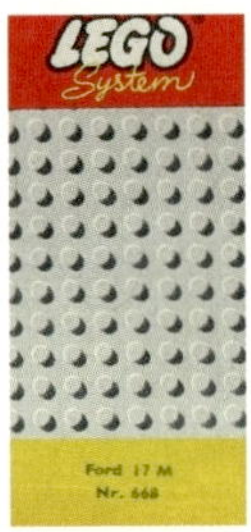

668 EU NA AU AS

Ford Taunus 17 M	
Ford Taunus 17 M	
Pcs: 1	1964–1967

670 EU NA AU AS

1:87 Jaguar E-Type	
1:87 Jaguar E-Type	
Pcs: 1	1964–1966

i		
659	Similar to: 259 (1958)	Ähnlich zu: 259 (1958)

671 EU AU

Vauxhall Victor Estate	
Vauxhall Victor Estate	
Pcs: 1	1964–1966

799 EU AU

Giant Base Plate 50 x 50 Studs	
Bauplatte, groß	
Pcs: 1	1964–1979

801 NA

Space Rocket	
Rakete	
Pcs: 112	1964

802 NA

Player Piano	
Spielklavier	
Pcs: -	1964

803 NA

Seesaw	
Wippe	
Pcs: -	1964

804 NA

Building Crane	
Baukran	
Pcs: -	1964

805 NA

Indians	
Indianer	
Pcs: -	1964

806 NA

Cowboy and Pony	
Cowboy mit Pferd	
Pcs: 84	1964

905 NA

Doll Set	
Puppenset	
Pcs: 278	1964

799	Similar to: 079 (1965)	Ähnlich zu: 079 (1965)

Lego-Geschenkkarton

1965

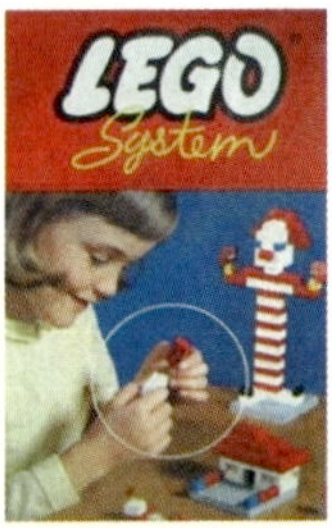

005	EU
Basic Building Set in Cardboard	
Geschenkkarton	
Pcs: -	1965–1967

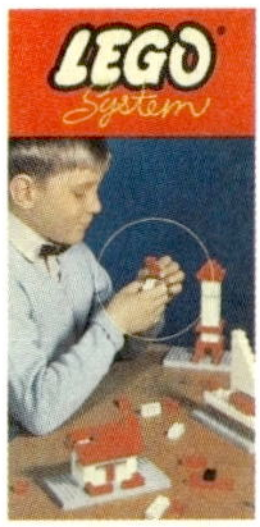

010	EU
Basic Building Set in Cardboard	
Geschenkkarton	
Pcs: 77	1965–1971

020	EU
Basic Building Set in Cardboard	
Geschenkkarton	
Pcs: 175	1965–1968

022	NA
Doll Furniture Set	
Puppenmöbelgarnitur	
Pcs: 301	1965

030	EU
Basic Building Set in Cardboard	
Geschenkkarton	
Pcs: 174	1965–1968

060	EU
Basic Building Set in Cardboard	
Geschenkkarton	
Pcs: -	1965–1968

i	010	Re-released in 1968	Neuauflage in 1968

079	EU **NA** AU AS	
Giant Base Plate		
Bauplatte, groß		
Pcs: 1	1965	
Rating: 5/6		

319	**EU** **NA** AU AS	
Truck with Trailer		
Lkw mit Anhänger		
Pcs: 72	1965–1966	
Rating: 5/6		

320	**EU** NA AU AS	
Two-engine Plane		
Flugzeug		
Pcs: 120	1965–1966	
Rating: 5/6		

321	**EU** NA AU **AS**	
Clowns		
Clowns		
Pcs: -	1965–1966	
Rating: 6/6		

326	**EU** NA AU AS	
Little House		
Kleines Haus		
Pcs: 60	1965–1970	
Rating: 4/6		

409	**EU** NA **AU** AS	
Slimbricks, Assorted Sizes		
Dünne Bausteine, versch. Größen		
Pcs: 38	1965–1972	
Rating: 4/6		

414	**EU** NA **AU** AS	
Windows Parts Pack		
9 verschiedene Fenster, 1 Tür		
Pcs: 10	1965–1969	
Rating: 3/6		

509	EU **NA** **AU** AS	
Slimbricks, Assorted Sizes		
Dünne Bausteine, versch. Größen		
Pcs: 38	1965	
Rating: 4/6		

510	**EU** **NA** AU AS	
Tiles		
Abdecksteine		
Pcs: 52	1965–1965	
Rating: 4/6		

i	079	Similar to: 799 (1964); in grey or green	Ähnlich zu: 799 (1964); in grau oder grün
i	414	Available in: red, white; similar to: 914 (1969)	Verfügbar in: rot, weiß; ähnlich zu: 914 (1969)
i	509	Available in: red, white, blue, yellow, clear, black	Verfügbar in: rot, weiß, blau, gelb, klar, schwarz
i	510	Similar to: 471 (1966), 971 (1969)	Ähnlich zu: 471 (1966), 971 (1969)

603	EU	NA	AU	AS
Citroën DS 19				
Citroën DS 19				
Pcs: 1	1965–1967			

605	EU	NA	AU	AS
Fiat 1800				
Fiat 1800				
Pcs: 1	1965–1967			

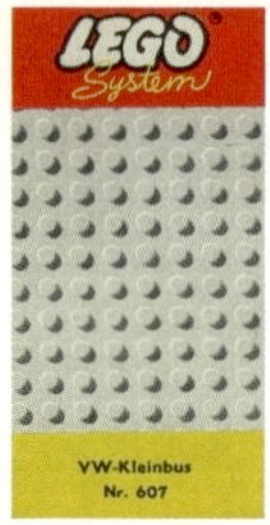

607	EU	NA	AU	AS
VW Bus				
VW Bus				
Pcs: 1	1965–1967			

610	EU	NA	AU	AS
Super Wheel Toy				
Großes Räder-Bauset				
Pcs: 297	1965			

698	EU	NA	AU	AS
1:87 Cars				
Modellautos (1:87)				
Pcs: 12	1965–1966			

699	EU	NA	AU	AS
8 Sorted Trucks				
8 Lastwagen sortiert im Karton				
Pcs: 8	1965–1967			

i		
610	Only released in Canada; also as Tall Box	Nur in Kanada veröffentlicht; auch als Tall Box

1966

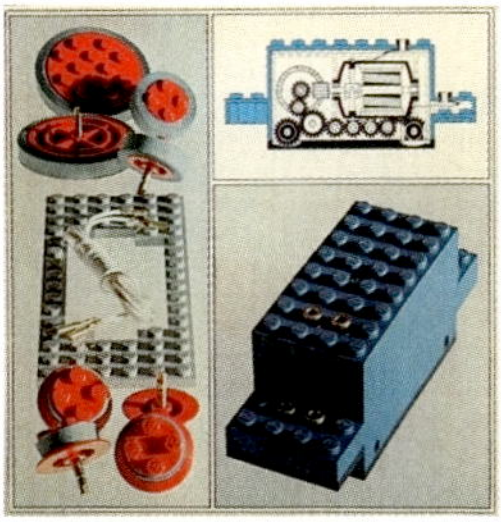

ⓘ 100	EU NA AU AS	
4.5V Motor with Wheels		
4,5V Motor mit Zuleitung u. Rädern		
Pcs: 27	1966–1968	

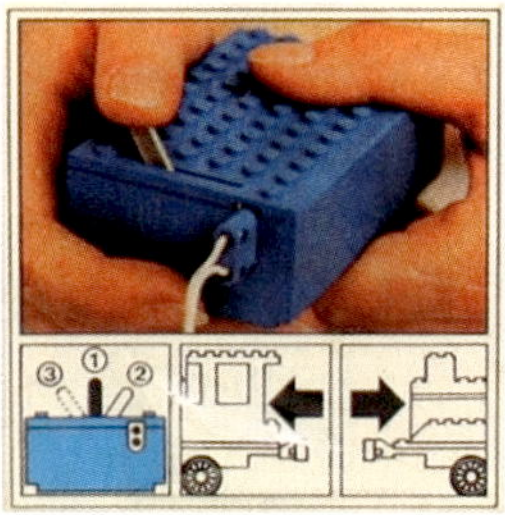

ⓘ 101	EU NA AU AS	
Battery Box		
Batteriekasten		
Pcs: 1	1966–1975	

ⓘ 111	EU NA AU AS	
Starter Train Set without Motor		
Kleiner Zug ohne Motor		
Pcs: 117	1966–1968	

ⓘ 112	EU NA AU AS	
Locomotive with Motor		
Lokomotive mit Motor		
Pcs: 76	1966–1969	

ⓘ 113	EU NA AU AS	
Motorized Train Set		
Großer Zug (mit Motor)		
Pcs: 271	1966–1967	

ⓘ 114	EU NA AU AS	
Small Train Set		
Kleiner Zug		
Pcs: 88	1966–1969	

ⓘ	111	Similar to: 118 (1968)	Ähnlich zu: 118 (1968)

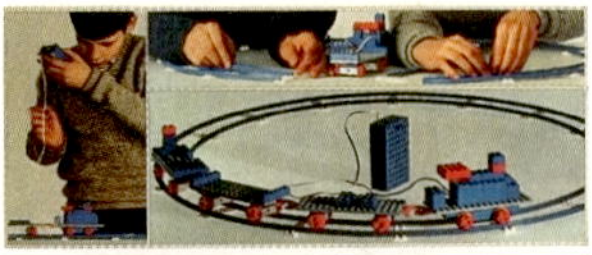

115 — EU, AU
Starter Train Set with Motor
Zug mit Motor
Pcs: 122 | 1966–1969
Rating: 5/6

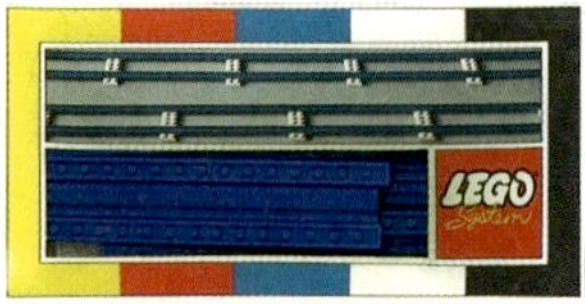

150 — EU
Straight Tracks
Gerade Schienen
Pcs: 25 | 1966–1976
Rating: 2/6

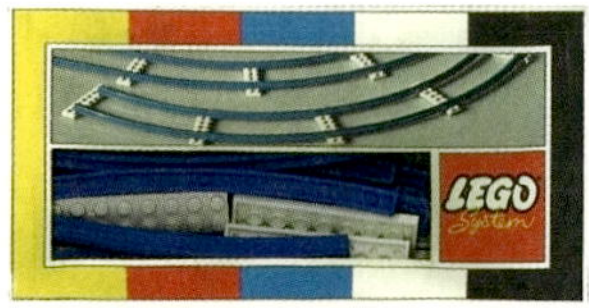

151 — EU
Curved Tracks
Gebogene Schienen
Pcs: 25 | 1966–1976
Rating: 2/6

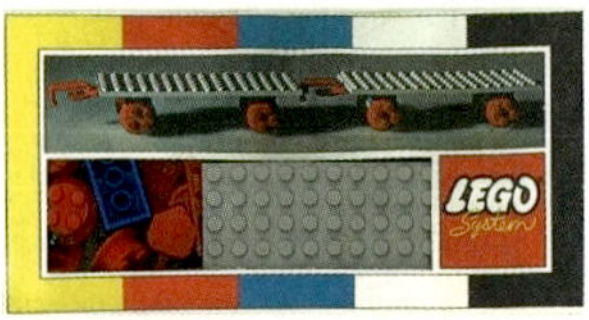

152 — EU
Two Train Wagons
2 kleine Fahrgestelle
Pcs: 22 | 1966–1969
Rating: 3/6

153 — EU
Large Train Wagon
Großes Fahrgestell
Pcs: 15 | 1966–1969
Rating: 3/6

239 — EU
Wir bauen mit LEGO
Wir bauen mit LEGO
Pcs: 1 | 1966–1968
Rating: 3/6

301 — NA
Wheel Toy Set
Fahrzeugset
Pcs: 301 | 1966
Rating: 5/6

325 — EU, AU
Shell Service Station
Shell Tankstelle
Pcs: 97 | 1966–1970
Rating: 4/6

415 — EU
2x8, 2x10 Bricks
2x8, 2x10 Bausteine
Pcs: 9 | 1966–1969
Rating: 3/6

i	415	Available in: red, white, blue/yellow; similar to: 915 (1969)	Verfügbar in: rot, weiß, blau/gelb; ähnlich zu: 915 (1969)
i	416	Available in: red, white, blue/yellow	Verfügbar in: rot, weiß, blau/gelb
i	417	Available in: blue/yellow, red/white	Verfügbar in: blau/gelb, rot/weiß

416	EU NA AU AS
2x8, 2x10 Bricks	
2x8, 2x10 Bausteine	
Pcs: 6	1966–1971

417	EU NA AU AS
4x4 L-shaped Bricks	
4x4 L-Winkelsteine	
Pcs: 10	1966–1972

418	EU NA AU AS
2x4 Bricks	
2x4 Bausteine	
Pcs: 21	1966–1972

419	EU NA AU AS
2x3 Bricks	
2x3 Bausteine	
Pcs: 25	1966–1971

420	EU NA AU AS
2x2 Bricks	
2x2 Bausteine	
Pcs: 33	1966–1972

421	EU NA AU AS
1x2 Bricks	
1x2 Bausteine	
Pcs: 44	1966–1969

421	EU NA AU AS
2x4, 2x3, 2x2, 2x1, 1x1 Plates	
2x4, 2x3, 2x2, 2x1, 1x1 Platten	
Pcs: 20	1966

422	EU NA AU AS
1x1, 1x2, 1x4, 1x6, 1x8 Bricks	
1x1, 1x2, 1x4, 1x6, 1x8 Bausteine	
Pcs: 28	1966–1969

423	EU NA AU AS
Curved Bricks and Cylinders	
Gebogene und runde Bausteine	
Pcs: 50	1966–1972

418	Available in: yellow, clear, red, black, white, blue	Verfügbar in: gelb, klar, rot, schwarz, weiß, blau
419	Available in: yellow, clear, red, black, white, blue	Verfügbar in: gelb, klar, rot, schwarz, weiß, blau
420	Available in: yellow, clear, red, black, white, blue	Verfügbar in: gelb, klar, rot, schwarz, weiß, blau
421	Available in: clear/black, red, white, blue/yellow	Verfügbar in: klar/schwarz, rot, weiß, blau/gelb
422	Available in: yellow, clear, blue, black, white, red	Verfügbar in: gelb, klar, blau, schwarz, weiß, rot
423	Available in: clear/black, red/white, blue/yellow	Verfügbar in: klar/schwarz, rot/weiß, blau/gelb

424	EU **NA** AU AS
Curved Bricks, assorted Colours	
Gebogene Steine, versch. Farben	
Pcs: -	1966

425	EU **NA** AU AS
1x6 & 1x8 Beams, assorted Colours	
1x6 & 1x8 Balken, versch. Farben	
Pcs: 5	1966–1972

426	**EU** NA **AU** AS
Named Beams	
Beschriftete Steine	
Pcs: 7	1966–1972

427	EU **NA** AU AS
4x8 assorted Base Plates	
4x8 Bodenplatten	
Pcs: 8	1966

428	**EU** NA **AU** AS
4x8 Plates	
4x8 Platten	
Pcs: 5	1966–1972

429	**EU** NA **AU** AS
6x8 Plates	
6x8 Platten	
Pcs: 4	1966–1972

430	**EU** **NA** **AU** AS
Trees and Bushes	
Bäume und Büsche	
Pcs: 6	1966–1972

431	EU **NA** AU AS
Garage Door and Esso Pumps	
Garagentor und Esso Zapfsäule	
Pcs: 5	1966–1972

432	**EU** NA **AU** AS
Road Signs	
Verkehrsschilder	
Pcs: 8	1966–1972

424	Available in: black, blue, red, clear, white, yellow	Verfügbar in: schwarz, blau, rot, klar, weiß, gelb
430	Canadian version includes 12 pieces	Kanadische Version enthielt 12 Teile

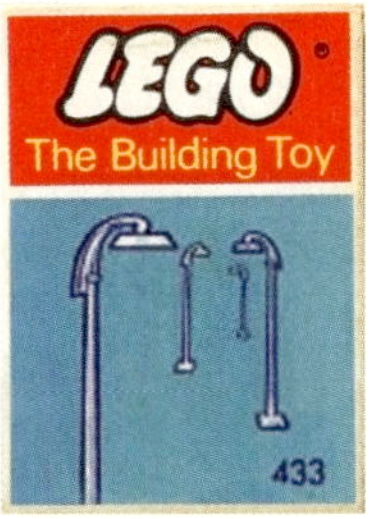

433	EU, AU	
Street Lamps		
Straßenlaternen		
Pcs: 6	1966–1972	
5/6		

434	EU, AU	
Lettered Bricks		
Buchstabensteine		
Pcs: 50	1966–1972	
4/6		

435	EU, AU	
Garage Plate and Door		
Garagenplatte und Tür		
Pcs: 3	1966–1968	
4/6		

437	EU, AU	
Numbered Bricks		
Zahlensteine		
Pcs: 50	1966–1972	
4/6		

445	EU, AU	
Light Brick with Wire and Light		
Leuchtstein mit Kabel und Lampe		
Pcs: 2	1966–1972	
4/6		

456	NA	
Lighting Device		
Leuchtstein		
Pcs: 8	1966	Special
4/6		

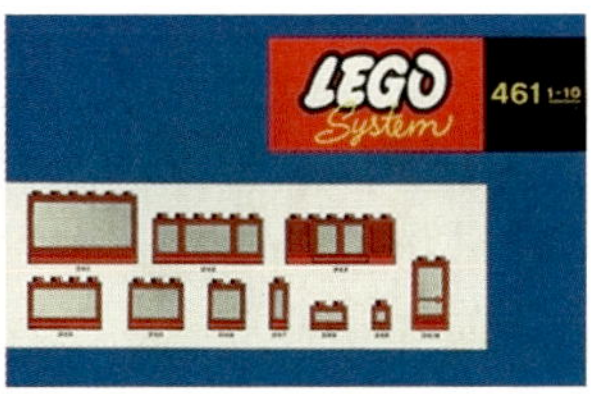

461	EU	
Windows and Doors, Retailer Pack		
Fenster und Türen, Händlerpackung		
Pcs: 375	1966	
4/6		

462	EU	
2x8 Plates, white		
Bauplatten, weiß		
Pcs: 16	1966–1969	
3/6		

463	EU	
4x8 Plates, white		
Bauplatten, weiß		
Pcs: 8	1966–1969	
3/6		

i			
i	437	Similar to: 237 (1960)	Ähnlich zu: 237 (1960)
i	456	Similar to: 050 (1969), 245 (1958), 485 (1966)	Ähnlich zu: 050 (1969), 245 (1958), 485 (1966)
i	461	Includes 451-460 (Servicepacks)	Enthält 451-460 (Servicepacks)

464	EU
6x8 Plates, white	
Bauplatten, weiß	
Pcs: 6	1966–1969

470	EU NA
1x1, 1x2, 2x2, 2x3, 2x4 Plates	
1x1, 1x2, 2x2, 2x3, 2x4 Platten	
Pcs: 39	1966–1969

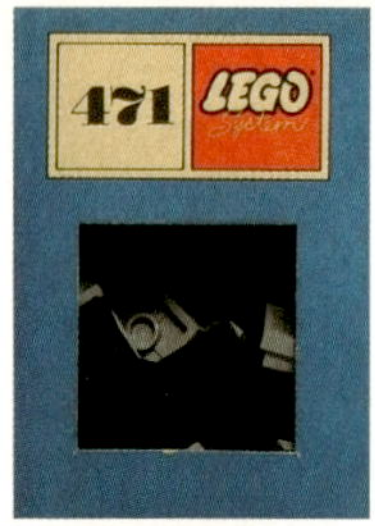

471	EU
Tiles	
Fliesen	
Pcs: 52	1966–1969

480	EU AU
Sloped Bricks, Regular, Peaks	
Dachsteine	
Pcs: 23	1966–1972

481	EU AU
Sloped Bricks, Gables, Corners	
Dachsteine	
Pcs: 34	1966–1972

482	EU NA
Bevelled Bricks	
Schräge Bausteine	
Pcs: 22	1966–1972

483	EU AU
Angle Valley and Corner Bricks	
Dachecken und Eck-Bausteine	
Pcs: 20	1966–1972

485	EU NA
Electrical Brick	
Leuchtstein mit Lampe	
Pcs: 8	1966–1969

487	EU
1x1 Bricks with Numbers	
1x1 Zahlensteine	
Pcs: 44	1966–1969

i	Set	English	Deutsch
i	470	Available in: red, white, blue, yellow, clear, black, grey	Verfügbar in: rot, weiß, blau, gelb, klar, schwarz, grau
i	471	Similar to: 510 (1965), 971 (1969)	Ähnlich zu: 510 (1965), 971 (1969)
i	480	Similar to: 280 (1958)	Ähnlich zu: 280 (1958)
i	481	Similar to: 281 (1959)	Ähnlich zu: 281 (1959)
i	482	Similar to: 282 (1958)	Ähnlich zu: 282 (1958)
i	483	Similar to: 283 (1959)	Ähnlich zu: 283 (1959)

488 EU NA AU AS

1x1 Bricks with Letters	
1x1 Buchstabensteine	
Pcs: 44	1966–1969

489 EU NA AU AS

Traffic Signs	
Verkehrszeichen	
Pcs: 14	1966–1969

490 EU NA AU AS

Trees and Bushes	
Bäume und Büsche	
Pcs: 9	1966–1969

491 EU NA AU AS

Shell Station Brick and Sign	
Shell Zapfstelle mit Schild	
Pcs: 21	1966–1969

492 EU NA AU AS

Nordic and American Flags	
Nordische und amerik. Flaggen	
Pcs: 8	1966–1969

493 EU NA AU AS

European Flags	
Europäische Flaggen	
Pcs: 8	1966–1969

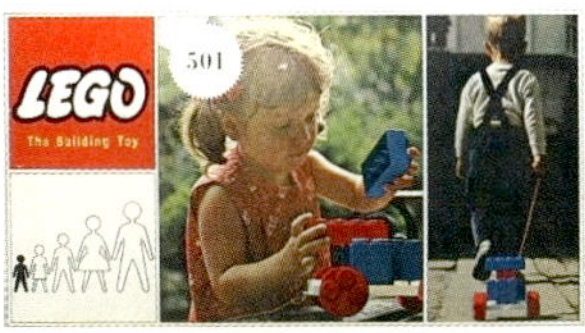

501 EU NA AU AS

JUMBO Pull Toy	
JUMBO Zugspielzeug	
Pcs: 9	1966–1968

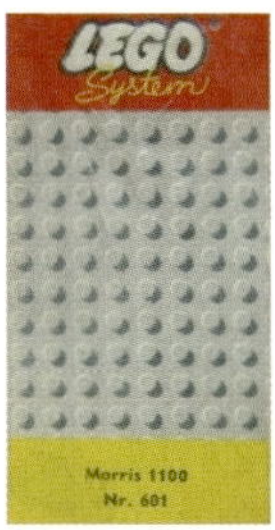

601 EU NA AU AS

Morris 1100	
Morris 1100	
Pcs: 1	1966–1967

649 EU NA AU AS

Shell Fuel Waggon	
Shell Tanklastwagen	
Pcs: 1	1966–1967

485	Similar to: 050 (1969), 245 (1958), 456 (1966)	Ähnlich zu: 050 (1969), 245 (1958), 456 (1966)
488	Similar to: 988 (1969)	Ähnlich zu: 988 (1969)

695	**EU** NA AU AS
6 Classic Cars with Garage	
6 Fahrzeuge sortiert im Karton	
Pcs: 7	1966

696	**EU** NA AU AS
6 Classic Cars with Garage	
6 Fahrzeuge sortiert im Karton	
Pcs: 6	1966–1967

700	**EU** **NA** AU AS
10x20 Brickplate	
10x20 Grundplatte	
Pcs: 1	1966–1970

704	EU **NA** AU AS
Master Discovery Set	
Große Entdeckerpackung	
Pcs: 704	1966

835	EU **NA** AU AS
Advanced Builders Set	
Baukasten für Fortgeschrittene	
Pcs: 565	1966

i	700	Available in red, blue, yellow, grey, green, white	Verfügbar in rot, blau, gelb, grau, grün, weiß
i	704	Similar to: 004 (1963)	Ähnlich zu: 004 (1963)
i	835	FAO Black (toys department store) exclusive-set	FAO Schwarz (Spielwaren-Kaufhaus) Exklusiv-Set

1967

ⓘ 1	EU **NA** AU AS	
Velveeta Promotional No. 1		
Velveeta Promo-Set Nr. 1		
Pcs: 74	1967	Special

ⓘ 2	EU **NA** AU AS	
Velveeta Promotional No. 2		
Velveeta Promo-Set Nr. 2		
Pcs: 141	1967	Special

ⓘ 3	EU **NA** AU AS	
Velveeta Promotional No. 3		
Velveeta Promo-Set Nr. 3		
Pcs: 300	1967	Special

ⓘ 4	EU **NA** AU AS	
Velveeta Promotional No. 4		
Velveeta Promo-Set Nr. 4		
Pcs: 321	1967	Special

ⓘ 5	EU **NA** AU AS	
Velveeta Promotional No. 5		
Velveeta Promo-Set Nr. 5		
Pcs: 156	1967	Special

ⓘ 005	EU **NA** AU AS	
Discovery Set		
Entdeckerset		
Sets: 2	1967	Special

ⓘ			
ⓘ	1-5	Unofficial Numbering of the Velveeta promo-sets	Inoffizielle Nummerierung der Velveeta-Sets
ⓘ	005	Includes: 001 (1963), 285 (1963); USA FAO Schwarz Exclusive	Enthält: 001 (1963), 285 (1963); USA FAO Schwarz Exklusivset

6	EU **NA** AU AS	
Velveeta Promotional No. 6		
Velveeta Promo-Set Nr. 6		
Pcs: 101	1967	Special
Rating: 5/6		

070	**EU** NA AU AS	
Universal Building Set		
Universalbaukasten		
Pcs: -	1967–1972	
Rating: 6/6		

080	**EU** NA AU AS	
Basic Building Set with Train		
Grundbaukasten mit Zug		
Pcs: 700	1967–1970	
Rating: 5/6		

116	**EU** NA AU AS	
Starter Train Set with Motor		
Zug mit Motor und Batteriekasten		
Pcs: 365	1967–1971	
Rating: 4/6		

117	**EU** NA AU AS	
Locomotive without Motor		
Lokomotive ohne Motor		
Pcs: 95	1967–1969	
Rating: 4/6		

154	**EU** NA **AU** AS	
Switch Tracks		
Weichenpaar (links/rechts)		
Pcs: 4	1967–1980	
Rating: 3/6		

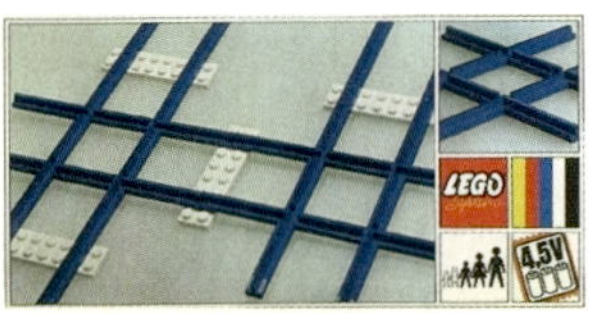

155	**EU** NA AU AS	
Track and Rail Compilation		
2 Kreuzungen		
Pcs: 14	1967–1976	
Rating: 2/6		

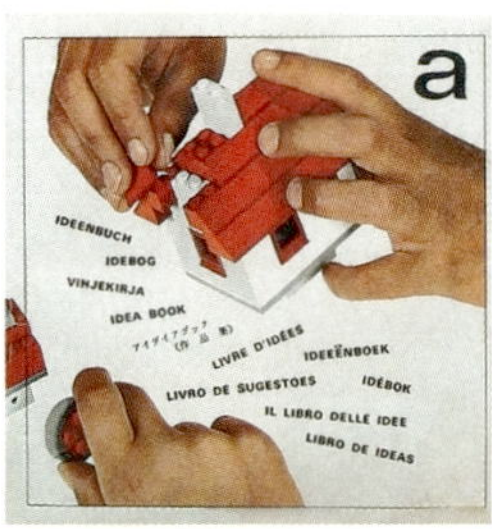

240	**EU** NA AU AS	
Idea Book		
Baubuch		
Pcs: 1	1967–1970	
Rating: 3/6		

328	**EU** NA AU AS	
Biplane		
Doppeldecker		
Pcs: 44	1967–1971	
Rating: 3/6		

6	Unofficial numbering of the Velveeta promo-sets	Inoffizielle Nummerierung der Velveeta-Sets
116	Similar to: 127 (1971)	Ähnlich zu: 127 (1971)

329	**EU** NA AU AS
Antique Car	
Oldtimer mit Speichenrädern	
Pcs: 111	1967–1970

331	**EU** NA AU AS
Dump Truck	
Lkw mit Kipperaufbau	
Pcs: 46	1967–1970

332	**EU** **NA** AU AS
Tow Truck	
Abschleppauto	
Pcs: 57	1967–1970

333	**EU** NA AU AS
Delivery Truck	
Geschlossener Transportwagen	
Pcs: 69	1967–1970

334	**EU** NA AU AS
Truck with Flatbed	
Sattelschlepper mit Pritsche	
Pcs: 73	1967–1968

335	**EU** NA AU AS
Transport Truck	
Sattelschlepper mit Aufbau	
Pcs: 100	1967–1970

371	EU **NA** AU AS
Motorized Truck Set	
Lkw mit Anhänger	
Pcs: 312	1967

403	**EU** NA **AU** AS
Train Couplers and Wheels	
Eisenbahnräder und Kupplungen	
Pcs: 11	1967–1972

404	**EU** NA AU AS
Hubs and Tires	
Triebräder für Motor	
Pcs: 12	1967–1969

ⓘ 403	Similar to: 903 (1969)	Ähnlich zu: 903 (1969)

(i) 494	EU NA AU AS	
Gates and Fences		
Zaunteile mit Pforte		
Pcs: 15	1967–1972	

(i) 536	EU NA AU AS	
Designer Set		
Universalbaukasten		
Pcs: 536	1967	Special

(i)	494	Available in: red, white	Verfügbar in: rot, weiß
(i)	536	USA FAO Schwarz and Sears Exclusive	USA FAO Schwarz und Sears Exklusivset

1968

010	EU NA AU AS
Basic Building Set	
Grundbaukasten	
Pcs: 77	1968–1972

011	EU NA AU AS
Basic Building Set	
Grundbaukasten	
Pcs: 143	1968–1972

022	EU NA AU AS
Basic Building Set	
Grundbaukasten	
Pcs: 162	1968–1972

033	EU NA AU AS
Basic Building Set	
Grundbaukasten	
Pcs: 188	1968–1972

044	EU NA AU AS
Basic Building Set	
Grundbaukasten	
Pcs: 410	1968–1972

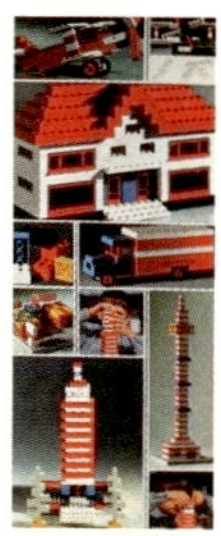

055	EU NA AU AS
Basic Building Set	
Grundbaukasten	
Pcs: -	1968–1972

066	EU
Basic Building Set	
Grundbaukasten	
Pcs: -	1968–1972

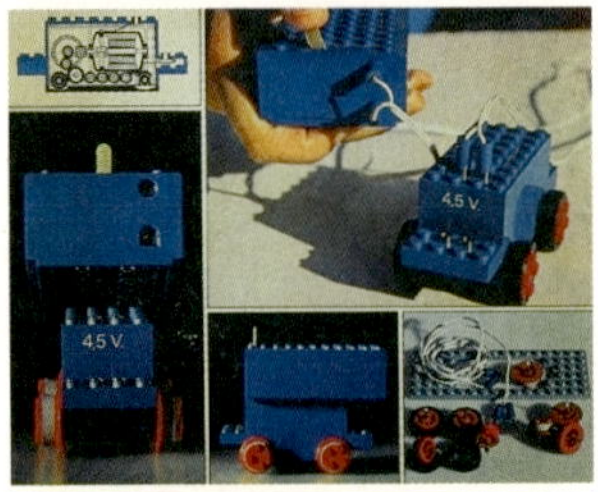

102	EU
Motor with Battery Box	
Motor mit Batteriekasten	
Pcs: 20	1968–1969

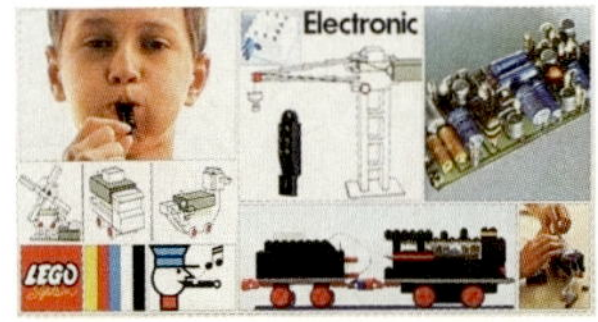

118	EU
Electronic Train (Forward-Stop)	
Electronic-Lok mit Tender	
Pcs: 99	1968

119	EU
Super Train Set	
Super-Zug	
Pcs: 404	1968–1971

156	EU
Signals with Automatic Stop & Go	
Signale	
Pcs: 4	1968–1971

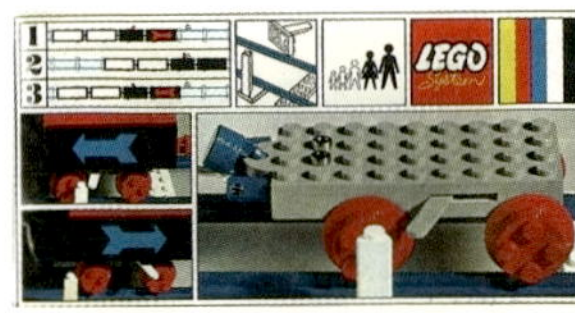

157	EU
Automatic Direction Changer	
Pol-Umschalter	
Pcs: 10	1968–1970

158	EU
Railroad Crossing Gate	
Bahnübergang mit Schranken	
Pcs: 8	1968–1975

160	EU
Magnetic Couplings	
Magnetkupplungen	
Pcs: 6	1968–1976

223	NA
Adventure Set	
Abenteuer-Baukasten	
Pcs: 225	1968

i 118	Similar to: 111 (1966)	Ähnlich zu: 111 (1966)

239	EU
The Big LEGO Book	
Das große LEGO Buch	
Pcs: 1	1968–1969

244	NA	
Explorer Set		
Entdecker-Baukasten		
Pcs: -	1968	Special

310	NA
Motorized Truck Set	
Motorisierter Lkw	
Pcs: 177	1968

330	EU
Jeep	
Jeep	
Pcs: 65	1968–1970

336	EU
Fire Engine	
Feuerwehrauto mit Leiter	
Pcs: 77	1968–1970

340	EU, NA
Blockhouse	
Stellwerkhäuschen	
Pcs: 74	1968–1969

341	EU
Warehouse	
Lagerhaus	
Pcs: 123	1968–1969

342	EU
Station	
Stationsgebäude	
Pcs: 191	1968–1969

343	EU, NA
Ferry Boat	
Fähre	
Pcs: 147	1968–1970

ⓘ	310	Instructions from 331 (1967), 332 (1967), 333 (1967) are included	Anleitungen von 331 (1967), 332 (1967), 333 (1967) sind enthalten

1968

502	EU
Pre-School Set Medium	
Vorschul-Anfängerset, mittel	
Pcs: 8	1968

502	NA	
Deluxe Set with Storage Case		
Luxusset mit Sortierkoffer		
Pcs: 450	1968	Special

503	EU, AU	
Pre-School Set Large		
Großes Vorschulset		
Pcs: 16	1968	Special

i	502	Deluxe Set with Storage Case; similar to: 450 (1963)	Luxusset mit Sortierkoffer; ähnlich zu: 450 (1963)

1969

ⓘ 1	EU NA AU AS	
Quaker/Life Cereal Promotional		
Quaker/Life Cereal Promoset		
Pcs: 301	1969	Special

ⓘ 2	EU NA AU AS	
Quaker/Life Cereal Promotional		
Quaker/Life Cereal Promoset		
Pcs: 159	1969	Special

ⓘ 3	EU NA AU AS	
Quaker/Life Cereal Promotional		
Quaker/Life Cereal Promoset		
Pcs: 156	1969	Special

ⓘ 044	EU NA AU AS	
JUMBO Bricks		
JUMBO Steine		
Pcs: 30	1969	

ⓘ 050	EU NA AU AS	
Lighting Device Pack		
Leuchtsteine		
Pcs: 9	1969–1970	

ⓘ 060	EU NA AU AS	
Jumbo Brick School Set		
Jumbo Steine		
Pcs: 60	1969	

ⓘ	1-3	Unofficial numbering of the Quaker promo-sets	Inoffizielle Numerierung der Quaker-Sets
ⓘ	050	Similar to: 245 (1958), 485 (1966), 456 (1969)	Ähnlich zu: 245 (1958), 485 (1966), 456 (1969)

ⓘ 102	EU **NA** AU AS	
Super Value Set		
Vorteilspackung		
Pcs: 102	1969	Special

ⓘ 103	**EU** NA AU AS	
4.5V Motor		
4,5V Batteriemotor		
Pcs: 24	1969–1975	

ⓘ 118	EU **NA** AU AS	
Motorized Freight/Passenger Train		
Passagier- und Güterzug mit Motor		
Pcs: 451	1969	

ⓘ 120	**EU** NA AU AS	
Freight Train Set, Tipper Wagons		
Lokomotive mit Kohlewaggons, 4,5V		
Pcs: 161	1969–1972	

ⓘ 122	**EU** NA AU AS	
Locomotive and Tender		
Lokomotive		
Pcs: 90	1969–1971	

ⓘ 123	**EU** NA AU AS	
Passenger Coach		
Personenwagen		
Pcs: 98	1969–1971	

ⓘ 124	**EU** NA AU AS	
Goods Wagon		
Blauer Güterwaggon		
Pcs: 56	1969–1971	

ⓘ 125	**EU** NA AU AS	
Tipping Wagon		
Kippwaggon		
Pcs: 20	1969–1971	

ⓘ 138	**EU** NA AU AS	
Electronic Train		
Electronik-Lok		
Pcs: 107	1969–1971	

ⓘ 103	Similar to: 900 (1973)	Ähnlich zu: 900 (1973)

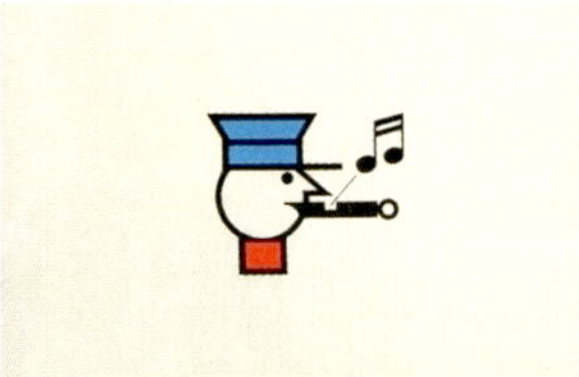

139	**EU** **NA** AU AS	
Electronic Control Unit		
Elektr. Steuerung für Bahn, Pfeife		
Pcs: 13	1969–1971	

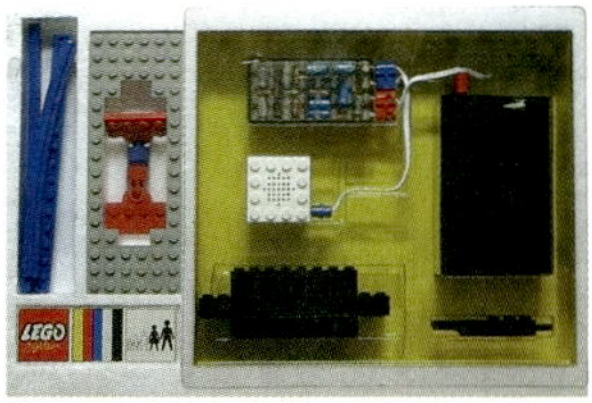

139A	**EU** NA AU AS	
Electr. Control Unit (only forward)		
Elektr. Steuerung, nur vorwärts		
Pcs: 13	1969–1971	

157	EU **NA** AU AS	
Four Car Auto Transport		
Autotransporter		
Pcs: 65	1969	Special

241	**EU** NA AU AS	
Idea Book		
Baubuch		
Pcs: 1	1969–1972	

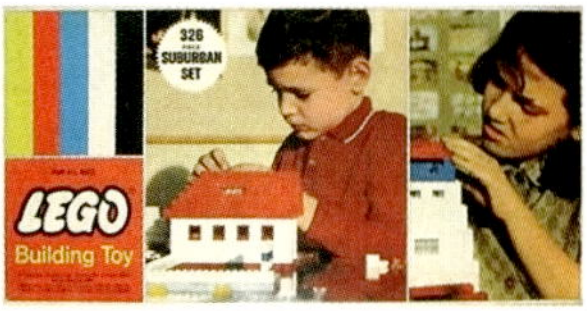

326	EU **NA** AU AS	
Suburban Set		
Vorstadt		
Pcs: 326	1969	Special

337	**EU** NA AU AS	
Truck with Crane		
Tieflader mit Kran		
Pcs: 93	1969–1970	

344	**EU** NA AU AS	
Bungalow		
Sommerhaus		
Pcs: 77	1969–1971	

345	**EU** NA AU AS	
House with Mini Wheel Car		
Bungalow mit Garage und PKW		
Pcs: 132	1969–1971	

346	**EU** NA AU AS	
House with Car		
Villa mit Garage und PKW		
Pcs: 167	1969–1971	

i	241	Exists in 3 different versions	Es existieren 3 verschiedene Versionen
i	326	USA Fao Schwarz Exclusive Promo	USA Fao Schwarz Promo

443	EU NA AU AS
Doors & Windows	
Türen und Fenster	
Pcs: 22	1969

445	EU NA AU AS
Roof Bricks	
Dachsteine	
Pcs: 68	1969

446	EU NA AU AS
Special Building Bricks	
Spezial-Bausteine	
Pcs: 72	1969

447	EU NA AU AS
Garage Kit & Street Signs	
Garage und Zubehör	
Pcs: -	1969

449	EU NA AU AS
Giant Base Plate 20x20 inch	
Riesengrundplatte 50x50	
Pcs: 1	1969

510	EU NA AU AS
Building Set	
Baukasten	
Pcs: 17	1969–1970

511	EU NA AU AS
Building Set	
Baukasten	
Pcs: 27	1969–1970

702	EU NA AU AS
12V Engine, demountable	
12V Elektromotor, zerlegbar	
Pcs: 1	1969–1972

720	EU NA AU AS
Train with 12V Electric Motor	
12V Elektro-Güterzug	
Pcs: 277	1969–1973

i	Set	English	Deutsch
i	447	Only released in Canada	Wurde nur in Kanada veröffentlicht
i	510	Re-release in 1970-1974, with new design	Neuauflage in anderem Design von 1970 bis 1974

721	EU NA AU AS	
Steam Locomotive		
Tenderlok mit 12V Elektromotor		
Pcs: 114	1969–1973	

740	EU NA AU AS	
220V Transformer		
220V Transformator		
Pcs: 1	1969–1973	

750	EU NA AU AS	
8 Straight 12V Rails		
8 Gerade Stromschienen		
Pcs: 8	1969–1980	

751	EU NA AU AS	
8 Curved 12V Conducting Rails		
8 Gebogene Stromschienen		
Pcs: 8	1969–1980	

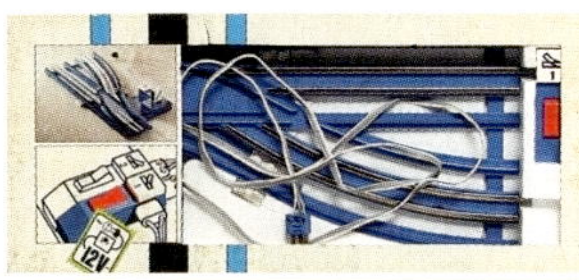

753	EU NA AU AS	
Automatic Right Electric Switch		
Elektrische Rechtsweiche		
Pcs: 5	1969–1974	

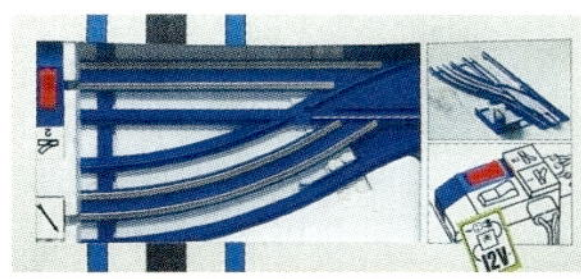

754	EU NA AU AS	
Automatic Left Electric Switch		
Elektrische Linksweiche		
Pcs: 5	1969–1974	

842	EU NA AU AS	
Townplan Set		
Spielplanset		
Pcs: -	1969	Special

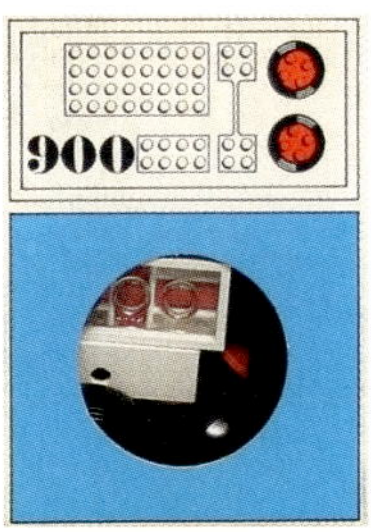

900	EU NA AU AS	
4 Small Wheels with Accessories		
Kleine Räder		
Pcs: 12	1969–1972	

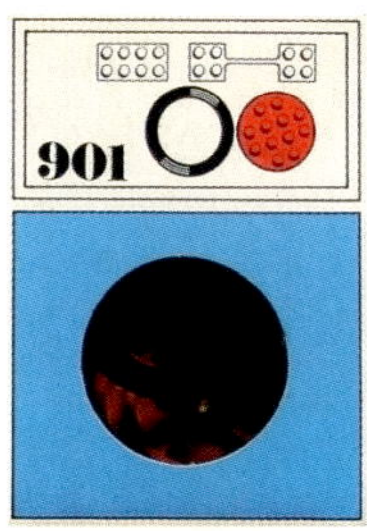

901	EU NA AU AS	
2 Large Wheels with Accessories		
Große Räder		
Pcs: 7	1969–1972	

i	Set	English	Deutsch
i	740	Exists in blue and grey	Gab es in blau und in grau
i	900	Similar to: 400 (1962)	Ähnlich zu: 400 (1962)
i	901	Similar to: 401 (1964)	Ähnlich zu: 401 (1964)

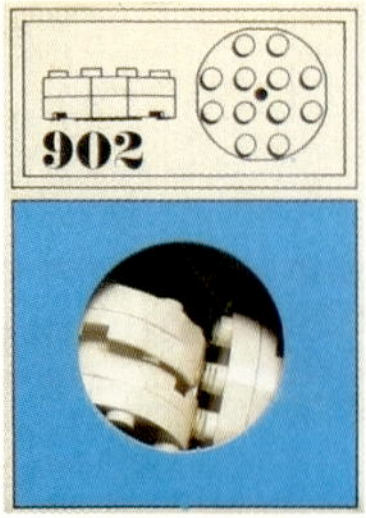

902	EU NA AU AS
5 Turntables	
Drehscheiben	
Pcs: 5	1969–1972

903	EU NA AU AS
Train Wheels and Couplers	
Zugräder und Kupplungen	
Pcs: 10	1969–1972

906	EU NA AU AS
12 Doors and 5 Hinges	
Schwenkbare Türen	
Pcs: 17	1969–1972

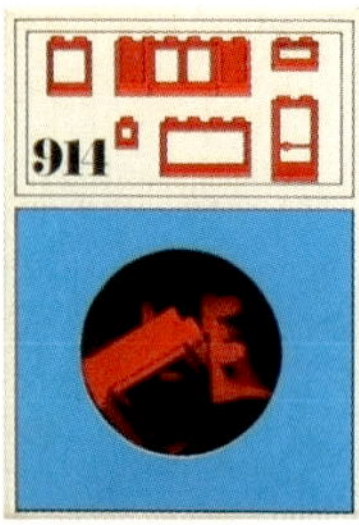

914	EU NA AU AS
Windows and Door	
Verschiedene Fenster, eine Tür	
Pcs: 10	1969–1972

915	EU NA AU AS
Assorted Bricks	
Balken und Winkelsteine	
Pcs: 9	1969–1972

918	EU NA AU AS
Bricks with 8 Studs	
Bausteine mit 8 Knöpfen	
Pcs: 21	1969–1972

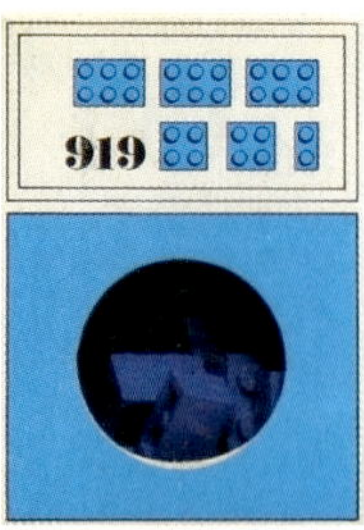

919	EU NA AU AS
Bricks with 2, 4 and 6 Studs	
Bausteine mit 2, 4 und 6 Knöpfen	
Pcs: 31	1969–1972

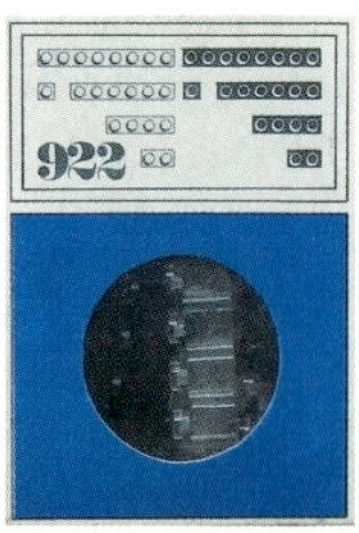

922	EU NA AU AS
Bricks with 1, 2, 4, 6 and 8 Studs	
Bausteine mit 1, 2, 4, 6 und 8 Knöpfen	
Pcs: 28	1969–1972

923	EU NA AU AS
Curved and Round Bricks	
Runde u. gebogene Bausteine	
Pcs: 50	1969–1972

i	Set	English	Deutsch
i	902	Similar to: 402 (1964)	Ähnlich zu: 402 (1964)
i	903	Similar to: 403 (1967)	Ähnlich zu: 403 (1967)
i	915	Similar to: 415 (1966); available in red/white	Ähnlich zu: 415 (1966); verfügbar in rot/weiß
i	918	Similar to: 418 (1966); available in: red, white, blue, transparent, black	Ähnlich zu: 418 (1966); verfügbar in: rot, weiß, gelb, transparent, schwarz
i	919	Available in: red, white, yellow, transparent, black	Verfügbar in: rot, weiß, gelb, transparent, schwarz

964
EU NA AU AS

Building Plates 2x8, 4x8, 6x8

Bauplatten 2x8, 4x8, 6x8

Pcs: 10 | 1969–1972

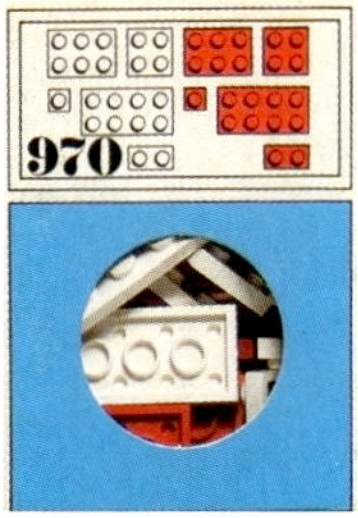

970
EU NA AU AS

1/3 Elements (Plates)

Verschiedene Flachsteine

Pcs: 47 | 1969–1972

971
EU NA AU AS

Flat Tile Bricks

Fliesen

Pcs: 52 | 1969–1972

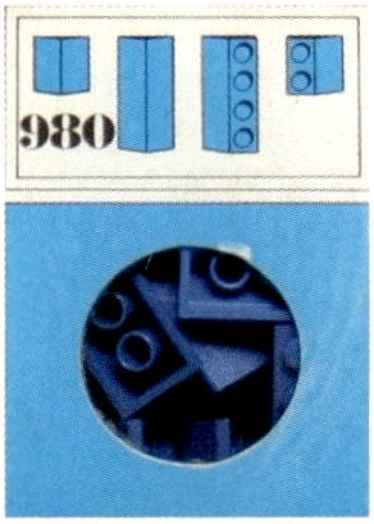

980
EU NA AU AS

Sloping and Roof Peak Bricks

Schräg- und Firststeine

Pcs: 23 | 1969–1972

981
EU NA AU AS

Sloping and Profile Peak Bricks

Kehl-, Grat- und Firststeine

Pcs: 34 | 1969–1972

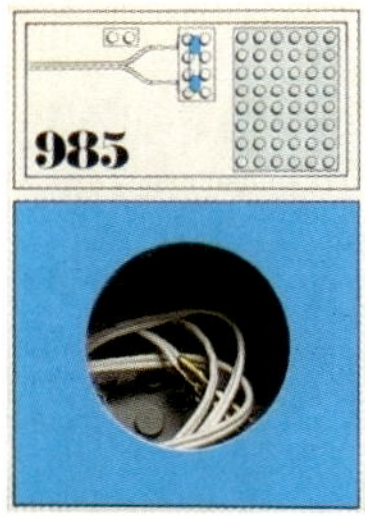

985
EU NA AU AS

Lighting Device Parts Pack

Leuchtstein mit Kabel, Bauplatte

Pcs: 4 | 1969–1972

987
EU NA AU AS

Number Bricks

Zahlensteine

Pcs: 10 | 1969–1972

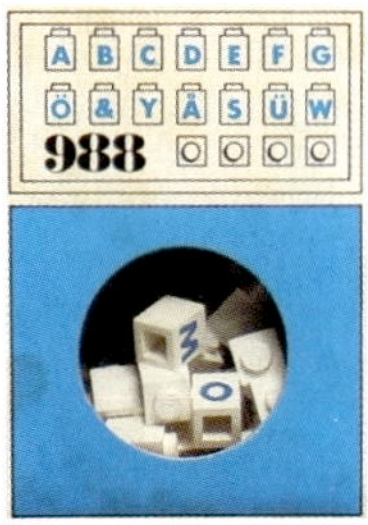

988
EU NA AU AS

Alphabet Bricks

Buchstabensteine

Pcs: 27 | 1969–1972

989
EU NA AU AS

10 Traffic Signs

Verkehrszeichen

Pcs: 10 | 1969–1972

i	Set	English	Deutsch
i	922	Similar to: 422 (1966); av. in: red/white, blue/yellow	Ähnlich zu: 422 (1966); verfügb. in:rot/weiß, blau/gelb
i	923	Similar to: 423 (1966); av. in: blue/yellow, transp./black	Ähnlich zu: 423 (1966); verfügb. in:rot/weiß, blau/gelb
i	970	Available in: blue/yellow, black/grey	Verfügbar in: blau/gelb, schwarz/grau
i	971	Similar to: 471 (1966), 510 (1965); available in: blue/yellow, transperant/black	Ähnlich zu: 471 (1966), 510 (1965); verfügbar in: blau/gelb, transparent/schwarz
i	980	Available in: red, blue	Verfügbar in: rot, blau

990	EU NA AU AS
Trees and Signs	
Bäume und Schilder	
Pcs: 12	1969–1972

994	EU NA AU AS
Fences with Garden Gates	
Zaunteile, 2 schwenkbare Pforten	
Pcs: 19	1969–1972

995	EU NA AU AS
Lighting Set	
Leuchtsteine, Namenbalken	
Pcs: 15	1969–1977

	EU NA AU AS	
Puppet Set		
Puppenset		
Pcs: 89	1969	Special

i	981	Available in: red, blue	Verfügbar in: rot, blau
i	988	Similar to: 488 (1966)	Ähnlich zu: 488 (1966)
i		Quaker Cereal Promo	Quaker Cereal Promo

1970

078	EU NA AU AS
Roadway Base Plate	
Straßen-Grundplatte	
Pcs: 1	1970

088	EU NA AU AS
Super Set	
Superset	
Pcs: -	1970–1972

102A	EU NA AU AS
Front-End Loader	
Planierraupe	
Pcs: 57	1970

103	EU NA AU AS
Imagination Standard Set 3	
Imagination Standardset 3	
Pcs: 568	1970

104	EU NA AU AS
4.5V Replacement Motor	
4,5V Austauschmotor	
Pcs: 1	1970–1976

126	EU NA AU AS
Steam Locomotive	
Dampflokomotive	
Pcs: 60	1970–1974

140	EU
Basic Set with Motor	
Grundbaukasten mit Motor	
Pcs: 96	1970–1973

242	EU
Big Model Book	
Modellbuch, groß	
Pcs: 1	1970–1976

311	NA	
Remote Control Car Set		
Fahrzeuge mit Fernbedienung		
Pcs: 175	1970	Special

312	NA
Remote Control Supplement	
Ersatz-Fernbedienung	
Pcs: 1	1970

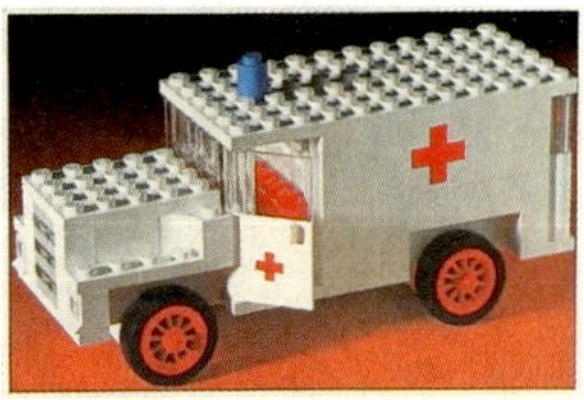

338	EU
Ambulance	
Krankenwagen	
Pcs: 74	1970

346	NA
Jumbo Jet	
Jumbo Jet	
Pcs: 117	1970

347	EU
Fire Station with Mini Cars	
Feuerwache mit Fahrzeugen	
Pcs: 206	1970–1972

348	EU NA
Mini-Wheel Car and Truck Set	
Mehrere Autos	
Pcs: 185	1970

367	NA
Mini Airport and Vehicles	
Kleinflughafen und Fahrzeuge	
Pcs: -	1970

510 EU NA AU AS

Building Set	
Baukasten	
Pcs: 17	1970–1974

512 EU NA AU AS

Building Set	
8-Knopf-Steine, 1 Fahrgestell	
Pcs: 20	1970–1974

513 EU NA AU AS

Building Set	
8-Knopf-Steine, 2 Fahrgestelle	
Pcs: 29	1970–1974

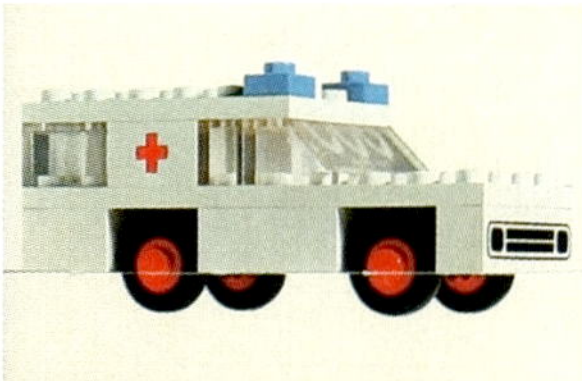

600 EU NA AU AS

Ambulance	
Krankenwagen	
Pcs: 21	1970–1971

601 EU NA AU AS

Tow Truck	
Abschleppauto	
Pcs: 21	1970–1971

602 EU NA AU AS

Fire Truck	
Lkw mit 4 schwenkbaren Türen	
Pcs: 24	1970

603 EU NA AU AS

Vintage Car	
Oldtimer	
Pcs: 35	1970

620 EU NA AU AS

Fire Truck	
Feuerwehr mit Ausziehleiter	
Pcs: 40	1970

621 EU NA AU AS

Shell Tanker Truck	
Shell Tankwagen	
Pcs: 43	1970

i	512	Similar to: 010 (1973)	Ähnlich zu: 010 (1973)
i	600	Similar to: 360 (1971)	Ähnlich zu: 360 (1971)
i	601	Similar to: 361 (1971)	Ähnlich zu: 361 (1971)
i	602	Similar to: 362 (1971)	Ähnlich zu: 362 (1971)
i	603	Similar to: 363 (1971)	Ähnlich zu: 363 (1971)

622 EU NA AU AS

Baggage Carts

Gepäckkarre mit 2 Anhängern

Pcs: 45 | 1970

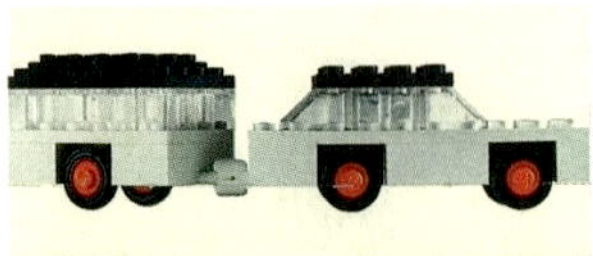

623 EU NA AU AS

White Car and Camper

Personenwagen mit Wohnwagen

Pcs: 38 | 1970

703 EU NA AU AS

12V Replacement Motor

12V Austauschmotor

Pcs: 1 | 1970–1976

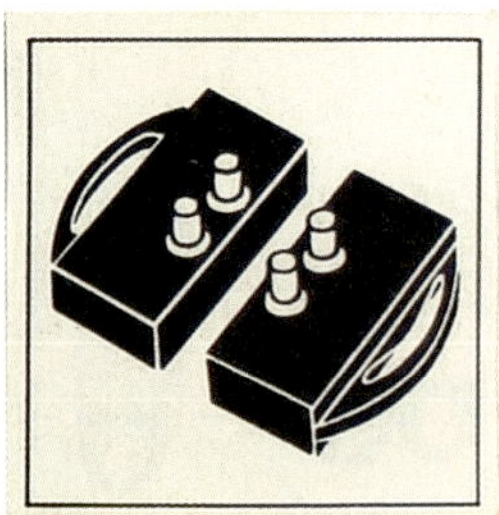

704 EU NA AU AS

12V Sleeper (Track) Contacts

1 Paar Schleifkontakte

Pcs: 2 | 1970–1976

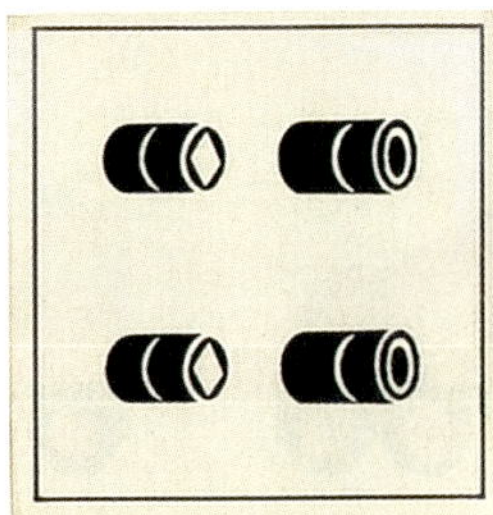

705 EU NA AU AS

Motor Bushings

4 Radbuchsen

Pcs: 4 | 1970–1976

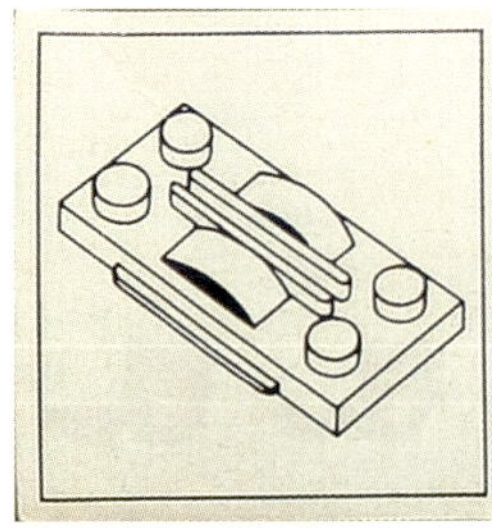

706 EU NA AU AS

Rail Contact Wires

Schienenkontaktplatte

Pcs: 1 | 1970–1976

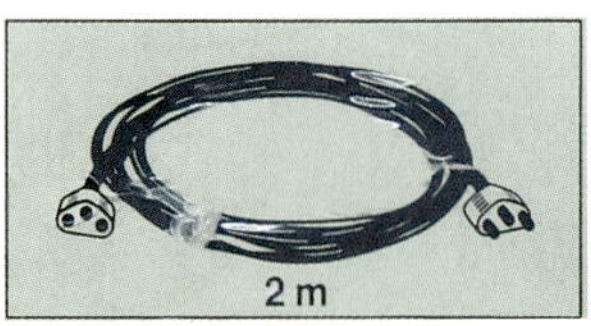

708 EU NA AU AS

2m Extension Cord for Points

2m Verlängerungskabel für Weichen

Pcs: 1 | 1970–1974

722 EU NA AU AS

12V Electric Train with 2 Wagons

12V Elektrozug mit 2 Kippwagen

Pcs: 151 | 1970–1973

723 EU NA AU AS

Diesel Locomotive

Rangierlokomotive

Pcs: 95 | 1970–1974

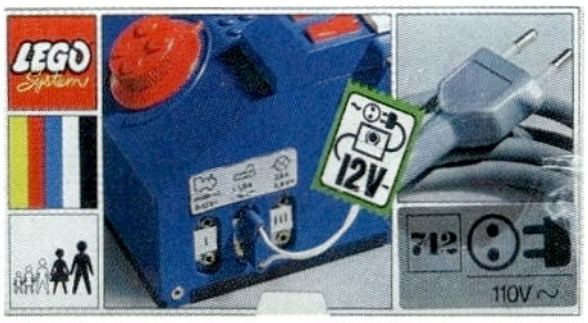

742	EU NA AU AS
110V Transformer	
110V Transformator	
Pcs: 1	1970–1973

800	EU NA AU AS
Gears, Motor and Bricks	
Zahnräder mit Motor	
Pcs: 120	1970–1973

801	EU NA AU AS
Gear Set	
Zahnräder, Lager, Achsstifte	
Pcs: 115	1970–1973

802	EU NA AU AS
Gear Supplement	
Zahnrad-Ergänzungsschachtel	
Pcs: 30	1970–1973

	EU NA AU AS	
Weetabix Castle		
Weetabix Burg		
Pcs: 471	1970	Special

i		Weetabix Promo	Weetabix Promo

1971

i 1	Region: EU	
Minitalia Set No. 1		
Minitalia Set Nr. 1		
Pcs: -	1971	Special

i 1	Region: NA	
Kraft Set No. 1 - Mini Wheeler		
Kraft Set Nr. 1 - Kleine Autos		
Pcs: 82	1971–1974	Special

i 2	Region: EU	
Minitalia Set No. 2		
Minitalia Set Nr. 2		
Pcs: -	1971	Special

i 2	Region: NA	
Kraft Set No. 2 - Mini Wheeler		
Kraft Set Nr. 2 - Kleine Autos		
Pcs: 74	1971–1974	Special

i 3	Region: EU	
Kraft Set No. 3 - Mini Wheeler		
Kraft Set Nr. 3 - Kleine Autos		
Pcs: 65	1971	Special

i 3	Region: NA	
Minitalia Set No. 3		
Minitalia Set Nr. 3		
Pcs: -	1971–1974	Special

i 1-3	Unofficial numbering of the Kraft promo-sets	Inoffizielle Nummerierung der Kraft-Sets

4	EU
Minitalia Set No. 4	
Minitalia Set Nr. 4	
Pcs: -	1971–1974	Special

21	EU
Minitalia Set No. 21	
Minitalia Set Nr. 21	
Pcs: -	1971–1974	Special

22	EU
Minitalia Set No. 22	
Minitalia Set Nr. 22	
Pcs: -	1971–1974	Special

23	EU
Minitalia Set No. 23	
Minitalia Set Nr. 23	
Pcs: -	1971–1974	Special

24	EU
Minitalia Set No. 24	
Minitalia Set Nr. 24	
Pcs: 73	1971–1974	Special

077	EU
Large Basic Set	
Grundbaukasten	
Pcs: -	1971–1972	

105	NA
Imagination Master Set 5	
Imagination Master Set 5	
Pcs: 917	1971	

107	NA
4.5V Reversible Power Unit (Motor)	
4,5V Motor	
Pcs: 24	1971	

110	NA
Vehicles Accessory Pack	
Fahrzeugzubehör	
Pcs: 61	1971	

i 110	Similar to: 166 (1971)	Ähnlich zu: 166 (1971)

1971

111 EU NA AU AS

Building Accessory Pack	
Bauzubehör	
Pcs: 111	1971

127 EU NA AU AS

Complete Train Set with 3 Wagons	
Vollständiger Zug mit 3 Waggons	
Pcs: 300	1971

128 EU NA AU AS

Mobile Crane	
Eisenbahnwaggon mit Kran	
Pcs: 25	1971–1974

166 EU NA AU AS

Vehicles Accessory Pack	
Fahrzeug-Zusatzpackung	
Pcs: 55	1971

167 EU NA AU AS

House and Garden Extra Parts Kit	
Zubehör für Haus und Garten	
Pcs: 111	1971

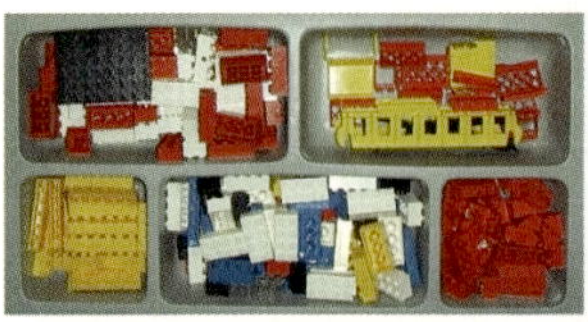

248 EU NA AU AS

Factory with Conveyor Belt	
Fabrik mit Förderband	
Pcs: 210	1971

260 EU NA AU AS

Dolls Living Room	
Puppenstube	
Pcs: 173	1971–1973

261 EU NA AU AS

Dolls Kitchen	
Puppenküche	
Pcs: 156	1971–1973

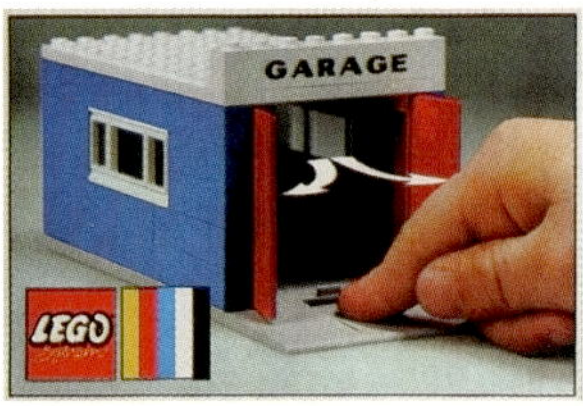

348 EU NA AU AS

Garage with Automatic Doors	
Garage mit automatischer Tür	
Pcs: 38	1971–1975

111	Similar to: 167 (1971)	Ähnlich zu: 167 (1971)
127	Similar to: 116 (1967)	Ähnlich zu: 116 (1967)
166	Similar to: 110 (1971)	Ähnlich zu: 110 (1971)
167	Similar to: 111 (1971)	Ähnlich zu: 111 (1971)
248	Was packed in brown cardboard box	War in brauner Pappschachtel verpackt

i 349	EU **NA** AU AS
Mini-Wheel Construction Set	
Fahrzeuge-Zusatzset	
Pcs: 181	1971–1974

i 349	**EU** **NA** AU AS
Swiss Chalet	
Tiroler Haus	
Pcs: 81	1971–1974

i 350	**EU** NA AU AS
Spanish Villa	
Villa Romana	
Pcs: 126	1971–1973

i 351	**EU** **NA** **AU** AS
Loader Hopper with Truck	
Schotterwerk mit Förderanlage	
Pcs: 170	1971–1974

i 360	EU **NA** AU AS
Ambulance	
Krankenwagen	
Pcs: 21	1971

i 361	EU **NA** AU AS
Tow Truck	
Abschleppwagen	
Pcs: 21	1971

i 362	EU **NA** AU AS
Delivery Van	
Lieferwagen	
Pcs: 30	1971

i 363	EU **NA** AU AS
Antique Car	
Oldtimer	
Pcs: 35	1971

i 371	**EU** NA AU AS
Tipper Truck	
Kipplader	
Pcs: 48	1971–1973

i			
i	351	Similar to: 545 (1973)	Ähnlich zu: 545 (1973)
i	360	Similar to: 600 (1970)	Ähnlich zu: 600 (1970)
i	361	Similar to: 601 (1970)	Ähnlich zu: 601 (1970)
i	362	Similar to: 602 (1970)	Ähnlich zu: 602 (1970)
i	363	Similar to: 603 (1970)	Ähnlich zu: 603 (1970)

372 EU NA AU AS

Tow Truck

Abschleppauto

Pcs: 54 | 1971–1972

373 EU NA AU AS

Ambulance

Krankenwagen

Pcs: 65 | 1971–1972

374 EU NA AU AS

Fire Engine

Löschwagen m. Drehleiter

Pcs: 74 | 1971–1973

375 EU NA AU AS

Refrigerator Truck and Trailer

Kühlwagen mit Anhänger

Pcs: 128 | 1971–1973

376 EU NA AU AS

Low-loader with Excavator

Tieflader mit Planierraupe

Pcs: 92 | 1971–1973

377 EU NA AU AS

Crane with Float Truck

Kran mit Sattelschlepper

Pcs: 91 | 1971–1973

380 EU NA AU AS

Village Set

Dorfanlage

Pcs: 485 | 1971

426 EU NA AU AS

7 Named Beams

7 beschriftete Balken

Pcs: 7 | 1971

427 EU NA AU AS

4x8 Assorted Base Plates

4x8 Bodenplatten

Pcs: 8 | 1971–1972

431	**EU** NA **AU** AS	
Petrol Pump and Sign		
Tanksäule und Schild		
Pcs: 12	1971–1972	

442A	EU **NA** AU AS	
International Flags		
Internationale Fahnen		
Pcs: 6	1971	

604	**EU** **NA** **AU** AS	
Excavator		
Frontlader		
Pcs: 28	1971–1973	

605	**EU** NA AU AS	
Taxi		
Taxi		
Pcs: 18	1971–1972	

608	**EU** NA AU AS	
Kiosk		
Kiosk mit Fernsprechzelle		
Pcs: 33	1971	

630	EU **NA** AU AS	
Diplomat Set		
Diplomatenset		
Pcs: 633	1971	Special

640	**EU** NA AU AS	
Fire Truck		
Feuerwehr mit Drehleiter & Anhänger		
Pcs: 45	1971–1973	

642	**EU** NA AU AS	
Double Excavator		
Löffelbagger		
Pcs: 33	1971–1973	

643	**EU** NA AU AS	
Mobile Crane		
Fahrbarer Kran		
Pcs: 35	1971–1972	

i	604	Similar to: 410 (1973)	Ähnlich zu: 410 (1973)

644	EU NA AU AS
Double Tanker	
Silowagen	
Pcs: 61	1971–1972

645	EU NA AU AS
Milk Float & Trailer	
Milchwagen mit Anhänger	
Pcs: 57	1971

646	EU NA AU AS
Mobile Site Office	
Lkw mit Bauwagen	
Pcs: 51	1971

647	EU NA AU AS
Lorry with Griders	
Sattelschlepper mit Stahlträgern	
Pcs: 52	1971

648	EU NA AU AS
Shell Service Station	
Shell Station	
Pcs: 55	1971–1973

680	EU NA AU AS
Low-loader and Crane	
Tieflader mit fahrbarem Kran	
Pcs: 61	1971

681	EU NA AU AS
Low-loader with 4 Wheel Excavator	
Tieflader mit Bagger, 4-achsig	
Pcs: 62	1971–1973

682	EU NA AU AS
Low-loader and Tractor	
Tieflader mit Frontlader	
Pcs: 57	1971–1973

683	EU NA AU AS
Articulated Lorry	
Thermowagen	
Pcs: 58	1971

795	EU NA AU AS
2 Large Baseplates, Red/Blue	
Bauplatten, Rot/Blau	
Pcs: 2	1971–1979

796	EU NA AU AS
2 Large Baseplates, Green/Yellow	
Bauplatten, Grün/Gelb	
Pcs: 2	1971–1979

797	EU NA AU AS
2 Large Baseplates, Grey/White	
Bauplatten, Grau/Weiß	
Pcs: 2	1971–1975

798	EU NA AU AS
2 Medium Baseplates, Green	
Bauplatten	
Pcs: 2	1971–1979

795	Similar to: 747 (1978), 842 (1980)	Ähnlich zu: 747 (1978), 842 (1980)
796	Similar to: 841 (1980), 746 (1978)	Ähnlich zu: 841 (1980), 746 (1978)

1972

130	EU NA AU AS
Wagon with Double Tippers	
Muldenkippwaggon	
Pcs: 20	1972–1975

Rating: 4 of 6 bricks; regions highlighted: EU

131	EU NA AU AS
Passenger Coach	
Personenwaggon	
Pcs: 67	1972–1974

Rating: 4 of 6 bricks; regions highlighted: EU

132	EU NA AU AS
Port Crane and Flat Waggon	
Torkran mit Güterwaggon	
Pcs: 60	1972–1974

Rating: 4 of 6 bricks; regions highlighted: EU

161	EU NA AU AS
Battery Wagon	
Batteriewagen	
Pcs: 8	1972–1976

Rating: 4 of 6 bricks; regions highlighted: EU

170	EU NA AU AS
Push-along Play Train	
Märchenzug zum Schieben	
Pcs: 93	1972–1974

Rating: 5 of 6 bricks; regions highlighted: EU

171	EU NA AU AS
Complete Train Set without Motor	
Güterzug mit 3 Waggons	
Pcs: 147	1972–1980

Rating: 3 of 6 bricks; regions highlighted: EU, AU

180	EU		
4.5V Train with 5 Wagons			
Güterzug mit 5 Waggons			
Pcs: 228	1972–1974		
Rating: 5 of 6			

181	EU		
Train Set with Motor, Signals			
Güterzug mit 3 Waggons			
Pcs: 148	1972–1975		
Rating: 4 of 6			

220	EU		
Play Book			
Baubuch			
Pcs: 1	1972		
Rating: 2 of 6			

262	EU NA AU		
Complete Children's Room Set			
Kinderzimmer			
Pcs: 259	1972–1973		
Rating: 5 of 6			

300	NA		
Jumbo Bricks			
Große Bausteine			
Pcs: 30	1972		
Rating: 5 of 6			

352	EU		
Windmill and Lorry			
Windmühle			
Pcs: 142	1972–1974		
Rating: 4 of 6			

353	EU NA		
Terrace House with Car & Garage			
Reihenhaus mit Pkw & Garage			
Pcs: 152	1972–1973		
Rating: 4 of 6			

354	EU NA AU		
Police Heliport			
Polizeistation			
Pcs: 168	1972–1975		
Rating: 3 of 6			

355	EU		
Town Centre Set with Roadways			
Stadt mit Gebäuden und Stadtplan			
Pcs: 336	1972–1974		
Rating: 5 of 6			

i	354	Similar to: 560 (1973)	Ähnlich zu: 560 (1973)

359	EU NA AU AS
Environment Plate	
Stadtplan	
Pcs: 1	1972–1974

378	EU NA AU AS
Tractor	
Traktor mit Frontlader und Kipplore	
Pcs: 36	1972–1974

379	EU NA AU AS
Car and Caravan	
Pkw mit Wohnwagen	
Pcs: 93	1972–1974

514	EU NA AU AS
Pre-School Building Set	
Bogensteine und 4er-Steinen	
Pcs: 17	1972–1974

606	EU NA AU AS
Tipper Lorry	
Lkw mit Kippvorrichtung	
Pcs: 22	1972

609	EU NA AU AS
Aeroplane	
Flugzeug	
Pcs: 28	1972–1973

649	EU NA AU AS
Low-loader with Excavator	
Sattelschlepper mit Bagger	
Pcs: 35	1972–1973

650	EU NA AU AS
Car with Trailer and Racing Car	
Pkw mit Rennwagen	
Pcs: 40	1972–1973

651	EU NA AU AS
Tow Truck and Car	
Kranwagen mit Pkw	
Pcs: 30	1972–1974

652 — EU NA AU

Fork Lift Truck and Trailer

Gabelstapler mit Hänger

Pcs: 42 | 1972–1974

684 — EU

Low-loader with Fork Lift Truck

Sattelschlepper mit Gabelstapler

Pcs: 52 | 1972–1973

685 — EU

Truck with Trailer

Lkw mit Anhänger

Pcs: 51 | 1972–1974

724 — EU

Locomotive, Crane and Wagon

12V Diesellok mit 2 Waggons

Pcs: 155 | 1972–1974

791 — EU

Red Storage Box

Tragebox, rot

Pcs: 1 | 1972–1983

792 — EU

White Storage Box

Tragebox, weiß

Pcs: 1 | 1972–1974

793 — EU

Blue Storage Box

Tragebox, blau

Pcs: 1 | 1972–1975

794 — EU

Yellow Storage Box

Tragebox, gelb

Pcs: 1 | 1972–1974

803 — EU

Gears, Bricks and Heavy Tires

Zahnräder, Steine, Gummireifen

Pcs: 163 | 1972–1973

652	Similar to: 450 (1973)	Ähnlich zu: 450 (1973)
685	Also without stickers (Rating: 5)	Gab es auch ohne Aufkleber (Rating: 5)

1512	EU NA AU AS	
Thinking with LEGO		
Denken mit LEGO		
Pcs: 250	1972–1974	

1513	EU NA AU AS	
Thinking with LEGO		
Denken mit LEGO		
Pcs: 900	1972–1974	

1550	EU NA AU AS	
Sterling Super Caravelle		
Sterling Super Caravelle		
Pcs: 50	1972–1976	Special

1551	EU NA AU AS	
Sterling Luggage Carrier		
Sterling Gepäckwagen		
Pcs: 49	1972–1976	Special

15102	EU NA AU AS	
Thinking with LEGO		
Denken mit LEGO		
Pcs: -	1972	

15103	EU NA AU AS	
Thinking with LEGO		
Denken mit LEGO		
Pcs: -	1972	

16197	EU NA AU AS	
Book “Thinking with LEGO”		
Spielbuch „Denken mit LEGO“		
Pcs: 1	1972	

16221	EU NA AU AS	
Thinking with LEGO / Rules		
Regelkärtchen und Spielpläne		
Pcs: -	1972	

i	1513	Exists with and without book	Gab es mit und ohne Buch
i	1550	Sterling Promo Set	Promoset von Sterling
i	1551	Sterling Promo Set	Promoset von Sterling
i	16197	Book for Sets: 1512 (1972), 1513 (1972)	Buch zu den Sets: 1512 (1972), 1513 (1972)

1973

1	EU NA AU AS	
Basic Set		
Grundbaukasten		
Pcs: 107	1973–1975	

2	EU NA AU AS	
Basic Set		
Grundbaukasten		
Pcs: 184	1973–1975	

3	EU NA AU AS	
Basic Set		
Grundbaukasten		
Pcs: 184	1973–1975	

4	EU NA AU AS	
Basic Set		
Grundbaukasten		
Pcs: 230	1973–1975	

5	EU NA AU AS	
Basic Set		
Grundbaukasten		
Pcs: 349	1973–1975	

5	EU NA AU AS	
Minitalia Set No. 5		
Minitalia Set Nr. 5		
Pcs: -	1973–1975	Special

i	3	Similar to: 115 (1973)	Ähnlich zu: 115 (1973)
i	4	Similar to: 125 (1974)	Ähnlich zu: 125 (1974)

6	**EU** NA AU AS
Basic Set	
Grundbaukasten	
Pcs: 349	1973–1975

7	**EU** NA AU AS
Basic Set	
Grundbaukasten	
Pcs: 415	1973–1975

8	**EU** NA AU AS
Basic Set	
Grundbaukasten	
Pcs: 663	1973–1975

010	EU **NA** AU AS
Pre-School Set	
Vorschulset	
Pcs: 17	1973–1974

020	EU **NA** AU AS
Building Set	
Grundkasten	
Pcs: -	1973–1974

030	EU **NA** AU AS
Building Set	
Grundkasten	
Pcs: 29	1973–1974

101	EU **NA** AU AS
Imagination Beginner Set 1	
Imagination Anfängerset 1	
Pcs: 298	1973

102	EU **NA** AU AS
Imagination Set 2	
Imaginationset 2	
Pcs: 414	1973

104	EU **NA** AU AS
Imagination Deluxe Set 4	
Imagination Luxusset 4	
Pcs: 737	1973

i	6	Similar to: 135 (1973)	Ähnlich zu: 135 (1973)
i	7	Similar to: 145 (1974)	Ähnlich zu: 145 (1974)
i	010	Similar to: 512 (1970)	Ähnlich zu: 512 (1970)

105	**NA**	
Building Set		
Grundkasten		
Pcs: 147	1973–1976	

112	**NA**	
40x40 Giant Base Plate		
40x40 Riesenbodenplatte		
Pcs: 2	1973	

115	**NA**	
Building Set		
Grundkasten		
Pcs: 186	1973–1976	

135	**NA**	
Building Set		
Grundkasten		
Pcs: 338	1973–1976	

270	**EU** **AU**	
Grandfather Clock, Chair, Table		
Standuhr, Sessel, Tisch, Lampe		
Pcs: 47	1973	

271	**EU** **AU**	
Baby's Cot and Cabinet		
Kinderbett und Nachttisch		
Pcs: 49	1973–1976	

272	**EU** **AU**	
Dressing Table with Mirror		
Frisierkommode mit Spiegel		
Pcs: 32	1973–1974	

273	**EU** **AU**	
Bureau		
Bücherschrank		
Pcs: 23	1973	

290	**EU** **AU**	
Dining Suite		
Esstisch mit 4 Stühlen		
Pcs: 114	1973	

i	Set	English	Deutsch
i	115	Similar to: 3 (1973)	Ähnlich zu: 3 (1973)
i	135	Similar to: 6 (1973)	Ähnlich zu: 6 (1973)

291	**EU** NA **AU** AS
Blackboard and School Desk	
Schreibtisch mit Stuhl und Tafel	
Pcs: 88	1973–1974

292	**EU** NA **AU** AS
Kitchen Sink and Cupboards	
Spültisch mit Geschirrschrank	
Pcs: 51	1973

293	**EU** NA **AU** AS
Piano	
Klavier mit Klavierbank und Noten	
Pcs: 90	1973–1976

310	**EU** NA AU AS
Tug	
Fischerboot	
Pcs: 46	1973–1975

311	**EU** **NA** AU AS
Ferry	
Frachtschiff	
Pcs: 83	1973–1975

312	**EU** NA AU AS
Tanker	
Tanker	
Pcs: 111	1973–1975

356	**EU** **NA** **AU** AS
Swiss Villa	
Ferienhaus mit Fensterläden	
Pcs: 150	1973–1975

357	**EU** **NA** **AU** AS
Fire Station	
Feuerwache	
Pcs: 242	1973–1975

358	**EU** NA AU AS
Rocket Base	
Raketenstation	
Pcs: 276	1973–1974

i	Set	Similar to	Ähnlich zu
i	356	Similar to: 540 (1973)	Ähnlich zu: 540 (1973)
i	357	Similar to: 570 (1973)	Ähnlich zu: 570 (1973)
i	382	Similar to: 710 (1973)	Ähnlich zu: 710 (1973)

381	EU
Lorry and Fork Lift Truck	
Pritschenwagen mit Gabelstapler	
Pcs: 80	1973–1975

382	EU NA AU
Breakdown Truck and Car	
Abschleppwagen mit Pkw	
Pcs: 92	1973–1975

383	EU NA AU
Low-loader and Excavator	
Tieflader mit Hochlöffelbagger	
Pcs: 103	1973–1975

384	EU NA AU
London Bus/Double Decker Bus	
Doppeldeckeromnibus	
Pcs: 111	1973–1976

410	NA
Payloader	
Frontlader	
Pcs: 28	1973–1975

420	EU NA
Police Car	
Polizeiauto	
Pcs: 19	1973–1975

450	EU NA
Fork Lift	
Gabelstapler	
Pcs: 42	1973–1975

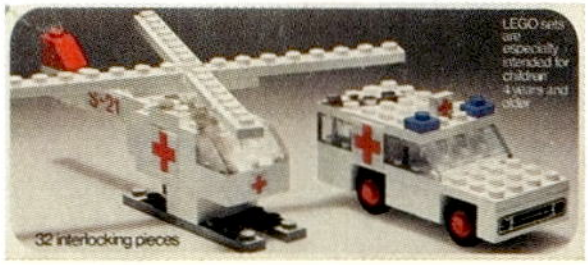

460	EU NA
Rescue Units	
Krankenwagen mit Hubschrauber	
Pcs: 37	1973–1975

515	EU
Building Set	
Steine & Fahrgestelle	
Pcs: 31	1973–1974

i	383	Similar to: 730 (1973)	Ähnlich zu: 730 (1973)
i	384	Similar to: 760 (1975)	Ähnlich zu: 760 (1975)
i	410	Similar to: 604 (1971)	Ähnlich zu: 604 (1971)
i	420	Similar to: 611 (1973)	Ähnlich zu: 611 (1973)
i	450	Similar to: 652 (1972)	Ähnlich zu: 652 (1972)
i	460	Similar to: 653 (1973)	Ähnlich zu: 653 (1973)

1973

ⓘ 540	EU **NA** AU AS
Swiss Villa	
Italienische Villa	
Pcs: 150	1973–1975

ⓘ 545	EU **NA** AU AS
Conveyor Station	
Schotterwerk mit Förderanlage	
Pcs: 164	1973–1975

ⓘ 560	EU **NA** AU AS
Police Heliport	
Polizeistation	
Pcs: 169	1973–1975

ⓘ 570	EU **NA** AU AS
Fire House	
Feuerwache	
Pcs: 242	1973–1976

610	**EU** NA AU AS
Vintage Car	
Oldtimer	
Pcs: 39	1973–1974

ⓘ 611	**EU** **NA** **AU** AS
Police Car	
Polizeiauto	
Pcs: 19	1973–1975

ⓘ 653	**EU** **NA** **AU** AS
Ambulance and Helicopter	
Krankenwagen mit Hubschrauber	
Pcs: 37	1973–1976

654	**EU** NA AU AS
Crane Lorry	
Lkw mit Kran	
Pcs: 34	1973–1974

655	**EU** NA AU AS
Mobile Hydraulic Joist	
Lkw mit Arbeitsbühne	
Pcs: 33	1973–1975

ⓘ	540	Similar to: 356 (1973)	Ähnlich zu: 356 (1973)
ⓘ	545	Similar to: 351 (1971)	Ähnlich zu: 351 (1971)
ⓘ	560	Similar to: 354 (1972)	Ähnlich zu: 354 (1972)
ⓘ	570	Similar to: 357 (1973)	Ähnlich zu: 357 (1973)
ⓘ	611	Similar to: 420 (1973)	Ähnlich zu: 420 (1973)
ⓘ	653	Similar to: 460 (1973)	Ähnlich zu: 460 (1973)

686	EU NA AU AS
Tipper Trucks and Loader	
Trecker mit 2 Loren und Bagger	
Pcs: 70	1973–1975

687	EU NA AU AS
Caravelle Plane	
Jet	
Pcs: 49	1973–1975

688	EU NA AU AS
Shell Tank Truck	
Shell Tanklastzug	
Pcs: 63	1973–1975

710	EU NA AU AS
Wrecker with Car	
Abschleppwagen mit Pkw	
Pcs: 92	1973–1978

730	EU NA AU AS
Steam Shovel with Carrier	
Sattelschlepper mit Bagger	
Pcs: 103	1973–1978

900	EU NA AU AS
Universal Motor Set	
Universal-Motor	
Pcs: 24	1973–1975

930	EU NA AU AS
Assorted Red Bricks	
Steinesortiment, rot	
Pcs: 45	1973–1979

931	EU NA AU AS
Assorted White Bricks	
Steinesortiment, weiß	
Pcs: 45	1973–1979

932	EU NA AU AS
Assorted Blue and Yellow Bricks	
Steinesortiment, blau und gelb	
Pcs: 45	1973–1979

i	710	Similar to: 382 (1973)	Ähnlich zu: 382 (1973)
i	730	Similar to: 383 (1973)	Ähnlich zu: 383 (1973)
i	900	Similar to: 103 (1969)	Ähnlich zu: 103 (1969)

933 EU NA AU AS

Windows and Doors	
Türen und Fenster	
Pcs: 38	1973–1979

934 EU NA AU AS

Red Roof Bricks	
45° Dachsteine, rot	
Pcs: 55	1973–1979

935 EU NA AU AS

Red Roof Bricks	
22° Dachsteine, rot	
Pcs: 43	1973–1979

936 EU NA AU AS

Large and Small Wheels	
Große und kleine Räder	
Pcs: 20	1973–1979

937 EU NA AU AS

Fences and Doors	
Zäune und Türen	
Pcs: 34	1973–1979

938 EU NA AU AS

Plates, Hinges and Turntables	
Platten, Scharniere und Drehteller	
Pcs: 17	1973–1976

939 EU NA AU AS

Road Signs, Flags and Trees	
Schilder, Fahnen und Bäume	
Pcs: 17	1973–1979

940 EU NA AU AS

Road Signs, Flags and Trees	
Schilder, Fahnen und Bäume	
Pcs: 19	1973–1979

i	939	Similar to: 940 (1973)	Ähnlich zu: 940 (1973)
i	940	Similar to: 939 (1973)	Ähnlich zu: 939 (1973)

1974

11	EU NA AU AS
Minitalia Set No. 11	
Minitalia Set Nr. 11	
Pcs: 31	1974–1976

12	EU NA AU AS
Minitalia Set No. 12	
Minitalia Set Nr. 12	
Pcs: -	1974–1976

13	EU NA AU AS
Minitalia Set No. 13	
Minitalia Set Nr. 13	
Pcs: -	1974–1976

14	EU NA AU AS
Minitalia Set No. 14	
Minitalia Set Nr. 14	
Pcs: -	1974–1976

15	EU NA AU AS
Minitalia Set No. 15	
Minitalia Set Nr. 15	
Pcs: 157	1974–1976

16	EU NA AU AS
Minitalia Set No. 16	
Minitalia Set Nr. 16	
Pcs: -	1974–1976

1974

17	**EU** NA AU AS
Minitalia Set No. 17	
Minitalia Set Nr. 17	
Pcs: -	1974–1976

30	**EU** NA AU AS
Minitalia Set No. 30	
Minitalia Set Nr. 30	
Pcs: 26	1974–1976

31	**EU** NA AU AS
Minitalia Set No. 31	
Minitalia Set Nr. 31	
Pcs: -	1974–1976

32	**EU** NA AU AS
Minitalia Set No. 32	
Minitalia Set Nr. 32	
Pcs: -	1974–1976

125	EU **NA** AU AS
Building Set	
Grundkasten	
Pcs: 233	1974

145	EU **NA** AU AS
Building Set	
Grundkasten	
Pcs: 415	1974

196	EU **NA** AU AS
Antique Car	
Auto mit Chauffeur und Frau	
Pcs: 115	1974–1978

200	**EU** **NA** AU AS
Family	
Familie	
Pcs: 78	1974–1977

221	**EU** NA AU AS
Idea Book	
Baubuch	
Pcs: 1	1974–1975

i	125	Similar to: 4 (1973)	Ähnlich zu: 4 (1973)
i	145	Similar to: 7 (1973)	Ähnlich zu: 7 (1973)

243	**EU** NA AU AS	
Book "Mach mehr aus LEGO"		
Buch „Mach mehr aus LEGO"		
Pcs: 1	1974–1976	
Rating: 3/6		

250	**EU** **NA** **AU** AS	
Aeroplane and Pilot		
Flugzeug mit einem Piloten		
Pcs: 89	1974–1975	
Rating: 2/6		

251	**EU** NA **AU** AS	
Windmill with Miller and his Wife		
Windmühle mit 2 Figuren		
Pcs: 90	1974	
Rating: 3/6		

252	**EU** NA **AU** AS	
Locomotive with Driver & Passenger		
Lokomotive mit 2 Figuren		
Pcs: 118	1974–1975	
Rating: 3/6		

263	**EU** NA **AU** AS	
Complete Kitchen with 2 figures		
Küche mit 2 Figuren		
Pcs: 174	1974–1977	
Rating: 3/6		

264	**EU** NA **AU** AS	
Livingroom with 2 Figures		
Wohnzimmer mit 2 Figuren		
Pcs: 238	1974–1977	
Rating: 3/6		

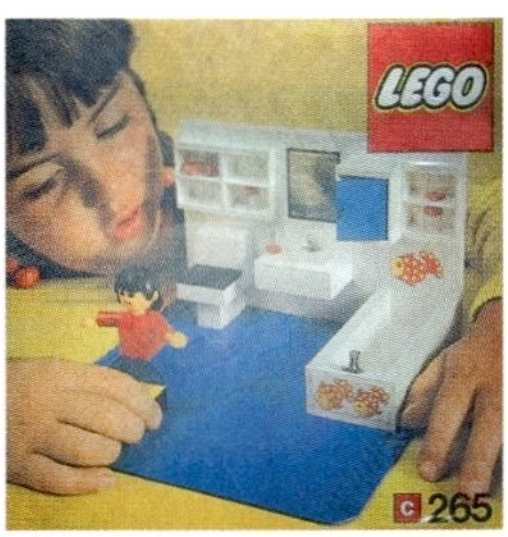

265	**EU** NA **AU** AS	
Complete Bathroom with 1 Figure		
Badezimmer mit 1 Figur		
Pcs: 148	1974–1977	
Rating: 3/6		

266	**EU** NA **AU** AS	
Children's Room		
Kinderzimmer		
Pcs: 146	1974–1976	
Rating: 3/6		

274	**EU** NA **AU** AS	
Colour TV and Chair		
Fernseher mit Tisch und Sessel		
Pcs: 46	1974–1976	
Rating: 3/6		

i	250	Similar to: 195 (1975)	Ähnlich zu: 195 (1975)

275 EU NA AU AS
Table and Chairs
Tisch mit zwei Stühlen
Pcs: 63 | 1974–1976

294 EU NA AU AS
Wall Unit
Anbauschrank mit Radio
Pcs: 57 | 1974–1976

295 EU NA AU AS
Secretary's Desk
Büro
Pcs: 85 | 1974–1976

360 EU NA AU AS
Gravel Quarry
Kieswerk mit Drehkran
Pcs: 212 | 1974–1976

361 EU NA AU AS
Tea Garden Café with Baker's Van
Café
Pcs: 211 | 1974–1976

612 EU NA AU AS
Tipper Truck
Zweiseitenkipper
Pcs: 23 | 1974–1976

613 EU NA AU AS
Biplane
Doppeldecker
Pcs: 18 | 1974–1975

614 EU NA AU AS
Excavator
Planierraupe
Pcs: 31 | 1974–1976

656 EU NA AU AS
Car and Caravan
Pkw mit Wohnwagen
Pcs: 49 | 1974–1976

ⓘ	Set	English	Deutsch
ⓘ	360	Similar to: 580 (1975)	Ähnlich zu: 580 (1975)
ⓘ	612	Similar to: 435 (1976)	Ähnlich zu: 435 (1976)
ⓘ	613	Similar to: 430 (1975)	Ähnlich zu: 430 (1975)

657 — EU

Executive Jet

Düsenflugzeug

Pcs: 37 | 1974–1975

658 — EU

Fire Engine

Löschfahrzeug mit Leiter

Pcs: 38 | 1974

689 — EU NA AU

Truck & Shovel

Lkw mit Greifbagger

Pcs: 46 | 1974–1975

690 — EU NA AU

Shell Station

Shell Tankstelle

Pcs: 73 | 1974–1976

691 — EU NA AU

Rescue Helicopter

Lastenhubschrauber

Pcs: 62 | 1974–1976

723 — EU

Diesel Locomotive

Rangierlokomotive

Pcs: 94 | 1974–1976

725 — EU

12V Freight Train and Track

12V Elektrozug mit 4 Waggons

Pcs: 317 | 1974–1980

741 — EU

12V Transformer

12V Transformator

Pcs: 1 | 1974–1982

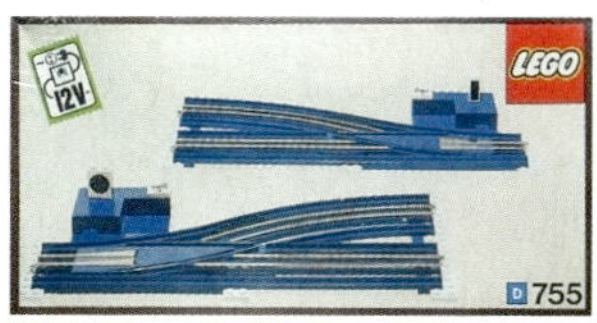

755 — EU

Left and Right Switches

Links- und Rechtsweiche

Pcs: 12 | 1974–1980

i	689	Similar to: 490 (1975)	Ähnlich zu: 490 (1975)
i	691	Similar to: 480 (1975)	Ähnlich zu: 480 (1975)
i	723	Re-release with Stickers (DB)	Neuauflage mit Aufklebern (DB)

756 EU NA AU AS
Electric Crossing
Elektrische Kreuzung

Pcs: 5	1974–1980	

789 EU NA AU AS
Suitcase with Trays, red
Koffer mit Einsatz, rot

Pcs: 1	1974	

790 EU NA AU AS
Suitcase with Trays, Blue
Koffer mit Einsatz, blau

Pcs: 1	1974	

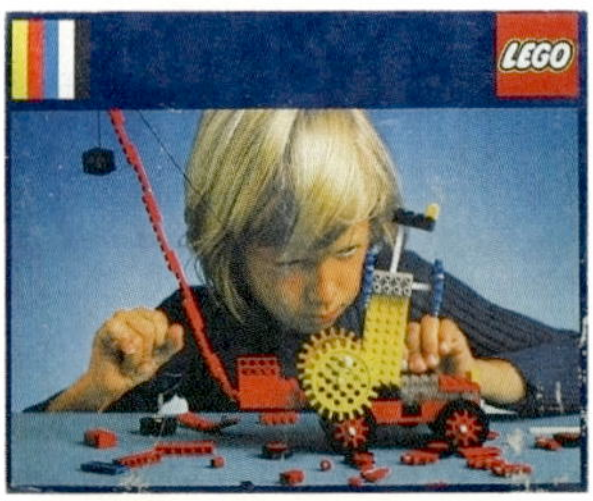

810 EU NA AU AS
Gear Set
Zahnräder und Gummireifen

Pcs: 111	1974–1975	

811 EU NA AU AS
Gear Set
Zahnräder und Kettenglieder

Pcs: 173	1974–1975	

812 EU NA AU AS
Gears, Axels & Bricks
Räder und Gelenke

Pcs: 122	1974–1976	

813 EU NA AU AS
Tractor with Trailer
Traktor mit Anhänger

Pcs: 102	1974–1975	

941 EU NA AU AS
Assorted Black and Transparent Bricks
Steinesortiment (schwarz, transp.)

Pcs: 48	1974–1976	

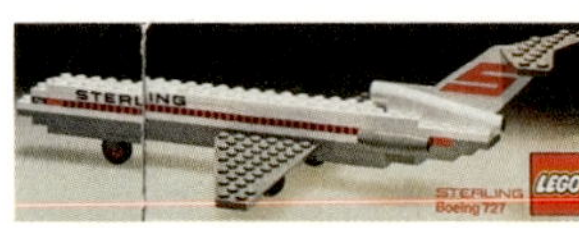

1552 EU NA AU AS
Sterling Boeing 727
Sterling Boeing 727

Pcs: 46	1974–1979	Special

1650	EU NA AU AS	
Maersk Line Container Ship		
Maersk Line Containerschiff		
Pcs: 219	1974–1975	Special

1975

i 075	EU **NA** AU AS
Pre-School Set	
Vorschulset	
Pcs: 16	1975–1976

i 077	EU **NA** AU AS
Pre-School Set	
Vorschulset	
Pcs: 20	1975–1976

i 078	EU **NA** AU AS
Pre-School Set	
Vorschulset	
Pcs: 32	1975

i 88	EU **NA** AU AS
Building Toy	
Kleiner Grundkasten	
Pcs: 88	1975

i 133	**EU** NA AU AS
Locomotive	
Lokomotive	
Pcs: 75	1975–1976

i 134	**EU** NA AU AS
Mobile Crane and Waggon	
2 Waggons	
Pcs: 59	1975–1976

136	EU, AU	
Tanker Waggon		
Shell Wagen		
Pcs: 83	1975–1976	
Rating: 3/6		

137	EU	
Passenger Sleeping Car		
Schlafwagen		
Pcs: 84	1975–1976	
Rating: 3/6		

148	EU, AU	
Central Station		
Bahnhofsgebäude		
Pcs: 273	1975–1980	
Rating: 4/6		

182	EU, AU	
4.5V Train Set with Signal		
4,5V Passagierzug		
Pcs: 374	1975–1980	
Rating: 3/6		

190	NA	
Farm Set		
Bauernhof		
Pcs: 526	1975–1978	
Rating: 3/6		

195	EU, NA	
Airplane		
Flugzeug		
Pcs: 68	1975–1978	
Rating: 3/6		

253	EU, AU	
Helicopter and Pilot		
Hubschrauber mit Pilot		
Pcs: 49	1975–1976	
Rating: 3/6		

254	EU, NA, AU	
Family		
Mutter u. Tochter m. Kinderwagen		
Pcs: 92	1975–1977	
Rating: 3/6		

255	EU, NA, AU	
Farming Scene		
Bauernhoffiguren		
Pcs: 120	1975–1976	
Rating: 3/6		

i	Set	English	Deutsch
i	195	Similar to: 250 (1974)	Ähnlich zu: 250 (1974)
i	254	Similar to: 194 (1976)	Ähnlich zu: 194 (1976)

362	EU NA AU AS
Windmill	
Bockmühle mit Transporter	
Pcs: 204	1975–1976

363	EU NA AU AS
Hospital with Figures	
Unfallstation mit Rettungswagen	
Pcs: 220	1975–1977

364	EU NA AU AS
Harbour Scene	
Hafen mit Schiffen	
Pcs: 515	1975–1976

365	EU NA AU AS
Wild West Scene	
Westernstadt	
Pcs: 589	1975–1976

367	EU NA AU AS
Moon Landing	
Mondlandefähre	
Pcs: 375	1975–1977

390	EU NA AU AS
1913 Cadillac	
1913 Cadillac	
Pcs: 200	1975–1978

391	EU NA AU AS
1926 Renault	
1926 Renault	
Pcs: 236	1975–1977

392	EU NA AU AS
Formula 1	
Formel 1-Rennwagen	
Pcs: 216	1975–1977

430	EU NA AU AS
Biplane	
Doppeldecker	
Pcs: 18	1975–1978

i	362	Similar to: 550 (1976)	Ähnlich zu: 550 (1976)
i	363	Similar to: 555 (1976)	Ähnlich zu: 555 (1976)
i	367	Similar to: 565 (1976)	Ähnlich zu: 565 (1976)
i	430	Similar to: 613 (1974)	Ähnlich zu: 613 (1974)

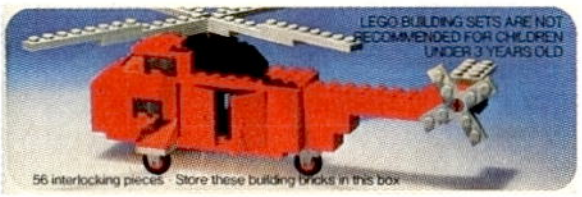

480	NA
Rescue Helicopter	
Lastenhubschrauber	
Pcs: 62	1975–1978

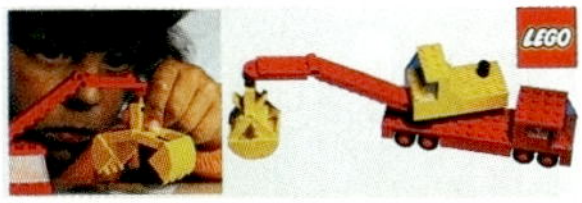

490	NA
Mobile Crane	
Lkw mit Greifbagger	
Pcs: 46	1975–1978

516	EU
Bricks and Half Bricks	
Acht- und Vierknopfsteine	
Pcs: 16	1975–1976

517	EU
Bricks, Half Bricks and Arches	
Acht-, Vierknopf- und Bogensteine	
Pcs: 14	1975–1976

518	EU
Bricks, Half Bricks and Trolley	
Acht- u. Vierknopfsteine, Fahrgestell	
Pcs: 15	1975–1976

519	EU
Bricks, Half Bricks, Arches, Trolley	
Steine, Bogensteine, Fahrgestell	
Pcs: 22	1975

520	EU
Bricks, Halfbricks, 2 Trolleys	
Acht-, Vierknopfsteine, 2 Fahrgestelle	
Pcs: 20	1975–1976

521	EU, NA, AU
All Bricks in all Colours	
Alle Steine in allen Farben	
Pcs: 30	1975–1976

580	NA
Brick Yard	
Kieswerk	
Pcs: 217	1975–1978

ⓘ	Set		
ⓘ	480	Similar to: 691 (1974)	Ähnlich zu: 691 (1974)
ⓘ	490	Similar to: 689 (1974)	Ähnlich zu: 689 (1974)
ⓘ	580	Similar to: 360 (1974)	Ähnlich zu: 360 (1974)

ⓘ 615 EU NA AU AS
Fork Lift with Driver
Gabelstapler
Pcs: 21 | 1975–1977

ⓘ 659 EU NA AU AS
Police Patrol with Policemen
Funk- und Verkehrstreife
Pcs: 41 | 1975–1977

ⓘ 660 EU NA AU AS
Car with Plane Transporter
Transporter für Sportflugzeuge
Pcs: 41 | 1975–1976

ⓘ 692 EU NA AU AS
Road Repair Crew
Transporter mit Planierraupe
Pcs: 57 | 1975–1977

ⓘ 693 EU NA AU AS
Fire Engine with Firemen
Feuerwehr mit Leiter
Pcs: 72 | 1975–1976

ⓘ 694 EU NA AU AS
Transport Truck
Sattelschlepper (Container)
Pcs: 65 | 1975–1976

ⓘ 760 EU NA AU AS
London Bus
London-Bus
Pcs: 111 | 1975–1978

ⓘ 814 EU NA AU AS
Tractor
Traktor mit Kreiselmäher
Pcs: 87 | 1975

ⓘ	615	Similar to: 425 (1976)	Ähnlich zu: 425 (1976)
ⓘ	659	Similar to: 445 (1976)	Ähnlich zu: 445 (1976)
ⓘ	692	Similar to: 492 (1977)	Ähnlich zu: 492 (1977)
ⓘ	693	Similar to: 485 (1976)	Ähnlich zu: 485 (1976)
ⓘ	760	Similar to: 384 (1973)	Ähnlich zu: 384 (1973)

1976

10	EU NA AU AS
Universal Building Set	
Universalkasten	
Pcs: 152	1976–1980

20	EU NA AU AS
Universal Building Set	
Universalkasten	
Pcs: 302	1976–1980

30	EU NA AU AS
Universal Building Set	
Universalkasten	
Pcs: 258	1976–1980

40	EU NA AU AS
Universal Building Set	
Universalkasten	
Pcs: 258	1976–1980

50	EU NA AU AS
Universal Building Set	
Universalkasten	
Pcs: 377	1976–1980

074	EU NA AU AS
Pre-School Set	
Vorschulset	
Pcs: 20	1976

i	10	Similar to: 110 (1977)	Ähnlich zu: 110 (1977)
i	20	Similar to: 111 (1977)	Ähnlich zu: 111 (1977)
i	30	Similar to: 112 (1977)	Ähnlich zu: 112 (1977)
i	40	Similar to: 113 (1977)	Ähnlich zu: 113 (1977)
i	50	Similar to: 114 (1977)	Ähnlich zu: 114 (1977)

1976

080	EU NA AU AS
Police Station	
Polizeistation	
Pcs: 23	1976

081	EU NA AU AS
Train Station	
Bahnhof	
Pcs: 51	1976

082	EU NA AU AS
LEGOVILLE	
LEGOVILLE	
Pcs: 52	1976

107	EU NA AU AS
Universal Motor	
4,5V Motor mit Batteriekasten	
Pcs: 31	1976–1985

108	EU NA AU AS
4.5V Battery Box	
4,5V Batteriekasten	
Pcs: 1	1976

146	EU NA AU AS
Level Crossing	
Bahnübergang	
Pcs: 64	1976–1980

147	EU NA AU AS
Refrigerated Wagon with Forklift	
Kühlwagen mit Gabelstapler	
Pcs: 107	1976–1980

149	EU NA AU AS
Fuel Refinery	
Füllstation für Tanklastwagen	
Pcs: 327	1976–1978

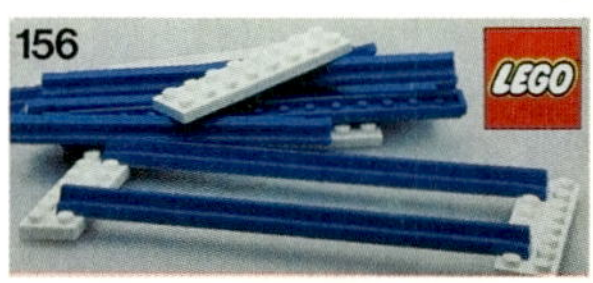

156	EU NA AU AS
Straight Tracks	
Gerade Schienenteile u. Schwellen	
Pcs: 25	1976–1980

i			
i	080	Similar to: 522 (1977)	Ähnlich zu: 522 (1977)
i	081	Similar to: 523 (1977)	Ähnlich zu: 523 (1977)
i	082	Similar to: 524 (1977)	Ähnlich zu: 524 (1977)
i	107	Similar to: 901 (1976)	Ähnlich zu: 901 (1976)
i	156	Similar to: 150 (1966)	Ähnlich zu: 150 (1966)

183	**EU** NA AU AS
Train Set with Motor and Signal	
Lok mit Batterie- und Kranwagen	
Pcs: 186	1976–1977

194	EU **NA** AU AS
Family	
Mutter u. Tochter m. Kinderwagen	
Pcs: 89	1976–1978

197	EU **NA** AU AS
Farm Vehicle and Animals	
Bauernhoffiguren	
Pcs: 120	1976–1978

210	**EU** **NA** **AU** AS
Cowboys	
Zwei Cowboys	
Pcs: 39	1976–1978

211	**EU** **NA** **AU** AS
Mother and Baby with Dog	
Mutter mit Kind und Hund	
Pcs: 44	1976–1977

212	**EU** NA **AU** AS
Scooter	
Vater mit Kind und Motorroller	
Pcs: 41	1976–1978

222	**EU** **NA** **AU** AS
Idea Book	
Baubuch	
Pcs: 1	1976–1980

256	**EU** **NA** **AU** AS
Police Officers and Motorcycle	
Polizeistreife mit Motorrad	
Pcs: 85	1976–1978

258	**EU** NA **AU** AS
Zoo with Baseboard	
Zoo	
Pcs: 474	1976–1977

i	194	Similar to: 254 (1975)	Ähnlich zu: 254 (1975)
i	210	Similar to: 198 (1977)	Ähnlich zu: 198 (1977)
i	212	Similar to: 199 (1977)	Ähnlich zu: 199 (1977)
i	256	Similar to: 192 (1977)	Ähnlich zu: 192 (1977)

314	EU NA AU AS
Police Boat	
Wasserschutzboot	
Pcs: 53	1976–1981

315	EU NA AU AS
Container Ship	
Container-Frachter	
Pcs: 86	1976–1977

368	EU NA AU AS
Taxi Station	
Garage mit Taxi und Tanksäule	
Pcs: 156	1976–1978

369	EU NA AU AS
Coast Guard Station	
Rettungsstation mit Helikopter	
Pcs: 275	1976–1978

370	EU NA AU AS
Police Headquarters	
Autobahn-Polizei	
Pcs: 280	1976–1978

385	EU NA AU AS
Jeep CJ-5	
Jeep mit Hänger	
Pcs: 57	1976–1977

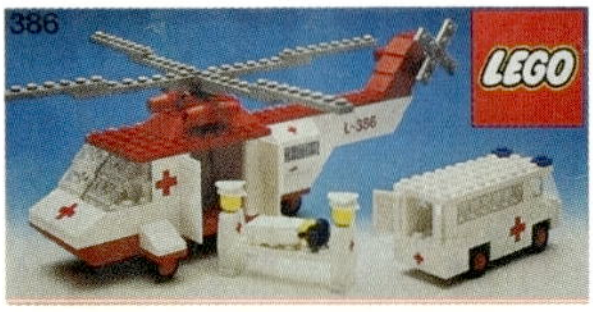

386	EU NA AU AS
Helicopter and Ambulance	
Hubschrauber mit Krankenwagen	
Pcs: 132	1976–1979

387	EU NA AU AS
Excavator and Dumper	
Planierraupe und Hinterkipper	
Pcs: 159	1976–1979

393	EU NA AU AS
Norton Motorcycle	
Motorrad „Norton“	
Pcs: 131	1976–1977

314	Similar to: 709 (1976)	Ähnlich zu: 709 (1976)
369	Similar to: 575 (1978)	Ähnlich zu: 575 (1978)
370	Similar to: 585 (1976)	Ähnlich zu: 585 (1976)
385	Similar to: 711 (1977)	Ähnlich zu: 711 (1977)
386	Similar to: 770 (1976)	Ähnlich zu: 770 (1976)
387	Similar to: 780 (1976)	Ähnlich zu: 780 (1976)

394	EU AU
Harley-Davidson 1000cc	
Motorrad „Harley-Davidson“	
Pcs: 151	1976–1978

395	EU AU
1909 Rolls-Royce	
1909 Rolls-Royce	
Pcs: 288	1976–1978

396	EU AU
Thatcher Perkins Locomotive	
Western-Lok „Thatcher Perkins“	
Pcs: 438	1976–1977

425	NA
Fork Lift	
Gabelstapler	
Pcs: 21	1976–1978

435	NA
Tipper Truck	
Seitenkipper	
Pcs: 23	1976–1978

445	NA
Police Units	
Funk- und Verkehrsstreife	
Pcs: 49	1976–1978

455	NA
Lear Jet	
Lear Jet	
Pcs: 46	1976–1978

485	NA
Fire Truck	
Feuerwehr mit Leiter	
Pcs: 72	1976–1978

530	EU AU
Puppy	
Hund	
Pcs: 10	1976–1978

i	396	With poster	Mit Poster
i	425	Similar to: 615 (1975)	Ähnlich zu: 615 (1975)
i	435	Similar to: 612 (1974)	Ähnlich zu: 612 (1974)
i	445	Similar to: 659 (1975)	Ähnlich zu: 659 (1975)
i	485	Similar to: 693 (1975)	Ähnlich zu: 693 (1975)
i	530	Similar to: 061 (1978)	Ähnlich zu: 061 (1978)

531	**EU** NA **AU** AS	
Elephants		
Elefanten		
Pcs: 20	1976–1977	

532	**EU** NA **AU** AS	
Ducks		
Entenfamilie		
Pcs: 20	1976–1978	

550	EU **NA** AU AS	
Windmill		
Windmühle		
Pcs: 211	1976–1978	

555	EU **NA** AU AS	
Hospital		
Krankenhaus		
Pcs: 230	1976–1978	

565	EU **NA** AU AS	
Moon Landing		
Mondlandefähre		
Pcs: 375	1976–1978	

585	EU **NA** AU AS	
Police Headquarters		
Autobahnpolizei		
Pcs: 300	1976–1978	

616	**EU** NA AU AS	
Cargo Ship		
Küstenmotorschiff		
Pcs: 31	1976	

617	**EU** NA AU AS	
Cowboys		
Cowboys mit Pferd und Gatter		
Pcs: 41	1976–1977	

661	**EU** **NA** **AU** AS	
Spirit of St. Louis		
Spirit of St. Louis		
Pcs: 50	1976–1977	

i	Set	English	Deutsch
i	532	Similar to: 063 (1978)	Ähnlich zu: 063 (1978)
i	550	Similar to: 362 (1975)	Ähnlich zu: 362 (1975)
i	555	Similar to: 363 (1975)	Ähnlich zu: 363 (1975)
i	565	Similar to: 367 (1975)	Ähnlich zu: 367 (1975)
i	585	Similar to: 370 (1976)	Ähnlich zu: 370 (1976)
i	661	Similar to: 456 (1977)	Ähnlich zu: 456 (1977)

662 — EU NA AU AS

Dumper Lorry		
Hinterkipper mit Drehschemel		
Pcs: 27	1976–1977	

695 — EU NA AU AS

Racing Car		
Formel 1-Rennwagen		
Pcs: 67	1976–1977	

696 — EU NA AU AS

Bus Stop		
Bushaltestelle		
Pcs: 80	1976–1977	

697 — EU NA AU AS

Stagecoach		
Postkutsche mit 2 Pferden		
Pcs: 83	1976–1977	

726 — EU NA AU AS

12V Western Train		
12V Westernzug		
Pcs: 291	1976–1977	

770 — EU NA AU AS

Rescue Set		
Hubschrauber mit Krankenwagen		
Pcs: 143	1976–1978	

780 — EU NA AU AS

Road Construction Set		
Planierraupe und Hinterkipper		
Pcs: 159	1976–1978	

901 — EU NA AU AS

4.5V Universal Motor		
4,5V Motor mit Batteriekasten		
Pcs: 31	1976–1984	

910 — EU NA AU AS

Universal Building Set		
Universalkasten f. Fortgeschrittene		
Pcs: 268	1976–1979	

i	Set	English	Deutsch
i	695	Similar to: 491 (1977)	Ähnlich zu: 491 (1977)
i	770	Similar to: 386 (1976)	Ähnlich zu: 386 (1976)
i	780	Similar to: 387 (1976)	Ähnlich zu: 387 (1976)
i	901	Similar to: 107 (1976)	Ähnlich zu: 107 (1976)
i	910	Similar to: 400 (1977)	Ähnlich zu: 400 (1977)

1976

911	EU
Universal Building Set	
Universalkasten f. Fortgeschrittene	
Pcs: 396	1976–1979

912	EU
Universal Building Set	
Universalkasten f. Fortgeschrittene	
Pcs: 437	1976–1979

1560	EU	
Lufthansa Boeing 727		
Lufthansa Passagierflugzeug		
Pcs: 45	1976–1979	Special

1561	EU	
Lufthansa Flight Crew		
Lufthansa Bordpersonal		
Pcs: 59	1976–1979	Special

1562	EU	
Lufthansa Double-decker		
Lufthansa Doppeldecker		
Pcs: 51	1976–1979	Special

1601	EU NA	
Conveyance		
Spedition		
Pcs: 181	1976	Special

	EU	
Windmill		
Windmühle		
Pcs: 119	1976	Special

	EU	
House 1		
Haus 1		
Pcs: 143	1976	Special

	EU	
House 2		
Haus 2		
Pcs: 140	1976	Special

i	911	Similar to: 402 (1977)	Ähnlich zu: 402 (1977)
i	912	Similar to: 404 (1977)	Ähnlich zu: 404 (1977)
i		Weetabix Promo; only in UK	Weetabix Promo; nur in UK

1977

2	EU NA AU AS	
Medium Basic Set		
Mittlerer Grundbaukasten		
Pcs: 128	1977–1979	Special

085	EU NA AU AS	
Racer		
Rennwagen		
Pcs: 4	1977–1979	

087	EU NA AU AS	
Taxi		
Taxi		
Pcs: 4	1977–1979	

088	EU NA AU AS	
Camping		
Pkw mit Wohnwagen		
Pcs: 9	1977–1979	

089	EU NA AU AS	
Mary's House		
Das Haus von Mary		
Pcs: 15	1977–1979	

110	EU NA AU AS	
Universal Building Set		
Universalkasten		
Pcs: 131	1977–1981	

085	Similar to: 533 (1977), 2401 (1984)	Ähnlich zu: 533 (1977), 2401 (1984)
087	Similar to: 535 (1977)	Ähnlich zu: 535 (1977)
088	Similar to: 537 (1977)	Ähnlich zu: 536 (1977)
089	Similar to: 537 (1977)	Ähnlich zu: 537 (1977)
110	Similar to: 10 (1976)	Ähnlich zu: 10 (1976)

111	Regions: EU
Universal Building Set	
Universalkasten	
Pcs: 156	1977–1981

112	Regions: NA
Universal Building Set	
Universalkasten	
Pcs: 195	1977–1982

113	Regions: EU
Universal Building Set	
Universalkasten	
Pcs: 264	1977–1981

114	Regions: NA
Universal Building Set	
Universalkasten	
Pcs: 379	1977–1981

157	Regions: EU, AU
Curved Track	
Gebogene Schienen u. Schwellen	
Pcs: 25	1977–1980

159	Regions: EU, AU
Crossover, Straight Rails	
Kreuzungen und Schienen	
Pcs: 30	1977–1980

162	Regions: EU, AU
Locomotive without Motor	
Lokomotive ohne Motor	
Pcs: 210	1977–1980

163	Regions: EU, AU
Cargo Wagon	
Waggons	
Pcs: 106	1977–1980

192	Regions: NA
Policemen	
Polizeistreife mit Motorrad	
Pcs: 85	1977–1978

111	Similar to: 20 (1976)	Ähnlich zu: 20 (1976)
112	Similar to: 30 (1976)	Ähnlich zu: 30 (1976)
113	Similar to: 40 (1976)	Ähnlich zu: 40 (1976)
114	Similar to: 50 (1976)	Ähnlich zu: 50 (1976)
157	Similar to: 151 (1966)	Ähnlich zu: 151 (1966)
192	Similar to: 256 (1976)	Ähnlich zu: 256 (1976)

198	EU **NA** AU AS	
Cowboys		
Zwei Cowboys		
Pcs: 39	1977	

199	EU **NA** AU AS	
Scooter		
Vater mit Kind und Motorroller		
Pcs: 41	1977	

213	**EU** NA **AU** AS	
Airplane Ride		
Propeller-Flugzeug mit 2 Figuren		
Pcs: 44	1977–1978	

214	**EU** NA **AU** AS	
Road Repair Crew		
Planierraupe und Bauarbeiter		
Pcs: 63	1977–1978	

215	**EU** **NA** **AU** AS	
Red Indians		
Indianer		
Pcs: 75	1977–1978	

217	**EU** NA AU AS	
Service Station		
Tankstelle		
Pcs: 210	1977–1978	

218	**EU** NA **AU** AS	
Firemen		
Feuerwehrfahrzeuge		
Pcs: 276	1977–1978	

225	EU **NA** AU AS	
Idea Book		
Baubuch		
Pcs: 1	1977–1980	

246	**EU** NA AU AS	
Santa with Sleigh and Reindeer		
Nikolaus mit Rentierschlitten		
Pcs: 70	1977–1980	Special

198	Similar to: 210 (1976)	Ähnlich zu: 210 (1976)
199	Similar to: 212 (1976)	Ähnlich zu: 212 (1976)
218	Similar to: 340 (1978)	Ähnlich zu: 340 (1978)

i 276	**EU** NA **AU** AS
Nurse	
Krankenschwester	
Pcs: 96	1977–1981

i 277	**EU** NA **AU** AS
Fireplace	
Kamin	
Pcs: 86	1977–1978

i 296	**EU** NA **AU** AS
Ladies' Hairdressers	
Damensalon	
Pcs: 166	1977–1981

i 371	**EU** **NA** **AU** AS
Seaplane	
Wasserflugzeug	
Pcs: 115	1977–1979

i 372	**EU** NA AU AS
Texas Rangers	
Texas Rangers	
Pcs: 259	1977–1978

i 373	**EU** NA **AU** AS
Offshore Rig with Fuel Tanker	
Bohrinsel mit Öltanker	
Pcs: 467	1977–1978

i 400	EU **NA** AU AS
Universal Building Set	
Universalkasten f. Fortgeschrittene	
Pcs: 290	1977–1979

i 402	EU **NA** AU AS
Universal Building Set	
Universalkasten f. Fortgeschrittene	
Pcs: 374	1977–1979

i 404	EU **NA** AU AS
Universal Building Set	
Universalkasten f. Fortgeschrittene	
Pcs: 482	1977–1979

i	371	Similar to: 712 (1977)	Ähnlich zu: 712 (1977)
i	400	Similar to: 910 (1976)	Ähnlich zu: 910 (1976)
i	402	Similar to: 911 (1976)	Ähnlich zu: 911 (1976)
i	404	Similar to: 912 (1976)	Ähnlich zu: 912 (1976)

ⓘ 456	EU **NA** AU AS
Spirit of St. Louis	
Spirit of St. Louis	
Pcs: 50	1977

ⓘ 491	EU **NA** AU AS
Formula 1 Racer	
Formel 1-Rennwagen	
Pcs: 67	1977

ⓘ 492	EU **NA** AU AS
Truck & Payloader	
Transporter mit Planierraupe	
Pcs: 57	1977

ⓘ 522	**EU** **NA** **AU** AS
Police Station	
Polizeistation	
Pcs: 26	1977–1980

ⓘ 523	**EU** **NA** **AU** AS
Locomotive and Station	
Lokomotive mit 2 Anhängern	
Pcs: 51	1977–1980

ⓘ 524	**EU** **NA** **AU** AS
LEGOVILLE	
Eine kleine Stadt	
Pcs: 61	1977–1980

ⓘ 533	**EU** NA **AU** AS
Racer	
Rennwagen	
Pcs: 4	1977–1979

ⓘ 535	**EU** **NA** **AU** AS
Taxi	
Taxi	
Pcs: 5	1977–1981

ⓘ 536	**EU** **NA** **AU** AS
Camping	
Pkw mit Wohnwagen	
Pcs: 8	1977–1979

ⓘ	456	Similar to: 661 (1976)	Ähnlich zu: 661 (1976)
ⓘ	491	Similar to: 695 (1976)	Ähnlich zu: 695 (1976)
ⓘ	492	Similar to: 692 (1975)	Ähnlich zu: 692 (1975)
ⓘ	522-524	Similar to: 080 (1976), 081 (1976), 082 (1976)	Ähnlich zu: 080 (1976), 081 (1976), 082 (1976)
ⓘ	533	Similar to: 085 (1977), 2401 (1984)	Ähnlich zu: 085 (1977), 2401 (1984)
ⓘ	535-536	Similar to: 087 (1977), 088 (1977)	Ähnlich zu: 087 (1977), 088 (1977)

1977

ⓘ 537	**EU** **NA** **AU** AS
Mary's House	
Das Haus von Mary	
Pcs: 15	1977–1981

ⓘ 618	**EU** NA AU AS
Police Helicopter	
Helikopter	
Pcs: 39	1977

ⓘ 619	**EU** NA AU AS
Rally Car	
Rallyefahrzeug	
Pcs: 23	1977

ⓘ 663	**EU** NA AU AS
Hovercraft	
Hovercraft	
Pcs: 61	1977

ⓘ 664	**EU** NA AU AS
TV Crew	
Ü-Wagen mit Fernsehkamera	
Pcs: 48	1977

ⓘ 698	**EU** NA AU AS
Boeing 727	
Boeing 727	
Pcs: 46	1977

ⓘ 699	**EU** NA AU AS
Photo Safari	
Fotosafari	
Pcs: 130	1977

ⓘ 711	EU **NA** AU AS
Jeep CJ-5	
Jeep mit Hänger	
Pcs: 57	1977

ⓘ 712	EU **NA** AU AS
Sea Plane	
Wasserflugzeug	
Pcs: 115	1977–1978

ⓘ	537	Similar to: 089 (1977)	Ähnlich zu: 089 (1977)
ⓘ	618	Similar to: 628 (1978)	Ähnlich zu: 628 (1978)
ⓘ	711	Similar to: 385 (1976)	Ähnlich zu: 385 (1976)
ⓘ	712	Similar to: 371 (1977)	Ähnlich zu: 371 (1977)
ⓘ	787	Similar to: 789 (1987)	Ähnlich zu: 789 (1987)

727 EU NA AU AS

12V Locomotive		
12V Lokomotive		
Pcs: 134	1977–1980	

787 EU NA AU AS

Storage Cloth		
Spiel- und Sammelbeutel		
Pcs: 1	1977–1990	

850 EU NA AU AS

Fork Lift Truck		
Gabelstapler		
Pcs: 210	1977–1983	

851 EU NA AU AS

Farm Tractor		
Traktor		
Pcs: 320	1977–1980	

852 EU NA AU AS

Helicopter		
Mehrzweck-Hubschrauber		
Pcs: 364	1977–1978	

853 EU NA AU AS

Auto Chassis		
Auto-Chassis		
Pcs: 601	1977–1979	

870 EU NA AU AS

4.5V Supplementary Set		
4,5V Motor mit Batteriekasten		
Pcs: 24	1977–1982	

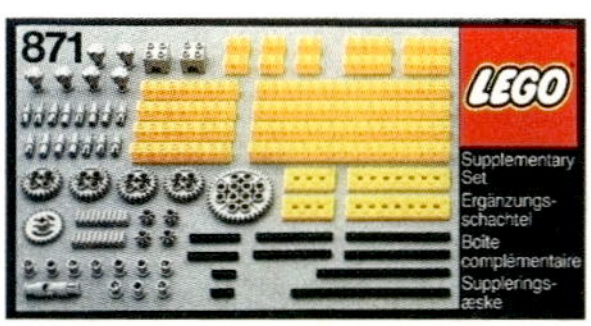

871 EU NA AU AS

Supplementary Set		
Zahnräder, Achsen, Balken		
Pcs: 78	1977–1981	

1575 EU NA AU AS

Finnjet Ferry		
Finnjet Fährschiff		
Pcs: 502	1977–1980	Special

850	Similar to: 950 (1979)	Ähnlich zu: 950 (1979)
851	Similar to: 952 (1978)	Ähnlich zu: 952 (1978)
852	Similar to: 954 (1978)	Ähnlich zu: 954 (1978)
853	Similar to: 956 (1978)	Ähnlich zu: 956 (1978)
870	Similar to: 960 (1978)	Ähnlich zu: 960 (1978)
871	Similar to: 961 (1978)	Ähnlich zu: 961 (1978)

1580	EU NA AU AS	
Silja Line Ferry		
Silja Line Fährschiff		
Pcs: 416	1977–1980	Special

1978

ⓘ 8	EU NA AU AS
Universal Building Set	
Universalkasten	
Pcs: 422	1978–1980

ⓘ 9	EU NA AU AS
Universal Building Set	
Universalkasten	
Pcs: 116	1978–1980

ⓘ 061	EU NA AU AS
Puppy	
Hund	
Pcs: 8	1978–1979

ⓘ 063	EU NA AU AS
Ducks	
Entenfamilie	
Pcs: 18	1978–1980

ⓘ 086	EU NA AU AS
Tub Boat	
Matrose mit Boot	
Pcs: 3	1978–1983

ⓘ 164	EU NA AU AS
Passenger Wagon	
Bahnpostwagen	
Pcs: 140	1978–1980

ⓘ			
ⓘ	061	Similar to: 530 (1976)	Ähnlich zu: 530 (1976)
ⓘ	063	Similar to: 532 (1976)	Ähnlich zu: 532 (1976)
ⓘ	086	Similar to: 534 (1978)	Ähnlich zu: 534 (1978)

165	EU
Cargo Station	
Güterbahnhof	
Pcs: 266	1978–1980

166	EU
Flat Wagon	
Rungenwaggon	
Pcs: 44	1978–1979

167	EU
Car Transport Wagon	
Auffahrrampe mit Waggon	
Pcs: 102	1978–1979

205	EU AU
Universal Figure Set	
Figuren-Universalkasten	
Pcs: 120	1978–1979

208	EU NA
Mother with Baby Carriage	
Mädchen mit Puppenwagen	
Pcs: 47	1978

230	EU NA AU
Hairdressing Salon	
Kosmetik-Salon	
Pcs: 235	1978–1981

231	EU NA AU
Hospital	
Krankenhaus	
Pcs: 420	1978–1981

232	EU AU
Bungalow	
Reihenhaus	
Pcs: 479	1978–1981

278	EU AU
TV Room	
Fernsehzimmer	
Pcs: 110	1978–1979

i	Set	English	Deutsch
i	205	Wedding; with poster	Hochzeit; mit Poster
i	300	Similar to: 551 (1979)	Ähnlich zu: 551 (1979)

297 EU NA AU AS

Nursery	
Kinderzimmer	
Pcs: 168	1978–1981

300 EU NA AU AS

T Road Plates	
T-Kreuzungen	
Pcs: 2	1978–1985

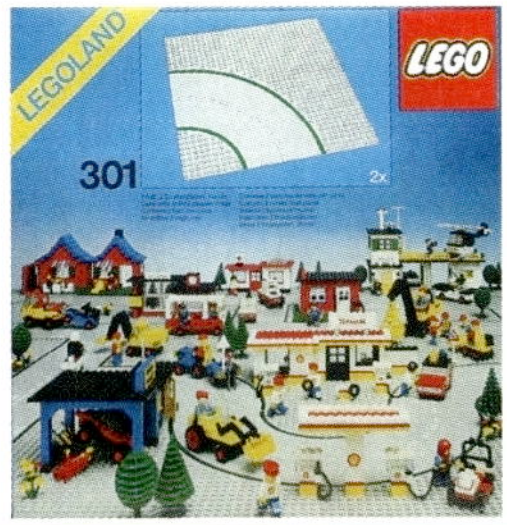

301 EU NA AU AS

Curved Road Plates	
Kurven	
Pcs: 2	1978–1985

302 EU NA AU AS

Straight Road	
Gerade Straßen	
Pcs: 2	1978–1985

316 EU NA AU AS

Fire Fighter	
Feuerlöschboot	
Pcs: 132	1978–1981

330 EU NA AU AS

Gas Station	
Tankstelle	
Pcs: 211	1978

340 EU NA AU AS

Fire Trucks	
Mehrere Feuerwehrwagen	
Pcs: 276	1978

374 EU NA AU AS

Fire Station	
Feuerwache	
Pcs: 336	1978–1980

375 EU NA AU AS

Castle	
Ritterburg	
Pcs: 779	1978–1983

i	301	Ähnlich zu: 551 (1979)	Ähnlich zu: 552 (1979)
i	302	Similar to: 553 (1979)	Ähnlich zu: 553 (1979)
i	316	Similar to: 775 (1978)	Ähnlich zu: 775 (1978)
i	330	Similar to: 217 (1977)	Ähnlich zu: 217 (1977)
i	340	Similar to: 218 (1977)	Ähnlich zu: 218 (1977)
i	375	Similar to: 6075 (1981)	Ähnlich zu: 6075 (1981)

376	EU NA AU AS
Town House with Garden	
Wochenendhaus mit Garten	
Pcs: 248	1978–1984

377	EU NA AU AS
Shell Service Station	
Shell Service-Station	
Pcs: 190	1978–1982

398	EU NA AU AS
U.S.S. Constellation	
U.S.S. Constellation	
Pcs: 1033	1978–1979

462	EU NA AU AS
Rocket Launcher	
Mobile Raketen-Abschussrampe	
Pcs: 76	1978–1983

483	EU NA AU AS
Alpha-1 Rocket Base	
Raketen-Abschussbasis	
Pcs: 186	1978–1983

487	EU NA AU AS
Space Cruiser	
Raumtransporter	
Pcs: 172	1978–1980

493	EU NA AU AS
Space Command Center	
Kommandozentrale	
Pcs: 170	1978–1979

528	EU NA AU AS
Building Set	
Universalkasten	
Pcs: 20	1978–1982

529	EU NA AU AS
Animals	
Phantasietiere	
Pcs: 39	1978–1980

i	Set	English	Deutsch
i	376	Similar to: 560 (1979)	Ähnlich zu: 560 (1979)
i	398	With poster; re-released as: 10021 (2003)	Mit Poster; neu aufgelegt als: 10021 (2003)
i	462	Similar to: 897 (1979)	Ähnlich zu: 897 (1979)
i	483	Similar to: 920 (1979)	Ähnlich zu: 920 (1979)
i	487	Similar to: 924 (1979)	Ähnlich zu: 924 (1979)
i	493	Similar to: 926 (1978); handbuilt craters or crater plate	Ähnlich zu: 926 (1978); gebauter Krater o. Kraterplatte

ⓘ 534	**EU** NA **AU** **AS**
Tub Boat	
Matrose mit Boot	
Pcs: 3	1978–1989

ⓘ 575	EU **NA** AU AS
Coast Guard Station	
Rettungsstation	
Pcs: 305	1978–1979

ⓘ 590	EU **NA** AU AS
Engine Co. No. 9	
Feuerwehrwache	
Pcs: 361	1978–1980

ⓘ 600	**EU** **NA** AU AS
Police Patrol	
Verkehrsstreife	
Pcs: 20	1978–1980

ⓘ 601	**EU** NA **AU** AS
Shell Gas Pump	
Shell Tanksäule mit Tankwart	
Pcs: 13	1978–1979

ⓘ 602	**EU** **NA** **AU** AS
Fire Chief's Car	
Feuerwehr-Hauptmann	
Pcs: 29	1978–1980

ⓘ 603	**EU** NA AU AS
Sidecar	
Motorrad mit Beiwagen	
Pcs: 26	1978

ⓘ 604	**EU** NA **AU** AS
Shell Service Car	
Shell Servicewagen	
Pcs: 22	1978–1979

ⓘ 605	**EU** NA AU AS
Street Sweeper	
Straßenkehrer	
Pcs: 19	1978

ⓘ	528	Similar to: 071 (1979)	Ähnlich zu: 071 (1979)
ⓘ	534	Similar to: 086 (1978)	Ähnlich zu: 086 (1978)
ⓘ	575	Similar to: 369 (1976)	Ähnlich zu: 369 (1976)
ⓘ	590	Similar to: 374 (1978)	Ähnlich zu: 374 (1978)
ⓘ	600	Similar to: 6600 (1981)	Ähnlich zu: 6600 (1981)
ⓘ	602	Similar to: 6602 (1981)	Ähnlich zu: 6602 (1981)

606	EU NA AU AS
Ambulance	
Krankenwagen mit Fahrer	
Pcs: 26	1978–1980

620	EU NA AU AS
Fireman's Car	
Feuermeldewagen m. Brandmeister	
Pcs: 33	1978

621	EU NA AU AS
Police Car	
Polizist mit Einsatzwagen	
Pcs: 35	1978–1979

622	EU NA AU AS
Tipper Truck	
Lkw mit Seitenkipper	
Pcs: 33	1978–1980

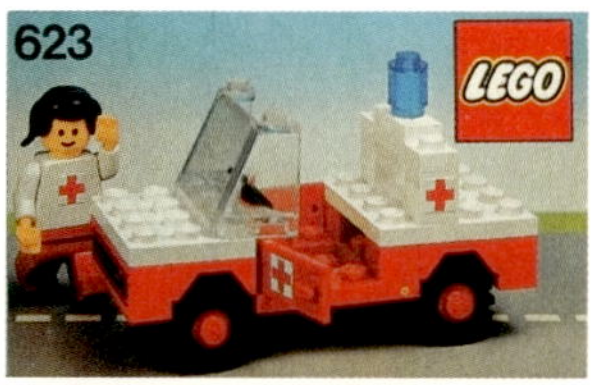

623	EU NA AU AS
Medic's Car	
Rot-Kreuz-Einsatzwagen	
Pcs: 34	1978–1979

625	EU NA AU AS
Tractor	
Traktor mit Vordergabel	
Pcs: 31	1978–1981

626	EU NA AU AS
Red Cross Helicopter	
Rettungshubschrauber	
Pcs: 37	1978–1980

628	EU NA AU AS
Police Helicopter	
Polizeihubschrauber	
Pcs: 39	1978–1980

640	EU NA AU AS
Fire Truck and Trailer	
Feuerwehr mit Anhänger	
Pcs: 48	1978–1979

i	626	Similar to: 6626 (1981)	Ähnlich zu: 6626 (1981)
i	628	Canadian version of 618 (1977)	Kanada-Version von 618 (1977)

641	EU
Excavator	
Hochlöffelbagger	
Pcs: 41	1978–1979

642	EU
Tow Truck and Car	
Shell Abschleppwagen	
Pcs: 42	1978–1980

643	EU
Flatbed Truck	
Pritschenwagen	
Pcs: 39	1978

644	EU NA AU
Police Mobile Patrol	
Autobahnpolizei	
Pcs: 45	1978–1980

670	EU NA AU
Mobile Crane	
Kranwagen mit Bauarbeiter	
Pcs: 55	1978–1979

671	EU NA AU
Shell Fuel Pumper	
Shell Tanklastzug mit Fahrer	
Pcs: 73	1978–1982

672	EU NA AU
Fire Engine	
Feuerwehr mit Löschgerät	
Pcs: 66	1978–1979

673	EU
Rally Repair Crew	
Rallye-Fahrzeug mit Polizist	
Pcs: 61	1978–1980

674	EU
Forklift & Truck	
Transporter mit Gabelstapler	
Pcs: 55	1978

i	644	Similar to: 540 (1979)	Ähnlich zu: 540 (1979)
i	670	Similar to: 558 (1979)	Ähnlich zu: 558 (1979)
i	671	Similar to: 554 (1979)	Ähnlich zu: 554 (1979)
i	672	Similar to: 556 (1979)	Ähnlich zu: 556 (1979)

709	EU NA AU AS
Police Boat	
Polizeiboot	
Pcs: 49	1978–1981

745	EU NA AU AS
Big Baseplate	
Große Bauplatte	
Pcs: 1	1978–1986

746	EU NA AU AS
Baseplates Green/Yellow	
Bauplatten, grün/gelb	
Pcs: 2	1978–1984

747	EU NA AU AS
Baseplates Red/Blue	
Bauplatten, rot/blau	
Pcs: 2	1978–1984

775	EU NA AU AS
Fire Fighter	
Feuerlöschboot	
Pcs: 133	1978–1981

854	EU NA AU AS
Go-Cart	
Go-Kart	
Pcs: 206	1978–1985

855	EU NA AU AS
Mobile Crane	
Kranwagen mit Bergungskran	
Pcs: 512	1978–1981

872	EU NA AU AS
Gear Blocks	
Getriebe	
Pcs: 77	1978–1989

948	EU NA AU AS
Go-Cart	
Go-Kart	
Pcs: 206	1978–1983

i	709	Updated version of: 314 (1976)	Neue Version von: 314 (1976)
i	745	Similar to: 813 (1986), 626 (1996), 840 (1980)	Ähnlich zu: 813 (1986), 626 (1996), 840 (1980)
i	746	Similar to: 796 (1971), 841 (1980)	Ähnlich zu: 796 (1971), 841 (1980)
i	747	Similar to: 795 (1971), 842 (1980)	Ähnlich zu: 795 (1971), 842 (1980)
i	775	Similar to: 316 (1978)	Ähnlich zu: 316 (1978)
i	854	Similar to: 948 (1978)	Ähnlich zu: 948 (1978)

952 (NA)

Farm Tractor
Traktor

Pcs: 314	1978–1980	

954 (NA)

Sky Copter
Hubschrauber

Pcs: 364	1978	

956 (NA)

Auto Chassis
Auto-Chassis

Pcs: 599	1978–1980	

960 (NA)

Expert Builder Power Pack
Experten Bauset

Pcs: 22	1978–1981	

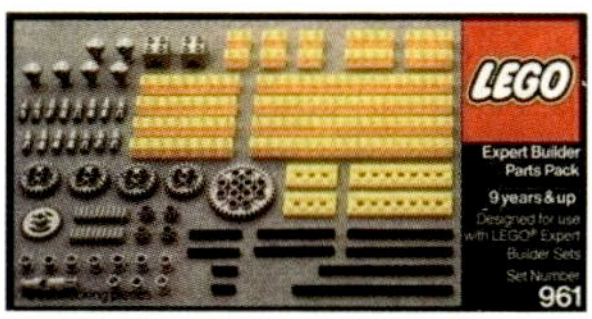

961 (NA)

Expert Builder Parts Pack
Bauset für Experten

Pcs: 78	1978–1980	

970 (EU) (NA) (AU) (AS)

Lighting Bricks
Leuchtsteine

Pcs: 17	1978–1986	

1555 (EU)

Sterling Airways Biplane
Sterling Airways Doppeldecker

Pcs: -	1978–1980	Special

1589 (EU)

Town Square
Altstadt

Pcs: 444	1978	Special

1610 (EU)

Martinair Cessna
Martinair Cessna

Pcs: 81	1978–1983	Special

855	Similar to: 955 (1979)	Ähnlich zu: 955 (1979)
948	Similar to: 854 (1978)	Ähnlich zu: 854 (1978)
952	Similar to: 851 (1977)	Ähnlich zu: 851 (1977)
954	Similar to: 852 (1977)	Ähnlich zu: 852 (1977)
956	Similar to: 853 (1977)	Ähnlich zu: 853 (1977)
960	Similar to: 870 (1977)	Ähnlich zu: 870 (1977)

1611	EU NA AU AS	
Martinair DC-9		
Martinair DC-9		
Pcs: 64	1978–1983	Special

1620	EU NA AU AS	
Factory		
Fabrik		
Pcs: 231	1978	Special

i	961	Similar to: 871 (1977)	Ähnlich zu: 871 (1977)
i	1589	Available from Weetabix	Weetabix-Set
i	1620	Chocomel Promo	Chocomel Promo

1979

7 — EU

Universal Building Set		
Universalkasten		
Pcs: 64	1979	

0011 — NA

Town Mini-Figures		
Stadtfiguren		
Pcs: 3	1979	

0012 — NA

Space Mini-Figures		
Astronauten		
Pcs: 4	1979	

0013 — NA

Space Mini-Figures		
Astronauten		
Pcs: 4	1979	

0014 — NA

Space Mini-Figures		
Astronauten		
Pcs: 14	1979	Special

0016 — NA

Castle Mini Figures		
Ritterfiguren		
Pcs: 12	1979	

i	Set	English	Deutsch
i	0012	Sold since 1979, wrong label on package	Erst ab 1979 verkauft, obwohl 1978 aufgedruckt ist
i	0013	Sold since 1979, wrong label on package	Erst ab 1979 verkauft, obwohl 1978 aufgedruckt ist
i	0014	Sold since 1979, wrong label on package	Erst ab 1979 verkauft, obwohl 1978 aufgedruckt ist
i	0016	Sold since 1979, wrong label on package	Erst ab 1979 verkauft, obwohl 1978 aufgedruckt ist

028	EU NA AU AS
Nursery Furniture	
Kinderzimmer	
Pcs: 7	1979–1981

032	EU NA AU AS
Living Room	
Wohnzimmer	
Pcs: 14	1979–1981

033	EU NA AU AS
Farm Set Animals	
Bauer mit Wagen und Tieren	
Pcs: 21	1979–1984

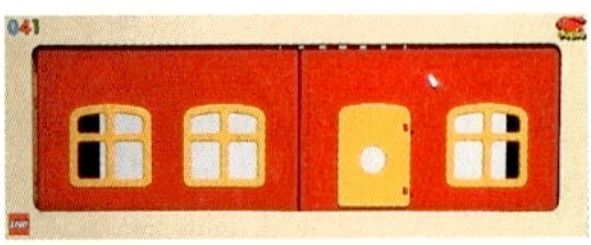

041	EU NA AU AS
Playhouse	
Spielhaus, aufklappbar	
Pcs: 24	1979–1984

045	EU NA AU AS
Farm	
Kompletter Bauernhof	
Pcs: 68	1979–1984

071	EU NA AU AS
Block Box	
Steineschachtel	
Pcs: 24	1979–1982

121	EU NA AU AS
Roadster	
Supercabrio	
Pcs: 23	1979

128	EU NA AU AS
Taxi Station	
Taxistation	
Pcs: 33	1979–1981

132	EU NA AU AS
Cottage	
Traumvilla	
Pcs: 113	1979–1981

i	Set	English	Deutsch
i	032	Similar to: 2630 (1980)	Ähnlich zu: 2630 (1980)
i	041	Similar to: 2643 (1980)	Ähnlich zu: 2643 (1980)
i	121	Similar to: 328 (1979)	Ähnlich zu: 328 (1979)
i	128	Similar to: 338 (1979)	Ähnlich zu: 338 (1979)
i	132	Similar to: 341 (1979)	Ähnlich zu: 341 (1979)

ⓘ 134	EU NA AU AS
Service Station	
Werkstatt	
Pcs: 41	1979–1981

ⓘ 137	EU NA AU AS
Hospital	
Krankenhaus	
Pcs: 19	1979–1981

ⓘ 140	EU NA AU AS
Town Hall	
Rathaus	
Pcs: 144	1979–1981

261	EU NA AU AS
Bathroom	
Bad	
Pcs: 179	1979–1983

268	EU NA AU AS
Family Room	
Wohnzimmer	
Pcs: 248	1979–1983

269	EU NA AU AS
Kitchen	
Küche	
Pcs: 212	1979–1983

ⓘ 305	EU NA AU AS
Crater Plates	
Basisplatten mit Krater	
Pcs: 2	1979–1989

ⓘ 306	EU NA AU AS
Landing Plates	
Basisplatten mit Landekreuz	
Pcs: 2	1979–1990

308	EU NA AU AS
Bracelet	
Armband mit Schmuckelementen	
Pcs: 38	1979–1981

ⓘ	134	Similar to: 344 (1979)	Ähnlich zu: 344 (1979)
ⓘ	137	Similar to: 347 (1979)	Ähnlich zu: 347 (1979)
ⓘ	140	Similar to: 350 (1979)	Ähnlich zu: 350 (1979)
ⓘ	305	Similar to: 453 (1979)	Ähnlich zu: 453 (1979)
ⓘ	306	Similar to: 454 (1979)	Ähnlich zu: 454 (1979)

309 — EU NA AU AS

Bracelet	
Armband mit Schmuckelementen	
Pcs: 38	1979–1981

310 — EU NA AU AS

Necklace	
Halskette mit Schmuckelementen	
Pcs: 29	1979–1981

311 — EU NA AU AS

Necklace	
Halskette mit Schmuckelementen	
Pcs: 25	1979–1981

312 — EU NA AU AS

Bracelet and Necklace	
Armband und Halskette	
Pcs: 59	1979–1981

313 — EU NA AU AS

Bracelet and Necklace	
Armband und Halskette	
Pcs: 59	1979–1981

324 — EU NA AU AS

Ricky Racoon on his Scooter	
Willie Waschbär auf Rennroller	
Pcs: 2	1979–1981

325 — EU NA AU AS

Percy Pig's Wheelbarrow	
Henry das Schwein mit Schubkarre	
Pcs: 4	1979–1981

328 — EU NA AU AS

Moe Mouse's Roadster	
Moe Maus' Supercabrio	
Pcs: 23	1979–1980

329 — EU NA AU AS

Bernard Bear and Pickup Truck	
Bernhard Bärs Eiltransporter	
Pcs: 27	1979–1980

i	Set	English	Deutsch
i	324	Similar to: 3605 (1980)	Ähnlich zu: 3605 (1980)
i	325	Similar to: 3615 (1980)	Ähnlich zu: 3615 (1980)
i	328	Similar to: 121 (1979)	Ähnlich zu: 121 (1979)
i	338	Similar to: 128 (1979)	Ähnlich zu: 128 (1979)

ⓘ 338 EU NA AU AS

Blondi the Pig and Taxi Station	
Blondi Schweins Taxistation	
Pcs: 37	1979–1981

ⓘ 341 EU NA AU AS

Cathy Cat's & Morty Mouse's Cottage	
Cathy Katzes & Morty Maus' Traumvilla	
Pcs: 114	1979–1981

ⓘ 344 EU NA AU AS

Service Station	
Olli Zieges & Mike Affes Großgarage	
Pcs: 41	1979–1981

ⓘ 347 EU NA AU AS

Doc David's Hospital	
Doc Davids Krankenhaus	
Pcs: 19	1979–1981

ⓘ 350 EU NA AU AS

Town Hall with Leonard Lion & Friends	
Leo Löwes Rathaus	
Pcs: 145	1979–1981

ⓘ 361 EU NA AU AS

Garage	
Garage mit Wärter	
Pcs: 79	1979–1982

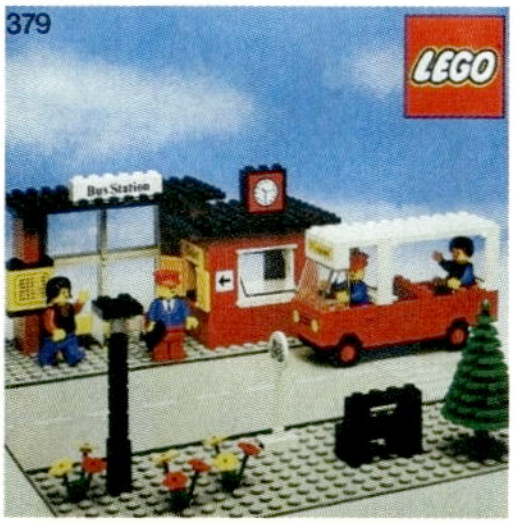

ⓘ 379 EU NA AU AS

Bus Station	
Omnibus-Station	
Pcs: 182	1979–1982

ⓘ 381 EU NA AU AS

Police Headquartes	
Polizeizentrale	
Pcs: 396	1979–1982

ⓘ 383 EU NA AU AS

Knight's Tournament	
Ritterturnier	
Pcs: 213	1979–1982

ⓘ	Set	Similar to	Ähnlich zu
ⓘ	341	Similar to: 132 (1979)	Ähnlich zu: 132 (1979)
ⓘ	344	Similar to: 134 (1979)	Ähnlich zu: 134 (1979)
ⓘ	347	Similar to: 137 (1979)	Ähnlich zu: 137 (1979)
ⓘ	350	Similar to: 140 (1979)	Ähnlich zu: 140 (1979)
ⓘ	381	Similar to: 588 (1979)	Ähnlich zu: 588 (1979)
ⓘ	383	Similar to: 6083 (1981)	Ähnlich zu: 6083 (1981)

ⓘ 442	EU NA AU AS
Space Shuttle	
Raumpatrouille	
Pcs: 39	1979–1980

ⓘ 452	EU NA AU AS
Mobile Tracking Station	
Mobile Funkstation	
Pcs: 78	1979–1980

ⓘ 453	EU NA AU AS
Crater Plates	
Basisplatten mit Krater	
Pcs: 2	1979–1983

ⓘ 454	EU NA AU AS
Landing Plates	
Basisplatten mit Landekreuz	
Pcs: 2	1979–1990

ⓘ 497	EU NA AU AS
Galaxy Explorer	
Raumkreuzer mit Funkzentrale	
Pcs: 346	1979–1983

ⓘ 540	EU NA AU AS
Police Units	
Autobahnpolizei	
Pcs: 45	1979–1980

ⓘ 542	EU NA AU AS
Street Crew	
Straßenarbeiter	
Pcs: 44	1979–1980

ⓘ 551	EU NA AU AS
T Road Plates	
Einfache Kreuzung	
Pcs: 2	1979–1983

ⓘ 552	EU NA AU AS
Curved Road Plates	
Kurven	
Pcs: 2	1979–1985

ⓘ	Set	English	Deutsch
ⓘ	442	USA version of: 891 (1979)	USA Version von: 891 (1979)
ⓘ	452	Similar to: 894 (1979)	Ähnlich zu: 894 (1979)
ⓘ	453	Similar to: 305 (1979)	Ähnlich zu: 305 (1979)
ⓘ	454	Similar to: 306 (1979)	Ähnlich zu: 306 (1979)
ⓘ	497	Similar to: 928 (1979)	Ähnlich zu: 928 (1979)
ⓘ	540	Similar to: 644 (1978)	Ähnlich zu: 644 (1978)

553	EU **NA** AU AS
Straight Road Plates	
Gerade Straße	
Pcs: 2	1979–1985

554	EU **NA** AU AS
Fuel Pumper	
Tanklastzug	
Pcs: 75	1979–1983

556	EU **NA** AU AS
Fire Emergency Van	
Feuerwehr mit Löschgerät	
Pcs: 66	1979–1980

558	EU **NA** AU AS
Road Crane	
Kranwagen mit Bauarbeiter	
Pcs: 55	1979–1980

560	EU **NA** AU AS
Town House with Garden	
Wochenendhaus mit Garten	
Pcs: 253	1979–1981

588	EU **NA** AU AS
Police Headquarters	
Polizeizentrale	
Pcs: 372	1979–1983

607	**EU** NA AU AS
Mini Loader	
Bagger mit Fahrer	
Pcs: 22	1979–1981

608	**EU** NA **AU** AS
Taxi	
Taxi mit Fahrer	
Pcs: 25	1979–1981

645	**EU** NA AU AS
Police Helicopter	
Polizeihubschrauber mit Pilot	
Pcs: 56	1979–1981

551	Similar to: 300 (1978)	Ähnlich zu: 300 (1978)
552	Similar to: 301 (1978)	Ähnlich zu: 301 (1978)
553	Similar to: 301 (1978)	Ähnlich zu: 301 (1978)
554	Similar to: 671 (1978)	Ähnlich zu: 671 (1978)
556	Similar to: 672 (1978)	Ähnlich zu: 672 (1978)
558	Similar to: 670 (1978)	Ähnlich zu: 670 (1978)

646	EU NA AU AS	
Auto Service Truck		
Reparaturwagen mit Mechaniker		
Pcs: 43	1979–1981	

675	EU NA AU AS	
Snack Bar		
Snack-Bar		
Pcs: 64	1979–1982	

677	EU NA AU AS	
Knight's Procession		
Ritter		
Pcs: 48	1979–1982	

856	EU NA AU AS	
Bulldozer		
Bulldozer		
Pcs: 370	1979–1983	

857	EU NA AU AS	
Motorcycle		
Motorrad mit Beiwagen, blau		
Pcs: 401	1979–1980	

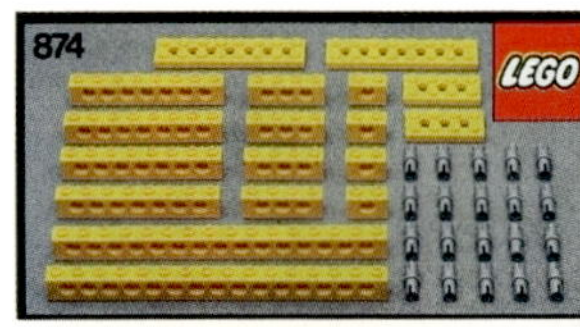

874	EU NA AU AS	
Supplementary Set Yellow		
Gelbe Technik Elemente		
Pcs: 38	1979–1981	

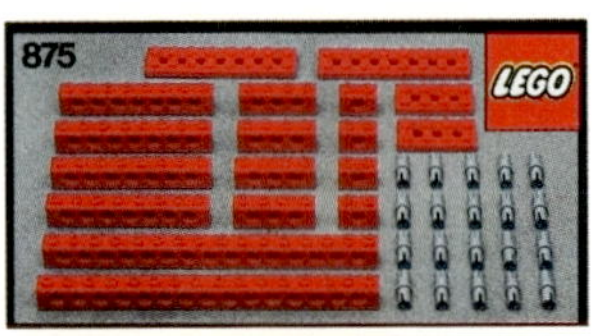

875	EU NA AU AS	
Supplementary Set Red		
Rote Technik Elemente		
Pcs: 38	1979–1981	

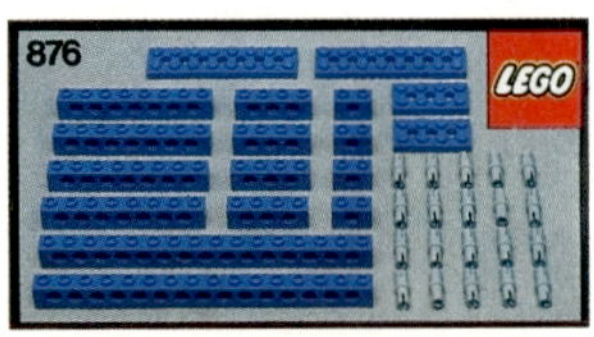

876	EU NA AU AS	
Supplementary Set Blue		
Blaue Technik Elemente		
Pcs: 38	1979–1981	

877	EU NA AU AS	
Supplementary Set Red/Black		
Lenkkonstruktionen Rot/Schwarz		
Pcs: 24	1979–1981	

i	Set	English	Deutsch
i	560	Similar to: 376 (1978)	Ähnlich zu: 376 (1978)
i	588	Similar to: 381 (1979)	Ähnlich zu: 381 (1979)
i	677	Similar to: 6077 (1981)	Ähnlich zu: 6077 (1981)
i	856	Similar to: 951 (1979)	Ähnlich zu: 951 (1979)
i	857	Similar to: 8857 (1980)	Ähnlich zu: 8857 (1980)
i	886	Included in: 1983 (1984)	Enthalten in: 1983 (1984)

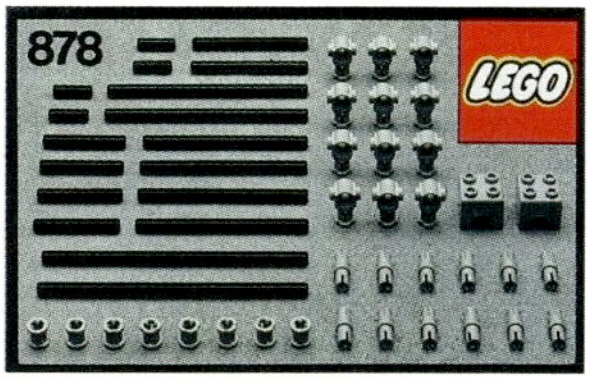

878	EU NA AU AS
Supplementary Set Black	
Schwarze Technik Elemente	
Pcs: 51	1979–1981

879	EU NA AU AS
Supplementary Set	
Zahnräder, Achsen, Kettenglieder	
Pcs: 87	1979–1981

885	EU NA AU AS
Space Scooter	
Raumgleiter mit Astronaut	
Pcs: 19	1979–1980

886	EU NA AU AS
Space Buggy	
Astronautenauto	
Pcs: 20	1979–1983

889	EU NA AU AS
Radar Truck	
Radarwagen	
Pcs: 29	1979–1980

891	EU NA AU AS
Two-Man Scooter	
Raumpatrouille	
Pcs: 39	1979–1983

894	EU NA AU AS
Mobile Tracking Station	
Mobile Funkstation	
Pcs: 78	1979–1980

897	EU NA AU AS
Rocket Launcher	
Mobile Raketen-Abschussrampe	
Pcs: 76	1979–1983

918	EU NA AU AS
Space Transport	
Raumfähre	
Pcs: 82	1979–1981

	Set	English	Deutsch
(i)	889	Included in: 1983 (1984)	Enthalten in: 1983 (1984)
(i)	891	Non-USA version of 442 (1979)	Nicht-USA Version von 442 (1979)
(i)	894	Similar to: 452 (1979)	Ähnlich zu: 452 (1979)
(i)	897	Similar to: 462 (1978)	Ähnlich zu: 462 (1978)
(i)	918	Released in Canada, not in USA	Veröffentlicht in Kanada, nicht in USA
(i)	920	Similar to: 483 (1978)	Ähnlich zu: 483 (1978)

920 EU NA AU AS

Alpha-1 Rocket Base

Raketen-Abschussbasis

Pcs: 186 | 1979–1982

924 EU NA AU AS

Space Cruiser

Raumtransporter

Pcs: 172 | 1979–1980

926 EU NA AU AS

Space Command Center

Kommando-Zentrale

Pcs: 173 | 1979

928 EU NA AU AS

Galaxy Explorer

Raumkreuzer mit Funkzentrale

Pcs: 340 | 1979–1983

950 EU NA AU AS

Fork Lift

Gabelstapler

Pcs: 210 | 1979–1981

951 EU NA AU AS

Bulldozer

Bulldozer

Pcs: 368 | 1979–1980

955 EU NA AU AS

Mobile Crane

Kranwagen mit Bergungskran

Pcs: 512 | 1979–1981

i	Set	English	Deutsch
i	924	Similar to: 487 (1978)	Ähnlich zu: 487 (1978)
i	926	Similar to: 493 (1978), exclusively on crater plate	Ähnlich zu: 493 (1978), ausschließlich auf Kraterplatte
i	928	Similar to: 497 (1979)	Ähnlich zu: 497 (1979)
i	950	Similar to: 850 (1977)	Ähnlich zu: 850 (1977)
i	951	Similar to: 856 (1979)	Ähnlich zu: 856 (1979)
i	955	Similar to: 855 (1978)	Ähnlich zu: 855 (1978)

1980

722	EU NA AU AS
Universal Building Set	
Universalkasten f. Fortgeschrittene	
Pcs: 299	1980–1985

733	EU NA AU AS
Universal Building Set	
Universalkasten f. Fortgeschrittene	
Pcs: 524	1980–1985

744	EU NA AU AS
Universal Building Set	
Universalkasten f. Fortgeschrittene	
Pcs: 518	1980–1985

820	EU NA AU AS
Assorted Red Plates	
Rote Platten	
Pcs: 34	1980–1986

822	EU NA AU AS
Assorted Blue Plates	
Blaue Platten	
Pcs: 34	1980–1986

830	EU NA AU AS
Assorted Red Bricks	
Rote Elemente	
Pcs: 46	1980–1986

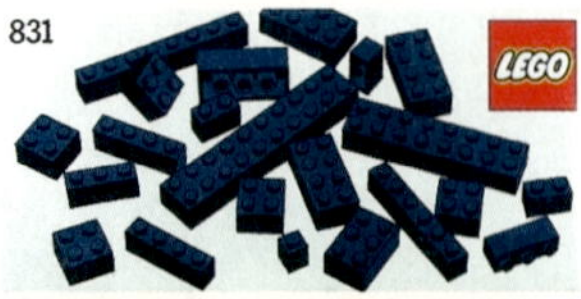

831 EU NA AU AS

Assorted Black Bricks	
Schwarze Elemente	
Pcs: 46	1980–1986

832 EU NA AU AS

Assorted Blue Bricks	
Blaue Elemente	
Pcs: 46	1980–1986

833 EU NA AU AS

Assorted White Bricks	
Weiße Elemente	
Pcs: 46	1980–1986

834 EU NA AU AS

Assorted Yellow Bricks	
Gelbe Elemente	
Pcs: 46	1980–1986

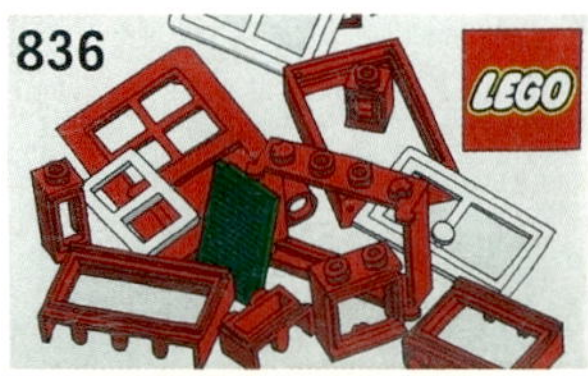

836 EU NA AU AS

Doors and Windows	
Türen und Fenster	
Pcs: 35	1980–1986

837 EU NA AU AS

Wheels and Tires	
Radelemente	
Pcs: 28	1980–1996

838 EU NA AU AS

45 Degree Roof Tiles	
Dachelemente 45°	
Pcs: 58	1980–1986

839 EU NA AU AS

22.5 Degree Roof Tiles	
Dachelemente 22,5°	
Pcs: 42	1980–1986

840 EU NA AU AS

32x32 Base Plate Green	
32x32 Bauplatte, grün	
Pcs: 1	1980–1985

i	840	Similar to: 813 (1986), 626 (1996), 745 (1978)	Ähnlich zu: 813 (1986), 626 (1996), 745 (1978)

841 EU NA AU AS

10x20 Baseplates Green/Yellow

10x20 Bauplatten, grün/gelb

Pcs: 2 | 1980–1985

842 EU NA AU AS

10x20 Baseplates Red/Blue

10x20 Bauplatten, rot/blau

Pcs: 2 | 1980–1985

843 EU NA AU AS

48x48 Baseplate Grey

48x48 Riesenbauplatte, grau

Pcs: 1 | 1980–1986

858 EU NA AU AS

Auto Engines

Motoren-Modelle

Pcs: 242 | 1980

1591 EU NA AU AS

Danone Truck

Danone Lkw

Pcs: 39 | 1980 | Special

1592 EU NA AU AS

Town Square - Castle Scene

Englische Stadt

Pcs: 491 | 1980

1651 EU NA AU AS

Maersk Line Container Truck

Maersk Line Container-Lkw

Pcs: 339 | 1980 | Special

2053 EU NA AU AS

Rattle-n-Roll

Fantasie-Auto zum Ziehen

Pcs: 5 | 1980–1984

2056 EU NA AU AS

Rock-A-Bye Pull-Toy

Wippwagen zum Ziehen

Pcs: 9 | 1980–1984

i	Set	English	Deutsch
i	841	Similar to: 796 (1971), 746 (1978)	Ähnlich zu: 796 (1971), 746 (1978)
i	842	Similar to: 747 (1978), 795 (1971)	Ähnlich zu: 747 (1978), 795 (1971)
i	843	Similar to: 628 (1996), 815 (1986), 1085 (1982)	Ähnlich zu: 628 (1996), 815 (1986), 1085 (1982)
i	858	Similar to: 8858 (1980)	Ähnlich zu: 8858 (1980)
i	1591	Only available in France; Danone Promo	Nur in Frankreich erhältlich; Danone Promo
i	1592	Similar to: 1592 (1983)	Ähnlich zu: 1592 (1983)

2620	EU NA AU AS
Sports Car	
Rennwagen	
Pcs: 3	1980–1984

2623	EU NA AU AS
Delivery Truck	
Lieferwagen mit Waren	
Pcs: 7	1980–1991

2625	EU NA AU AS
Car with Boat and Trailer	
Auto mit Anhänger und Boot	
Pcs: 7	1980–1991

2627	EU NA AU AS
Rodeo	
Auto mit Pferdetransporter	
Pcs: 6	1980–1991

2630	EU NA AU AS
Family Room	
Wohnzimmer	
Pcs: 14	1980–1981

2640	EU NA AU AS
Grocery Store	
Supermarkt mit Klingelkasse	
Pcs: 23	1980–1984

2643	EU NA AU AS
Playhouse	
Spielhaus, aufklappbar	
Pcs: 1	1980–1982

2645	EU NA AU AS
School	
Klassenzimmer mit Schulglocke	
Pcs: 35	1980–1991

2650	EU NA AU AS
Farm	
Kompletter Bauernhof	
Pcs: 68	1980–1984

i	2630	Similar to: 032 (1979)	Ähnlich zu: 032 (1979)

3602 — **EU** **NA** AU AS

Bianca Lamb and Stroller

Kinderwagen

Pcs: 4 | 1980–1981

3604 — **EU** **NA** AU AS

Marc Monkey and Wheelbarrow

Obststand

Pcs: 4 | 1980–1981

3605 — EU **NA** AU AS

Ricky Raccoon and his Scooter

Willie Waschbär auf Rennroller

Pcs: 2 | 1980–1982

3634 — **EU** **NA** AU AS

Charlie Crow's Carry-All

Müllwagen

Pcs: 18 | 1980–1983

3665 — **EU** **NA** AU AS

Ice Cream with Scooter

Eisdiele und Eiswagen

Pcs: 39 | 1980–1981

4306 — **EU** NA AU AS

Finger Rings

Fingerringe

Pcs: 15 | 1980–1981

4307 — **EU** NA AU AS

Finger Rings

Fingerringe

Pcs: 15 | 1980–1981

4336 — **EU** NA AU AS

Mirror

Universal-Rahmen

Pcs: 52 | 1980–1981

5233 — EU **NA** AU AS

Bedroom

Kinderzimmer

Pcs: 164 | 1980–1983

i		
3605	Similar to: 324 (1979)	Ähnlich zu: 324 (1979)

6000 EU NA AU AS
LEGOLAND Idea Book
LEGOLAND Baubuch
Pcs: 1 | 1980–1985

6304 EU NA AU AS
Cross Roads
Kreuzungen
Pcs: 2 | 1980–1985

6305 EU NA AU AS
Trees and Flowers
Bäume und Blumen
Pcs: 24 | 1980–1987

6306 EU NA AU AS
Road Signs
Verkehrsschilder
Pcs: 12 | 1980–1987

6363 EU NA AU AS
Auto Service Station
Autowerkstatt
Pcs: 141 | 1980–1984

6364 EU NA AU AS
Paramedic Unit
Erste-Hilfe-Station
Pcs: 140 | 1980–1983

6375 EU NA AU AS
Gas Station
Tankstelle
Pcs: 274 | 1980–1984

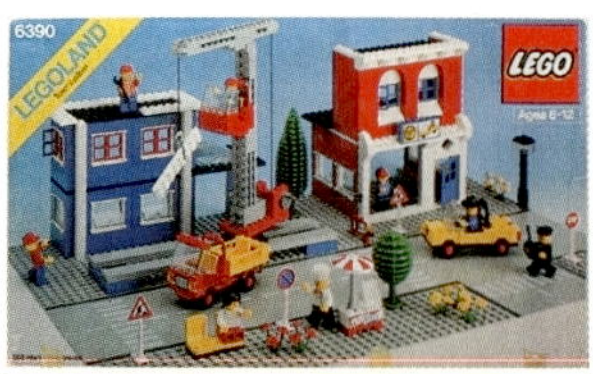

6390 EU NA AU AS
Main Street
Hauptstraße
Pcs: 606 | 1980–1983

6609 EU NA AU AS
Race Car
Buggy mit Rennfahrer
Pcs: 17 | 1980–1984

i	6390	Re-released as: 10041 (2003)	Neu aufgelegt als 10041: (2003)

6627	EU AU
Convertible	
Geländewagen mit Fahrer	
Pcs: 37	1980–1982
■■■□□□	

6647	EU NA AU AS
Highway Repair	
Traktor mit Hänger und Arbeiter	
Pcs: 55	1980–1982
■■■□□□	

6648	NA
Dump Truck	
Kipplaster	
Pcs: 42	1980–1983
■■■□□□	

6678	EU NA AU AS
Pneumatic Crane	
Greifbagger mit Fahrer	
Pcs: 60	1980–1983
■■■□□□	

6679	NA
Tow Truck	
Abschleppwagen	
Pcs: 65	1980–1983
■■■■□□	

6690	EU NA AU AS
Snorkel Pumper	
Löschfahrzeug mit Steiger	
Pcs: 102	1980–1983
■■■■□□	

6821	EU NA AU AS
Shovel Buggy	
Forscherfahrzeug	
Pcs: 28	1980–1983
■■■□□□	

6841	EU
Mineral Detector	
Fahrzeug für Bodenerkundung	
Pcs: 44	1980–1982
■■■□□□	

6861	NA
X-1 Patrol Craft	
X-1 Patrol Craft	
Pcs: 53	1980–1984
■■■■□□	

6901	EU NA AU AS
Mobile Lab	
Mobiles Laboratorium	
Pcs: 139	1980–1983

7710	EU NA AU AS
Train Set without Motor	
Personenzug mit Haltestelle	
Pcs: 468	1980–1986

7720	EU NA AU AS
Battery Train Set	
Güterzug mit Verladerampe	
Pcs: 429	1980–1986

7730	EU NA AU AS
12V Goods Train	
12V Güterzug mit Tenderlokomotive	
Pcs: 524	1980–1982

7740	EU NA AU AS
12V Passenger Train	
12V TEE-Zug	
Pcs: 787	1980–1986

7750	EU NA AU AS
12V Steam Locomotive	
12V Schnellzuglokomotive	
Pcs: 267	1980–1982

7760	EU NA AU AS
12V Diesel Locomotive	
12V Lokomotive	
Pcs: 153	1980–1982

7810	EU NA AU AS
Locomotive without Motor	
Dampflokomotive ohne Motor	
Pcs: 97	1980–1982

7814	EU NA AU AS
Brakedown Cran	
Kranwagen mit drehbarem Kran	
Pcs: 111	1980–1985

7816 EU NA AU AS

Shell Tanker Wagon

Shell Tankwagen

Pcs: 116 | 1980–1982

7818 EU NA AU AS

Passenger Coach

Personenwagen

Pcs: 116 | 1980–1983

7820 EU NA AU AS

Mail Van

Postwagen mit Türen zum Öffnen

Pcs: 212 | 1980–1982

7822 EU NA AU AS

Railway Station

Bahnhofsgebäude

Pcs: 382 | 1980–1982

7834 EU NA AU AS

Level Crossing

Bahnübergang

Pcs: 96 | 1980–1985

7850 EU NA AU AS

Straight Rails

Gerade Schienen

Pcs: 48 | 1980–1993

7851 EU NA AU AS

Curved Rails

Gebogene Schienen

Pcs: 48 | 1980–1997

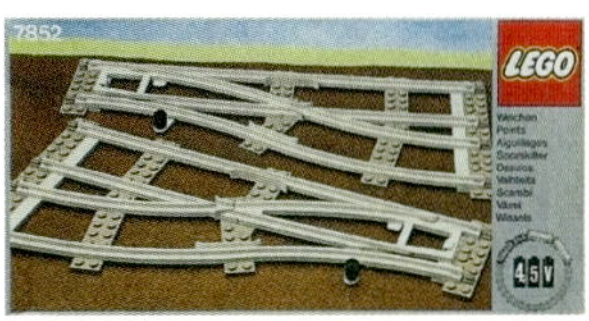

7852 EU NA AU AS

Points

Weichenpaar

Pcs: 14 | 1980–1996

7853 EU NA AU AS

Rail Crossings

Kreuzung

Pcs: 5 | 1980–1983

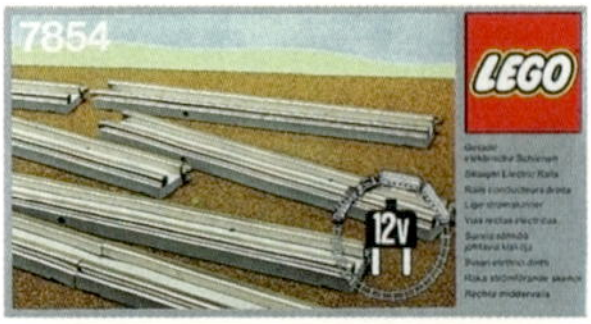

7854 EU NA AU AS

Straight Electric Rails

Gerade Stromführungen

Pcs: 8 | 1980–1993

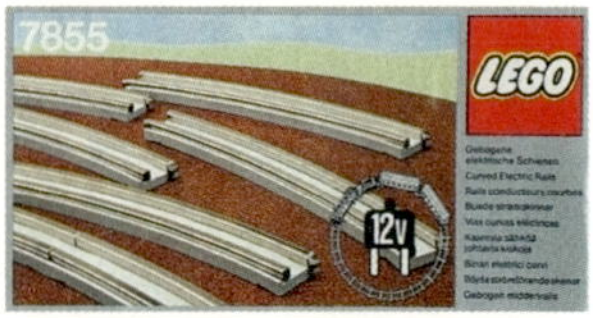

7855 EU NA AU AS

Curved Electric Rails

Gebogene Stromführungen

Pcs: 8 | 1980–1993

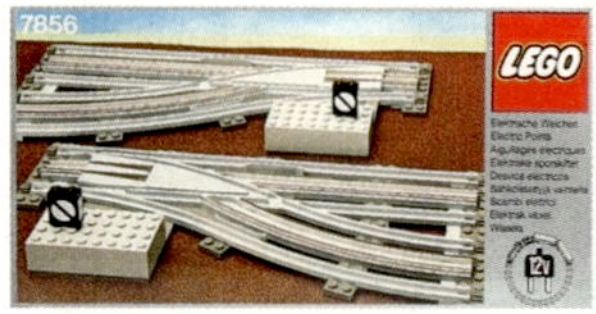

7856 EU NA AU AS

Electric Points

Weichenpaar

Pcs: 16 | 1980–1993

7857 EU NA AU AS

Electric Crossing

Kreuzung

Pcs: 5 | 1980–1993

7858 EU NA AU AS

Remote-Controlled Points, right

Ferngesteuerte Rechtsweiche

Pcs: 15 | 1980–1993

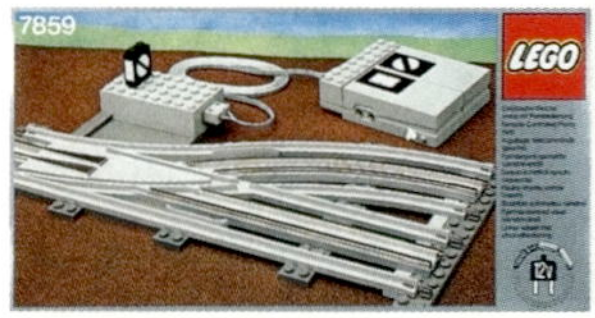

7859 EU NA AU AS

Remote-Controlled Points, left

Ferngesteuerte Linksweiche

Pcs: 15 | 1980–1993

7860 EU NA AU AS

Remote-Controlled Signal

Ferngesteuertes Lichtsignal

Pcs: 20 | 1980–1993

7861 EU NA AU AS

Electric Lighting Set

Beleuchtungsset

Pcs: 32 | 1980–1993

7863 EU NA AU AS

Magnetic Unit for Remote Control

Elektromagnetische Schalteinheit

Pcs: 6 | 1980–1993

7864	EU, AU, AS
12V Transformer	
12V Universaltrafo	
Pcs: 28	1980–1993
Rating: 3/6	

7865	EU, AU, AS
12V Motor	
12V Zug-Einbaumotor	
Pcs: 19	1980–1993
Rating: 3/6	

8857	NA
Motorcycle	
Motorrad mit Beiwagen	
Pcs: 419	1980–1981
Rating: 5/6	

8858	NA
Auto Engines	
Motoren-Modelle	
Pcs: 242	1980–1982
Rating: 5/6	

8860	EU, NA, AU, AS
Auto Chassis	
Auto-Chassis	
Pcs: 669	1980–1988
Rating: 3/6	

8888	EU, NA, AU, AS
Expert Builder Idea Book	
Technik-Baubuch	
Pcs: 1	1980–1984
Rating: 3/6	

i	8857	Similar to: 857 (1979)	Ähnlich zu: 857 (1979)
i	8858	AUS/CAN-edition was sold with Box No. 858; exists with grey and chromed taps; similar to: 858 (1980)	AUS/KAN-Variante wurde mit Box Nr. 858 verkauft; existiert sowohl mit grauen als auch mit verchromten Wasserhähnen; ähnlich zu: 858 (1980)

1981

ⓘ 1	EU NA AU AS	
Basic Souvenir Box		
Mini-Geschenkgrundkasten		
Pcs: 32	1981–1991	Special

ⓘ 226	EU NA AU AS	
Idea Book		
Baubuch		
Pcs: 1	1981–1985	

ⓘ 322	EU NA AU AS	
Basic Set		
Grundbaukasten		
Pcs: 86	1981–1991	

ⓘ 333	EU NA AU AS	
Basic Set		
Grundbaukasten		
Pcs: 104	1981–1991	

ⓘ 355	EU NA AU AS	
Basic Set		
Grundbaukasten		
Pcs: 144	1981–1990	

ⓘ 366	EU NA AU AS	
Basic Set		
Grundbaukasten		
Pcs: 191	1981–1991	

ⓘ 322	Similar to: 1932 (1993)	Ähnlich zu: 1932 (1993)

544	EU NA AU AS	
Basic Set		
Grundbaukasten		
Pcs: 145	1981–1991	

555	EU NA AU AS	
Basic Set		
Grundbaukasten		
Pcs: 223	1981–1991	

566	EU NA AU AS	
Basic Set		
Grundbaukasten		
Pcs: 274	1981–1990	

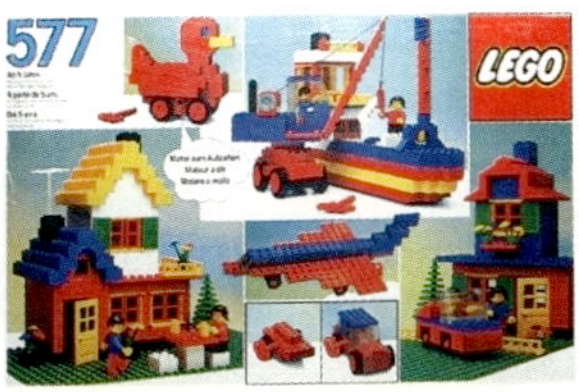

577	EU NA AU AS	
Basic Set		
Grundbaukasten		
Pcs: 409	1981–1991	

890	EU NA AU AS	
Wind-Up Motor		
Motor zum Aufziehen		
Pcs: 10	1981–1985	

1581	EU NA AU AS	
Silja Line Ferry		
Silja Line Fährschiff		
Pcs: 181	1981–1985	Special

2330	EU NA AU AS	
Basic Set		
Grundbaukasten		
Pcs: 9	1981–1984	

2340	EU NA AU AS	
Basic Set		
Grundbaukasten		
Pcs: 17	1981–1984	

2350	EU NA AU AS	
Basic Set		
Grundbaukasten		
Pcs: 24	1981–1984	

544	Similar to: 1944 (1983), 1954 (1984)	Ähnlich zu: 1944 (1983), 1954 (1984)
890	Similar to: 895 (1985)	Ähnlich zu: 895 (1985)
1581	Sold only on Silja Line Ferries	Wurde nur auf Silja Line Fähren verkauft

2360	EU NA AU AS	
Basic Set		
Grundbaukasten		
Pcs: 35	1981–1984	
Rating: 5/6		

2370	EU NA AU AS	
Basic Set		
Grundbaukasten		
Pcs: 48	1981–1984	
Rating: 5/6		

2621	EU (NA AU AS greyed)	
Tractor		
Traktor mit Fahrer		
Pcs: 3	1981–1982	
Rating: 5/6		

2624	EU (NA AU AS greyed)	
Helicopter		
Hubschrauber mit Pilot		
Pcs: 3	1981–1982	
Rating: 5/6		

2644	EU (NA AU AS greyed)	
Service Station		
Tankstelle mit Abschleppwagen		
Pcs: 17	1981–1984	
Rating: 5/6		

3601	EU NA (AU AS greyed)	
Elton Elephant / Edward Elephant		
Edward Elefant am Gartentisch		
Pcs: 7	1981	
Rating: 4/6		

3603	EU NA (AU AS greyed)	
Boris Bulldog and Mailbox		
Boris Bulldogge am Briefkasten		
Pcs: 5	1981	
Rating: 4/6		

3615	NA (EU AU AS greyed)	
Percy Pig's Wheelbarrow		
Henry das Schwein mit Schubkarre		
Pcs: 4	1981	
Rating: 5/6		

3628	EU NA (AU AS greyed)	
Perry Panda & Chester Chimp		
Leiter-Roller		
Pcs: 5	1981–1983	
Rating: 4/6		

i	3615	Similar to: 325 (1979)	Ähnlich zu: 325 (1979)

3629 EU NA AU AS

Barney Bear

Bruno Bärs Reparaturwagen

Pcs: 17	1981–1982	

3635 EU NA AU AS

Bonnie Bunny's Camper

Bonnie Kaninchens Wohnmobil

Pcs: 30	1981–1983	

6075 EU NA AU AS

Castle

Burg

Pcs: 775	1981–1983	

6077 EU NA AU AS

Knight's Procession

Ritter

Pcs: 48	1981–1983	

6083 EU NA AU AS

Knight's Tournament

Ritterturnier

Pcs: 211	1981–1983	

6365 EU NA AU AS

Summer Cottage

Sommerhaus

Pcs: 152	1981–1989	

6382 EU NA AU AS

Fire Station

Feuerwache

Pcs: 395	1981–1985	

6383 EU NA AU AS

Public Works Center

Bauhof mit Doppelgarage

Pcs: 414	1981–1984	

6600 EU NA AU AS

Police Patrol

Verkehrsstreife

Pcs: 20	1981–1983	

i	6075	Similar to: 375 (1978)	Ähnlich zu: 375 (1978)
i	6077	Similar to: 677 (1979)	Ähnlich zu: 677 (1979)
i	6083	Similar to: 383 (1979)	Ähnlich zu: 383 (1979)
i	6600	Similar to: 600 (1978)	Ähnlich zu: 600 (1978)

6602	EU NA AU AS
Fire Unit 1	
Feuerwehrhauptmann	
Pcs: 25	1981–1983

6610	EU NA AU AS
Gas Pumps	
Tanksäule	
Pcs: 29	1981–1982

6611	EU NA AU AS
Fire Chief's Car	
Feuerwehrhauptmann	
Pcs: 20	1981–1984

6626	EU NA AU AS
Rescue Helicopter	
Rettungshubschrauber	
Pcs: 37	1981–1982

6628	EU NA AU AS
Shell Tow Truck	
Shell Abschleppwagen	
Pcs: 38	1981–1983

6629	EU NA AU AS
Ambulance	
Erste-Hilfe-Wagen	
Pcs: 39	1981–1984

6630	EU NA AU AS
Bucket Loader	
Traktor mit Planierschild	
Pcs: 34	1981–1989

6650	EU NA AU AS
Fire and Rescue Van	
Löschfahrzeug	
Pcs: 46	1981–1983

6680	EU NA AU AS
Ambulance	
Ambulanz-Wagen	
Pcs: 63	1981–1983

i	Set	English	Deutsch
i	6602	Similar to: 602 (1978)	Ähnlich zu: 602 (1978)
i	6611	Included in: 1976 (1984)	Enthalten in: 1976 (1984)
i	6626	Similar to: 626 (1978)	Ähnlich zu: 626 (1978)
i	6628	Also included in: 1979 (1985)	Auch enthalten in: 1979 (1985)
i	6629	Also included in: 1976 (1984)	Auch enthalten in: 1976 (1984)

6681	EU NA AU AS	
Police Van		
Radar-Kontrolle		
Pcs: 82	1981–1983	

6691	EU NA AU AS	
Red Cross Helicopter		
Rettungshubschrauber		
Pcs: 108	1981–1983	

6801	EU NA AU AS	
Space Scooter (Rocket Sled)		
Planeten-Scooter		
Pcs: 23	1981–1984	

6822	EU NA AU AS	
Space Shuttle		
Schubgleiter		
Pcs: 33	1981–1985	

6842	EU NA AU AS	
Shuttle Craft		
Schwerer Schubgleiter		
Pcs: 46	1981–1984	

6870	EU NA AU AS	
Space Probe Launcher		
Weltraum-Traktor		
Pcs: 60	1981–1983	

6927	EU NA AU AS	
All-Terrain Vehicle		
Mobile Messstation		
Pcs: 172	1981–1983	

6929	EU NA AU AS	
Starfleet Voyager		
Transplanetarischer Raumtransporter		
Pcs: 247	1981–1997	

6970	EU NA AU AS	
Beta-1 Command Base		
Kommandozentrale		
Pcs: 270	1981–1983	

ⓘ	6801	Also included in: 1977 (1983)	Auch enthalten in: 1977 (1983)
ⓘ	6822	Also included in: 1977 (1983), 1999 (1985)	Auch enthalten in: 1977 (1983), 1999 (1985)

7725	EU NA AU AS
12V Passenger Train Set	
12V Schnelltriebwagen	
Pcs: 496	1981–1986

7777	EU NA AU AS
Trains Idea Book	
Eisenbahn-Baubuch	
Pcs: 1	1981–1985

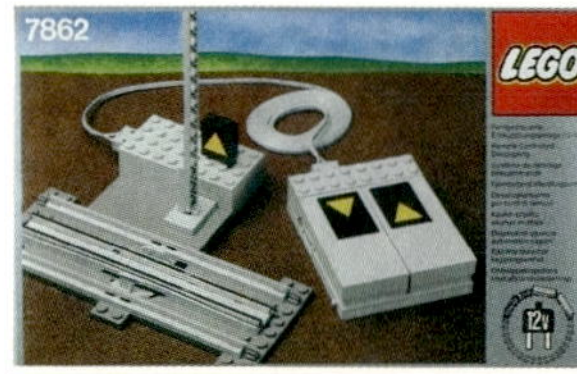

7862	EU NA AU AS
Remote-Controlled Decoupler	
Ferngesteuerte Entkupplungsanlage	
Pcs: 14	1981–1983

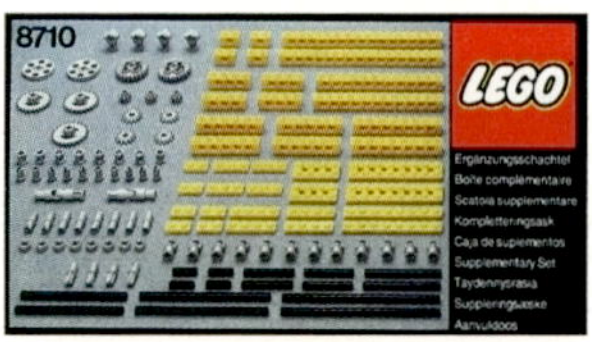

8710	EU NA AU AS
Supplementary Set	
Ergänzungsset Gerätebau	
Pcs: 124	1981–1989

8844	EU NA AU AS
Helicopter	
Verkehrs-Helikopter	
Pcs: 318	1981–1985

8845	EU NA AU AS
Dune Buggy	
Geländewagen	
Pcs: 179	1981–1985

8848	EU NA AU AS
Power Truck	
Lastkraftwagen	
Pcs: 398	1981–1985

8859	EU NA AU AS
Tractor	
Traktor mit Lenkung	
Pcs: 615	1981–1985

1982

599	EU NA AU AS	
Super Basic Set		
Super Grundbaukasten		
Pcs: -	1982–1985	

1590	EU NA AU AS	
ANWB Breakdown Assistance		
ANWB Pannenhilfe		
Pcs: 270	1982–1984	Special

1600	EU NA AU AS	
Pampers Gift Pack		
Pampers Gratisset		
Pcs: 5	1982–1985	Special

1656	EU NA AU AS	
Viking Line Ferry		
Viking Line Fährschiff		
Pcs: 178	1982–1985	Special

1658	EU NA AU AS	
Viking Line Ferry		
Viking Line Fährschiff		
Pcs: -	1982–1985	Special

1905	EU NA AU AS	
Mini Basic Set		
Mini Grundbaukasten		
Pcs: 36	1982–1985	

i	1590	Similar to: 1589 (1986); Promo set only in Netherlands	Ähnlich zu: 1589 (1986); Promo, gab es nur in NL
i	1600	Available only in the Netherlands	Gab es nur in Holland
i	1656	Sold only on Viking Line Ferries	Wurde nur auf Viking Line Fähren verkauft
i	1658	Sold only on Viking Line Ferries	Wurde nur auf Viking Line Fähren verkauft
i	1905	Similar to: 1901 (1984), 1 (1981)	Ähnlich zu: 1901 (1984), 1 (1981)

1910	EU NA AU AS	
Promo Basic Set		
Promo Grundbaukasten		
Pcs: 84	1982–1984	Special

1920	EU NA AU AS	
Promo Basic Set		
Promo Grundbaukasten		
Pcs: 115	1982–1984	Special

1922	EU NA AU AS	
Basic Building Set w. Storage Case		
Grundbaukasten mit Sortierkoffer		
Pcs: 52	1982–1983	Special

2302	EU NA AU AS	
Building Plate 24x24		
Bauplatte 24x24		
Pcs: 1	1982–1984	

2306	EU NA AU AS	
Supplementary Bricks		
Ergänzungskasten		
Pcs: 18	1982–1984	

2308	EU NA AU AS	
Supplementary Bricks		
Ergänzungskasten		
Pcs: -	1982–1984	

2622	EU NA AU AS	
Little Plane		
Flugzeug		
Pcs: 2	1982–1984	

2635	EU NA AU AS	
Fire Engine		
Feuerwehrauto		
Pcs: 4	1982–1984	

2641	EU NA AU AS	
Barnyard		
Bauernhof		
Pcs: 21	1982–1984	

i	2302	Similar to: 2305 (1984), 2598 (2005), 2306 (1991)	Ähnlich zu: 2305 (1984), 2598 (2005), 2306 (1991)

2642	EU NA AU AS
Living Room	
Wohnzimmer	
Pcs: 26	1982–1984

2648	EU NA AU AS
House with Garage	
Spielhaus mit Garage	
Pcs: 18	1982–1984

3654	EU NA AU AS
Country Cottage	
Gartenlaube	
Pcs: 44	1982–1986

3666	EU NA AU AS
Petrol Station	
Tankstelle	
Pcs: 32	1982–1983

3667	EU NA AU AS
Bakery	
Zucker-Bäckerei	
Pcs: 65	1982–1985

3669	EU NA AU AS
Police-/Fire Station	
Polizei- und Brandwache	
Pcs: 30	1982–1983

3672	EU NA AU AS
Hotel/Restaurant	
Gartenhotel	
Pcs: 57	1982–1984

3678	EU NA AU AS
The Fabuland House	
Terrassenhaus	
Pcs: 135	1982–1985

3701	EU NA AU AS
Fisherman Cornelius Cat	
Sportangler Charlie Kater	
Pcs: 3	1982–1983

3703	EU NA AU AS
Peter Pig the Cook	
Koch Pierre Schwein	
Pcs: 3	1982–1983

3704	EU NA AU AS
Majorie Mouse	
Raumpflegerin Moe Maus	
Pcs: 3	1982–1983

3706	EU NA AU AS
Elmer Elefant	
Straßenfeger Ernie Elefant	
Pcs: 3	1982–1984

3707	EU NA AU AS
Clover Cow	
Gärtnerin Clara Kuh	
Pcs: 3	1982–1983

3708	EU NA AU AS
Rufus Rabbit	
Eilbote Robby Hase	
Pcs: 4	1982–1983

3781	EU NA AU AS
Maximilian Mouse, the Handyman	
Max Maus mit Hobbywagen	
Pcs: 5	1982–1983

3782	EU NA AU AS
Photographer Patrick Parrot	
Fotoreporter Paul Papagei	
Pcs: 5	1982–1984

3784	EU NA AU AS
Hugo Hog the Tinker	
Henry Schweins Marktstand	
Pcs: 5	1982–1983

3786	EU NA AU AS
Buzzy Bulldog the Postman	
Briefträger Boris Bulldogge	
Pcs: 7	1982–1984

4005 EU NA AU AS

Tug Boat		
Bugsierschlepper		
Pcs: 66	1982–1986	

4015 EU NA AU AS

Cargo Steamer		
Stückgutfrachter		
Pcs: 80	1982–1986	

4025 EU NA AU AS

Fire Boat		
Feuerlöschboot		
Pcs: 151	1982–1986	

5235 EU (faded) NA AU (faded) AS (faded)

Schoolroom		
Klassenzimmer		
Pcs: 234	1982–1983	

6302 EU NA AU AS

6 Figures		
6 Figuren		
Pcs: 31	1982–1985	

6308 EU NA AU (faded) AS (faded)

Policemen		
Polizisten		
Pcs: 20	1982–1985	

6362 EU NA (faded) AU AS

Post Office		
Postamt mit Paketwagen		
Pcs: 138	1982–1984	

6372 EU NA AU AS

Town House		
Einfamilienhaus mit Garten		
Pcs: 233	1982–1984	

6607 EU NA AU AS

Service Truck		
Straßenkehrmaschine		
Pcs: 25	1982–1984	

1982

6608	EU NA AU AS
Tractor	
Traktor	
Pcs: 21	1982–1988

6651	EU NA AU AS
Post Office Van	
Postauto mit Briefkasten	
Pcs: 47	1982–1984

6653	EU NA AU AS
Highway Emergency Van	
Autobahn-Verkehrswacht	
Pcs: 56	1982–1989

6685	EU NA AU AS
Fire Copter 1	
Mehrzweck-Hubschrauber	
Pcs: 99	1982–1989

6880	EU NA AU AS
Surface Explorer	
Planetenfahrzeug	
Pcs: 82	1982–1984

6890	EU NA AU AS
Cosmic Cruiser	
Raumfähre	
Pcs: 115	1982–1984

6950	EU NA AU AS
Mobile Rocket Transport	
Fahrbare Startrampe	
Pcs: 209	1982–1985

8030	EU NA AU AS
Universal Box	
Universalkasten	
Pcs: 141	1982–1985

8050	EU NA AU AS
Universal Box	
Universalkasten	
Pcs: 151	1982–1985

6653	Included in: 1997 (1985)	Enthalten in: 1997 (1985)

8090	EU NA AU AS
Universal Box	
Universalkasten	
Pcs: 266	1982–1983

8700	EU NA AU AS
4.5V Expert Builder Power Pack	
4,5V Technik Motor	
Pcs: 27	1982–1990

8846	EU NA AU AS
Tow Truck	
Abschleppwagen	
Pcs: 379	1982–1983

1983

710	EU NA AU AS	
Universal Building Set		
Universalkasten m. Dekorelementen		
Pcs: 364	1983–1985	

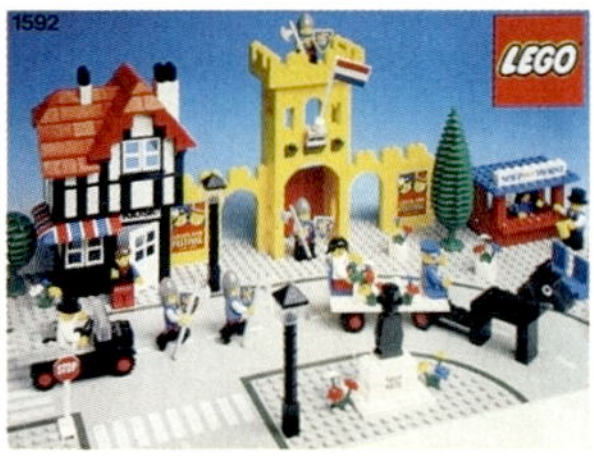

1592	EU	
Town Square - Castle Scene		
Stadtmilieu		
Pcs: 491	1983–1984	Special

1593	EU	
Delta Spacecraft		
Delta-Fähre		
Pcs: 313	1983–1984	Special

1907	EU	
Crecer Feliz Giftbox		
Crecer Feliz Geschenkkasten		
Pcs: 2	1983–1984	Special

1911	NA	
Basic Set		
Grundbaukasten		
Pcs: 34	1983–1984	Special

1912	EU NA AS	
Car		
Auto		
Pcs: 20	1983	Special

i	1592	Dutch Version of 1592 (1980)	Niederländische Version von 1592 (1980)
i	1593	Sold until 12/31/1983 in GB as Persil promo, only in UK, D, DK, F	Bis 31.12.1983 in GB als Persil-Promo, nur in GB, D, DK, F
i	1911	Similar to: 311 (1984)	Ähnlich zu: 311 (1984)
i	1912	McDonald's Promo	McDonald's Promo

1913	EU NA AU AS	
Ship		
Schiff		
Pcs: 27	1983	Special

1914	EU NA AU AS	
Helicopter		
Hubschrauber		
Pcs: 20	1983	Special

1915	EU NA AU AS	
Airplane		
Flugzeug		
Pcs: 20	1983	Special

1918	EU NA AU AS	
Bird		
Vogel		
Pcs: 5	1983–1992	Special

1919	EU NA AU AS	
Boat		
Boot		
Pcs: 5	1983–1989	Special

1924	EU NA AU AS	
Motorcycle		
Motorrad		
Pcs: 103	1983–1984	Special

1944	EU NA AU AS	
Basic Set with Storage Case		
Grundbaukasten mit Koffer		
Pcs: 139	1983–1984	Special

1977	EU NA AU AS	
Space Value Pack		
Raumfahrt-Kombiset		
Sets: 3	1983	Special

1978	EU NA AU AS	
Town Value Pack		
Stadt-Kombiset		
Sets: 3	1983	Special

i			
i	1913-1919	McDonald's Promo	McDonald's Promo
i	1944	Similar to: 544 (1981), 1954 (1984)	Ähnlich zu: 544 (1981), 1954 (1984)
i	1977	Includes: 6801 (1981), 6822 (1981), 6823 (1983)	Enthält: 6801 (1981), 6822 (1981), 6823 (1983)
i	1978	Includes: 6611 (1981), 6623 (1983), 6624 (1983)	Enthält: 6611 (1981), 6623 (1983), 6624 (1983)

2015 EU NA AU AS

Rattle "Oval"

Rassel mit Greifring

Pcs: 1 | 1983–1987

2023 EU NA AU AS

Rattle "Square"

Rassel mit Greifrahmen

Pcs: 1 | 1983–1987

2024 EU NA AU AS

Rattle "Figure"

Rassel mit Greifring und Figur

Pcs: 1 | 1983–1987

2037 EU NA AU AS

Spin-A-Coaster

Greif-Karussell

Pcs: 2 | 1983–1987

2038 EU NA AU AS

Activity Water Toy

Schwimm-Insel

Pcs: 2 | 1983–1987

2365 EU NA AU AS

Basic Set "Safari"

Grundbaukasten „Safari"

Pcs: 32 | 1983–1991

2634 EU NA AU AS

Truck

Lastwagen zum Kippen mit Fahrer

Pcs: 7 | 1983–1990

2646 EU NA AU AS

Crane Set

Kran mit Silo

Pcs: 23 | 1983–1986

2700 EU NA AU AS

Freight Train Set

Lokomotive mit 2 Kipploren

Pcs: 38 | 1983–1989

i	2015	Similar to: 2014 (1987)	Ähnlich zu: 2014 (1987)
i	2024	Similar to: 2020 (1987); included in: 9004 (1988)	Ähnlich zu: 2020 (1987); enthalten in: 9004 (1988)
i	2037	Similar to: 2051 (1987)	Ähnlich zu: 2051 (1987)
i	2038	Similar to: 2059 (1987)	Ähnlich zu: 2059 (1987)

2705	EU NA AU AS
Passenger Train	
Personenzug	
Pcs: 14	1983–1992

2711	EU NA AU AS
Straight Rails	
Gerade Schienen	
Pcs: 4	1983–1993

2712	EU NA AU AS
Curved Rails	
Gebogene Schienen	
Pcs: 4	1983–1993

3626	EU NA AU AS
Roger Raccoon's Sports Car	
Rennfahrer Wuschi Waschbär	
Pcs: 17	1983–1984

3627	EU NA AU AS
Bonnie Rabbit's Flower Truck	
Bonnie Kaninchens Blumenwagen	
Pcs: 25	1983–1984

3637	EU NA AU AS
Gertrude Goat's Painter's Truck	
Malerin Zensie Ziege	
Pcs: 15	1983–1984

3638	EU NA AU AS
Buster Bulldog's Fire Engine	
Bello Bulldogges Feuerwehr	
Pcs: 18	1983–1984

3709	EU NA AU AS
Harry Horse, Carpenter	
Bastler Harry Pferd	
Pcs: 3	1983–1984

3710	EU NA AU AS
Peter Panda Takes a Bath	
Percy Bär mit Badewanne	
Pcs: 3	1983–1984

(i)	3627	Similar to: 3624 (1985)	Ähnlich zu: 3624 (1985)
(i)	3638	Similar to: 3642 (1985)	Ähnlich zu: 3642 (1985)

3787 EU NA AU AS

Hannah Hippopotamus, Gardener

Gärtnerin Nessy Nilpferd

Pcs: 13	1983–1984	

3788 EU NA AU AS

Paulette Poodle's Living Room

Paula Pudels Wohnzimmer

Pcs: 15	1983–1984	

6002 EU NA AU AS

Town Figures

Stadtfiguren

Pcs: 8	1983–1986	

6002 EU NA AU AS

Castle Figures

Burgfiguren

Pcs: 18	1983–1986	

6307 EU NA AU AS

Firemen

Feuerwehrmänner

Pcs: 22	1983–1985	

6371 EU NA AU AS

Service Station

Tankstelle

Pcs: 269	1983–1986	

6374 EU NA AU AS

Holiday Home

Ferienvilla

Pcs: 270	1983–1989	

6384 EU NA AU AS

Police Station

Polizei-Einsatz-Zentrale

Pcs: 399	1983–1987	

6606 EU NA AU AS

Road Repair Set

Straßenarbeiter

Pcs: 26	1983–1985	

ⓘ 6623	EU NA AU AS
Police Car	
Streifenwagen	
Pcs: 40	1983–1987

ⓘ 6624	EU NA AU AS
Delivery Van	
Lieferwagen	
Pcs: 41	1983–1989

ⓘ 6652	EU NA AU AS
Construction Truck	
Traktor mit Hinterkipper	
Pcs: 45	1983–1989

ⓘ 6654	EU NA AU AS
Motorcycle Transport	
Motorradtransporter	
Pcs: 54	1983–1988

ⓘ 6683	EU NA AU AS
Burger Stand	
Schnellimbiss	
Pcs: 69	1983–1984

ⓘ 6692	EU NA AU AS
Tractor Trailer	
Schwerlastzug	
Pcs: 102	1983–1985

ⓘ 6701	EU NA AU AS
Space Mini-Figures	
Raum-Crew	
Pcs: 36	1983–1985

ⓘ 6711	EU NA AU AS
Space Figures	
Weltraumfiguren	
Pcs: 24	1983–1986

ⓘ 6803	EU NA AU AS
Space Patrol	
Kleiner Raumgleiter	
Pcs: 25	1983–1985

ⓘ	Set	Also included in	Auch enthalten in
ⓘ	6623	Also included in: 1978 (1983)	Auch enthalten in: 1978 (1983)
ⓘ	6624	Also included in: 1978 (1983)	Auch enthalten in: 1978 (1983)

1983

6823 EU NA AU AS
Surface Transport
Geo-Traktor
Pcs: 27 | 1983–1984

6844 EU NA AU AS
Seismologic Vehicle
Seismobil
Pcs: 46 | 1983–1985

6930 EU NA AU AS
Space Supply Station
Raumversorgungsbasis
Pcs: 206 | 1983–1986

6980 EU NA AU AS
Galaxy Commander
Interplanetarisches Raumschiff
Pcs: 443 | 1983–1985

7727 EU NA AU AS
12V Goods Train
12V Güterzug mit Dampflok
Pcs: 570 | 1983–1985

7755 EU NA AU AS
12V Diesel Locomotive
12V Diesellokomotive
Pcs: 156 | 1983–1985

7815 EU NA AU AS
Sleeping Car
Schlafwagen
Pcs: 228 | 1983–1985

7819 EU NA AU AS
Mail Van
Post- und Gepäckwagen
Pcs: 183 | 1983–1985

7821 EU NA AU AS
Service Wagon
Reparaturwagen
Pcs: 90 | 1983–1985

ⓘ	6823	Also included in: 1977 (1983)	Auch enthalten in: 1977 (1983)

7824	EU NA AU AS
Railway Station	
Bahnhof	
Pcs: 473	1983–1991

7838	EU NA AU AS
Goods Station	
Güterbahnhof	
Pcs: 328	1983–1985

7866	EU NA AU AS
Remote-Controlled Level Crossing	
Ferngesteuerter Bahnübergang	
Pcs: 192	1983–1990

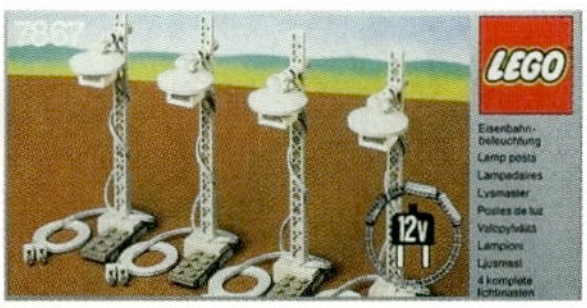

7867	EU NA AU AS
Light Posts	
Eisenbahnbeleuchtung	
Pcs: 52	1983–1993

8841	EU NA AU AS
Desert Racer	
Buggy	
Pcs: 180	1983–1988

8847	EU NA AU AS
Dragster	
Dragster	
Pcs: 252	1983–1986

1984

ⓘ 105 — NA

Canada Post Truck		
Kanada Postauto		
Pcs: 64	1984	Special

ⓘ 311 — EU NA AU AS

Basic Set		
Grundbaukasten		
Pcs: 35	1984–1988	

ⓘ 533 — EU NA AU AS

Basic Set		
Grundbaukasten		
Pcs: 83	1984–1991	

ⓘ 757 — EU NA AU

Red Storage Tray		
Sortiereinsatz, rot		
Pcs: 1	1984–1994	

ⓘ 758 — EU NA AU

Blue Storage Tray		
Sortiereinsatz, blau		
Pcs: 1	1984–1994	

ⓘ 759 — EU NA AU

Storage Cabinet		
Sammelkabinett		
Pcs: 1	1984–1994	

ⓘ	311	Similar to: 1911 (1983)	Ähnlich zu: 1911 (1983)
ⓘ	760	Same as 759 (1984), but with four plastic trays	Wie 759 (1984), aber mit vier Sortiereinschüben
ⓘ	1901	Similar to: 1 (1981), 1905 (1982)	Ähnlich zu: 1 (1981), 1905 (1982)

760	EU NA AU AS	
Storage Cabinet		
Aufbewahrungsregal		
Pcs: 5	1984	

1900	EU NA AU AS	
Special Trial Pack "Duck"		
Schnupperpackung „Ente"		
Pcs: 6	1984–1985	Special

1901	EU NA AU AS	
Mini Basic Set		
Mini Grundbaukasten		
Pcs: 31	1984	Special

1932	EU NA AU AS	
Basic Building Set + Storage Case		
Grundbaukasten mit Sortierkoffer		
Pcs: 83	1984–1985	Special

1954	EU NA AU AS	
Basic Set with Storage Case		
Grundbaukasten mit Sortierkoffer		
Pcs: 137	1984–1985	Special

1976	EU NA AU AS	
Town 3-Pack		
Stadt 3er-Pack		
Sets: 3	1984	Special

1979	EU NA AU AS	
Town Value Pack		
Stadt Kombiset		
Sets: 3	1984	Special

1983	EU NA AU AS	
Space Value Pack		
Weltraum Kombiset		
Sets: 3	1984	Special

2054	EU NA AU AS	
Squirrel		
Eichkätzchen mit Rassel		
Pcs: 2	1984–1987	

1932	Similar to: 322 (1981)	Ähnlich zu: 322 (1981)
1954	Similar to: 1944 (1983), 544 (1981)	Ähnlich zu: 1944 (1983), 544 (1981)
1976	Includes: 6611 (1981), 6628 (1981), 6629 (1981)	Enthält: 6611 (1981), 6628 (1981), 6629 (1981)
1979	Includes: 6621 (1984), 6605 (1984), 6628 (1981)	Enthält: 6621 (1984), 6605 (1984), 6628 (1981)
1983	Includes: 889 (1979), 886 (1979), 6824 (1984)	Enthält: 889 (1979), 886 (1979), 6824 (1984)
2054	Similar to: 2050 (1987)	Ähnlich zu: 2050 (1987)

1984

2055 EU NA AU AS
Rocking Horse
Schaukelpferd
Pcs: 3 | 1984–1987

2305 EU NA AU AS
Building Plate 24x24
Bauplatte 24x24
Pcs: 1 | 1984–1997

2307 EU NA AU AS
Supplementary Bricks
Ergänzungskasten
Pcs: 18 | 1984–1989

2309 EU NA AU AS
Supplementary Bricks
Ergänzungskasten
Pcs: 25 | 1984–1987

2335 EU NA AU AS
Basic Set "Animal"
Grundbaukasten „Tiere"
Pcs: 9 | 1984–1991

2345 EU NA AU AS
Basic Set "House"
Grundbaukasten „Haus"
Pcs: 17 | 1984–1991

2355 EU NA AU AS
Basic Set "Vehicles"
Grundbaukasten „Autos"
Pcs: 26 | 1984–1991

2375 EU NA AU AS
Basic Building Set "Town"
Grundbaukasten „Stadt"
Pcs: 32 | 1984–1991

2401 EU NA AU AS
Racer
Rennfahrer
Pcs: 3 | 1984

ⓘ	2055	Similar to: 2057 (1987)	Ähnlich zu: 2057 (1987)
ⓘ	2305	Similar to: 2302 (1982), 2598 (2005), 2306 (1991)	Ähnlich zu: 2302 (1982), 2598 (2005), 2306 (1991)
ⓘ	2401	Similar to: 085 (1977), 533 (1977)	Ähnlich zu: 085 (1977), 533 (1977)

2402	EU NA AU AS
Police Car	
Polizeiauto	
Pcs: 5	1984–1986

2411	EU NA AU AS
Camping	
Auto mit Wohnmobil	
Pcs: 11	1984–1986

2618	EU NA AU AS
Deep Sea Diver	
Schlauchboot mit Taucher	
Pcs: 3	1984–1990

2619	EU NA AU AS
Helicopter	
Hubschrauber	
Pcs: 3	1984–1992

2636	EU NA AU AS
Tow Truck	
Abschleppwagen	
Pcs: 6	1984–1987

2639	EU NA AU AS
Petrol Station	
Tankstelle mit Tankwagen	
Pcs: 14	1984–1989

2649	EU NA AU AS
Sea Explorer	
Fährschiff	
Pcs: 43	1984–1988

2713	EU NA AU AS
Points	
Weichen	
Pcs: 10	1984–1992

2717	EU NA AU AS
Bridge	
Eisenbahnbrücke	
Pcs: 6	1984–1992

3630	EU NA AU AS
Sports Airplane	
Albert Albatros' Sport-Flugzeug	
Pcs: 11	1984

3639	EU NA AU AS
Police Car	
Arrestwagen	
Pcs: 11	1984

3664	EU NA AU AS
Police Station	
Polizeistation	
Pcs: 63	1984–1986

3670	EU NA AU AS
Service Station	
Tankstelle	
Pcs: 53	1984–1986

3671	EU NA AU AS
Airport	
Flughafen	
Pcs: 59	1984–1988

3711	EU NA AU AS
Pierre Pig and his Tube	
Pierre Schwein mit Tuba	
Pcs: 5	1984

3712	EU NA AU AS
Robby Rabbit and Accordion	
Robby Hase und Akkordeon	
Pcs: 5	1984

3713	EU NA AU AS
Drummer Gabriel Monkey	
Gabriel Affe mit Trommel	
Pcs: 8	1984

3789	EU NA AU AS
Police Motorcylcle	
Inspektor Dogge mit Motorrad	
Pcs: 6	1984

i	3630	Similar to: 3625 (1985)	Ähnlich zu: 3625 (1985)
i	3639	Similar to: 3643 (1985)	Ähnlich zu: 3643 (1985)

3791 EU NA AU AS

Wally Walrus	
Willem Walross mit Spezial-Roller	
Pcs: 7	1984

6010 EU NA AU AS

Supply Wagon	
Landsknecht	
Pcs: 35	1984–1986

6021 EU NA AU AS

Jousting Knights	
Turnierritter	
Pcs: 41	1984–1986

6022 EU NA AU AS

Horse Cart	
Turnierwagen	
Pcs: 42	1984–1987

6030 EU NA AU AS

Catapult	
Steinschleuder	
Pcs: 83	1984–1991

6040 EU NA AU AS

Blacksmith Shop	
Burgschmiede	
Pcs: 92	1984–1985

6061 EU NA AU AS

Siege Tower	
Belagerungsturm	
Pcs: 218	1984–1987

6073 EU NA AU AS

Knight's Castle	
Kleine Ritterburg	
Pcs: 418	1984–1985

6080 EU NA AU AS

King's Castle	
Große Ritterburg	
Pcs: 687	1984–1991

6103	EU NA AU AS	
Knights		
Ritter		
Pcs: 21	1984	

6366	EU NA AU AS	
Fire & Rescue Squad		
Feuerwehr mit Einsatzwagen		
Pcs: 116	1984–1986	

6367	EU NA AU AS	
Truck		
Truck		
Pcs: 156	1984–1985	

6373	EU NA AU AS	
Motorcycle Shop		
Motorrad-Center		
Pcs: 187	1984–1986	

6391	EU NA AU AS	
Cargo Center		
Spedition		
Pcs: 563	1984–1986	

6605	EU NA AU AS	
Road Racer		
Go-Kart		
Pcs: 20	1984–1986	

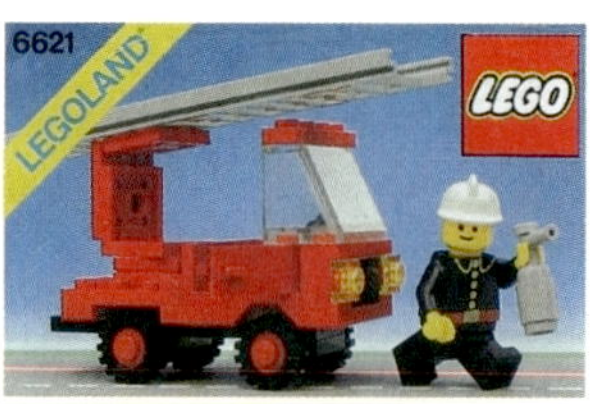

6621	EU NA AU AS	
Fire Truck		
Feuerwehr-Rettungswagen		
Pcs: 38	1984–1986	

6622	EU NA AU AS	
Mailman on Motorcycle		
Postbote mit Motorrad		
Pcs: 30	1984–1988	

6628	EU NA AU AS	
Construction Workers		
Bauarbeiter		
Pcs: 8	1984	Special

i	6605	Also included in: 1979 (1985)	Auch enthalten in: 1979 (1985)
i	6621	Also included in: 1979 (1985)	Auch enthalten in: 1979 (1985)
i	6622	Also included in: 1997 (1985)	Auch enthalten in: 1997 (1985)

6655	EU NA AU AS
Auto & Tire Repair	
Pkw mit Wagenheber	
Pcs: 58	1984–1986

6684	EU NA AU AS
Police Patrol Squad	
Polizei-Arrestwagen	
Pcs: 81	1984–1989

6686	EU NA AU AS
Backhoe	
Traktor für Straßenbau	
Pcs: 87	1984–1987

6694	EU NA AU AS
Car with Camper	
Pkw mit Wohnwagen	
Pcs: 109	1984–1986

6695	EU NA AU AS
Shell Tanker	
Shell Tanklastzug	
Pcs: 106	1984–1986

6696	EU NA AU AS
Fuel Tanker	
Tanklastzug	
Pcs: 104	1984–1985

6804	EU NA AU AS
Surface Rover	
Lunar-Taxi	
Pcs: 21	1984–1987

6824	EU NA AU AS
Space Dart-I	
Strato-Flitzer	
Pcs: 48	1984–1985

6846	EU NA AU AS
Tri-Star Voyager	
Schubdüsen-Controller	
Pcs: 69	1984–1985

i 6824	Also included in: 1983 (1984)	Auch enthalten in: 1983 (1984)

6871 EU NA AU AS

Star-Patrol Launcher

Planetenmobil

Pcs: 70	1984–1985	

6881 EU NA AU AS

Lunar Rocket Launcher

Radiosonden-Transporter

Pcs: 98	1984–1991	

6928 EU NA AU AS

Uranium Search Vehicle

Mobile Licht- und Schallmessstation

Pcs: 201	1984–1985	

6951 EU NA AU AS

Robot Command Center

Sonnenobservatorium

Pcs: 295	1984–1986	

6971 EU NA AU AS

Inter-Galactic Command Base

Lunar-Zentrum

Pcs: 328	1984–1991	

8020 EU NA AU AS

Building Set

Universalkasten

Pcs: 121	1984–1988	

8040 EU NA AU AS

Building Set

Universalkasten „Pneumatik“

Pcs: 163	1984–1988	

8843 EU NA AU AS

Fork Truck

Gabelstapler

Pcs: 259	1984–1987	

8851 EU NA AU AS

Excavator

Bagger

Pcs: 357	1984–1988	

8889	EU NA AU AS
Idea Book	
Baubuch	
Pcs: 1	1984–1987

1985

106		
UNICEF Van		
UNICEF Geländewagen		
Pcs: 58	1985	Special

107		
Canada Post Mail Truck		
Canada Post Sattelschlepper		
Pcs: 137	1985	Special

200		
Idea Book		
Baubuch		
Pcs: 1	1985–1987	

293		
Basic Building Set		
Grundbaukasten		
Pcs: -	1985–1989	Special

304		
Basic Building Set		
Grundbaukasten		
Pcs: 31	1985–1987	

308		
Basic Building Set		
Grundbaukasten		
Pcs: 30	1985–1986	

200	Available with other covers	Mit unterschiedlichen Titelbildern erhältlich

310 EU NA AU AS

Basic Building Set

Grundbaukasten

Pcs: 46 | 1985–1989

320 EU NA AU AS

Basic Building Set

Grundbaukasten

Pcs: 78 | 1985–1989

330 EU NA AU AS

Basic Building Set

Grundbaukasten

Pcs: 160 | 1985–1989

340 EU NA AU AS

Basic Building Set

Grundbaukasten

Pcs: 216 | 1985–1989

350 EU NA AU AS

Basic Building Set

Grundbaukasten

Pcs: 309 | 1985–1989

504 EU NA AU AS

Basic Building Set

Grundbaukasten

Pcs: 41 | 1985–1987

508 EU NA AU AS

Basic Building Set

Grundbaukasten

Pcs: 62 | 1985–1986

510 EU NA AU AS

Basic Building Set

Grundbaukasten

Pcs: 106 | 1985–1989

520 EU NA AU AS

Basic Building Set

Grundbaukasten

Pcs: 174 | 1985–1989

ⓘ 530	EU NA AU AS
Basic Building Set	
Grundbaukasten	
Pcs: 275	1985–1989

ⓘ 540	EU NA AU AS
Basic Building Set	
Grundbaukasten	
Pcs: 429	1985–1989

ⓘ 550	EU NA AU AS
Basic Building Set	
Grundbaukasten	
Pcs: 498	1985–1989

ⓘ 720	EU NA AU AS
Basic Building Set	
Grundbaukasten	
Pcs: 321	1985–1989

ⓘ 730	EU NA AU AS
Basic Building Set	
Grundbaukasten	
Pcs: 429	1985–1989

ⓘ 740	EU NA AU AS
Basic Building Set	
Grundbaukasten	
Pcs: 529	1985–1990

ⓘ 783	EU NA AU AS
Storage Case	
Sortierkoffer	
Pcs: 1	1985–1994

ⓘ 810	EU NA AU AS
4.5V Motor	
4,5V Motor mit Batteriekasten	
Pcs: 33	1985–1991

ⓘ 895	EU NA AU AS
Wind-Up Motor	
Aufziehmotor	
Pcs: 10	1985–1989

ⓘ	530	Similar to: 537 (1987)	Ähnlich zu: 537 (1987)
ⓘ	540	Similar to: 1662 (1989), 547 (1987)	Ähnlich zu: 1662 (1989), 547 (1987)
ⓘ	550	Similar to: 557 (1987)	Ähnlich zu: 557 (1987)
ⓘ	895	Similar to: 890 (1981)	Ähnlich zu: 890 (1981)

ⓘ 1512	EU NA AU AS	
Basic Set with Storage Case		
Grundbaukasten mit Sortierkoffer		
Pcs: 250	1985	Special

ⓘ 1520	EU NA AU AS	
Basic Set with Storage Case		
Grundbaukasten mit Sortierkoffer		
Pcs: 204	1985–1988	Special

ⓘ 1537	EU NA AU AS	
Rattle Round with Ball		
Rassel mit Greifring		
Pcs: 1	1985	Special

ⓘ 1538	EU NA AU AS	
Building Bricks		
Bausteine		
Pcs: 10	1985–1988	Special

ⓘ 1539	EU NA AU AS	
Building Bricks & Figure		
Bausteine & Figur		
Pcs: 10	1985–1988	Special

ⓘ 1548	EU NA AU AS	
Helicopter		
Helikopter		
Pcs: 36	1985	Special

ⓘ 1550	EU NA AU AS	
Basic Set		
Grundbaukasten		
Pcs: 6	1985–1986	Special

ⓘ 1551	EU NA AU AS	
Build-a-Duck		
Bau eine Ente		
Pcs: 6	1985–1997	Special

ⓘ 1552	EU NA AU AS	
Container Truck		
Container-Lkw		
Pcs: 441	1985	Special

ⓘ	1520	Similar to: 1962 (1985), 1963 (1985)	Ähnlich zu: 1962 (1985), 1963 (1985)
ⓘ	1548	McDonald's Promo	McDonald's Promo
ⓘ	1552	Maersk Line Promo	Maersk Line Promo

1560	NA
Crest Basic Building Set	
Crest Basic-Set	
Pcs: 27	1985	Special

1562	NA
Basic Building Set	
Grundbaukasten	
Pcs: 32	1985	Special

1655	EU
Viking Line Ferry	
Viking Line Fährschiff	
Pcs: 172	1985–1986	Special

1957	EU NA AU AS
Building Set with Storage Bunny	
Bauset mit Hasentasche	
Pcs: 29	1985–1986	Special

1958	EU NA AU AS
Basic Model	
Grundbaukasten	
Pcs: 5	1985	Special

1959	EU NA AU AS
Basic Model	
Grundbaukasten	
Pcs: -	1985	Special

1960	EU NA AU AS
Basic Building Set	
Grundbaukasten	
Pcs: -	1985–1986	Special

1961	EU NA AU AS
Basic Set with Storage Case	
Grundbaukasten mit Sortierkoffer	
Pcs: -	1985	Special

1962	EU NA AU AS
Basic Building Set	
Grundbaukasten	
Pcs: 211	1985–1987	Special

i	Set	English	Deutsch
i	1562	Crest/Pepsi Promo	Crest/Pepsi Promo
i	1655	Sold only on Viking Line Ferries	Wurde nur auf Viking Line Fähren verkauft
i	1958	Included in: 1975 (1985)	Enthalten in: 1975 (1985)
i	1959	Included in: 1975 (1985)	Enthalten in: 1975 (1985)
i	1962	Similar to: 1520 (1985), 1963 (1985)	Ähnlich zu: 1520 (1985), 1963 (1985)

ⓘ 1964 — EU NA AS

Basic Building Set		
Grundbaukasten		
Pcs: 27	1985–1986	Special

ⓘ 1965 — EU NA AS

Basic Building Set		
Grundbaukasten		
Pcs: 38	1985–1986	Special

ⓘ 1966 — EU

Car Repair Shop		
Autowerkstatt		
Pcs: 303	1985–1986	Special

ⓘ 1967 — NA

Town Value Pack		
Stadt Kombiset		
Sets: 3	1985	Special

ⓘ 1968 — EU NA AS

Spacecraft		
Raumschiff		
Pcs: 183	1985–1986	Special

ⓘ 1969 — NA

Space Value Pack		
Raumfahrt Kombiset		
Sets: 3	1985	Special

ⓘ 1972 — EU NA AS

Go-Cart		
Go-Kart		
Pcs: 98	1985–1987	Special

ⓘ 1975 — EU NA AU AS

Combi Pack		
Kombi-Pack		
Sets: 2	1985	Special

ⓘ 1997 — EU NA AU AS

Town Value Pack		
Stadt Kombiset		
Sets: 3	1985	Special

ⓘ		
1964	Similar to: 1523 (1986), 1588 (1987)	Ähnlich zu: 1523 (1986), 1588 (1987)
1965	Similar to: 1598 (1987), 1524 (1986)	Ähnlich zu: 1598 (1987), 1524 (1986)
1967	Includes: 6633 (1985), 6656 (1985), 6653 (1982)	Enthält: 6633 (1985), 6656 (1985), 6653 (1982)
1969	Includes: 6825 (1985), 6848 (1985), 6847 (1985)	Enthält: 6825 (1985), 6848 (1985), 6847 (1985)
1975	Includes: 1958 (1985), 1959 (1985)	Enthält: 1958 (1985), 1959 (1985)
1997	Includes: 6604 (1985), 6622 (1984), 6633 (1985)	Enthält: 6604 (1985), 6622 (1984), 6633 (1985)

1999	EU NA AU AS	
Space Value Pack		
Raumfahrt Kombiset		
Sets: 3	1985	Special

2033	EU NA AU AS	
Shape Sorter		
Puzzle-Clown		
Pcs: 7	1985–1987	

2301	EU NA AU AS	
Building Plates 6x12		
Bauplatten 6x12		
Pcs: 2	1985–1990	

2315	EU NA AU AS	
Pre-School Basic Building Set		
Vorschul-Bauset		
Pcs: 6	1985–1987	Special

2403	EU NA AU AS	
Fire Chief Building Set		
Feuerwehrauto		
Pcs: 4	1985–1989	

2412	EU NA AU AS	
Boat Yard Building Set		
Hafen		
Pcs: 10	1985–1987	

2610	EU NA AU AS	
Car		
Personenwagen		
Pcs: 3	1985–1989	

2611	EU NA AU AS	
Fire Engine		
Feuerwehr		
Pcs: 3	1985–1991	

2629	EU NA AU AS	
Tractor and Farm Tools		
Trecker		
Pcs: 7	1985–1997	

1999	Includes: 6807 (1985), 6822 (1981), 6823 (1983)	Enthält: 6807 (1985), 6822 (1981), 6823 (1983)
2033	Similar to: 2052 (1987)	Ähnlich zu: 2052 (1987)

2631 EU NA AU AS

Stunt Pilot and Plane

Flugzeug

Pcs: 2 | 1985–1989

2647 EU NA AU AS

Farm Animals

Bauer mit Tieren

Pcs: 7 | 1985–1995

2655 EU NA AU AS

Play Farm

Bauernhof

Pcs: 52 | 1985–1996

3624 EU NA AU AS

Flower Car

Blumenwagen

Pcs: 25 | 1985

3625 EU NA AU AS

Aeroplane

Sportflugzeug

Pcs: 11 | 1985–1997

3631 EU NA AU AS

Orchestra

Zwei-Mann-Kapelle

Pcs: 32 | 1985–1988

3641 EU NA AU AS

Car & Camper

Wohnmobil

Pcs: 25 | 1985–1986

3642 EU NA AU AS

Fire Engine

Feuerwehr

Pcs: 18 | 1985

3643 EU NA AU AS

Police Car

Arrestwagen

Pcs: 11 | 1985–1986

i	3624	Similar to: 3627 (1983)	Ähnlich zu: 3627 (1983)
i	3625	Similar to: 3630 (1984)	Ähnlich zu: 3630 (1984)
i	3642	Similar to: 3638 (1983)	Ähnlich zu: 3638 (1983)
i	3643	Similar to: 3639 (1984)	Ähnlich zu: 3639 (1984)

3660	EU NA AU AS
Fisherman's Cottage	
Wochenendhaus	
Pcs: 29	1985–1986

3673	EU NA AU AS
Steamboat	
Raddampfer	
Pcs: 66	1985–1987

3681	EU NA AU AS
Amusement Park	
Freizeitpark	
Pcs: 107	1985–1988

3714	EU NA AU AS
Bricklayer Oscar Orangutan	
Maurer Arnolds Affe	
Pcs: 7	1985–1986

3715	EU NA AU AS
Flower Stand	
Nessy Nilpferds Blumenstand	
Pcs: 24	1985–1987

3716	EU NA AU AS
Office	
Freddy Fuchs am Schreibtisch	
Pcs: 10	1985–1986

3717	EU NA AU AS
Fisherman	
Morty Maus mit Angel	
Pcs: 10	1985

3792	EU NA AU AS
Bedroom	
Sofie Lamm im Schlafzimmer	
Pcs: 17	1985–1988

3793	EU NA AU AS
Buzzy Bulldog's Mailbox	
Briefträger Boris Bulldogge	
Pcs: 12	1985

3794	EU NA AU AS
Police Motorcycle	
Polizeimotorrad	
Pcs: 15	1985–1986

3795	EU NA AU AS
Kitchen	
Cathy Katzes Küche	
Pcs: 27	1985–1987

6011	EU NA AU AS
Black Knight's Treasure	
Ritter mit Schatztruhe	
Pcs: 26	1985–1986

6055	EU NA AU AS
Prisoner Convoy	
Gefangenenkutsche	
Pcs: 117	1985–1991

6102	EU NA AU AS
Castle Mini-Figures	
6 Ritter	
Pcs: 36	1985–1988

6368	EU NA AU AS
Jet Airliner	
Zweistrahliger Verkehrs- u. Reisejet	
Pcs: 138	1985–1987

6369	EU NA AU AS
Garage	
Autowerkstatt	
Pcs: 134	1985–1987

6370	EU NA AU AS
Weekend Home	
Reihenhaus	
Pcs: 187	1985–1987

6377	NA
Delivery Center	
Luftfracht-Verladezentrum	
Pcs: 305	1985–1986

1985

6385	EU NA AU AS
Fire House-I	
Feuerwache	
Pcs: 419	1985–1989

6392	EU NA AU AS
Airport	
Flughafen	
Pcs: 545	1985–1990

6601	EU NA AU AS
Ice Cream Cart	
Eiswagen mit Verkäufer	
Pcs: 31	1985–1987

6603	EU NA AU AS
Shovel Truck	
Traktor mit Planierschild	
Pcs: 27	1985–1986

6604	EU NA AU AS
Formula-I Racer	
Formel I Rennwagen	
Pcs: 31	1985–1991

6631	EU NA AU AS
Steam Shovel	
Löffelbagger	
Pcs: 48	1985–1989

6632	EU NA AU AS
Tactical Patrol Truck	
Polizeigerätewagen	
Pcs: 44	1985–1987

6633	EU NA AU AS
Family Car	
Familienauto	
Pcs: 46	1985

6656	EU NA AU AS
Tow Truck	
Reparatur- und Abschleppwagen	
Pcs: 53	1985–1987

i	6604	Also included in: 1997 (1985)	Auch enthalten in: 1997 (1985)
i	6633	Included in: 1997 (1985), 1967 (1985)	Enthalten in: 1997 (1985), 1967 (1985)
i	6656	Also included in: 1997 (1985)	Auch enthalten in: 1997 (1985)

6657	EU NA AU AS
Fire Patrol Copter	
Feuerlöschhubschrauber	
Pcs: 66	1985–1987

6682	EU NA AU AS
Cement Mixer	
Betonmischer	
Pcs: 91	1985–1989

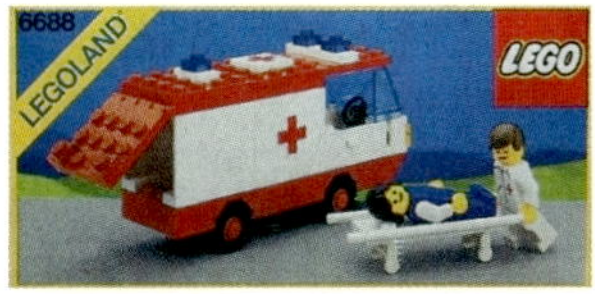

6688	EU NA AU AS
Ambulance	
Krankenwagen	
Pcs: 70	1985–1989

6689	EU NA AU AS
Post-Station	
Postamt	
Pcs: 53	1985–1987

6697	EU NA AU AS
Rescue-I Helicopter	
Rettungshubschrauber	
Pcs: 87	1985–1989

6805	EU NA AU AS
Astro Dasher	
F1-Flügelgleiter	
Pcs: 31	1985–1986

6806	EU NA AU AS
Surface Hopper	
Vertikal-Scooter	
Pcs: 25	1985–1986

6807	EU NA AU AS	
Space Scooter with Robot		
Raumgleiter mit Roboter		
Pcs: 24	1985–1988	Special

6825	EU NA AU AS
Cosmic Comet	
F2-Flügelgleiter	
Pcs: 42	1985–1989

i	6807	Included in: 1999 (1985)	Enthalten in: 1999 (1985)
i	6825	Included in: 1969 (1985)	Enthalten in: 1969 (1985)

6826	EU NA AU AS
Crater Crawler	
System-Controller	
Pcs: 34	1985–1986

6847	EU NA AU AS
Space Dozer	
Geobil	
Pcs: 49	1985–1989

6848	EU NA AU AS
Interplanetary Shuttle	
Interplanetarisches Shuttle	
Pcs: 54	1985

6872	EU NA AU AS
Lunar Patrol Craft	
Iono-Fähre	
Pcs: 68	1985–1991

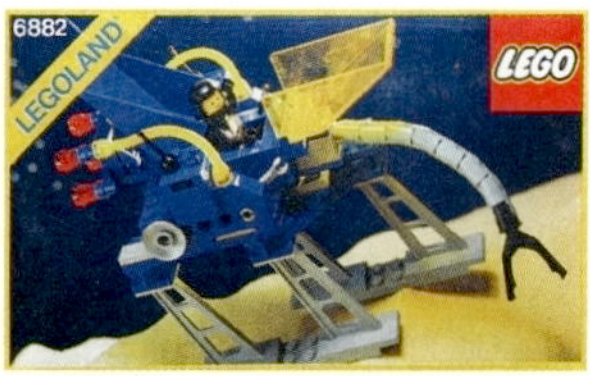

6882	EU NA AU AS
Walking Astro Grappler	
Oberflächen-Kontroll-Center	
Pcs: 94	1985–1987

6891	EU NA AU AS
Gamma-V Laser Craft	
Ultraschall-Transporter	
Pcs: 137	1985–1991

6931	EU NA AU AS
FX-Star Patroller	
Zweistufen-Space-Cruiser	
Pcs: 232	1985–1991

6952	EU NA AU AS
Solar Power Transporter	
Multifunktionaler Planeten-Truck	
Pcs: 313	1985–1989

7715	EU NA AU AS
Passenger Train without Motor	
Personenzug	
Pcs: 445	1985–1991

ⓘ	6847	Also included in: 1969 (1985)	Auch enthalten in: 1969 (1985)
ⓘ	6848	Included in: 1969 (1985)	Enthalten in: 1969 (1985)

7722 EU NA AU AS

4.5V Train with Steam Engine

4,5V Güterzug mit Dampflok

Pcs: 500 | 1985–1991

7735 EU NA AU AS

12V Mixed Train Set

12V Güterzug mit Herkuleslok

Pcs: 524 | 1985–1990

7745 EU NA AU AS

12V High Speed Train

12V Super-Passagierzug

Pcs: 737 | 1985–1990

7817 EU NA AU AS

Crane Waggon

Kranwagen mit Stückgut

Pcs: 152 | 1985–1991

7835 EU NA AU AS

Level Crossing

Beschrankter Bahnübergang

Pcs: 133 | 1985–1991

1986

390	EU NA AU AS
Helicopter	
Hubschrauber	
Pcs: 26	1986–1987

391	EU NA AU AS
Police Car	
Polizeiauto	
Pcs: 22	1986–1987

392	EU NA AU AS
Fire Engine	
Feuerwehr	
Pcs: 30	1986–1987

393	EU NA AU AS
Tow Truck	
Abschlepper	
Pcs: 30	1986–1987

800	EU NA AU AS
Red Bricks	
Rote Steine	
Pcs: 62	1986–1995

801	EU NA AU AS
Blue Bricks	
Blaue Steine	
Pcs: 62	1986–1994

802	EU NA AU AS
White Bricks	
Weiße Steine	
Pcs: 62	1986–1995

803	EU NA AU AS
Yellow Bricks	
Gelbe Steine	
Pcs: 62	1986–1994

804	EU NA AU AS
Black Bricks	
Schwarze Steine	
Pcs: 62	1986–1994

805	EU NA AU AS
Grey Bricks	
Graue Steine	
Pcs: 62	1986–1994

806	EU NA AU AS
Blue Plates	
Blaue Platten	
Pcs: 42	1986–1990

807	EU NA AU AS
Red Plates	
Rote Platten	
Pcs: 42	1986–1990

808	EU NA AU AS
Wheels	
Radelemente	
Pcs: 34	1986–1995

809	EU NA AU AS
Doors and Windows	
Türen und Fenster	
Pcs: 39	1986–1995

811	EU NA AU AS
Roof Tiles 45°	
Dachelemente 45°	
Pcs: 59	1986–1995

ⓘ 812	EU NA AU AS	
Roof Tiles 25°		
Dachelemente 25°		
Pcs: 60	1986–1995	

ⓘ 813	EU NA AU AS	
Base Plate Green 32x32		
Grüne Bauplatte 32x32		
Pcs: 1	1986–1996	

ⓘ 814	EU NA AU AS	
Building Plates Red/Green/Yellow		
Bauplatten, rot/grün/gelb		
Pcs: 3	1986–1995	

ⓘ 815	EU NA AU AS	
Building Plate Grey 48x48		
Große graue Bauplatte 48x48		
Pcs: 1	1986–1996	

ⓘ 816	EU NA AU AS	
Lighting Bricks		
Leuchtsteine 4,5V		
Pcs: 21	1986–1991	

ⓘ 1502	EU NA AU AS	
Basic Set + Duffle Bag		
Grundbaukasten + Tragetasche		
Pcs: 1	1986–1987	Special

ⓘ 1503	EU NA AU AS	
Car Building Set		
Baukasten „Auto“		
Pcs: 7	1986–1987	Special

ⓘ 1504	EU NA AU AS	
House Building Set		
Baukasten „Haus“		
Pcs: 14	1986–1987	Special

ⓘ 1505	EU NA AU AS	
Combi Pack		
Doppelpack		
Sets: 2	1986–1987	Special

ⓘ	813	Similar to: 626 (1996), 840 (1980), 745 (1978)	Ähnlich zu: 626 (1996), 840 (1980), 745 (1978)
ⓘ	814	Similar to: 629 (1996)	Ähnlich zu: 629 (1996)
ⓘ	815	Similar to: 628 (1996), 843 (1980)	Ähnlich zu: 628 (1996), 843 (1980)
ⓘ	1505	Includes: 1503 (1986), 1504 (1986)	Enthält: 1503 (1986), 1504 (1986)

ⓘ 1506	EU NA AU AS	
Town Value Pack		
Stadt Kombiset		
Sets: 2	1986–1987	Special

ⓘ 1507	EU NA AU	
Space Value Pack		
Raumfahrt Kombiset		
Sets: 2	1986–1987	Special

ⓘ 1511	EU NA AU AS	
Basic Set with Storage Case		
Grundbaukasten mit Sortierkoffer		
Pcs: -	1986–1987	Special

ⓘ 1523	EU NA AU AS	
Basic Set Trial Size		
Grundbaukasten Probepackung		
Pcs: 24	1986	Special

ⓘ 1524	EU NA AU AS	
Basic Set Trial Size		
Grundbaukasten Probepackung		
Pcs: 38	1986	Special

ⓘ 1525	EU NA AS	
Container Lorry		
Container-Laster		
Pcs: 154	1986–1987	Special

ⓘ 1528	EU NA	
Dragster		
Dragster		
Pcs: 24	1986–1987	Special

ⓘ 1554	EU	
Silja Line Ferry		
Silja Line Fährschiff		
Pcs: 169	1986	Special

ⓘ 1555	EU NA AU AS	
Father Christmas		
Weihnachtsmann		
Pcs: 19	1986–1996	Special

ⓘ	1506	Includes: 1528 (1986), 1572 (1986)	Enthält: 1528 (1986), 1572 (1986)
ⓘ	1507	Includes: 1557 (1986), 1558 (1986)	Enthält: 1557 (1986), 1558 (1986)
ⓘ	1523	Similar to: 1964 (1985), 1588 (1987)	Ähnlich zu: 1964 (1985), 1588 (1987)
ⓘ	1524	Similar to: 1965 (1985), 1598 (1987)	Ähnlich zu: 1965 (1985), 1598 (1987)
ⓘ	1528	Included in: 1506 (1986)	Enthalten in: 1506 (1986)
ⓘ	1554	Sold only on Silja Line Ferries	Wurde nur auf Silja Line Fähren verkauft

1556	EU NA AU AS	
Christmas Hearts		
Weihnachtsherzen		
Pcs: 10	1986–1992	Special

1557	EU NA AU AS	
Space Scooter		
Orbitalgleiter		
Pcs: 28	1986–1987	Special

1558	EU NA AU AS	
Mobile Command Trailer		
Geoprobentransporter		
Pcs: 72	1986–1987	Special

1570	EU NA AU AS	
Fabuland Figure		
Fabulandfigur		
Pcs: 4	1986	Special

1572	EU NA AU AS	
Super Tow Truck		
Schwerer Abschleppwagen		
Pcs: 72	1986–1987	Special

1580	EU NA AU AS	
Lunar Scout		
Bodenerkundungs-Rover		
Pcs: 76	1986	Special

1589	EU NA AU AS	
TCS Breakdown Assistance		
TCS Pannenhilfe		
Pcs: 261	1986–1989	Special

1618	EU NA AU AS	
Storage Bucket		
Aufbewahrungstonne		
Pcs: 47	1986–1987	Special

1619	EU NA AU AS	
Storage Bucket		
Aufbewahrungstonne		
Sets: 260	1986–1987	Special

1557	Included in: 1507 (1986)	Enthalten in: 1507 (1986)
1558	Included in: 1507 (1986)	Enthalten in: 1507 (1986)
1572	Included in: 1506 (1986)	Enthalten in: 1506 (1986)
1589	Touring Club Suisse promo set	Touring Club Schweiz Promoset

1926	EU NA AU AS
Combi Pack	
Kombiset	
Pcs: 8	1986 | Special

1963	EU NA AU AS
Basic Set with Storage Case	
Grundbaukasten mit Sortierkoffer	
Pcs: 212	1986–1987 | Special

2750	EU NA AU AS
Family	
Familie	
Pcs: 7	1986–1990

2752	EU NA AU AS
Bedroom	
Schlafzimmer	
Pcs: 30	1986–1990

2754	EU NA AU AS
Bathroom	
Badezimmer	
Pcs: 11	1986–1990

2756	EU NA AU AS
Kitchen	
Küche	
Pcs: 22	1986–1990

2758	EU NA AU AS
Living Room	
Wohnzimmer	
Pcs: 30	1986–1990

2760	EU NA AU AS
House Supplementary	
Spielhaus	
Pcs: 11	1986–1990

2770	EU NA AU AS
Play House	
Spielhaus (komplett)	
Pcs: 69	1986–1990

1963	Similar to: 1962 (1985), 1520 (1985)	Ähnlich zu: 1962 (1985), 1520 (1985)

3633 EU NA AU AS

Motor Boat	
Willem Walross' Motorboot	
Pcs: 13	1986–1988

3644 EU NA AU AS

Mayor's Car	
Leo Löwes Dienstlimousine	
Pcs: 12	1986–1988

3668 EU NA AU AS

Merry-Go-Round	
Karussell	
Pcs: 52	1986–1988

3679 EU NA AU AS

Mill with Shop	
Mühle	
Pcs: 79	1986–1988

3718 EU NA AU AS

Small Café	
Kleines Eis-Café	
Pcs: 7	1986–1988

3796 EU NA AU AS

Small Bakery	
Kleine Bäckerei	
Pcs: 31	1986–1987

5510 EU NA AU AS

Off-Road 4x4	
Off-Roader	
Pcs: 288	1986–1992

5540 EU NA AU AS

Formula I Racer	
Formel I-Rennwagen	
Pcs: 447	1986–1991

5580 EU NA AU AS

Highway Truck	
Highway Truck	
Pcs: 670	1986–1992

i		
5540	With poster	Mit Poster

6012	EU NA AU AS
Siege Cart	
Ambrust-Streitwagen	
Pcs: 54	1986–1988

6023	EU NA AU AS
Maiden's Cart	
Einspänner mit Burgfräulein	
Pcs: 42	1986–1991

6041	EU NA AU AS
Armor Shop	
Ausrüstungsdepot	
Pcs: 114	1986–1990

6067	EU NA AU AS
Guarded Inn	
Wachhaus	
Pcs: 246	1986–1990

6074	EU NA AU AS
Black Falcon's Fortress	
Ritterschloss	
Pcs: 457	1986–1990

6301	EU NA AU AS
Town Mini-Figures	
6 Figuren	
Pcs: 33	1986–1988

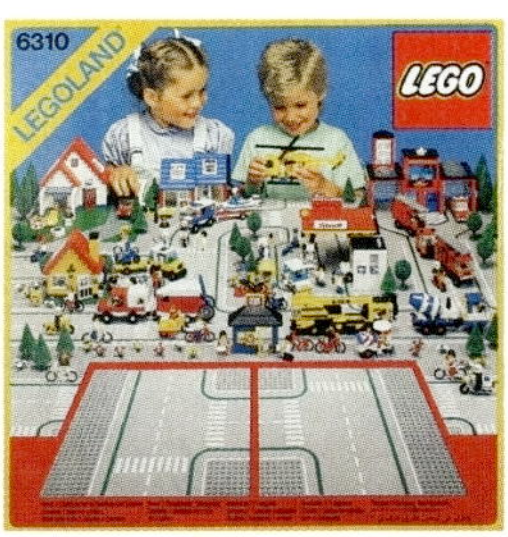

6310	EU NA AU AS
"T" Road Plates	
T-Kreuzungen m. Fahrradweg	
Pcs: 2	1986–1996

6311	EU NA AU AS
Curved Road Plates	
Kurven mit Fahrradweg	
Pcs: 2	1986–1996

6312	EU NA AU AS
Straight Road Plates	
Gerade Straßen mit Fahrradweg	
Pcs: 2	1986–1996

	Set	Re-released	Neu aufgelegt
i	6067	Re-released as: 10000 (2001)	Neu aufgelegt als: 10000 (2001)
i	6074	Re-released as: 10039 (2002)	Neu aufgelegt als: 10039 (2002)

1986

6313 — EU NA AU AS

Cross-Roads Plates

Kreuzungen mit Fahrradweg

Pcs: 2 | 1986–1996

6359 — EU NA AU AS

Horse Trailer

Rennpferd-Transporter

Pcs: 144 | 1986–1988

6360 — EU NA AU AS

Weekend Cottage

Wochenendhaus

Pcs: 117 | 1986–1988

6361 — EU NA AU AS

Mobile Crane

Dreiachsiger Telekran

Pcs: 165 | 1986–1989

6378 — EU NA AU AS

Service Station

Tank-Service-Station

Pcs: 291 | 1986–1988

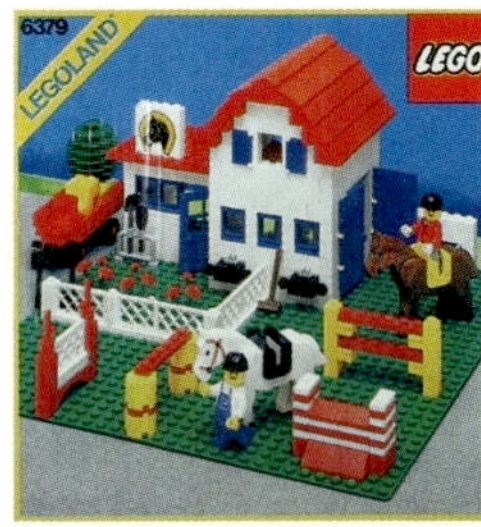

6379 — EU NA AU AS

Riding Stable

Reiterhof

Pcs: 285 | 1986–1989

6386 — EU NA AU AS

Police Command Base

Polizeidirektion

Pcs: 402 | 1986–1992

6450 — EU NA AU AS

Mobile Police Truck

Polizeieinsatzwagen

Pcs: 83 | 1986–1990

6480 — EU NA AU AS

Hook and Ladder Truck

Feuerwehr mit Leiter

Pcs: 104 | 1986–1990

(i)	6450	Was supposed to be released in 1985 originally	Sollte ursprünglich 1985 erscheinen
(i)	6480	Was supposed to be released in 1985 originally	Sollte ursprünglich 1985 erscheinen

6612 EU NA AU AS

Fire Chief's Car	
Feuerwehr-Kommandowagen	
Pcs: 29	1986–1987

6613 EU NA AU AS

Telephone Booth	
Telefonzelle	
Pcs: 24	1986–1987

6634 EU NA AU AS

Stock Car	
Rallye-Auto	
Pcs: 47	1986–1988

6658 EU NA AU AS

Bulldozer	
Schaufel-Radlader	
Pcs: 65	1986–1988

6659 EU NA AU AS

TV Camera Crew	
TV-Kamerawagen	
Pcs: 64	1986–1988

6676 EU NA AU AS

Mobile Command Unit	
Radar-Kontrolle	
Pcs: 102	1986–1989

6677 EU NA AU AS

Motocross Racing	
Rennmaschinen-Transporter	
Pcs: 77	1986–1991

6698 EU NA AU AS

RV with Speedboat	
Geländewagen mit Motorboot	
Pcs: 132	1986–1989

6702 EU NA AU AS

Space Mini-Figures	
Space-Team	
Pcs: 47	1986–1987

6780 EU NA AU AS

XT-Starship	
Stufen-Exosphären-Orbiter	
Pcs: 204	1986–1988

6783 EU NA AU AS

Sonar Transmitting Cruiser	
Geo-Galaxis Fähre	
Pcs: 354	1986–1990

6802 EU NA AU AS

Space Probe	
Mobile Mikro-Sonde	
Pcs: 28	1986–1987

6820 EU NA AU AS

Starfire I	
Space-Scooter	
Pcs: 37	1986–1997

6845 EU NA AU AS

Cosmic Charger	
Raumpatrouille	
Pcs: 53	1986–1987

6874 EU NA AU AS

Moonrover	
Mehrzweck-Explorer	
Pcs: 68	1986–1989

6892 EU NA AU AS

Modular Space Transport	
Service-Transporter	
Pcs: 150	1986–1987

6926 EU NA AU AS

Mobile Recovery Vehicle	
High-Speed-Feuer-Truck	
Pcs: 150	1986–1987

6940 EU NA AU AS

Alien Moon Stalker	
Mobiles Space-Center	
Pcs: 268	1986–1990

6985 EU NA AU AS

Cosmic Fleet Voyager

Flottenkreuzer

Pcs: 413 | 1986–1989

7813 EU NA AU AS

Shell Wagon

Shell Waggon

Pcs: 123 | 1986–1990

7823 EU NA AU AS

Container Crane

Container-Bahnhof

Pcs: 487 | 1986–1990

7839 EU NA AU AS

Car Carrier Platform

Auto-Verlade-Bahnhof

Pcs: 333 | 1986–1990

8035 EU NA AU AS

Universal Set

Universalkasten

Pcs: 176 | 1986–1988

8055 EU NA AU AS

Universal Set

Universalkasten

Pcs: 196 | 1986–1988

8620 EU NA AU AS

Snow Scooter

Pistenfahrzeug

Pcs: 101 | 1986–1989

8640 EU NA AU AS

Polar Copter

Helikopter

Pcs: 244 | 1986–1989

8660 EU NA AU AS

Arctic Rescue Unit

Expeditions-Fahrzeug

Pcs: 387 | 1986–1989

i	6985	"Party Cruiser"	„Partykreuzer"

8680	EU NA AU AS	
Arctic Rescue Base		
Forschungsstation		
Pcs: 523	1986–1987	

8842	EU NA AU AS	
Go-Cart		
Go-Kart		
Pcs: 283	1986–1990	

8849	EU NA AU AS	
Tractor		
Traktor		
Pcs: 355	1986–1989	

1987

0011	EU NA AU AS	
Castle 2 for 1 Bonus Offer		
Burg Bonusset		
Sets: 2	1987	Special

250	EU NA AU AS	
Idea Book		
Baubuch		
Pcs: 1	1987–1989	

303	EU NA AU AS	
Basic Building Set		
Grundbaukasten		
Pcs: 33	1987–1989	

307	EU NA AU AS	
Basic Building Set		
Grundbaukasten		
Pcs: -	1987–1989	

317	EU NA AU AS	
Basic Building Set		
Grundbaukasten		
Pcs: 68	1987–1989	

327	EU NA AU AS	
Basic Building Set		
Grundbaukasten		
Pcs: 102	1987–1989	

0011	Includes: 6016 (1987), 6041 (1986)	Enthält: 6016 (1987), 6041 (1986)

337	EU NA AU AS
Basic Building Set	
Grundbaukasten	
Pcs: 212	1987–1989

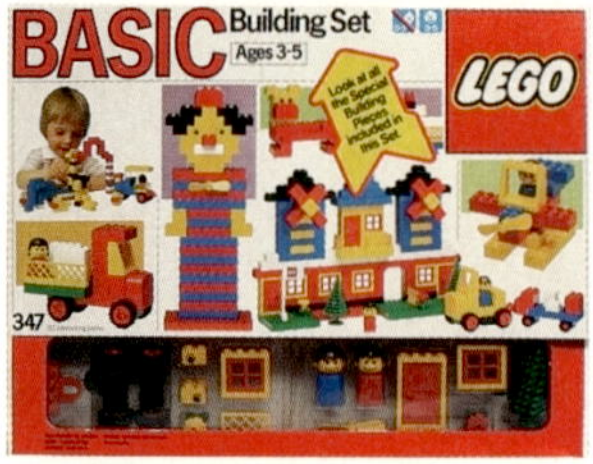

347	EU NA AU AS
Basic Building Set	
Grundbaukasten	
Pcs: 318	1987–1988

357	EU NA AU AS
Basic Building Set	
Grundbaukasten	
Pcs: 681	1987–1988

503	EU NA AU AS
Basic Building Set	
Grundbaukasten	
Pcs: 31	1987–1989

507	EU NA AU AS
Basic Building Set	
Grundbaukasten	
Pcs: 56	1987–1989

517	EU NA AU AS
Basic Building Set	
Grundbaukasten	
Pcs: 125	1987–1989

527	EU NA AU AS
Basic Building Set	
Grundbaukasten	
Pcs: 199	1987–1989

537	EU NA AU AS
Basic Building Set	
Grundbaukasten	
Pcs: 206	1987–1989

547	EU NA AU AS
Basic Building Set	
Grundbaukasten	
Pcs: 616	1987–1988

537	Similar to: 530 (1985)	Ähnlich zu: 530 (1985)
547	Similar to: 1662 (1989), 540 (1985)	Ähnlich zu: 1662 (1989), 540 (1985)

ⓘ 557	EU NA (AU AS)	
Basic Building Set		
Grundbaukasten		
Pcs: 561	1987–1989	
4/6		

ⓘ 610	NA (EU AU AS)	
Rescue Helicopter		
Rettungshubschrauber		
Pcs: 35	1987	Special
6/6		

ⓘ 789	EU NA AU AS	
Storage Cloth		
Spiel- und Sammelbeutel		
Pcs: 1	1987–1992	
4/6		

ⓘ 1467	EU (NA AU AS)	
Shell Race Car		
Shell Rennwagen		
Pcs: 45	1987–1990	Special
6/6		

ⓘ 1468	EU (NA AU AS)	
Shell Tanker		
Shell Tankwagen		
Pcs: 33	1987–1990	Special
6/6		

ⓘ 1469	EU (NA AU AS)	
Shell Helicopter		
Shell Helikopter		
Pcs: 40	1987–1990	Special
6/6		

ⓘ 1470	EU (NA AU AS)	
Shell Station		
Shell Tankstelle		
Pcs: 26	1987–1990	Special
6/6		

ⓘ 1472	EU NA AS (AU)	
Holiday Home		
Ferienvilla mit Wohnmobil		
Pcs: 369	1987	Special
6/6		

ⓘ 1473	EU NA AS (AU)	
Combi Pack		
Kombi-Pack		
Pcs: -	1987	Special
6/6		

ⓘ	Set	English	Deutsch
ⓘ	557	Similar to: 550 (1985)	Ähnlich zu: 550 (1985)
ⓘ	610	Air Canada promo set	Air Canada Promo-Set
ⓘ	789	Similar to: 787 (1977)	Ähnlich zu: 787 (1977)
ⓘ	1472	Similar to: 6388 (1989)	Ähnlich zu: 6388 (1989)

1484	Regions: EU
Weetabix Town House	
Weetabix Reihenhaus	
Pcs: 200	1987	Special
Rating: 4/6	

1488	Regions: EU, NA, AS
Building Set	
Baukasten	
Pcs: -	1987–1988	Special
Rating: 6/6	

1496	Regions: NA, AU
Rally Car	
Rallye-Auto	
Pcs: 52	1987	Special
Rating: 5/6	

1497	Regions: AU
Rally and Pitcrew Team	
Boxencrew mit Auto	
Pcs: 124	1987	Special
Rating: 5/6	

1498	Regions: AU
Spy-Bot	
Info-Roboter	
Pcs: 66	1987	Special
Rating: 5/6	

1499	Regions: EU, NA, AU, AS
Twin Starfire	
Doppelkanzel-Explorer	
Pcs: 91	1987–1988	Special
Rating: 5/6	

1501	Regions: EU, NA, AU, AS
Large Storage Bucket	
Großer Eimer	
Pcs: -	1987–1991	
Rating: 3/6	

1509	Regions: EU, NA, AU, AS
Town Value Pack	
Stadt Kombiset	
Sets: 2	1987	Special
Rating: 5/6	

1510	Regions: EU, NA
Space Value Pack	
Raumfahrt Kombiset	
Sets: 2	1987	Special
Rating: 6/6	

i	1496	Included in: 1509 (1987), 1502 (1987)	Enthalten in: 1509 (1987), 1502 (1987)
i	1497	Included in: 1509 (1987)	Enthalten in: 1509 (1987)
i	1498	Included in: 1510 (1987)	Enthalten in: 1510 (1987)
i	1499	Included in: 1510 (1987)	Enthalten in: 1510 (1987)
i	1509	Includes: 1496 (1987), 1497 (1987)	Enthält: 1496 (1987), 1497 (1987)
i	1510	Contains: 1498 (1987), 1499 (1987)	Enthält: 1498 (1987), 1499 (1987)

1516	EU NA AU AS	
Theatre with Play-Scenes		
Theaterbühne		
Pcs: 23	1987	Special

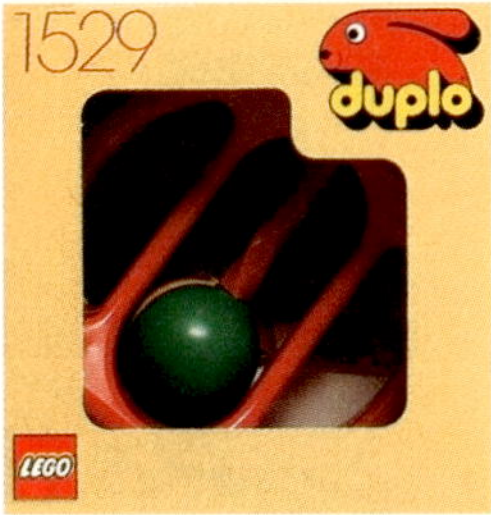

1529	EU NA AU AS	
Rattle (Assorted)		
Rasseln gemischt		
Pcs: 1	1987	Special

1573	EU NA AU AS	
Basic Building Set		
Grundbaukasten		
Pcs: -	1987–1988	Special

1575	EU NA AU AS	
Basic Set with Board Game		
Grundbaukasten mit Brettspiel		
Pcs: 230	1987–1988	Special

1585	EU NA AU AS	
Combi Pack		
Kombi-Paket		
Pcs: -	1987	Special

1586	EU NA AU AS	
Basic Set with Storage Case		
Grundbaukasten mit Sortierkoffer		
Pcs: -	1987	Special

1587	EU NA AU AS	
Basic Set with Storage Case		
Grundbaukasten mit Sortierkoffer		
Pcs: -	1987	Special

1588	EU NA AU AS	
Basic Set		
Grundbaukasten		
Pcs: 27	1987	

1598	EU NA AU AS	
Basic Set		
Grundbaukasten		
Pcs: 33	1987	Special

ⓘ	1575	Possibly released only in Australia	Wahrscheinlich nur in Australien veröffentlicht
ⓘ	1588	Similar to: 1523 (1986), 1964 (1985)	Ähnlich zu: 1523 (1986), 1964 (1985)
ⓘ	1598	Similar to: 1965 (1985), 1524 (1986)	Ähnlich zu: 1965 (1985), 1524 (1986)

1599	EU, AU	
Britannia Airways		
Britannia Airways		
Pcs: 98	1987–1992	Special

1601	EU, NA, AS	
Basic Set with Storage Case		
Grundbaukasten mit Sortierkoffer		
Pcs: -	1987	Special

1602	EU, NA, AU, AS	
Giraffe		
Giraffe		
Pcs: 16	1987–1994	Special

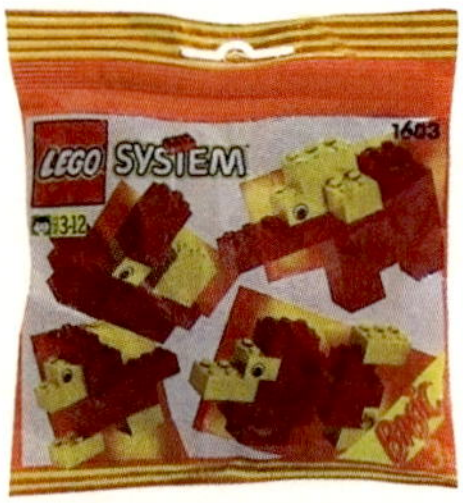

1603	EU, NA, AU, AS	
Elephant		
Elefant		
Pcs: 13	1987–1994	Special

1604	EU, NA, AU, AS	
Lion		
Löwe		
Pcs: 17	1987–1996	Special

1605	EU, NA, AU, AS	
Snail		
Schnecke		
Pcs: 14	1987–1996	Special

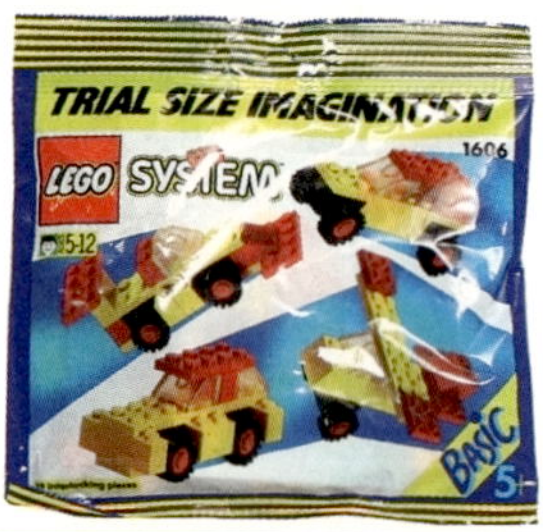

1606	EU, NA, AU, AS	
Car		
Auto		
Pcs: 23	1987–1994	Special

1607	EU, NA, AU, AS	
Helicopter		
Helikopter		
Pcs: 26	1987–1994	Special

1608	EU, NA, AU, AS	
Aeroplane		
Flugzeug		
Pcs: -	1987–1990	Special

ⓘ	Set	Included in	Enthalten in
ⓘ	1602	Included in: 4774 (1987)	Enthalten in: 4774 (1987)
ⓘ	1603	Included in: 4774 (1987)	Enthalten in: 4774 (1987)

1609	EU NA AU AS	
Ship		
Schiff		
Pcs: 27	1987–1990	Special

1613	EU NA AU AS	
Basic Set in Bucket		
Großer Eimer		
Pcs: 383	1987–1990	

1615	EU NA AU AS	
Basic Set in Bucket		
Großer Eimer		
Pcs: 382	1987–1991	

1685	EU NA AU AS	
Pre-School Building Set		
Vorschul-Baukasten		
Pcs: 67	1987	Special

1927	EU NA AU AS	
Parents' Pack		
Eltern-Set		
Pcs: -	1987–1988	Special

1928	EU NA AU AS	
Parents' Pack		
Eltern-Set		
Pcs: -	1987–1988	Special

1981	EU NA AU AS	
Rattle		
Rassel		
Pcs: 1	1987–1988	Special

2014	EU NA AU AS	
Oval Rattle		
Rassel		
Pcs: 1	1987–1990	

2020	EU NA AU AS	
Duck Rattle with Handles		
Rassel		
Pcs: 1	1987–1996	

2014	Similar to: 2015 (1983)	Ähnlich zu: 2015 (1983)
2020	Similar to: 2024 (1983)	Ähnlich zu: 2024 (1983)

ⓘ 2050	EU NA AU AS
Squirrel	
Eichhörnchen	
Pcs: 2	1987–1991

ⓘ 2051	EU NA AU AS
Spin-A-Coaster	
Greifkarussell	
Pcs: 2	1987–1988

ⓘ 2052	EU NA AU AS
Shape Sorter	
Puzzle-Clown	
Pcs: 7	1987–1990

ⓘ 2057	EU NA AU AS
Rocking Horse	
Schaukelpferd	
Pcs: 3	1987–1988

ⓘ 2059	EU NA AU AS
"Activity and Water Toy"	
„Schwimminsel“	
Pcs: 2	1987

ⓘ 2070	EU NA AU AS
Telephone	
Telefon	
Pcs: 4	1987–1996

ⓘ 2072	EU NA AU AS
Learn and Build Centre	
Lern-, Spiel- und Bauset	
Pcs: 7	1987–1996

ⓘ 2310	EU NA AU AS
Supplementary Set	
Ergänzungskasten	
Pcs: 28	1987–1990

ⓘ 2312	EU NA AU AS
Supplementary Set	
Ergänzungskasten	
Pcs: -	1987–1990

ⓘ	Set	English	Deutsch
ⓘ	2050	Similar to: 2054 (1984)	Ähnlich zu: 2054 (1984)
ⓘ	2051	Similar to: 2037 (1983)	Ähnlich zu: 2037 (1983)
ⓘ	2052	Similar to: 2033 (1985)	Ähnlich zu: 2033 (1985)
ⓘ	2057	Similar to: 2055 (1984)	Ähnlich zu: 2055 (1984)
ⓘ	2059	Similar to: 2038 (1983)	Ähnlich zu: 2038 (1983)
ⓘ	2070	Also included in: 9004 (1988)	Auch enthalten in: 9004 (1988)

2333 EU NA AU AS

Animal

Grundbaukasten „Ente“

Pcs: 11 | 1987–1990

2344 EU NA AU AS

Circus

Grundbaukasten „Clown“

Pcs: 19 | 1987–1997

2366 EU NA AU AS

House with Car

Grundbaukasten „Haus“

Pcs: 27 | 1987–1990

2377 EU NA AU AS

Safari

Grundbaukasten „Safari“

Pcs: 45 | 1987–1990

2385 EU NA AU AS

Street Enviroment

Grundbaukasten „Straßen“

Pcs: - | 1987–1990

2388 EU NA AU AS

Harbour

Grundbaukasten „Hafen“

Pcs: 46 | 1987–1990

2395 EU NA AU AS

Railway Station

Grundbaukasten „Bahnhof“

Pcs: - | 1987–1989

2399 EU NA AU AS

Town

Grundbaukasten „Stadt“

Pcs: 68 | 1987–1996

2404 EU NA AU AS

Windmill Building Set

Windmühle

Pcs: 11 | 1987–1989

2414 EU NA AU AS
Airport Building Set
Flughafen
Pcs: 15 | 1987

2628 EU NA AU AS
Horse Transport
Lastwagen mit Pferd
Pcs: 5 | 1987–1992

2632 EU NA AU AS
Container Transport
Möbellastwagen
Pcs: 5 | 1987–1989

2637 EU NA AU AS
Fire Engine
Feuerwehr
Pcs: 8 | 1987–1993

2638 EU NA AU AS
Truck with Crane
Kranwagen
Pcs: 14 | 1987–1990

2714 EU NA AU AS
Crossings
Kreuzungen
Pcs: 4 | 1987–1992

3636 EU NA AU AS
Bedroom
Schlafzimmer
Pcs: 21 | 1987–1988

3645 EU NA AU AS
Classroom
Klassenzimmer
Pcs: 26 | 1987–1990

3659 EU NA AU AS
Play Ground
Spielplatz
Pcs: 19 | 1987–1990

3662	EU NA AU AS
Bus	
Bus und Haltestelle	
Pcs: 34	1987–1989

3674	EU NA AU AS
Bonnie Bunny's New House	
Traumvilla	
Pcs: 47	1987–1990

3675	EU NA AU AS
General Store	
Einkaufs-Zentrum mit Poststation	
Pcs: 105	1987–1990

3682	EU NA AU AS
Fire Station	
Feuerwache	
Pcs: 149	1987–1989

3719	EU NA AU AS
Busstop	
Bushaltestelle	
Pcs: 5	1987–1988

3797	EU NA AU AS
Fire Chief Barty Bulldog	
Feuerwehr-Einsatzwagen	
Pcs: 9	1987–1989

4010	EU NA AU AS
Police Rescue Boat	
Polizeischnellboot	
Pcs: 92	1987–1990

4020	EU NA AU AS
Fire Fighting Boat	
Feuerlöschboot	
Pcs: 214	1987–1990

4030	EU NA AU AS
Cargo Carrier	
Container-Frachter	
Pcs: 325	1987–1990

4774	EU NA AU AS	
Imagination 2-Pack		
Kreativität 2er Kombiset		
Sets: 2	1987	Special

6016	EU NA AU AS	
Knight's Arsenal		
Streitwagen		
Pcs: 37	1987–1991	

6017	EU NA AU AS	
King's Oarsmen		
Kurierschiff		
Pcs: 45	1987–1989	

6035	EU NA AU AS	
Castle Guard		
Turnierwache		
Pcs: 54	1987–1992	

6049	EU NA AU AS	
Viking Voyager		
Ruderschiff		
Pcs: 100	1987–1992	

6062	EU NA AU AS	
Battering Ram		
Belagerungsturm		
Pcs: 240	1987–1989	

6066	EU NA AU AS	
Camouflaged Outpost		
Geheimquartier		
Pcs: 240	1987–1992	

6358	EU NA AU AS	
Snorkel Squad		
Hochhaus-Feuerwehr		
Pcs: 153	1987–1991	

6380	EU NA AU AS	
Emergency Treatment Center		
Stadtklinik		
Pcs: 315	1987–1991	

i	4774	Includes: 1602 (1987), 1603 (1987)	Enthält: 1602 (1987), 1603 (1987)
i	6016	Also included in: 0011 (1987)	Auch enthalten in: 0011 (1987)

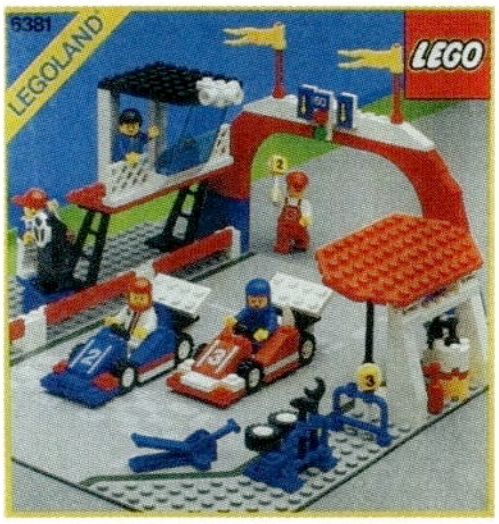

6381 EU NA AU AS

Motor Speedway

Rennpiste

Pcs: 206 | 1987–1992

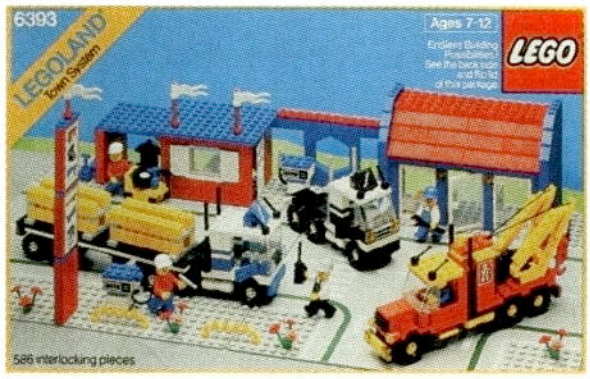

6393 EU NA AU AS

Big Rig Truck Stop

Fernfahrer-Raststätte

Pcs: 641 | 1987–1989

6501 EU NA AU AS

Sport Convertible

Einkaufsflitzer

Pcs: 30 | 1987–1991

6502 EU NA AU AS

Turbo Racer

Strandbuggy

Pcs: 24 | 1987–1988

6521 EU NA AU AS

Emergency Repair Truck

Autobahn-Servicewagen

Pcs: 59 | 1987–1988

6522 EU NA AU AS

Highway Patrol

Motorradstreife

Pcs: 40 | 1987–1990

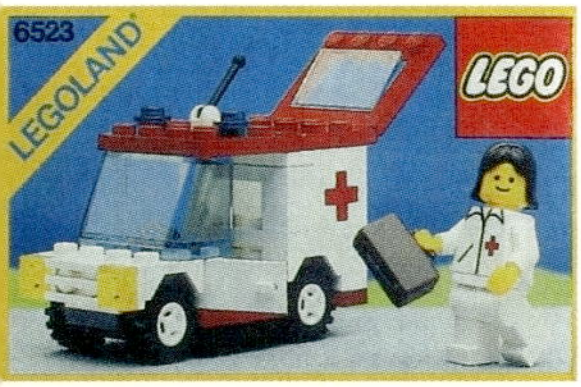

6523 EU NA AU AS

Red Cross

Erste-Hilfe-Pkw

Pcs: 52 | 1987–1991

6641 EU NA AU AS

4-Wheelin' Truck

Expeditions-Jeep

Pcs: 83 | 1987–1991

6687 EU NA AU AS

Turbo Prop I

Geschäftsflugzeug

Pcs: 78 | 1987–1990

6693 EU NA AU AS

Refuse Collection Truck	
Müllabfuhrwagen	
Pcs: 117	1987–1991

6699 EU NA AU AS

Cycle Fix-It Shop	
Zweirad-Shop	
Pcs: 80	1987–1988

6750 EU NA AU AS

Sonic Robot	
Galaxis-Roboter	
Pcs: 111	1987

6808 EU NA AU AS

Galaxy Trekkor	
Asteroiden-Controller	
Pcs: 31	1987–1989

6809 EU NA AU AS

XT-5 and Droid	
Schubsessel	
Pcs: 39	1987–1989

6827 EU NA AU AS

Strato Scooter	
Space-Kurier	
Pcs: 39	1987–1988

6849 EU NA AU AS

Satellite Patroller	
Weltraumfahrzeug	
Pcs: 50	1987–1988

6883 EU NA AU AS

Terrestrial Rover	
Satelliten-Transporter	
Pcs: 115	1987–1990

6884 EU NA AU AS

Aero-Module	
Galaxis-Jäger	
Pcs: 116	1987–1989

i	6808	Also included in: 1530 (1988)	Auch enthalten in: 1530 (1988)

6893	EU NA AU AS
Orion II Hyperspace	
Sternenschiff	
Pcs: 167	1987–1990
4/6	

6894	EU NA AU AS
Invader	
Strato-Kreuzer „Centaurus“	
Pcs: 167	1987–1990
3/6	

6932	EU NA AU AS
Stardefender 200	
Space-Fregatte	
Pcs: 253	1987–1989
3/6	

6941	EU NA AU AS
Battrax	
Galaxis-Galeere	
Pcs: 288	1987–1991
3/6	

6953	EU NA AU AS
Cosmic Laser Launcher	
Intergalaktische Raumbasis	
Pcs: 206	1987–1989
3/6	

6954	NA
Renegade	
Subkorsal-Kurier „Cerberus“	
Pcs: 328	1987–1989
4/6	

6972	EU NA AU AS
Polaris-I Space Lab	
Space-Boden-Basis	
Pcs: 397	1987–1990
3/6	

6990	EU NA AU AS
Monorail Transport System	
Galax-Star-Express	
Pcs: 740	1987–1991
3/6	

8852	EU NA AU AS
Robot	
Roboter	
Pcs: 332	1987–1990
3/6	

8890	EU NA AU AS
Idea Book	
Baubuch	
Pcs: 1	1987–1989

1988

ⓘ 611	EU NA AU AS	
Air Canada Jet Plane		
Air Canada Düsenflugzeug		
Pcs: 92	1988	Special

ⓘ 1490	EU NA AU AS	
Town Bank		
Bank		
Pcs: 197	1988–1990	Special

ⓘ 1495	EU NA AU AS	
Basic Building Set Trial Size		
Grundbaukasten Probepackung		
Pcs: 26	1988	Special

ⓘ 1500	EU NA AU AS	
Oval Bricks		
Ovale Steine		
Pcs: 2	1988–1991	Special

ⓘ 1514	EU NA AU AS	
Basic Building Set Trial Size		
Grundbaukasten Probepackung		
Pcs: 46	1988	Special

ⓘ 1530	EU NA AU AS	
Space Bonus Pack		
Raumfahrt Doppelpack		
Pcs: 2	1988	Special

ⓘ	Set	English	Deutsch
ⓘ	611	Air Canada promotional set	Air Canada Promoset
ⓘ	1530	Includes: 6808 (1987), 6848 (1988)	Enthält: 6808 (1987), 6848 (1988)

1988

1544	EU NA AU AS
Medium Bucket	
Mittelgroßer Eimer	
Pcs: 57	1988–1991

1571	EU NA AU AS
Basic Building Set Gift Item	
Grundbaukasten Geschenkset	
Pcs: -	1988–1992	Special

1577	EU NA AU AS
Medium Bucket	
Mittelgroßer Eimer	
Pcs: 217	1988–1992

1584	EU NA AU AS
Knight's Challenge	
Ritterturnier	
Pcs: 172	1988–1989	Special

1612	EU NA AU AS
Race Car	
Rennwagen	
Pcs: 30	1988–1989	Special

1617	EU NA AU AS
Small Bucket	
Kleiner Eimer	
Pcs: 149	1988–1991	Special

1622	EU NA AU AS
Pre-School Bucket	
Großer Vorschul-Eimer	
Pcs: 114	1988–1989	Special

1623	EU NA AU AS
Small Bucket	
Kleiner Eimer	
Pcs: -	1988–1991	Special

1929	EU NA AU AS
Guardsman	
Wachsoldat	
Pcs: 13	1988–1991	Special

i	1584	Similar to: 6060 (1989)	Ähnlich zu: 6060 (1989)
i	1612	Exists with and without building instruction	Gab es mit und ohne Bauanleitung
i	1929	Availabe only in Denmark	War nur in Dänemark erhältlich

2316
EU NA AU AS

Building Bricks
Bausteine
Pcs: 6 | 1988–1992

2612
EU NA AU AS

Motorbike
Motorrad
Pcs: 2 | 1988–1997

2614
EU NA AU AS

Mother with Pram
Mutter und Kind
Pcs: 2 | 1988–1996

2626
EU NA AU AS

Car and Boat Vacation Trailer
Auto mit Boot
Pcs: 5 | 1988–1991

2641
EU NA AU AS

Jumbo Plane
Flugzeug mit Pilot
Pcs: 21 | 1988–1992

2652
EU NA AU AS

Circus Caravane
Zirkus
Pcs: 17 | 1988–1992

2701
EU NA AU AS

Play Train Large
Lokomotive mit 3 Waggons
Pcs: 46 | 1988–1996

2706
EU NA AU AS

Goods Train
Güterzug
Pcs: 11 | 1988–1992

2720
EU NA AU AS

Cargo Center
Güterbahnhof
Pcs: 37 | 1988–1989

1988

3622 EU NA AU AS

Rowboat	
Ruderboot	
Pcs: 14	1988–1990

3623 EU NA AU AS

Beauty Salon	
Frisiersalon	
Pcs: 25	1988–1989

3646 EU NA AU AS

Kitchen	
Küche	
Pcs: 57	1988–1989

3680 EU NA AU AS

Camping Caravan	
Wohnwagengespann	
Pcs: 35	1988–1989

3683 EU NA AU AS

Amusement Park	
Vergnügungspark	
Pcs: 95	1988–1990

3721 EU NA AU AS

Clive Crocodile on Skateboard	
Skateboard-Meister	
Pcs: 13	1988–1990

3798 EU NA AU AS

Hanna's Garden	
Gartenlaube	
Pcs: 25	1988–1990

6039 EU NA AU AS

Twin Arm Launcher	
Zwillingsschleuder	
Pcs: 77	1988–1992

6054 EU NA AU AS

Forestmen's Hideout	
Baumhöhle	
Pcs: 206	1988–1992

6085	EU NA AU AS
Black Monarch's Castle	
Schwarze Drachenburg	
Pcs: 696	1988–1992

6103	EU NA AU AS
Castle Mini Figures	
6 Burgfiguren	
Pcs: 42	1988–1993

6309	EU NA AU AS
Town Mini-Figures	
6 Stadtfiguren	
Pcs: 42	1988–1992

6315	EU NA AU AS
Road Signs	
Verkehrsschilder	
Pcs: 11	1988–1996

6316	EU NA AU AS
Flags and Fences	
Flaggen, Zäune, Absperrgitter	
Pcs: 38	1988–2001

6317	EU NA AU AS
Trees and Flowers	
Bäume und Blumen	
Pcs: 48	1988–1992

6349	EU NA AU AS
Vacation House	
Einfamilienhaus	
Pcs: 216	1988–1990

6356	EU NA AU AS
Med-Star Rescue Plane	
Viermotoriges Rettungsflugzeug	
Pcs: 162	1988–1991

6357	EU NA AU AS
Stunt 'Copter N' Truck	
Helikopter-Transporter	
Pcs: 180	1988–1992

6394 EU NA AU AS

Metro Park & Service Tower

Parkhaus

Pcs: 640	1988–1990	

6395 EU NA AU AS

Victory Lap Raceway

Formel 1 Start-Ziel Boxen Center

Pcs: 618	1988–1990	

6503 EU NA AU AS

Sprint Racer

Formel 1 Rennwagen

Pcs: 32	1988–1990	

6504 EU NA AU AS

Tractor

Traktor mit Frontschaufel

Pcs: 25	1988–1989	

6505 EU NA AU AS

Fire Chief's Car

Feuerwehrjeep

Pcs: 31	1988–1989	

6524 EU NA AU AS

Blizzard Blazer

Räum- und Planiertrecker

Pcs: 50	1988–1990	

6590 EU NA AU AS

Vacation Camper

Pkw mit Caravan

Pcs: 117	1988–1992	

6642 EU NA AU AS

Police Helicopter

Verkehrs-Helikopter

Pcs: 71	1988–1990	

6643 EU NA AU AS

Fire Truck

Feuerwehr-Mannschaftswagen

Pcs: 79	1988–1991	

6674	EU NA AU AS	
Tow Truck		
Abschleppwagen		
Pcs: 100	1988–1990	

6675	EU NA AU AS	
Road & Trail 4x4		
Allrad-Pick-Up		
Pcs: 83	1988–1992	

6703	EU NA AU AS	
Space Mini-Figures		
6 Raumfahrtfiguren		
Pcs: 42	1988–1991	

6770	EU NA AU AS	
Lunar Transport Patroller		
Space-Explorer		
Pcs: 117	1988–1997	

6828	EU NA AU AS	
Twin-Winged Spoiler		
Fly-Walker		
Pcs: 57	1988–1990	

6830	EU NA AU AS	
Space Patroller		
Space-Patrouille		
Pcs: 55	1988–1990	

6848	EU NA AU AS	
Strategic Pursuer		
Krater-Roboter		
Pcs: 70	1988–1990	

6875	EU NA AU AS	
Hovercraft		
Raum-Clipper		
Pcs: 97	1988–1989	

6876	EU NA AU AS	
Alienator		
Space-Rider		
Pcs: 88	1988–1991	

6848	Included in: 1530 (1988)	Enthalten in: 1530 (1988)

6885 EU NA AU AS

Crater Crawler

Meteoriten-Truck

Pcs: 104 | 1988–1989

6921 EU NA AU AS

Monorail Accessory Track

Leitschienen

Pcs: 46 | 1988–1990

6925 EU NA AU AS

Interplanetary Rover

Galax-Rover

Pcs: 215 | 1988–1989

6987 EU NA AU AS

Message Intercept Base

Galax-Palast

Pcs: 576 | 1988–1991

8712 EU NA AU AS

Technic Figures

3 Technic Action-Figuren

Pcs: 15 | 1988–1992

8832 EU NA AU AS

Roadster

Mini-Kart

Pcs: 86 | 1988–1990

8853 EU NA AU AS

Excavator

Schaufelradlader

Pcs: 327 | 1988–1991

8855 EU NA AU AS

Prop Plane

Amphibienflugzeug

Pcs: 573 | 1988–1991

8865 EU NA AU AS

Test Car

Pkw-Chassis

Pcs: 909 | 1988–1992

1989

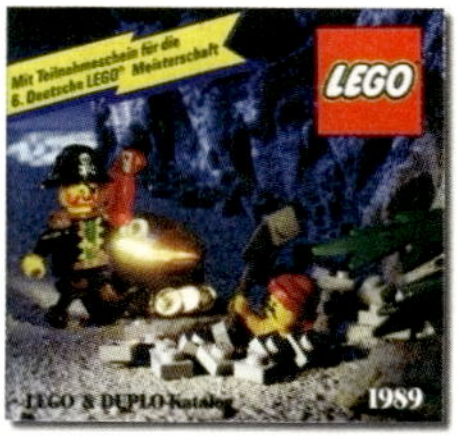

1489	EU NA AU AS	
Mobile Car Crane		
Schwerer Autokran		
Pcs: 174	1989–1991	Special

1513	EU NA AU AS	
Basic Building Set Gift Item		
Grundbaukasten Geschenkset		
Pcs: -	1989–1990	Special

1515	EU NA AU AS	
Town Value Pack		
Stadt Kombiset		
Sets: 2	1989	Special

1517	EU NA AU AS	
Race Car		
Rennauto		
Pcs: 32	1989	Special

1518	EU NA AU AS	
Race Car Repair		
Rennauto-Service-Wagen		
Pcs: 82	1989	Special

1521	EU NA AU AS	
Basic Building Set Trial Size		
Grundbaukasten Probepackung		
Pcs: 24	1989–1990	Special

1515	Includes: 1517 (1989), 1518 (1989)	Enthält: 1517 (1989), 1518 (1989)
1517	Included in: 1515 (1989)	Enthalten in: 1515 (1989)
1518	Included in: 1515 (1989)	Enthalten in: 1515 (1989)

1989

1522 EU NA AU AS

Basic Building Set Trial Size		
Grundbaukasten Probepackung		
Pcs: 44	1989	Special

1616 EU NA AU AS

Space Combi-Pack		
Raumfahrt Doppelpack		
Sets: 2	1989	Special

1620 EU NA AU AS

Astro Dart		
Schwingflügel-Gleiter		
Pcs: 35	1989	Special

1621 EU NA AU AS

Lunar MPV Vehicle		
Quattro-Explorer-Fahrzeug		
Pcs: 97	1989	Special

1625 EU NA AU AS

Snowman		
Schneemann		
Pcs: 40	1989–1990	Special

1626 EU NA AU AS

Angel		
Engel		
Pcs: 33	1989–1990	Special

1627 EU NA AU AS

Santa		
Nikolaus		
Pcs: 36	1989–1990	Special

1628 EU NA AU AS

Santa's Reindeer Sleigh		
Rentierschlitten mit Nikolaus		
Pcs: 64	1989–1991	Special

1640 EU NA AU AS

Tuttle the Turtle		
Tuttle the Turtle		
Pcs: 6	1989	Special

1616	Includes: 1620 (1989), 1621 (1989)	Enthält: 1620 (1989), 1621 (1989)
1620	Included in: 1616 (1989)	Enthalten in: 1616 (1989)
1621	Included in: 1616 (1989)	Enthalten in: 1616 (1989)
1626	Similar to: 10080 (2003)	Ähnlich zu: 10080 (2003)
1640	Similar to: 1800 (1998); McDonald's Promo	Ähnlich zu: 1800 (1998); McDonald's Promo

1641	EU NA AU AS	
Giddy the Gator		
Giddy the Gator		
Pcs: 6	1989–2001	Special
★★★★★☆		

1642	EU	
Sea Eagle		
Sea Eagle		
Pcs: 15	1989–1994	Special
★★★★☆☆		

1643	NA	
Lightning Striker		
Lightning Striker		
Pcs: 14	1989	Special
★★★★★☆		

1644	EU	
Wind Whirler		
Wind Whirler		
Pcs: 17	1989–1994	Special
★★★★☆☆		

1645	NA	
Gyro Bird		
Gyro Bird		
Pcs: 19	1989	Special
★★★★★☆		

1646	EU	
Land Laser		
Land Laser		
Pcs: 17	1989–1994	Special
★★★★☆☆		

1647	NA	
Turbo Force		
Turbo Force		
Pcs: 14	1989	Special
★★★★★☆		

1648	NA	
Swamp Stinger		
Swamp Stinger		
Pcs: 16	1989	Special
★★★★★☆		

1649	EU	
Sea Skimmer		
Sea Skimmer		
Pcs: 17	1989–1994	Special
★★★★☆☆		

1641-1649	McDonald's Promo	McDonald's Promo

ⓘ 1653	EU NA AU AS	
Container		
Container		
Pcs: 38	1989–1990	Special

ⓘ 1661	EU NA AU AS	
Basic Building Set in Bucket		
Grundbaukasten in Eimer		
Pcs: 407	1989	Special

ⓘ 1662	EU NA AU AS	
Basic Building Set in Bucket		
Grundbaukasten in Eimer		
Pcs: 635	1989–1990	Special

ⓘ 1663	EU NA AU AS	
Basic Building Set in Bucket		
Grundbaukasten in Eimer		
Pcs: 451	1989–1990	Special

ⓘ 1681	EU NA AU AS	
Rattle		
Rassel		
Pcs: -	1989–1990	Special

ⓘ 1898	EU NA AU AS	
Weetabix Dragster		
Weetabix Dragster		
Pcs: 27	1989	Special

ⓘ 1899	EU NA AU AS	
Weetabix Racer		
Weetabix Rennwagen		
Pcs: 24	1989	Special

ⓘ 1923	EU NA AU AS	
Viking Line Ferry		
Viking Line Fährschiff		
Pcs: 170	1989–1991	Special

ⓘ 1952	EU NA AU AS	
Dairy Tanker		
Molkereitankwagen		
Pcs: 131	1989	Special

ⓘ	Set	English	Deutsch
ⓘ	1662	Similar to: 540 (1985), 547 (1987)	Ähnlich zu: 540 (1985), 547 (1987)
ⓘ	1898	Weetabix Promo	Weetabix Promo
ⓘ	1899	Weetabix Promo	Weetabix Promo
ⓘ	1923	Sold only on Viking Line Ferries	Wurde nur auf Viking Line Fähren verkauft
ⓘ	1952	Promo set for MD, only released in Denmark	MD Promo, nur in Dänemark veröffentlicht

1953	EU NA AU AS	
Catch the Mouse		
Fang die Maus		
Pcs: 14	1989–1994	Special

1973	EU NA AU AS	
Emirates Airliner		
Emirates Airliner		
Pcs: 138	1989–1991	Special

1974	EU NA AU AS	
LEGOLAND Triple Pack		
LEGOLAND Dreierpack		
Sets: 3	1989	Special

2040	EU NA AU AS	
Rock 'n' Roller		
Wippwagen		
Pcs: 3	1989–1997	

2066	EU NA AU AS	
Bath-Tub Bunnies		
Badewannenfreunde		
Pcs: 2	1989–1996	

2073	EU NA AU AS	
Baby Gift Package		
Baby Geschenkset		
Pcs: 5	1989–1994	

2074	EU NA AU AS	
Rattle and Activity Gift Set		
Großes Baby Geschenkset		
Pcs: 10	1989–1996	

2424	EU NA AU AS	
Basic Building Bucket		
Grundbaukasten in Eimer		
Pcs: 82	1989	

2426	EU NA AU AS	
Farm Bucket		
Bauernhof Eimer		
Pcs: 56	1989–1990	

i 1974	Includes: 3 sets with number 1974	Enthält: 3 Sets mit Nummer 1974

2430 EU NA AU AS

Clown Parade

Clown-Parade

Pcs: 16 | 1989

2617 EU NA AU AS

Tow Truck

Abschleppwagen

Pcs: 4 | 1989–1996

2643 EU NA AU AS

Fishing Boat

Fischkutter

Pcs: 17 | 1989–1996

2650 EU NA AU AS

Cannon Ball Clowns

Clowns

Pcs: 5 | 1989–1996

2651 EU NA AU AS

Circus Artists

Zirkusartisten

Pcs: 9 | 1989–1997

2656 EU NA AU AS

Family House

Eigenheim

Pcs: 28 | 1989–1996

2657 EU NA AU AS

Gas Station

Autowerkstatt

Pcs: 48 | 1989–1992

2658 EU NA AU AS

Fire Station

Feuerwache

Pcs: 63 | 1989–1994

3647 EU NA AU AS

School Room

Schule

Pcs: 45 | 1989

3663	EU NA AU AS	
Max Mouse's Carousel		
Karussell		
Pcs: 25	1989	

3676	EU NA AU AS	
Catherine Cat's Fun Park		
Cathy Katzes Spielparadies		
Pcs: 44	1989	

6060	EU NA AU AS	
Knight's Challenge		
Ritterturnier		
Pcs: 172	1989–1991	

6077	EU NA AU AS	
Forestmen's River Fortress		
Flussturm		
Pcs: 365	1989–1992	

6235	EU NA AU AS	
Buried Treasure		
Pirat mit Schatztruhe		
Pcs: 27	1989–1992	

6245	EU NA AU AS	
Harbor Sentry		
Ruderboot mit Kanonier		
Pcs: 26	1989–1991	

6251	EU NA AU AS	
Pirate Mini Figures		
Piraten und Kolonialbeamte		
Pcs: 40	1989–1996	

6255	EU NA AU AS	
Pirate Comic		
Piratenbuch		
Pcs: 13	1989–1991	

6257	EU NA AU AS	
Castaway's Raft		
Piratenspähtrupp		
Pcs: 54	1989–1992	

6060	Similar to: 1584 (1988)	Ähnlich zu: 1584 (1988)
6255	„Der Schatz der halben Münze“ (D), „La ghinea d'oro“ (ITA), “The golden Sovereign” (UK), “The Golden Medaillon” (US)	„Der Schatz der halben Münze“ (D), „La ghinea d'oro“ (ITA), “The golden Sovereign”(UK), “The Golden Medaillon” (US)

6260 — EU NA AU AS
Shipwreck Island
Piratenschatzinsel
Pcs: 79 | 1989–1992
Rating: 3/6 bricks

6265 — EU NA AU AS
Sabre Island
Gouverneurs-Vorposten
Pcs: 92 | 1989–1992
Rating: 4/6 bricks

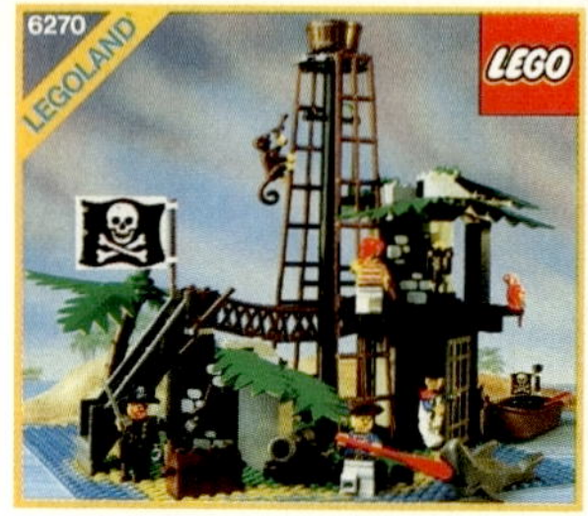

6270 — EU NA AU AS
Forbidden Island
Pirateninsel
Pcs: 194 | 1989–1992
Rating: 3/6 bricks

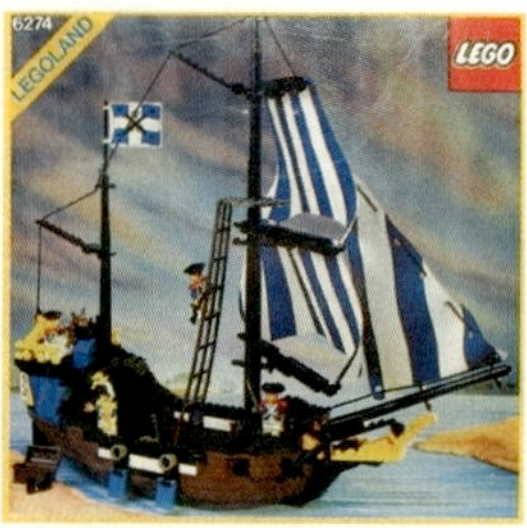

6274 — EU NA AU AS
Caribbean Clipper
Gouverneurskogge
Pcs: 393 | 1989–1992
Rating: 3/6 bricks

6276 — EU NA AU AS
Eldorado Fortress
Gouverneurskastell
Pcs: 517 | 1989–1992
Rating: 4/6 bricks

6285 — EU NA AU AS
Black Seas Barracuda
Piratenbrigantine
Pcs: 925 | 1989–1992
Rating: 3/6 bricks

6355 — EU NA AU AS
Derby Trotter
Rennstall
Pcs: 144 | 1989–1991
Rating: 3/6 bricks

6387 — EU NA (AU AS greyed)
Coastal Rescue Base
Station der Küstenwacht
Pcs: 351 | 1989–1991
Rating: 4/6 bricks

6388 — EU NA AU AS
Holiday Home with Caravan
Ferienvilla mit Wohnmobil
Pcs: 374 | 1989–1992
Rating: 4/6 bricks

i	Set	English	Deutsch
i	6285	Re-released as: 10040 (2002)	Neu aufgelegt als: 10040 (2002)
i	6388	Similar to: 1472 (1987)	Ähnlich zu: 1472 (1987)

6481 EU NA AU AS

Construction Crew	
Schaufelradlader	
Pcs: 183	1989–1992

Rating: 3 of 6

6482 EU NA AU AS

Rescue Helicopter	
Bergungshelikopter	
Pcs: 201	1989–1992

Rating: 3 of 6

6506 EU NA AU AS

Precinct Cruiser	
Cityflitzer	
Pcs: 32	1989–1991

Rating: 3 of 6

6507 EU NA AU AS

Mini Dumper	
Muldenkipper	
Pcs: 31	1989–1991

Rating: 3 of 6

6526 EU NA AU AS

Red Line Racer	
Dragster	
Pcs: 50	1989–1993

Rating: 3 of 6

6527 EU NA AU AS

Tipper Truck	
Kleinlaster mit Kipp-Pritsche	
Pcs: 43	1989–1990

Rating: 3 of 6

6528 EU NA AU AS

Sand Storm Racer	
Geländerennwagen	
Pcs: 39	1989–1991

Rating: 3 of 6

6591 EU (grey) NA AU (grey) AS (grey)

Nitro Dragsters	
Dragster-Rennen	
Pcs: 144	1989–1990

Rating: 4 of 6

6660 EU NA AU AS

Hook & Haul Wrecker	
Abschlepptruck	
Pcs: 54	1989–1996

Rating: 3 of 6

6661	EU NA AU AS
Mobile TV Studio	
Fernsehübertragungswagen	
Pcs: 84	1989–1991

6671	EU NA AU AS
Utility Repair Lift	
Reparaturwagen mit Scherenlift	
Pcs: 109	1989–1996

6781	EU NA AU AS
SP-Striker	
Galax-Police-Patrol	
Pcs: 230	1989–1991

6810	EU NA AU AS
Laser Ranger	
Space-Hornisse	
Pcs: 43	1989–1990

6831	EU NA AU AS
Message Decoder	
Space-Police-Scooter	
Pcs: 36	1989–1992

6850	EU NA AU AS
Auxilary Patroller	
Space-Hummel	
Pcs: 50	1989–1990

6886	EU NA AU AS
Galactic Peace Keeper	
Galax-Police-Hopper	
Pcs: 125	1989–1992

6895	EU NA AU AS
Spy-Trak I	
Galax-Police-Giant-Wheeler	
Pcs: 150	1989–1991

6955	EU NA AU AS
Space Lock-Up Isolation Base	
Galax-Police-Basisstation	
Pcs: 253	1989–1991

6986	EU NA AU AS
Mission Commander	
Galax-Police-Cruiser	
Pcs: 488	1989–1997

8024	EU NA AU AS
Universal Set	
Universalkasten	
Pcs: 113	1989–1992

8034	EU NA AU AS
Universal Set	
Universalkasten	
Pcs: 195	1989–1993

8044	EU NA AU AS
Universal Pneumatic Set	
Universalkasten „Pneumatic“	
Pcs: 196	1989–1992

8054	EU NA AU AS
Universal Motor Set	
Universalkasten mit Motor	
Pcs: 194	1989–1990

8835	EU NA AU AS
Forklift	
Gabelstapler	
Pcs: 240	1989–1992

8854	EU NA AU AS
Power Crane	
Kranwagen	
Pcs: 520	1989–1992

8862	EU NA AU AS
Backhoe Grader	
Schaufelbagger	
Pcs: 674	1989–1993

i	8862	With poster	Mit Poster

1990

260	EU NA AU AS
Idea Book	
Baubuch	
Pcs: 1	1990–1996

315	EU NA AU AS
Basic Building Set	
Grundbaukasten in Sammelbox	
Pcs: 62	1990–1996

325	EU NA AU AS
Basic Building Set	
Grundbaukasten in Sammelbox	
Pcs: 103	1990–1996

335	EU NA AU AS
Basic Building Set	
Grundbaukasten in Sammelbox	
Pcs: 245	1990–1999

365	EU NA AU AS
Build-N-Store Chest 3+	
Bau- und Sortierkoffer	
Pcs: 45	1990–1996

385	EU NA AU AS
Build-N-Store Chest	
Bau- und Sortierkoffer	
Pcs: 434	1990–1996

395	EU NA AU AS
Build-N-Store Chest	
Bau- und Sortierkoffer	
Pcs: 535	1990–1991

515	EU NA AU AS
Basic Building Set	
Grundbaukasten in Sammelbox	
Pcs: 117	1990–1996

525	EU NA AU AS
Basic Building Set	
Grundbaukasten in Sammelbox	
Pcs: 187	1990–1999

535	EU NA AU AS
Basic Building Set	
Grundbaukasten in Sammelbox	
Pcs: 357	1990–1996

545	EU NA AU AS
Build-N-Store Chest	
Bau- und Sortierkoffer	
Pcs: 426	1990–1996

565	EU NA AU AS
Build-N-Store Chest	
Bau- und Sortierkoffer	
Pcs: 682	1990–1996

715	EU NA AU AS
Basic Building Set	
Grundbaukasten „Fahrzeuge"	
Pcs: 409	1990–1996

725	EU NA AU AS
Basic Building Set	
Grundbaukasten „Stadt"	
Pcs: 426	1990–1996

735	EU NA AU AS
Basic Building Set	
Grundbaukasten „Feuerwehr"	
Pcs: 538	1990–1996

i	525	Available as box and cardboard version	Auch im Karton erhältlich
i	535	Available as box and cardboard version	Auch im Karton erhältlich
i	545	Available as box and cardboard version	Auch im Karton erhältlich

818	EU NA AU AS
Wheel-Wind Motor	
Traktionsmotor	
Pcs: 8	1990–1996

821	EU NA AU AS	
Brick Separator		
Trennhilfe		
Pcs: 1	1990–1996	Special

1482	EU NA AU AS	
Panda and Friends		
Promoset Japan Panda mit Freunden		
Pcs: 26	1990–1991	Special

1559	EU NA AU AS	
Clown Car		
Clownsauto		
Pcs: 4	1990–1992	Special

1560	EU NA AU AS	
Glory Glider		
Gleiter		
Pcs: 22	1990–1992	Special

1561	EU NA AU AS	
Stunt Chopper		
Hubschrauber		
Pcs: 31	1990–1992	Special

1562	EU NA AU AS	
Wave Jumper		
Motorboot		
Pcs: 25	1990–1992	Special

1563	EU NA AU AS	
Track Blaster		
Rennwagen		
Pcs: 30	1990–1992	Special

1581	EU NA AU AS	
Delivery Truck		
Molkereilaster		
Pcs: 119	1990	Special

1559-1563	Kellogg's Promo	Kellogg's Promo
1581	Arla Dairies Promo (Sweden)	Arla Dairies Promo (Schweden)

1630	EU NA AU AS	
Helicopter		
Helikopter		
Pcs: 30	1990–1991	Special

1631	EU NA AU AS	
Black Racer		
Schwarzer Rennwagen		
Pcs: 23	1990–1991	Special

1632	EU NA AU AS	
Motor Boat		
Motorboot		
Pcs: 30	1990–1991	Special

1633	EU NA AU AS	
Loader Tractor		
Traktor mit Frontschaufel		
Pcs: 24	1990–1991	Special

1636	EU NA AU AS	
Small Bucket		
Kleiner Eimer		
Pcs: 194	1990–1991	Special

1637	EU NA AU AS	
Large Bucket		
Großer Eimer		
Pcs: 503	1990–1991	

1638	EU NA AU AS	
Large Bucket		
Großer Eimer		
Pcs: 450	1990–1991	Special

1639	EU NA AU AS	
Large Bucket		
Großer Eimer		
Pcs: -	1990–1991	Special

1657	EU NA AU AS	
Bird		
Vogel		
Pcs: 6	1990–1995	Special

1630	Similar to: 1690 (1990)	Ähnlich zu: 1690 (1990)
1631	Similar to: 1691 (1990)	Ähnlich zu: 1691 (1990)

1665	EU NA AU AS	
Dual FX Racers		
Rennduell		
Pcs: 108	1990	Special

1672	EU NA AU AS	
Building Set "Circus"		
Baukasten „Circus"		
Pcs: -	1990–1991	Special

1674	EU NA AU AS	
Pre-School Bucket		
Vorschul-Eimer		
Pcs: 100	1990	Special

1675	EU NA AU AS	
Special Offer Value Pack		
Angebots Kombiset		
Sets: 3	1990	Special

1676	EU NA AU AS	
Basic Building Set		
Grundbaukasten		
Pcs: 22	1990–1993	

1677	EU NA AU AS	
Build-a-Bunny		
Osterhase		
Pcs: 26	1990–1998	Special

1679	EU NA AU AS	
Basic Building Set		
Grundbaukasten		
Pcs: 43	1990–1992	

1680	EU NA AU AS	
Hay Cart with Smugglers		
Heuwagen mit Schmugglern		
Pcs: 67	1990	Special

1682	EU NA AU AS	
Space Shuttle		
Space Shuttle		
Pcs: 426	1990–1992	

1675	Includes: 1875 (1990), 1876 (1990), 1877 (1990)	Enthält: 1875 (1990), 1876 (1990), 1877 (1990)
1677	Similar to: 10071 (2003)	Ähnlich zu: 10071 (2003)
1680	Similar to: 1877 (1990); with one additional figure	Ähnlich zu: 1877 (1990); mit einer zusätzlichen Figur

1684	EU NA AU AS	
Large Bucket		
Großer Eimer		
Pcs: 49	1990	

1685	EU NA AU AS	
XL Bucket		
Riesen Eimer		
Pcs: 69	1990–1991	Special

1690	EU NA AU AS	
Helicopter		
Helikopter		
Pcs: 29	1990	Special

1691	EU NA AU AS	
Racer		
Rennwagen		
Pcs: -	1990	Special

1692	EU NA AU AS	
Loader Tractor		
Bagger		
Pcs: -	1990	Special

1875	EU NA AU AS	
Meteor Monitor		
Meteor Monitor		
Pcs: 36	1990	Special

1876	EU NA AU AS	
Soil Scooper		
Schaufelbagger		
Pcs: 73	1990	Special

1877	EU NA AU AS	
Crusader's Cart		
Heuwagen mit Schmugglern		
Pcs: 61	1990	Special

1883	EU NA AU AS	
Rabbit Rattle		
Hasenrassel		
Pcs: 1	1990–1995	Special

i			
i	1690	Similar to: 1630 (1990); Colgate Promo	Ähnlich zu: 1630 (1990); Colgate Promo
i	1691	Similiar to: 1631 (1990); Colgate Promo	Ähnlich zu: 1631 (1990); Colgate Promo
i	1692	Colgate Promo	Colgate Promo
i	1875	Included in: 1675 (1990)	Enthalten in: 1675 (1990)
i	1876	Included in: 1675 (1990)	Enthalten in: 1675 (1990)
i	1877	Included in: 1675 (1990)	Enthalten in: 1675 (1990)

ⓘ 1998	EU	
Silja Line Ferry		
Silja Line Fährschiff		
Pcs: 354	1990–1993	Special

2442	EU NA AU AS	
School Room		
Schulklasse		
Pcs: 7	1990	

2446	EU NA AU AS	
Windmill		
Windmühle		
Pcs: 12	1990	

2450	EU NA AU AS	
Airport		
Flugplatz		
Pcs: 15	1990	

2454	NA	
Harbour		
Hafen		
Pcs: 15	1990	

2458	NA	
Farm		
Bauernhof		
Pcs: 20	1990	Special

2550	EU	
Tom's Adventure		
Ulis kleine Reise		
Pcs: 4	1990–1991	Special

2609	EU NA AU AS	
Racer		
Rennwagen		
Pcs: 2	1990–1996	

2613	EU NA AU AS	
Refuse Truck		
Müllabfuhr		
Pcs: 4	1990–1996	

ⓘ 1998	Sold only on Silja Line Ferries	Nur auf Silja Line Fähren im Verkauf

2615 EU NA AU AS

Nursery

Kinderzimmer

Pcs: 8 | 1990–1996

2630 EU NA AU AS

Camping Set

Wohnwagengespann

Pcs: 11 | 1990–1994

2661 EU NA AU AS

Animal Transporter

Raubtiertransporter

Pcs: 4 | 1990–1995

2662 EU NA AU AS

Crocodile and Sea Lion

Krokodil und Seelöwe

Pcs: 15 | 1990–1997

2664 EU NA AU AS

Tiger Enclosure

Tigerfamilie und Panda

Pcs: 26 | 1990–1996

2666 EU NA AU AS

Mini Zoo

Giraffen und Eisbären

Pcs: 26 | 1990–1997

2668 EU NA AU AS

Zoo

Tierpark

Pcs: 43 | 1990–1996

2669 EU NA AU AS

Maxi Zoo

Großer Zoo

Pcs: 71 | 1990–1996

5590 EU NA AU AS

Whirl N' Wheel Super Truck

Heli-Truck

Pcs: 1064 | 1990–1996

ⓘ 6018	EU NA AU AS
Battle Dragon	
Drachenschiff	
Pcs: 56	1990–1992

ⓘ 6034	EU NA AU AS
Black Monarch's Ghost	
Leuchtender Schlossgeist	
Pcs: 48	1990–1996

ⓘ 6042	EU NA AU AS
Dungeon Hunters	
Gefangenenkutsche	
Pcs: 113	1990–1992

ⓘ 6059	EU NA AU AS
Knight's Stronghold	
Burgtor	
Pcs: 229	1990–1996

ⓘ 6071	EU NA AU AS
Forestmen's Crossings	
Flussbrücke	
Pcs: 214	1990–1992

ⓘ 6081	EU NA AU AS
King's Mountain Fortress	
Spukschloss	
Pcs: 442	1990–1992

ⓘ 6354	EU NA AU AS
Pursuit Squad	
Polizei-Spezialisten-Team	
Pcs: 179	1990–1996

ⓘ 6375	EU NA AU AS
Trans Air Carrier	
Frachtflugzeug	
Pcs: 215	1990–1993

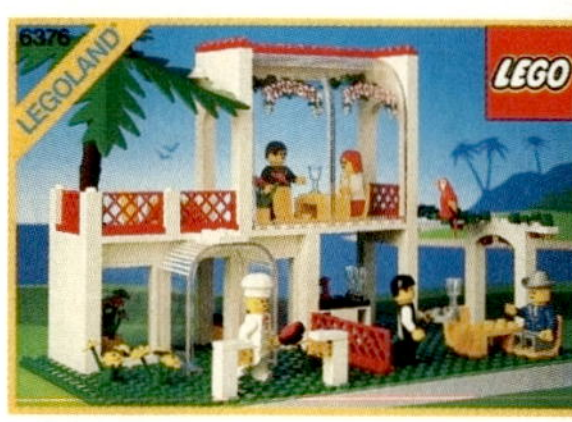

ⓘ 6376	EU NA AU AS
Breezeway Café	
Ristorante	
Pcs: 195	1990–1992

ⓘ 6376	Re-released as: 10037 (2002)	Neu aufgelegt als: 10037 (2002)

6389 EU NA AU AS
Fire Control Center
Feuerwehr-Einsatz-Zentrale
Pcs: 564 | 1990–1996

6396 EU NA AU AS
International Jetport
Insel-Flughafen
Pcs: 560 | 1990–1993

6399 EU NA AU AS
Airport Shuttle
Airport Shuttle
Pcs: 791 | 1990–1996

6508 EU NA AU AS
Wave Racer
Rennkatamaran
Pcs: 39 | 1990–1992

6529 EU NA AU AS
Ultra Light I
Ultraleichtflieger
Pcs: 40 | 1990–1992

6530 EU NA AU AS
Sport Coupé
Einkaufsflitzer
Pcs: 46 | 1990–1992

6592 EU NA AU AS
Vacation Hideaway
Ferienhaus
Pcs: 125 | 1990–1992

6644 EU NA AU AS
Road Rebel
Sportcabriolet mit Trailer
Pcs: 72 | 1990–1992

6672 EU NA AU AS
Safari Off Road Vehicle
Safari Off-Roader
Pcs: 69 | 1990–1992

6673	EU NA AU AS
Solo Trainer	
Turbo-Prop Sportflugzeug	
Pcs: 69	1990–1992

6811	EU NA AU AS
Pulsar Charger	
Space Wespe	
Pcs: 26	1990–1992

6833	EU NA AU AS
Beacon Tracer	
Space Buggy	
Pcs: 40	1990–1992

6877	EU NA AU AS
Vector Detector	
Space Single-Gleiter	
Pcs: 62	1990–1992

6896	EU NA AU AS
Celestial Foragier	
Space-Carrier	
Pcs: 94	1990–1992

6923	EU NA AU AS
Particle Ionizer	
Space Exo-Copter	
Pcs: 193	1990–1992

6956	EU NA AU AS
Stellar Recon Voyager	
Space Rettungsraumer	
Pcs: 233	1990–1992

6989	EU NA AU AS
Mega Core Magnetizer	
Mobiles Space Rescue-Center	
Pcs: 498	1990–1992

8064	EU NA AU AS
Universal Motor Set 9V	
Universalkasten mit Motor	
Pcs: 230	1990–1996

i	Set		
i	6833	Also included in: 1999 (1985)	Auch enthalten in: 1999 (1985)
i	6989	With poster	Mit Poster

8094 (EU) (NA) (AU) (AS)

Control Center

Steuerzentrale

Pcs: 561	1990–1994	

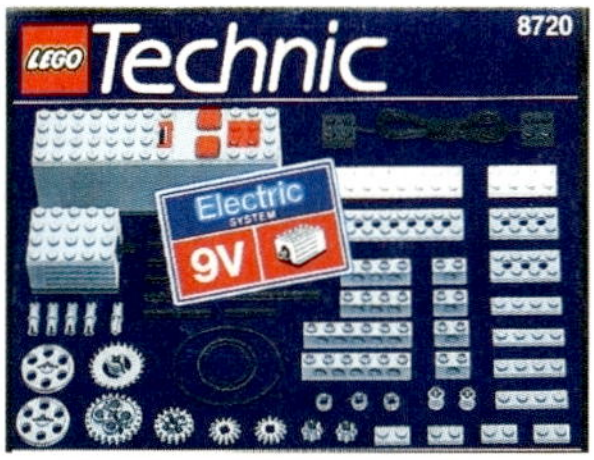

8720 (EU) (NA) (AU) (AS)

9V Motor Set

9V Motor-Set

Pcs: 57	1990–1999	

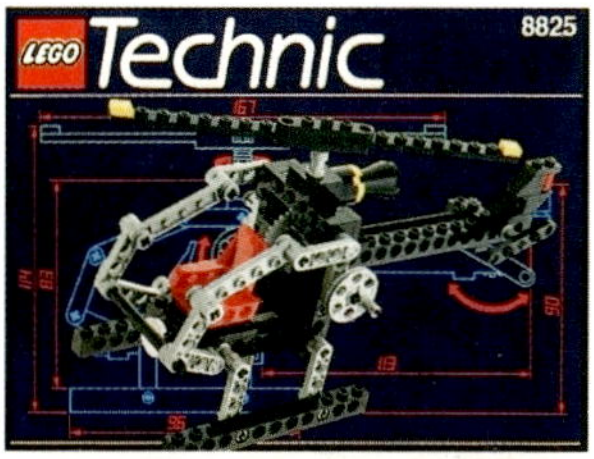

8825 (EU) (NA) (AU) (AS)

Night Chopper

Minicopter

Pcs: 113	1990–1993	

8830 (EU) (NA) (AU) (AS)

Rally 6-Wheeler

Rallye Wheeler

Pcs: 169	1990–1993	

8840 (EU) (NA) (AU) (AS)

Rally Shock n' Roll Racer

Geländerennwagen

Pcs: 225	1990–1993	

8850 (EU) (NA) (AU) (AS)

Rally Support Truck

Off-Roader

Pcs: 364	1990–1992	

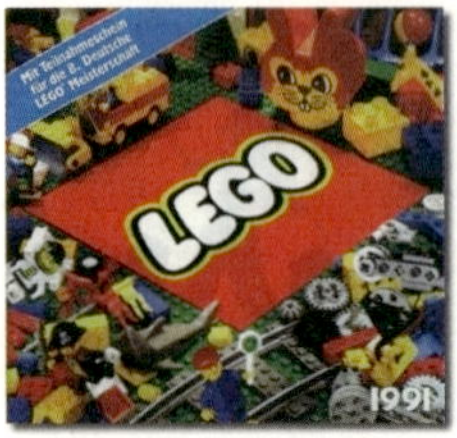

1991

ⓘ 819	EU NA AU AS	
Baseplate Blue 32x32		
Blaue Bauplatte 32x32		
Pcs: 1	1991–1997	

ⓘ 1474	EU NA AU AS	
Basic Building Set with Gift Item		
Geschenkkasten		
Pcs: 61	1991–1993	Special

ⓘ 1475	EU NA AU AS	
Airport Security Squad		
Helikopter mit Einweiser		
Pcs: 133	1991	Special

ⓘ 1476	EU NA AU AS	
5 Set Bonus Pack		
Fünffachpack		
Sets: 5	1991	Special

ⓘ 1483	EU NA AU AS	
Sailor and Parrot		
Seefahrer und Papagei		
Pcs: 19	1991–1992	Special

ⓘ 1548	EU NA AU AS	
Stena Line Ferry		
Stena Line Fährschiff		
Pcs: 180	1991–1996	Special

ⓘ			
ⓘ	819	Similar to: 627 (1996)	Ähnlich zu: 627 (1996)
ⓘ	1476	Includes: 1477, 1478, 1479, 1480, 1481	Enthält: 1477, 1478, 1479, 1480, 1481
ⓘ	1548	Sold only on Stena Line Ferries	Wurde nur auf Stena Line Fähren verkauft

1591 EU NA AU AS

Small Bucket		
Kleiner Eimer		
Pcs: 34	1991–1994	Special

1610 EU NA AU AS

Police Car		
Polizeiauto		
Pcs: 24	1991–1992	Special

1611 EU NA AU AS

Dune Buggy		
Strandbuggy		
Pcs: 21	1991–1992	Special

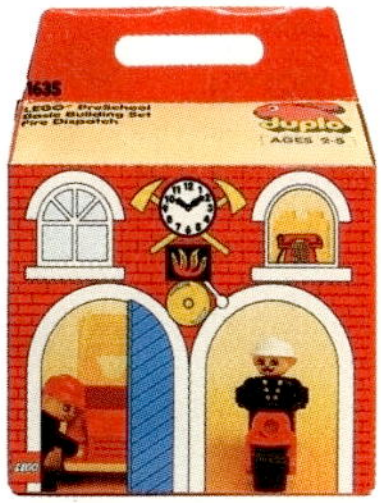

1635 EU NA AU AS

Fire Dispatch		
Feuerwache		
Pcs: 18	1991	Special

1656 EU NA AU AS

Evacuation Team		
Feuerwehr-Sondereinsatz-Team		
Pcs: 244	1991–1992	Special

1666 EU NA AU AS

Brick Vac		
Bausteinsammler (zum Aufräumen)		
Pcs: 140	1991–1992	

1678 EU NA AU AS

Basic Building Set Trial Size		
Probepackung		
Pcs: 48	1991	Special

1698 EU NA AU AS

Basic Building Set Trial Size		
Probepackung		
Pcs: 24	1991	Special

1772 EU NA AU AS

Airport Container Truck		
Flughafen-Lkw		
Pcs: 77	1991–1995	Special

1773	EU NA AU AS	
Airline Maintenance Vehicle		
Flughafenfahrzeug mit Anhänger		
Pcs: 98	1991–1994	Special

1774	EU NA AU AS	
Aircraft		
Flugzeug		
Pcs: 139	1991–1996	Special

1878	EU NA AU AS	
Small Bucket		
Kleiner Eimer		
Pcs: 393	1991–1996	Special

1881	EU NA AU AS	
Small Bucket		
Kleiner Eimer		
Pcs: 288	1991–1996	

1882	EU NA AU AS	
Large Bucket		
Großer Eimer		
Pcs: 459	1991–1992	

1977	EU NA AU AS	
Pre-School Building Set (XL)		
Vorschul-Eimer		
Pcs: 99	1991–1993	Special

1978	EU NA AU AS	
Build-A-Santa		
Weihnachtsmann		
Pcs: 39	1991–1992	Special

1979	EU NA AU AS	
Build-A-Snowman		
Schneemann		
Pcs: 43	1991–1992	Special

1980	EU NA AU AS	
Build-A-Pair of Elves		
Weihnachtselfen		
Pcs: 29	1991–1992	Special

1978	Similar to: 1127 (1999), 10068 (2002)	Ähnlich zu: 1127 (1999), 10068 (2002)
1979	Similar to: 10079 (2003)	Ähnlich zu: 10079 (2003)

ⓘ 2303	EU NA AU AS
Building Plates	
Bauplatten	
Pcs: 2	1991–1998

ⓘ 2306	EU NA AU AS
Large Building Plate	
Große Bauplatte	
Pcs: 1	1991–1999

ⓘ 2313	EU NA AU AS
Supplementary Set	
Kleiner Ergänzungskasten	
Pcs: 29	1991–1993

ⓘ 2314	EU NA AU AS
Large Supplementary Set	
Großer Ergänzungskasten	
Pcs: 38	1991–1996

ⓘ 2318	EU NA AU AS
Pullback Motor	
Traktionsmotor	
Pcs: 1	1991–1993

ⓘ 2331	EU NA AU AS
Barney, the Skateboard Bear	
Bär mit Skateboard	
Pcs: 8	1991–1996

ⓘ 2341	EU NA AU AS
Peter's Holiday Building Set	
Grundkasten „Reise“	
Pcs: 17	1991–1999

ⓘ 2361	EU NA AU AS
Matt and Mutt Building Set	
Grundkasten „Herr und Hund“	
Pcs: 21	1991–1996

ⓘ 2371	EU NA AU AS
Flying School	
Grundkasten „Flughafen“	
Pcs: 29	1991–1996

ⓘ	2306	Similar to: 2302 (1982), 2305 (1984), 2598 (2005)	Ähnlich zu: 2302 (1982), 2305 (1984), 2598 (2005)

2376	EU NA AU AS
Play Bucket	
Spieleimer	
Pcs: 36	1991–1999

2381	EU NA AU AS
Small Bucket	
Kleiner Eimer „Stein auf Stein“	
Pcs: 64	1991–1999

2386	EU NA AU AS
Large Bucket	
Großer Eimer „Circus“	
Pcs: 53	1991

2391	EU NA AU AS
Farm in a Bucket	
Großer Eimer „Bauernhof“	
Pcs: 60	1991–1992

2392	EU NA AU AS
Farmyard	
Grundkasten „Bauernhof“	
Pcs: 63	1991–1999

2443	EU NA AU AS
Lil' Skipper	
Der kleine Kapitän	
Pcs: 6	1991–1993

2447	EU NA AU AS
Speedway	
Rennstrecke	
Pcs: 9	1991–1992

2451	EU NA AU AS
Police Squad	
Polizeieinheit	
Pcs: 13	1991–1992

2455	EU NA AU AS
Corral	
Bauernhaus	
Pcs: 24	1991–1993

i	2391	Similar to: 2392 (1991)	Ähnlich zu: 2392 (1991)
i	2392	Similar to: 2391 (1991)	Ähnlich zu: 2391 (1991)

2459	EU NA AU AS
Express Train	
Schnellzug	
Pcs: 38	1991–1992

2654	EU NA AU AS
Police Emergency Unit	
Polizeirevier	
Pcs: 12	1991–1996

2660	EU NA AU AS
Zoo Nursery	
Tierkinder	
Pcs: 5	1991–1996

2671	EU NA AU AS
Racing Team	
Rennteam	
Pcs: 9	1991–1993

2672	EU NA AU AS
Police Station	
Polizei-Einsatzzentrale	
Pcs: 19	1991–1996

2771	EU NA AU AS
Family	
Familie	
Pcs: 8	1991–1996

2772	EU NA AU AS
World People	
Leute aus aller Welt	
Pcs: 12	1991–1997

2773	EU NA AU AS
Barbecue	
Grillfest	
Pcs: 15	1991–1996

2775	EU NA AU AS
Bathroom	
Badezimmer	
Pcs: 7	1991–1993

2776	EU NA AU AS
Bedroom	
Schlafzimmer	
Pcs: 15	1991–1993

2777	EU NA AU AS
Living Room	
Wohnzimmer	
Pcs: 12	1991–1997

2778	EU NA AU AS
Kitchen	
Küche	
Pcs: 11	1991–1993

2779	EU NA AU AS
Unfurnished Play House	
Spielhaus, unmöbliert	
Pcs: 11	1991–1997

2780	EU NA AU AS
Complete Play House	
Spielhaus mit Einrichtung	
Pcs: 55	1991–1996

4011	EU NA AU AS
Cabin Cruiser	
Motoryacht mit Hochseeangler	
Pcs: 101	1991–1995

4021	EU NA AU AS
Police Patrol	
Wasserschutzpolizei	
Pcs: 195	1991–1996

4031	EU NA AU AS
Fire Rescue	
Schweres Feuerlöschboot	
Pcs: 372	1991–1996

4515	EU NA AU AS
Straight Rails	
Gerade Gleisstücke	
Pcs: 8	1991–2006

4520
EU NA AU AS

Curved Rails	
Gebogene Gleisstücke	
Pcs: 8	1991–2006

4531
EU NA AU AS

Manual Points	
Weichenpaar für Handbetrieb	
Pcs: 7	1991–2006

4536
EU NA AU AS

Hopper Car	
Schüttgutwagen	
Pcs: 171	1991–1992

4539
EU NA AU AS

Level Crossing	
Bahnübergang	
Pcs: 117	1991–1997

4543
EU NA AU AS

Railroad Tractor Flatbed	
Niederbordwagen	
Pcs: 188	1991–1993

4546
EU NA AU AS

Road N' Rail Maintenance	
Schienen- und Straßenfahrzeug	
Pcs: 83	1991–1997

4548
EU NA AU AS

Transformer and Speed Regulator	
9V Transformator	
Pcs: 3	1991–2006

4551
EU NA AU AS

Crocodile Locomotive	
Schwere Güterzug-E-Lok	
Pcs: 314	1991–1993

4554
EU NA AU AS

Metro Station	
Großer Stadtbahnhof	
Pcs: 612	1991–1994

4558	EU NA AU AS
Metro Liner	
Moderner Hochgeschwindigkeitszug	
Pcs: 762	1991–1996

4563	EU NA AU AS
Load N' Haul Railroad	
Eisenbahn-Komplett-Set	
Pcs: 490	1991–1996

5550	EU NA AU AS
Custom Rally Van	
Rallye-Service-Wagen	
Pcs: 527	1991–1993

6234	EU NA AU AS
Renegade's Raft	
Schiffbrüchiger Pirat	
Pcs: 40	1991–1996

6259	EU NA AU AS
Broadside's Brig	
Gefängnis	
Pcs: 69	1991–1996

6267	EU NA AU AS
Lagoon Lock-up	
Hafenschänke	
Pcs: 194	1991–1996

6273	EU NA AU AS
Rock Island Refuge	
Piratennest	
Pcs: 391	1991–1996

6347	EU NA AU AS
Monorail Accessory Track	
Weichen, Leitschienen, Pfeiler	
Pcs: 54	1991–1993

6352	EU NA AU AS
Cargomaster Crane	
Teleskopkranwagen	
Pcs: 151	1991–1993

i	4558	Re-released as: 10001 (2001)	Neu aufgelegt als: 10001 (2001)
i	6234	Also included in: 9206 (1994)	Auch enthalten in: 9206 (1994)

6353 EU NA AU AS

Coastal Cutter

Küsten-Patrouillenkreuzer

Pcs: 193	1991–1996	

6430 EU NA AU AS

Night Patroller

Polizei-Spezialeinsatzwagen

Pcs: 140	1991–1996	

6440 EU NA AU AS

Jetport Fire Squad

Flughafen-Löschgigant

Pcs: 165	1991–1996	

6509 EU NA AU AS

Red Devil Racer

Formel 1 Rennwagen

Pcs: 39	1991–1996	

6510 EU NA AU AS

Mud Runner

Wüsten-Buggy

Pcs: 34	1991–1992	

6531 EU NA AU AS

Flame Chaser

Löschhubschrauber

Pcs: 58	1991–1996	

6532 EU NA AU AS

Diesel Dumper

Straßenbautraktor

Pcs: 48	1991–1993	

6540 EU NA AU AS

Pier Police

Hafenpolizei-Station

Pcs: 375	1991–1996	

6541 EU NA AU AS

Intercoastal Seaport

Stückguthafen

Pcs: 553	1991–1996	

1991

6542 EU NA AU AS

Launch & Load Seaport

Containerterminal

Pcs: 1102 | 1991–1996

6593 EU NA AU AS

Blaze Battler

Feuerwehr-Drehleiterwagen

Pcs: 126 | 1991–1996

6645 EU NA AU AS

Street Sweeper

Straßenkehrmaschine

Pcs: 65 | 1991

6646 EU NA AU AS

Screaming Patriot

California Fun Car

Pcs: 65 | 1991–1993

6669 EU NA AU AS

Diesel Daredevil

Königstruck

Pcs: 92 | 1991–1996

6679 EU NA AU AS

Dark Shark

Schmuggler-Speedboat

Pcs: 84 | 1991–1996

6704 EU NA AU AS

Space Mini Figures

6 verschiedene Astronauten

Pcs: 44 | 1991–1996

6710 EU NA AU AS

Space Landing Pads

Start- und Landeplatten

Pcs: 2 | 1991–1996

6812 EU NA AU AS

Grid Trekkor

Blacktron Spektrobiler

Pcs: 25 | 1991–1993

6832	EU NA AU AS	
Super Nova II		
Blacktron Deltaswinger		
Pcs: 42	1991–1993	

6851	EU NA AU AS	
Tri-Wheeled Tyrax		
Blacktron Cross-Rauh Walze		
Pcs: 38	1991–1996	

6862	EU NA AU AS	
Secret Space Voyager		
Supermodell-Bauanleitung		
Pcs: -	1991	Special

6878	EU NA AU AS	
Sub Orbital Guardian		
Blacktron Moskito		
Pcs: 69	1991–1993	

6887	EU NA AU AS	
Allied Avenger		
Blacktron Kugellibelle		
Pcs: 100	1991–1996	

6933	EU NA AU AS	
Spectral Starguider		
Blacktron Mobil		
Pcs: 208	1991–1993	

6981	EU NA AU AS	
Aerial Intruder		
Blacktron Spy Intruder		
Pcs: 266	1991–1996	

6988	EU NA AU AS	
Alpha Centauri Outpost		
Blacktron Informationszentrale		
Pcs: 406	1991–1993	

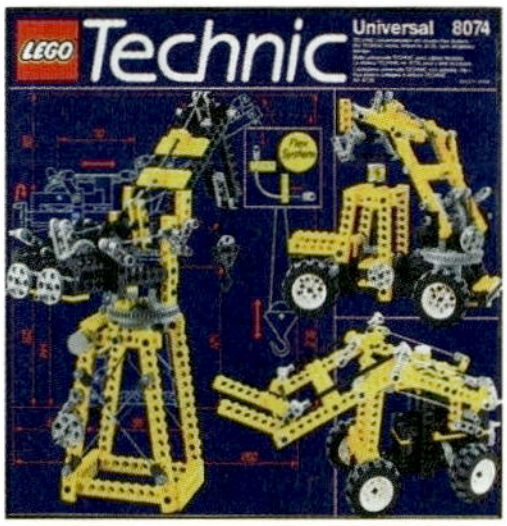

8074	EU NA AU AS	
Universal Set with Flex System		
Universalkasten		
Pcs: 320	1991–1993	

i	6851	Also included in: 4741 (1993)	Auch enthalten in: 4741(1993)
i	6862	Only building instruction	Nur Bauanleitung
i	6878	Included in: 4741 (1993)	Enthalten in: 4741 (1993)
i	6887	Also included in: 4741 (1993)	Auch enthalten in: 4741(1993)

8810	EU NA AU AS
Cafe Racer	
1-Zylinder-Motorrad	
Pcs: 80	1991–1994

8815	EU NA AU AS
Speedway Bandit	
Go-Kart	
Pcs: 78	1991–1993

8820	EU NA AU AS
Mountain Rambler	
Cross-Roadster	
Pcs: 139	1991–1993

8838	EU NA AU AS
Shock Cycle	
Enduro	
Pcs: 251	1991–1995

8856	EU NA AU AS
Whirlwind Rescue	
Rettungshubschrauber	
Pcs: 522	1991–1994

8891	EU NA AU AS
Idea Book	
Baubuch	
Pcs: 1	1991–1994

1992

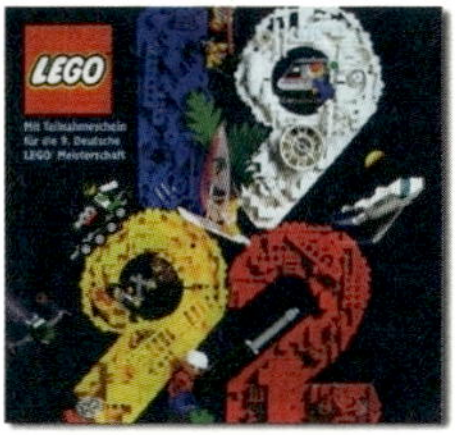

845	EU NA AU AS	
9V Battery Motor		
9V Motor		
Pcs: 27	1992–1996	

1461	NA	
Turbo Force		
Turbo Force		
Pcs: 33	1992–1993	Special

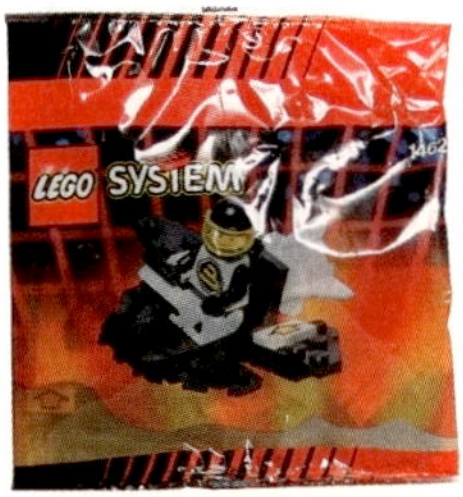

1462	NA	
Galactic Scout		
Galaxis-Späher		
Pcs: 23	1992–1993	Special

1463	NA	
Treasure Cart		
Schatztransport		
Pcs: 22	1992–1993	Special

1464	NA	
Pirate Lookout		
Pirateninsel		
Pcs: 17	1992–1993	Special

1491	NA	
Dual Defender		
Doppelschleuder		
Pcs: 50	1992–1993	Special

1461	Similar to: 1693 (1992)	Ähnlich zu: 1693 (1992)
1462	Similar to: 1694 (1992)	Ähnlich zu: 1694 (1992)
1463	Similar to: 2889 (1997), 1695 (1992)	Ähnlich zu: 2889 (1997), 1695 (1992)
1464	Similar to: 1696 (1992)	Ähnlich zu: 1696 (1992)

1492 EU NA AU AS

Battle Cove

Geschützstellung

Pcs: 30	1992–1993	Special

1545 EU NA AU AS

Build-A-Rabbit

Bau einen Hasen

Pcs: 30	1992	Special

1549 EU NA AU AS

Santa with Chimney

Weihnachtsmann am Schornstein

Pcs: 67	1992	Special

1583 EU NA AU AS

Clown Bucket

Eimer „Clown"

Pcs: 30	1992–1996	Special

1594 EU NA AU AS

Rabbit with Bear Friend

Hase und Bär

Pcs: 13	1992–1993	Special

1659 EU NA AU AS

Tote Pack

Tragebox

Pcs: 30	1992	Special

1664 EU NA AU AS

Bird

Vogel

Pcs: 2	1992–1994	Special

1668 EU NA AU AS

Basic Building Set Trial Size

Probepackung

Pcs: 30	1992	Special

1670 EU NA AU AS

Basic Building Set Trial Size

Probepackung

Pcs: 28	1992	Special

1671	EU NA AU AS	
Basic Building Set Trial Size		
Probepackung		
Pcs: -	1992–1995	Special

1673	EU NA AU AS	
Zoo Train Special Offer		
Zoo-Zug Spezialangebot		
Pcs: 8	1992–1993	Special

1693	EU NA AU AS	
Turbo Force		
Turbo Force		
Pcs: 26	1992–1993	Special

1694	EU NA AU AS	
Galactic Scout		
Galaxis-Späher		
Pcs: 29	1992	Special

1695	EU NA AU AS	
Treasure Cart		
Schatztransport		
Pcs: 22	1992–1993	Special

1696	EU NA AU AS	
Pirate Lookout		
Pirateninsel		
Pcs: 17	1992–1996	Special

1750	EU NA AU AS	
Renault Formula 1 Racer		
Renault Formel 1 Rennwagen		
Pcs: 31	1992	Special

1769	EU NA AU AS	
Aircraft		
Flugzeug		
Pcs: 23	1992–1996	Special

1879	EU NA AU AS	
Large Bucket		
Großer Eimer		
Pcs: 432	1992–1994	

1693	Similar to: 1461 (1992); included in: 1900 (1994)	Ähnlich zu: 1461 (1992); enthalten in: 1900 (1994)
1694	Similar to: 1462 (1992)	Ähnlich zu: 1462 (1992)
1695	Similar to: 1463 (1992), 2889 (1997)	Ähnlich zu: 1463 (1992), 2889 (1997)
1696	Similar to: 1464 (1992); incl. in: 1900 (1994), 9206 (1994)	Ähnlich zu: 1464 (1992); ent. in: 1900 (1994), 9206 (1994)

1880	EU NA AU AS	
XL Bucket		
Riesen Eimer		
Pcs: 536	1992–1994	Special

1884	EU NA AU AS	
Small Bucket		
Kleiner Eimer		
Pcs: 197	1992–1996	

1885	EU NA AU AS	
XL Bucket		
Riesen Eimer		
Pcs: 465	1992–1996	

1891	EU NA AU AS	
4 Set Value Pack		
4er Kombiset		
Sets: 4	1992	Special

1893	EU NA AU AS	
Bucket with Bonus Animals		
Dschungel-Eimer mit Bonus-Tieren		
Pcs: 37	1992	Special

1895	EU NA AU AS	
Sky Patrol		
Polizeiflugzeug		
Pcs: 84	1992	Special

1896	EU NA AU AS	
Trauma Team		
Einsatzrettungskräfte		
Pcs: 304	1992–1993	Special

1924	EU NA AU AS	
Viking Line Ferry		
Viking Line Fährschiff		
Pcs: 201	1992–1998	Special

1994	EU NA AU AS	
Turtle Bucket with Motor		
Mittlerer Eimer mit Motor		
Pcs: 182	1992–1994	

1891	Includes four sets, nummbered as 1887-1890, they don't exist besides this set	Enthält vier Sets, mit den Nummern 1887-1890, Sets sind aber nicht außerhalb der 1891 erschienen
1924	Sold only on Viking Line Ferries	Wurde nur auf Viking Line Fähren verkauft

2304	**EU** **NA** **AU** **AS**	
Large Green Building Plate		
Große grüne Bauplatte		
Pcs: 1	1992–1994	
■■■□□□		

2374	EU **NA** AU AS	
Bucket		
Eimer		
Pcs: 59	1992–1996	
■■■■■■		

2383	EU **NA** AU AS	
Bucket		
Eimer		
Pcs: 61	1992–1993	
■■■■■■		

2384	EU **NA** AU AS	
Farm Bucket		
Großer Eimer „Bauernhof“		
Pcs: -	1992	
■■■■■■		

2387	**EU** **NA** **AU** **AS**	
Playtime Bucket		
Großer Eimer „Dicke Freunde“		
Pcs: 49	1992–1999	
■■■■□□		

2551	EU **NA** AU AS	
Grandma's Kitchen		
Omas Küche		
Pcs: 41	1992–1994	Special
■■■■■□		

2552	**EU** **NA** **AU** **AS**	
Family Home Bucket		
Eimer „Meine Familie“		
Pcs: 49	1992–1996	
■■■■□□		

2910	**EU** **NA** **AU** **AS**	
Dumper Truck		
Schaufelradlader		
Pcs: 18	1992–1996	
■■■□□□		

2920	**EU** **NA** **AU** **AS**	
Digger		
Muldenkipper		
Pcs: 20	1992–1995	
■■■□□□		

2930 EU NA AU AS
Mobile Crane
Kranwagen
Pcs: 29 | 1992–1996

2940 EU NA AU AS
Fire Truck
Löschzug
Pcs: 34 | 1992–1996

6009 EU NA AU AS
Black Knight
Turnierritter
Pcs: 22 | 1992–1996

6038 EU NA AU AS
Wolfpack Renegades
Wegelagerer
Pcs: 97 | 1992–1996

6057 EU NA AU AS
Sea Serpent
Einmast-Seedrache
Pcs: 142 | 1992–1996

6075 EU NA AU AS
Wolfpack Tower
Räuberhöhle
Pcs: 241 | 1992–1996

6086 EU NA AU AS
Black Knight's Castle
Ritterburg
Pcs: 599 | 1992–1996

6247 EU NA AU AS
Bounty Boat
Ruderboot
Pcs: 41 | 1992–1996

6258 EU NA AU AS
Smuggler's Shanty
Beutehöhle
Pcs: 75 | 1992–1996

i		
6086	With poster	Mit Poster

6261 EU NA AU AS

Raft Raiders	
Piratenfloß	
Pcs: 86	1992–1996

6271 EU NA AU AS

Imperial Flagship	
Admiralskaravelle	
Pcs: 331	1992–1996

6277 EU NA AU AS

Imperial Trading Post	
Historischer Freihafen	
Pcs: 631	1992–1996

6314 EU NA AU AS

City People	
6 Figuren	
Pcs: 34	1992–1997

6346 EU NA AU AS

Shuttle Launching Crew	
Space Shuttle-Eskorte	
Pcs: 425	1992–1996

6351 EU NA AU AS

Surf N' Sail Camper	
Wohnmobil mit Bootsanhänger	
Pcs: 192	1992–1994

6397 EU NA AU AS

Gas N' Wash Express	
Octan Tank- und Service-Station	
Pcs: 477	1992–1996

6401 EU NA AU AS

Seaside Cabana	
Paradisa Strandoase	
Pcs: 49	1992–1996

6405 EU NA AU AS

Sunset Stables	
Turnierteam	
Pcs: 133	1992–1999

i	6397	Similar to: 6472 (2001)	Ähnlich zu: 6472 (2001)

6411	EU NA AU AS
Sand Dollar Café	
Paradisa Strandcafé	
Pcs: 176	1992–1996

6416	EU NA AU AS
Poolside Paradise	
Traumstrand-Palast	
Pcs: 243	1992–1996

6419	EU NA AU AS
Rolling Acres Ranch	
Reit- und Fahrschule	
Pcs: 366	1992–1996

6511	EU NA AU AS
Rescue Runabout	
Feuerwehreinsatzwagen	
Pcs: 40	1992–1996

6512	EU NA AU AS
Landscape Loader	
Ladefahrzeug	
Pcs: 43	1992–1997

6533	EU NA AU AS
Police 4x4	
Polizei-Pick-Up	
Pcs: 63	1992–1996

6534	EU NA AU AS
Beach Bandit	
Strandbuggy	
Pcs: 44	1992–1996

6551	EU NA AU AS
Checkered Flag 500	
Cross Country Rallye	
Pcs: 194	1992–1996

6594	EU NA AU AS
Gas Transit	
Octan Tank-Truck	
Pcs: 129	1992–1997

6411	With poster	Mit Poster

6648	EU NA AU AS
Mag Racer	
Cross-Cart	
Pcs: 62	1992–1996

6662	EU NA AU AS
Backhoe	
Frontlader mit Heckschaufel	
Pcs: 85	1992–1996

6668	EU NA AU AS
Recycle Truck	
Recycling-Container Truck	
Pcs: 109	1992–1994

6897	EU NA AU AS
Rebel Hunter	
Space Police Quick-Hunter	
Pcs: 146	1992–1996

6957	EU NA AU AS
Solar Snooper	
Space Police Gefangenentruck	
Pcs: 253	1992–1996

6984	EU NA AU AS
Galactic Mediator	
Space Police Commander-Corvette	
Pcs: 408	1992–1996

8826	EU NA AU AS
ATX Sport Cycle	
All Terrain Vehicle	
Pcs: 95	1992–1994

8828	EU NA AU AS
Front End Loader	
Frontschaufellader	
Pcs: 177	1992–1994

8836	EU NA AU AS
Sky Ranger	
Sportflugzeug	
Pcs: 273	1992–1996

8837	EU NA AU AS
Pneumatic Excavator	
Löffelbagger	
Pcs: 242	1992–1996

8839	EU NA AU AS
Supply Ship	
Bergungsschlepper	
Pcs: 563	1992–1993

8868	EU NA AU AS
Air Tech Claw Rig	
Truck	
Pcs: 970	1992–1996

1993

345	EU NA AU AS	
Small Bucket for Her		
Kleiner Eimer „Fröhliche Familie“		
Pcs: 135	1993–1996	

1504	EU NA AU AS	
Family Bucket		
Eimer „Familie“		
Pcs: 1	1993–1996	

1540	EU NA AU AS	
Betsy's Bedroom		
Betsys Schlafzimmer		
Pcs: 39	1993–1994	

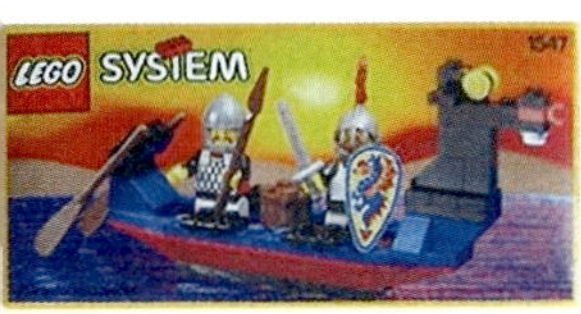

1547	EU NA AU AS	
Black Knight's Boat		
Drachenboot		
Pcs: 62	1993	

1579	EU NA AU AS	
Funny Animals		
Sammelbox „Maskottchen“		
Pcs: 30	1993–1996	

1595	EU NA AU AS	
Girl with Cat		
Mädchen mit Katze		
Pcs: 17	1993	

1547	Included in: 1597 (1993)	Enthalten in: 1597 (1993)

1596	EU NA AU AS
Ghostly Hideout	
Geist mit Wolfsbandit	
Pcs: 37	1993

1597	EU NA AU AS
Castle 3-Pack	
Burg Dreierpack	
Sets: 3	1993

1614	EU NA AU AS
Build-a-Farm	
Spielbox „Bauernhof“	
Pcs: 26	1993

1624	EU NA AU AS
King's Archer	
Bogenschütze	
Pcs: 22	1993

1651	EU NA AU AS
Basic Building Set Trial Size	
Probierpackung	
Pcs: 30	1993–1996

1652	EU NA AU AS	
Basic Building Set Trial Size		
Probierpackung		
Pcs: 43	1993–1996	Special

1687	EU NA AU AS
Midnight Transport	
Goldtransport	
Pcs: 278	1993–1994

1688	EU NA AU AS
Large Bucket for Her	
Großer Eimer „Fröhliche Familie“	
Pcs: 216	1993–1996

1699	EU NA AU AS
Small Bucket	
Kleiner Eimer	
Pcs: 179	1993–1996

ⓘ	1596	Included in: 1597 (1993)	Enthalten in: 1597 (1993)
ⓘ	1597	Includes: 1547 (1993), 1596 (1993), 1624 (1993)	Enthält: 1547 (1993), 1596 (1993), 1624 (1993)
ⓘ	1624	Included in: 1597 (1993)	Enthalten in: 1597 (1993)

1707 EU NA AU AS

20th Anniversary Jackpot Bucket	
20th Anniversary Jackpot Bucket	
Pcs: 400	1993

1735 EU NA AU AS

20th Anniversary Jackpot Bucket	
20th Anniversary Jackpot Bucket	
Pcs: 50	1993

1816 EU NA AU AS

20th Anniversary Jackpot Bucket	
20th Anniversary Jackpot Bucket	
Pcs: 90	1993

1830 EU NA AU AS

Large Bucket	
Großer Eimer	
Pcs: -	1993–1994

1845 EU NA AU AS

20th Anniversary Jackpot Bucket	
20th Anniversary Jackpot Bucket	
Pcs: 714	1993

1874 EU NA AU AS

Polly Pick-Up	
Lora Steinpick	
Pcs: 141	1993–1996

1903 EU NA AU AS

Medium Bucket	
Mittlerer Eimer	
Pcs: -	1993–1996

1908 EU NA AU AS

Small Bucket	
Kleiner Eimer	
Pcs: 39	1993

1916 EU NA AU AS

Starion Patrol	
Space Police Streife	
Pcs: 25	1993

i	1735	Was released due to 20th Anniversary of LEGO USA	Zum 20. Jubiläum von LEGO USA veröffentlicht
i	1916	Similar to: 3015 (1998); included in: 1900 (1994)	Ähnlich zu: 3015 (1998); enthalten in: 1900 (1994)

1917	EU NA AU AS	
King's Catapult		
Katapult		
Pcs: 22	1993–1996	

1932	EU NA AU AS	
Medium Bucket		
Mittlerer Eimer		
Pcs: -	1993	

1955	EU NA AU AS	
Color Line Ferry		
Color Line Fährschiff		
Pcs: 255	1993–1999	Special

1967	EU NA AU AS	
System Value Pack		
System Kombiset		
Sets: 4	1993	

1990	EU NA AU AS	
F1 Race Car		
Formel 1 Rennwagen		
Pcs: 35	1993	

1991	EU NA AU AS	
Racing Pickup		
Renn-Service-Wagen		
Pcs: 81	1993	

1992	EU NA AU AS	
Dragsters		
Dragsters		
Pcs: 108	1993	

1993	EU NA AU AS	
Race Value Pack		
Rennen Kombiset		
Sets: 3	1993	

2311	EU NA AU AS	
Clown		
Grundkasten „Clown"		
Pcs: 16	1993–1994	

i	1917	Similar to: 1890 (1997); included in: 1900 (1994)	Ähnlich zu: 2890 (1997); enth. in: 1900 (1994)
i	1955	Sold only on Color Line Ferries	Wurde nur auf Color Line Fähren verkauft
i	1967	Includes: 1959 (1993), 1969 (1993), 1970 (1993), 1971 (1993)	Enthält: 1959 (1993), 1969 (1993), 1970 (1993), 1971 (1993)
i	1990	Included in: 1993 (1993)	Enthalten in: 1993 (1993)
i	1991	Included in: 1993 (1993)	Enthalten in: 1993 (1993)
i	1992	Included in: 1993 (1993)	Enthalten in: 1993 (1993)

2369 EU NA AU AS

Racing Bucket

Kleiner Eimer „Rennen“

Pcs: 38 | 1993–1994

2372 EU NA AU AS

Zoo Bucket

Eimer „Zoo“

Pcs: 41 | 1993–1999

2378 EU NA AU AS

Farm Bucket

Großer Eimer „Bauernhof“

Pcs: 53 | 1993

2382 EU NA AU AS

Train Bucket

Großer Eimer „Eisenbahn“

Pcs: 41 | 1993–1994

2389 EU NA AU AS

Animal Bucket

Großer Eimer „Tiere“

Pcs: 43 | 1993

2452 EU NA AU AS

Choo Choo Train

Tuff-tuff-Eisenbahn

Pcs: 13 | 1993–1994

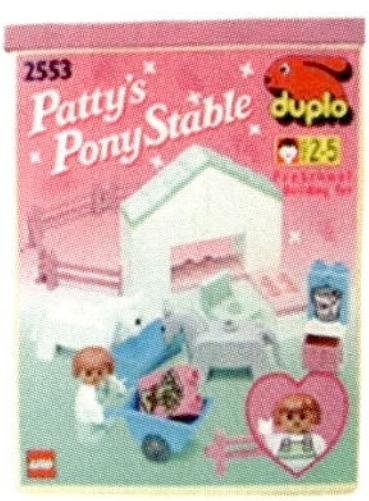

2553 EU NA AU AS

Patty's Pony Stable

Pattys Ponystall

Pcs: 28 | 1993–1994

2675 EU NA AU AS

Police Helicopter

Polizeihubschrauber

Pcs: 4 | 1993–1997

2676 EU NA AU AS

Bertie the Little Red Plane

Privatflugzeug

Pcs: 10 | 1993–2000

i 1993	Includes: 1990 (1993), 1991 (1993), 1992 (1993)	Enthält: 1990 (1993), 1991 (1993), 1992 (1993)

2677	EU NA AU AS
Fire Helicopter	
Feuerlöschhubschrauber	
Pcs: 11	1993–1999

2678	EU NA AU AS
Jumbo Jet	
Düsenjet	
Pcs: 15	1993–1996

2679	EU NA AU AS
Airport	
Flugplatz	
Pcs: 26	1993–1997

2730	EU NA AU AS
Electric Play Train Set	
Eisenbahn mit Batteriemotor	
Pcs: 61	1993–1996

2732	EU NA AU AS
Push-Along Play Train Set	
Schiebezug	
Pcs: 50	1993–1996

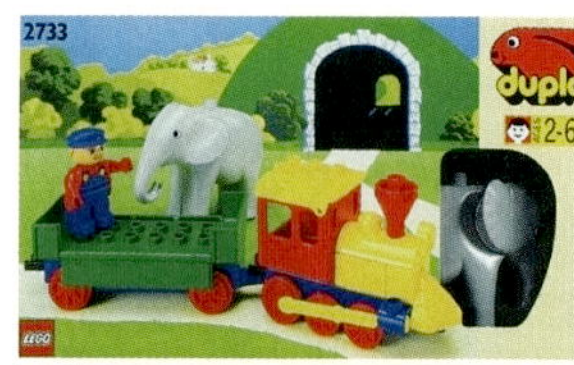

2733	EU NA AU AS
Push-Along Play Train	
Lokomotive mit Elefantenwaggon	
Pcs: 12	1993–1996

2734	EU NA AU AS
Straight Rails	
Gerade Schienen	
Pcs: 6	1993–2005

2735	EU NA AU AS
Curved Rails	
Gebogene Schienen	
Pcs: 6	1993–2005

2736	EU NA AU AS
Points	
Weichen	
Pcs: 4	1993–2005

i	Set	Note	Hinweis
i	2734	Re-release 2004	Neuauflage 2004
i	2735	Re-release 2004	Neuauflage 2004

2737 EU NA AU AS

Diamond Crossing and Tracks

Schienen und Kreuzung

Pcs: 9 | 1993–2004

2740 EU NA AU AS

Level Crossing

Bahnübergang

Pcs: 7 | 1993–2000

2905 EU NA AU AS

Supplementary Set

Ergänzungskasten

Pcs: 19 | 1993–1997

2950 EU NA AU AS

Construction Site

Baustelle

Pcs: 51 | 1993–1994

4537 EU NA AU AS

Twin Tank Transport

Octan Tankwagen

Pcs: 176 | 1993–1996

4547 EU NA AU AS

Club Car

Doppeldeckerpanoramawagen

Pcs: 295 | 1993–1994

4549 EU NA AU AS

Container Double Stack

Containertransportwagen

Pcs: 454 | 1993–1996

5521 EU NA AU AS

Sea Jet

Hochsee-Powerboot

Pcs: 403 | 1993–1999

5581 EU NA AU AS

Magic Flash

Rennboot-Gespann

Pcs: 791 | 1993–1996

(i) 4547	Re-released as: 10002 (2001)	Neu aufgelegt als: 10002 (2001)

6020	EU NA AU AS
Magic Shop	
Cerlin, der Zauberer	
Pcs: 45	1993–1995

ⓘ 6043	EU NA AU AS
Dragon Defender	
Drachenkatapult	
Pcs: 148	1993–1996

6048	EU NA AU AS
Majisto's Magical Workshop	
Hexenmeisterwerkstatt	
Pcs: 193	1993–1996

6056	EU NA AU AS
Dragon Wagon	
Karren mit Raubtierkäfig	
Pcs: 108	1993–1995

ⓘ 6076	EU NA AU AS
Dark Dragon's Den	
Drachenhöhle	
Pcs: 218	1993–1996

ⓘ 6082	EU NA AU AS
Fire Breathing Fortress	
Burg Drachenstein	
Pcs: 402	1993–1996

6105	EU NA AU AS
Medieval Knights	
Verschiedene Ritter	
Pcs: 37	1993–1996

6237	EU NA AU AS
Pirates' Plunder	
Schatzsucher	
Pcs: 29	1993–1995

6252	EU NA AU AS
Sea Mates	
Piraten, Rotröcke und Zubehör	
Pcs: 41	1993–1995

ⓘ	6043	Included in: 1960 (1993)	Enthalten in: 1960 (1993)
ⓘ	6076	With poster	Mit Poster
ⓘ	6082	With poster	Mit Poster

6266	EU NA AU AS
Cannon Cove	
Felsenkerker	
Pcs: 114	1993–1996

6268	EU NA AU AS
Renegade Runner	
Einmast-Piratensegler	
Pcs: 187	1993–1996

6286	EU NA AU AS
Skull's Eye Schooner	
Piraten-Dreimastbark	
Pcs: 929	1993–1996

6319	EU NA AU AS
Trees and Fences	
Bäume, Blumen und Zäune	
Pcs: 49	1993–1996

6342	EU NA AU AS
Beach Rescue Chopper	
Seenot-Rettungshubschrauber	
Pcs: 155	1993–1995

6344	EU NA AU AS
Jet Speed Justice	
Umweltschutzpolizei	
Pcs: 158	1993–1995

6345	EU NA AU AS
Aerial Acrobats	
Kunstflugakrobaten	
Pcs: 348	1993–1996

6398	EU NA AU AS
Central Precinct HQ	
Polizeihauptquartier	
Pcs: 638	1993–1995

6403	EU NA AU AS
Paradise Playground	
Spielplatz	
Pcs: 99	1993–1996

i	Set	English	Deutsch
i	6268	With poster	Mit Poster
i	6286	With poster	Mit Poster
i	6398	With poster	Mit Poster

6409 EU NA AU AS
Island Arcade
Freizeitpark
Pcs: 157 | 1993–1996

6513 EU NA AU AS
Glade Runner
Air-Boat
Pcs: 32 | 1993–1996

6536 EU NA AU AS
Aero Hawk
Kurierflugzeug
Pcs: 48 | 1993–1996

6539 EU NA AU AS
Victory Cup Racers
Go-Kart-Center
Pcs: 461 | 1993–1996

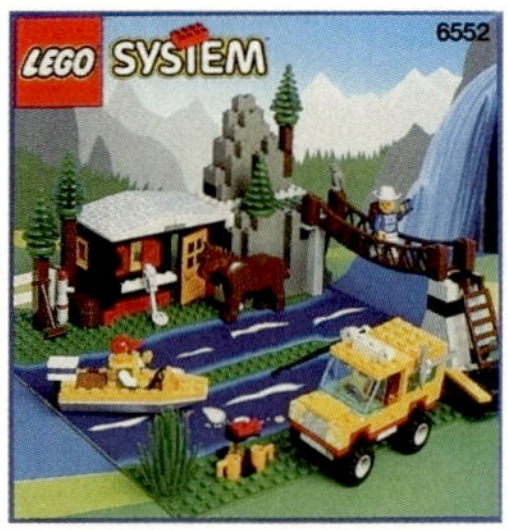

6552 EU NA AU AS
Rocky River Retreat
Canadian Mountain Camp
Pcs: 250 | 1993–1996

6595 EU NA AU AS
Surf Shack
Windsurfer-Schule
Pcs: 94 | 1993–1996

6663 EU NA AU AS
Wave Rebel
Off-Roader mit Sportboot
Pcs: 79 | 1993–1996

6664 EU NA AU AS
Chopper Cops
Highway Patrol
Pcs: 76 | 1993–1996

6667 EU NA AU AS
Road Repair Car
Straßenbau-Reparaturwagen
Pcs: 96 | 1993–1995

	Set	English	Deutsch
i	6409	With poster	Mit Poster
i	6539	With poster	Mit Poster

6670	EU NA AU AS
Wrecker	
Bergungs- und Abschlepptruck	
Pcs: 115	1993–1996

6813	EU NA AU AS
Galactic Chief	
Space Police Cop-Hopper	
Pcs: 24	1993–1996

6814	EU NA AU AS
Ice Tunnelator	
Ice Planet Connector	
Pcs: 25	1993–1996

6834	EU NA AU AS
Celestial Sled	
Ice Planet Bob	
Pcs: 55	1993–1995

6852	EU NA AU AS
Sonar Security	
Space Police Satmobil	
Pcs: 62	1993–1996

6861	EU NA AU AS	
Super Model Building Instruction		
Supermodell-Bauanleitung		
Pcs: -	1993	Special

6879	EU NA AU AS
Blizzard Baron	
Ice Planet Deltagleiter	
Pcs: 82	1993–1995

6898	EU NA AU AS
Ice-Sat V	
Ice Planet Raketen-Transporter	
Pcs: 139	1993–1996

6973	EU NA AU AS
Deep Freeze Defender	
Ice Planet Tripel-Raumtransporter	
Pcs: 420	1993–1995

i	6861	Shop at Home Nr. 4741, only building instruction	Shop at Home Nr. 4741, nur Bauanleitung
i	6973	With poster	Mit Poster

6983	EU NA AU AS
Ice Station Odyssey	
Ice Planet Forschungszentrum	
Pcs: 352	1993–1996

8022	EU NA AU AS
Starter Set	
Mini-Set	
Pcs: 118	1993–1996

8042	EU NA AU AS
Pneumatic Set	
Pneumatic-Set	
Pcs: 232	1993–1996

8082	EU NA AU AS
Multi Control Set	
Multi-Control-Set	
Pcs: 461	1993–1994

8714	EU NA AU AS
Technic Team	
Technic Figuren	
Pcs: 9	1993–1999

8818	EU NA AU AS
Baja Blaster	
Gelände-Buggy	
Pcs: 120	1993–1996

8824	EU NA AU AS
Hovercraft	
Luftkissenboot	
Pcs: 196	1993–1996

8857	EU NA AU AS
Street Chopper	
Trike	
Pcs: 384	1993–1996

8872	EU NA AU AS
Forklift Transporter	
Sattelzugmaschine m. Gabelstapler	
Pcs: 763	1993–1996

1994

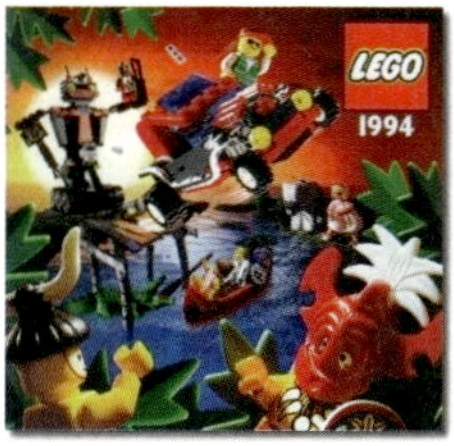

1576	EU NA AU AS	
Happy Face Carry Case		
Ovaler Koffer „Knollennase"		
Pcs: 32	1994–1999	

1701	EU NA AU AS	
Basic Building Set Trial Size		
Probierpackung		
Pcs: 26	1994–1996	Special

1703	EU NA AS (AU faded)	
Dalmatian Station Building Set		
Dalmatiner Bauset		
Pcs: 164	1994	

1705	NA (EU AU AS faded)	
Large Dinosaur Bucket		
Großer Eimer „Dinosaurier"		
Pcs: 329	1994	

1706	NA (EU AU AS faded)	
Small Bucket		
Kleiner Eimer		
Pcs: -	1994	

1708	NA (EU AU AS faded)	
Large Bucket		
Großer Eimer		
Pcs: 669	1994–1996	

1709 EU NA AU AS

Small Bucket

Kleiner Eimer

Pcs: - | 1994

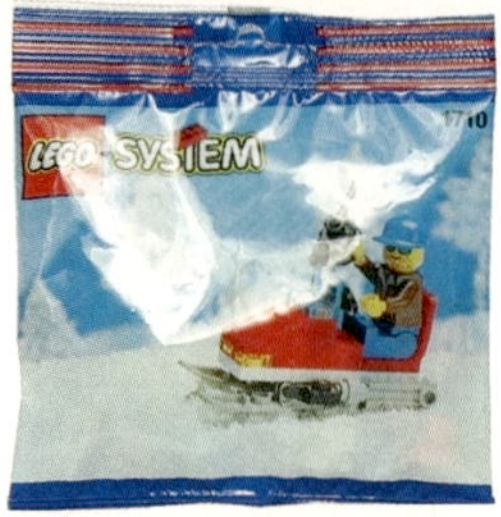

1710 EU NA AU AS

Snow Scooter

Schneemobil

Pcs: 24 | 1994

1711 EU NA AU AS

Ice Planet Scooter

Eismobil

Pcs: 14 | 1994

1712 EU NA AU AS

Crossbow Cart

Armbrustwagen

Pcs: 20 | 1994

1713 EU NA AU AS

Shipwrecked Pirate

Schiffbrüchiger Pirat

Pcs: 23 | 1994–1995

1716 EU NA AU AS

Starter Set with Building Plates

Starterset mit Bauplatten

Pcs: 201 | 1994

1720 EU NA AU AS

Cactus Canyon Value Pack

Cactus Canyon Kombiset

Sets: 3 | 1994

1721 EU NA AU AS

Sandypoint Marina Value Pack

Sandypoint Marina Kombiset

Sets: 3 | 1994

1722 EU NA AU AS

Rescue/Ice Planet Combi Pack

Feuerwehr/Ice-Planet-Kombipack

Sets: 2 | 1994–1995

i	Set	English	Deutsch
i	1710	Similar to: 1730 (1994)	Ähnlich zu: 1730 (1994)
i	1711	Similar to: 1731 (1994), 3014 (1998)	Ähnlich zu: 1731 (1994), 3014 (1998)
i	1712	Similar to: 1732 (1994)	Ähnlich zu: 1732 (1994)
i	1713	Similar to: 1733 (1994)	Ähnlich zu: 1733 (1994)
i	1720	Includes: 1740 (1994), 1741 (1994), 1742 (1994)	Enthält: 1740 (1994), 1741 (1994), 1742 (1994)
i	1721	Includes: 1790 (1994), 1791 (1994), 1792 (1994)	Enthält: 1790 (1994), 1791 (1994), 1792 (1994)

1723 EU NA AU AS

Castle/Pirates Combi Pack		
Burg/Piraten-Kombiset		
Sets: 2	1994	Special

1724 EU NA AU AS

Buddy "Bird"		
Kamerad „Vogel"		
Pcs: 9	1994–1996	

1725 EU NA AU AS

Buddy "Dinosaur"		
Kamerad „Dinosaurier"		
Pcs: 11	1994–1996	

1726 EU NA AU AS

Buddy "Girl"		
Kamerad „Mädchen"		
Pcs: 7	1994–1996	

1727 EU NA AU AS

Buddy "Pony"		
Kamerad „Pony"		
Pcs: 10	1994–1996	

1729 EU NA AU AS

Barnacle Bay Value Pack		
Seepockenbucht Kombiset		
Sets: 3	1994	

1730 EU NA AU AS

Snow Scooter		
Schneemobil		
Pcs: 24	1994–1996	

1731 EU NA AU AS

Ice Planet Scooter		
Ice Planet Scooter		
Pcs: 19	1994–1996	

1732 EU NA AU AS

Crossbow Cart		
Armbrustwagen		
Pcs: 19	1994–1997	

1722	Includes: 1702 (1994), 1704 (1994)	Enthält: 1702 (1994), 1704 (1994)
1723	Includes: 1794 (1994), 1795 (1994)	Enthält: 1794 (1994), 1795 (1994)
1729	Includes: 1871 (1994), 1872 (1994), 1873 (1994)	Enthält: 1871 (1994), 1872 (1994), 1873 (1994)
1730	Similar to: 1710 (1994)	Ähnlich zu: 1710 (1994)
1731	Similar to: 1711 (1994), 3014 (1998)	Ähnlich zu: 1711 (1994), 3014 (1998)
1732	Similar to: 1711 (1994), 3014 (1998)	Ähnlich zu: 1712 (1994)

1733	EU NA AU AS	
Shipwrecked Pirate		
Schiffbrüchiger Pirat		
Pcs: 23	1994–1996	

1738	EU NA AU AS	
Bulk Box		
Steinebox		
Pcs: -	1994–1995	

1755	EU NA AU AS	
Medium Bulk Bucket		
Mittlerer Steineeimer		
Pcs: 60	1994	

1757	EU NA AU AS	
Large Bulk Bucket		
Großer Steineeimer		
Pcs: -	1994	

1775	EU NA AU AS	
Jet		
Düsenflugzeug		
Pcs: 166	1994–2001	

1798	EU NA AU AS	
Building Table		
Spieltisch		
Pcs: 1	1994–1995	

1865	EU NA AU AS	
Sky Hopper		
Propellerflugzeug		
Pcs: 28	1994–2001	Special

1900	EU NA AU AS	
Special Bonus Pack		
Bonuspackung		
Sets: 4	1994	

1904	EU NA AU AS	
Bulk Box		
Steinebox		
Pcs: -	1994–1995	

i	Set	English	Deutsch
i	1733	Similar to: 1713 (1994)	Ähnlich zu: 1713 (1994)
i	1798	Similar to: 637 (1996)	Ähnlich zu: 637 (1996)
i	1900	Includes: 1917 (1993), 1696 (1992), 1693 (1992), 1916 (1993)	Enthält: 1917 (1993), 1696 (1992), 1693 (1992), 1916 (1993)

1906 — Regions: NA

Majisto's Tower	
Cerlins Turm	
Pcs: 196	1994–1995

1922 — Regions: NA

Medium Bucket	
Mittlerer Eimer	
Pcs: 50	1994

1935 — Regions: EU, NA, AS

Robin Rabbit Building Set	
Bauset „Häschen“	
Pcs: -	1994–1995

1945 — Regions: EU, NA, AU, AS

Playmates Building Set	
Bauset „Spielkameraden“	
Pcs: -	1994–1995

2317 — Regions: EU, NA, AU, AS

Police Building Set	
Grundkasten „Polizei“	
Pcs: 12	1994–1997

2327 — Regions: EU, NA, AU, AS

Supplementary Bricks	
Ergänzungsbausteine	
Pcs: 19	1994–1997

2337 — Regions: EU, NA, AU, AS

Mutt's Building Set	
Grundkasten „Hund“	
Pcs: 32	1994–1996

2347 — Regions: EU, NA, AU, AS

Barnaby Bear's Building Set	
Grundkasten „Bär“	
Pcs: 41	1994–1996

2352 — Regions: AS

Giraffe Bucket	
Großer Eimer „Giraffe“	
Pcs: -	1994

2359 EU NA AU AS
Elephant Bucket
Großer Eimer „Elefant“
Pcs: - | 1994

2380 EU NA AU AS
Panda's Building Bonanza
Riesen-Grundkasten
Pcs: 78 | 1994–1996

2390 EU NA AU AS
Build and Learn Bucket
Eimer „Lernen und bauen“
Pcs: 29 | 1994–1996

2393 EU NA AU AS
Building Bucket
Eimer „Pfiffiger Baumeister“
Pcs: 40 | 1994–1996

2394 EU NA AU AS
Farm Bucket
Eimer „Fleißiger Bauer“
Pcs: 52 | 1994–1996

2396 EU NA AU AS
Zoo Bucket
Eimer „Großer Tierfreund“
Pcs: 55 | 1994

2397 EU NA AU AS
Circus Bucket
Eimer „Bau einen Zirkus“
Pcs: 41 | 1994

2398 EU NA AU AS
Building Bucket
Eimer „Bausteine“
Pcs: - | 1994

2444 EU NA AU AS
Lil' Circus
Kleiner Zirkus
Pcs: 8 | 1994

2445 — EU NA AU AS

Farm Yard		
Bauernhof		
Pcs: 19	1994	

2608 — EU NA AU AS

Family		
Großfamilie		
Pcs: 11	1994–1998	

2616 — EU NA AU AS

Mini Safari		
Elefantenbaby mit Wildhüter		
Pcs: 5	1994–1997	

2621 — EU NA AU AS

Motorbike Transport		
Motorradtransporter		
Pcs: 5	1994–1996	

2680 — EU NA AU AS

Doctor's Surgery		
Behandlungszimmer		
Pcs: 13	1994–1996	

2681 — EU NA AU AS

Lion Safari		
Fotosafari		
Pcs: 16	1994–1996	

2682 — EU NA AU AS

Ambulance		
Krankenwagen		
Pcs: 8	1994–1997	

2688 — EU NA AU AS

Doctor's House		
Arztpraxis		
Pcs: 40	1994–1997	

2689 — EU NA AU AS

Savannah Animals		
Safaripark		
Pcs: 33	1994–1996	

2738	EU NA AU AS
Train Bridge	
Eisenbahnbrücke	
Pcs: 11	1994–2005

2784	EU NA AU AS
Mother and Baby	
Mutter und Baby	
Pcs: 4	1994–1998

2786	EU NA AU AS
Utility Room	
Waschtag	
Pcs: 9	1994–1996

2787	EU NA AU AS
Sleepy Dreams Nursery	
Babys Kuschelecke	
Pcs: 14	1994–1997

2788	EU NA AU AS
Katie's Kitchen	
Küche	
Pcs: 20	1994–1996

2789	EU NA AU AS
Bathroom	
Badezimmer	
Pcs: 19	1994–1995

2790	EU NA AU AS
Play Room	
Kinderzimmer	
Pcs: 32	1994–1996

2792	EU NA AU AS
Grandma's House	
Stadthaus	
Pcs: 45	1994–1997

2794	EU NA AU AS
My House	
Einfamilienhaus	
Pcs: 79	1994–1997

ⓘ 2795	EU NA AU AS	
Vacation Cottage Bucket		
Eimer „Ferienhaus“		
Pcs: 36	1994–1996	

ⓘ 4525	EU NA AU AS	
Road N' Rail Repair		
Schaufelbagger		
Pcs: 93	1994–1998	

ⓘ 4544	EU NA AU AS	
Car Transport Wagon		
Niederflurwagen		
Pcs: 147	1994–1997	

ⓘ 4564	EU NA AU AS	
Freight Rail Runner		
Großes Güterzug-Starter-Set		
Pcs: 595	1994–1996	

ⓘ 5591	EU NA AU AS	
Mach II Red Bird Rig		
US-Haubertruck mit Düsenjet		
Pcs: 1181	1994–1996	

ⓘ 5860	EU NA AU AS	
Love 'N Lullabies		
Babyzimmer		
Pcs: 54	1994–2001	

ⓘ 5870	EU NA AU AS	
Pretty Playland		
Spielplatz		
Pcs: 110	1994–1995	

ⓘ 5880	EU NA AU AS	
Prize Pony Stables		
Ponyclub		
Pcs: 136	1994–1996	

ⓘ 5890	EU NA AU AS	
Pretty Wishes Playhouse		
Traumhaus		
Pcs: 225	1994–1995	

ⓘ	5860	With poster	Mit Poster
ⓘ	5870	With poster	Mit Poster
ⓘ	5880	With poster	Mit Poster
ⓘ	5890	With poster	Mit Poster

6236 EU NA AU AS

King Kahuka

Häuptlingsthron

Pcs: 49 | 1994–1996

6246 EU NA AU AS

Crocodile Cage

Tropenkerker

Pcs: 61 | 1994–1997

6256 EU NA AU AS

Islander Catamaran

Zwillingskanu

Pcs: 64 | 1994–1996

6262 EU NA AU AS

King Kahuka's Throne

Voodoohütte

Pcs: 154 | 1994–1995

6264 EU NA AU AS

Forbidden Cove

Tropenhöhle

Pcs: 223 | 1994–1996

6278 EU NA AU AS

Enchanted Island

Tropenlagune

Pcs: 438 | 1994–2001

6340 EU NA AU AS

Hook & Ladder

Feuerwehrtruck

Pcs: 179 | 1994–1996

6341 EU NA AU AS

Gas N' Go Flyer

Überwachungsflugzeug

Pcs: 102 | 1994–1997

6348 EU NA AU AS

Surveillance Squad

Mobile Polizei-Einsatzzentrale

Pcs: 322 | 1994–1996

i	6262	With poster	Mit Poster
i	6264	With poster	Mit Poster
i	6278	Re-released as: 6292 (2001)	Neu aufgelegt als: 6292 (2001)
i	6348	With poster	Mit Poster

ⓘ 6350	EU NA AU AS
Pizza To Go	
Pizza-Paules Lieferservice	
Pcs: 152	1994–1996

ⓘ 6402	EU NA AU AS
Sidewalk Café	
Tonis Eis-Shop	
Pcs: 48	1994–1996

ⓘ 6410	EU NA AU AS
Cabana Beach	
Paradisa Beach Party	
Pcs: 156	1994–1996

ⓘ 6483	EU NA AU AS
Coastal Patrol	
Polizeischnellboot	
Pcs: 249	1994–1997

ⓘ 6514	EU NA AU AS
Trail Ranger	
4-Wheeler	
Pcs: 37	1994–1995

ⓘ 6515	EU NA AU AS
Stunt Copter	
Octan Miniheli	
Pcs: 39	1994–1997

ⓘ 6537	EU NA AU AS
Hydro Racer	
Racingboot	
Pcs: 51	1994–1997

ⓘ 6538	EU NA AU AS
Rebel Roadster	
City-Dragster	
Pcs: 61	1994–1997

ⓘ 6543	EU NA AU AS
Sail N' Fly Marina	
Yachthafen	
Pcs: 721	1994–1996

ⓘ	6350	Re-released as: 10036 (2002)	Neu aufgelegt als: 10036 (2002)
ⓘ	6402	Included in: 22 (1995)	Enthalten in: 22 (1995)

6561 EU NA AU AS

Hot Rod Club	
Dragster Tuning Shop	
Pcs: 244	1994–1996

6571 EU NA AU AS

Flame Fighters	
Feuerwache	
Pcs: 439	1994–1996

6597 EU NA AU AS

Century Skyway	
City Airport	
Pcs: 910	1994–1996

6665 EU NA AU AS

River Runners	
Raftingboot	
Pcs: 79	1994–1997

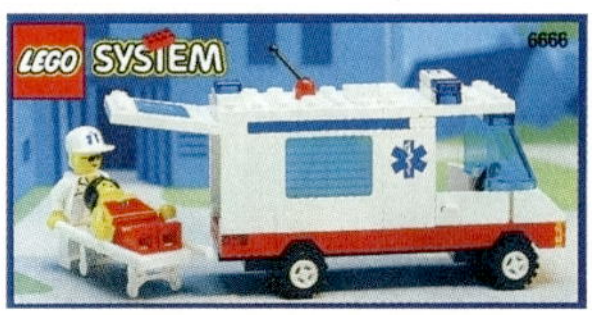

6666 EU NA AU AS

Ambulance	
Rettungswagen	
Pcs: 84	1994–1997

6705 EU NA AU AS

Space Explorers	
Raumfahrtfiguren	
Pcs: 40	1994–1996

6835 EU NA AU AS

Saucer Scout	
Spyrius Single Observer	
Pcs: 47	1994–1996

6889 EU NA AU AS

Recon Robot	
Spyrius Multifunktionsroboter	
Pcs: 137	1994–1996

6939 EU NA AU AS

Saucer Centurion	
Spyrius Mega Spy Ufo	
Pcs: 222	1994–1996

i	Set	English	Deutsch
i	6597	Re-released as: 10159 (2004)	Neu aufgelegt als: 10159 (2004)
i	6665	Included in: 23 (1995)	Enthalten in: 23 (1995)
i	6939	With poster	Mit Poster

6949	EU NA AU AS	
Robo-Guardian		
Spyrius Titan Monster Robot		
Pcs: 373	1994–1996	

6959	EU NA AU AS	
Lunar Launch Site		
Spyrius Berg der Mutanten		
Pcs: 297	1994–1996	

6991	EU NA AU AS	
Monorail Transport Base		
Experimental-Astro-Express		
Pcs: 578	1994–1996	

8032	EU NA AU AS	
Universal Set		
Universalkasten		
Pcs: 215	1994–1997	

8062	EU NA AU AS	
Universal Set with Storage Case		
Sortierkoffer		
Pcs: 410	1994–1997	

8808	EU NA AU AS	
FI Racer		
Formel 1 Racer		
Pcs: 94	1994–1996	

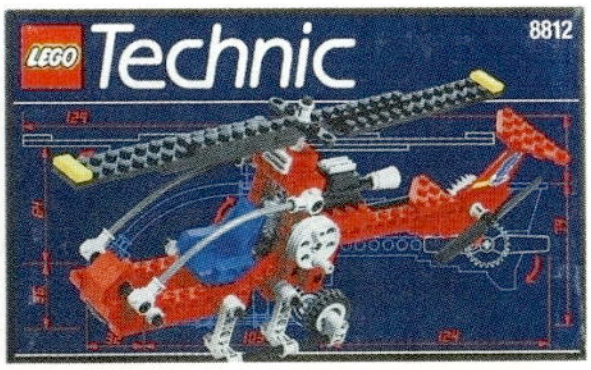

8812	EU NA AU AS	
Aero Hawk II		
High-Speed-Helikopter		
Pcs: 152	1994–1996	

8816	EU NA AU AS	
Off-Road Rambler		
Offroader		
Pcs: 185	1994–1996	

8829	EU NA AU AS	
Dune Blaster		
Moto-Cross-Renner		
Pcs: 278	1994–1996	

i	Set	English	Deutsch
i	6949	With poster	Mit Poster
i	8829	With poster	Mit Poster

8858	EU NA AU AS
Rebel Wrecker	
„Big Foot“ Bergungstruck	
Pcs: 451	1994–1996

8880	EU NA AU AS
Super Car	
Super Car	
Pcs: 1425	1994–1997

1995

ⓘ 22	EU	
Value Pack Italy		
Kombiset Italien		
Sets: 3	1995	Special

ⓘ 23	EU	
Value Pack Italy		
Kombiset Italien		
Sets: 3	1995	Special

ⓘ 1660	EU	
DSB Ferry "Kronprins Frederik"		
DSB Fähre „Kronprins Frederik"		
Pcs: 165	1995–1996	Special

ⓘ 1714	NA	
Surveillance Scooter		
Spyrius Aufklärer		
Pcs: 25	1995	

ⓘ 1715	NA	
Standard Bricks		
Grundelemente		
Pcs: 400	1995–1996	

ⓘ 1719	EU NA AU AS	
FreeStyle Bricks and Plates		
FreeStyle Steine und Bauplatten		
Pcs: 194	1995–1997	

ⓘ	22	Includes: 1761 (1995), 6402 (1994), 5810 (1995)	Enthält: 1761 (1995), 6402 (1994), 5810 (1995)
ⓘ	23	Includes: 1760 (1995), 6665 (1994), 6649 (1995)	Enthält: 1760 (1995), 6665 (1994), 6649 (1995)
ⓘ	1660	Sold only on DSB Ferries	Nur auf DSB Fähren im Verkauf
ⓘ	1714	Similar to: 3013 (1998), 1954 (1995)	Ähnlich zu: 3013 (1998), 1954 (1995)

1734 — EU NA AU AS

Large Clown Bucket	
Großer Eimer „Clown"	
Pcs: 77	1995–1996

1736 — EU AU AS

Merlin's Magic Box	
Merlins Zaubertruhe	
Pcs: 18	1995–1996

1743 — EU NA AU AS

Standard Bricks	
Standardelemente	
Pcs: 400	1995–1998

1744 — NA

Medium Bucket	
Mittlerer Eimer	
Pcs: 51	1995–1997

1745 — EU NA AU AS

Standard Bricks	
Grundelemente	
Pcs: 404	1995

1746 — NA

Wizard's Cart	
Merlins Zaubertruhe	
Pcs: 18	1995

1756 — EU NA AU AS

Animals	
Tiere	
Pcs: 8	1995–1997

1758 — EU NA AU AS

Animals	
Tiere	
Pcs: 7	1995–1997

1759 — EU NA AU AS

Parrot	
Papagei	
Pcs: 7	1995–2002

1736	Similar to: 1746 (1995), 2891 (1997)	Ähnlich zu: 1746 (1995), 2891 (1997)
1746	Similar to: 2891 (1997), 1736 (1995)	Ähnlich zu: 2891 (1997), 1736 (1995)

ⓘ 1760	EU NA AU AS
Go-Cart	
Go-Kart	
Pcs: 22	1995–1996

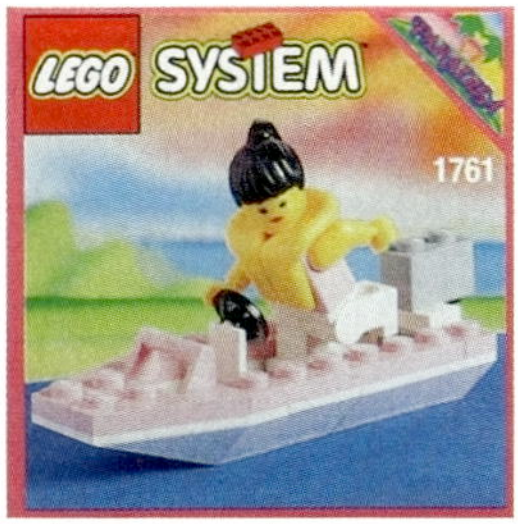

ⓘ 1761	EU NA AU AS
Paradisa Speedboat	
Motorboot	
Pcs: 23	1995–1997

ⓘ 1762	EU NA AU AS
Go-Cart	
Go-Kart	
Pcs: 22	1995–1996

ⓘ 1764	EU NA AU AS
Birthday Building Set	
Grundbaukasten	
Pcs: 100	1995–1997

ⓘ 1765	EU NA AU AS
Small Bucket	
Kleiner Eimer	
Pcs: 34	1995–1998

ⓘ 1766	EU NA AU AS
Small FreeStyle Bucket	
Kleiner FreeStyle Eimer	
Pcs: 109	1995–1998

ⓘ 1767	EU NA AU AS
Animals	
Tiere	
Pcs: 6	1995–1997

ⓘ 1768	EU NA AU AS
Animals	
Tiere	
Pcs: 10	1995–1997

ⓘ 1785	EU NA AU AS
Crater Critters	
Kraterkriecher	
Pcs: 151	1995

ⓘ	Set	English	Deutsch
ⓘ	1760	Similar to: 1762 (1995); included in: 23 (1995)	Ähnlich zu: 1762 (1995); enthalten in: 23 (1995)
ⓘ	1761	Included in: 22 (1995)	Enthalten in: 22 (1995)
ⓘ	1762	Similar to: 1760 (1995)	Ähnlich zu: 1760 (1995)

1786 EU NA AU AS
Jailbreak Joe
Ede, der Ausbrecherkönig
Pcs: 193 | 1995

1787 EU NA AU AS
Crater Cruiser
Unitron Krater-Cruiser
Pcs: 183 | 1995–1996

1788 EU NA AU AS
Treasure Chest
Schatztruhe
Pcs: 163 | 1995–1996

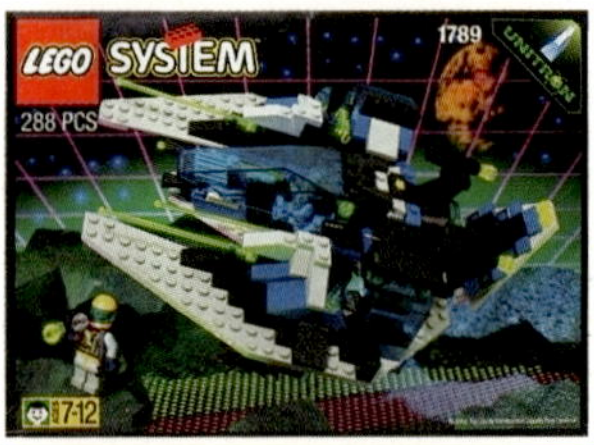

1789 EU NA AU AS
Star Hawk II
Unitron Gabelgleiter
Pcs: 293 | 1995–1996

1793 EU NA AU AS
Space Station Zenon
Unitron Hyper-Echo-Basis
Pcs: 344 | 1995

1805 EU NA AU AS
Small Bucket
Kleiner Eimer
Pcs: 32 | 1995–1996

1807 EU NA AU AS
Santa Claus with Sleigh
Weihnachtsmann mit Schlitten
Pcs: 17 | 1995–2001

1808 EU NA AU AS
Cloud Hopper
Propellerflugzeug
Pcs: 116 | 1995–1999 | Special

1811 EU NA AU AS
Safari
Safari
Pcs: 27 | 1995–1996

1814	NA	
Toolo Box		
Toolo Box		
Pcs: 23	1995	

1819	NA	
Large Bucket		
Großer Eimer		
Pcs: 950	1995	

1820	EU NA AS	
Primo Sampling		
Primo Probeexemplar		
Pcs: -	1995	

1822	EU NA AU AS	
Sea Claw 7		
Neptune III		
Pcs: 196	1995–2001	

1828	EU NA AU AS	
Animals		
Tiere		
Pcs: -	1995–1997	

1831	EU AU AS	
Truck		
Truck		
Pcs: 211	1995–1998	Special

1836	EU NA AU AS	
FreeStyle Cat		
FreeStyle Katze		
Pcs: 9	1995–1999	

1837	EU NA AU AS	
FreeStyle Duck		
FreeStyle Ente		
Pcs: 11	1995–1999	

1838	EU NA AU AS	
FreeStyle Bird		
FreeStyle Vogel		
Pcs: 20	1995–1999	

1831	Maersk Line Promo	Maersk Line Promo

1839	**EU** **NA** **AU** **AS**
FreeStyle Fish	
FreeStyle Fisch	
Pcs: 19	1995–1999

1840	EU **NA** AU AS
FreeStyle Set	
FreeStyle Set	
Pcs: 24	1995–1996

1844	EU **NA** AU AS
Large Bucket	
Großer Eimer	
Pcs: 90	1995

1850	EU **NA** AU AS
FreeStyle Set	
FreeStyle Set	
Pcs: 27	1995

1852	**EU** **NA** **AU** **AS**
Alligator Bucket	
Alligator-Eimer	
Pcs: 43	1995–1996

1860	EU **NA** AU AS
FreeStyle Set	
FreeStyle Set	
Pcs: 30	1995

1863	EU **NA** AU AS	
FreeStyle Trial Set		
FreeStyle Probierpackung		
Pcs: 11	1995	Special

1870	EU **NA** AU AS
FreeStyle Set	
FreeStyle Set	
Pcs: 36	1995

1954	**EU** **NA** **AU** **AS**
Surveillance Scooter	
Spyrius Aufklärer	
Pcs: 25	1995–1996

i 1954	Similar to: 3013 (1998), 1714 (1995)	Ähnlich zu: 3013 (1998), 1714 (1995)

2080 EU NA AU AS
Small Stack 'n' Learn
Primo „Dicke Brummer"
Pcs: 9 | 1995–1997

2082 EU NA AU AS
Medium Stack 'n' Learn
Primo „Jumbo auf Entdeckungstour"
Pcs: 10 | 1995–1997

2084 EU NA AU AS
Large Stack 'n' Learn
Primo „Spielplatzbesuch"
Pcs: 15 | 1995–1996

2086 EU NA AU AS
XL Stack 'n' Learn
Primo „Besuch im Tierpark"
Pcs: 20 | 1995–1996

2090 EU NA AU AS
Storage Bear
Behälter „Bär"
Pcs: 21 | 1995–1997

2320 NA
Small Basic Box
Kleiner Grundbaukasten
Pcs: 10 | 1995–1996

2324 EU NA AS
Large Giraffe Bucket
Großer Eimer „Giraffen"
Pcs: - | 1995–1996

2326 AS
XL Elefant Bucket
Riesen Eimer „Elefanten"
Pcs: 66 | 1995–1997

2338 EU NA AU AS
Kitty Cat's Building Set
Grundkasten „Kater Carlo"
Pcs: 36 | 1995–1996

2342	EU NA AU AS
Small Animals Bucket	
Kleiner Eimer „Tiere“	
Pcs: -	1995–1996

2362	EU NA AU AS
Large Circus Bucket	
Großer Eimer „Clowns“	
Pcs: 57	1995

2364	EU NA AU AS
Medium Circus Bucket	
Mittlerer Eimer „Stars in der Manege“	
Pcs: -	1995–1996

2368	EU NA AU AS
Extra Large Monkeys Bucket	
Extra großer Eimer „Affentheater“	
Pcs: 71	1995–1996

2659	EU NA AU AS
Baby Animals	
Tierbabys	
Pcs: 8	1995–1997

2663	EU NA AU AS
Water Animals	
Polartiere	
Pcs: 23	1995–1996

2665	EU NA AU AS
Wild Cats	
Wildkatzen	
Pcs: 22	1995–1997

2667	EU NA AU AS
Animals Park	
Tiergarten	
Pcs: 45	1995–1996

2670	EU NA AU AS
Water Park	
Aqua-Park „Polarkreis“	
Pcs: 53	1995–1997

2690	EU NA AU AS
Fire Chief	
Feuerwehr-Blitzeinsatzgespann	
Pcs: 7	1995–1998

2691	EU NA AU AS
My First Fire Engine	
Feuerwehrtruck	
Pcs: 14	1995–1999

2692	EU NA AU AS
Fire Heliport	
Feuerwehr-Spezialeinheit	
Pcs: 24	1995–1996

2693	EU NA AU AS
Fire Station	
Feuerwehrstation	
Pcs: 45	1995–1997

2783	EU NA AU AS
Ironing Set	
Bügelzimmer	
Pcs: 8	1995–1996

2785	EU NA AU AS
Living Room	
Wohnzimmer	
Pcs: 9	1995–1996

2796	EU NA AU AS
Play House Carry Case	
Ovaler Koffer „Babysitting“	
Pcs: 32	1995–1996

2915	EU NA AU AS
Mini Digger	
Löffelbagger	
Pcs: 17	1995–1998

2925	EU NA AU AS
Helicopter	
Hubschrauber	
Pcs: 21	1995–1996

1995

2945	EU NA AU AS
Space Center	
Raumfahrtcenter	
Pcs: 49	1995–1996

2960	EU NA AU AS
Tool Box	
Werkzeugkoffer	
Pcs: 45	1995–1998

4130	EU NA AU AS
FreeStyle Building Set	
FreeStyle Tierchen Allerei	
Pcs: 37	1995–1997

4131	EU NA AU AS
FreeStyle Building Set	
FreeStyle Schnupperlieschen	
Pcs: 68	1995–1998

4132	EU NA AU AS
FreeStyle Building Set	
FreeStyle Pelle Rollili	
Pcs: 119	1995–1996

4133	EU NA AU AS
Small FreeStyle Bucket	
FreeStyle Eimer Ida Sausefant	
Pcs: 137	1995–1998

4134	EU NA AU AS
Large FreeStyle Bucket	
FreeStyle Eimer Flotte Lotte	
Pcs: 252	1995–1997

4142	EU NA AU AS
FreeStyle Building Set	
FreeStyle Funny Fantasie	
Pcs: 95	1995–1996

4143	EU NA AU AS
FreeStyle Building Set	
FreeStyle Doggy Elefant	
Pcs: 196	1995–1996

4144 EU NA AU AS

FreeStyle Brick Vac Bus

FreeStyle Magic Bus

Pcs: 146 | 1995–1996

4145 EU NA AU AS

FreeStyle Playcase

FreeStyle Happy Kids

Pcs: 249 | 1995–1997

4146 EU NA AU AS

Extra Large FreeStyle Bucket

FreeStyle Eimer Dicke Molly

Pcs: 410 | 1995–1997

4150 EU NA AU AS

FreeStyle Building Set

FreeStyle Flinke Flieger

Pcs: 92 | 1995–1997

4151 EU NA AU AS

Girl's FreeStyle Set

FreeStyle Lady Lustig

Pcs: 272 | 1995–1998

4152 EU NA AU AS

Large FreeStyle Bucket

FreeStyle Eimer Fit und Fun

Pcs: 418 | 1995–1997

4153 EU NA AU AS

Large FreeStyle Playcase

FreeStyle Jumbo Junior

Pcs: 688 | 1995–1997

4161 EU NA AU AS

Girl's Freestlye Suitcase

FreeStyle Lillie Wunderschön

Pcs: 297 | 1995–1996

4162 EU NA AU AS

FreeStyle Multibox

FreeStyle Multibox

Pcs: 611 | 1995–1997

4163	EU NA AU AS
Electric Freestyle Set	
FreeStyle Electric Power Pack	
Pcs: 349	1995–1997

4552	EU NA AU AS
Cargo Crane	
Servicewaggon mit Teleskopkran	
Pcs: 295	1995–1998

4555	EU NA AU AS
Cargo Station	
Container-Verladestation	
Pcs: 401	1995–1998

5541	EU NA AU AS
Blue Fury	
Hot Rod Speedster	
Pcs: 429	1995–1996

5810	EU NA AU AS
Vanity Fun	
Beautyset	
Pcs: 25	1995–1996

5830	EU NA AU AS
Fun-Day Sundaes	
Eisvergnügen	
Pcs: 35	1995–1996

5840	EU NA AU AS
Garden Playmates	
Hundetraum	
Pcs: 93	1995–1998

6008	EU NA AU AS
Royal King	
König Richard	
Pcs: 13	1995–1997

6036	EU NA AU AS
Skeleton Surprise	
Burgverlies	
Pcs: 74	1995–1996

i	5541	Re-released as: 10151 (2004)	Neu aufgelegt als: 10151 (2004)
i	5810	Included in: 22 (1995)	Enthalten in: 22 (1995)

6044	EU NA AU AS
King's Carriage	
Prunk-Kutsche	
Pcs: 127	1995–1996

6078	EU NA AU AS
Royal Drawbridge	
Wachturm mit Brücke	
Pcs: 272	1995–1996

6090	EU NA AU AS
Royal Knight's Castle	
Burg Königstolz	
Pcs: 771	1995–1998

6115	EU NA AU AS
Shark Scout	
Aquashark Propeller-Scooter	
Pcs: 30	1995–1997

6125	EU NA AU AS
Sea Sprint 9	
Aquanaut Minitauchboot	
Pcs: 32	1995–1997

6155	EU NA AU AS
Deep Sea Predator	
Aquashark Seeungeheuer	
Pcs: 104	1995–1997

6175	EU NA AU AS
Crystal Explorer Sub	
Aquanaut U-Boot „Deep Sea“	
Pcs: 167	1995–1997

6195	EU NA AU AS
Neptune Discovery Lab	
Aquanaut Station „Palais Neptun“	
Pcs: 506	1995–1997

6254	EU NA AU AS
Rocky Reef	
Schatzinsel	
Pcs: 107	1995–1996

	Set	English	Deutsch
i	6078	With poster	Mit Poster
i	6155	With poster	Mit Poster
i	6175	With poster	Mit Poster

6263	EU NA AU AS
Imperial Outpost	
Gefängnisinsel	
Pcs: 223	1995–1996

6279	EU NA AU AS
Skull Island	
Totenkopfhöhle	
Pcs: 390	1995–1996

6336	EU NA AU AS
Launch Response Unit	
Space Port Truck	
Pcs: 188	1995–1997

6338	EU NA AU AS
Hurricane Harbor	
Küstenwache	
Pcs: 371	1995–1996

6339	EU NA AU AS
Shuttle Launch Pad	
Weltraumbahnhof	
Pcs: 562	1995–1997

6414	EU NA AU AS
Dolphin Point	
Ferieninsel	
Pcs: 211	1995–1996

6484	EU NA AU AS
F1 Hauler	
Formel 1 Bergungskran	
Pcs: 278	1995–1997

6516	EU NA AU AS
Moon Walker	
Planetenflitzer	
Pcs: 36	1995–1997

6525	EU NA AU AS
Blaze Commander	
Feuerwehrkommandowagen	
Pcs: 50	1995–1997

i	6339	With poster	Mit Poster

6535 EU NA AU AS

Dumper

Minikipper

Pcs: 42 | 1995–1997

6544 EU NA AU AS

Shuttle Transcon 2

Space Shutle mit „Huckepack-Jet“

Pcs: 346 | 1995–1997

6562 EU NA AU AS

Gas Stop Shop

Octan Tankstation

Pcs: 228 | 1995–1996

6596 EU NA AU AS

Wave Master

Abenteurergespann

Pcs: 136 | 1995–1998

6614 EU NA AU AS

Launch Evac 1

Space Port Löschfahrzeug

Pcs: 123 | 1995–1997

6639 EU NA AU AS

Raven Racer

Speedking Turbo-Dragster

Pcs: 72 | 1995–1996

6649 EU NA AU AS

Street Sweeper

Straßenkehrmaschine

Pcs: 68 | 1995–1998

8210 EU NA AU AS

Nitro GTX Bike

Rennmaschine

Pcs: 92 | 1995–1998

8225 EU NA AU AS

Road Rally V

Go-Kart

Pcs: 97 | 1995–1998

i	6544	With poster	Mit Poster
i	6649	Included in: 23 (1995)	Enthalten in: 23 (1995)
i	8225	With poster	Mit Poster

8235	EU NA AU AS
Front End Loader	
Frontlader	
Pcs: 173	1995–1997

8280	EU NA AU AS
Fire Engine	
Flughafenlöschgigant	
Pcs: 464	1995–1997

8412	EU NA AU AS
Nighthawk	
Beobachtungshelikopter	
Pcs: 288	1995–1997

8422	EU NA AU AS
Circuit Shock Racer	
TT Superbike	
Pcs: 319	1995–1997

8440	EU NA AU AS
Formula Flash	
Formel 1 Bolide	
Pcs: 435	1995–1997

8460	EU NA AU AS
Pneumatic Crane Truck	
3-Achs-Kranwagen	
Pcs: 856	1995–1999

8485	EU NA AU AS
Control Center II	
Super Control Center	
Pcs: 1093	1995–1997

i	8235	With poster	Mit Poster
i	8280	With poster	Mit Poster
i	8460	Similar to: 8431 (2002), 8438 (2003)	Ähnlich zu: 8431 (2002), 8438 (2003)

1996

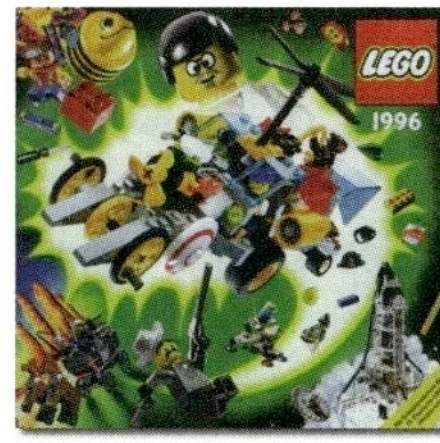

624	EU NA AU AS	
9V Motor		
9V Motor		
Pcs: 27	1996–2000	

626	EU NA AU AS	
Green Building Plate		
Bauplatte „Rasen“		
Pcs: 1	1996–2006	

627	EU NA AU AS	
Sea Building Plate		
Bauplatte „Wasser“		
Pcs: 1	1996–2002	

628	EU NA AU AS	
Grey Building Plate		
Bauplatte „Asphalt“		
Pcs: 1	1996–2006	

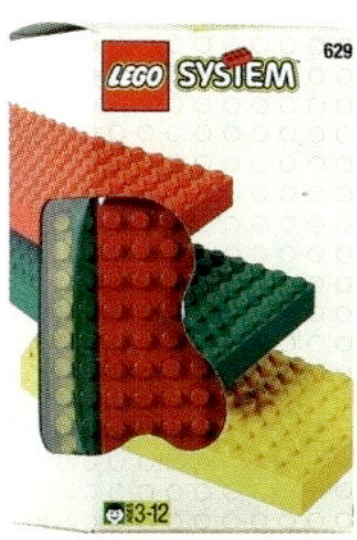

629	EU NA AU AS	
Building Plates (8x16 studs each)		
Bauplattenset		
Pcs: 3	1996–1999	

630	EU NA AU AS	
Brick Separator		
Elementetrenner		
Pcs: 1	1996–2007	

	Similar to	Ähnlich zu
626	Similar to: 813 (1986), 840 (1980), 745 (1978)	Ähnlich zu: 813 (1986), 840 (1980), 745 (1978)
627	Similar to: 819 (1991)	Ähnlich zu: 819 (1991)
628	Similar to: 843 (1980), 815 (1986)	Ähnlich zu: 843 (1980), 815 (1986)
629	Similar to: 814 (1986)	Ähnlich zu: 814 (1986)

1996

631	EU NA AU AS
Doors and Windows	
Fenster und Türen	
Pcs: 52	1996–1999

632	EU NA AU AS
Wheels	
Räder	
Pcs: 60	1996–1999

633	EU NA AU AS
Roof Tiles	
Dachsteine 22,5°	
Pcs: 50	1996–2002

634	EU NA AU AS
Extra Bricks in Red	
Rote Elemente	
Pcs: 62	1996–1999

635	EU NA AU AS
Extra Bricks in White	
Weiße Elemente	
Pcs: 62	1996–1999

636	EU NA AU AS
Pull-Back Motor	
Motorflitzer mit Figur	
Pcs: 14	1996–1998

637	EU NA AU AS
Play Table	
Spieltisch	
Pcs: 1	1996–2002

638	EU NA AU AS
Bin with Bricks	
Classic Box Grundelemente	
Pcs: 404	1996–1998

639	EU NA AU AS
Bin with Bricks	
Classic Box Grundelemente	
Pcs: 400	1996–1998

637	Similar to: 1798 (1994)	Ähnlich zu: 1798 (1994)

1728 EU NA AU AS

Crystal Crawler

Aquanaut Amphibienwalze

Pcs: 95 | 1996

1737 EU NA AU AS

Scorpion Detector

Exploriens Magno-Carrier

Pcs: 198 | 1996–1997

1747 EU NA AU AS

Treasure Surprise

Schatzversteck

Pcs: 26 | 1996

1749 EU NA AU AS

Paravane

Aquanaut Ein-Mann-Scooter

Pcs: 16 | 1996–1997

1751 EU NA AU AS

Small Bulk Bucket

Kleiner Steineeimer

Pcs: 27 | 1996–1998

1752 EU NA AU AS

Crossbow Boat

Ruderboot mit Armbrustschützen

Pcs: 21 | 1996–1997

1753 EU NA AU AS

Medium Bulk Bucket

Mittlerer Steineeimer

Pcs: - | 1996

1754 EU NA AU AS

Supplementary

Zubehör

Pcs: 100 | 1996–1997

1776 EU NA AU AS

Large Bulk Bucket

Großer Steineeimer

Pcs: 950 | 1996–1998

i	1728	Similar to: 6145 (1996)	Ähnlich zu: 6145 (1996)
i	1737	Similar to: 6938 (1996)	Ähnlich zu: 6938 (1996)
i	1747	Similar to: 1802 (1996)	Ähnlich zu: 1802 (1996)
i	1749	Similar to: 1806 (1996)	Ähnlich zu: 1806 (1996)
i	1752	Similar to: 1804 (1996), 2892 (1997)	Ähnlich zu: 1804 (1996), 2892 (1997)

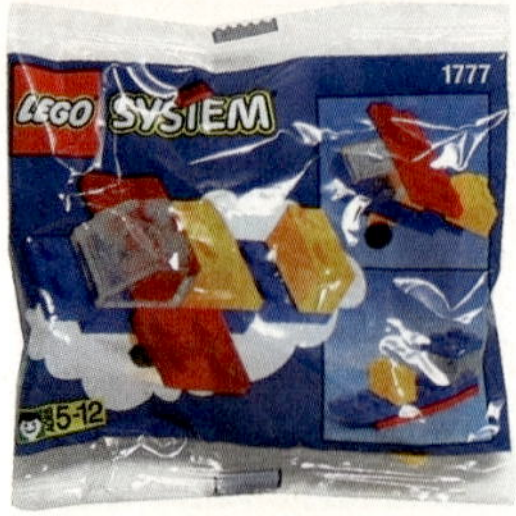

1777 EU NA AU AS

Small Aeroplane		
Kleines Flugzeug		
Pcs: 10	1996–1998	Special

1778 EU NA AU AS

Small Ship		
Kleines Schiff		
Pcs: 9	1996–1998	Special

1779 EU NA AU AS

Small Helicopter		
Kleiner Hubschrauber		
Pcs: 10	1996–1998	Special

1784 EU NA AU AS

Animals Bulk Box		
Steine Box „Tiere“		
Pcs: -	1996–1998	

1796 EU NA AU AS

FreeStyle Large Monster Bucket		
Großer FreeStyle Eimer		
Pcs: 656	1996–2000	

1797 EU NA AU AS

Large Bulk Bucket		
Großer Steineeimer		
Pcs: 90	1996–1998	

1802 EU NA AU AS

Tidy Treasure		
Schatzversteck		
Pcs: 25	1996	

1804 EU NA AU AS

Crossbow Boat		
Ruderboot mit Armbrustschütze		
Pcs: 21	1996	

1806 EU NA AU AS

Underwater Scooter		
Aquanaut Ein-Mann-Scooter		
Pcs: 16	1996–1997	

i	1777	Sabah Promo; was sold with a turkish newspaper	Sabah Promo; wurde einer türkischen Zeitung beigelegt
i	1778	Sabah Promo; was sold with a turkish newspaper	Sabah Promo; wurde einer türkischen Zeitung beigelegt
i	1779	Sabah Promo; was sold with a turkish newspaper	Sabah Promo; wurde einer türkischen Zeitung beigelegt
i	1802	Similar to: 1747 (1996)	Ähnlich zu: 1747 (1996)
i	1804	Similar to: 1752 (1996), 2892 (1997)	Ähnlich zu: 1752 (1996), 2892 (1997)
i	1806	Similar to: 1749 (1996)	Ähnlich zu: 1749 (1996)

1809	EU NA AU AS	
Small Amphibian		
Wasserflugzeug		
Pcs: 29	1996–2001	Special

1815	EU NA AU AS	
Paradisa Lifeguard		
Rettungsschwimmer		
Pcs: 43	1996–1997	

1817	EU NA AU AS	
Canadian Lake District		
Wasserflugzeug mit Fischerhütte		
Pcs: 140	1996–2001	Special

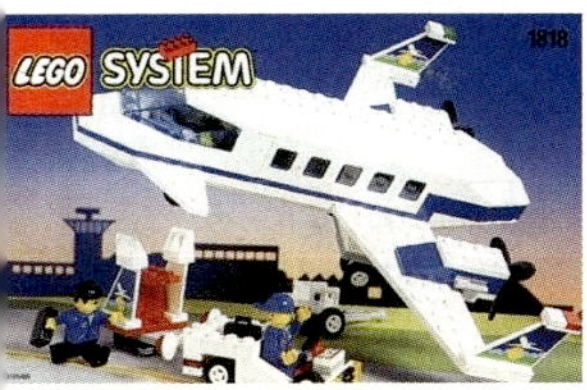

1818	EU NA AU AS	
Canard Starliner		
Entenflügler		
Pcs: 204	1996–1999	Special

1821	EU NA AU AS	
Rally Racers		
Renntrucks		
Pcs: 198	1996	

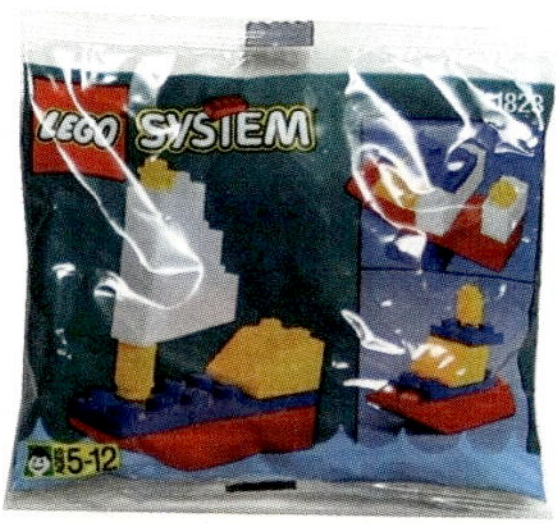

1823	EU NA AU AS	
Yacht		
Yacht		
Pcs: 10	1996–1998	Special

1843	EU NA AU AS	
Space/Castle Value Pack		
Raumfahrt/Burg-Kombiset		
Sets: 2	1996	

1846	EU NA AU AS	
FreeStyle Set		
FreeStyle Set		
Pcs: 25	1996	

1847	EU NA AU AS	
FreeStyle Set		
FreeStyle Set		
Pcs: 33	1996	

1823	Sabah Promo	Sabah Promo

1853	EU NA AU AS	
Hypno Cruiser		
Time Cruiser Navigator		
Pcs: 161	1996	

1854	EU NA AU AS	
VELUX House		
VELUX Haus		
Pcs: 157	1996	Special

1856	EU NA AU AS	
Water Park Tub		
Eimer „Aquazoo“		
Pcs: 71	1996–1997	

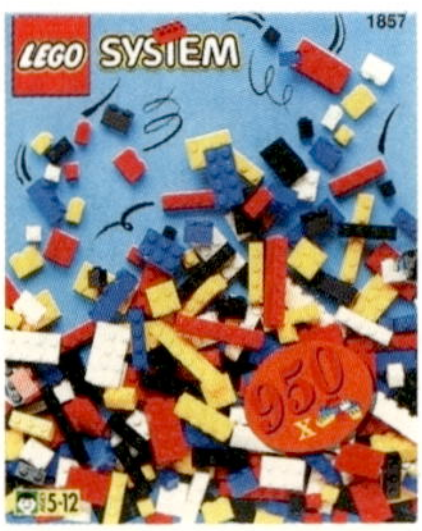

1857	EU NA AU AS	
Basic Bricks		
Standardelemente		
Pcs: 950	1996–1998	

1858	EU NA AU AS	
Cloud Cruiser		
Exploriens Ein-Mann-Flieger		
Pcs: 23	1996–1997	

1859	EU NA AU AS	
Small Prop Plane		
Kleines Flugzeug		
Pcs: 9	1996–1998	Special

1861	EU NA AU AS	
Box of Bricks		
Steinebox		
Pcs: -	1996	

1866	EU NA AU AS	
Stack-n-Learn Sampling		
Stecken und Lernen Probepack		
Pcs: -	1996–1997	

1868	EU NA AU AS	
Freestyle Box		
FreeStyle Hottehüh		
Pcs: 220	1996–1997	

1853	Similar to: 6492 (1996)	Ähnlich zu: 6492 (1996)
1854	Available at Velux after 1996	Bei Velux auch nach 1996 noch erhältlich
1859	Sabah Promo	Sabah Promo

1869	EU NA AU AS	
South African Flag		
Flagge Südafrikas		
Pcs: 80	1996	Special

2002	EU NA AU AS	
Jumbo Building Bag		
Primo Steinesack		
Pcs: 80	1996–1998	

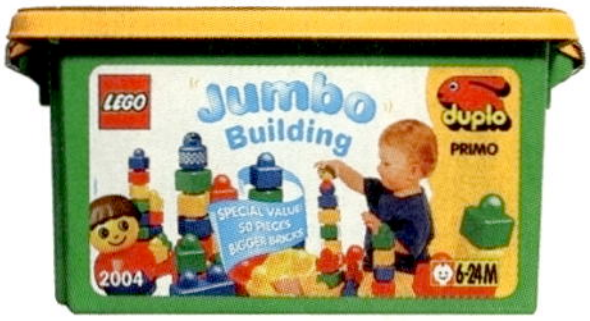

2004	EU NA AU AS	
Jumbo Building Tub		
Primo Steineeimer		
Pcs: 51	1996–1997	

2005	EU NA AU AS	
Primo Box		
Primo Box		
Pcs: 19	1996	

2006	EU NA AU AS	
Primo Box		
Primo Box		
Pcs: 24	1996	

2078	EU NA AU AS	
Mini Set		
Miniset		
Pcs: 4	1996–1997	

2091	EU NA AU AS	
Primo Tumbler "Walrus"		
Primo „Großer Seehund"		
Pcs: 20	1996	

2092	EU NA AU AS	
Primo Canister		
Primo „Ausflug"		
Pcs: 11	1996–1999	

2100	EU NA AU AS	
Souvenir Box		
Geschenkbox		
Pcs: -	1996–2000	

ⓘ 1869	Was sold in South Africa only	Wurde nur in Südafrika angeboten

2119	EU NA AS
Small FreeStyle Bucket	
Kleiner FreeStyle Eimer	
Pcs: -	1996

2120	EU NA AU AS
FreeStyle Set	
FreeStyle Hoppsalarifari	
Pcs: -	1996–1997

2140	EU
ANWB Roadside Assistance Crew	
ANWB Abschleppdienst	
Pcs: 272	1996

2146	NA
FreeStyle with Storage Case	
FreeStyle mit Sortierkoffer	
Pcs: 803	1996–1998

2150	EU NA AS
Railway Station	
Großer Stadtbahnhof	
Pcs: 617	1996–1998

2220	EU NA AU AS
Build N' Play Fire Theme	
Grundkasten „Feuerwehr"	
Pcs: 57	1996–1997

2221	EU NA AU AS
Build N' Play Circus	
Grundkasten „Circus"	
Pcs: -	1996

2321	EU NA AU AS
Basic Building Set	
Grundbaukasten	
Pcs: 33	1996

2339	EU NA AU AS
Supplementary	
Ergänzungsbox	
Pcs: 49	1996

2220	With poster	Mit Poster

2346	EU NA AU AS
Train Oval Suitcase	
Ovaler Koffer „Zug“	
Pcs: 54	1996–1997

2349	EU NA AU AS
Green Suitcase	
Ovaler Koffer „Panda“	
Pcs: 41	1996

2356	EU NA AU AS
Zoo Tub	
Eimer „Zoo“	
Pcs: 117	1996–2006

2673	EU NA AU AS
Motorcycle Patrol	
Motorradstreife	
Pcs: 6	1996–2000

2674	EU NA AU AS
Racing Team	
Rennteam	
Pcs: 9	1996–1998

2683	EU NA AU AS
Police Station	
Polizeiwache	
Pcs: 37	1996–1998

2685	EU NA AU AS
Water Park	
Delphinarium	
Pcs: 47	1996

2694	EU NA AU AS
Mini Farm	
Kleine Farm	
Pcs: 43	1996–2001

2695	EU NA AU AS
Pony Carriage	
Kutschwagen	
Pcs: 4	1996–2000

2349	With poster	Mit Poster
2683	With poster	Mit Poster
2694	With poster	Mit Poster

2696 EU NA AU AS
Farm Tractor
Trecker mit Hänger
Pcs: 11 | 1996–2000

2697 EU NA AU AS
Farm Animals
Tiere vom Bauernhof
Pcs: 18 | 1996–2000

2699 EU NA AU AS
Farm Yard
Großer Bauernhof
Pcs: 72 | 1996–2002

2731 EU NA AU AS
Push-Along Play Train
Schiebezug
Pcs: 10 | 1996–2000

2739 EU NA AU AS
Tip Wagon
Kipplore
Pcs: 10 | 1996–2000

2741 EU NA AU AS
Electric Train Starter Set
Eisenbahn Starterset
Pcs: 37 | 1996–2000

2745 EU NA AU AS
Deluxe Electric Train Set
Eisenbahn Superset
Pcs: 89 | 1996–2000

2781 EU NA AU AS
Bathroom
Badezimmer
Pcs: 27 | 1996

2791 EU NA AU AS
Playground
Spielplatz
Pcs: 33 | 1996–1997

2917 EU NA AU AS

Aeroplane
Flugzeug
Pcs: 20 | 1996–1998

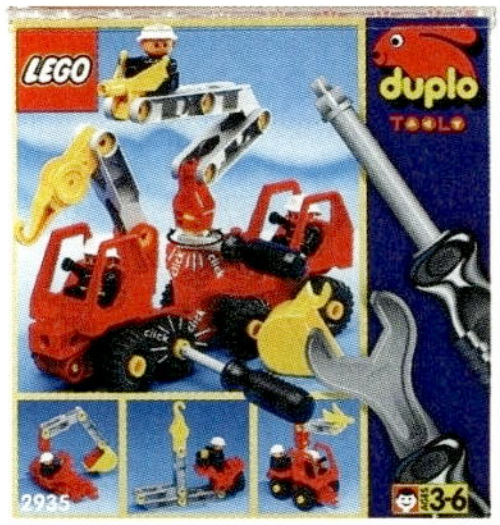

2935 EU NA AU AS

Fire Engine
Löschzug
Pcs: 37 | 1996–1998

4002 EU NA AU AS

Powerboat
Powerboat
Pcs: 56 | 1996–1998

4012 EU NA AU AS

Wave Cops
Polizeischnellboot
Pcs: 107 | 1996–1998

4022 EU NA AU AS

C26 Sea Cutter
Coast Guard
Pcs: 195 | 1996–1998

4135 EU NA AU AS

FreeStyle Garden Friends
FreeStyle Kleinergernegroß
Pcs: 113 | 1996–1998

4147 EU NA AU AS

FreeStyle Elefant Villa
FreeStyle Elemonkeyflitz
Pcs: 182 | 1996

4532 EU NA AU AS

Level Crossing
Bahnübergang
Pcs: 136 | 1996–1998

4559 EU NA AU AS

Cargo Railway
Shuttle Express 2011
Pcs: 854 | 1996–1999

4565 EU NA AU AS

Freight and Crane Railway

Schwerer Güterzug

Pcs: 928 | 1996–2002

5571 EU NA AU AS

Giant Truck

„Black Cat" Muscle Truck

Pcs: 1769 | 1996–1997

5820 EU NA AU AS

Garden Fun

Schaukelspaß

Pcs: 29 | 1996–1998

5835 EU NA AU AS

Dance Studio

Primaballerina

Pcs: 40 | 1996–1998

5875 EU NA AU AS

Hospital Ward

Kinderklinik

Pcs: 108 | 1996–2001

5876 EU NA AU AS

Hospital Ward & Booklet

Kinderklinik mit Büchlein

Pcs: 109 | 1996–1998

5895 EU NA AU AS

House

Traumvilla

Pcs: 319 | 1996–1998

6024 EU NA AU AS

Bandit Ambush

Hinterhalt im Wald

Pcs: 64 | 1996–1998

6046 EU NA AU AS

Hemlock Stronghold

Räuber in der Felsschlucht

Pcs: 221 | 1996–1997

i	5875	Similar to: 5876 (1996); with Poster	Ähnlich zu: 5876 (1996); mit Poster
i	5876	Similar to: 5875 (1996)	Ähnlich zu: 5875 (1996)
i	5895	With poster	Mit Poster

ⓘ 6079	EU NA AU AS
Dark Forest Fortress	
Waldfestung	
Pcs: 503	1996–1997

ⓘ 6104	EU NA AU AS
Aquanauts & Aquasharks	
Aquazone Ergänzungsset	
Pcs: 26	1996–1998

ⓘ 6135	EU NA AU AS
Spy Shark	
Aquashark Kristalljäger	
Pcs: 62	1996–1997

ⓘ 6145	EU NA AU AS
Crystal Crawler	
Aquanaut Amphibienwalze	
Pcs: 97	1996–1998

ⓘ 6190	EU NA AU AS
Shark's Crystal Cave	
Aquashark Skorpion	
Pcs: 256	1996–1997

ⓘ 6232	EU NA AU AS
Skeleton Crew	
Skeletthöhle	
Pcs: 31	1996–1997

ⓘ 6244	EU NA AU AS
Armada Sentry	
Speicherturm	
Pcs: 74	1996

ⓘ 6248	EU NA AU AS
Volcano Island	
Totenkopf-Vulkan	
Pcs: 124	1996–1997

ⓘ 6280	EU NA AU AS
Armada Flagship	
Gouverneurs-Galeone	
Pcs: 291	1996–1997

ⓘ	6145	Similar to: 1728 (1996)	Ähnlich zu: 1728 (1996)
ⓘ	6190	With poster	Mit Poster
ⓘ	6280	Re-released as: 6291 (2001)	Neu aufgelegt als: 6291 (2001)

6289	EU NA AU AS
Red Beard Runner	
Piratenbrigg	
Pcs: 709	1996–1997

6296	EU NA AU AS
Shipwreck Island	
Piratenversteck mit Schiffswrack	
Pcs: 226	1996–1997

6318	EU NA AU AS
Flowers, Trees and Fences	
Bäume, Blumen und Zäune	
Pcs: 74	1996–1998

6331	EU NA AU AS
Patriot Jet	
Kurierjet „Flying Eagle“	
Pcs: 168	1996–1997

6334	EU NA AU AS
Wave Jump Racers	
Wassersport-Center	
Pcs: 181	1996–1997

6335	EU NA AU AS
Indy Transport	
Formel 1-Transporttruck	
Pcs: 409	1996–1998

6337	EU NA AU AS
Fast Track Finish	
Formel 1-Startbox	
Pcs: 350	1996–1998

6404	EU NA AU AS
Carriage Ride	
Ausflugskutsche	
Pcs: 64	1996–1997

6418	EU NA AU AS
Country Club	
Landhaus	
Pcs: 293	1996–1997

i	Set	English	Deutsch
i	6289	Re-released as: 6290 (2001)	Neu aufgelegt als: 6290 (2001)
i	6296	With poster	Mit Poster
i	6335	With poster	Mit Poster

ⓘ 6491	EU NA AU AS
Rocket Racer	
Time Cruiser Scooty	
Pcs: 60	1996–1998

ⓘ 6492	EU NA AU AS
Hypno Cruiser	
Time Cruiser Navigator	
Pcs: 161	1996–1998

ⓘ 6493	EU NA AU AS
Flying Time Vessel	
Time Cruiser Flybo	
Pcs: 246	1996–1998

ⓘ 6494	EU NA AU AS
Mystic Mountain Time Lab	
Time Cruiser Labo	
Pcs: 523	1996–1997

ⓘ 6517	EU NA AU AS
Water Jet	
Jet-Ski-Freak	
Pcs: 28	1996–1998

ⓘ 6518	EU NA AU AS
Baja Buggy	
Beachbuggy	
Pcs: 37	1996–1998

ⓘ 6545	EU NA AU AS
Search N' Rescue	
Polizeisonderkommando	
Pcs: 296	1996–1997

ⓘ 6546	EU NA AU AS
Slick Racer	
Formel 1-Racer	
Pcs: 39	1996–1998

ⓘ 6563	EU NA AU AS
Gator Landing	
Schmugglerversteck	
Pcs: 242	1996–1997

ⓘ			
ⓘ	6492	First edition with radio play tape; similar to: 1853 (1996)	Erste Aufl. mit Hörspielkassette; ähnlich zu: 1853 (1996)
ⓘ	6493	First edition with audio tape	Erste Auflage mit Hörspielkassette
ⓘ	6494	First edition with audio tape	Erste Auflage mit Hörspielkassette

6581 EU NA AU AS
Dig N' Dump
Schwerer Muldenkipper
Pcs: 129 | 1996–1998

6598 EU NA AU AS
Metro PD Station
Polizeidirektion
Pcs: 570 | 1996–1997

6615 EU NA AU AS
Eagle Stunt Flyer
Doppeldecker „Red Eagle"
Pcs: 75 | 1996–1998

6625 EU NA AU AS
Speed Tracker
Polizeistreife
Pcs: 69 | 1996–1997

6706 EU NA AU AS
Frontier Patrol
Kavallerie
Pcs: 30 | 1996–2000

6712 EU NA AU AS
Sheriff's Showdown
Sheriff und Bandit
Pcs: 28 | 1996–1998

6716 EU NA AU AS
Covered Wagon
Planwagen
Pcs: 64 | 1996–1998

6755 EU NA AU AS
Sheriff's Lock-up
Sheriff's Office
Pcs: 182 | 1996–1998

6761 EU NA AU AS
Bandits' Secret Hideout
Alte Goldmine m. Banditenversteck
Pcs: 254 | 1996–1997

i	6598	With poster	Mit Poster
i	6755	Re-released as: 6764 (2002)	Neu aufgelegt als: 6764 (2002)
i	6761	With poster	Mit Poster

6765	EU NA AU AS
Gold City Junction	
Main Street	
Pcs: 353	1996–1998

6769	EU NA AU AS
Fort LEGOREDO	
Fort LEGOREDO	
Pcs: 692	1996–1998

6815	EU NA AU AS
Hovertron	
Exploriens Untertasse	
Pcs: 29	1996–1998

6854	EU NA AU AS
Alien Fossilizer	
Exploriens Bodenkontakter	
Pcs: 53	1996–1997

6856	EU NA AU AS
Planetary Decoder	
Exploriens Datatransmitter	
Pcs: 80	1996–1997

6899	EU NA AU AS
Nebula Outpost	
Exploriens Mobilab	
Pcs: 161	1996–1997

6938	EU NA AU AS
Scorpion Detector	
Exploriens Magno-Cruiser	
Pcs: 199	1996–1997

6958	EU NA AU AS
Android Base	
Exploriens Planeten-Laboratorium	
Pcs: 269	1996–1997

6982	EU NA AU AS
Explorien Starship	
Exploriens Athmo Cruiser	
Pcs: 678	1996–1997

6769	Re-released as: 6762 (2002)	Neu aufgelegt als: 6762 (2002)
6938	With poster; similar to: 1737 (1996)	Mit Poster; ähnlich zu: 1737 (1996)
6958	With poster	Mit Poster

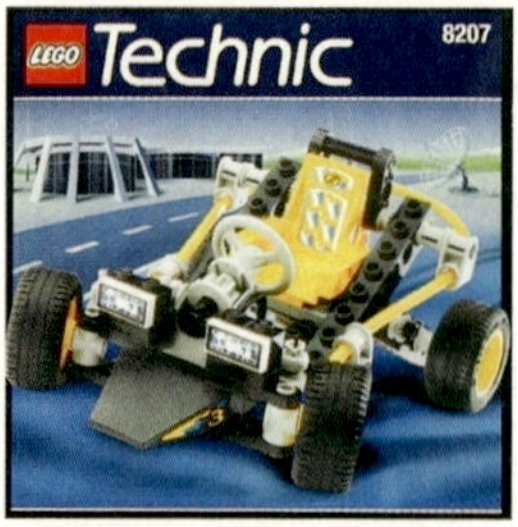

8207	EU NA AU AS
Dune Duster	
Strandflitzer	
Pcs: 85	1996–1998

8223	EU NA AU AS
Hydrofoil 7	
Rennboot	
Pcs: 130	1996–1998

8230	EU NA AU AS
Coastal Cop Buggy	
Polizeioffroader	
Pcs: 176	1996–1998

8244	EU NA AU AS
Convertibles	
Modulset	
Pcs: 281	1996–1998

8286	EU NA AU AS
3-In-1 Car	
Powergespann	
Pcs: 736	1996–1998

8408	EU NA AU AS
Desert Ranger	
Cross Hunter	
Pcs: 288	1996–1998

8425	EU NA AU AS
Black Hawk	
Turboprop-Flugzeug	
Pcs: 485	1996–1997

8443	EU NA AU AS
Pneumatic Log Loader	
Forsttraktor	
Pcs: 339	1996–1998

8456	EU NA AU AS
Fiber Optic Multi Set	
Fiber Optic Multiset	
Pcs: 420	1996–1998

i	8230	With poster	Mit Poster

8480	EU NA AU AS
Space Shuttle	
Space Shuttle	
Pcs: 1409	1996–1998

1997

54	EU NA AU AS	
U.F.O. Action Pack		
U.F.O. Kombiset		
Pcs: 93	1997	Special

697	EU NA AU AS	
Idea Book		
Baubuch		
Pcs: 1	1997–1999	

1739	EU NA AU AS	
Penguin		
Pinguin		
Pcs: 8	1997–2001	Special

1781	EU NA AU AS	
Dino Babies		
Dinobabys		
Pcs: 90	1997–1998	

1782	EU NA AU AS	
Discovery Station		
Meeresforschungsstation		
Pcs: 332	1997–1998	

1783	EU NA AU AS	
Rattle		
Rassel		
Pcs: 2	1997–2000	

54	Includes: 6800 (1997), 6818 (1997), 6836 (1997)	Enthält: 6800 (1997), 6818 (1997), 6836 (1997)
1739	McDonald's Promo	McDonald's Promo
1783	Similar to: 2168 (1997)	Ähnlich zu: 2168 (1997)

1824	EU NA (AU) AS
Flying Duck	
Fliegende Ente	
Pcs: 14	1997–1999
Rating: 4/6	

1825	EU NA (AU) AS
Racing Car	
Rennwagen	
Pcs: 18	1997–1999
Rating: 4/6	

1826	EU NA (AU) AS
Bird, Boat or Plane	
Vogel, Boot oder Flugzeug	
Pcs: 16	1997–1999
Rating: 6/6	

1827	EU NA (AU) AS
Helicopter	
Hubschrauber	
Pcs: 20	1997–1999
Rating: 4/6	

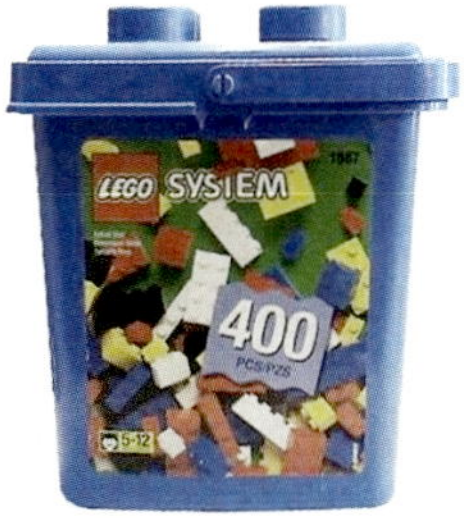

1867	(EU) NA (AU) (AS)
Medium Bulk Bucket	
Mittlerer Steineeimer	
Pcs: 400	1997–1998
Rating: 4/6	

2003	EU NA (AU) AS
Jumbo Building Bag	
Großer Bauspaß	
Pcs: 80	1997–1999
Rating: 6/6	

2009	EU NA AU AS
Large Bulk Box	
Große Steinebox	
Pcs: 25	1997
Rating: 5/6	

2010	EU NA AU AS
Baby Walker	
Lauflernvergnügen	
Pcs: 23	1997–2003
Rating: 5/6	

2081	EU NA AU AS
Ladybird Stacker	
Marienkäfer-Spielerei	
Pcs: 6	1997–1999
Rating: 5/6	

2083	EU NA AU AS	
Medium Stack 'N' Learn		
Stecken und lernen		
Pcs: 9	1997–1998	

2085	EU NA AU AS	
Storage Frog		
Riesenfrosch		
Pcs: 14	1997–1998	

2087	EU NA AU AS	
Storage Bird		
Riesenvogel		
Pcs: 18	1997	

2089	EU NA AU AS	
Stack 'N' Learn Gift Set		
Jumbo entdeckt die Welt		
Pcs: 24	1997–1998	

2093	EU NA AU AS	
Lady Bird		
Marienkäferrassel		
Pcs: 1	1997–1998	

2094	EU NA AU AS	
Cozy Duck		
Versteck-Spiel-Ente		
Pcs: 2	1997–1998	

2095	EU NA AU AS	
Pee-Po Ball		
Figurenball		
Pcs: 2	1997–2000	

2096	EU NA AU AS	
Stack-a-Mouse		
Kreisel-Bär		
Pcs: 6	1997–1999	

2097	EU NA AU AS	
Clarence Caterpillar and Friends		
Raupe „Löwenzahn“		
Pcs: 3	1997–2000	

2098 EU NA AU AS

Tub Boat Tommy

Dampfer mit „Pfiff"

Pcs: 4 | 1997–2000

2099 EU NA AU AS

Fun Shape Sorter

Sortier- und Stapelspaß

Pcs: 10 | 1997–2000

2121 EU NA AU AS

Stomper

Stomper

Pcs: 11 | 1997–1999 | Special

2122 EU NA AU AS

Bob

Bob

Pcs: 14 | 1997–1999 | Special

2123 EU NA AU AS

Spinner

Spinner

Pcs: 12 | 1997–1999 | Special

2124 EU NA AU AS

Medium Bucket

Mittlerer Eimer

Pcs: 40 | 1997–1998

2125 EU NA AU AS

Large Bucket

Großer Eimer

Pcs: 70 | 1997

2126 EU NA AU AS

Train Cars

Güterwaggon-Set

Pcs: 385 | 1997–1998

2127 EU NA AU AS

FreeStyle Friendly Monsters

Freundliche Monster

Pcs: 13 | 1997–1999 | Special

i	2121	Jack-In-The-Box Promo	Jack-In-The-Box Promo
i	2122	Jack-In-The-Box Promo	Jack-In-The-Box Promo
i	2123	Jack-In-The-Box Promo	Jack-In-The-Box Promo
i	2127	Jack-In-The-Box Promo	Jack-In-The-Box Promo

2129	EU NA AU AS	
Dragster		
Dragster		
Pcs: 65	1997–1998	

2135	EU NA AU AS	
Aircraft		
Flugzeug		
Pcs: 9	1997	Special

2136	EU NA AU AS	
Aeroplane		
Flugzeug		
Pcs: 12	1997	Special

2137	EU NA AU AS	
Prop Boat		
Propellerboot		
Pcs: 8	1997	Special

2138	EU NA AU AS	
Helicopter		
Hubschrauber		
Pcs: 8	1997	Special

2139	EU NA AU AS	
Ship		
Schiff		
Pcs: 12	1997	

2147	EU NA AU AS	
Dragon Fly Team		
Drachenfliegerteam		
Pcs: 198	1997–2000	

2148	EU NA AU AS	
Show Truck		
Show Truck		
Pcs: 108	1997–1999	Special

2149	EU NA AU AS	
Color Line Container Truck		
Color Line Container-Lkw		
Pcs: 190	1997–1999	Special

i	2135	Sabah Promo; was added to a turkish newspaper	Sabah Promo; wurde einer türkischen Zeitung beigel.
i	2136	Similar to: 2708 (1999); Sabah Promo; was added to a turkish newspaper	Ähnlich zu: 2708 (1999); Sabah Promo; wurde einer türkischen Zeitung beigelegt
i	2137-2139	Sabah Promo; was added to a turkish newspaper	Sabah Promo; wurde einer türkischen Zeitung beigelegt
i	2148	Re-rel. as: 10156 (2004); LEGO Truck Tour 2004 Promo	Neu aufgel. als: 10156 (2004); LEGO Truck Tour 2004 Promo

2151	EU NA AU AS
Robo Raider	
Robo Raider	
Pcs: 141	1997–1998

2152	EU NA AU AS
Robo Raptor	
Robo Raptor	
Pcs: 227	1997–1998

2153	EU NA AU AS
Robo Stalker	
Robo Stalker	
Pcs: 273	1997–1999

2154	EU NA AU AS
Robo Master	
Robo Master	
Pcs: 349	1997–1998

2155	EU NA AU AS
Waterplane	
Wasserflugzeug	
Pcs: 18	1997–2000

2156	EU NA AU AS
Racer	
Rennwagen	
Pcs: 17	1997–2000

2157	EU NA AU AS
Speed Boat	
Schnellboot	
Pcs: 16	1997–2000

2160	EU NA AU AS
Crystal Scavenger	
Aquaraiders Kristallschürfer	
Pcs: 109	1997–1998

2161	EU NA AU AS
Aqua Dozer	
Aquaraiders Tiefseeschaufler	
Pcs: 137	1997–1998

i	2155	Was re-released as a Kabaya promo in 2000	Wurde 2000 als Kabaya Promo neu aufgelegt
i	2156	Was re-released as a Kabaya promo in 2000	Wurde 2000 als Kabaya Promo neu aufgelegt
i	2157	Was re-released as a Kabaya promo in 2000	Wurde 2000 als Kabaya Promo neu aufgelegt

2162	EU NA AU AS	
Hydro Reef Wrecker		
Aquaraiders Riffpanzer		
Pcs: 292	1997–1998	

2163	EU NA AU AS	
Toucan		
Tukan		
Pcs: 9	1997–2000	Special

2164	EU NA AU AS	
Whale		
Wal		
Pcs: 9	1997–2000	Special

2165	EU NA AU AS	
Rhinoceros		
Nashorn		
Pcs: 10	1997–2000	Special

2166	EU NA AU AS	
Elephant		
Elefant		
Pcs: 10	1997–2000	Special

2167	EU NA AU AS	
Penguin		
Pinguin		
Pcs: 8	1997–2000	Special

2168	EU NA AU AS	
Rattle		
Rassel		
Pcs: 2	1997–2001	

2181	EU NA AU AS	
Infomaniac		
Infomaniac		
Pcs: 3	1997	

2184	EU NA AU AS	
XL Bulk Bucket		
Riesen Steineeimer		
Pcs: 1000	1997–1999	

i			
i	2163-2167	Sabah Promo; was added to a turkish newspaper	Sabah Promo; wurde einer türkischen Zeitung beigelegt
i	2168	Similar to: 1783 (1997)	Ähnlich zu: 1783 (1997)

2186	EU NA AU AS	
Seaplane		
Wasserflugzeug		
Pcs: -	1997–1999	Special

2187	EU NA AU AS	
Racer		
Rennwagen		
Pcs: -	1997–1999	Special

2188	EU NA AU AS	
Speedboat		
Rennboot		
Pcs: -	1997–1999	Special

2189	EU NA AU AS	
Pony		
Pony		
Pcs: -	1997–1998	Special

2195	EU NA AU AS	
Small FreeStyle Bucket		
FreeStyle Eimer kleine Biester		
Pcs: 228	1997–1998	

2199	EU NA AU AS	
Large Bulk Bucket		
Großer Steineeimer		
Pcs: 466	1997–1998	

2241	EU NA AU AS	
Basic Set		
Grundbaukasten „Apfelbaum“		
Pcs: 32	1997–1998	

2242	EU NA AU AS	
Brick Starters		
Steine-Box		
Pcs: 52	1997–2007	

2245	EU NA AU AS	
Farmhouse Bucket		
Eimer „Haus und Hof“		
Pcs: 46	1997	

i	2186	Mars Promo	Mars Promo
i	2187	Mars Promo	Mars Promo
i	2188	Mars Promo	Mars Promo
i	2242	Included in: 66151 (2006)	Enthalten in: 66151 (2006)

2246 EU NA AU AS

Large Basic Set

Großer Grundbaukasten m. Bauplatte

Pcs: -	1997–1998	

2247 EU NA AU AS

Extra Bricks

Große Steine-Box

Pcs: 99	1997–1998	

2249 EU NA AU AS

Basic Set

Grundbaukasten

Pcs: -	1997	

2251 EU NA AU AS

Large Basic Set

Riesen Grundbaukasten

Pcs: 80	1997	

2252 EU NA AU AS

Basic Set

Grundbaukasten mit Bauplatte

Pcs: 36	1997–1998	

2261 EU NA AU AS

Small Basic Set

Kleiner Grundbaukasten

Pcs: 11	1997–1998	

2262 EU NA AU AS

Basic Set

Grundbaukasten

Pcs: 20	1997–1998	

2264 EU NA AU AS

Medium Bucket

Mittlerer Steineeimer

Pcs: 48	1997–1998	

2265 EU NA AU AS

Large Puppy Clearpack

Kleiner Hund

Pcs: 71	1997–1998	

2266 EU NA AU AS
XL Bulk Bucket
Riesen Steineimer
Pcs: 92 | 1997–1998

2581 EU NA AU AS
Animal Bus
Schulbus
Pcs: - | 1997

2601 EU NA AU AS
T-Rex Dinosaurs
Roter Hüpfdino mit Kind
Pcs: 7 | 1997–1998

2602 EU NA AU AS
Dinosaurs Family Home
Dinodorf
Pcs: 29 | 1997–1998

2603 EU NA AU AS
Dinosaurs Tub
Großer Dinoeimer
Pcs: 70 | 1997–1998

2604 EU NA AU AS
Dino World
Dinowelt
Pcs: 62 | 1997–1998

2605 EU NA AU AS
Dinosaurs Park
Dinopark
Pcs: 46 | 1997–1998

2606 EU NA AU AS
Dump Truck
Kipplaster
Pcs: 7 | 1997–1999

2607 EU NA AU AS
Catapult Racer
Rennflitzer mit Katapultantrieb
Pcs: 4 | 1997–2000

2684	
Dinghy	
Schlauchboot	
Pcs: 3	1997–2000

2687	
Habor	
Hafen	
Pcs: 53	1997–1998

2707		
Glider		
Flugzeug		
Pcs: 9	1997	Special

2708		
Aircraft		
Flugzeug		
Pcs: 12	1997	Special

2709		
Snow Mobile		
Schneemobil		
Pcs: 8	1997	Special

2710		
Helicopter		
Hubschrauber		
Pcs: 8	1997	Special

2722		
Ship		
Schiff		
Pcs: 12	1997	Special

2761	
Pony Stable Oval Suitcase	
Ovaler Koffer „Ponystall“	
Pcs: 43	1997

2762	
Family Fun Playground	
Kindergarten	
Pcs: 49	1997

2707	Bandai Promo; similar to: 2135 (1997)	Bandai Promo; ähnlich zu: 2135 (1997)
2708	Bandai Promo; similar to: 2136 (1997)	Bandai Promo; ähnlich zu: 2136 (1997)
2709	Promo: Frestis Ice Cream (Sweden), Bandai (Japan)	Promo: Frestis Eiscreme (Schweden), Bandai (Japan)
2710	Bandai Promo; similar to: 2138 (1997)	Bandai Promo; ähnlich zu: 2138 (1997)
2722	Bandai Promo; similar to: 2139 (1997)	Bandai Promo; ähnlich zu: 2139 (1997)

2805	EU NA AU AS
Pony Club	
Pony-Reitturnier	
Pcs: 15	1997–1998

2806	EU NA AU AS
Mini Dinosaur	
Flugdino	
Pcs: 4	1997–1998

2840	EU NA AU AS	
Girl		
Mädchen		
Pcs: 10	1997–2000	Special

2841	EU NA AU AS	
Boy		
Junge		
Pcs: 9	1997–2000	Special

2844	EU NA AU AS	
Doggy		
Hündchen		
Pcs: 8	1997–2000	Special

2845	EU NA AU AS
Indian Chief	
Medizinmann mit Totempfahl	
Pcs: 21	1997–1998

2846	EU NA AU AS
Indian Kayak	
Indianerkajak	
Pcs: 19	1997–1998

2847	EU NA AU AS
U.F.O. Flyer	
U.F.O. Alien	
Pcs: 16	1997–1998

2848	EU NA AU AS
Fright Knight's Flying Machine	
Flugmaschine	
Pcs: 19	1997–1998

2840	Sabah Promo	Sabah Promo
2841	Sabah Promo	Sabah Promo
2844	Sabah Promo	Sabah Promo

1997

2849	EU NA AU AS	
Gyrocopter		
Hubschrauber		
Pcs: 25	1997–2001	

2851	AS	
Medium Dino Bucket		
Mittlerer Dinoeimer		
Pcs: 31	1997–1998	

2852	AS	
Large Dino Bucket		
Großer Dinoeimer		
Pcs: 57	1997–1998	

2870	EU NA AU AS	
Barbecue		
Grillfest		
Pcs: 24	1997–1998	

2871	EU NA AU AS	
The white Shark		
Der weiße Hai		
Pcs: 17	1997–1998	

2872	EU NA AU AS	
Witch's Fireplace		
Hexenofen		
Pcs: 22	1997–1998	

2874	EU NA AS	
Christmas		
Weihnachten		
Pcs: 9	1997–1998	Special

2878	EU NA AS	
Santa Claus		
Weihnachtsmann		
Pcs: -	1997–2002	Special

2880	EU NA AU AS	
Open Top Jeep		
Sportcabriolet		
Pcs: 30	1997–2001	

i	2849	Similar to: 1068 (1999)	Ähnlich zu: 1068 (1999)
i	2878	Shipped with 3 gift boxes; Hawaiian Shirt, Tuxedo, Soccer Santa; from „Mos Burger“; M&M/Mars Candy Promo	Ausgel. m. 3 Geschenkpackungen:Hawaiian Shirt, Tuxedo, Soccer Santa; von „Mos Burger“; M&M/ Mars Candy Promo

2881 EU NA AU AS

Parking Guard
Parkplatzwächter

Pcs: 22	1997–1998	

2882 EU NA AU AS

Speed Boat
Motorboot

Pcs: 23	1997–1998	

2883 EU NA AU AS

Swamp Racer
Sumpfboot

Pcs: 26	1997–1998	

2884 EU NA AU AS

White Mini Plane
Kleinstflugzeug

Pcs: 21	1997–2001	

2885 EU NA AU AS

Ice Cream Stand
Eisverkäuferin

Pcs: 30	1997–1998	

2886 EU NA AU AS

Formula 1 Racer
Formel 1-Wagen

Pcs: 25	1997–2001	

2887 EU NA AU AS

Petrol Pump
Tankstation

Pcs: 15	1997–1998	

2889 EU NA AU AS

Treasure Cart
Schatztransport

Pcs: 22	1997–1998	Special

2890 EU NA AU AS

King's Catapult
Katapult

Pcs: 22	1997–1998	Special

2882	Similar to: 1069 (1999)	Ähnlich zu: 1069 (1999)
2884	Similar to: 1070 (1999)	Ähnlich zu: 1070 (1999)
2886	Similar to: 1088 (1999)	Ähnlich zu: 1088 (1999)
2889	Similar to: 1463 (1992), 1695 (1992); Kabaya Promo	Ähnlich zu: 1463 (1992), 1695 (1992); Kabaya Promo
2890	Similar to: 1917 (1993); Kabaya Promo	Ähnlich zu: 1917 (1993); Kabaya Promo

ⓘ 2891	EU NA AU AS	
Wizard's Cart		
Cerlins Zaubertruhe		
Pcs: 13	1997	Special

ⓘ 2892	EU NA AU AS	
Crossbow Boat		
Ruderboot mit Armbrustschütze		
Pcs: 18	1997–1998	Special

ⓘ 3200	EU NA AU AS	
Beauty Studio		
Beautystudio		
Pcs: 32	1997–1998	

ⓘ 3201	EU NA AU AS	
Living Room		
Wohnzimmer		
Pcs: 33	1997–1998	

ⓘ 3202	EU NA AU AS	
Laundry Room		
Waschtag		
Pcs: 40	1997–1998	

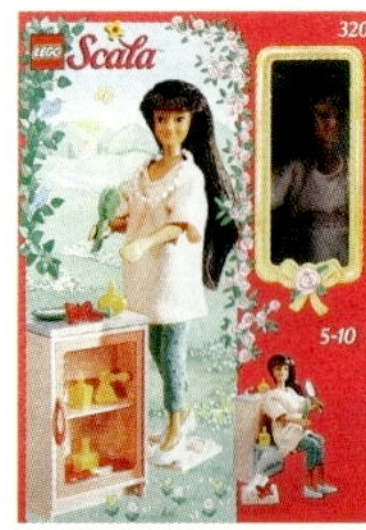

ⓘ 3203	EU NA AU AS	
Dressing Table		
Lauras Schminktisch		
Pcs: 19	1997–1998	

ⓘ 3240	EU NA AU AS	
Ashley's Miniature Garden		
Garten		
Pcs: 50	1997–1998	

ⓘ 3241	EU NA AU AS	
Nursery		
Kinderzimmer		
Pcs: 55	1997–1998	

ⓘ 3242	EU NA AU AS	
Bathroom		
Bad		
Pcs: 73	1997–1998	

ⓘ	2891	Similar to: 1746 (1995), 1736 (1995); Kabaya Promo	Ähnlich zu: 1746 (1995), 1736 (1995); Kabaya Promo
ⓘ	2892	Similar to: 1752 (1996), 1804 (1996); Kabaya Promo	Ähnlich zu: 1752 (1996), 1804 (1996); Kabaya Promo

3243 EU NA AU AS

Kitchen	
Küche	
Pcs: 96	1997–1998

Rating: 4/6

3270 EU NA AU AS

Dream Cottage	
Katharinas Appartement	
Pcs: 116	1997–1998

Rating: 4/6

3290 EU NA AU AS

The Big Family House	
Großes Haus	
Pcs: 279	1997–1998

Rating: 4/6

4055 EU NA AU AS

Medium Bucket	
Mittelgroßer Eimer	
Pcs: 328	1997–1999

Rating: 3/6

4128 EU NA AU AS

XL FreeStyle Bucket	
Riesen FreeStyle Eimer	
Pcs: 664	1997–1998

Rating: 3/6

4129 EU NA AU AS

FreeStyle Trial Size	
FreeStyle Probepackung	
Pcs: 27	1997

Rating: 5/6

4137 EU NA AU AS

Small FreeStyle Clearpack	
FreeStyle Probierspaß	
Pcs: 120	1997–1998

Rating: 4/6

4138 EU NA AU AS

Value Set with Storage Bag	
FreeStyle ab 5 mit Tasche	
Pcs: 400	1997

Rating: 5/6

4139 EU NA AU AS

FreeStyle Bucket	
FreeStyle Eimer Flitzeblitz	
Pcs: 249	1997–1998

Rating: 4/6

4148 — NA
Large FreeStyle Clearpack
Großer FreeStyle Probierspaß
Pcs: 249 | 1997

4157 — NA
FreeStyle Trial Size
FreeStyle Probepackung
Pcs: 38 | 1997

4158 — EU NA
Small FreeStyle Box
Kleine FreeStyle Box
Pcs: 128 | 1997

4168 — EU NA AU AS
Large FreeStyle Clearpack
Großer FreeStyle Probierspaß
Pcs: - | 1997

4169 — EU NA AU AS
FreeStyle Gift Item
FreeStyle Geschenkset
Pcs: - | 1997

5561 — EU NA AU AS
Big Foot 4x4
Trans-Continental Big Foot
Pcs: 762 | 1997–1998

5821 — EU NA AU AS
Pamela's Picnic Time
Picknickset
Pcs: 9 | 1997–2001

5822 — EU NA AU AS
Jennifer's Foal
Pferdefreundin
Pcs: 7 | 1997–1998

5853 — EU NA AU AS
Lucinda and Cressida
Zirkusprinzessin
Pcs: 6 | 1997–1999

ⓘ 5854	EU NA AU AS
Pony Trekking	
Sommercamp	
Pcs: 56	1997–1998

ⓘ 5855	EU NA AU AS
Riding Stables	
Reitschule	
Pcs: 168	1997–1998

5874	EU NA AU AS
Nursery	
Babystation	
Pcs: 64	1997–1998

6004	EU NA AU AS
Crossbow Cart	
Armbrustkarren	
Pcs: 21	1997–1998

6007	EU NA AU AS
Bat Lord	
Graf Fledermaus	
Pcs: 16	1997–1998

6027	EU NA AU AS
Bat Lord's Catapult	
Steinschleuderfuhrwerk	
Pcs: 56	1997–1998

6037	EU NA AU AS
Witch's Windship	
Hexengondel „Grüner Drache“	
Pcs: 60	1997–1998

ⓘ 6047	EU NA AU AS
Prison Transport	
Kutsche der bitterbösen Buben	
Pcs: 145	1997–1998

ⓘ 6087	EU NA AU AS
Witch's Magic Manor	
Hexengrotte „Zum Magischen Felsen“	
Pcs: 255	1997–1998

ⓘ	5854	With stationery	Mit Briefpapier
ⓘ	5855	With stationery; similar to: 5871 (2002)	Mit Briefpapier; ähnlich zu: 5871 (2002)
ⓘ	6047	Similar to: 6099 (1997)	Ähnlich zu: 6099 (1997)
ⓘ	6087	With poster	Mit Poster

6097	EU NA AU AS	
Night Lord's Castle		
Burg des Grafen Fledermaus		
Pcs: 598	1997–1998	
Rating: 3/6		

6099	NA	
Traitor Transport		
Kutsche der bitterbösen Buben		
Pcs: 146	1997	
Rating: 4/6		

6204	NA	
Buccaneers		
5 Piratenfiguren		
Pcs: 43	1997	
Rating: 4/6		

6249	NA	
Pirates Ambush		
Piratenfort		
Pcs: 159	1997	
Rating: 4/6		

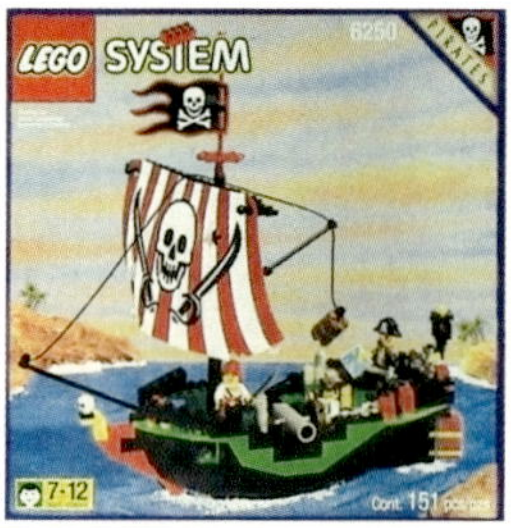

6250	NA	
Cross Bone Clipper		
Küstenschaluppe		
Pcs: 160	1997	
Rating: 4/6		

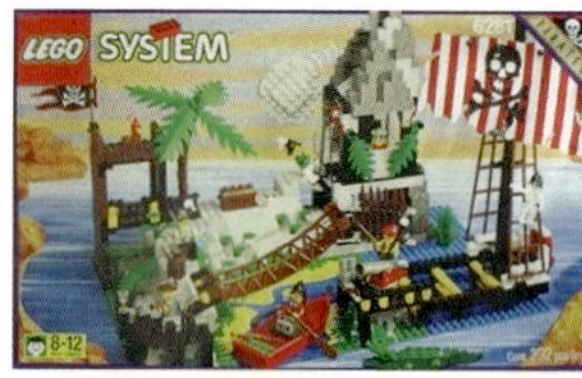

6281	NA	
Pirates Perilous Pitfall		
Piratenbucht mit Schiffswrack		
Pcs: 408	1997	
Rating: 4/6		

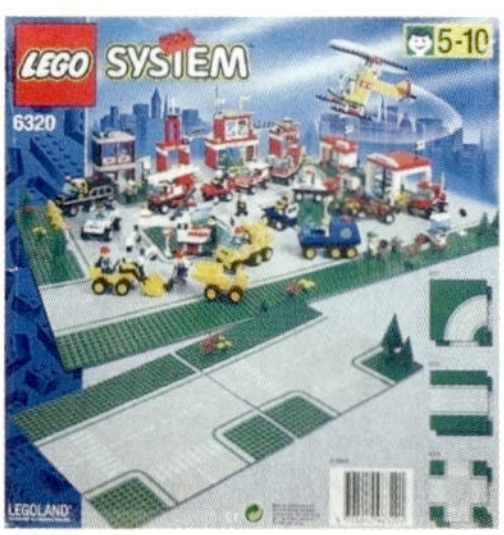

6320	EU NA AU AS	
T-Road Plates		
T-Kreuzungen		
Pcs: 2	1997–2002	
Rating: 2/6		

6321	EU NA AU AS	
Curved Road Plates		
Kurven		
Pcs: 2	1997–2002	
Rating: 2/6		

6322	EU NA AU AS	
Straight Road Plates		
Gerade Straßen		
Pcs: 2	1997–2002	
Rating: 2/6		

ⓘ	6097	With poster	Mit Poster
ⓘ	6099	Similar to: 6047 (1997); comes with plastic cave	Ähnlich zu: 6047 (1997); mit Plastikhöhle

6323	EU NA AU AS
Cross Road Plates	
Kreuzungen	
Pcs: 2	1997–2002

6400	EU NA AU AS
Go-Cart	
Go-Kart	
Pcs: 24	1997–1998

6406	EU NA AU AS
Go-Cart	
Go-Kart	
Pcs: 23	1997

6407	EU NA AU AS
Fire Chief	
Feuerwehrauto	
Pcs: 26	1997–1998

6417	EU NA AU AS
Jumping Course	
Springreiten	
Pcs: 45	1997

6441	EU NA AU AS
Deep Reef Refuge	
Unterwasser Forschungsstation	
Pcs: 454	1997–1998

6442	EU NA AU AS
Sting Ray Explorer	
Unterwasserfilmteam	
Pcs: 155	1997–1998

6444	EU NA AU AS
Outback Airstrip	
Outbackflugplatz	
Pcs: 166	1997–1998

6486	EU NA AU AS
Fire Engine	
Feuerwehrlöschwagen	
Pcs: 67	1997–1998

i	6400	Similar to: 6406 (1997), 1096 (1999)	Ähnlich zu: 6406 (1997), 1096 (1999)
i	6406	Similar to: 6400 (1997), 1096 (1999)	Ähnlich zu: 6400 (1997), 1096 (1999)
i	6441	With poster	Mit Poster

6487 EU NA AU AS

Mountain Rescue

Bergrettungshubschrauber

Pcs: 70 | 1997–1998

6489 EU NA AU AS

Seaside Holiday Cottage

Strandbad

Pcs: 89 | 1997

6490 EU NA AU AS

Amazon Crossing

Wüstenflitzer

Pcs: 121 | 1997–1998

6495 EU NA AU AS

Time Tunnelator

Time Cruisers Fledermausflieger

Pcs: 85 | 1997–1998

6496 EU NA AU AS

Whirling Time Warper

Time Cruisers Geisterbus

Pcs: 156 | 1997–1998

6497 EU NA AU AS

Twisted Time Train

Time Cruisers Gruselexpress

Pcs: 305 | 1997–1998

6499 NA AS

Time Tunnelator

Time Cruisers Fledermausflieger

Pcs: 83 | 1997

6547 EU NA AU AS

Fun Fair

Spielpark

Pcs: 207 | 1997

6548 EU NA AU AS

Octan Gas Station

Tankstelle

Pcs: 131 | 1997–1998

i	6495	Similar to: 6499 (1997)	Ähnlich zu: 6499 (1997)
i	6499	Similar to: 6495 (1997); with time machine	Ähnlich zu: 6495 (1997); mit Zeitmaschine

6549	EU NA AU AS
Roadblock Runners	
Verfolgungsjagd	
Pcs: 195	1997–1998
■■■□□□	

6550	EU NA AU AS
Outback Racer	
Rallyesportwagen	
Pcs: 51	1997–1998
■■■□□□	

6553	EU NA AU AS
Crisis News Crew	
TV-Kamerateam	
Pcs: 139	1997–1998
■■■□□□	

6554	EU NA AU AS
Blaze Brigade	
Feuerwache	
Pcs: 258	1997–1998
■■■□□□	

6555	EU NA AU AS
Sea Hunter	
Schlauchboot	
Pcs: 37	1997–1998
■■■□□□	

6556	EU NA AU AS
Scuba Squad	
Bootsgespann	
Pcs: 79	1997–1998
■■■□□□	

6557	EU NA AU AS
Treasure Hunters	
Schiff mit Minitauchboot	
Pcs: 152	1997–1998
■■■■■□	

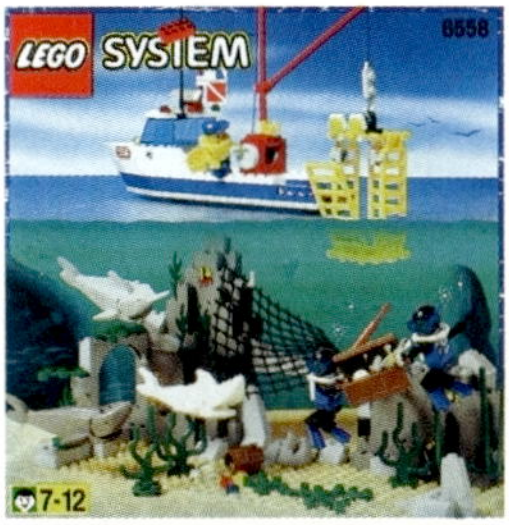

6558	EU NA AU AS
Shark Cage Cove	
Rifftaucher	
Pcs: 205	1997–1998
■■■□□□	

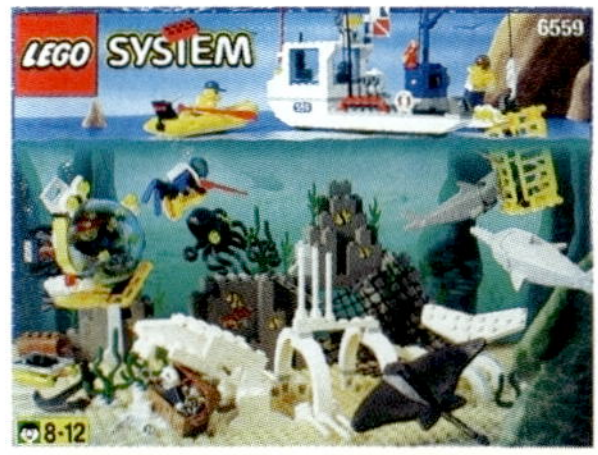

6559	EU NA AU AS
Deep Sea Bounty	
Unterwasserexpedition	
Pcs: 375	1997–1998
■■■□□□	

(i) 6554	With poster	Mit Poster

6560	EU NA AU AS
Diving Expedition Explorers	
Schatzsucher der 7 Weltmeere	
Pcs: 492	1997–1998

6564	EU NA AU AS
Recycle Truck	
Müllwagen	
Pcs: 35	1997–1998

6565	EU NA AU AS
Construction Crew	
Drei Baufahrzeuge	
Pcs: 78	1997–1998

6566	EU NA AU AS
Bank	
Bank	
Pcs: 107	1997–1998

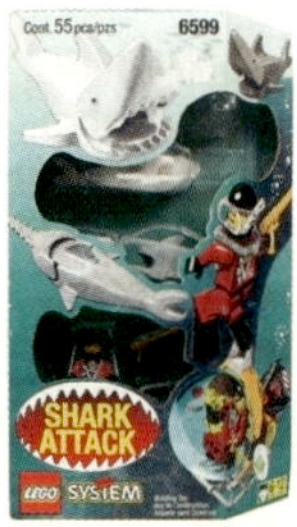

6599	EU NA AU AS
Shark Attack	
Haiangriff	
Pcs: 63	1997

6709	EU NA AU AS
Tribal Chief	
Häuptling	
Pcs: 16	1997–1998

6718	EU NA AU AS
Raindance Ridge	
Medizinmann	
Pcs: 74	1997–1998

6746	EU NA AU AS
Chief's Tipi	
Häuptlingstipi	
Pcs: 135	1997–1998

6748	EU NA AU AS
Boulder Cliff Canyon	
Tipi des Medizinmanns	
Pcs: 257	1997–1998

i	Set	English	Deutsch
i	6559	With poster	Mit Poster
i	6746	With poster	Mit Poster

6766 EU NA AU AS
Rapid River Village
Indianerlager
Pcs: 353 | 1997–1998

6790 EU NA AU AS
Bandit's Wheelgun
Bandit mit Geschützwagen
Pcs: 21 | 1997–2001

6791 EU NA AU AS
Bandit's Wheelgun
Bandit mit Geschützwagen
Pcs: 20 | 1997–1998

6799 EU NA AU AS
Showdown Canyon
Lohngeldkutsche
Pcs: 73 | 1997

6800 EU NA AU AS
Cyber Blaster
U.F.O. Hover Transporter
Pcs: 20 | 1997–1998

6816 EU NA AU AS
Cyber Blaster
U.F.O. Hover Transporter
Pcs: 20 | 1997

6818 EU NA AU AS
Cyborg Scout
U.F.O. Planetensprinter
Pcs: 36 | 1997–2001

6829 EU NA AU AS
Radon Rover
U.F.O. Mob Moon Traveller
Pcs: 53 | 1997–1998

6836 EU NA AU AS
V-Wing Fighter
U.F.O. Sky Surfer
Pcs: 40 | 1997–1998

i	6766	With poster; re-released as: 6763 (2002)	Mit Poster; neu aufgelegt als: 6763 (2002)
i	6790	Similar to: 6791 (1997)	Ähnlich zu: 6791 (1997)
i	6791	Similar to: 6790 (1997)	Ähnlich zu: 6790 (1997)
i	6800	Similar to: 6816 (1997), 3012 (1998); also in: 54 (1997)	Ähnlich zu: 6816 (1997), 3012 (1998); auch in: 54 (1997)
i	6816	Similar to: 6800 (1997), 3012 (1998)	Ähnlich zu: 6800 (1997), 3012 (1998)
i	6818	Similar to: 4305 (1998); also included in: 54 (1997)	Ähnlich zu: 4305 (1998); auch enthalten in: 54 (1997)

6900	EU NA AU AS
Cyber Saucer	
U.F.O. Diskus	
Pcs: 114	1997–1998

6915	EU NA AU AS
Warp Wing Fighter	
U.F.O. Schwesterschiff	
Pcs: 238	1997–1998

6975	EU NA AU AS
Alien Avenger	
U.F.O. Docking Disc	
Pcs: 367	1997–1998

6979	EU NA AU AS
Interstellar Starfighter	
U.F.O. Mutterschiff	
Pcs: 291	1997–1998

6999	EU NA AU AS
Cyber Saucer	
U.F.O. Diskus	
Pcs: 114	1997

8205	EU NA AU AS
Bungee Blaster	
Dragster	
Pcs: 65	1997–1999

8215	EU NA AU AS
Gyro Copter	
Mini-Heli	
Pcs: 110	1997–1999

8216	EU NA AU AS
Turbo 1	
Formel 1-Racer	
Pcs: 97	1997–1999

8222	EU NA AU AS
VTOL	
Senkrechtstarter	
Pcs: 141	1997–1998

i	Set	English	Deutsch
i	6836	Also included in: 54 (1997)	Auch enthalten in: 54 (1997)
i	6900	With poster; similar to: 6999 (1997)	Mit Poster; ähnlich zu: 6999 (1997)
i	6979	With poster	Mit Poster
i	6999	With poster; similar to: 6900 (1997)	Mit Poster; ähnlich zu: 6900 (1997)

8229	EU NA AU AS	
Tread Trekker		
High-Speed-Raupe		
Pcs: 189	1997–1999	

8232	EU NA AU AS	
Chopper Force		
Helikopter		
Pcs: 294	1997–1998	

ⓘ 8250	EU NA AU AS	
Search Sub		
U-Boot		
Pcs: 383	1997–1998	

8277	EU NA AU AS	
Giant Model Set		
Großer Universalkasten		
Pcs: 553	1997–1998	

ⓘ 8299	EU NA AU AS	
Search Sub with CD-ROM		
U-Boot mit CD-ROM		
Pcs: 383	1997–1998	

8414	EU NA AU AS	
Mountain Rambler		
Geländeraupe		
Pcs: 247	1997–1999	

8437	EU NA AU AS	
Future Car		
Offroad-Racer		
Pcs: 420	1997–1998	

ⓘ 8459	EU NA AU AS	
Pneumatic Front-End Loader		
Schaufelradlader „Gigant“		
Pcs: 594	1997–1999	

8479	EU NA AU AS	
Barcode Multi Set		
Truck „Barcode Control“		
Pcs: 1298	1997–1999	

ⓘ	8250	Similar to: 8299 (1997)	Ähnlich zu: 8299 (1997)
ⓘ	8299	Similar to: 8250 (1997)	Ähnlich zu: 8250 (1997)
ⓘ	8459	Similar to: 8439 (2004), 8464 (2001)	Ähnlich zu: 8439 (2004), 8464 (2001)

8735	EU NA AU AS
Motor Set 9V	
9V Power-Motor	
Pcs: 60	1997–2003

1998

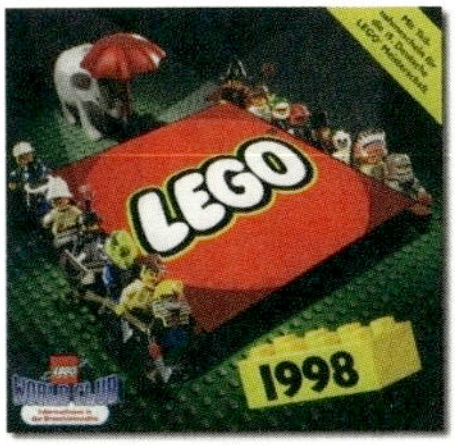

1298	EU NA AU AS	
Christmas Calendar		
Weihnachtskalender		
Pcs: 217	1998–1999	Special

1800	EU NA AU AS	
Turtle		
Schildkröte		
Pcs: 6	1998–2001	Special

2000	EU NA AU AS	
Sally Starfish		
Seesternchen		
Pcs: 1	1998–2001	

2001	EU NA AU AS	
Three-In-One Play Set		
Quietschepalme		
Pcs: 3	1998–2001	

2007	EU NA AU AS	
Musical Cuthbert and Friend		
Spieluhr „Kamel“		
Pcs: 2	1998–1999	

2011	EU NA AU AS	
Molly's Stack 'n' Learn Set		
Ferienhaus		
Pcs: 6	1998–1999	

1800	Similar to: 1640 (1989)	Ähnlich zu: 1640 (1989)

2012 EU NA AU AS

Lucy Ladybug		
Marienkäfer		
Pcs: 13	1998–1999	Special

Rating: 4 of 6

2013 EU NA AU AS

Choo-choo Train		
Tierexpress		
Pcs: 9	1998–2000	

Rating: 3 of 6

2017 NA

Choo-choo Train		
Zug		
Pcs: 12	1998–1999	Special

Rating: 4 of 6

2018 EU NA AU AS

Timmy's Stack 'n' Learn Set		
Baumeister		
Pcs: 20	1998–1999	

Rating: 3 of 6

2021 EU NA AU AS

Clarence Caterpillar and Friends		
Rasselbande		
Pcs: 7	1998–1999	

Rating: 3 of 6

2022 EU NA AU AS

Edward Elephant		
Elefantenrutscher		
Pcs: 12	1998–1999	

Rating: 4 of 6

2028 EU NA AU AS

Try-Me-Set with Bee		
Biene		
Pcs: 5	1998–1999	Special

Rating: 3 of 6

2130 EU

Duck		
Ente		
Pcs: 7	1998	Special

Rating: 5 of 6

2131 EU

Hippo		
Nilpferd		
Pcs: 9	1998	Special

Rating: 5 of 6

i	2130	Danone Promo; available only in Belgium	Danone Promo; verfügbar nur in Belgien
i	2131	Danone Promo; available only in Belgium	Danone Promo; verfügbar nur in Belgien

ⓘ 2132 EU NA AU AS

Cow		
Kuh		
Pcs: 10	1998	Special

ⓘ 2133 EU NA AU AS

Bull		
Stier		
Pcs: 12	1998	Special

ⓘ 2134 EU NA AU AS

Bison		
Bison		
Pcs: 10	1998	Special

2222 EU NA AU AS

Tunnel Fun		
Abenteuerspielplatz		
Pcs: 33	1998–2000	

2223 EU NA AU AS

Spooky House		
Geisterbahn		
Pcs: 40	1998–1999	

2224 EU NA AU AS

Tubular Chest		
Eimer „Röhrenbahn“		
Pcs: 116	1998–2003	Special

ⓘ 2226 EU NA AU AS

Medium Bucket		
Mittlerer Eimer		
Pcs: 50	1998–1999	Special

2229 EU NA AU AS

Bucketful of Fun		
Eimer „Spielspaß“		
Pcs: 201	1998–2000	

2234 EU NA AU AS

Police Chase		
Polizei-Verfolgungsjagd		
Pcs: 161	1998–2001	Special

ⓘ	Set	English	Deutsch
ⓘ	2132	Danone Promo; available only in Belgium	Danone Promo; verfügbar nur in Belgien
ⓘ	2133	Danone Promo; available only in Belgium	Danone Promo; verfügbar nur in Belgien
ⓘ	2134	Danone Promo; available only in Belgium	Danone Promo; verfügbar nur in Belgien
ⓘ	2226	Similar to: 1450 (2000), 2272 (1998)	Ähnlich zu: 1450 (2000), 2272 (1998)

2268	EU NA AU AS
Medium Bucket	
Eimer „Schmusekatze“	
Pcs: 50	1998–1998

2269	EU NA AU AS
Large Bucket	
Großer Eimer „Babyelefant“	
Pcs: 89	1998–1999

2270	EU NA AU AS	
Puppy		
Hündchen		
Pcs: -	1998–1998	Special

2271	EU NA AU AS	
Boy with Barrow		
Junge mit Schubkarre		
Pcs: 4	1998–1998	Special

2272	EU NA AU AS	
Medium Bucket		
Mittlerer Eimer		
Pcs: 50	1998–1998	Special

2275	EU NA AU AS
Sarah's Flower Garden	
Sarahs Blumengarten	
Pcs: 19	1998–1999

2276	EU NA AU AS
Train with Oval Case	
Koffer „Eisenbahn“	
Pcs: 52	1998–1999

2277	EU NA AU AS
Boy with Cat	
Haustiere	
Pcs: 8	1998–1999

2278	EU NA AU AS	
Large Bucket		
Großer Eimer		
Pcs: 91	1998–1999	Special

i	2268	Similar to: 2493 (1998)	Ähnlich zu: 2493 (1998)
i	2272	Similar to: 1450 (2000), 2226 (1998)	Ähnlich zu: 1450 (2000), 2226 (1998)

2279	EU NA AU AS	
Tubular Motion		
Eimer „Kugelbahn“		
Pcs: 74	1998–1999	

2431	EU NA AU AS	
Big Chief Brown Bear		
Indianerhäuptling		
Pcs: 3	1998–1999	

2432	EU NA AU AS	
Big Chief's Tipi		
Häuptlingstipi		
Pcs: 18	1998–1999	

2433	EU NA AU AS	
Stagecoach		
Westernkutsche		
Pcs: 10	1998–1999	

2434	EU NA AU AS	
Sheriff Jake		
Sheriff		
Pcs: 31	1998–1999	

2435	EU NA AU AS	
Western Town		
Western-Stadt		
Pcs: 37	1998–1999	Special

2436	EU NA AU AS	
Big Chief's Camp		
Indianerlager		
Pcs: 45	1998–1999	

2437	EU NA AU AS	
Sheriff Jake		
Sheriff		
Pcs: 69	1998–1998	Special

2438	EU NA AU AS	
Big Western Set		
Indianerlager und Siedlertreck		
Pcs: 68	1998–1998	Special

2449	EU NA AU AS	
Classic Bulk		
Box mit Grundelementen		
Pcs: 466	1998–1999	Special
■■■■■■		

2453	EU NA AU AS	
Large Bulk Bucket		
Großer Steineeimer		
Pcs: 950	1998–1999	Special
■■■■■□		

2456	EU NA AU AS	
Big Bulk Box		
Box mit Grundelementen		
Pcs: -	1998–1998	Special
■■■■■□		

2490	EU NA AU AS	
Insectoids Combi Set		
Insectoids Kombiset		
Pcs: 167	1998–1998	Special
■■■■■■		

2493	EU NA AU AS	
Medium Bucket		
Mittelgroßer Eimer		
Pcs: 50	1998–1999	Special
■■■■■□		

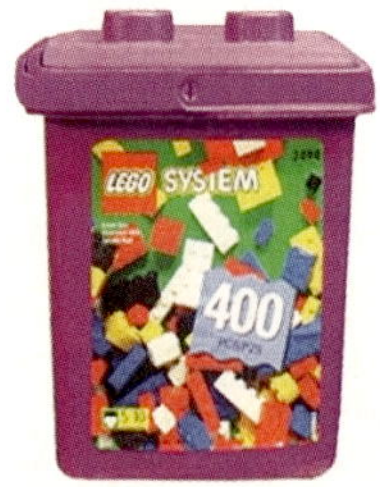

2494	EU NA AU AS	
400-piece Purple Bucket		
Lila 400-Teile-Eimer		
Pcs: 400	1998–1999	Special
■■■■□□		

2531	EU NA AU AS	
Rescue Chopper		
Luftrettung		
Pcs: 107	1998–2001	Special
■■■■□□		

2532	EU NA AU AS	
Aircraft and Ground Crew		
Flugzeug mit Bodencrew		
Pcs: 148	1998–1998	Special
■■■■■□		

2535	EU NA AU AS	
Formula 1 Racer		
Formel-1-Rennwagen		
Pcs: 29	1998–1999	Special
■■■□□□		

i			
i	2490	Woolworth's UK promo	Woolworths UK Promo
i	2493	Similar to: 2268 (1998)	Ähnlich zu: 2268 (1998)
i	2535	Shell Promo	Shell Promo

ⓘ 2536	EU NA AU AS	
Jetski		
Jetski		
Pcs: 25	1998–2000	Special

ⓘ 2537	EU NA AU AS	
Raft		
Floß		
Pcs: 21	1998–2000	Special

ⓘ 2538	EU NA AU AS	
Crossbow Flamer		
Flammenwerfer		
Pcs: 21	1998–2000	Special

ⓘ 2539	EU NA AU AS	
Batwing Flyer		
Flugdrache		
Pcs: 22	1998–2000	Special

ⓘ 2540	EU NA AU AS	
Catapult		
Katapult		
Pcs: 28	1998–2000	Special

ⓘ 2541	EU NA AU AS	
Adventurer Car		
Abenteurerbuggy		
Pcs: 27	1998–2000	Special

ⓘ 2542	EU NA AU AS	
Adventurer Plane		
Abenteurerflugzeug		
Pcs: 23	1998–2000	Special

ⓘ 2543	EU NA AU AS	
Spacecraft		
Mini-UFO		
Pcs: 21	1998–2000	Special

ⓘ 2544	EU NA AU AS	
Motorcycle		
Motorrad		
Pcs: 33	1998–2000	Special

ⓘ	2536-2544	Shell Promo	Shell Promo

2554	EU NA AU AS	
Pit Stop		
Pit Stop		
Pcs: 177	1998–2000	Special

2555	EU NA AU AS	
Beach Swing		
Strandschaukel		
Pcs: 58	1998–2000	Special

2583	EU NA AU AS	
Fire Truck		
Feuerwehrwagen		
Pcs: -	1998–1999	

2584	EU NA AU AS	
Biker Bob		
Biker Bob		
Pcs: 24	1998–1999	Special

2585	EU NA AU AS	
Handcar		
Draisine		
Pcs: 28	1998–1999	Special

2586	EU NA AU AS	
Chess King		
Der Schachkönig		
Pcs: 29	1998–1999	Special

2599	EU NA AU AS	
Racing Team		
Renn-Team		
Pcs: 13	1998–1999	Special

2600	EU NA AU AS	
Brontosaurus Family		
Familie Brontosaurus		
Pcs: 32	1998–1998	Special

2704	EU NA AU AS	
Fire Vehicle		
Feuerwehrwagen		
Pcs: 90	1998–1998	Special

2554	Shell Promo	Shell Promo
2555	Shell Promo	Shell Promo

2718	EU NA AU AS	
Inflight Air 2000		
Flugzeug mit Bodencrew		
Pcs: 130	1998–2002	Special

2815	EU NA AU AS	
Me and My Bike		
Dreiradtour		
Pcs: 6	1998–1998	

2817	EU NA AU AS	
Me and My Birthday		
Kindergeburtstag		
Pcs: 33	1998–1998	

2818	EU NA AU AS	
Me and My House		
Spielhaus		
Pcs: 68	1998–1998	

2838	EU NA AU AS	
Big Chief's Family		
Indianerfamilie		
Pcs: 80	1998–1998	Special

2853	EU NA AU AS	
Classic Bulk		
Grundelemente		
Pcs: -	1998–1998	Special

2854	EU NA AU AS	
Bungee Chopper		
Aufzieh-Trike		
Pcs: 73	1998–1998	Special

2855	EU NA AU AS	
Baby Tiger		
Tigerbaby		
Pcs: -	1998–1998	Special

2858	EU NA AU AS	
Girl with Cats		
Mädchen mit Katzen		
Pcs: 6	1998–1999	Special

2858	World Children's Day Promotion	Promotion zum Weltkindertag

2862	EU NA AU AS	
Baby Animals		
Tierkinder		
Pcs: 8	1998–1999	

2864	EU NA AU AS	
Animal Friends		
Tiergehege		
Pcs: 16	1998–2000	

2865	EU NA AU AS	
Children's Zoo		
Kinderzoo		
Pcs: 25	1998–1998	Special

2866	EU NA AU AS	
Animal Playground		
Tierpark		
Pcs: 46	1998–2000	

2879	EU NA AU AS	
Treasure Raiders		
Schatzräuber		
Pcs: 205	1998–1998	Special

2893	EU NA AU AS	
Ghost Boy		
Geisterjunge		
Pcs: 3	1998–1999	Special

2894	EU NA AU AS	
Dino Baby		
Dino-Baby		
Pcs: 3	1998–1998	Special

2895	EU NA AU AS	
Rooster on Wheels		
Hahn auf Rädern		
Pcs: 19	1998–1998	Special

2898	EU NA AU AS	
Flower		
Blume		
Pcs: -	1998–2000	Special

i	2879	Similar to: 5948 (1998), 5909 (1998)	Ähnlich zu: 5948 (1998), 5909 (1998)
i	2893	World Children's Day Promotion	Promotion zum Weltkindertag

2899	EU NA AU AS	
Flower & Bee		
Blumen und Bienen		
Pcs: -	1998–1999	Special

2907	EU NA AU AS	
Play Desk, Blue		
Blauer Spieltisch		
Pcs: 303	1998–1998	

2922	EU NA AU AS	
Dinosaur Blocks		
Dinosaurier		
Pcs: 28	1998–1998	Special

2923	EU NA AU AS	
Nursery		
Kinderzimmer		
Pcs: -	1998–1998	Special

2924	EU NA AU AS	
Car with Trailer		
Auto mit Anhänger		
Pcs: -	1998–1998	Special

2962	EU NA AU AS	
Res-Q Lifeguard		
Res-Q Strandwacht		
Pcs: 71	1998–1999	Special

2963	EU NA AU AS	
Desert Racer		
X-Treme Wüstenflitzer		
Pcs: 82	1998–2000	Special

2964	EU NA AU AS	
Space Spider		
Spider Wheeler		
Pcs: 46	1998–1999	Special

2965	EU NA AU AS	
Hornet Scout		
Hornet Scout		
Pcs: 74	1998–1999	Special

i 2907	Similar to: 4254 (1998)	Ähnlich zu: 4254 (1998)

2995	EU NA AU AS	
Adventurers Car		
Abenteurerauto		
Pcs: 75	1998–1999	Special

2996	EU NA AU AS	
The Lost Tomb		
Der Tempel des Osiris		
Pcs: 82	1998–1998	Special

2997	EU NA AU AS	
Small Bucket		
Kleiner Eimer		
Pcs: 40	1998–2002	

2998	EU	
Stena Line Catamaran		
Stena Line Katamaran		
Pcs: 200	1998–2001	Special

3012	AS	
Space Hover		
Space Hover		
Pcs: 20	1998–1998	Special

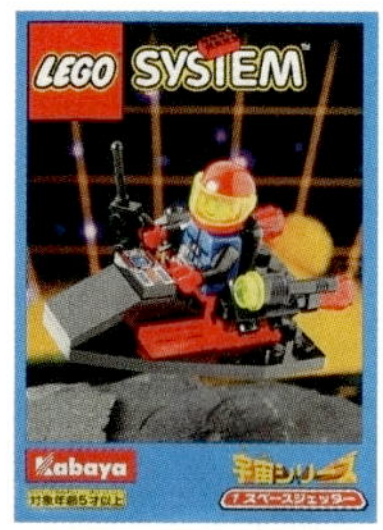

3013	AS	
Space Jet		
Space Jet		
Pcs: 18	1998–1998	Special

3014	AS	
Ice Planet Scooter		
Ice Planet Scooter		
Pcs: 19	1998–1998	Special

3015	AS	
Space Police Car		
Space Police Car		
Pcs: 19	1998–1998	Special

3016	AS	
Ninja Blaster		
Ninja Blaster		
Pcs: 24	1998–1998	Special

i	Set	English	Deutsch
i	2998	Sold only on Stena Line Ferries	Nur auf Stena Line Fähren im Verkauf
i	3012	Similar to: 6800 (1997), 6816 (1997); Kabaya Promo	Ähnlich zu: 6800 (1997), 6816 (1997); Kabaya Promo
i	3013	Similar to: 1714 (1995), 1954 (1995); Kabaya Promo	Ähnlich zu: 1714 (1995), 1954 (1995); Kabaya Promo
i	3014	Similar to: 1731 (1994), 1711 (1994); Kabaya Promo	Ähnlich zu: 1731 (1994), 1711 (1994); Kabaya Promo
i	3015	Similar to: 1916 (1993); Kabaya Promo	Ähnlich zu: 1916 (1993); Kabaya Promo
i	3016	Similar to: 1184 (1999), 1099 (1999); Kabaya Promo	Ähnlich zu: 1184 (1999), 1099 (1999); Kabaya Promo

ⓘ 3017		EU NA AU **AS**
Water Spider		
Water Spider		
Pcs: 25	1998–1999	Special

ⓘ 3018		EU NA AU **AS**
Shogun		
Shogun		
Pcs: 26	1998–1998	Special

ⓘ 3019		EU NA AU **AS**
Big Bat		
Big Bat		
Pcs: 23	1998–2001	Special

ⓘ 3020		EU NA AU **AS**
Raft of Johnse		
Raft of Johnse		
Pcs: 20	1998–1998	Special

ⓘ 3021		EU NA AU **AS**
King Pharaoh the Third		
King Pharaoh the Third		
Pcs: 19	1998–1998	Special

ⓘ 3022		EU NA AU **AS**
Plane of Hurrykain		
Plane of Hurrykain		
Pcs: 24	1998–1999	Special

ⓘ 3023		EU NA AU **AS**
Slyboot Car		
Slyboot Car		
Pcs: 24	1998–1999	Special

ⓘ 3024		EU **NA** AU AS
Building Table		
Spieltisch		
Pcs: 21	1998–2000	

ⓘ 3025		EU **NA** AU AS
25th Anniversary Silver Bucket		
25-Jahre-Jubiläumseimer		
Pcs: 601	1998–1998	Special

ⓘ	3017	Similar to: 1185 (1999); Kabaya Promo	Ähnlich zu: 1185 (1999); Kabaya Promo
ⓘ	3018	Similar to: 1186 (1999); Kabaya Promo	Ähnlich zu: 1186 (1999); Kabaya Promo
ⓘ	3019	Similar to: 1187 (1999); Kabaya Promo	Ähnlich zu: 1187 (1999); Kabaya Promo
ⓘ	3020	Similar to: 1182 (1999); Kabaya Promo	Ähnlich zu: 1182 (1999); Kabaya Promo
ⓘ	3021	Similar to: 1183 (1999); Kabaya Promo	Ähnlich zu: 1183 (1999); Kabaya Promo
ⓘ	3022	Similar to: 3039 (1999); Kabaya Promo	Ähnlich zu: 3039 (1999); Kabaya Promo

3026	EU NA AU AS	
25th Anniversary Silver Tub		
25-Jahre-Jubiläumseimer		
Pcs: 1201	1998–1998	Special

3027	EU NA AU AS	
25th Anniversary Silver Bucket		
25-Jahre-Jubiläumseimer		
Pcs: 411	1998–1998	Special

3028	EU NA AU AS	
25th Anniversary Silver Tub		
25-Jahre-Jubiläumseimer		
Pcs: 836	1998–1998	Special

3029	EU NA AU AS	
25th Anniversary Silver Bucket		
25-Jahre-Jubiläumseimer		
Pcs: 71	1998–1998	Special

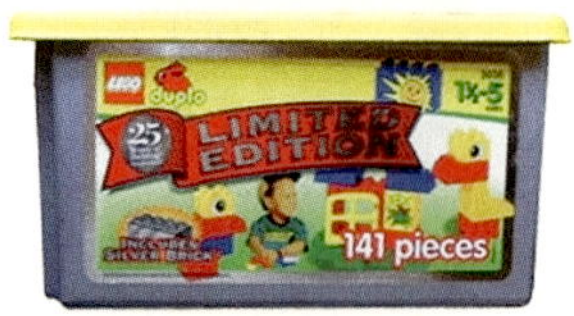

3030	EU NA AU AS	
25th Anniversary Silver Tub		
25-Jahre-Jubiläumseimer		
Pcs: 141	1998–1998	Special

3033	EU NA AU AS	
Basic Bulk Tub		
Steineeimer		
Pcs: 1200	1998–2005	Special

3034	EU NA AU AS	
25th Anniversary Silver Bucket		
25-Jahre-Jubiläumseimer		
Pcs: -	1998	Special

3037	EU NA AU AS	
Strata Tub		
Strata-Kiste		
Pcs: 140	1998–1999	Special

3038	EU NA AU AS	
Competition Multi Set with Motor		
Competition Multiset mit Motor		
Pcs: 376	1998	Special

i	3023	Kabaya Promo	Kabaya Promo
i	3033	American Version	Amerikanische Ausgabe
i	3038	Similar to: 8266 (1998)	Ähnlich zu: 8266 (1998)

3039 — EU NA AS

Adventurer Plane		
Abenteurer-Flugzeug		
Pcs: 24	1998–2001	Special

Rating: 4/6

3040 — EU NA AU AS

Challenger Set 200		
„Häuser Box“		
Pcs: 160	1998–2000	

Rating: 4/6

3041 — EU NA AU AS

Big Bucket of Fun		
Großer Eimer „Baumeister“		
Pcs: 470	1998–2000	

Rating: 3/6

3047 — NA

Halloween Bucket		
Halloween-Eimer		
Pcs: 250	1998–1999	Special

Rating: 5/6

3054 — EU

Motor Cycle		
Motorrad		
Pcs: 29	1998–2000	Special

Rating: 5/6

3055 — EU

Adventurers Car		
Abenteurerauto		
Pcs: 21	1998–1998	Special

Rating: 5/6

3056 — EU NA

Go-Cart		
Go-Kart		
Pcs: 23	1998	Special

Rating: 5/6

3066 — AS

Cosmos Glider		
Weltraumgleiter		
Pcs: 15	1998–1999	Special

Rating: 5/6

3067 — AS

Test Shuttle		
Test-Shuttle		
Pcs: 21	1999–1999	Special

Rating: 5/6

ⓘ	3039	Similar to: 3022 (1998); Nestlé Promo	Ähnlich zu: 3022 (1998); Nestlé Promo
ⓘ	3041	Similar to: 4267 (1998)	Ähnlich zu: 4267 (1998)
ⓘ	3054	Kellogg's Promo	Kellogg's Promo
ⓘ	3055	Kellogg's Promo	Kellogg's Promo
ⓘ	3056	Kabaya Promo	Kabaya Promo
ⓘ	3066	Kabaya Promo	Kabaya Promo

3068	AS
Radar Buggy	
Radar-Buggy	
Pcs: 18	1998–1999	Special

3069	AS
Cosmic Wing	
Cosmic Wing	
Pcs: 29	1998–1999	Special

3078	EU NA AS
Racing Car	
Rennauto	
Pcs: 18	1998–1999	Special

3079	EU NA AS
Bird Plane	
Flugzeug	
Pcs: 14	1998–1999	Special

3080	EU NA AS
Prop Plane	
Propellerflugzeug	
Pcs: 16	1998–1999	Special

3081	EU NA AS
Helicopter	
Hubschrauber	
Pcs: 16	1998–1999	Special

3100	EU NA AU AS
Girls' Sportswear	
Sportmode	
Pcs: 14	1998–1999	

3101	EU NA AU AS
Dressing Up	
Carolines Cocktailkleid	
Pcs: 11	1998–1999	

3102	EU NA AU AS
Leisure Wear for Christian	
Christians Urlaubsmode	
Pcs: 11	1998–1999	

i	3067	Kabaya Promo	Kabaya Promo
i	3068	Similar to: 1265 (1999), 1180 (1999); Kabaya Promo	Ähnlich zu: 1265 (1999), 1180 (1999); Kabaya Promo
i	3069	Similar to: 1181 (1999), 1266 (1999); Kabaya Promo	Ähnlich zu: 1181 (1999), 1266 (1999); Kabaya Promo
i	3078	Similar to: 3330 (1998); Kellogg's Promo	Ähnlich zu: 3330 (1998); Kellogg's Promo
i	3079	Similar to: 3331 (1998); Kellogg's Promo	Ähnlich zu: 3331 (1998); Kellogg's Promo
i	3080	Similar to: 3332 (1998); Kellogg's Promo	Ähnlich zu: 3332 (1998); Kellogg's Promo

3103 EU NA AU AS

Christian in Blue Blazer

Christian im Freizeitdress

Pcs: 11	1998–1999	

3104 EU NA AU AS

Caroline in Red Dress

Caroline - die Frau in Rot

Pcs: 8	1998–1999	

3105 EU NA AU AS

Emma in Flower Dress

Emma im Blumenkleid

Pcs: 9	1998–1999	

3106 EU NA AU AS

Marie in Rainbow Skirt

Marie im Spicy Look

Pcs: 11	1998–1999	

3107 EU NA AU AS

Andrea in Sun Dress

Andrea im Sommerkleid

Pcs: 9	1998–1998	

3108 EU NA AU AS

Happy Birthday

Geburtstag

Pcs: 29	1998–1999	

3110 EU NA AU AS

Fuzzy Friends

Kleine Tierfreunde

Pcs: 18	1998–2000	

3112 EU NA AU AS

Giggly Nursery

Baby Wickelspaß

Pcs: 30	1998–1998	

3114 EU NA AU AS

Place for Me

Nur für mich

Pcs: 50	1998–1998	

3081	Kellogg's Promo	Kellogg's Promo

3115	EU NA AU AS
Spicy Kitchen	
Bunte Spielküche	
Pcs: 41	1998–2000

3116	EU NA AU AS
Poolside Café	
Cool Eiscafé	
Pcs: 75	1998–1998

3117	EU NA AU AS
Flashy Pool	
Plantschy Pool	
Pcs: 91	1998–1999

3118	EU NA AU AS
Fun Fashion Boutique	
Fashion Shop	
Pcs: 115	1998–1999

3119	EU NA AU AS
Sunshine Home	
Villa Sonnenschein	
Pcs: 184	1998–2000

3120	EU NA AU AS
Moving In	
Anbau zur Villa Sonnenschein	
Pcs: 15	1998–1998

3204	EU NA AU AS
Auntie Jane and Cousin Sophie	
Stadtbummel	
Pcs: 29	1998–1998

3205	EU NA AU AS
Andrea's Picnic Lunch	
Picknick	
Pcs: 27	1998–1998

3206	EU NA AU AS
Emma Making Lunch	
Frühstück	
Pcs: 20	1998–1998

3210 EU NA AU AS

Ladies' Dress and Accessories

Ellens Ballkleid

Pcs: 22	1998–1998	

3211 EU NA AU AS

Girls' Dress and Accessories

Partykleid

Pcs: 20	1998–1998	

3220 EU NA AU AS

Christian with Gifts

Michaels Geburtstagsüberraschung

Pcs: 17	1998–1998	

3225 EU NA AU AS

Classic Train

Westernzug

Pcs: 288	1998–1998	Special

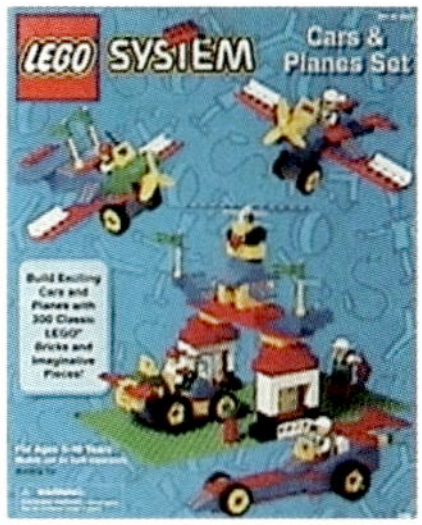

3226 EU NA AU AS

Cars and Planes

Autos und Flugzeuge

Pcs: 300	1998–1998	Special

3233 EU NA AU AS

Fantasy Bird

Fantasievogel

Pcs: 34	1998–2001	Special

3234 EU NA AU AS

Fantasy Boat

Fantasieboot

Pcs: 28	1998–2000	Special

3302 EU NA AU AS

Football Pitch

Fußballfeld

Pcs: 2	1998–1998	Special

3303 EU NA AU AS

Field Accessories

Tore und Schiedsrichter

Pcs: 52	1998–1998	Special

i	3233	SAS (Airline) Promo	SAS (Fluglinie) Promo
i	3234	SAS (Airline) Promo	SAS (Fluglinie) Promo
i	3302	Included in: 880002 (1998); Shell Promo	Enthalten in: 880002 (1998); Shell Promo
i	3303	Included in: 880002 (1998); Shell Promo	Enthalten in: 880002 (1998); Shell Promo

3304	EU NA AU AS	
Dutch International		
Nationalspieler, Niederlande		
Pcs: 4	1998–1998	Special

3305	EU NA AU AS	
World Team Player		
Weltteamspieler		
Pcs: 4	1998–1998	Special

3306	EU NA AU AS	
Goal Keepers		
Torhüter		
Pcs: 8	1998–1998	Special

3308	EU NA AU AS	
Tribune		
Fanblock		
Pcs: 83	1998–1998	Special

3309	EU NA AU AS	
Main Stand		
Haupttribüne		
Pcs: 95	1998–1998	Special

3310	EU NA AU AS	
Press Box		
Kommentator- und Pressekabine		
Pcs: 92	1998–1998	Special

3311	EU NA AU AS	
Television Tower		
Kameraturm		
Pcs: 94	1998–1998	Special

3312	EU NA AU AS	
Medic's Station		
Sanitätsstation		
Pcs: 80	1998–1998	Special

3313	EU NA AU AS	
Floodlight Masts		
Flutlichtmasten		
Pcs: 102	1998–1998	Special

3304	Shell Promo	Shell Promo
3305	Included in: 880002 (1998); Shell Promo	Enthalten in: 880002 (1998); Shell Promo
3306	Included in: 880002 (1998); Shell Promo	Enthalten in: 880002 (1998); Shell Promo
3308-3314	Shell Promo	Shell Promo
3317	Included in: 880002 (1998); Shell Promo	Enthalten in: 880002 (1998); Shell Promo

3314	**EU** **NA** AU **AS**	
Stadium Security		
Bereitschaftspolizei		
Pcs: 137	1998–1998	Special

3317	**EU** **NA** AU **AS**	
German International		
Nationalspieler, Deutschland		
Pcs: 4	1998–1998	Special

3318	**EU** **NA** AU **AS**	
English International		
Nationalspieler, England		
Pcs: 4	1998–1998	Special

3320	**EU** NA AU **AS**	
Austrian International		
Nationalspieler, Österreich		
Pcs: 4	1998–1998	Special

3323	**EU** NA AU AS	
Football Player with Football		
Fußballspieler mit Ball		
Pcs: 5	1998–1998	Special

3324	**EU** NA AU AS	
World Team Player with Football		
Fußballspieler mit Ball		
Pcs: 5	1998–1998	Special

3330	**EU** **NA** AU **AS**	
Blockbuster Racing Car		
Blockbuster Rennauto		
Pcs: 19	1998–2000	Special

3331	**EU** **NA** AU **AS**	
Blockbuster Bird Plane		
Blockbuster Flugzeug		
Pcs: 14	1998–2000	Special

3332	EU **NA** AU AS	
Blockbuster Prop Plane		
Blockbuster Propellerflugzeug		
Pcs: 16	1998–2000	Special

i	3318-3320	Shell Promo	Shell Promo
i	3323	Kaufhof Stores (Germany) promo	Kaufhof Läden (Deutschland) Promo
i	3324	Kaufhof Stores (Germany) promo	Kaufhof Läden (Deutschland) Promo
i	3330	Similar to: 3078 (1998)	Ähnlich zu: 3078 (1998)
i	3331	Similar to: 3079 (1998)	Ähnlich zu: 3079 (1998)
i	3332	Similar to: 3080 (1998)	Ähnlich zu: 3080 (1998)

3333	EU NA AU AS	
Blockbuster Helicopter		
Blockbuster Hubschrauber		
Pcs: 17	1998–2000	Special

3442	EU NA AU AS	
LEGOLAND California Truck		
LEGOLAND California Truck		
Pcs: 107	1998–1999	Special

3501	EU NA AU AS	
Jet-Car		
Fun Car		
Pcs: 26	1998–1999	

3502	EU NA AU AS	
Bi-Wing		
Jet Plane		
Pcs: 25	1998–1999	

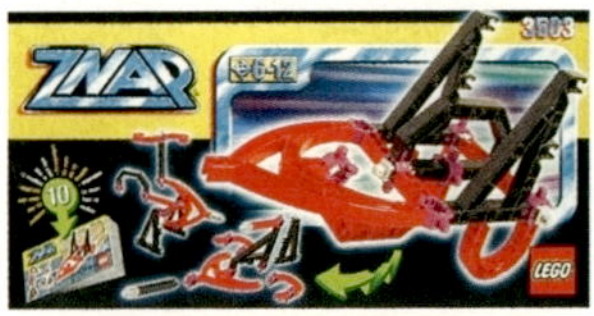

3503	EU NA AU AS	
Mini-Sonic		
Speed Boat		
Pcs: 22	1998–1999	

3504	EU NA AU AS	
Hook-Truck		
Truck		
Pcs: 30	1998–1999	

3510	EU NA AU AS	
Red Racer		
Flitzer		
Pcs: 25	1998–1999	Special

3531	EU NA AU AS	
Tri-Bike		
Bike		
Pcs: 29	1998–1999	

3532	EU NA AU AS	
Jet-Ski		
Aqua Scooter		
Pcs: 27	1998–1999	

3333	Similar to: 3081 (1998)	Ähnlich zu: 3081 (1998)

3551	EU NA AU AS
Dino-Jet	
Jet	
Pcs: 80	1998–1999

3552	EU NA AU AS
Hover Sub with Motor	
Helikopter mit Motor	
Pcs: 126	1998–1999

3555	EU NA AU AS
Jeep	
Jeep	
Pcs: 266	1998–1999

3571	EU NA AU AS
Blackmobile with Motor	
Black Racer mit Motor	
Pcs: 143	1998–1999

3581	EU NA AU AS
Formula Z Car in Storage Case	
F1-Renner mit Koffer	
Pcs: 171	1998–1999

3591	EU NA AU AS
Heli-Transport (Rota Beast)	
Helikopter-Transporter mit Motor	
Pcs: 242	1998–1999

3670	EU NA AU AS	
35th Anniversary Bucket		
35-Jahre-Jubiläumseimer		
Pcs: 410	1998	Special

3722	EU NA AU AS	
Treasure Tomb		
Das Tal der Könige		
Pcs: 161	1998–2001	Special

3758	EU NA AU AS	
35th Anniversary Bucket		
35-Jahre-Jubiläumseimer		
Pcs: 600	1998–1998	Special

3722	Similar to: 5919 (1998)	Ähnlich zu: 5919 (1998)

3759	EU NA AU AS	
35th Anniversary Tub		
35-Jahre-Jubiläumseimer		
Pcs: 1200	1998–1998	Special

3760	EU NA AU AS	
35th Anniversary Bucket		
35-Jahre-Jubiläumseimer		
Pcs: 418	1998–1998	Special

3761	EU NA AU AS	
35th Anniversary Tub		
35-Jahre-Jubiläumseimer		
Pcs: 835	1998–1998	Special

3762	EU NA AU AS	
Bucket		
Eimer		
Pcs: 70	1998–1998	Special

3763	EU NA AU AS	
Bucket		
Eimer		
Pcs: -	1998–1998	Special

3888	EU NA AU AS	
Three Eights		
Drei Achten		
Pcs: 182	1998–1998	Special

4211	EU NA AU AS	
Starter Set 100		
„Meine kleine Tierwelt“		
Pcs: 53	1998–2000	

4212	EU NA AU AS	
Starter Set 200		
Starterbox mit Grundelementen		
Pcs: 95	1998–2000	

4213	EU NA AU AS	
Super Set 200		
„Welt auf Rädern“		
Pcs: 200	1998–2000	

4214 EU NA AU AS

Medium Bucket

Mittlerer Eimer

Pcs: 257 | 1998–2000

4215 EU NA AU AS

Starter Set 300

„Tierpark“

Pcs: 264 | 1998–2000

4216 EU NA AU AS

Super Set 100

„Lustiger Zirkus“

Pcs: 480 | 1998–2000

4217 EU NA AU AS

Playdesk and Bricks

„Spielplatz“

Pcs: 203 | 1998–2000

4219 EU NA AU AS

Brick Pack 100

Box mit Grundelementen

Pcs: 288 | 1998–2000

4220 EU NA AU AS

Large Box of Bricks

Box mit Grundelementen

Pcs: 428 | 1998–1999

4221 EU NA AU AS

Challenger Set 100

„Fahrzeug Box“

Pcs: 66 | 1998–2000

4222 EU NA AU AS

Challenger Set 300

„Coole Flitzer“

Pcs: 361 | 1998–2000

4223 EU NA AU AS

Challenger Set 400 with Motor

„Motor Maniac“

Pcs: 549 | 1998–2000

4224	**EU** **NA** **AU** **AS**	
Medium Bucket		
Mittlerer Eimer		
Pcs: -	1998–2000	Special

4225	**EU** **NA** **AU** **AS**	
Challenger Set 350		
„Fantasiemobile“		
Pcs: 245	1998–2000	

4226	**EU** **NA** **AU** **AS**	
Building Monsters		
„Baue Monster“		
Pcs: 500	1998–1999	Special

4229	**EU** **NA** **AU** **AS**	
Brick Pack 300		
XXL Steinebox m. Standardelementen		
Pcs: 812	1998–2000	

4232	EU **NA** AU AS	
FreeStyle Set		
FreeStyle Set		
Pcs: 30	1998–1999	Special

4239	EU **NA** AU AS	
FreeStyle Set		
FreeStyle Set		
Pcs: 37	1998–1999	Special

4244	EU NA AU **AS**	
Large Bulk Bucket		
Großer Steineeimer		
Pcs: 416	1998–2005	Special

4254	EU **NA** AU AS	
FreeStyle Playdesk		
FreeStyle Spieltisch		
Pcs: 300	1998–1999	Special

4255	EU **NA** AU AS	
Box with Bagpack		
Set mit Rucksack		
Pcs: 496	1998–1998	Special

i		
4254	Similar to: 2907 (1998)	Ähnlich zu: 2907 (1998)

4258	EU NA AU AS	
Big Box Play Scape		
Box mit Spiellandschaft		
Pcs: 1001	1998–1998	Special

4267	EU NA AU AS	
Large Bucket		
Großer Eimer		
Pcs: 470	1998–2006	Special

4271	EU NA AU AS	
FreeStyle Box		
FreeStyle Box		
Pcs: 180	1998–1999	Special

4274	EU NA AU AS	
FreeStyle Playdesk		
FreeStyle Spieltisch		
Pcs: 500	1998–1998	Special

4276	EU NA AU AS	
Big Box Store Pack		
Set mit Aufbewahrungsbox		
Pcs: 801	1998–1998	Special

4280	EU NA AU AS	
FreeStyle Trial Size		
FreeStyle Probierpackung		
Pcs: 39	1998–1998	Special

4533	EU NA AU AS	
Train Track Snow Remover		
Schnee- und Geröllfräse		
Pcs: 63	1998–2001	

4541	EU NA AU AS	
Rail and Road Service Truck		
Reparatur und Servicewagen		
Pcs: 115	1998–2000	

4553	EU NA AU AS	
Train Wash		
Zugwaschanlage		
Pcs: 190	1998–2001	

4267	Similar to: 3041 (1998)	Ähnlich zu: 3041 (1998)

ⓘ 4556	EU NA AU AS
Train Station	
Bahnhof	
Pcs: 242	1998–2002

ⓘ 4560	EU NA AU AS
Railway Express	
Personen- u. Autoreisezug	
Pcs: 674	1998–2002

ⓘ 5542	EU NA AU AS
Black Thunder	
Personen- und Transporthelikopter	
Pcs: 498	1998–1999

ⓘ 5600	EU NA AU AS
Radio Control Racer	
Crazy Car	
Pcs: 295	1998–2000

ⓘ 5841	EU NA AU AS
Beach Fun	
Bootsausflug	
Pcs: 44	1998–1998

ⓘ 5844	EU NA AU AS
Dolphin Windsurfer	
Surfspaß	
Pcs: 16	1998–1999

ⓘ 5845	EU NA AU AS
Dolphin Show	
Delphin Show	
Pcs: 50	1998–1999

ⓘ 5846	EU NA AU AS
Desert Island	
Schatzinsel	
Pcs: 97	1998–1999

ⓘ 5847	EU NA AU AS
Surfer's Paradise	
Strandcafé	
Pcs: 133	1998–1998

ⓘ	Set	English	Deutsch
ⓘ	4560	Without speed regulator; similar to: 4561 (1999)	Ohne Trafo; ähnlich zu: 4561 (1999)
ⓘ	5600	Similar to: 5599 (1998)	Ähnlich zu: 5599 (1998)

5848	EU NA AU AS	
Luxury Cruiser		
Traumyacht		
Pcs: 227	1998–1999	

5900	EU NA AU AS	
Johnny Thunder		
Johnny Thunder		
Pcs: 14	1998–1999	Special

5909	EU NA AU AS	
Treasure Raiders with Sarcophagus		
Schatzräuber mit Sarkophag		
Pcs: 205	1998–1998	Special

5918	EU NA AU AS	
Scorpion Tracker		
Expeditionsmobil		
Pcs: 36	1998–1999	

5919	EU NA AU AS	
The Valley of the Kings		
Das Tal der Könige		
Pcs: 166	1998–1998	Special

5928	EU NA AU AS	
Bi-Wing Baron		
Doppeldecker		
Pcs: 73	1998–1999	

5938	EU NA AU AS	
Oasis Ambush		
Das Grabmal des Anubis		
Pcs: 82	1998–1999	

5948	EU NA AU AS	
Desert Expedition		
Wüstenexpedition		
Pcs: 203	1998–1999	Special

5958	EU NA AU AS	
Mummy's Tomb		
Mumiengrab		
Pcs: 261	1998–1999	Special

i	Set	English	Deutsch
i	5900	Similar to: 1094 (1999)	Ähnlich zu: 1094 (1999)
i	5909	Similar to: 5948 (1998), 2879 (1998)	Ähnlich zu: 2879 (1998), 5948 (1998)
i	5919	Similar to: 3722 (1998)	Ähnlich zu: 3722 (1998)
i	5948	Similar to: 2879 (1998), 5909 (1998)	Ähnlich zu: 2879 (1998), 5909 (1998)

5978	EU NA AU AS	
Sphynx Secret Surprise		
Das Geheimnis der Sphinx		
Pcs: 351	1998–1999	

5988	EU NA AU AS	
Pharaoh's Forbidden Ruins		
Der Schatz des Pharaonentempels		
Pcs: 737	1998–1999	

6013	EU NA AU AS	
Samurai Swordsman		
Der mächtige Shogun		
Pcs: 14	1998–1999	

6028	EU NA AU AS	
Treasure Transport		
Schatztransport		
Pcs: 26	1998–1998	Special

6029	EU NA AU AS	
Treasure Transport		
Schatztransport		
Pcs: 25	1998–1998	Special

6031	EU NA AU AS	
Fright Force		
Figuren mit Ausrüstung		
Pcs: 32	1998–1998	

6033	EU NA AU AS	
Treasure Transport		
Schatztransport		
Pcs: 61	1998–1999	

6045	EU NA AU AS	
Ninja Surprise		
Schlupfwinkel der Banditen		
Pcs: 113	1998–1999	

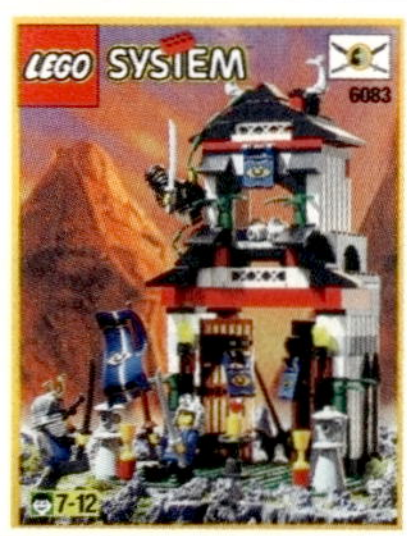

6083	EU NA AU AS	
Samurai Stronghold		
Shoguns Festung		
Pcs: 199	1998–1999	

i	6028	Cardbox edition of: 6029 (1998)	Kartonversion von: 6029 (1998)
i	6029	Polybag edition of: 6028 (1998)	Tütchenversion von: 6028 (1998)

6088 EU NA AU AS

Robber's Retreat

Das Versteck der Ninja

Pcs: 281 | 1998–1999

6089 EU NA AU AS

Stone Tower Bridge

Die Brücke der Shogun

Pcs: 396 | 1998–1999

6093 EU NA AU AS

Flying Ninja Fortress

Palast der Shogun

Pcs: 702 | 1998–1999

6100 EU NA AU AS

Aquashark Dart

Aquashark Dart

Pcs: 24 | 1998–1998 | Special

6107 EU NA AU AS

Recon Ray

Stingray Scout

Pcs: 20 | 1998–1999 | Special

6109 EU NA AU AS

Sea Creeper

Stingray Fighter

Pcs: 80 | 1998–1998 | Special

6110 EU NA AU AS

Solo Sub

Aquaprotector

Pcs: 26 | 1998–1999

6140 EU NA AU AS

Sea Creaper

Stingray Fighter

Pcs: 79 | 1998–1998

6150 EU NA AU AS

Crystal Detector

Kristalldetektor

Pcs: 105 | 1998–1999

i	6100	Similar to: 1095 (1999)	Ähnlich zu: 1095 (1999)
i	6109	Similar to: 6140 (1998)	Ähnlich zu: 6140 (1998)
i	6140	Similar to: 6109 (1998)	Ähnlich zu: 6109 (1998)
i	6150	Similar to: 6159 (1998)	Ähnlich zu: 6159 (1998)

6159	EU NA AU AS	
Crystal Detector		
Kristalldetektor		
Pcs: 105	1998	Special

6160	EU NA AU AS	
Sea Scorpion		
Stingray Lobster		
Pcs: 306	1998–1999	

6180	EU NA AU AS	
Hydro Search Sub		
Aqua-Voyager		
Pcs: 297	1998–1998	

6198	EU NA AU AS	
Stingray Stormer		
Stingray Super-Rochen		
Pcs: 405	1998–1999	

6199	EU NA AU AS	
Hydro Crystalization Station		
Aqua-Dome		
Pcs: 493	1998–1998	

6324	EU NA AU AS	
Chopper Cop		
Polizei-Trike		
Pcs: 25	1998–1999	

6325	EU NA AU AS	
Package Pick-Up		
Lieferwagen		
Pcs: 29	1998–1999	

6326	EU NA AU AS	
Town People		
6 verschiedene Figuren		
Pcs: 39	1998–2000	

6327	EU NA AU AS	
Turbo Champs		
Rennteam		
Pcs: 59	1998–1999	

i	6159	Similar to: 6150 (1998)	Ähnlich zu: 6150 (1998)
i	6324	Similar to: 4304 (1998)	Ähnlich zu: 4304 (1998)

6328	EU NA AU AS	
Helicopter Transport		
Polizei-Tieflader		
Pcs: 102	1998–1999	

6329	EU NA AU AS	
Truck Stop		
Schwertransport		
Pcs: 144	1998–1999	

6330	EU NA AU AS	
Cargo Center		
Frachtflughafen		
Pcs: 239	1998–1999	

6332	EU NA AU AS	
Command Post Central		
Polizei-Hauptquartier		
Pcs: 290	1998–2001	

6333	EU NA AU AS	
Race and Chase		
Polizeikontrolle		
Pcs: 54	1998–1998	Special

6415	EU NA AU AS	
Jet Ski		
RES-Q Jetski		
Pcs: 19	1998–1999	Special

6420	EU NA AU AS	
Mail Carrier		
Postbote		
Pcs: 13	1998–1998	Special

6422	EU NA AU AS	
Telephone Repair		
Telefonnotdienst		
Pcs: 48	1998–1999	

6424	EU NA AU AS	
Rig Racers		
Renntrucks		
Pcs: 106	1998–1999	

6332	Similar to: 6636 (2002)	Ähnlich zu: 6636 (2002)
6415	Similar to: 1097 (1999), 6428 (1998)	Ähnlich zu: 1097 (1999), 6428 (1998)

6426	EU NA AU AS	
Super Cycle Center		
Motorradshop		
Pcs: 165	1998–1999	

6428	EU NA AU AS	
Wave Saver		
RES-Q Jetski		
Pcs: 19	1998–1998	Special

6431	EU NA AU AS	
Road Rescue		
RES-Q Off-Roader		
Pcs: 52	1998–1999	

6445	EU NA AU AS	
Emergency Evac		
RES-Q Bergungstruck		
Pcs: 106	1998–1999	

6451	EU NA AU AS	
River Response		
RES-Q Speedboot		
Pcs: 154	1998–1999	

6462	EU NA AU AS	
Aerial Recovery		
RES-Q Helikopter		
Pcs: 207	1998–1999	

6473	EU NA AU AS	
RES-Q Cruiser		
RES-Q Hovercraft		
Pcs: 301	1998–1999	

6479	EU NA AU AS	
Emergency Response Center		
RES-Q Hauptquartier		
Pcs: 449	1998–1999	

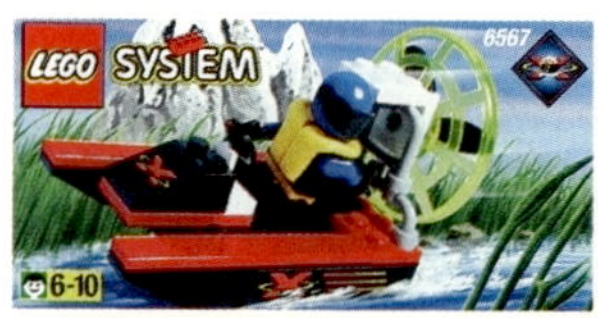

6567	EU NA AU AS	
Speed Splash		
X-Treme Air Boat		
Pcs: 28	1998–1999	

i 6428	Similar to: 6415 (1998), 1097 (1999)	Ähnlich zu: 6415 (1998), 1097 (1999)

6568	EU NA AU AS	
Drag Race Rally		
X-Treme Dragster Race		
Pcs: 303	1998–1999	

6572	EU NA AU AS	
Wind Runners		
X-Treme Beach Buggy		
Pcs: 55	1998–1999	

6580	EU NA AU AS	
Land Jet 7		
X-Treme Raketenwagen		
Pcs: 113	1998–1999	

6582	EU NA AU AS	
Daredevil Flight Squad		
X-Treme Fliegerstaffel		
Pcs: 285	1998–1999	Special

6584	EU NA AU AS	
Extreme Team Challenge		
X-Treme Action Trophy		
Pcs: 363	1998–1999	

6585	EU NA AU AS	
Hang Glider		
X-Treme Drachenflieger		
Pcs: 19	1998–1999	Special

6589	EU NA AU AS	
Radical Racer		
X-Treme Cross Country Racer		
Pcs: 83	1998–1998	Special

6817	EU NA AU AS	
Beta Buzzer		
Mosquito Scout		
Pcs: 33	1998–1999	

6837	EU NA AU AS	
Cosmic Creeper		
Formicola Collector		
Pcs: 58	1998–1999	

6585	Similar to: 1098 (1999)	Ähnlich zu: 1098 (1999)
6589	With raised Canyon Play Plate	Mit Canyon-Bodenplatte

ⓘ 6901	EU NA AU AS	
Small Droid Space Ship		
U.F.O. Robo-Intruder		
Pcs: 20	1998–1998	Special

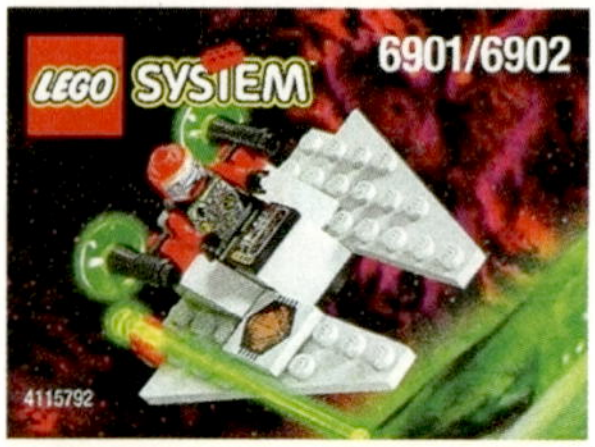

ⓘ 6902	EU NA AU AS	
Small Droid Space Ship		
U.F.O. Robo-Intruder		
Pcs: 20	1998–1998	Special

ⓘ 6903	EU NA AU AS	
Bug Blaster		
Mono Motte		
Pcs: 25	1998–1999	

ⓘ 6905	EU NA AU AS	
Bi-Wing Blaster		
Duo-Insect Flyer		
Pcs: 115	1998–1999	Special

ⓘ 6907	EU NA AU AS	
Sonic Stinger		
Vespular Stinger		
Pcs: 96	1998–1999	

ⓘ 6909	EU NA AU AS	
Sonic Stinger		
Vespular Stinger		
Pcs: 97	1998–1998	Special

ⓘ 6919	EU NA AU AS	
Planetary Prowler		
Gryllo Hopper		
Pcs: 251	1998–1999	

ⓘ 6969	EU NA AU AS	
Celestial Stinger		
Hornet Protector		
Pcs: 258	1998–1999	

ⓘ 6977	EU NA AU AS	
Arachnoid Star Base		
Arachno Base		
Pcs: 448	1998–1999	

ⓘ	6901	Similar to: 6902 (1998)	Ähnlich zu: 6902 (1998)
ⓘ	6902	Similar to: 6901 (1998)	Ähnlich zu: 6901 (1998)
ⓘ	6907	Similar to: 6909 (1998)	Ähnlich zu: 6909 (1998)
ⓘ	6909	Similar to: 6907 (1998)	Ähnlich zu: 6907 (1998)

8202 EU NA AU AS

Bungee Chopper		
Trike		
Pcs: 74	1998–1999	

8203 EU NA AU AS

Rover Discovery		
Buggy		
Pcs: 41	1998–1998	Special

8204 EU NA AU AS

Sky Flyer 1		
Flugzeug		
Pcs: 41	1998–1998	Special

8208 EU NA AU AS

Custom Cruiser		
Chopper		
Pcs: 53	1998–1998	Special

8209 EU NA AU AS

Future F1		
Rennbolide		
Pcs: 49	1998–1999	Special

8213 EU NA AU AS

Spy Runner		
Flugracer		
Pcs: 105	1998–1999	

8217 EU NA AU AS

The Wasp		
Hubschrauber		
Pcs: 67	1998–1998	Special

8218 EU NA AU AS

Trike Tourer		
Dreirad		
Pcs: 70	1998–1999	Special

8219 EU NA AU AS

Go-Cart		
Go-Kart		
Pcs: 101	1998–1998	Special

ⓘ 8226	EU NA AU AS	
Mud Masher		
Off-Roader		
Pcs: 126	1998–2000	

ⓘ 8233	EU NA AU AS	
Blue Thunder versus The Sting		
Motorrad gegen Scorpion		
Pcs: 120	1998–1999	

ⓘ 8239	EU NA AU AS	
Cyber Slam Spider		
Motorrad gegen Skorpion		
Pcs: 120	1998–1998	Special

ⓘ 8245	EU NA AU AS	
Robot's Revenge		
Robots Rache		
Pcs: 224	1998–1999	Special

ⓘ 8248	EU NA AU AS	
Forklift		
Gabelstapler		
Pcs: 233	1998–1999	Special

ⓘ 8257	EU NA AU AS	
Cyber Strikers		
Teleskopboxer		
Pcs: 384	1998–1999	

ⓘ 8266	EU NA AU AS	
Spider Slayer		
Competition Multiset		
Pcs: 376	1998–1999	

ⓘ 8417	EU NA AU AS	
Mag Wheel Master		
Rennbike		
Pcs: 324	1998–1999	

ⓘ 8428	EU NA AU AS	
Turbo Command with CD-ROM		
Prototyp mit CD-ROM		
Pcs: 477	1998–1999	

ⓘ	8233	Similar to: 8239 (1998)	Ähnlich zu: 8239 (1998)
ⓘ	8239	Similar to: 8233 (1998); with storage case	Ähnlich zu: 8233 (1998); mit Plastikkoffer
ⓘ	8248	Similar to: 8463 (2001)	Ähnlich zu: 8463 (2001)
ⓘ	8266	Similar to: 3038 (1998)	Ähnlich zu: 3038 (1998)
ⓘ	8417	Similar to: 8430 (2002)	Ähnlich zu: 8430 (2002)
ⓘ	8428	Similar to: 8432 (1998)	Ähnlich zu: 8432 (1998)

8432	EU NA AU AS	
Turbo Command without CD-ROM		
Prototyp ohne CD-ROM		
Pcs: 476	1998–1998	Special

8462	EU NA AU AS	
Tow Truck		
Abschlepptruck		
Pcs: 785	1998–1999	

8482	EU NA AU AS	
Cyber Master		
Cyber Master		
Pcs: 898	1998–2000	

8483	EU	
Cyber Master with Metal Case		
Cyber Master mit Metallkoffer		
Pcs: 898	1998–2000	

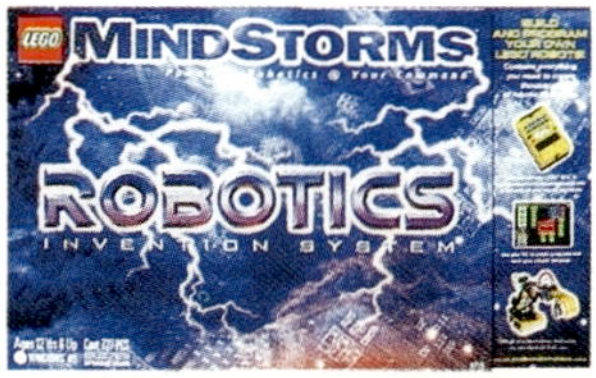

9719	EU NA AU AS	
Robotics Invention System		
Robotics Invention System		
Pcs: 733	1998-1999	Special

9730	EU NA AU AS	
Robo Sports		
Robo Sports		
Pcs: 90	1998-1999	Special

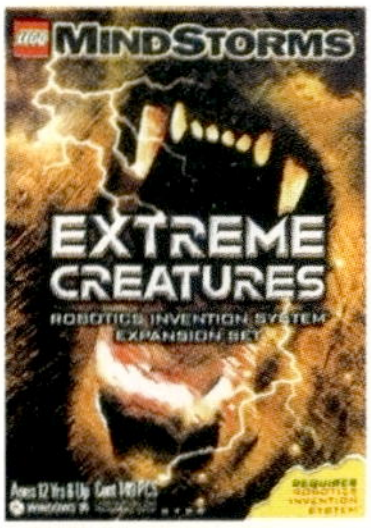

9732	EU NA AU AS	
Extreme Creatures		
Extreme Creatures		
Pcs: 153	1998-1999	Special

880002	EU	
Shell - Soccer World Cup		
Shell - Fußball-Einstiegsset		
Sets: 7	1998	Special

8432	Similar to: 8428 (1998)	Ähnlich zu: 8428 (1998)
8482	Similar to: 8483 (1998)	Ähnlich zu: 8483 (1998)
8483	Similar to: 8482 (1998)	Ähnlich zu: 8482 (1998)
880002	Includes: 3302 (1998), 3303 (1998), 2x3305 (1998), 3306 (1998), 2x3317 (1998)	Enthält: 3302 (1998), 3303 (1998), 2x3305 (1998), 3306 (1998), 2x3317 (1998)

1999

ⓘ 1029	EU	
Milk Delivery Truck		
Milchtransporter		
Pcs: 91	1999	Special
Rating: 4/6		

ⓘ 1061	NA	
Slizer Disc		
Slizer Disk		
Pcs: 1	1999	Special
Rating: 5/6		

ⓘ 1068	NA	
Air Patrol		
Hubschrauber		
Pcs: 214	1999–2001	Special
Rating: 4/6		

ⓘ 1068	EU	
Stena Line Ferry		
Stena Line Fährschiff		
Pcs: 25	1999–2001	Special
Rating: 4/6		

ⓘ 1069	NA	
Speed Boat		
Motorboot		
Pcs: 22	1999	Special
Rating: 4/6		

ⓘ 1070	NA	
Stunt Flyer		
Kleinstflugzeug		
Pcs: 20	1999	Special
Rating: 4/6		

ⓘ	Set	English	Deutsch
ⓘ	1029	Tine Dairies (Norway) Promo	Tine Dairies (Norwegen) Promo
ⓘ	1061	Includes one random slizer disc	Enthält eine zufällige Slizer Disk
ⓘ	1068	Similar to: 2849 (1997)	Ähnlich zu: 2849 (1997)
ⓘ	1068	Only sold on the route Dover-Calais	Nur auf der Strecke Dover-Calais verkauft
ⓘ	1069	Similar to: 2882 (1997)	Ähnlich zu: 2882 (1997)
ⓘ	1070	Similar to: 2884 (1997)	Ähnlich zu: 2884 (1997)

1076 EU NA AU AS

Advent Calendar

Adventskalender

Pcs: 240 | 1999 | Special

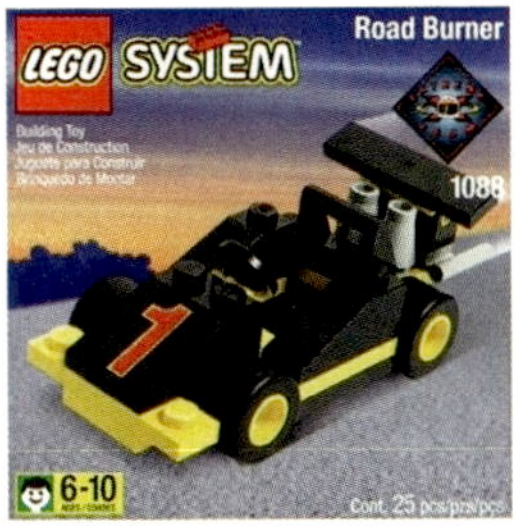

1088 EU NA AU AS

Road Burner

Formel-1-Wagen

Pcs: 25 | 1999–2000 | Special

1094 EU NA AU AS

Johnny Thunder

Joe Freeman

Pcs: 13 | 1999 | Special

1095 EU NA AU AS

Super Sub

Aquashark Dart

Pcs: 24 | 1999 | Special

1096 EU NA AU AS

Race Buggy

Go-Kart

Pcs: 23 | 1999–2000 | Special

1097 EU NA AU AS

RES-Q Runner

RES-Q Jetski

Pcs: 19 | 1999 | Special

1098 EU NA AU AS

Hang Glider

X-Treme Drachenflieger

Pcs: 19 | 1999 | Special

1099 EU NA AU AS

Ninja Blaster

Ninja Katapult

Pcs: 24 | 1999–2001 | Special

1106 EU NA AU AS

Basic Building Set

„Heiße Kisten“

Pcs: 428 | 1999 | Special

1088	Similar to: 2886 (1997)	Ähnlich zu: 2886 (1997)
1094	Similar to: 5900 (1998)	Ähnlich zu: 5900 (1998)
1095	Similar to: 6100 (1998)	Ähnlich zu: 6100 (1998)
1096	Similar to: 6400 (1997), 6406 (1997)	Ähnlich zu: 6400 (1997), 6406 (1997)
1097	Similar to: 6415 (1998), 6428 (1998)	Ähnlich zu: 6415 (1998), 6428 (1998)
1098	Similar to: 6585 (1998)	Ähnlich zu: 6585 (1998)

ⓘ 1127	EU NA AU AS	
Milka Santa Claus		
Milka Weihnachtsmann		
Pcs: 40	1999–2002	Special

ⓘ 1128	EU NA AU AS	
Milka Skiing Santa		
Milka Weihnachtsmann auf Skiern		
Pcs: 21	1999–2001	Special

ⓘ 1129	EU NA AU AS	
Milka Reindeer with Elf		
Milka Rentier und Wichtel		
Pcs: 34	1999–2001	

ⓘ 1180	EU NA AU AS	
Moon Buggy		
Mondfahrzeug		
Pcs: 27	1999	Special

ⓘ 1181	EU NA AU AS	
Space Probe		
Raumfahrzeug		
Pcs: 29	1999	Special

ⓘ 1182	EU NA AU AS	
Adventurers Raft		
Abenteurerfloß		
Pcs: 20	1999	Special

ⓘ 1183	EU NA AU AS	
Mummy		
Mumie		
Pcs: 19	1999	Special

ⓘ 1184	EU NA AU AS	
Ninja Blaster		
Ninja Katapult		
Pcs: 24	1999	Special

ⓘ 1185	EU NA AU AS	
River Ninja		
Ninja mit Floß		
Pcs: 25	1999	Special

ⓘ	Set	Similar to	Ähnlich zu
ⓘ	1099	Similar to: 3016 (1998), 1184 (1999)	Ähnlich zu: 3016 (1998), 1184 (1999)
ⓘ	1127	Similar to: 1978 (1991), 10068 (2002)	Ähnlich zu: 1978 (1991), 10068 (2002)
ⓘ	1180	Similar to: 1265 (1999), 3068 (1998)	Ähnlich zu: 1265 (1999), 3068 (1998)
ⓘ	1181	Similar to: 3069 (1998), 1266 (1999)	Ähnlich zu: 3069 (1998), 1266 (1999)
ⓘ	1182	Similar to: 3020 (1998)	Ähnlich zu: 3020 (1998)
ⓘ	1183	Similar to: 3021 (1998)	Ähnlich zu: 3021 (1998)

1186	EU NA AU AS	
Siege-Cart		
Angriffswagen		
Pcs: 26	1999	Special

1187	EU NA AU AS	
Flying Ninja		
Fliegender Ninja		
Pcs: 23	1999	Special

1188	EU NA AU AS	
Fire Formula		
Fire Formula		
Pcs: 38	1999	Special

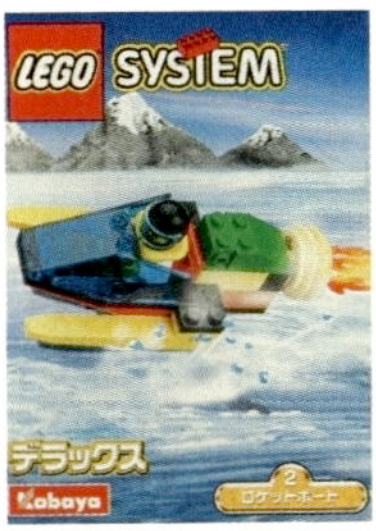

1189	EU NA AU AS	
Rocket Boat		
Rocket Boat		
Pcs: 30	1999	Special

1190	EU NA AU AS	
Retro Buggy		
Retro Buggy		
Pcs: 45	1999	Special

1191	EU NA AU AS	
Try Bird		
Try Bird		
Pcs: 35	1999	Special

1192	EU NA AU AS	
Stack N' Learn Gift Box		
Stapelspaß-Geschenkkasten		
Pcs: 40	1999–2001	Special

1193	EU NA AU AS	
Water Park Tub		
Eimer „Aqua-Park“		
Pcs: 42	1999–2000	Special

1194	EU NA AU AS	
Classic Building Table		
Classic Bautisch		
Pcs: 400	1999–2000	Special

1184	Similar to: 3016 (1998), 1099 (1999)	Ähnlich zu: 3016 (1998), 1099 (1999)
1185	Similar to: 3017 (1998)	Ähnlich zu: 3017 (1998)
1186	Similar to: 3018 (1998)	Ähnlich zu: 3018 (1998)
1187	Similar to: 3019 (1998)	Ähnlich zu: 3019 (1998)
1188-1191	Kabaya Promo	Kabaya Promo

ⓘ 1246		EU NA AU AS
Police Helicopter		
Polizeihubschrauber		
Pcs: 32	1999–2001	Special

ⓘ 1247		EU NA AU AS
Police Patrol Car		
Polizeiauto		
Pcs: 33	1999–2001	Special

ⓘ 1248		EU NA AU AS
Fire Boat		
Feuerwehrboot		
Pcs: 24	1999–2001	Special

ⓘ 1249		EU NA AU AS
Paramedic Trike		
Erste-Hilfe-Trike		
Pcs: 23	1999–2001	Special

ⓘ 1250		EU NA AU AS
Dragster		
Dragster		
Pcs: 24	1999–2001	Special

ⓘ 1251		EU NA AU AS
Go-Cart		
Go-Kart		
Pcs: 25	1999–2001	Special

ⓘ 1252		EU NA AU AS
Tanker		
Tankwagen		
Pcs: 107	1999–2001	Special

ⓘ 1253		EU NA AU AS
Ferrari Transport		
Ferrari-Transporter		
Pcs: 103	1999–2001	Special

ⓘ 1254		EU NA AU AS
Select Shop		
Select Shop		
Pcs: 171	1999–2001	Special

ⓘ	1246-1256	Shell Promo	Shell Promo

1255 EU NA AU AS

Car Wash		
Autowaschanlage		
Pcs: 139	1999–2001	Special

1256 EU NA AU AS

Petrol Pump		
Tankstation		
Pcs: 165	1999–2001	Special

1257 EU NA AU AS

Trike		
Trike		
Pcs: 37	1999–2000	Special

1258 EU NA AU AS

Propeller Buggy		
Propeller Buggy		
Pcs: 33	1999–2000	Special

1259 EU NA AU AS

Bike Blaster		
Bike Blaster		
Pcs: 34	1999–2000	Special

1260 EU NA AU AS

Piston Car		
Piston Car		
Pcs: 28	1999–2000	Special

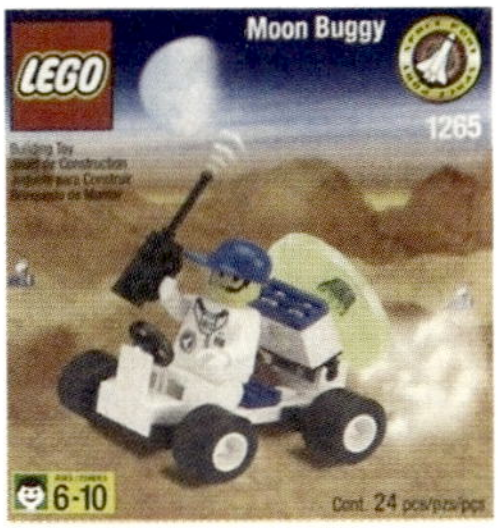

1265 EU NA AU AS

Moon Buggy		
Mondfahrzeug		
Pcs: 27	1999–2000	Special

1266 EU NA AU AS

Space Probe		
Raumfahrzeug		
Pcs: 29	1999–2000	Special

1268 EU NA AU AS

Bike Blaster		
Bike Blaster		
Pcs: 34	1999–2000	Special

i	1257	Similar to: 3000 (1999)	Ähnlich zu: 3000 (1999)
i	1258	Similar to: 3001 (1999)	Ähnlich zu: 3001 (1999)
i	1259	Similar to: 1268 (1999), 3003 (1999)	Ähnlich zu: 1268 (1999), 3003 (1999)
i	1260	Similar to: 3005 (1999)	Ähnlich zu: 3005 (1999)
i	1265	Similar to: 3068 (1998), 1180 (1999)	Ähnlich zu: 3068 (1998), 1180 (1999)
i	1266	Similar to: 3069 (1998), 1181 (1999)	Ähnlich zu: 3069 (1998), 1181 (1999)

1269 EU **NA** AU AS

White Ninja		
Weiße Ninja		
Pcs: 23	1999–2000	Special

1271 EU **NA** AU AS

Jungle Surprise		
Geheimnis des Dschungels		
Pcs: 33	1999–2000	Special

1274 EU NA AU **AS**

Light Hover		
Light Hover		
Pcs: 21	1999–2000	Special

1275 EU NA AU **AS**

Chainsaw Bulldozer		
Chainsaw Bulldozer		
Pcs: 15	1999–2000	Special

1276 EU NA AU **AS**

Helicopter Transport		
Helicopter Transport		
Pcs: 18	1999–2000	Special

1277 EU NA AU **AS**

Drill Craft		
Drill Craft		
Pcs: 23	1999–2000	Special

1841 EU **NA** AU AS

Plane		
Flugzeug		
Pcs: 15	1999	Special

1995 EU **NA** AU AS

Racer		
Rennwagen		
Pcs: 15	1999	Special

2025 EU **NA** AU AS

Boat		
Boot		
Pcs: 12	1999	Special

i	1268	Similar to: 1259 (1999), 3003 (1999)	Ähnlich zu: 1259 (1999), 3003 (1999)
i	1269	Similar to: 3076 (1999)	Ähnlich zu: 3076 (1999)
i	1271	Similar to: 5905 (1999)	Ähnlich zu: 5905 (1999)
i	1274-1277	Kabaya Promo	Kabaya Promo
i	1841-2025	McDonald's Promo	McDonald's Promo

2030	EU NA AU AS	
Freddie Frog		
Zwinker-Frosch		
Pcs: 1	1999–2001	

2031	EU NA AU AS	
Tiny Turtle		
Kleine Transport-Schildkröte		
Pcs: 3	1999–2000	

2032	EU NA AU AS	
Helicopter		
Hubschrauber		
Pcs: 18	1999	Special

2039	EU NA AU AS	
Paddleboat		
Schaufelradboot		
Pcs: 3	1999	

2044	EU NA AU AS	
Waterlily Princess and Friend		
Prinzessin auf der Seerose		
Pcs: 3	1999	

2045	EU NA AU AS	
Car		
Auto		
Pcs: 17	1999	Special

2046	EU NA AU AS	
Let's Go Fishing		
Petri Heil Fischerset		
Pcs: 5	1999–2001	

2047	EU NA AU AS	
Plane		
Flugzeug		
Pcs: 13	1999	Special

2048	EU NA AU AS	
Water Friends		
Badewannenfreunde		
Pcs: 11	1999	

2032	McDonald's Promo	McDonald's Promo
2045	McDonald's Promo	McDonald's Promo
2047	McDonald's Promo	McDonald's Promo

2069	EU NA AU AS	
Boat		
Boot		
Pcs: 15	1999	Special

2071	EU NA AU AS	
Roll N' Go Pilot		
Propellerflugzeug		
Pcs: 2	1999–2001	

2075	EU NA AU AS	
Prop Plane		
Porpellerflugzeug		
Pcs: 14	1999	Special

2076	EU NA AU AS	
Peek-A-Boo Playhouse		
Versteck-Spiel-Haus		
Pcs: 8	1999–2000	

2101	EU NA AU AS	
Circus Catapult		
Katapult		
Pcs: 7	1999	Special

2102	EU NA AU AS	
Storage Bee		
Große Biene		
Pcs: 19	1999	Special

2103	EU NA AU AS	
Busy Builder Starter Set		
Honigbienen-Spielerei		
Pcs: 8	1999–2000	

2104	EU NA AU AS	
Wilma Whale		
Walfisch		
Pcs: 13	1999	

2106	EU NA AU AS	
Lily Pad Deluxe Set		
Wasserspielzeug		
Pcs: 9	1999–2000	Special

2069	McDonald's Promo	McDonald's Promo
2075	McDonald's Promo	McDonald's Promo

2108	NA	
Perky Paddler		
Bootsspaß		
Pcs: 5	1999	Special

2117	EU NA AU AS	
Peek-A-Boo Playmat		
Baby entdeckt die Welt		
Pcs: 4	1999–2000	

2158	AS	
Helicopter		
Hubschrauber		
Pcs: 10	1999–2000	Special

2190	EU NA AS	
Storage Frog		
Großer Frosch		
Pcs: 13	1999–2005	Special

2198	EU NA AU AS	
3 Building Plates		
3 Bauplatten		
Pcs: 3	1999–	

2253	EU NA AU AS	
Big Tubular Playtime		
Großes Rutschvergnügen		
Pcs: 90	1999–2000	

2280	EU NA AU AS	
Circus Freeway		
Baustein-Flitzer-Anlage		
Pcs: 30	1999–2000	Special

2281	EU NA AU AS	
Deluxe Harbor Highway		
Große Baustein-Flitzer-Anlage		
Pcs: 49	1999–2000	

2284	EU NA AU AS	
Clown Go Round		
Baustein-Flitzer-Kreisel		
Pcs: 14	1999–2000	

2158	Was re-released as a Kabaya promo in 2000	Wurde 2000 als Kabaya Promo neu aufgelegt

2294	EU NA AU AS	
Ladybug		
Marienkäfer		
Pcs: 9	1999–2000	Special

2295	EU NA AU AS	
Clown		
Clown		
Pcs: 6	1999	Special

2299	EU NA AU AS	
Pingo		
Pinguin		
Pcs: 11	1999	Special

2300	EU NA AU AS	
Small Bucket		
Kleiner Eimer		
Pcs: 48	1999–2002	

2467	EU NA AU AS	
Large Bucket		
Großer Eimer		
Pcs: 85	1999	

2488	NA	
Happy Hippo Build n' Store		
Großes Nilpferd		
Pcs: 80	1999–2000	Special

2588	EU NA AU AS	
Safari Hippo		
Großes Nilpferd „Safari“		
Pcs: 78	1999	

2719	EU AS	
Heli Monster		
Heli Monster		
Pcs: 9	1999	Special

2728	EU AS	
The Chopper		
Hubschrauber		
Pcs: 12	1999	Special

i	Set	English	German
i	2719	McDonald's Promo	McDonald's Promo
i	2728	McDonald's Promo	McDonald's Promo

2729	EU NA AU AS	
Quattro Leg		
Quattro Leg		
Pcs: 17	1999	Special

2742	EU NA AU AS	
Loudspeaker		
Loudspeaker		
Pcs: 9	1999	Special

2743	EU NA AU AS	
Pendulum Nose		
Pendulum Nose		
Pcs: 21	1999	Special

2744	EU NA AU AS	
Propeller Man		
Propeller-Mann		
Pcs: 10	1999	Special

2757	EU NA AU AS	
Bad Monkey		
Bad Monkey		
Pcs: 9	1999	Special

2759	EU NA AU AS	
Rotor Head		
Rotor Head		
Pcs: 13	1999	Special

2769	EU NA AU AS	
Swamp Flyer		
Sumpfboot und Wasserflugzeug		
Pcs: 107	1999–2002	Special

2774	EU NA AU AS	
Red Tiger Airshow		
„Red Tiger" Flugschau		
Pcs: 148	1999–2001	Special

2803	EU NA AU AS	
Dinosaur Babies		
Dinobabys		
Pcs: 19	1999	Special

2729-2759	McDonald's Promo	McDonald's Promo

2807	EU NA AU AS
Big Wheels Digger	
Schaufelradlader	
Pcs: 6	1999–2002

2808	EU NA AU AS
Big Wheels Tipper Truck	
Baustellen-Schwerlaster	
Pcs: 12	1999–2000

2811	EU NA AU AS
Rescue Station	
Rettungsstation	
Pcs: 57	1999–2001

2814	EU NA AU AS
Big Wheels Road Works Set	
Baustellenfahrzeuge	
Pcs: 37	1999–2000

2819	EU NA AU AS
Brick Mixer	
Betonmischer mit Steinen	
Pcs: 70	1999–2002

2821	EU NA AU AS	
Dinosaurs Fun Forest		
Dino-Wald		
Pcs: 37	1999	Special

2828	EU NA AU AS
Trouble Toadstool & Jangle Bluebell	
Picknick im Wald	
Pcs: 6	1999

2829	EU NA AU AS
M. Strawberry & D. Meadowsweet	
Schlummerblatt	
Pcs: 6	1999

2830	EU NA AU AS
The Strawberries	
Rote Erdbeeren auf Taxifahrt	
Pcs: 13	1999–2000

i	2828	With listening-tape	Mit Hörspielkassette
i	2829	With listening-tape	Mit Hörspielkassette

2831 EU NA AU AS

The Toadstools	
Grüne Blätterpilze	
Pcs: 13	1999–2000

2832 EU NA AU AS

The Bluebells	
Lila Perlblumen	
Pcs: 13	1999–2000

2833 EU NA AU AS

Bluebell Girl and Friends	
Große lila Perlblume	
Pcs: 34	1999–2000

2834 EU NA AU AS

The Meadowsweets' Home	
Maiglöckchen-Hügel	
Pcs: 46	1999–2000

2981 EU NA AU AS

Pooh's Corner	
Pooh's Corner	
Pcs: 8	1999–2000

2982 EU NA AU AS

Pooh's Birthday	
Winnie Poohs Geburtstagsparty	
Pcs: 9	1999–2000

2983 EU NA AU AS

Pooh and Tigger	
Poohs & Tiggers Versteckspiel	
Pcs: 14	1999–2000

2984 EU NA AU AS

Pooh and Piglet go Honey-Hunting	
Pooh & Ferkel sammeln Honig	
Pcs: 22	1999–2000

2985 EU NA AU AS

Tigger's Slippery Slide	
Poohs & Tiggers Spiel ohne Ende	
Pcs: 20	1999–2000

1999

2987	EU NA AU AS	
The Hundred Acre Wood		
Im Hundert-Morgen-Wald		
Pcs: 37	1999–2000	
Rating: 3/6		

2988	EU NA AU AS	
Surprise for Eeyore		
Überraschung für I-aah		
Pcs: 32	1999–2000	Special
Rating: 5/6		

3000	AS	
Trike		
Trike		
Pcs: 37	1999–2000	Special
Rating: 5/6		

3001	AS	
Propeller Buggy		
Propeller Buggy		
Pcs: 33	1999–2000	Special
Rating: 5/6		

3003	AS	
Bike Blaster		
Bike Blaster		
Pcs: 34	1999–2000	Special
Rating: 5/6		

3005	AS	
Piston Car		
Piston Car		
Pcs: 28	1999–2000	Special
Rating: 5/6		

3032	NA	
Medium Bucket		
Mittlerer Eimer		
Pcs: 600	1999	Special
Rating: 5/6		

3035	EU	
FreeStyle Tub		
FreeStyle Eimer		
Pcs: -	1999	
Rating: 6/6		

3036	EU NA AU AS	
Large Bucket		
Großer Eimer		
Pcs: 71	1999–2002	
Rating: 4/6		

	Set	English	Deutsch
i	3000	Similar to: 1257 (1999); Kabaya Promo	Ähnlich zu: 1257 (1999); Kabaya Promo
i	3001	Similar to: 1258 (1999); Kabaya Promo	Ähnlich zu: 1258 (1999); Kabaya Promo
i	3003	Similar to: 1268 (1999), 1259 (1999); Kabaya Promo	Ähnlich zu: 1268 (1999), 1259 (1999); Kabaya Promo
i	3005	Similar to: 1260 (1999); Kabaya Promo	Ähnlich zu: 1260 (1999); Kabaya Promo

3050		EU NA AU AS
Shanghai Surprise		
Schiff der roten Ninja		
Pcs: 109	1999–2000	Special

3051		EU NA AU AS
Blaze Attack		
Angriff des roten Drachens		
Pcs: 145	1999–2000	Special

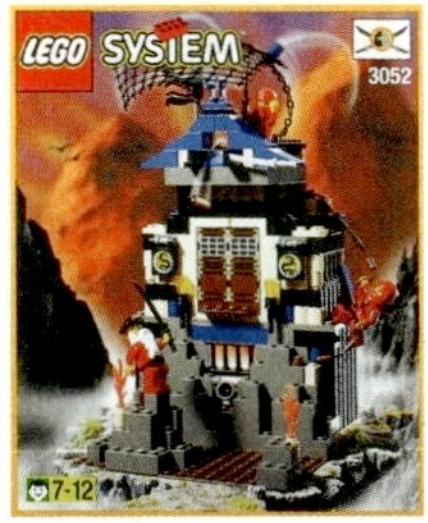

3052		EU NA AU AS
Ninja's Fire Fortress		
Turm der roten Ninja		
Pcs: 173	1999–2001	Special

3053		EU NA AU AS
Emperor's Stronghold		
Festung des Tenno		
Pcs: 338	1999–2000	Special

3070		EU NA AU AS
Mosquito		
Mosquito		
Pcs: 20	1999	Special

3071		EU NA AU AS
Light Flyer		
Light Flyer		
Pcs: 21	1999	Special

3072		EU NA AU AS
Mega Tack		
Mega Tack		
Pcs: 24	1999	Special

3073		EU NA AU AS
Booster		
Booster		
Pcs: 20	1999	Special

3074		EU NA AU AS
Red Ninja's Dragon Glider		
Roter Ninja mit Drachengleiter		
Pcs: 20	1999–2000	Special

3070-3074	Kabaya Promo	Kabaya Promo

3075	EU NA AU AS	
Ninja Master's Boat		
Boot des Ninja-Meisters		
Pcs: 21	1999–2000	Special

3076	EU NA AU AS	
White Ninja's Attack Cart		
Angriff der weißen Ninja		
Pcs: 23	1999–2000	Special

3077	EU NA AU AS	
Ninja Shogun's Small Fort		
Kleine Bastion des Shoguns		
Pcs: 22	1999–2000	Special

3130	EU NA AU AS	
Swinging Stroller		
Baby-Buggy		
Pcs: 19	1999–2000	

3132	EU NA AU AS	
Emma		
Emma im Frühlingskleid		
Pcs: 11	1999–2000	

3133	EU NA AU AS	
Andrea in Jogging Suit		
Andrea im Jogginganzug		
Pcs: -	1999	Special

3134	EU NA AU AS	
Marie in Happy Flowers		
Marie in fröhlichen Blumen		
Pcs: 10	1999–2000	

3135	EU NA AU AS	
Olivia in Fancy Wear		
Olivia in roter Seidenjacke		
Pcs: 11	1999–2000	

3136	EU NA AU AS	
Christian in Blue Jeans		
Christian in Jeans		
Pcs: 9	1999–2000	

3075	Kabaya Promo	Kabaya Promo
3076	Kabaya Promo; similar to: 1269 (1999)	Kabaya Promo; ähnlich zu: 1269 (1999)
3077	Kabaya Promo	Kabaya Promo

3137	EU NA AU AS
Casual Wear for Men	
Herrenmode	
Pcs: 3	1999–2000

3138	EU NA AU AS
Fashion Wear for Ladies	
Damenmode	
Pcs: 3	1999–2000

3139	EU NA AU AS
Outdoor Wear for Girls	
Windjacke für Mädchen	
Pcs: 3	1999–2000

3140	EU NA AU AS
Dancing Circle Dress for Girls	
Tanzdress für Mädchen	
Pcs: 4	1999–2000

3141	EU NA AU AS
Snuggly Baby Wear	
Babymode	
Pcs: 4	1999–2000

3142	EU NA AU AS
Marie's Creative Corner	
Maries Künstleratelier	
Pcs: 117	1999–2000

3143	EU NA AU AS
Ridin' Camp Out	
Pferdecamp	
Pcs: 64	1999–2002

3144	EU NA AU AS
Wilderness Waterstop	
Pferdetränke	
Pcs: 32	1999–2002

3146	EU NA AU AS
Carry and Shopping Accessories	
Shopping	
Pcs: 12	1999–2000

3438 EU NA AU AS
McDonald's Restaurant
McDonald's Restaurant
Pcs: 96 | 1999–2000 | Special

3505 EU NA AU AS
Sky-Fly
Flugzeug
Pcs: 23 | 1999–2001 | Special

3506 EU NA AU AS
Road Ripper
Motocrossbike
Pcs: 27 | 1999 | Special

3520 EU NA AU AS
Fork-Truck
Gabelstapler
Pcs: 39 | 1999 | Special

3521 EU NA AU AS
Red Racer
Fun-Racer
Pcs: 35 | 1999 | Special

3554 EU NA AU AS
Helicopter
Hubschrauber
Pcs: 90 | 1999 | Special

3582 EU NA AU AS
Ant
Ameise
Pcs: 254 | 1999 | Special

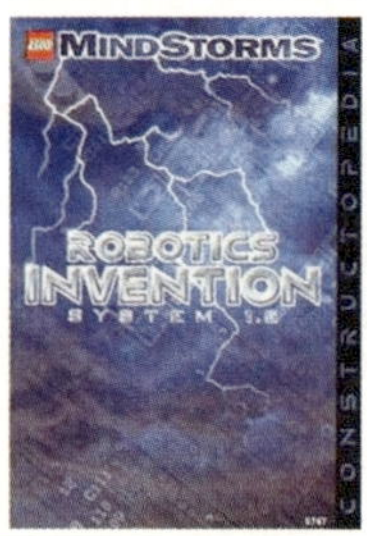

3803 EU NA AU AS
RIS 1.5 Upgrade Kit
RIS 1,5 Upgrade-Kit
Pcs: 69 | 1999–2000

4281 EU NA AU AS
Classic Trial Size
Classic Probepackung
Pcs: 25 | 1999–2000 | Special

3803	Robotics Invention System	Robotics Invention System

4282

EU **NA** AU AS

Classic Trial Size

Classic Probepackung

Pcs: 37	1999–2000	Special

Rating: 4 of 6 bricks

4283

EU **NA** AU AS

Classic Trial Size

Classic Probepackung

Pcs: 53	1999–2000	Special

Rating: 4 of 6 bricks

4284

EU **NA** AU AS

Classic Trial Size

Classic Probepackung

Pcs: 124	1999–2000	Special

Rating: 4 of 6 bricks

4285

EU **NA** **AU** **AS**

Small Bucket

Kleiner Eimer

Pcs: 256	1999–2002	

Rating: 3 of 6 bricks

4288

EU **NA** AU AS

Large Bucket

Großer Eimer

Pcs: 403	1999–2001	

Rating: 4 of 6 bricks

4291

EU **NA** AU AS

Classic Build & Store Tub

Classic Eimer mit Grundplatte

Pcs: 771	1999	Special

Rating: 5 of 6 bricks

4293

EU **NA** AU AS

Classic Value Pack

Classic Vorteilspackung

Pcs: 822	1999–2000	Special

Rating: 5 of 6 bricks

4519

EU **NA** **AU** **AS**

Cross Track

Kreuzung

Pcs: 1	1999–2006	

Rating: 2 of 6 bricks

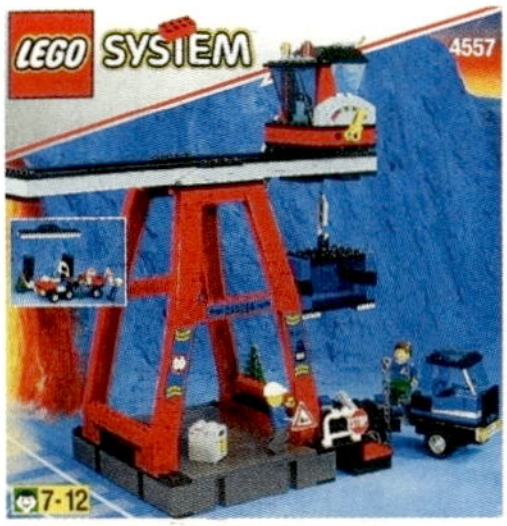

4557

EU **NA** **AU** **AS**

Freight Loading Station

Container-Verladekran

Pcs: 215	1999–2001	

Rating: 2 of 6 bricks

4285	Similar to: 4810 (2001)	Ähnlich zu: 4810 (2001)

ⓘ 4561	EU NA AU AS	
Railway Express		
Personen- und Autoreisezug		
Pcs: 679	1999–2002	

ⓘ 4805	EU NA AU AS	
5 Ninja Warriors		
5 Ninja Kämpfer		
Pcs: 31	1999–2000	

ⓘ 4910	EU NA AU AS	
Hover Scout		
Hover Scout		
Pcs: 44	1999–2000	

ⓘ 4920	EU NA AU AS	
Rapid Rider		
Rapid Rider		
Pcs: 40	1999–2000	

ⓘ 4930	EU NA AU AS	
The Rock Raiders		
Rock Raiders Team		
Pcs: 55	1999–2000	

ⓘ 4940	EU NA AU AS	
Granite Grinder		
Granit Grinder Minen-Bohrer		
Pcs: 113	1999–2000	

ⓘ 4950	EU NA AU AS	
Loader Dozer		
Loader-dozer Schaufellader		
Pcs: 93	1999–2000	

ⓘ 4970	EU NA AU AS	
Chrome Crusher		
Chrome Crusher Power Bohrer		
Pcs: 172	1999–2000	

ⓘ 4980	EU NA AU AS	
Tunnel Transport		
Tunnel Transport Senkrechtstarter		
Pcs: 353	1999–2000	

ⓘ 4561	With Trafo; similar to: 4560 (1998)	Mit Trafo; ähnlich zu: 4560 (1998)

4990	EU NA AU AS
The Rock Raiders HQ	
Rock Raiders Headquarter	
Pcs: -	1999–2000

5533	EU NA AU AS
Red Fury	
Dragster und Traktor Pulling	
Pcs: 395	1999–2000

5563	EU NA AU AS
Racing Truck	
Racing Truck	
Pcs: 806	1999–2000

5801	EU NA AU AS
Millimy the Fairy	
Die kleine Zauberfee	
Pcs: 14	1999–2000

5802	EU NA AU AS
Princess Rosaline	
Die Prinzessin	
Pcs: 10	1999–2000

5803	EU NA AU AS
Iris	
Das Schlossmädchen	
Pcs: 7	1999

5804	EU NA AU AS
Witch's Cottage	
Hexenküche	
Pcs: 42	1999–2000

5805	EU NA AU AS
Princess Rosaline's Room	
Schlafgemach der Prinzessin	
Pcs: 72	1999–2001

5807	EU NA AU AS
The Royal Stables	
Königlicher Pferdestall	
Pcs: 59	1999–2000

5808	EU NA AU AS	
The Enchanted Palace		
Märchenschloss		
Pcs: 217	1999–2001	

5811	EU NA AU AS	
Prince Justin		
Der Prinz		
Pcs: 6	1999–2000	

5812	EU NA AU AS	
Old King Alfred		
Der König		
Pcs: 6	1999–2000	

5827	EU NA AU AS	
The Royal Coach		
Die Hochzeitskutsche		
Pcs: 87	1999–2002	

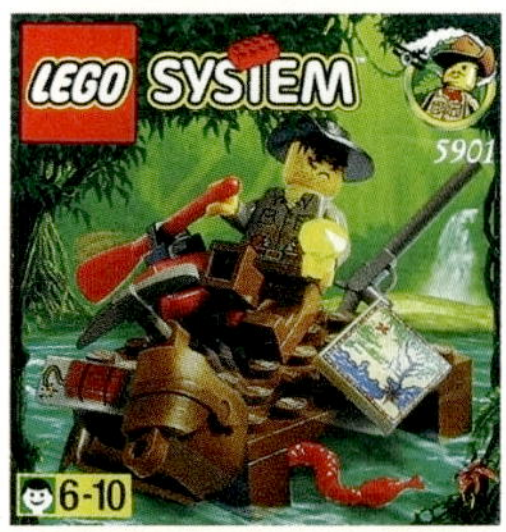

5901	EU NA AU AS	
River Raft		
Flussfloß		
Pcs: 19	1999	Special

5902	EU NA AU AS	
River Raft		
Flussfloß		
Pcs: 19	1999–2000	

5905	EU NA AU AS	
Hidden Treasure		
Geheimnis des Dschungels		
Pcs: 33	1999	Special

5906	EU NA AU AS	
Ruler of the Jungle		
Herr des Dschungels		
Pcs: 24	1999	Special

5925	EU NA AU AS	
Pontoon Plane		
Wasserflugzeug		
Pcs: 78	1999–2000	

i	Set	English	Deutsch
i	5901	Similar to: 5902 (1999)	Ähnlich zu: 5902 (1999)
i	5902	Similar to: 5901 (1999)	Ähnlich zu: 5901 (1999)
i	5905	Similar to: 1271 (1999)	Ähnlich zu: 1271 (1999)

5936 EU NA AU AS

Spider's Secret

Señor Gomez' Expedition

Pcs: 131 | 1999–2000

5956 EU NA AU AS

Air Zeppelin

Abenteuer-Zeppelin

Pcs: 176 | 1999

5976 EU NA AU AS

River Expedition

Fluss-Expedition

Pcs: 325 | 1999–2000

5986 EU NA AU AS

Amazon Ancient Ruins

Dschungeltempel

Pcs: 471 | 1999–2000

6425 EU NA AU AS

TV Chopper

Hubschrauber

Pcs: 45 | 1999–2001

6427 EU NA AU AS

Road Signs

Verkehrsschilder

Pcs: 43 | 1999–2000

6429 EU NA AU AS

Blaze Responder

Feuer-Löschboot

Pcs: 46 | 1999–2001

6432 EU NA AU AS

Speedway Transport

Rennwagentransporter

Pcs: 147 | 1999–2000

6433 EU NA AU AS

Coast Watch

Polizeischnellboot

Pcs: 90 | 1999–2000

6434	EU NA AU AS	
Roadside Repair		
Autowerkstatt		
Pcs: 232	1999	

6435	EU NA AU AS	
Coast Guard HQ		
Küstenwache		
Pcs: 231	1999	

6436	EU NA AU AS	
Go-Kart		
Go-Kart		
Pcs: 23	1999–2000	

6437	EU NA AU AS	
Beach Buggy		
Buggy		
Pcs: 28	1999–2001	

6439	EU NA AU AS	
Mini Dumper		
Mini-Kipper		
Pcs: 30	1999	Special

6446	EU NA AU AS	
Crane Truck		
Abschleppwagen		
Pcs: 26	1999	Special

6447	EU NA AU AS	
Dumper		
Muldenkipper		
Pcs: 46	1999	Special

6452	EU NA AU AS	
Mini Rocket Launcher		
Raketen-Testlabor		
Pcs: 35	1999	Special

6453	EU NA AU AS	
Com-Link Cruiser		
Radarmobil		
Pcs: 62	1999–2000	

i	6436	Similar to: 6498 (1999)	Ähnlich zu: 6498 (1999)
i	6452	Also included in: 6469 (1999)	Auch enthalten in: 6469 (1999)

6454	EU NA AU AS
Countdown Corner	
Raketenstartrampe	
Pcs: 135	1999–2000

6455	EU NA AU AS
Space Simulation Station	
Astronauten-Trainings-Camp	
Pcs: 267	1999–2000

6456	EU NA AU AS
Mission Control	
Space Shuttle Weltraumbahnhof	
Pcs: 488	1999–2000

6457	EU NA AU AS
Astronaut	
Weltraumspaziergänger	
Pcs: 25	1999–2000

6458	EU NA AU AS
Satellite with Astronaut	
Telekommunikationssatellit	
Pcs: 34	1999–2000

6459	EU NA AU AS
Fuel Truck	
Raketen-Tanktruck	
Pcs: 118	1999

6461	EU NA AU AS	
Surveillance Chopper		
Beobachtungs-Helikopter		
Pcs: 32	1999	Special

6463	EU NA AU AS
Lunar Buggy	
Moon Racer	
Pcs: 40	1999–2000

6464	EU NA AU AS
Super Rescue Complex	
City Polizei und Feuerwehr	
Pcs: 347	1999

ⓘ 6458	Also included in: 6469 (1999)	Auch enthalten in: 6469 (1999)

6465	EU NA AU AS	
Space Port Jet		
Testflugzeug		
Pcs: 65	1999	Special

6467	EU NA AU AS	
Power Pitstop		
Pit-Stop		
Pcs: 74	1999–2000	

6468	EU NA AU AS	
Tow-n-Go		
City Doppelpack		
Pcs: 52	1999	Special

6469	EU NA AU AS	
Space Port Value Pack		
Space Port Kombiset		
Sets: 3	1999	Special

6498	EU NA AU AS	
Go-Kart		
Go-Kart		
Pcs: 23	1999–2001	

6942	EU NA AU AS	
Speed Sled		
Raumschlitten		
Pcs: 21	1999	Special

6943	EU NA AU AS	
Speed Sled		
Raumschlitten		
Pcs: 21	1999	Special

7101	EU NA AU AS	
Lightsaber™ Duel		
Lightsaber™ Duel		
Pcs: 52	1999–2000	

7110	EU NA AU AS	
Landspeeder™		
Landspeeder™		
Pcs: 49	1999–2000	

i	6465	Also included in: 6469 (1999)	Auch enthalten in: 6469 (1999)
i	6469	Contains: 6452 (1999), 6458 (1999), 6465 (1999)	Enthält: 6452 (1999), 6458 (1999), 6465 (1999)
i	6498	Similar to: 6436 (1999)	Ähnlich zu: 6436 (1999)
i	6942	Similar to: 6943 (1999)	Ähnlich zu: 6943 (1999)
i	6943	Similar to: 6942 (1999)	Ähnlich zu: 6942 (1999)

7111	EU NA AU AS
Droid Fighter™	
Droid Fighter™	
Pcs: 64	1999–2000

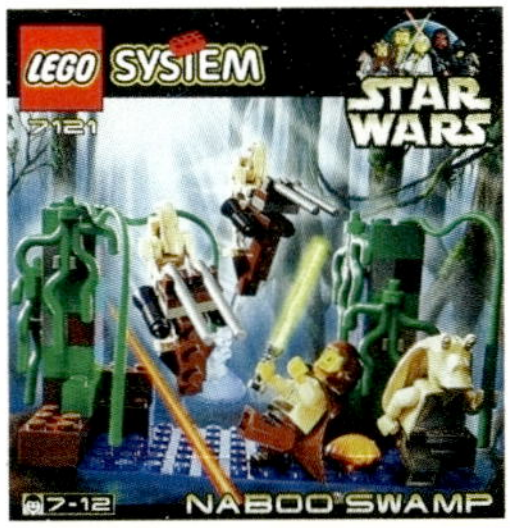

7121	EU NA AU AS
Naboo Swamp™	
Naboo Swamp™	
Pcs: 82	1999–2000

7128	EU NA AU AS
Speeder Bikes™	
Speeder Bikes™	
Pcs: 94	1999–2000

7130	EU NA AU AS
Snowspeeder™	
Snowspeeder™	
Pcs: 217	1999–2000

7131	EU NA AU AS
Anakin's Podracer™	
Anakin's Podracer™	
Pcs: 143	1999–2000

7140	EU NA AU AS
X-wing Fighter™	
X-wing Fighter™	
Pcs: 274	1999–2001

7141	EU NA AU AS
Naboo Fighter™	
Naboo Fighter™	
Pcs: 183	1999–2001

7150	EU NA AU AS
Y-wing™ & TIE Fighter™	
Y-wing™ & TIE Fighter™	
Pcs: 413	1999–2000

7151	EU NA AU AS
Sith Infiltrator™	
Sith Infiltrator™	
Pcs: 249	1999–2000

7121	Also included in: 65034 (2001)	Auch enthalten in: 65034 (2001)
7140	Similar to: 7142 (2002)	Ähnlich zu: 7142 (2002)
7141	Also included in: 65028 (2001)	Auch enthalten in: 65028 (2001)
7150	Similar to: 7152 (2002)	Ähnlich zu: 7152 (2002)

7161	EU NA AU AS	
Gungan Sub™		
Gungan Sub™		
Pcs: 382	1999–2000	

7171	EU NA AU AS	
Mos Espa Podrace™		
Mos Espa Podrace™		
Pcs: 926	1999–2000	

8246	EU NA AU AS	
Hydro Racer		
Air Boot		
Pcs: 52	1999–2000	Special

8247	EU NA AU AS	
Road Rebel		
Buggy		
Pcs: 48	1999–2000	Special

8251	EU NA AU AS	
Sonic Cycle		
Motorrad mit Federung		
Pcs: 94	1999–2000	

8252	EU NA AU AS	
Beach Buster		
Polizei Off-Roader		
Pcs: 184	1999–2000	

8253	EU NA AU AS	
Fire Helicopter		
Feuerlösch-Heli		
Pcs: 210	1999–2000	

8255	EU NA AU AS	
Rescue Bike		
Trick-Gespann		
Pcs: 204	1999–2000	

8268	EU NA AU AS	
Scorpion Attack		
Flieger jagt Hummer		
Pcs: 87	1999–2000	Special

7161	Also included in: 65034 (2001)	Auch enthalten in: 65034 (2001)

8269 EU NA AU AS

Cyber Stinger

Flight Action

Pcs: 345 | 1999–2000 | Special

8279 EU NA AU AS

4WD X-Track

4WD X-Track

Pcs: 456 | 1999–2001

8444 EU NA AU AS

Air Enforcer

Helikopter

Pcs: 309 | 1999–2000

8445 EU NA AU AS

Indy Storm

Rennbolide

Pcs: 454 | 1999–2001

8446 EU NA AU AS

Crane Truck

Monster Truck

Pcs: 583 | 1999–2000

8448 EU NA AU AS

Super Street Sensation

Design Car

Pcs: 1437 | 1999–2000

8450 EU NA AU AS

Mission Experience Pack

Cybermaster–The Mission

Pcs: 644 | 1999–2000

8500 EU NA AU AS

Fire Slizer

Feuer Slizer

Pcs: 36 | 1999–2000

8501 EU NA AU AS

Ice Slizer

Eis Slizer

Pcs: 37 | 1999–2000

8502	EU NA AU AS	
City Slizer		
City Slizer		
Pcs: 44	1999–2000	

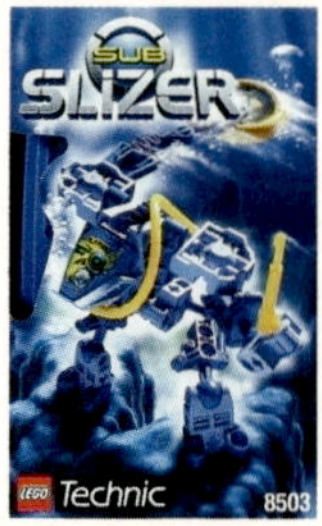

8503	EU NA AU AS	
Sub Slizer		
Tiefsee Slizer		
Pcs: 42	1999–2000	

8504	EU NA AU AS	
Judge Slizer		
Master Slizer		
Pcs: 47	1999–2000	Special

8505	EU NA AU AS	
Jungle Slizer		
Dschungel Slizer		
Pcs: 38	1999–2000	Special

8506	EU NA AU AS	
Rock Slizer		
Felsen Slizer		
Pcs: 32	1999–2000	

8507	EU NA AU AS	
Energy Slizer		
Energie Slizer		
Pcs: 38	1999–2000	

8508	EU NA AU AS	
Slizer Disc Pack		
Disk Box		
Pcs: 5	1999–2000	

8520	EU NA AU AS	
Millennium Slizer		
Millennium Slizer		
Pcs: 143	1999–2000	

9747	EU NA AU AS	
Robotics Invention System 1.5		
Robotics Invention System 1.5		
Pcs: 726	1999–2003	

9748 EU NA AU AS

Droid™ Developer Kit

Droid™ Developer Kit

Pcs: 665	1999–2001	

2000

1086	EU NA AU AS	
Bulk Bucket		
Steineeimer		
Pcs: 48	2000–2001	

1177	EU NA AU AS	
Santa's Truck		
Weihnachtsmann mit Auto		
Pcs: 26	2000–2002	Special

1196	EU NA AU AS	
Racing Cyclist		
Radrennfahrer		
Pcs: 6	2000	Special

1197	EU NA AU AS	
Motor Bike with Camera		
Motorradfahrer mit Kamera		
Pcs: 31	2000–2001	Special

1198	EU NA AU AS	
Bike Pit Stop		
Erfrischungsstand & Serviceteam		
Pcs: 78	2000	Special

1199	EU NA AU AS	
Car & Tribune		
Siegerehrung		
Pcs: 101	2000	Special

i	Set	English	German
i	1177	Coca-Cola Promo in Japan	Coca-Cola Promo in Japan
i	1196	Team Telekom Promo	Team Telekom Promo
i	1197	Team Telekom Promo	Team Telekom Promo
i	1198	Team Telekom Promo	Team Telekom Promo
i	1199	Team Telekom Promo	Team Telekom Promo

1237	EU NA AU AS
Honda Asimo Robot	
Honda Asimo Roboter	
Pcs: 61	2000–2001	Special

1261	EU NA AU AS
Picnic	
Picknick	
Pcs: 11	2000–2001	Special

1263	EU NA AU AS
Easter Bunny	
Der Osterhase	
Pcs: 31	2000–2002	Special

1264	EU NA AU AS
Hen with Chicken	
Osterküken	
Pcs: 28	2000–2001	Special

1272	EU NA AU AS
Turbo Racer	
Turbo Racer	
Pcs: 24	2000	Special

1273	EU NA AU AS
Rough Rider	
Rough Rider	
Pcs: 20	2000	Special

1278	EU NA AU AS
Johnny Thunder & Baby T	
Joe Freeman & Dinobaby	
Pcs: 23	2000	Special

1279	EU NA AU AS
Cunningham's Dinofinder	
Mr. Cunninghams Miniflieger	
Pcs: 17	2000	Special

1280	EU NA AU AS
Micro Copter	
Minicopter	
Pcs: 29	2000	Special

1272	Similar to: 1282 (2000), 6618 (2000)	Ähnlich zu: 1282 (2000), 6618 (2000)
1273	Similar to: 1283 (2000), 6619 (2000)	Ähnlich zu: 1283 (2000), 6619 (2000)
1278	Similar to: 5903 (2000); Kabaya Promo	Ähnlich zu: 5903 (2000); Kabaya Promo
1279	Kabaya Promo	Kabaya Promo
1280	Similar to: 5904 (2000); Kabaya Promo	Ähnlich zu: 5904 (2000); Kabaya Promo

1281	EU NA AU AS	
Mike's Dinohunter		
Mikes Kleinflugzeug		
Pcs: 20	2000	Special

1282	EU NA AU AS	
Blue Shark		
Blue Shark		
Pcs: 24	2000–2001	Special

1283	EU NA AU AS	
Red Scorpion		
Red Scorpion		
Pcs: 20	2000–2001	Special

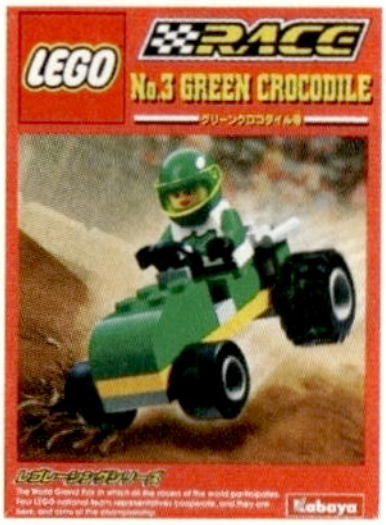

1284	EU NA AU AS	
Green Crocodile		
Green Crocodile		
Pcs: 23	2000–2001	Special

1285	EU NA AU AS	
Yellow Tiger		
Yellow Tiger		
Pcs: 23	2000–2001	Special

1286	EU NA AU AS	
King Richard		
König Richard		
Pcs: 22	2000	Special

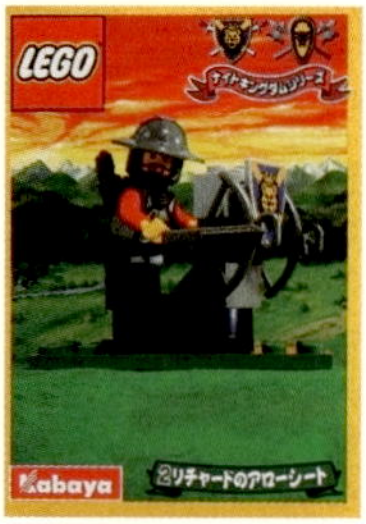

1287	EU NA AU AS	
Defense Archer		
Armbrustschütze		
Pcs: 15	2000	Special

1288	EU NA AU AS	
Fire Cart		
Feuerangriff		
Pcs: 22	2000	Special

1289	EU NA AU AS	
Catapult		
Steinschleuder		
Pcs: 22	2000	Special

1281	Kabaya Promo	Kabaya Promo
1282	Similar to: 1272 (2000), 6618 (2000); Kabaya Promo	Ähnlich zu: 1272 (2000), 6618 (2000); Kabaya Promo
1283	Similar to: 1273 (2000), 6619 (2000); Kabaya Promo	Ähnlich zu: 1273 (2000), 6619 (2000); Kabaya Promo
1284	Similar to: 6707 (2000); Kabaya Promo	Ähnlich zu: 6707 (2000); Kabaya Promo
1285/6	Kabaya Promo	Kabaya Promo
1287	Similar to: 4801 (2000), 4811 (2000); Kabaya Promo	Ähnlich zu: 4801 (2000), 4811 (2000); Kabaya Promo

ⓘ 1290	EU NA AU AS	
Volcano Climber		
Volcano Climber		
Pcs: 34	2000–2001	Special

ⓘ 1291	EU NA AU AS	
Dirt Bike		
Dirt Bike		
Pcs: 32	2000–2001	Special

ⓘ 1292	EU NA AU AS	
Ice Explorer		
Ice Explorer		
Pcs: 34	2000–2001	Special

ⓘ 1293	EU NA AU AS	
Swamp Craft		
Swamp Craft		
Pcs: 25	2000–2001	Special

ⓘ 1294	EU NA AU AS	
Fire Helicopter		
Feuerwehrhubschrauber		
Pcs: 26	2000–2001	Special

ⓘ 1295	EU NA AU AS	
Hovercraft		
Sumpfboot		
Pcs: 24	2000–2001	Special

ⓘ 1296	EU NA AU AS	
Excavator		
Schaufellader		
Pcs: 26	2000–2001	Special

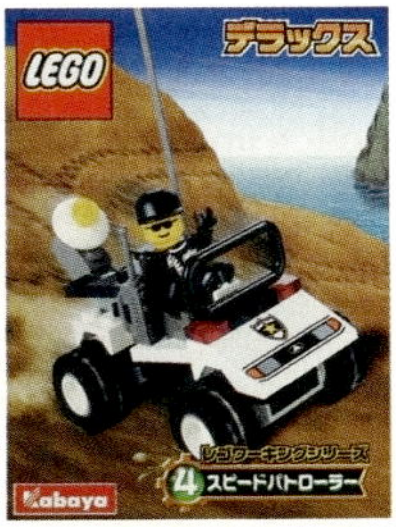

ⓘ 1297	EU NA AU AS	
Police Car		
Polizeibuggy		
Pcs: 34	2000–2001	Special

ⓘ 1349	EU NA AU AS	
Steven Spielberg MovieMaker Set		
Steven Spielberg MovieMaker Set		
Pcs: 459	2000–2002	

ⓘ	1288	Similar to: 4807 (2000); Kabaya Promo	Ähnlich zu: 4807 (2000); Kabaya Promo
ⓘ	1289	Kabaya Promo	Kabaya Promo
ⓘ	1290	Similar to: 8003 (2000); Kabaya Promo	Ähnlich zu: 8003 (2000); Kabaya Promo
ⓘ	1291	Similar to: 8004 (2000); Kabaya Promo	Ähnlich zu: 8004 (2000); Kabaya Promo
ⓘ	1292	Similar to: 8005 (2000); Kabaya Promo	Ähnlich zu: 8005 (2000); Kabaya Promo
ⓘ	1293	Similar to: 8006 (2000); Kabaya Promo	Ähnlich zu: 8006 (2000); Kabaya Promo

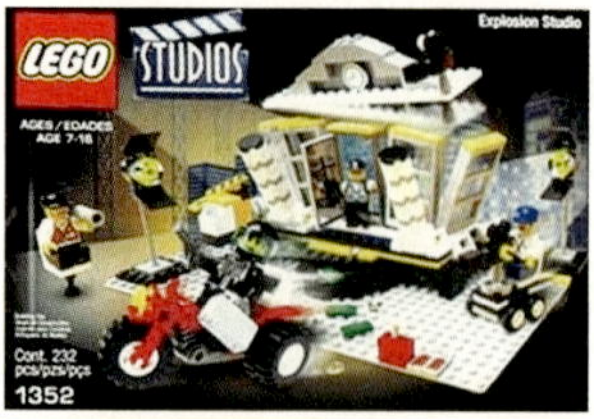

1352	EU NA AU AS	
Explosion Studio		
Banküberfall mit Explosion		
Pcs: 236	2000–2002	

1353	EU NA AU AS	
Car Stunt Studio		
Stuntautos		
Pcs: 166	2000–2002	

1354	EU NA AU AS	
Dino Head Attack		
Spezialeffekte-Dino		
Pcs: 94	2000–2001	

1355	EU NA AU AS	
Temple of Gloom		
Abenteuerdreh		
Pcs: 58	2000–2001	

1450	EU NA AU AS	
Small Bucket		
Kleiner Eimer		
Pcs: 50	2000–2001	Special

2077	EU NA AU AS	
My Bumble Bee		
Meine Hummel		
Pcs: 12	2000–2001	

2107	EU NA AU AS	
My Turtle Friend		
"Mein Freund die Schildkröte"		
Pcs: 37	2000–2001	

2225	EU NA AU AS	
Heavy Loader		
Muldenkipper		
Pcs: 70	2000–2002	

2250	EU NA AU AS	
Christmas Calendar		
Adventskalender		
Pcs: 240	2000	

i	Set	English	Deutsch
i	1294-1297	Kabaya Promo	Kabaya Promo
i	1450	Similar to: 2272 (1998), 2226 (1998)	Ähnlich zu: 2272 (1998), 2226 (1998)

2297	EU NA AU AS
Cute Animals	
Bau mit! Tolle Tierchen	
Pcs: 11	2000

2332	EU NA AU AS
XL Elephant Bucket	
Riesen Elafanten Eimer	
Pcs: 90	2000–2005

2400	EU NA AU AS
Cute Vehicles	
Bau mit! Bunte Brummer	
Pcs: 32	2000

2468	EU NA AU AS
My First Rattle	
Baby-Rassel	
Pcs: 2	2000–2001

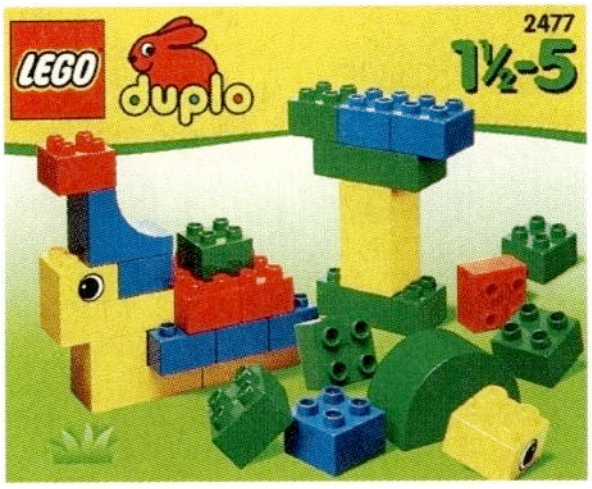

2477	EU NA AU AS
Basic Set	
Grundbaukasten	
Pcs: 30	2000

2503	EU NA AU AS
Musical Apple	
Musikapfel	
Pcs: 2	2000–2001

2514	EU NA AU AS
Activity Friends	
Erlebniskette	
Pcs: 9	2000–2003

2517	EU NA AU AS
Rattle Friends	
Kleine Rassel-Freunde	
Pcs: 3	2000

2522	EU NA AU AS
Play a Story	
Baby Spiel-Buch	
Pcs: 3	2000–2001

i	2503	Similar to: 2973 (2001)	Ähnlich zu: 2973 (2001)

2524	EU NA AU AS	
My Racing Bugs		
Flotte Käfer		
Pcs: 4	2000–2001	

2526	EU NA AU AS	
Tim & Tom's Adventure		
Tim & Toms Abenteuer		
Pcs: 2	2000	

2556	EU NA AU AS	
Ferrari Formula 1 Racing Car		
Ferrari Formel 1-Rennwagen		
Pcs: 580	2000–2000	Special

2587	EU NA AU AS	
My First Train		
Mein erster Zug		
Pcs: 7	2000–2001	

2589	EU NA AU AS	
Timmy on Tour		
Timmy auf Tour		
Pcs: 10	2000–2002	

2591	EU NA AU AS	
Happy Explorers		
Entdeckungsreise		
Pcs: 19	2000–2002	

2592	EU NA AU AS	
Disney's Baby Mickey & Minnie		
Disney Babies		
Pcs: 18	2000–2001	

2593	EU NA AU AS	
Disney's Baby Mickey		
Baby Mickey		
Pcs: 9	2000–2001	

2594	EU NA AU AS	
Disney's Baby Mickey & Minnie		
Baby Mickey & Baby Minnie		
Pcs: 11	2000–2002	

2556	Shell Promo	Shell Promo

2751	EU NA AU AS
Egg Fun	
Spiel-Eier	
Pcs: 9	2000

2797	EU NA AU AS
Happy Bucket	
Eimer Grundelemente	
Pcs: 49	2000–2001

2799	EU NA AU AS
XL Fun-time Bucket	
Riesen Eimer Haus und Hof	
Pcs: 90	2000

2825	EU NA AU AS
The Meadowsweets	
Die weißen Maiglöckchen	
Pcs: 16	2000

2827	EU NA AU AS
Read, Listen & Play Box	
Das Land der Roten Erdbeeren	
Pcs: 45	2000

2904	EU NA AU AS
Motorbike	
Motorrad	
Pcs: 12	2000–2002

2909	EU NA AU AS
Helicopter	
Hubschrauber	
Pcs: 19	2000–2002

2912	EU NA AU AS
Racing Car	
Rennwagen	
Pcs: 17	2000–2002

2913	EU NA AU AS
Tread Trackers	
Baufahrzeuge	
Pcs: 31	2000–2002

2914 EU NA AU AS

Rescue Base	
Rettungsstation	
Pcs: 47	2000

2916 EU NA AU AS

MyBot	
MyBot	
Pcs: 32	2000–2002

2931 EU NA AU AS

Push Locomotive	
Schiebezug	
Pcs: 11	2000–2005

2932 EU NA AU AS

Train Starter Set with Motor	
Eisenbahn Starterset	
Pcs: 33	2000–2002

2933 EU NA AU AS

Train Deluxe Set with Motor	
Eisenbahn Superset	
Pcs: 79	2000–2002

2936 EU NA AU AS

Station	
Bahnhof	
Pcs: 44	2000–2002

2937 EU NA AU AS

Supplementary Wagon	
Autotransportwaggon	
Pcs: 10	2000–2002

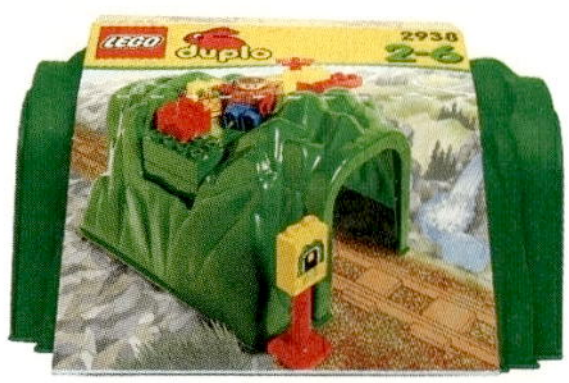

2938 EU NA AU AS

Train Tunnel	
Tunnel	
Pcs: 16	2000–2002

2942 EU NA AU AS

Playhouse	
Spielhaus	
Pcs: 91	2000–2002

i	2933	With poster	Mit Poster

2967	EU NA AU AS	
Special Tubes		
Röhren		
Pcs: 38	2000–2001	

2968	EU NA AU AS	
Basic Zoo		
Zoo		
Pcs: 49	2000	

2989	EU NA AU AS	
The Big Honeypot		
Der große Honigtopf		
Pcs: 50	2000–2001	

2990	EU NA AU AS	
Tigger's Treehouse		
Tiggers Baumhaus		
Pcs: 35	2000–2001	

3048	EU NA AU AS	
Medium Idea Bucket		
Mittlerer Ideeneimer		
Pcs: 49	2000–2002	Special

3049	EU NA AU AS	
XL Idea Bucket		
Riesen Ideeneimer		
Pcs: 78	2000–2002	Special

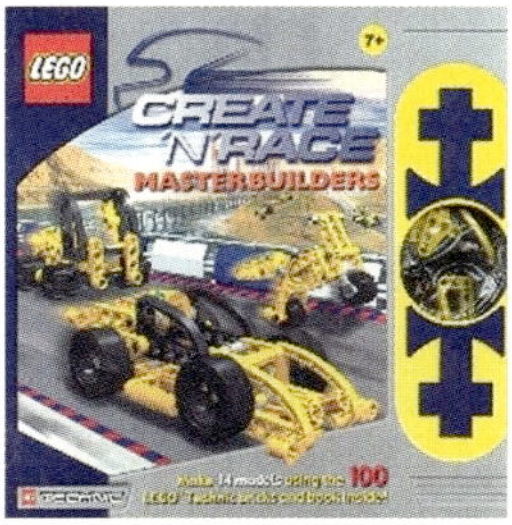

3057	EU NA AU AS	
Masterbuilders: Create 'n' Race		
Masterbuilders: Create 'n' Race		
Pcs: 105	2000–2002	Special

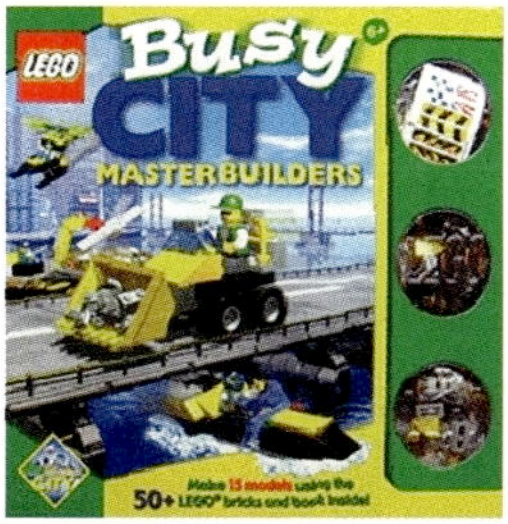

3058	EU NA AU AS	
Masterbuilders: Busy City		
Masterbuilders: Busy City		
Pcs: 78	2000–2002	Special

3059	EU NA AU AS	
Masterbuilders: Mars Mission		
Masterbuilders: Mars Mission		
Pcs: 92	2000–2002	Special

i 3048	Similar to: 4836 (2001), 4827 (2001)	Ähnlich zu: 4836 (2001), 4827 (2001)

3099 — EU NA AU AS

Storage Chest

Sammelkiste

Pcs: 142 | 2000–2004

3148 — EU NA AU AS

Carla and the Bear Cubs

Carla im Wintercamp

Pcs: 146 | 2000–2001

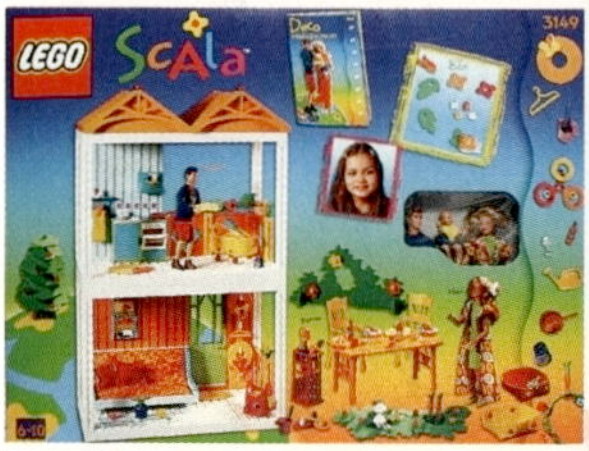

3149 — EU NA AU AS

Happy Home

Villa Sonnenschein

Pcs: 270 | 2000–2002

3150 — EU NA AU AS

Puppy Playground

Kleine Hundefreunde

Pcs: 106 | 2000–2002

3151 — EU NA AU AS

Emma on the Move

Emma auf Skitour

Pcs: 65 | 2000–2002

3152 — EU NA AU AS

Playroom for Baby Thomas

Baby Thomas' Kinderzimmer

Pcs: 88 | 2000–2002

3155 — EU NA AU AS

Olivia in Smooth Dress

Olivia im Superdress

Pcs: 8 | 2000–2001

3156 — EU NA AU AS

Hot Wear for Women

Schicke Damenmode

Pcs: 3 | 2000–2001

3157 — EU NA AU AS

Cool Wear for Girls

Coole Mode für Mädchen

Pcs: 2 | 2000–2001

3158	EU NA AU AS	
Christian in Tough Wear		
Christian im Freizeitlook		
Pcs: 8	2000–2001	

3159	EU NA AU AS	
Celebration		
Geburtstagsfeier		
Pcs: 45	2000–2001	

3336	EU NA AU AS	
Green Tub		
Grüne Bausteinebox		
Pcs: 90	2000	Special

3340	EU NA AU AS	
The Dark Side™		
The Dark Side™		
Pcs: 27	2000–2002	

3341	EU NA AU AS	
Luke™, Han Solo™ & Boba Fett™		
Luke™, Han Solo™ & Boba Fett™		
Pcs: 22	2000–2002	

3342	EU NA AU AS	
Chewbacca™ & 2 Biker Scouts™		
Chewbacca™ & 2 Biker Scouts™		
Pcs: 23	2000–2002	

3343	EU NA AU AS	
Battle Droids™		
Battle Droids™		
Pcs: 33	2000–2002	

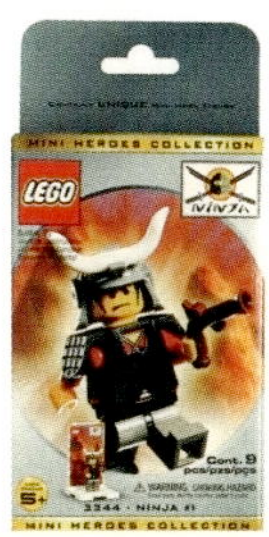

3344	EU NA AU AS	
Shogun Warlord		
Shogun Warlord		
Pcs: 11	2000–2002	

3345	EU NA AU AS	
Black Ninja & Samurai		
Schwarzer Ninja & Samurai		
Pcs: 21	2000–2002	

i	3336	Similar to: 5350 (2004)	Ähnlich zu: 5350 (2004)

3346 EU NA AU AS

Green Ninja & Samurai Lord

Green Ninja & Samurai Lord

Pcs: 23 | 2000–2002

3347 EU NA AU AS

Rock Raiders Chief

Rock Raiders Chief

Pcs: 10 | 2000–2002

3348 EU NA AU AS

Docs, Bandit & Sparks

Docs, Bandit & Sparks

Pcs: 21 | 2000–2002

3349 EU NA AU AS

Axel, Docs & Jet

Axel, Docs & Jet

Pcs: 24 | 2000–2002

3350 EU NA AU AS

Axel, Fred & Paula

Axel, Fred & Paula

Pcs: 27 | 2000–2002

3351 EU NA AU AS

Dave, Garry & Pete

Dave, Garry & Pete

Pcs: 19 | 2000–2002

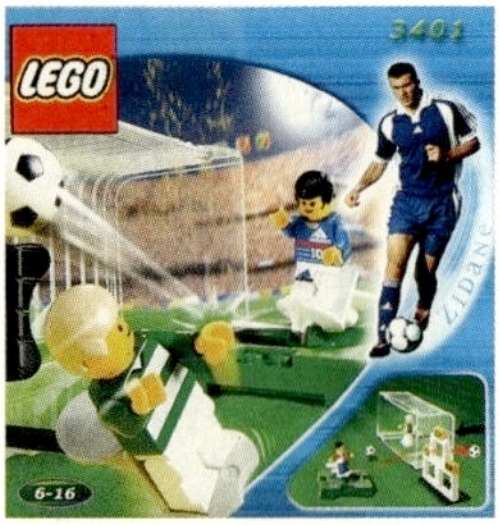

3401 EU NA AU AS

Kicker Box

Kicker-Box

Pcs: 24 | 2000–2001

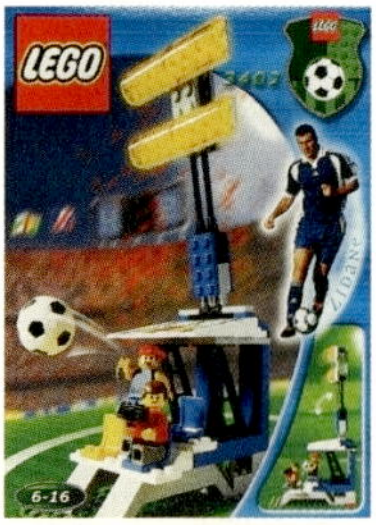

3402 EU NA AU AS

Grandstand

Zuschauertribüne

Pcs: 61 | 2000–2001

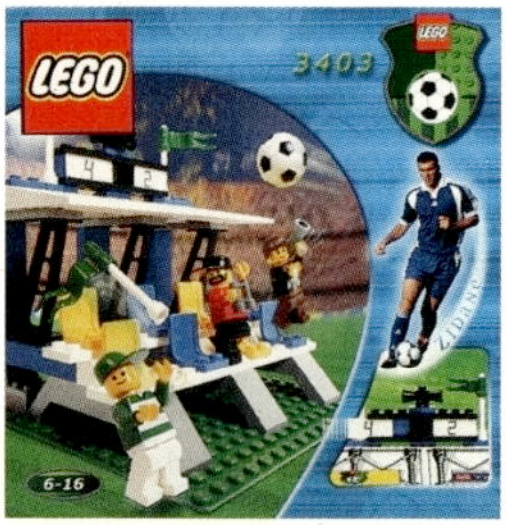

3403 EU NA AU AS

Grandstand with Scoreboard

Fantribüne mit Anzeigetafel

Pcs: 79 | 2000–2001

i	3401	Additional release with Zidane Figure	Gab es auch mit Zidane Minifigur

3404 EU NA AU AS

Football Team Coaches

Mannschaftsbus

Pcs: 132 | 2000–2002

3405 EU NA AU AS

Football Team Coaches

Mannschaftsbus

Pcs: 132 | 2000–2002

3406 EU NA AU AS

Football Team Coaches

Mannschaftsbus

Pcs: 132 | 2000–2002

3407 EU NA AU AS

Football Team Coaches

Mannschaftsbus

Pcs: 132 | 2000–2002

3408 EU NA AU AS

Main Entrance with Ground Staff

Haupteingang mit Stadion-Crew

Pcs: 224 | 2000–2002

3409 EU NA AU AS

Championship Challenge

Arena der Champions

Pcs: 304 | 2000–2001

3410 EU NA AU AS

Accessory Football Set

Fußball Ausbau-Set

Pcs: 53 | 2000–2001

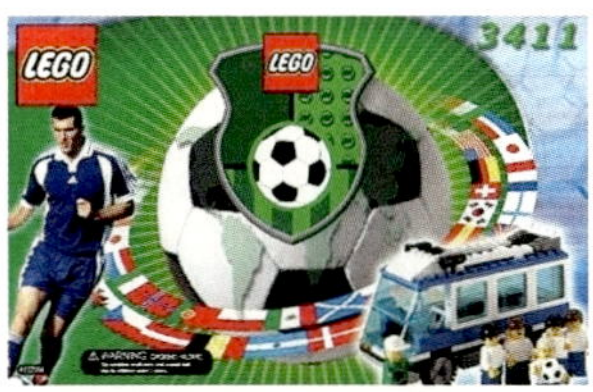

3411 EU NA AU AS

Team Transport with Soccer Ball

Mannschaftsbus mit Fußball

Pcs: 135 | 2000–2001

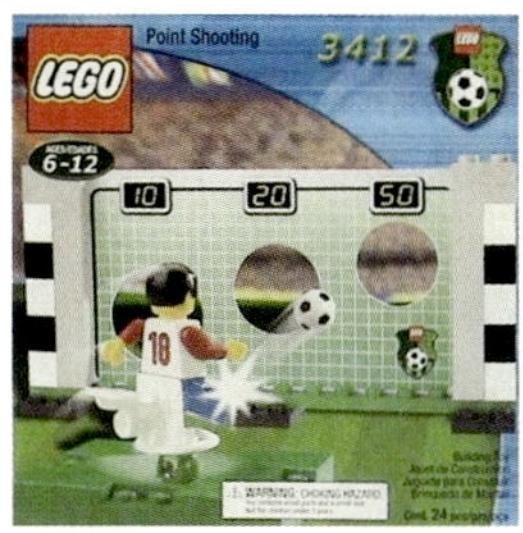

3412 EU NA AU AS

Point Shooting

Zielschießen

Pcs: 24 | 2000

i	3404	D, A, PL, RU, CZ	D, A, PL, RU, CZ
i	3405	Similar to: 3411 (2000); SF, ENG, SCO, S, NL	Ähnlich zu: 3411 (2000); SF, ENG, SCO, S, NL
i	3406	USA, CD, BRA, MEX , ARG	USA, CD, BRA, MEX , ARG
i	3407	CH, E, P	CH, E, P
i	3411	Similar to: 3405 (2000)	Ähnlich zu: 3405 (2000)
i	3412	Similar to: 3418 (2001)	Ähnlich zu: 3418 (2001)

3413	EU NA AU AS	
Goalkeeper		
Torwart		
Pcs: 30	2000	

3414	EU NA AU AS	
Precision Shooting		
Präzisionsschießen		
Pcs: 24	2000	

3439	EU NA AU AS	
Spy Runner		
Spy Runner		
Pcs: 120	2000–2001	

3443	EU NA AU AS	
Mosaic		
Mosaik		
Pcs: 2427	2000–2005	

3450	EU NA AU AS	
Statue of Liberty		
Freiheitsstatue		
Pcs: 2896	2000–2002	

3468	EU NA AU AS	
1x4 Bricks Black		
1x4 Steine, schwarz		
Pcs: 50	2000–2003	

3723	EU NA AU AS	
Minifigure		
Minifigur		
Pcs: 1857	2000–2002	

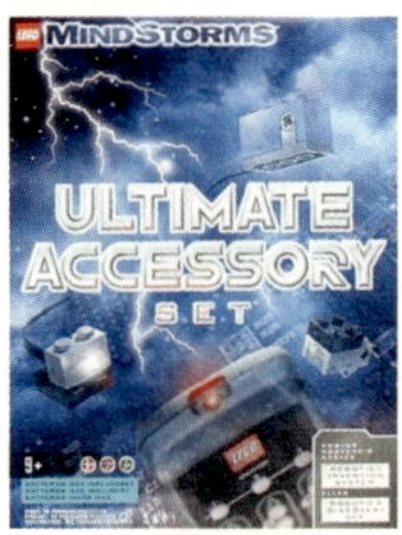

3801	EU NA AU AS	
Ultimate Accessory Set		
Ultimate Accessory Set		
Pcs: 45	2000–2002	

3900	EU NA AU AS	
Scala Bracelet		
Armband		
Pcs: 20	2000–2002	Special

i	3414	Similar to: 3419 (2001)	Ähnlich zu: 3419 (2001)

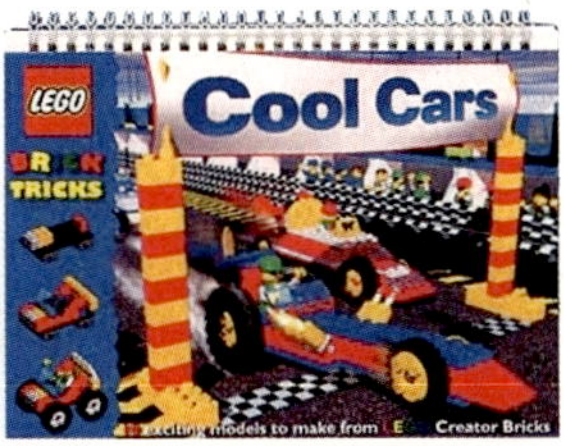

4006	EU NA AU AS	
Brick Tricks: Cool Cars		
Brick Tricks: Cool Cars		
Pcs: -	2000–2001	

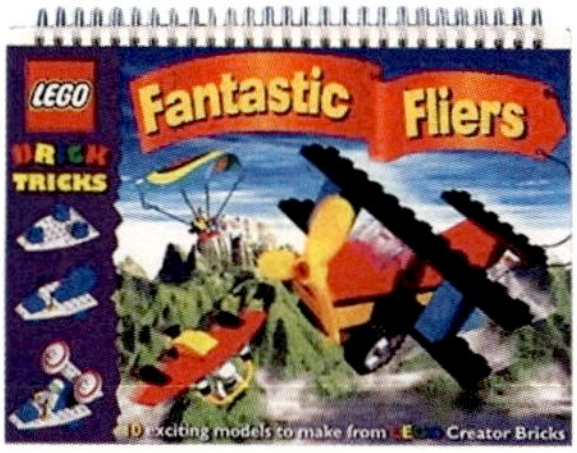

4007	EU NA AU AS	
Brick Tricks: Fantastic Fliers		
Brick Tricks, Fantastic Fliers		
Pcs: -	2000–2001	

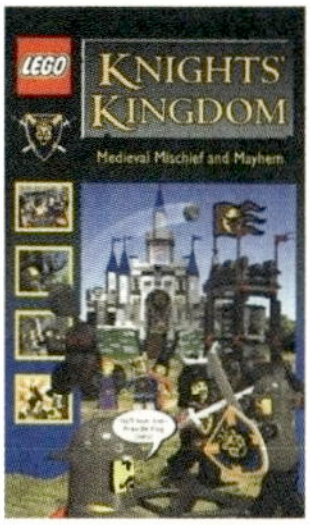

4008	EU NA AU AS	
Medieval Mischief and Mayhem		
Medieval Mischief and Mayhem		
Pcs: -	2000–2001	

4009	EU NA AU AS	
High Adventure Deep Underground		
High Adventure Deep Underground		
Pcs: 1	2000–2001	Special

4122	EU NA AU AS	
Creative with Bricks		
Kreativ mit Steinen		
Pcs: 201	2000–2001	Special

4164	EU NA AU AS	
Mickey's Fire Engine		
Mickeys Feuerwehrauto		
Pcs: 27	2000–2002	

4165	EU NA AU AS	
Minnie's Birthday Party		
Minnies Geburtstagsparty		
Pcs: 85	2000–2001	

4166	EU NA AU AS	
Mickey's Garage		
Mickeys Autowerkstatt		
Pcs: 94	2000–2002	

4167	EU NA AU AS	
Mickey's Mansion		
Mickeys Haus		
Pcs: 123	2000–2001	

4178	EU NA AU AS	
Mickey's Fishing Trip		
Mickeys Angelausflug		
Pcs: 107	2000–2001	

4249	EU NA AU AS	
Basic Suitcase		
Basic Koffer		
Pcs: -	2000–2001	Special

4801	EU NA AU AS	
Defense Archer		
Armbrustschütze		
Pcs: 15	2000	

4806	EU NA AU AS	
Axe Cart		
Axtkarren		
Pcs: 28	2000	

4807	EU NA AU AS	
Fire Attack		
Feuerangriff		
Pcs: 24	2000–2001	

4811	EU NA AU AS	
Defense Archer		
Armbrustschütze		
Pcs: 15	2000	Special

4816	EU NA AU AS	
Knight's Catapult		
Ritterkatapult		
Pcs: 52	2000	

4817	EU NA AU AS	
Dungeon		
Verlies		
Pcs: 39	2000	

4818	EU NA AU AS	
Dragon Rider		
Cedric, der Drachenreiter		
Pcs: 17	2000	

i	Set	English	Deutsch
i	4801	Similar to: 1287 (2000), 4811 (2000)	Ähnlich zu: 1287 (2000), 4811 (2000)
i	4807	Similar to: 1288 (2000)	Ähnlich zu: 1288 (2000)
i	4811	Similar to: 1287 (2000), 4801 (2000)	Ähnlich zu: 1287 (2000), 4801 (2000)

4819 EU NA AU AS

Rebel Chariot	
Kutsche der Rebellen	
Pcs: 50	2000

5206 EU NA AU AS

Speed Computer	
Speed Computer	
Pcs: 31	2000–2002

5218 EU NA

Pneumatic Pack	
Pneumatic Pack	
Pcs: 147	2000–2002

5219 EU NA

Tyres and Drives Pack	
Reifen Pack	
Pcs: 28	2000–2002

5220 EU NA

Styling Pack	
Styling Pack	
Pcs: 224	2000–2002

5221 EU NA

Motor Base Pack	
Motor Base Pack	
Pcs: 59	2000–2002

5222 EU NA

Chassis Pack	
Chassis Pack	
Pcs: 142	2000–2002

5823 EU NA AU AS

Millimy's Bedroom	
Die Stube der kleinen Fee	
Pcs: 37	2000–2001

5824 EU NA AU AS

Millimy's House	
Das Schloß der kleinen Fee	
Pcs: 73	2000–2001

5825	EU NA AU AS
Fairy Queen's Magical Place	
Die Feenkönigin	
Pcs: 53	2000–2001

5826	EU NA AU AS
The Queen's Chamber	
Das Gemach der Königin	
Pcs: 79	2000–2001

5903	EU NA AU AS
Johnny Thunder & Baby T	
Joe Freeman & Dinobaby	
Pcs: 23	2000–2001

5904	EU NA AU AS
Minicopter	
Minicopter	
Pcs: 29	2000–2001

5911	EU NA AU AS
Johnny Thunder's Plane	
Joe Freemans Flugzeug	
Pcs: 23	2000

5912	EU NA AU AS
Mike's Swamp Boat	
Mikes Sumpfboot	
Pcs: 19	2000

5913	EU NA AU AS
Dr. Kilroy's Car	
Prof. Kilroys Auto	
Pcs: 21	2000

5914	EU NA AU AS
Sam Sanister & Baby T	
Sam Sanister & Dino Baby	
Pcs: 23	2000

5920	EU NA AU AS
Island Racer	
Insel-Racer	
Pcs: 56	2000

i	5903	Similar to: 1278 (2000)	Ähnlich zu: 1278 (2000)
i	5904	Similar to: 1280 (2000)	Ähnlich zu: 1280 (2000)

5921 EU NA AU AS

Research Glider

Forschungs-Gleitflieger

Pcs: 58	2000–2001	

5934 EU NA AU AS

Track Master

Dino Fährtenleser

Pcs: 92	2000–2001	

5935 EU NA AU AS

Island Hopper

Insel-Hopper

Pcs: 210	2000–2002	

5955 EU NA AU AS

All Terrain Trapper

Universalfallen

Pcs: 193	2000–2001	

5975 EU NA AU AS

T-Rex Transport

T-Rex Transport

Pcs: 331	2000–2002	

5987 EU NA AU AS

Dino Research Compound

Dino-Forschungsstation

Pcs: 630	2000–2001	

6026 EU NA AU AS

King Leo

König Richard

Pcs: 21	2000–2001	

6032 EU NA AU AS

Catapult Crusher

Katapult-Zerstörer

Pcs: 58	2000–2001	

6091 EU NA AU AS

King Leo's Castle

Königsburg

Pcs: 541	2000–2001	

i	6091	US version of EU-6098 (2000); sometimes with Plan 6098; Not 6091/6098	US Version von EU-6098 (2000); teilweise mit Plan 6098, nicht 6091/6098

6094	EU NA AU AS
Guarded Treasury	
Bewachte Schatzkammer	
Pcs: 103	2000–2002

6095	EU NA AU AS
Royal Joust	
Königliches Tunier	
Pcs: 109	2000–2001

6096	EU NA AU AS
Bull's Attack	
Belagerer-Angriff	
Pcs: 320	2000–2003

6098	EU NA AU AS
King Leo's Castle	
Königsburg	
Pcs: 541	2000–2003

6423	EU NA AU AS
Tow-away Truck	
Abschlepptruck	
Pcs: 34	2000–2001

6470	EU NA AU AS
Mini-Dumper	
Mini-Kipper	
Pcs: 25	2000–2001

6471	EU NA AU AS
4WD Police Patrol	
4-Rad Polizei-Patrouille	
Pcs: 30	2000–2001

6474	EU NA AU AS
Wheeled Front Shovel	
Frontschaufellader	
Pcs: 48	2000–2001

6477	EU NA AU AS
Firefighter's Lift Truck	
Feuerwehr Lift-Truck	
Pcs: 114	2000–2001

i	6098	EU version of Set 6091 (2000) (USA); Includes Plan 6091/6098 (2000)	EU Version zu Set 6091 (2000) (USA); enthält Plan 6091/6098 (2000)

ⓘ 6478	EU NA AU AS
Fire Station	
Feuerwehr-Hauptquatier	
Pcs: 243	2000–2001

ⓘ 6519	EU NA AU AS
Turbo Tiger	
Turbo Tiger	
Pcs: 48	2000–2001

ⓘ 6520	EU NA AU AS
Mobile Outpost	
Mobiler Vorposten	
Sets: 231	2000–2001

ⓘ 6569	NA AU
Polar Scout	
Polar-Scout	
Sets: 2	2000	Special

ⓘ 6573	EU NA AU AS
Arctic Expedition	
Expedition	
Pcs: 123	2000–2001

ⓘ 6575	EU NA AU AS
Polar Base	
Polar-Basis	
Pcs: 453	2000–2001

ⓘ 6577	EU NA AU AS
Snow Scooter	
Schnee-Scooter	
Pcs: 22	2000–2001

ⓘ 6578	NA
Polar Explorer	
Polar-Explorer	
Pcs: 21	2000	Special

ⓘ 6579	EU NA AU AS
Ice Surfer	
Eis-Surfer	
Pcs: 43	2000–2001

ⓘ	6577	Similar to: 6626 (2000)	Ähnlich zu: 6626 (2000)

6586	EU NA AU AS	
Polar Scout		
Polar-Scout		
Pcs: 63	2000–2001	

6600	EU NA AU AS	
Highway Construction		
Highway-Konstruktion		
Pcs: 321	2000–2002	

6602	EU NA AU AS	
Scorpion Buggy		
Scorpion Buggy		
Pcs: 81	2000–2001	

6616	EU NA AU AS	
Rocket Dragster		
Rocket Dragster		
Pcs: 150	2000–2001	

6617	EU NA AU AS	
Tough Truck Rally		
Große Hindernis-Ralley		
Pcs: 393	2000–2001	

6618	EU NA AU AS	
Turbo Racer		
Turbo Racer		
Pcs: 24	2000–2001	

6619	EU NA AU AS	
Rough Rider		
Rough Rider		
Pcs: 20	2000–2001	

6626	EU NA AU AS	
Snow Scooter		
Schnee-Scooter		
Pcs: 21	2000	Special

6707	EU NA AU AS	
Speed Buggy		
Speed Buggy		
Pcs: 23	2000–2001	

i	Set	Similar to	Ähnlich zu
i	6618	Similar to: 1272 (2000), 1282 (2000)	Ähnlich zu: 1272 (2000), 1282 (2000)
i	6619	Similar to: 1273 (2000), 1283 (2000)	Ähnlich zu: 1273 (2000), 1283 (2000)
i	6626	Similar to: 6577 (2000)	Ähnlich zu: 6577 (2000)
i	6707	Similar to: 1284 (2000)	Ähnlich zu: 1284 (2000)

6713	EU NA AU AS
Grip 'n' Go Challenge	
Grip-and-Go-Wettkampf	
Pcs: 297	2000–2001

6714	EU NA AU AS
Speed Dragster	
Speed Dragster	
Pcs: 80	2000–2001

7104	EU NA AU AS
Desert Skiff™	
Desert Skiff™	
Pcs: 55	2000–2001

7115	EU NA AU AS
Gungan™ Patrol	
Gungan™ Patrol	
Pcs: 83	2000–2001

7124	EU NA AU AS
Flash Speeder™	
Flash Speeder™	
Pcs: 108	2000–2001

7134	EU NA AU AS
A-wing Fighter™	
A-wing Fighter™	
Pcs: 125	2000–2001

7144	EU NA AU AS
Slave I™	
Slave I™	
Pcs: 166	2000–2001

7155	EU NA AU AS
Trade Federation AAT™	
Trade Federation AAT™	
Pcs: 162	2000–2001

7159	EU NA AU AS
Podracing™ Bucket	
Podracing™-Eimer	
Pcs: 292	2000–2001

7104	Included in: 65030 (2001)	Enthalten in: 65030 (2001)
7115	Included in: 65028 (2001)	Enthalten in: 65028 (2001)
7124	Included in: 65028 (2001)	Enthalten in: 65028 (2001)
7144	Included in: 65030 (2001)	Enthalten in: 65030 (2001)

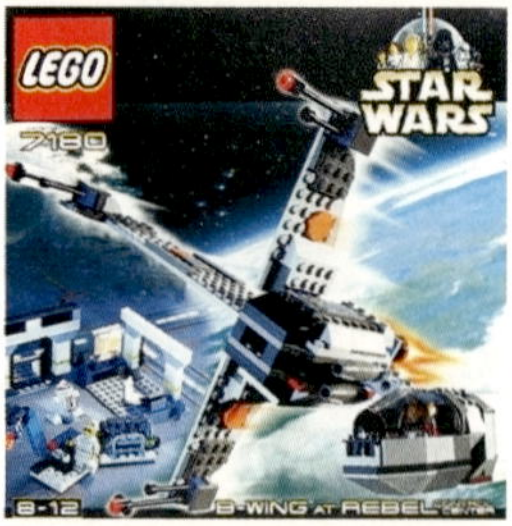

7180	EU NA AU AS
B-wing™ at Rebel Control Center	
B-wing™ & Rebel Control Center	
Pcs: 353	2000–2001
Rating: 2/6	

7181	EU NA AU AS
TIE Interceptor™	
TIE Interceptor™	
Pcs: 706	2000–2001
Rating: 2/6	

7184	EU NA AU AS
Trade Federation MTT™	
Trade Federation MTT™	
Pcs: 472	2000–2001
Rating: 2/6	

7190	EU NA AU AS
Millennium Falcon™	
Millennium Falcon™	
Pcs: 671	2000–2002
Rating: 2/6	

7191	EU NA AU AS
X-wing Fighter™	
X-wing Fighter™	
Pcs: 1316	2000–2002
Rating: 2/6	

7320	NA
Vega	
Vega	
Pcs: 5	2000–2001	Special
Rating: 4/6	

7321	NA
Mizar	
Mizar	
Pcs: 5	2000–2001	Special
Rating: 4/6	

7322	NA
Altair	
Altair	
Pcs: 5	2000–2001	Special
Rating: 4/6	

7323	NA
Guard	
Wächter	
Pcs: 5	2000–2001	Special
Rating: 4/6	

ⓘ 7975	EU NA AU AS	
Large Bucket		
Großer Eimer		
Pcs: 107	2000–2002	Special

ⓘ 8000	EU NA AU AS	
Pit Droid™		
Pit Droid™		
Pcs: 236	2000–2001	

ⓘ 8001	EU NA AU AS	
Battle Droid™		
Battle Droid™		
Pcs: 363	2000–2001	

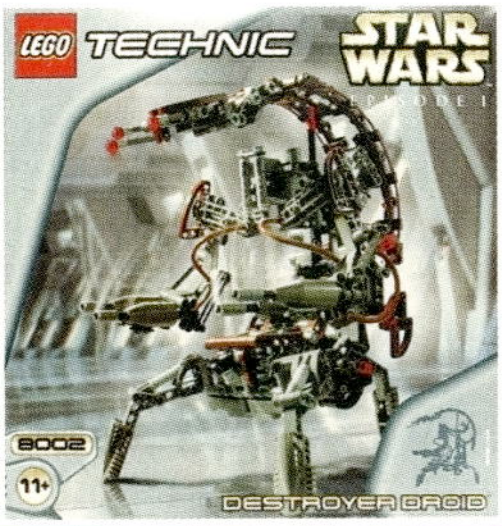

ⓘ 8002	EU NA AU AS	
Destroyer Droid™		
Destroyer Droid™		
Pcs: 654	2000–2001	

ⓘ 8003	EU NA AU AS	
Volcano Climber		
Vulcano Climber		
Pcs: 34	2000	Special

ⓘ 8004	EU NA AU AS	
Dirt Bike		
Dirt Bike		
Pcs: 32	2000	Special

ⓘ 8005	EU NA AU AS	
Ice Explorer		
Ice Explorer		
Pcs: 34	2000	Special

ⓘ 8006	EU NA AU AS	
Swamp Craft		
Swamp Craft		
Pcs: 25	2000	Special

ⓘ 8236	EU NA AU AS	
Bike Burner		
Bike Burner		
Pcs: 61	2000–2001	

ⓘ	7975	Similar to: 7969 (2001)	Ähnlich zu: 7969 (2001)
ⓘ	8003	Similar to: 1290 (2000)	Ähnlich zu: 1290 (2000)
ⓘ	8004	Similar to: 1291 (2000)	Ähnlich zu: 1291 (2000)
ⓘ	8005	Similar to: 1292 (2000)	Ähnlich zu: 1292 (2000)
ⓘ	8006	Similar to: 1293 (2000)	Ähnlich zu: 1293 (2000)

8237	EU NA AU AS
Slammer Racer	
Slammer Racer	
Pcs: 115	2000–2001

8238	EU NA AU AS
Slammer Dragsters	
Slammer Dragster	
Pcs: 201	2000–2001

8300	EU NA AU AS
Action Figures	
Action Figuren	
Pcs: 7	2000–2002

8305	EU NA AU AS
Duel Bikes	
Duel Bikes	
Pcs: 200	2000–2002

8307	EU NA AU AS
Turbo Racer	
Turbo Racer	
Pcs: 396	2000–2002

8457	EU NA AU AS
Power Puller	
Power Puller	
Pcs: 982	2000–2001

8458	EU NA AU AS
Silver Champion	
Silver Champion	
Pcs: 1443	2000–2002

8509	EU NA AU AS
Swamp	
Swamp	
Pcs: 45	2000–2001

8510	EU NA AU AS
Lava	
Lava	
Pcs: 32	2000–2001

8509	Included in: 880010 (2000)	Enthalten in: 880010 (2000)
8510	Included in: 880010 (2000)	Enthalten in: 880010 (2000)

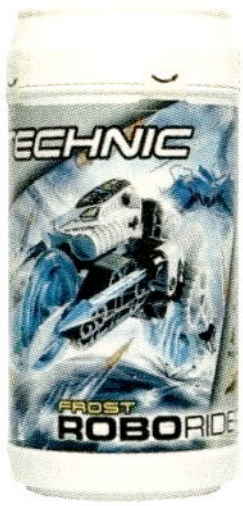

8511	EU NA AU AS
Frost	
Frost	
Pcs: 44	2000–2001

8512	EU NA AU AS
Onyx	
Onyx	
Pcs: 39	2000–2001

8513	EU NA AU AS
Dust	
Dust	
Pcs: 46	2000–2001

8514	EU NA AU AS
Power	
Power	
Pcs: 31	2000–2001

8515	EU NA AU AS
RoboRider Wheels	
RoboRider Räder	
Pcs: 4	2000–2001

8516	EU NA AU AS
The Boss	
The Boss	
Pcs: 128	2000–2001

8521	EU NA AU AS
Flare Slizer	
Flammen Slizer	
Pcs: 45	2000

8522	EU NA AU AS
Spark Slizer	
Blitz Slizer	
Pcs: 35	2000

8523	EU NA AU AS
Blaster Slizer	
Donner Slizer	
Pcs: 92	2000

78777	EU NA AU AS
Alien Discovery	
Alien Discovery	
Sets: 3	2000–2001	Special

79974	EU NA AU AS
Race Pack	
Race Pack	
Pcs: 28	2000	Special

2001

ⓘ 1100	EU NA AU AS	
Sky Pirates		
Schmugglerflugzeug		
Pcs: 108	2001–2002	Special

ⓘ 1149	EU NA AU AS	
Air Police		
Polizeihubschrauber		
Pcs: 24	2001–2002	Special

ⓘ 1166	EU NA AU AS	
Stack-n-Learn Gift Item		
Stapeln-und-Lernen-Geschenkbox		
Pcs: 42	2001–2002	

ⓘ 1195	NA	
Alien Encounter		
Alienangriff		
Pcs: 48	2001	Special

ⓘ 1201	EU NA AS	
Chicken Run		
Huhn		
Pcs: 6	2001–2002	Special

ⓘ 1202	EU	
Single Racers Figure Pack		
Rennfahrer Einzelfigur		
Pcs: 1	2001	Special

ⓘ	1195	Quaker Cereal Promo	Quaker Cereal Promo
ⓘ	1201	Similar to: 5437 (2002)	Ähnlich zu: 5437 (2002)

1238	EU NA AU AS	
Medium Bucket		
Mittlerer Eimer		
Pcs: -	2001–2002	

1239	EU NA AU AS	
Subzero		
Subzero		
Pcs: 4	2001	Special

1351	EU NA AU AS	
Moving Backdrop Studio		
Bewegungs-Simulationsset		
Pcs: 218	2001	

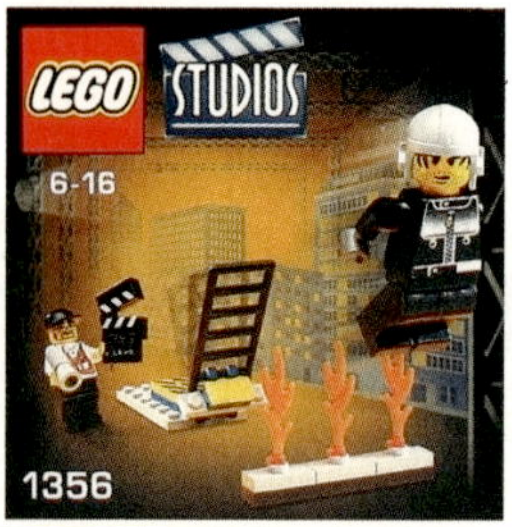

1356	EU NA AU AS	
Stuntman Catapult		
Stuntman-Katapult		
Pcs: 30	2001–2002	

1357	EU NA AU AS	
Cameraman		
Kameramann		
Pcs: 27	2001–2002	

1360	EU NA AU AS	
Director's Copter		
Regisseur und Hubschrauber		
Pcs: 23	2001–2002	

1361	EU NA AU AS	
Camera Car		
Kamerafahrzeug		
Pcs: 21	2001–2002	

1362	EU NA AU AS	
Air Boat		
Rennboot		
Pcs: 30	2001–2002	

1363	EU NA AU AS	
Stunt Go-Kart		
Stunt Go-Kart		
Pcs: 26	2001–2002	

i	Set	English	Deutsch
i	1360	Similar to: 1421 (2001)	Ähnlich zu: 1421 (2001)
i	1361	Similar to: 1422 (2001)	Ähnlich zu: 1422 (2001)
i	1362	Similar to: 1423 (2001)	Ähnlich zu: 1423 (2001)
i	1363	Similar to: 1424 (2001)	Ähnlich zu: 1424 (2001)

1370	EU NA AU AS	
Raptor Rumble Studio		
Kampf der Raptoren Studio		
Pcs: 162	2001–2002	

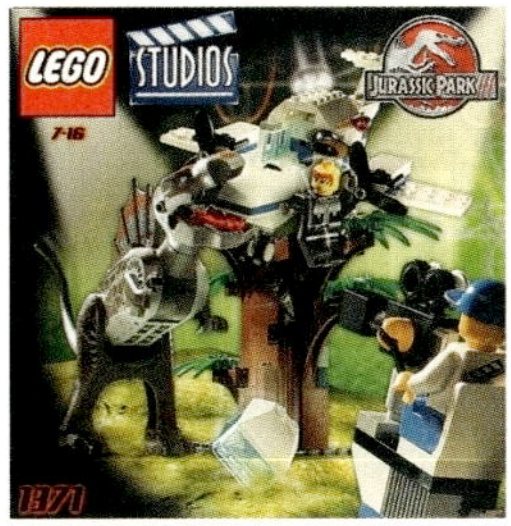

1371	EU NA AU AS	
Spinosaurus Attack Studio		
Spinosaurus Angriff Studio		
Pcs: 190	2001–2002	

1388	EU NA AU AS	
Huki		
Huki		
Pcs: 8	2001–2004	Special

1389	EU NA AU AS	
Onepu		
Onepu		
Pcs: 8	2001–2003	Special

1390	EU NA AU AS	
Maku		
Maku		
Pcs: 8	2001–2003	Special

1391	EU NA AU AS	
Jala		
Jala		
Pcs: 8	2001–2003	Special

1392	EU NA AU AS	
Kongu		
Kongu		
Pcs: 8	2001–2003	Special

1393	EU NA AU AS	
Matoro		
Matoro		
Pcs: 8	2001–2004	Special

1403	EU NA AU AS	
Racing Leopard		
Schwarzer Rennflitzer		
Pcs: 3	2001–2002	

1388	McDonald's Promo	McDonald's Promo
1389	McDonald's Promo	McDonald's Promo
1390	McDonald's Promo	McDonald's Promo
1391	McDonald's Promo	McDonald's Promo
1392	McDonald's Promo	McDonald's Promo
1393	McDonald's Promo	McDonald's Promo

1404 — EU NA AU AS

Racing Tiger		
Gelber Rennflitzer		
Pcs: 3	2001–2002	

1405 — EU NA AU AS

Racing Lion		
Blauer Rennflitzer		
Pcs: 3	2001–2002	

1406 — EU NA AU AS

Nursing the Baby		
Kinderwagen		
Pcs: 11	2001–2002	

1407 — EU NA AU AS

Cooking with Mummy		
Küche		
Pcs: 8	2001–2002	

1408 — EU NA AU AS

Walking the Dog with Daddy		
Bello		
Pcs: 6	2001–2002	

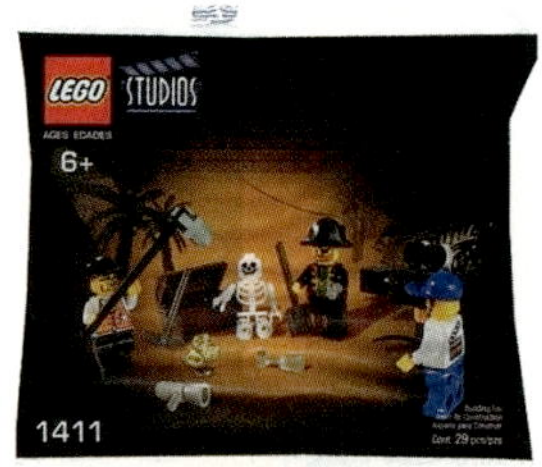

1411 — NA

Pirate and Treasure Chest		
Piraten-Filmszene		
Pcs: 41	2001	Special

1413 — AS

Rover		
Erkundungsfahrzeug		
Pcs: 32	2001	Special

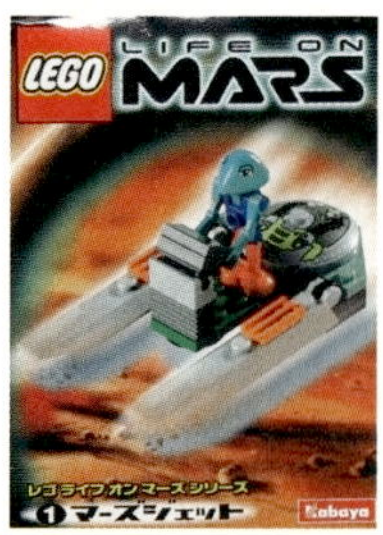

1414 — AS

Double Hover		
Double Hover		
Pcs: 22	2001	Special

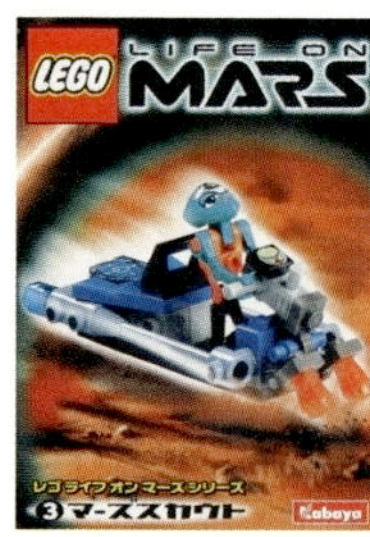

1415 — AS

Jet Scooter		
Jet-Scooter		
Pcs: 25	2001	Special

1413	Similar to: 7309 (2001), 7301 (2001)	Ähnlich zu: 7309 (2001), 7301 (2001)
1414	Similar to: 7308 (2001), 7300 (2001); Kabaya Promo	Ähnlich zu: 7308 (2001), 7300 (2001); Kabaya Promo
1415	Similar to: 7303 (2001); Kabaya Promo	Ähnlich zu: 7303 (2001); Kabaya Promo
1416	Similar to: 7302 (2001); Kabaya Promo	Ähnlich zu: 7302 (2001); Kabaya Promo
1417	Similar to: 8540 (2001); Kabaya Promo	Ähnlich zu: 8540 (2001); Kabaya Promo
1418	Similar to: 8541 (2001); Kabaya Promo	Ähnlich zu: 8541 (2001); Kabaya Promo

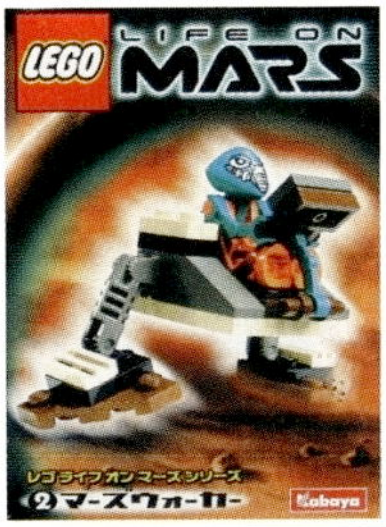

1416	EU NA AU AS	
Worker Robot		
Arbeitsroboter		
Pcs: 30	2001	Special

1417	EU NA AU AS	
Vakama		
Vakama		
Pcs: 30	2001–2003	Special

1418	EU NA AU AS	
Matau		
Matau		
Pcs: 29	2001–2002	Special

1419	EU NA AU AS	
Nokama		
Nokama		
Pcs: 31	2001–2002	Special

1420	EU NA AU AS	
Nuju		
Nuju		
Pcs: 33	2001–2002	Special

1421	EU NA AU AS	
Director's Copter		
Regisseur und Hubschrauber		
Pcs: 23	2001	Special

1422	EU NA AU AS	
Camera Car		
Kamerafahrzeug		
Pcs: 20	2001	Special

1423	EU NA AU AS	
Air Boat		
Rennboot		
Pcs: 30	2001	Special

1424	EU NA AU AS	
Stunt Go-Cart		
Stunt Go-Kart		
Pcs: 26	2001	Special

1419	Similar to: 8543 (2001); Kabaya Promo	Ähnlich zu: 8543 (2001); Kabaya Promo
1420	Similar to: 8544 (2001); Kabaya Promo	Ähnlich zu: 8544 (2001); Kabaya Promo
1421	Similar to: 1360 (2001); Kabaya Promo	Ähnlich zu: 1360 (2001); Kabaya Promo
1422	Similar to: 1361 (2001); Kabaya Promo	Ähnlich zu: 1361 (2001); Kabaya Promo
1423	Similar to: 1362 (2001); Kabaya Promo	Ähnlich zu: 1362 (2001); Kabaya Promo
1424	Similar to: 1363 (2001); Kabaya Promo	Ähnlich zu: 1363 (2001); Kabaya Promo

1452		
Flower		
Blume		
Pcs: 1	2001–2002	Special

1453		
Butterfly		
Schmetterling		
Pcs: -	2001	Special

1454		
Stack-n-Learn		
Stecken und lernen		
Pcs: -	2001–2002	Special

1456		
Squirt Frog		
Zwinker-Frosch		
Pcs: 1	2001–2002	

1457		
Caterpillar		
Raupe „Löwenzahn“		
Pcs: 3	2001–2002	

2580		
Friendly Animal Bus		
Tier Bus		
Pcs: 108	2001–2006	Special

2863		
Box of Bricks		
Jubelbox		
Pcs: 100	2001–2003	Special

2946		
MyBot Expansion Kit		
Mybot Erweiterungsbausatz		
Pcs: 16	2001–2002	

2947		
Pull Back Racer		
Turbo Bike		
Pcs: 14	2001–2003	

1456	Similar to: 5430 (2002)	Ähnlich zu: 5430 (2002)
1457	Similar to: 5432 (2002)	Ähnlich zu: 5432 (2002)

2949 EU NA AU AS

Remote Control Dozer

Remote Control Fahrzeug

Pcs: 23 | 2001–2003

2951 EU NA AU AS

Lisa

Lisa

Pcs: 6 | 2001–2002

2952 EU NA AU AS

Marie

Marie

Pcs: 8 | 2001–2002

2953 EU NA AU AS

Anna

Anna

Pcs: 6 | 2001–2002

2954 EU NA AU AS

Garden Party

Gartenparty

Pcs: 14 | 2001–2002

2955 EU NA AU AS

Sarah's Big Recipe

Sarahs Puppenküche

Pcs: 35 | 2001–2002

2961 EU NA AU AS

Bedroom

Kinderzimmer

Pcs: 20 | 2001–2002

2971 EU NA AU AS

Action Police Bike

Motorradstreife

Pcs: 6 | 2001–2002

2973 EU NA AU AS

Musical Apple

Musikapfel

Pcs: 1 | 2001–2002

i	2973	Similar to: 2503 (2000)	Ähnlich zu: 2503 (2000)

2974	EU NA AU AS	
Play Train		
Zug		
Pcs: 7	2001–2004	

2975	EU NA AU AS	
Bouncing with Tigger		
Tigger		
Pcs: 11	2001	

2976	EU NA AU AS	
Acorn Adventure with Piglet		
Ferkel		
Pcs: 11	2001	

2977	EU NA AU AS	
Eeyore and the Little Raincloud		
I-Aah		
Pcs: 9	2001	

2979	EU NA AU AS	
Winnie Pooh Build and Play		
Winnie Pooh Spiel- und Lernbuch		
Pcs: 14	2001	

2991	EU NA AU AS	
Pooh and the Honeybees		
Winnie Pooh		
Pcs: 11	2001	

2993	EU NA AU AS	
Surprise Birthday Party for Eeyore		
Geburtstagsparty		
Pcs: 28	2001	

3083	EU NA AU AS	
Flying Action		
Kleiner Flughafen		
Pcs: 12	2001–2002	

3085	EU NA AU AS	
Racing Action		
Autorennen		
Pcs: 50	2001–2002	

3087 EU NA AU AS

The Circus Princess
Circus Pony

Pcs: 8	2001–2002	

3088 EU NA AU AS

Growing Garden
Mein kleiner Garten

Pcs: 21	2001–2002	

3089 EU NA AU AS

Adventure Trip
Abenteuer-Tour

Pcs: 32	2001–2002	

3090 EU NA AU AS

Forest Picnic
Sonntagsausflug

Pcs: 28	2001–2002	

3091 EU NA AU AS

Big Gas Truck
Tankwagen

Pcs: 4	2001–2002	

3092 EU NA AU AS

Friendly Farm
Tiere vom Bauernhof

Pcs: 13	2001–2003	

3093 EU NA AU AS

Fun Playground
Spielplatz

Pcs: 30	2001–2002	

3095 EU NA AU AS

Wildlife Park
Safaripark

Pcs: 39	2001–2002	

3121 EU NA AU AS

Summer Day Out
Sommertag

Pcs: 21	2001–2002	

ⓘ 3122	EU NA AU AS
1, 2, 3 ... Marie	
1, 2, 3 ... Marie	
Pcs: 23	2001–2002

ⓘ 3123	EU NA AU AS
Emma's Chill-out Kitchen	
Emmas Küche	
Pcs: 70	2001

ⓘ 3124	EU NA AU AS
Indie's Stable	
Indies Stall	
Pcs: 117	2001–2002

ⓘ 3160	EU NA AU AS
Play Plane	
Propellerflugzeug	
Pcs: 2	2001–2002

ⓘ 3161	EU NA AU AS
Soft Stacking Hen	
Überraschungs-Henne	
Pcs: 2	2001–2002

ⓘ 3162	EU NA AU AS
Take Along Friend	
Blumenmädchen und Freunde	
Pcs: 2	2001–2002

ⓘ 3169	EU NA AU AS
Crib and Mirror Adventure	
Entdecken und Lernen	
Pcs: 2	2001–2002

ⓘ 3170	EU NA AU AS
Light and Sound Stacker	
Schmetterling, Rassel & Co.	
Pcs: 11	2001–2002

ⓘ 3172	EU NA AU AS
Soft Frog Rattle	
Klett-Frosch	
Pcs: 1	2001–2002

ⓘ	3160	Similar to: 5429 (2002)	Ähnlich zu: 5429 (2002)
ⓘ	3161	Similar to: 5425 (2002)	Ähnlich zu: 5425 (2002)
ⓘ	3162	Similar to: 5424 (2002)	Ähnlich zu: 5424 (2002)
ⓘ	3169	Similar to: 5423 (2002)	Ähnlich zu: 5423 (2002)
ⓘ	3172	Similar to: 5420 (2002)	Ähnlich zu: 5420 (2002)

ⓘ 3173	EU NA AU AS	
Caterpillar Teether		
Raupen-Beißring		
Pcs: 1	2001–2002	

ⓘ 3197	AS	
Blue Aeroplane		
Blaues Flugzeug		
Pcs: 16	2001–2002	Special

ⓘ 3212	EU NA AU AS	
Star Teether		
Seestern		
Pcs: 1	2001–2002	

ⓘ 3235	EU NA AU AS	
Soft Ladybird and Bee		
Marienkäfer und Biene		
Pcs: 1	2001	

ⓘ 3236	EU NA AU AS	
Roll-n-Play		
Figurenball		
Pcs: 3	2001–2002	

ⓘ 3237	EU NA AU AS	
Stacking Tower		
Stapelbär		
Pcs: 5	2001–2002	

ⓘ 3238	EU NA AU AS	
Shape and Colour Sorter		
Form- und Farben-Sortierer		
Pcs: 9	2001–2002	

ⓘ 3263	EU NA AU AS	
Goozle		
Goozle		
Pcs: 10	2001–2002	

ⓘ 3264	EU NA AU AS	
Tez		
Tez		
Pcs: 9	2001–2002	

ⓘ	3173	Similar to: 5422 (2002)	Ähnlich zu: 5422 (2002)
ⓘ	3197	Promo for japanese Airline	Promo für japanische Airline
ⓘ	3212	Similar to: 5421 (2002)	Ähnlich zu: 5421 (2002)
ⓘ	3236	Similar to: 5431 (2002)	Ähnlich zu: 5431 (2002)
ⓘ	3237	Similar to: 5433 (2002)	Ähnlich zu: 5433 (2002)
ⓘ	3238	Similar to: 5426 (2002)	Ähnlich zu: 5426 (2002)

3265	EU NA AU AS
Wazo	
Wazo mit Rekorderfunktion	
Pcs: 6	2001–2002

3266	EU NA AU AS
Tubes	
Röhren zum Experimentieren	
Pcs: 58	2001–2003

3267	EU NA AU AS
Brick Runner	
Rennbahn	
Pcs: 26	2001–2002

3271	EU NA AU AS
Bob's Workshop	
Bobs Werkstatt	
Pcs: 11	2001–2002

3272	EU NA AU AS
Scoop on the Road	
Baggi repariert die Straße	
Pcs: 21	2001–2004

3273	EU NA AU AS
Bob, Lofty and the Mice	
Bob, Heppo & die Mäusefamilie	
Pcs: 18	2001–2004

3274	EU NA AU AS
Bob and Muck Repair the Barn	
Bob & Buddel reparieren d. Scheune	
Pcs: 36	2001–2004

3275	EU NA AU AS
Bob's Big Building Box	
Bobs große Baufirma	
Pcs: 52	2001–2002

3276	EU NA AU AS
Muck and Scoop	
Waschtag für Baggi und Buddel	
Pcs: 54	2001–2002

3416	EU NA AU AS	
Women's Team		
Frauen-Fußball-Team		
Pcs: 69	2001–2002	

3418	EU NA AU AS	
Point Shooting		
Zielschießen		
Pcs: 24	2001	Special

3419	EU NA AU AS	
Precision Shooting		
Präzisionsschießen		
Pcs: 24	2001	Special

3451	EU NA AU AS	
Sopwith Camel		
Sopwith Camel		
Pcs: 589	2001–2003	

3724	EU NA AU AS	
Dragon		
Drache		
Pcs: 1540	2001–2002	

3731	EU NA AU AS	
Pumpkin Pack		
Kürbis		
Pcs: 87	2001–2005	

3740	EU NA AU AS	
Small Train Basis		
Kleine Lokomotive		
Pcs: 67	2001–2003	

3741	EU NA AU AS	
Large Train Basis		
Große Lokomotive		
Pcs: 92	2001–2003	

3742	EU NA AU AS	
Tender Basis		
Tender Lokomotive		
Pcs: 39	2001–2003	

3418	Similar to: 3412 (2000)	Ähnlich zu: 3412 (2000)
3419	Similar to: 3414 (2000)	Ähnlich zu: 3414 (2000)

3743	EU NA AS
Blue Bricks for Train	
Blaue Steine für Lok	
Pcs: 106	2001–2003

3744	EU NA AS
Green Bricks for Train	
Grüne Steine für Lok	
Pcs: 106	2001–2003

3745	EU NA AS
Black Bricks for Train	
Schwarze Steine für Lok	
Pcs: 106	2001–2003

3746	EU NA AS
Brown Bricks for Train	
Braune Steine für Lok	
Pcs: 106	2001–2003

3747	EU NA AS
Grey Bricks for Train	
Graue Steine für Lok	
Pcs: 106	2001–2003

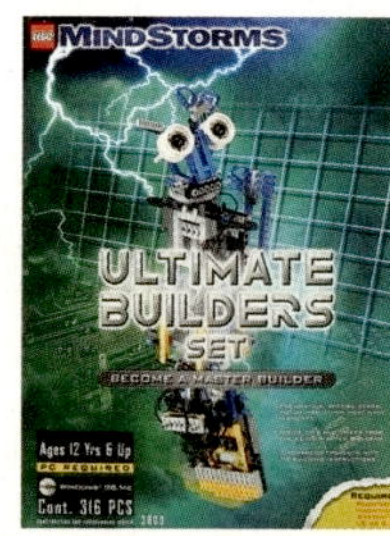

3800	EU NA AU AS
Ultimate Builders Set	
Ultimate Builders Set	
Pcs: 323	2001–2003

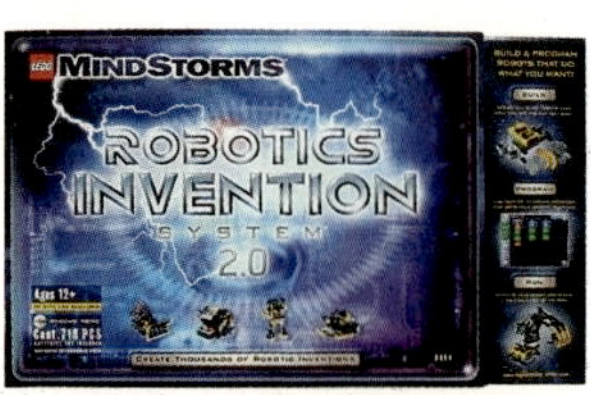

3804	EU NA AU AS
Robotics Invention System 2.0	
Robotics Invention System 2.0	
Pcs: 718	2001–2006

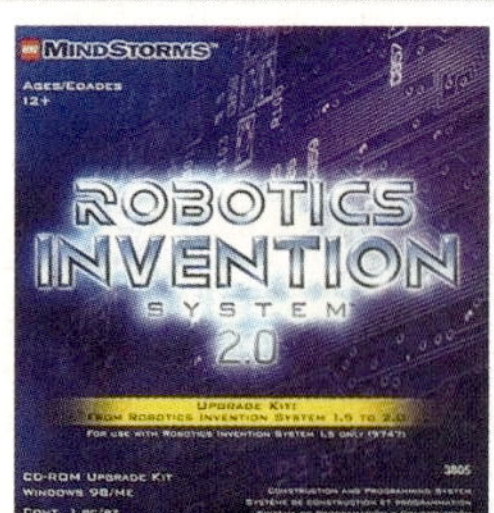

3805	EU NA AU
2.0 Upgrade Kit	
Robotic Invention Erweiterungsset	
Pcs: 1	2001–2002

4016	EU NA AS	
Racer		
Rennwagen		
Pcs: 21	2001–2002	Special

4017	EU NA AU AS	
Sea Helicopter		
Wasser-Hubschrauber		
Pcs: 13	2001–2002	Special

4018	EU NA AU AS	
Ship		
Schiff		
Pcs: 12	2001–2002	Special

4019	EU NA AU AS	
Aeroplane		
Flugzeug		
Pcs: 17	2001–2002	Special

4049	EU NA AU AS	
Film Set with Quiky		
Filmset mit Quiky		
Pcs: 30	2001–2003	Special

4051	EU NA AU AS	
Quiky		
Quiky		
Pcs: 4	2001	Special

4052	EU NA AU AS	
Director		
Regisseur		
Pcs: 4	2001–2003	Special

4053	EU NA AU AS	
Cameraman		
Kameramann		
Pcs: 5	2001–2003	Special

4056	EU NA AU AS	
Color Light		
Vierfarb-Spot		
Pcs: 15	2001	Special

4057	EU NA AU AS	
Spotlight with Red Light		
Rotlicht-Scheinwerfer		
Pcs: 8	2001	Special

4049	Nesquik Promo	Nesquik Promo
4051	Nesquik Promo	Nesquik Promo
4052-4057	Coca-Cola Promo	Coca-Cola Promo

ⓘ 4058	EU NA AU AS	
Cameraman		
Kameramann		
Pcs: 5	2001	Special

ⓘ 4059	EU NA AU AS	
Director		
Direktor		
Pcs: 5	2001	Special

ⓘ 4060	EU NA AU AS	
Gaffer		
Beleuchter		
Pcs: 5	2001	Special

ⓘ 4061	EU NA AU AS	
Assistant		
Regieassistentin		
Pcs: 5	2001	Special

ⓘ 4062	EU NA AU AS	
Actress		
Schauspielerin		
Pcs: 5	2001	Special

ⓘ 4063	EU NA AU AS	
Camera Assistant		
Kameraassistent		
Pcs: 5	2001	Special

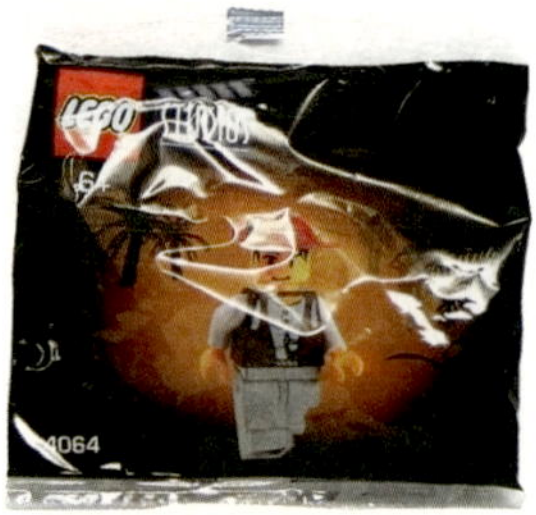

ⓘ 4064	EU NA AU AS	
Actor		
Schauspieler		
Pcs: 4	2001	Special

ⓘ 4065	EU NA AU AS	
Actor		
Schauspieler		
Pcs: 4	2001	Special

ⓘ 4066	EU NA AU AS	
Stuntman		
Stuntman		
Pcs: 5	2001	Special

ⓘ	4058-4066	Coca-Cola Promo	Coca-Cola Promo

ⓘ 4067	EU NA AU AS	
Small Car		
Setwägelchen		
Pcs: 17	2001	Special

ⓘ 4068	EU NA AU AS	
Camera		
Kamera		
Pcs: 7	2001	Special

ⓘ 4069	EU NA AU AS	
Clapperboard and Megaphone		
Setklappe mit Megaphon		
Pcs: 5	2001	Special

ⓘ 4070	EU NA AU AS	
Stand Camera		
Kameraständer		
Pcs: 10	2001	Special

ⓘ 4071	EU NA AU AS	
Crate of Coke		
Eine Kiste Cola		
Pcs: 7	2001	Special

ⓘ 4072	EU NA AU AS	
Skeleton		
Skelett		
Pcs: 7	2001	Special

ⓘ 4073	EU NA AU AS	
Jungle Tree		
Dschungelbaum		
Pcs: 6	2001	Special

ⓘ 4074	EU NA AU AS	
Rock with Spider		
Fels mit Spinne		
Pcs: 14	2001	Special

ⓘ 4075	EU NA AU AS	
Tree with Spider		
Baum mit Spinne		
Pcs: 13	2001	Special

ⓘ	4067-4075	Coca-Cola Promo	Coca-Cola Promo

4076	EU NA AU AS	
Pteranodon		
Pteranodon		
Pcs: 17	2001	Special

4077	EU NA AU AS	
Plesiosaur		
Plesiosaurier		
Pcs: 13	2001	Special

4078	EU NA AU AS	
Tyrannosaurus		
Tyrannosaurus		
Pcs: 18	2001	Special

4079	EU NA AU AS	
Baby T-Rex		
T-Rex-Baby		
Pcs: 4	2001	Special

4113	EU NA AU AS	
Brick Adventures		
Abenteuer mit Bausteinen		
Pcs: 124	2001–2002	

4115	EU NA AU AS	
All That Drives		
Fahrzeuge		
Pcs: 166	2001–2002	

4116	EU NA AU AS	
Animal Adventures		
Eimer Abenteuer mit Tieren		
Pcs: 211	2001–2002	

4117	EU NA AU AS	
Fantastic Flyers and Cool Cars		
Fantastische Flugzeuge, coole Autos		
Pcs: 259	2001–2002	

4118	EU NA AU AS	
Buildings, Mansions and Shops		
Eimer Gebäude und Geschäfte		
Pcs: 366	2001–2002	

ⓘ	4076-4079	Coca-Cola Promo	Coca-Cola Promo

4119	EU NA AU AS
Regular & Transparent Bricks	
Normale & durchsichtige Steine	
Pcs: 234	2001–2003

4120	EU NA AU AS
Fun and Cool Transportation	
Fun and Cool Transportation	
Pcs: 608	2001–2002

4121	EU NA AU AS
All Kinds of Animals	
Verschiedene Tiere	
Pcs: 174	2001–2002

4124	EU NA AU AS
Advent Calendar	
Weihnachtskalender	
Pcs: 275	2001–2002

4171	EU NA AU AS
Spot & Friends	
Spot & Freunde	
Pcs: 53	2001–2002

4172	EU NA AU AS
Tina's House	
Tinas Haus	
Pcs: 44	2001–2002

4173	EU NA AU AS
Max's Pit Stop	
Max' Boxenstop	
Pcs: 59	2001–2003

4174	EU NA AU AS
Max Goes Flying	
Max geht fliegen	
Pcs: 165	2001–2002

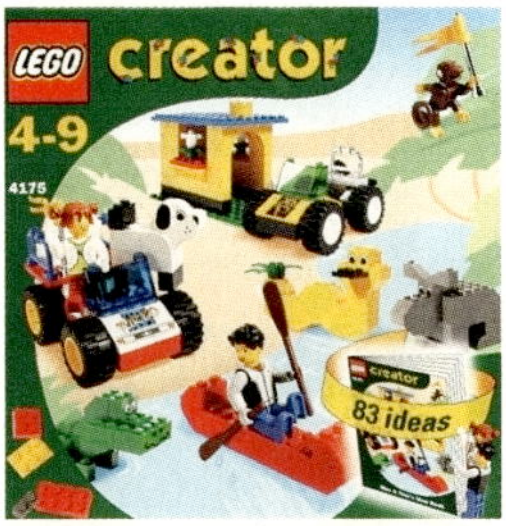

4175	EU NA AU AS
Adventures with Max & Tina	
Abenteuer mit Max & Tina	
Pcs: 219	2001–2003

4176	EU NA AU AS	
The Race of the Year		
Das Rennen des Jahres		
Pcs: 326	2001–2003	

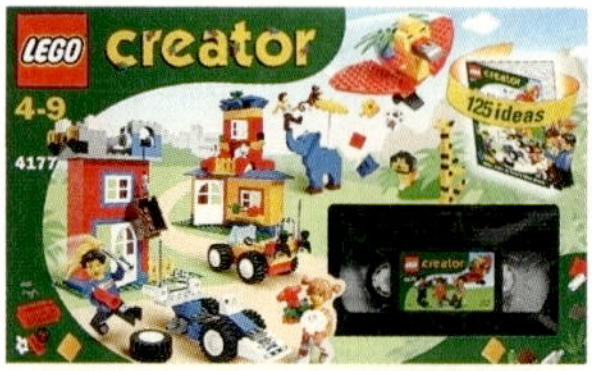

4177	EU NA AU AS	
Building Stories with NaNa Bird		
Der große Nana		
Pcs: 382	2001–2003	

4250	EU NA AU AS	
Creator Bulk (Exclusive)		
Creator Steinsammlung		
Pcs: -	2001–2002	Special

4566	EU NA AU AS	
Gear		
Gear		
Pcs: 9	2001	

4567	EU NA AU AS	
Surfer		
Surfer		
Pcs: 9	2001	

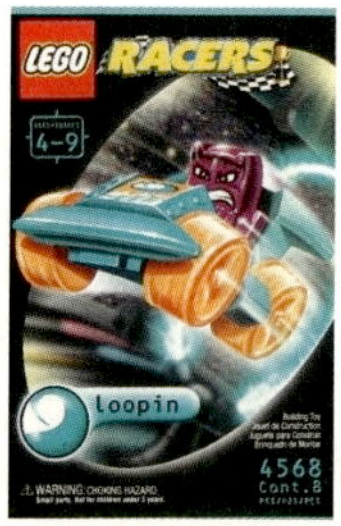

4568	EU NA AU AS	
Loopin		
Loopin		
Pcs: 9	2001	

4569	EU NA AU AS	
Warrior		
Warrior		
Pcs: 9	2001–2002	

4570	EU NA AU AS	
Shredd		
Shredd		
Pcs: 9	2001	

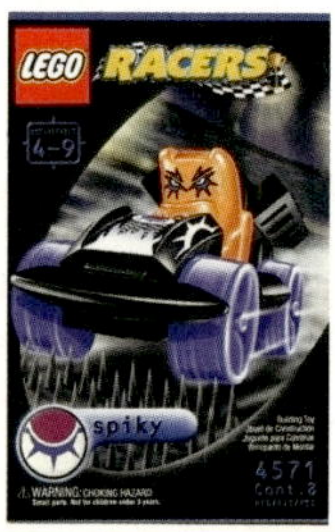

4571	EU NA AU AS	
Spiky		
Spiky		
Pcs: 9	2001	

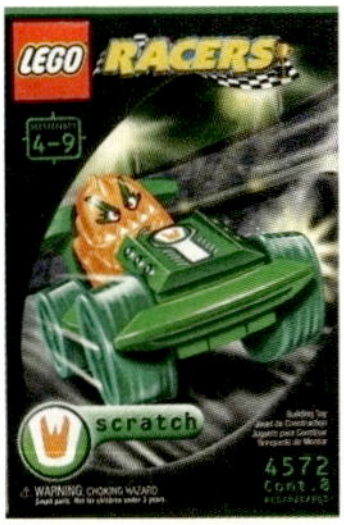

4572	EU NA AU AS
Scratch	
Scratch	
Pcs: 9	2001

4573	EU NA AU AS
Lightor	
Lightor	
Pcs: 9	2001–2002

4574	EU NA AU AS
Rip	
Rip	
Pcs: 9	2001–2002

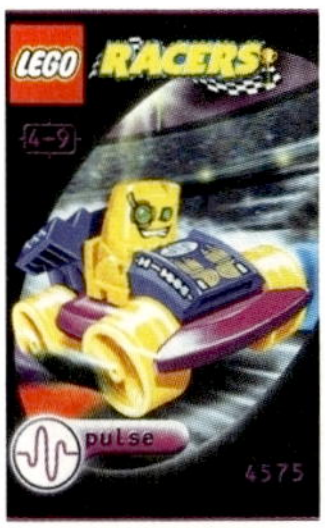

4575	EU NA AU AS
Pulse	
Pulse	
Pcs: 9	2001–2002

4576	EU NA AU AS
Duster	
Duster	
Pcs: 9	2001–2002

4577	EU NA AU AS
Snake	
Snake	
Pcs: 9	2001–2002

4578	EU NA AU AS
Ghost	
Ghost	
Pcs: 9	2001

4579	EU NA AU AS
Freeze - Chill	
Freeze - Chill	
Pcs: 114	2001–2002

4600	EU NA AU AS
Police Cruiser	
Polizei Streifenwagen	
Pcs: 26	2001–2002

4601 EU NA AU AS

Fire Cruiser

Kleines Feuerwehrauto

Pcs: 24 | 2001–2003

4603 EU NA AU AS

Res-Q Wrecker

Abschleppwagen

Pcs: 31 | 2001–2002

4604 EU NA AU AS

Police Copter

Polizei Hubschrauber

Pcs: 23 | 2001–2003

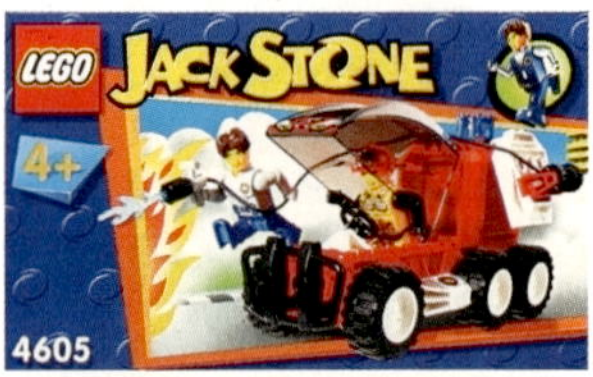

4605 EU NA AU AS

Fire Response SUV

Feuerwehrlöschzug

Pcs: 30 | 2001–2003

4606 EU NA AU AS

Aqua Res-Q Transport

Rettungsboot-Transport

Pcs: 40 | 2001–2002

4607 EU NA AU AS

Copter Transport

Hubschrauber-Transport

Pcs: 66 | 2001–2002

4608 EU NA AU AS

Bank Breakout

Polizei-Einsatz

Pcs: 68 | 2001–2002

4609 EU NA AU AS

Fire Attack Team

Feuerwehr-Mannschaft

Pcs: 92 | 2001–2002

4610 EU NA AU AS

Aqua Res-Q Super Station

Hauptquartier der Küstenwache

Pcs: 91 | 2001–2002

4611 EU NA AU AS

Police HQ

Polizeirevier mit Einsatzfahrzeugen

Pcs: 143	2001–2002	

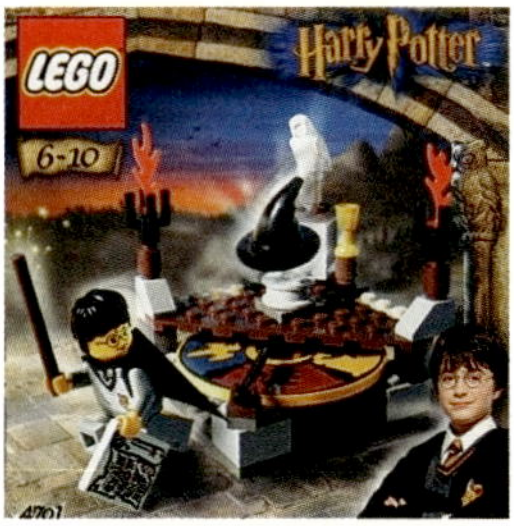

4701 EU NA AU AS

The Sorting Hat

Der Sprechende Hut

Pcs: 49	2001–2002	

4702 EU NA AU AS

The Final Challenge

Die letzte Herausforderung

Pcs: 64	2001–2002	

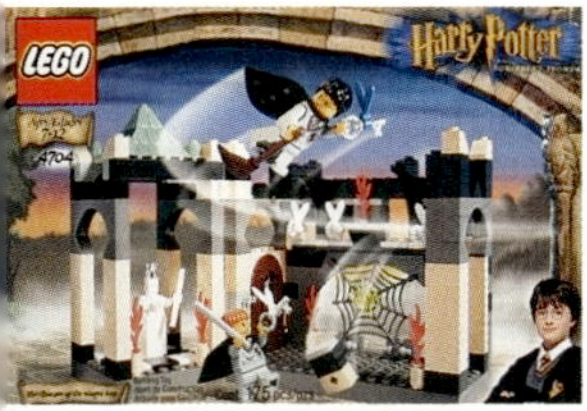

4704 EU NA AU AS

The Chamber of the Winged Keys

Die Gruft mit den gefl. Schlüsseln

Pcs: 180	2001–2002	

4705 EU NA AU AS

Snape's Class

Unterricht bei Snape

Pcs: 169	2001–2002	

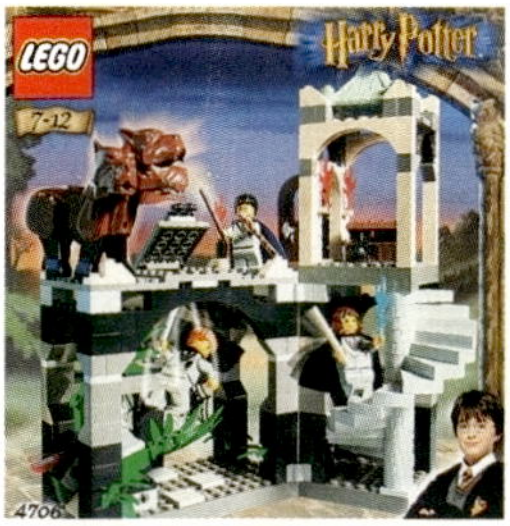

4706 EU NA AU AS

Forbidden Corridor

Der verbotene Gang

Pcs: 242	2001–2003	

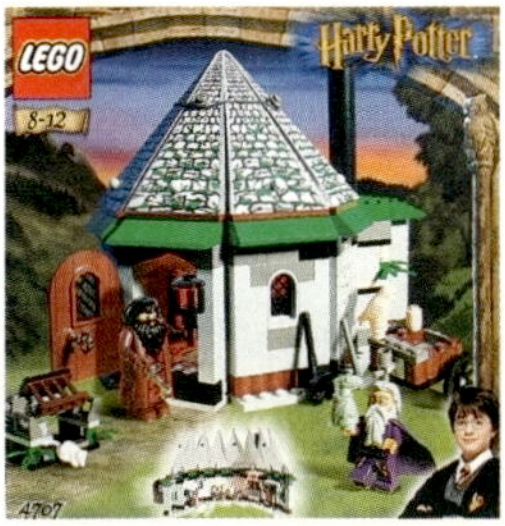

4707 EU NA AU AS

Hagrid's Hut

Hagrids Hütte

Pcs: 310	2001–2002	

4708 EU NA AU AS

Hogwarts Express

Hogwarts-Express

Pcs: 424	2001–2003	

4709 EU NA AU AS

Hogwarts Castle

Hogwarts

Pcs: 701	2001–2003	

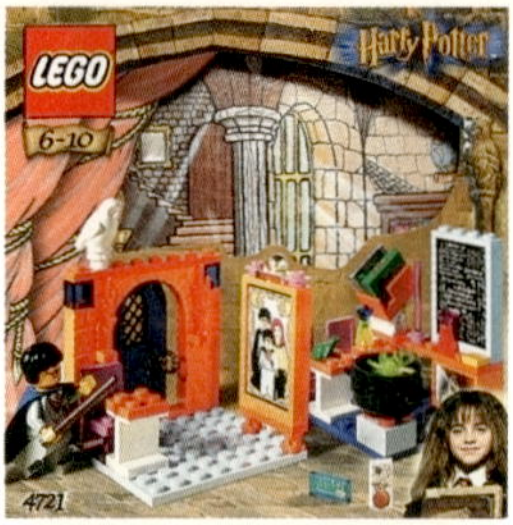

4721	EU NA AU AS
Hogwarts Classrooms	
Hogwarts Klassenzimmer	
Pcs: 78	2001–2002

4722	EU NA AU AS
Gryffindor	
Gryffindor	
Pcs: 71	2001–2002

4723	EU NA AU AS
Diagon Alley Shops	
Läden in der Winkelgasse	
Pcs: 89	2001–2002

4789	EU NA AU AS
Alpha Team Robot Sub	
Alpha Team Robot Sub	
Pcs: -	2001–2002

4810	NA	
Small Bucket		
Kleiner Eimer		
Pcs: 256	2001	Special

4827	EU NA AU AS	
Medium Bucket		
Mittlerer Eimer		
Pcs: -	2001–2002	Special

4830	EU	
Bucket		
Eimer		
Pcs: 51	2001	Special

4836	EU NA AU AS	
Medium Bucket		
Mittlerer Eimer		
Pcs: -	2001–2002	Special

5223	EU NA
Wind-up Motor	
Wind-up Motor	
Pcs: 41	2001–2003

i	4810	Similar to: 4285 (1999)	Ähnlich zu: 4285 (1999)
i	4827	Similar to: 3048 (2000), 4836 (2001)	Ähnlich zu: 3048 (2000), 4836 (2001)
i	4830	Similar to: 4827 (2001), 4836 (2001), 3048 (2000)	Ähnlich zu: 4827 (2001), 4836 (2001), 3048 (2000)
i	4836	Similar to: 3048 (2000), 4827 (2001)	Ähnlich zu: 3048 (2000), 4827 (2001)

5322 EU NA AU AS

Small Idea Bucket		
Kleiner Eimer		
Pcs: 60	2001–2002	Special

5324 EU NA AU AS

Small Bucket		
Kleiner Eimer		
Pcs: -	2001–2002	Special

5327 EU NA AU AS

Small Bucket		
Kleiner Eimer		
Pcs: 60	2001–2002	Special

5339 EU NA AU AS

Small Bucket		
Kleiner Eimer		
Pcs: 43	2001–2002	Special

5599 EU NA AU AS

Radio Control Racer		
Crazy Car		
Pcs: 295	2001	

5831 EU NA AU AS

Adventurous Puppy		
Kleines Hundebaby		
Pcs: 16	2001–2002	

5832 EU NA AU AS

Vanilla's Magic Tea Party		
Vanillas Tee-Party		
Pcs: 16	2001–2002	

5833 EU NA AU AS

Rosita's Wonderful Stable		
Rosita und das Zauberpony		
Pcs: 38	2001–2002	

5834 EU NA AU AS

The Enchanted Garden		
Flora & Elena im Zaubergarten		
Pcs: 103	2001–2002	

i	5322	Similar to: 5327 (2001)	Ähnlich zu: 5327 (2001)
i	5327	Similar to: 5322 (2001)	Ähnlich zu: 5322 (2001)
i	5599	Rerelease of: 5600 (1998)	Neuauflage von: 5600 (1998)

5950	EU
Baby Ankylosaurus	
Baby Ankylosaurus	
Pcs: 37	2001–2002	Special

5951	EU
Baby Iguanodon	
Baby Iguanodon	
Pcs: 23	2001–2002	Special

5952	EU
Baby Brachiosaurus	
Baby Brachiosaurus	
Pcs: 31	2001–2002	Special

5953	EU
Baby Dimetrodon	
Baby Dimetrodon	
Pcs: 20	2001–2002	Special

5977	
Bears on the Beach	
Bären am Strand	
Pcs: 17	2001–2002	Special

6290	EU NA AU AS
Pirate Battle Ship	
Piratenflaggschiff	
Pcs: 745	2001	

6291	EU NA AU AS
Spaniard Ship	
Gouverneurs-Fregatte	
Pcs: 298	2001	

6292	EU NA AU AS
Enchanted Island	
Tropenlagune	
Pcs: 444	2001	

6472	EU NA
Octan Gas Station	
Große Tank- und Service-Station	
Pcs: 489	2001	

i	5950	Similar to: 7000 (2001)	Ähnlich zu: 7000 (2001)
i	5951	Similar to: 7001 (2001)	Ähnlich zu: 7001 (2001)
i	5952	Similar to: 7002 (2001)	Ähnlich zu: 7002 (2001)
i	5953	Similar to: 7003 (2001)	Ähnlich zu: 7003 (2001)
i	5977	Airline Promo	Airline Promo
i	6290	Similar to: 6289 (1996)	Ähnlich zu: 6289 (1996)

6719 EU NA AU AS

Brachiosaurus

Brachiosaurus

Pcs: 27 | 2001–2002

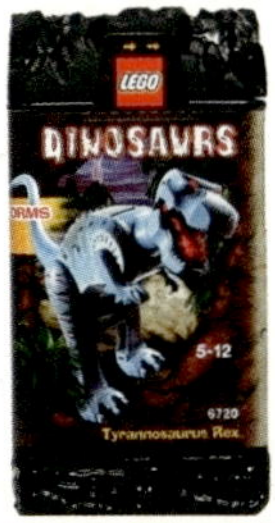

6720 EU NA AU AS

Tyrannosaurus Rex

Tyrannosaurus Rex

Pcs: 25 | 2001–2002

6721 EU NA AU AS

Mosasaurus

Mosasaurus

Pcs: 28 | 2001–2002

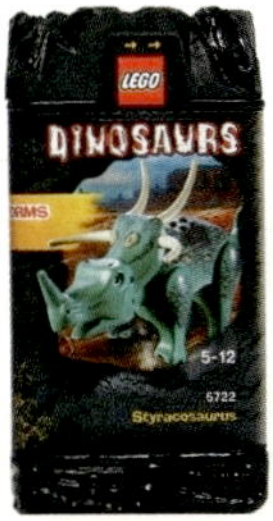

6722 EU NA AU AS

Styracosaurus

Styracosaurus

Pcs: 21 | 2001–2002

6771 EU NA AU AS

Ogel Command Striker

Ogel Command Striker

Pcs: 34 | 2001–2002

6772 EU NA AU AS

Alpha Team Cruiser

Alpha Team Cruiser

Pcs: 65 | 2001–2002

6773 EU NA AU AS

Alpha Team Helicopter

Alpha Team Helicopter

Pcs: 80 | 2001–2002

6774 EU NA AU AS

Alpha Team ATV

Alpha Team ATV

Pcs: 139 | 2001–2002

6775 EU NA AU AS

Alpha Team Bomb Squad

Alpha Team Bomb Squad

Pcs: 206 | 2001–2002

6291	Similar to: 6280 (1996)	Ähnlich zu: 6280 (1996)
6292	Similar to: 6278 (1994)	Ähnlich zu: 6278 (1994)
6472	Similar to: 6397 (1992)	Ähnlich zu: 6397 (1992)

2001

ⓘ **6776**	EU NA AU AS
Ogel Control Centre	
Ogel Control Center	
Pcs: 428	2001–2002

ⓘ **7000**	EU NA AU AS
Baby Ankylosaurus	
Baby Ankylosaurus	
Pcs: 39	2001–2002

ⓘ **7001**	EU NA AU AS
Baby Iguanodon	
Baby Iguanodon	
Pcs: 23	2001–2002

ⓘ **7002**	EU NA AU AS
Baby Brachiosaurus	
Baby Brachiosaurus	
Pcs: 31	2001–2002

ⓘ **7003**	EU NA AU AS
Baby Dimetrodon	
Baby Dimetrodon	
Pcs: 21	2001–2002

ⓘ **7106**	EU NA AU AS
Droid™ Escape	
Droid™ Escape	
Pcs: 48	2001

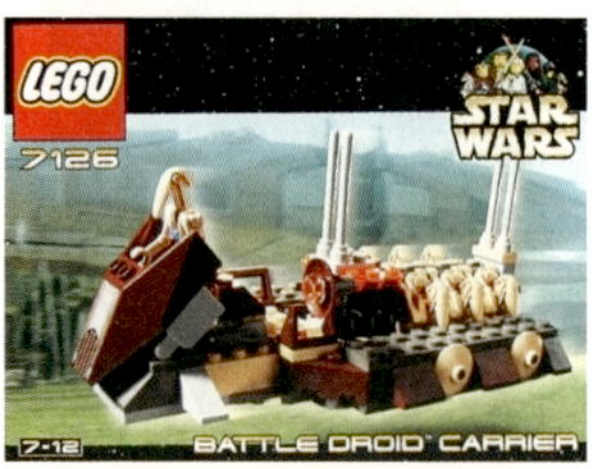

ⓘ **7126**	EU NA AU AS
Battle Droid™ Carrier	
Battle Droid™ Carrier	
Pcs: 136	2001

ⓘ **7127**	EU NA AU AS
Imperial AT-ST™	
Imperial AT-ST™	
Pcs: 109	2001–2002

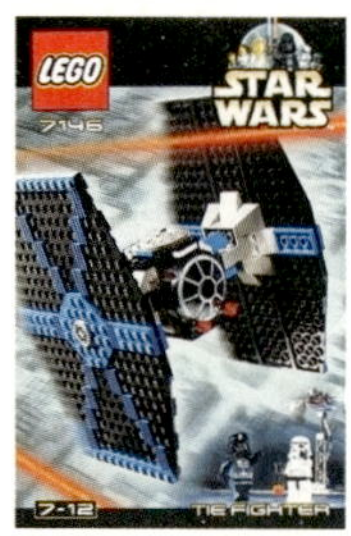

ⓘ **7146**	EU NA AU AS
TIE Fighter™	
TIE Fighter™	
Pcs: 174	2001–2002

ⓘ	Set		
ⓘ	7000	Similar to: 5950 (2001)	Ähnlich zu: 5950 (2001)
ⓘ	7001	Similar to: 5951 (2001)	Ähnlich zu: 5951 (2001)
ⓘ	7002	Similar to: 5952 (2001)	Ähnlich zu: 5952 (2001)
ⓘ	7003	Similar to: 5953 (2001)	Ähnlich zu: 5953 (2001)

7166	EU NA AU AS
Imperial Shuttle™	
Imperial Shuttle™	
Pcs: 242	2001–2002

7186	EU NA AU AS
Watto's™ Junkyard	
Watto's™ Junkyard	
Pcs: 455	2001

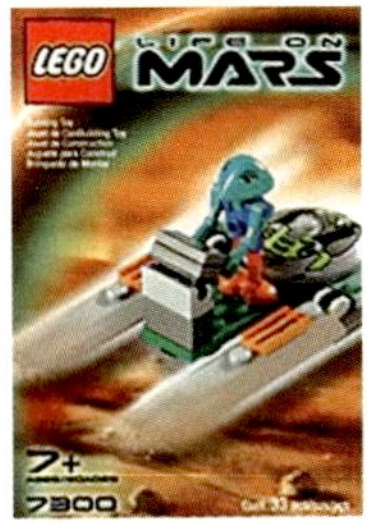

7300	EU NA AU AS
Double Hoover	
Double Hoover	
Pcs: 22	2001

7301	EU NA AU AS
Rover	
Rover	
Pcs: 32	2001

7302	EU NA AU AS
Worker Robot	
Worker Robot	
Pcs: 30	2001

7303	EU NA AU AS
Jet Scooter	
Jet Scooter	
Pcs: 25	2001

7308	EU NA AU AS
Double Hoover	
Double Hoover	
Pcs: 21	2001

7309	EU NA AU AS
Rover	
Rover	
Pcs: 30	2001

7310	EU NA AU AS
Mono Jet	
Mono Jet	
Pcs: 34	2001–2002

i	7300	Similar to: 7308 (2001), 1414 (2001)	Ähnlich zu: 7308 (2001), 1414 (2001)
i	7301	Similar to: 7309 (2001), 1413 (2001)	Ähnlich zu: 7309 (2001), 1413 (2001)
i	7302	Similar to: 1416 (2001)	Ähnlich zu: 1416 (2001)
i	7303	Similar to: 1415 (2001)	Ähnlich zu: 1415 (2001)
i	7308	Similar to: 1414 (2001), 7300 (2001)	Ähnlich zu: 1414 (2001), 7300 (2001)
i	7309	Similar to: 1413 (2001), 7301 (2001)	Ähnlich zu: 1413 (2001), 7301 (2001)

7311 EU NA AU AS

Red Planet Cruiser	
Red Planet Cruiser	
Pcs: 80	2001–2002

7312 EU NA AU AS

T3-Trike	
T3 Trike	
Pcs: 106	2001–2002

7313 EU NA AU AS

Red Planet Protector	
Red Planet Protector	
Pcs: 200	2001–2002

7314 EU NA AU AS

Recon-Mech RP	
Recon-Mech RP	
Pcs: 206	2001–2002

7315 EU NA AU AS

Solar Explorer	
Solar Explorer	
Pcs: 251	2001–2002

7316 EU NA AU AS

Excavation Searcher	
Explorer Station	
Pcs: 489	2001–2002

7317 EU NA AU AS

Aero Tube Hangar	
Vacuum Transport Station	
Pcs: 727	2001–2002

7951 EU NA AU AS

XL Bucket		
Riesen Eimer		
Pcs: 78	2001–2002	Special

7969 EU NA AU AS

XL Bucket		
Riesen Eimer		
Pcs: 106	2001–2002	Special

7969	Similar to: 7975 (2000)	Ähnlich zu: 7975 (2000)

8007	EU NA AU AS
C-3PO™	
C-3PO™	
Pcs: 355	2001–2002

8008	EU NA AU AS
Stormtrooper™	
Stormtrooper™	
Pcs: 368	2001–2002

8240	EU NA AU AS
Slammer Stunt Bike	
Slammer Stunt Bike	
Pcs: 161	2001–2002

8241	EU NA AU AS
Battle Cars	
Battle Cars	
Pcs: 123	2001–2002

8242	EU NA AU AS
Slammer Turbo	
Slammer Turbo	
Pcs: 255	2001–2002

8463	EU NA AU AS
Forklift Truck	
Gabelstapler	
Pcs: 232	2001

8464	EU NA AU AS
Pneumatic Front-End Loader	
Schaufelradlader „Gigant“	
Pcs: 590	2001

8465	EU NA AU AS
Extreme Off-Roader	
Extreme Off-Roader	
Pcs: 364	2001–2003

8466	EU NA AU AS
4x4 Off-Roader	
4x4 Offroader	
Pcs: 1117	2001–2003

8463	Similar to: 8248 (1998)	Ähnlich zu: 8248 (1998)
8464	Similar to: 8439 (2004), 8459 (1997)	Ähnlich zu: 8439 (2004), 8459 (1997)

8525	EU NA AU AS
Kanohi Box	
Masken Box	
Pcs: 6	2001–2002

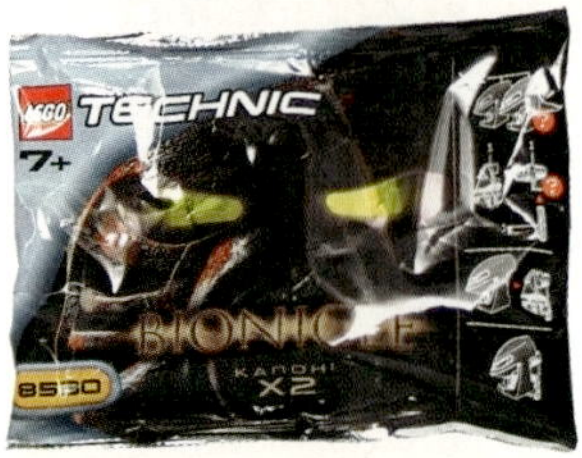

8530	EU NA AU AS
Kanohi	
Masken	
Pcs: 6	2001–2002

8531	EU NA AU AS
Pohatu	
Pohatu	
Pcs: 49	2001–2002

8532	EU NA AU AS
Onua	
Onua	
Pcs: 30	2001–2002

8533	EU NA AU AS
Gali	
Gali	
Pcs: 35	2001–2002

8534	EU NA AU AS
Tahu	
Tahu	
Pcs: 33	2001–2002

8535	EU NA AU AS
Lewa	
Lewa	
Pcs: 36	2001–2002

8536	EU NA AU AS
Kopaka	
Kopaka	
Pcs: 33	2001–2002

8537	EU NA AU AS
Nui-Rama	
Nui-Rama	
Pcs: 154	2001–2002

i	8525	Similar to: 8530 (2001)	Ähnlich zu: 8530 (2001)
i	8530	Similar to: 8525 (2001)	Ähnlich zu: 8525 (2001)

8538 EU NA AU AS

Muaka & Kane-Ra

Muaka & Kana-Ra

Pcs: 654 | 2001–2002

8539 EU NA AU AS

Manas

Manas

Pcs: 457 | 2001–2002

8540 EU NA AU AS

Vakama

Vakama

Pcs: 30 | 2001

8541 EU NA AU AS

Matau

Matau

Pcs: 29 | 2001

8542 EU NA AU AS

Onewa

Onewa

Pcs: 33 | 2001

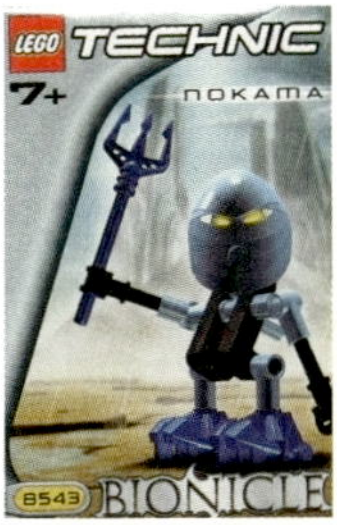

8543 EU NA AU AS

Nokama

Nokama

Pcs: 31 | 2001

8544 EU NA AU AS

Nuju

Nuju

Pcs: 33 | 2001

8545 EU NA AU AS

Whenua

Whenua

Pcs: 31 | 2001

8546 EU NA AU AS

Power Pack

Power Pack

Pcs: 9 | 2001–2002 | Special

ⓘ	8540	Similar to: 1417 (2001)	Ähnlich zu: 1417 (2001)
ⓘ	8541	Similar to: 1418 (2001)	Ähnlich zu: 1418 (2001)
ⓘ	8543	Similar to: 1419 (2001)	Ähnlich zu: 1419 (2001)
ⓘ	8544	Similar to: 1420 (2001)	Ähnlich zu: 1420 (2001)

8548 EU NA AU AS
Nui-Jaga
Nui-Jaga
Pcs: 228 | 2001–2002

8549 EU NA AU AS
Tarakava
Tarakava
Pcs: 411 | 2001–2002

10000 EU NA AU AS
Guarded Inn
Gasthaus mit Rittern
Pcs: 246 | 2001–2002

10001 EU NA AU AS
Metroliner
Metroliner
Pcs: 791 | 2001–2002

10002 EU NA AU AS
Club Car
Panoramawagen
Pcs: 295 | 2001–2002

10013 EU NA AU AS
Open Freight Wagon
Offener Frachtwaggon
Pcs: 121 | 2001–2003

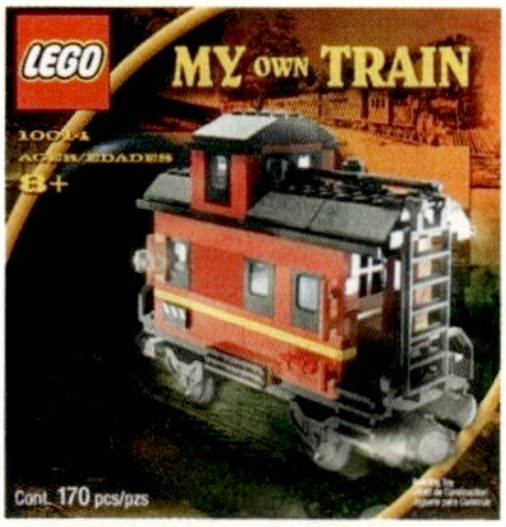

10014 EU NA AU AS
Caboose
Dienstwaggon
Pcs: 173 | 2001–2003

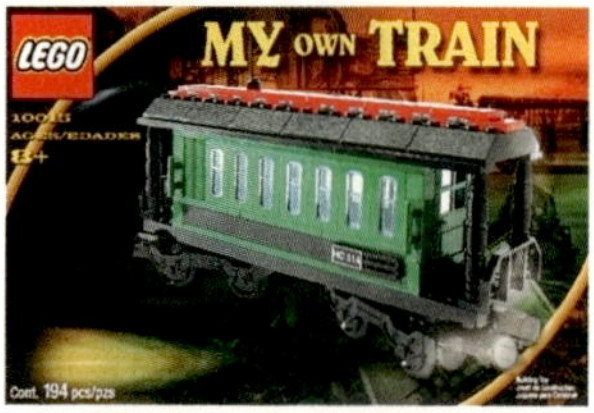

10015 EU NA AU AS
Passenger Wagon
Passagierwaggon
Pcs: 197 | 2001–2003

10016 EU NA AU AS
Tanker
Tankwaggon
Pcs: 128 | 2001–2003

i	10000	Re-release of: 6067 (1986)	Neuauflage von: 6067 (1986)
i	10001	Re-release of: 4558 (1991)	Neuauflage von: 4558 (1991)
i	10002	Re-release of: 4547 (1993)	Neuauflage von: 4547 (1993)

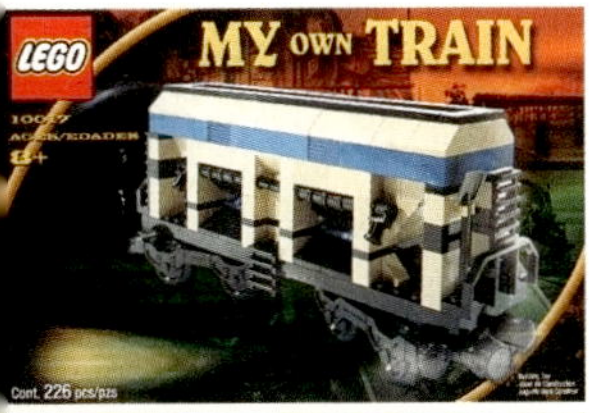

10017	EU NA AU AS
Hopper Wagon	
Selbstentladewagen	
Pcs: 229	2001–2003

10018	EU NA AU AS
Darth Maul™	
Darth Maul™	
Pcs: 1871	2001–2002

10019	EU NA AU AS	
Rebel Blockade Runner™		
Rebel Blockade Runner™		
Pcs: 1763	2001–2003	Special

65028	EU NA AU AS	
Star Wars™ Value Pack 1		
Star Wars™ Kombiset 1		
Sets: 3	2001	Special

65030	EU NA AU AS	
Star Wars™ Value Pack 3		
Star Wars™ Kombiset 3		
Sets: 2	2001	Special

65034	EU NA AU AS	
Star Wars™ Value Pack 4		
Star Wars™ Kombiset 4		
Sets: 2	2001	Special

78660	EU NA AU AS	
Road Racer Value Pack		
Road Racer Kombiset		
Sets: 3	2001	Special

78731	EU NA AU AS	
Star Wars™ Value Pack 2		
Star Wars™ Kombiset 2		
Sets: -	2001	Special

78732	EU NA AU AS	
Star Wars™ Value Pack 3		
Star Wars™ Kombiset 3		
Sets: 2	2001	Special

65028	Includes: 7115 (2000), 7124 (2000), 7141 (1999)	Enhält: 7115 (2000), 7124 (2000), 7141 (1999)
65030	ncludes: 7104 (2000), 7144 (2000)	Enthält: 7104 (2000), 7144 (2000)
65034	Includes: 7121 (1999), 7161 (1999)	Enhält: 7121 (1999), 7161 (1999)

78744	EU NA AU AS	
Star Wars™ Value Pack 8		
Star Wars™ Kombiset 8		
Sets: 2	2001	Special

78800	EU NA AU AS	
Soccer Bonus Set		
Fußball Bonusset		
Sets: 3	2001	Special

880001	EU NA AU AS	
Trike Race		
Trike-Rennen		
Pcs: -	2001	Special

880010	EU NA AU AS	
Roboriders Value Pack		
Roboriders Kombiset		
Sets: 2	2001	Special

880011	EU NA AU AS	
Roboriders Value Pack		
Roboriders Kombiset		
Sets: 2	2001	Special

880012	EU NA AU AS	
Roboriders Value Pack		
Roboriders Kombiset		
Sets: 2	2001	Special

1024601	EU NA AU AS	
Adventurers Value Pack		
Abenteurer Kombiset		
Sets: 2	2001	Special

i	78800	Includes: 3403 (2000), 3418 (2001), 3419 (2001)	Enthält: 3403 (2000), 3418 (2001), 3419 (2001)
i	880010	Includes: 8509 (2000), 8510 (2000)	Enthält: 8509 (2000), 8510 (2000)
i	880011	Includes: 8511 (2000), 8513 (2000)	Enthält: 8511 (2000), 8513 (2000)
i	880012	Includes: 8512 (2000), 8514 (2000)	Enthält: 8512 (2000), 8514 (2000)
i	1024601	Includes: 2995 (1998), 2996 (1998); Toys 'R' Us Promo	Enthält: 2995 (1998), 2996 (1998); Toys 'R' Us Promo

2002

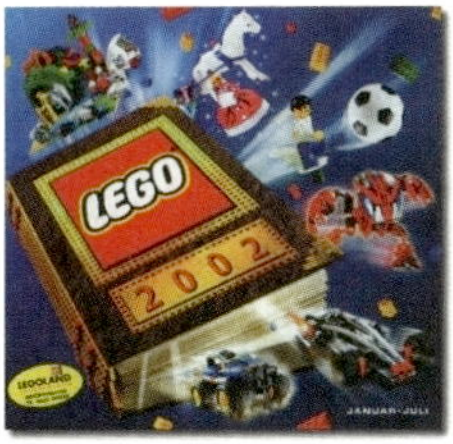

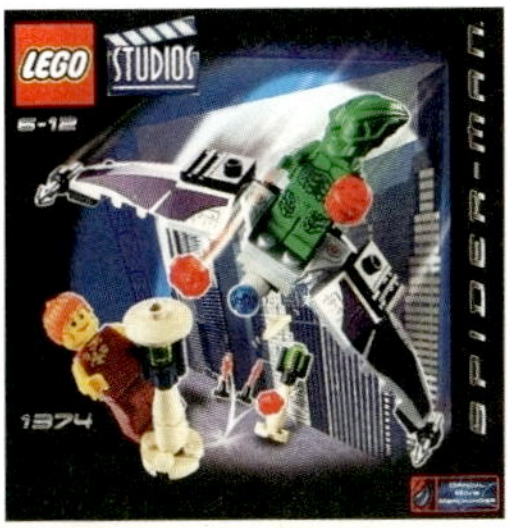

1374	EU NA AU AS
Green Goblin	
Der grüne Kobold	
Pcs: 55	2002–2003

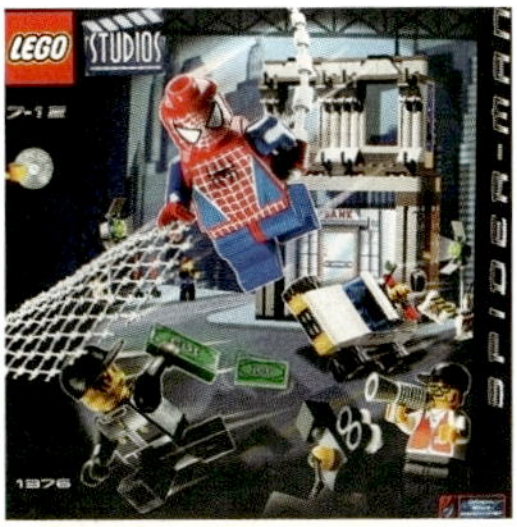

1376	EU NA AU AS
Action Studio	
Action Studio	
Pcs: 244	2002–2003

1380	EU NA AU AS
Werewolf Ambush	
Das Heulen des Werwolfs	
Pcs: 110	2002–2003

1381	EU NA AU AS
Vampire Crypt	
Die Gruft des Vampirs	
Pcs: 170	2002–2003

1382	EU NA AU AS
Scary Laboratory	
Die verrückte Gruselfabrik	
Pcs: 492	2002–2003

1383	EU NA AU AS
Curse of the Pharaoh	
Der Fluch des Pharao	
Pcs: 50	2002–2003

2002

1384	EU NA		
Colorful Bird			
Bunter Vogel			
Pcs: 6	2002	Special	

1425	AS		
Kabaya Dash Jet Sub			
Kabaya Dash Jet Sub			
Pcs: 23	2002	Special	

1426	AS		
Kabaya Cam Wing Diver			
Kabaya Cam Wing Diver			
Pcs: 21	2002	Special	

1427	AS		
Kabaya Ogel Marine Slizer			
Kabaya Ogel Marine Slizer			
Pcs: 21	2002	Special	

1428	AS		
Kabaya Free Kick Shooting			
Kabaya Freistoßschießen			
Pcs: 23	2002–2004	Special	

1429	AS		
Kabaya Point Shooting			
Kabaya Zielschießen			
Pcs: 22	2002–2004	Special	

1430	AS		
Kabaya Precision shooting			
Kabaya Präzisionsschießen			
Pcs: 14	2002–2004	Special	

1431	AS		
Kabaya Tahnok Va			
Kabaya Tahnok Va			
Pcs: 28	2002–2003	Special	

1432	AS		
Kabaya Nuhvok Va			
Kabaya Nuhvok Va			
Pcs: 27	2002–2003	Special	

i	1384	McDonald's Promo	McDonald's Promo
i	1425	Similar to: 4800 (2002); also available as Poly-Bag	Ähnlich zu: 4800 (2002); auch als Poly-Bag erhältlich
i	1426	Also available as polybag	Auch als Poly-Bag erhältlich
i	1427	Similar to: 4798 (2002)	Ähnlich zu: 4798 (2002)
i	1431	Similar to: 8554 (2002); also available as Poly-Bag	Ähnlich zu: 8554 (2002); auch als Poly-Bag erhältlich
i	1432	Similar to: 8555 (2002); also available as Poly-Bag	Ähnlich zu: 8555 (2002); auch als Poly-Bag erhältlich

ⓘ 1433		EU NA AU **AS**
Kabaya Gahlok Va		
Kabaya Gahlok Va		
Pcs: 27	2002–2003	Special

ⓘ 1434		EU NA AU **AS**
Kabaya Lehvak Va		
Kabaya Lehvak Va		
Pcs: 30	2002–2003	Special

ⓘ 1435		EU NA AU **AS**
Kabaya Super Glider		
Kabaya Drachenflieger		
Pcs: 7	2002	Special

ⓘ 1436		EU NA AU **AS**
Kabaya Ultralight Flyer		
Kabaya Ultraleichtflugzeug		
Pcs: 12	2002	Special

ⓘ 1437		EU NA AU **AS**
Kabaya Turbo Chopper		
Kabaya Turbo-Hubschrauber		
Pcs: 13	2002	Special

ⓘ 1441		**EU** NA AU AS
Fikou		
Fikou		
Pcs: 15	2002–2003	Special

ⓘ 3033		**EU** NA **AU** **AS**
Basic Bulk Tub (Overseas Version)		
Blauer 1200-Steine-Eimer		
Pcs: 1200	2002	Special

ⓘ 3125		EU **NA** AU AS
Preschool Playtable		
Spieltisch		
Pcs: 18	2002–2006	Special

ⓘ 3219		**EU** **NA** **AU** **AS**
Mini TIE Fighter™		
Mini TIE Fighter™		
Pcs: 29	2002–2003	Special

ⓘ	1433	Similar to: 8550 (2002)	Ähnlich zu: 8550 (2002)
ⓘ	1434	Similar to: 8552 (2002); also available as Poly-Bag	Ähnlich zu: 8552 (2002); auch als Poly-Bag
ⓘ	1435	Similar to: 4612 (2002)	Ähnlich zu: 4612 (2002)
ⓘ	1441	Promo set from Belgium	Belgisches Promo-Set
ⓘ	3033	"Noodle Box"	„Nudelbox"

3278 EU NA AU AS

Wallpaper Wendy

Wendy tapeziert

Pcs: 9 | 2002–2003

3279 EU NA AU AS

Bob at Work

Bob hat zu tun

Pcs: 9 | 2002–2003

3281 EU NA AU AS

Naughty Spud

Der unartige Knolle

Pcs: 10 | 2002–2003

3282 EU NA AU AS

Clock Tower Bob

Bob und der Uhrenturm

Pcs: 50 | 2002–2003

3283 EU NA AU AS

Dizzy's Birdwatch

Mixi bei der Vogelbeobachtung

Pcs: 45 | 2002–2004

3325 EU NA AU AS

Intelli-Train Gift Set

Eisenbahn Luxusset

Pcs: 98 | 2002–2005

3326 EU NA AU AS

Intelli-Train Cargo

Güterwagen

Pcs: 15 | 2002–2004

3327 EU NA AU AS

Intelli-Train Station

Eisenbahnstation

Pcs: 28 | 2002–2003

3334 EU NA AU AS

Intelli-Train Tunnel

Eisenbahntunnel

Pcs: 10 | 2002–2004

3335	EU NA AU AS	
Intelli-Train Starter Set		
Eisenbahn Starterset		
Pcs: 28	2002–2005	

3361	EU NA AU AS	
Music Twister		
Musik Twist		
Pcs: 4	2002–2003	

3362	EU NA AU AS	
Music Tapper		
Musik Komposition		
Pcs: 4	2002–2003	

3363	EU NA AU AS	
Music Roller		
Musik Roller		
Pcs: 4	2002–2003	

3364	EU NA AU AS	
Music Builder Composer		
Musik Orchester		
Pcs: 7	2002–2003	

3370	EU NA AU AS	
Music Extras		
Musik Extras 1		
Pcs: 6	2002–2003	

3371	EU NA AU AS	
Music Extras		
Musik Extras 2		
Pcs: 4	2002–2003	

3420	EU NA AU AS	
Championship Challenge II		
Arena der Champions II		
Pcs: 376	2002–2006	Special

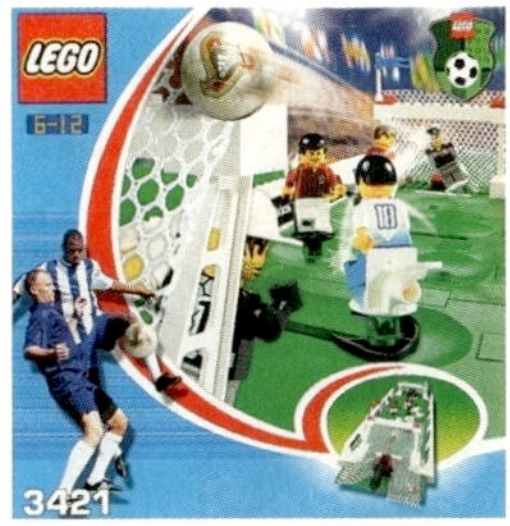

3421	EU NA AU AS	
3 vs. 3 Shootout		
Hallenfußball		
Pcs: 227	2002–2003	

3420	Also available with different teams; FC Bayern Promo	Auch mit anderen Mannschaften verfügbar; FC Bayern-Promo

3422	EU NA AU AS
Shoot-n-Save	
Elfmeterschießen	
Pcs: 107	2002–2003

3423	EU NA AU AS
Freekick Frenzy	
Präzisionsschießen	
Pcs: 51	2002–2004

3424	EU NA AU AS
Target Practice	
Zielschießen	
Pcs: 37	2002–2003

3425	EU NA AU AS
Grand Championship Cup	
Grand Championship Cup	
Pcs: 570	2002

3426	EU NA AU AS	
Adidas Team Transport		
Team Adidas		
Pcs: 125	2002	Special

3509	EU NA AU AS
Brickbuster Super Truck	
Brickbuster Super Truck	
Pcs: 43	2002–2006

3514	EU NA AU AS
Rhino and Lion	
Nashorn und Löwe	
Pcs: 29	2002–2004

3605	EU NA AU AS
Birthday Party	
Geburtstagsparty	
Pcs: 10	2002–2003

3606	EU NA AU AS
Tow Service	
Go-Kart Transport	
Pcs: 7	2002–2003

i	3422	Also available as FC Bayern München Promo	Auch als FC Bayern München Promo verfügbar

3607	EU NA AU AS
Police Action	
Polizei im Einsatz	
Pcs: 8	2002–2003

3608	EU NA AU AS
Playground	
Spielplatz	
Pcs: 25	2002–2003

3609	EU NA AU AS
Beach House	
Strandspaß	
Pcs: 9	2002

3610	EU NA AU AS
Campsite	
Camping-Abenteuer	
Pcs: 9	2002–2003

3611	EU NA AU AS
Road Worker Truck	
Baufahrzeug	
Pcs: 15	2002–2003

3612	EU NA AU AS
Wildlife Animals	
Welt der wilden Tiere	
Pcs: 35	2002–2003

3613	EU NA AU AS
Fire Rescue	
Feuerwehr	
Pcs: 31	2002–2003

3614	EU NA AU AS
Racing	
Rennstrecke	
Pcs: 37	2002–2003

3615	EU NA AU AS
Theatre Stories	
Theatergeschichten	
Pcs: 50	2002–2003

3616	EU NA AU AS
On the Move Police Station	
Polizeistation immer dabei	
Pcs: 17	2002–2003

3617	EU NA AU AS
On the Move Hospital	
Krankenhaus immer dabei	
Pcs: 19	2002–2003

3618	EU NA AU AS
Family Farm	
Bauernhof mit Familie	
Pcs: 57	2002–2004

3619	EU NA AU AS
Traffic City	
Verkehrsschule	
Pcs: 82	2002–2003

3621	EU NA AU AS
Polar Animals	
Polar-Abenteuer	
Pcs: 32	2002–2003

3650	EU NA AU AS
First Rollabout	
Stack-n-Learn Autospaß	
Pcs: 11	2002–2003

3651	EU NA AU AS
Friends	
Stack-n-Learn Freunde	
Pcs: 12	2002–2003

3652	EU NA AU AS
Ladybird Collection	
Stack-n-Learn Marienkäfer	
Pcs: 17	2002–2003

3739	EU NA AU AS
Blacksmith Shop	
Schmiedewerkstatt	
Pcs: 634	2002–2003

3739	Was designed by a LEGO fan	Wurde von einem LEGO Sammler entworfen

3763 EU NA AU AS

35 Year Anniversary Tub		
35-Jahre-Jubiläumseimer		
Pcs: 142	2002	Special

3806 EU NA AU AS

Gigamesh G60		
Gigamesh G60		
Pcs: 233	2002–2003	

3807 EU NA AU AS

Snaptrax S45		
Snaptrax S45		
Pcs: 193	2002–2004	

3808 EU NA AU AS

Shadowstrike S70		
Shadowstrike S70		
Pcs: 223	2002–2003	

3809 EU NA AU AS

Technojaw T55		
Technojaw T55		
Pcs: 246	2002–2004	

3928 EU NA AU AS

Astronaut Sandy		
Astronaut Sandy		
Pcs: 4	2002–2003	Special

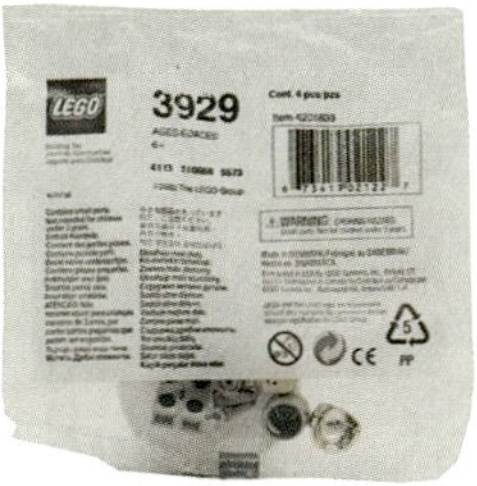

3929 EU NA AU AS

Astronaut Biff		
Astronaut Biff		
Pcs: 4	2002–2003	Special

4038 EU NA AU AS

Airplane		
Flugzeug		
Pcs: 37	2002–2004	Special

4040 EU NA AU AS

Nick		
Nick		
Pcs: 3	2002–2003	Special

3928	World Space Congress 2002	World Space Congress 2002
3929	World Space Congress 2002	World Space Congress 2002
4038	Airline Promo	Airline Promo
4040	McDonald's Promo	McDonald's Promo

4042	EU **NA** AU AS	
Jens		
Jens		
Pcs: 3	2002–2003	Special

4043	EU **NA** AU AS	
Gorm		
Gorm		
Pcs: 4	2002–2003	Special

4044	EU **NA** AU AS	
Euripides		
Euripides		
Pcs: 3	2002–2003	Special

4045	EU **NA** AU AS	
Nepol		
Nepol		
Pcs: 3	2002–2003	Special

4080	**EU** **NA** **AU** AS	
Small Bucket		
Kleiner Eimer		
Pcs: 45	2002–2006	

4081	**EU** NA **AU** AS	
Small Bucket		
Kleiner Eimer		
Pcs: 45	2002–2006	

4082	**EU** NA AU AS	
Small Bucket		
Kleiner Eimer		
Pcs: 45	2002–2005	Special

4083	**EU** NA AU AS	
Small Bucket		
Kleiner Eimer		
Pcs: 45	2002–2003	Special

4084	EU **NA** AU AS	
Bucket		
Eimer		
Pcs: 45	2002–2003	Special

i	Set	English	Deutsch
i	4042-4045	McDonald's Promo	McDonald's Promo
i	4081	Similar to: 4082 (2002)	Ähnlich zu: 4082 (2002)
i	4082	Similar to: 4081 (2002)	Ähnlich zu: 4081 (2002)

4085	**EU** NA AU AS	
Large Bucket		
Großer Eimer		
Pcs: 90	2002–2007	

4087	**EU** NA AU AS	
Bucket "Colourful World"		
Eimer „Farbenprächtige Welt"		
Pcs: 90	2002–2003	

ⓘ 4088	**EU** NA AU AS	
Clown Bucket		
Clown Eimer		
Pcs: 90	2002–2003	

ⓘ 4089	EU **NA** AU AS	
Large Bucket		
Großer Eimer		
Pcs: 90	2002–2003	Special

ⓘ 4103	**EU** **NA** AU AS	
Fun with Bricks		
Lustige Baumeister		
Pcs: 200	2002–2006	Special

4104	**EU** NA AU AS	
Small Bucket		
Kleiner Eimer		
Pcs: 200	2002–2006	Special

4105	**EU** NA AU AS	
Imagine and Build		
Fantasievolles Bauen		
Pcs: 500	2002–2007	

ⓘ 4106	**EU** NA AU AS	
Large Bucket		
Großer Eimer		
Pcs: 500	2002–2003	Special

4107	**EU** NA AU AS	
Build your Dreams		
Bau deine Träume		
Pcs: 1000	2002–2004	

ⓘ	Set	English	Deutsch
ⓘ	4088	Similar to: 4180 (2002), 4089 (2002)	Ähnlich zu: 4180 (2002), 4089 (2002)
ⓘ	4089	Similar to: 4180 (2002, 4088 (2002)	Ähnlich zu: 4180 (2002), 4088 (2002)
ⓘ	4103	2006: New release with figures	2006: Neuveröffentlichung mit Figuren
ⓘ	4106	Similar to: 4014 (2003), 4179 (2002), 7825 (2002)	Ähnlich zu: 4014 (2003), 4179 (2002), 7825 (2002)

ⓘ 4108	EU NA AU AS	
T-Junction Road Plates		
T-Kreuzungen		
Pcs: 2	2002–2006	

ⓘ 4109	EU NA AU AS	
Curved Road Plates		
Kurven		
Pcs: 2	2002–2006	

ⓘ 4110	EU NA AU AS	
Straight Road Plates		
Gerade Straßen		
Pcs: 2	2002–2005	

ⓘ 4111	EU NA AU AS	
Cross Road Plates		
Kreuzungen		
Pcs: 2	2002–2005	

ⓘ 4179	EU NA AU AS	
Large Box		
Große Box		
Pcs: 500	2002–2003	Special

ⓘ 4180	EU NA AU AS	
Animals		
Tiere		
Pcs: 90	2002–2003	Special

ⓘ 4294	EU NA AU AS	
Helicopter		
Hubschrauber		
Pcs: 16	2002–2004	Special

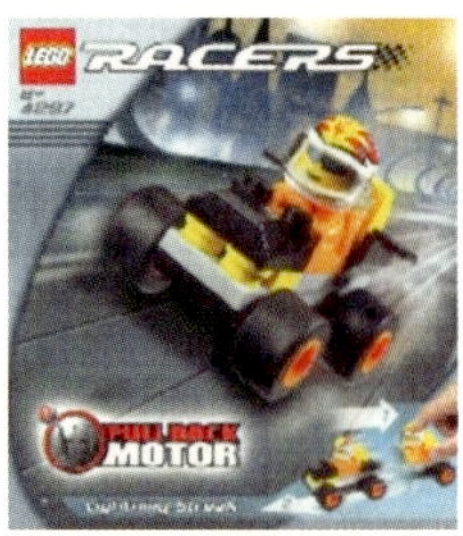

ⓘ 4297	EU NA AU AS	
Lightning Streak		
Lightning Streak		
Pcs: 20	2002–2003	Special

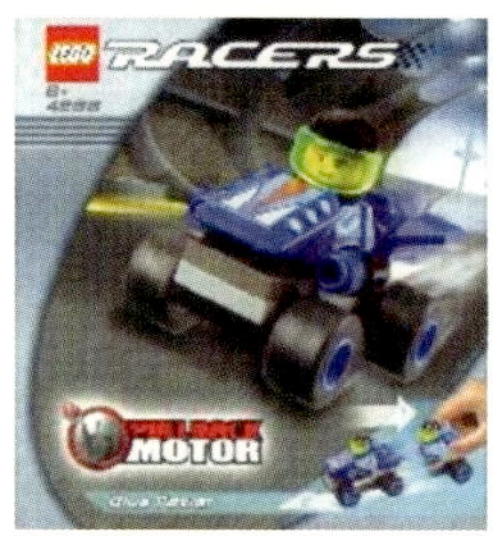

ⓘ 4298	EU NA AU AS	
Blue Power		
Blue Power		
Pcs: 25	2002–2003	Special

ⓘ	4179	Similar to: 4014 (2003), 4106 (2002), 7825 (2002)	Ähnlich zu: 4014 (2003), 4106 (2002), 7825 (2002)
ⓘ	4180	Similar to: 4088 (2002), 4089 (2002)	Ähnlich zu: 4088 (2002), 4089 (2002)
ⓘ	4294	Airline Promo	Airline Promo
ⓘ	4297	Duracell Promo	Duracell Promo
ⓘ	4298	Duracell Promo	Duracell Promo

4299	EU NA AU AS	
Quiky Racer		
Quiky Racer		
Pcs: 18	2002–2003	Special

4340	EU NA AU AS	
Storybuilder Jungle Jam		
Geschichtengestalter - Dschungel		
Pcs: 10	2002–2003	

4341	EU NA AU AS	
Storybuilder Farmyard Fun		
Erweiterungsset - Bauernhof		
Pcs: 9	2002–2003	

4342	EU NA AU AS	
Storybuilder Crazy Castle		
Erweiterungsset - Rittermärchen		
Pcs: 9	2002–2003	

4443	EU NA AU AS	
Defender 1		
Verteidiger 1		
Pcs: 4	2002	Special

4444	EU NA AU AS	
Defender 2		
Verteidiger 2		
Pcs: 4	2002	Special

4445	EU NA AU AS	
Midfielder 1		
Mittelfeldspieler 1		
Pcs: 4	2002	Special

4446	EU NA AU AS	
Forwarder 1		
Stürmer 1		
Pcs: 4	2002	Special

4447	EU NA AU AS	
Forwarder 2		
Stürmer 2		
Pcs: 4	2002	Special

i			
i	4299	Nesquik Promo	Nesquik Promo
i	4443-4447	Coca-Cola Promo	Coca-Cola Promo

ⓘ 4448	EU NA AU AS	
Defender 3		
Verteidiger 3		
Pcs: 4	2002	Special

ⓘ 4449	EU NA AU AS	
Defender 4		
Verteidiger 4		
Pcs: 4	2002	Special

ⓘ 4450	EU NA AU AS	
Midfielder 2		
Mittelfeldspieler 2		
Pcs: 4	2002	Special

ⓘ 4451	EU NA AU AS	
Forwarder 3		
Stürmer 3		
Pcs: 4	2002	Special

ⓘ 4452	EU NA AU AS	
Forwarder 4		
Stürmer 4		
Pcs: 4	2002	Special

ⓘ 4453	EU NA AU AS	
Goal Keeper		
Torwart		
Pcs: 4	2002	Special

ⓘ 4454	EU NA AU AS	
Referee		
Schiedsrichter		
Pcs: 6	2002	Special

ⓘ 4455	EU NA AU AS	
Hot Dog Girl		
Wurstverkäuferin		
Pcs: 6	2002	Special

ⓘ 4456	EU NA AU AS	
Doctor		
Mannschaftsarzt		
Pcs: 5	2002	Special

ⓘ	4448-4456	Coca-Cola Promo	Coca-Cola Promo

ⓘ 4457	EU NA AU AS	
TV Cameraman		
Kameramann		
Pcs: 4	2002	Special

ⓘ 4458	EU NA AU AS	
TV Camera		
Fernsehkamera		
Pcs: 11	2002	Special

ⓘ 4459	EU NA AU AS	
Kicker		
Kicker		
Pcs: 4	2002	Special

ⓘ 4460	EU NA AU AS	
Goal		
Tor		
Pcs: 7	2002	Special

ⓘ 4461	EU NA AU AS	
Substitute Bench		
Ersatzbank		
Pcs: 7	2002	Special

ⓘ 4462	EU NA AU AS	
Hot Dog Trolley		
Hotdog-Wagen		
Pcs: 18	2002	Special

ⓘ 4463	EU NA AU AS	
Light		
Licht		
Pcs: 16	2002	Special

ⓘ 4464	EU NA AU AS	
Bottle Case		
Getränkekiste		
Pcs: 7	2002	Special

ⓘ 4465	EU NA AU AS	
Vending Machine		
Getränkeautomat		
Pcs: 6	2002	Special

ⓘ	4457-4465	Coca-Cola Promo	Coca-Cola Promo

2002

4466	EU NA AU AS	
Sign Board		
Werbebande		
Pcs: 3	2002	Special

4467	EU NA AU AS	
Stretcher		
Krankentrage		
Pcs: 3	2002	Special

4468	EU NA AU AS	
Drink Stand 1		
Getränkestand 1		
Pcs: 9	2002	Special

4469	EU NA AU AS	
Drink Stand 2		
Getränkestand 2		
Pcs: 8	2002	Special

4470	EU NA AU AS	
Soccer Balls		
Fußbälle		
Pcs: 2	2002	Special

4471	EU NA AU AS	
Secret Substitute 1		
Geheimer Einwechselspieler 1		
Pcs: 4	2002	Special

4472	EU NA AU AS	
Secret Substitute 2		
Geheimer Einwechselspieler 2		
Pcs: 4	2002	Special

4524	EU NA AU AS	
Advent Calendar		
Adventskalender		
Pcs: 231	2002	Special

4534	EU NA AU AS	
Express		
Express		
Pcs: 487	2002	Special

i	4466-4472	Coca-Cola Promo	Coca-Cola Promo

4535	EU NA AU AS	
Express Deluxe		
Express Deluxe		
Pcs: 776	2002	Special

4582	EU NA AU AS	
Red Bullet		
Red Bullet		
Pcs: 31	2002–2003	

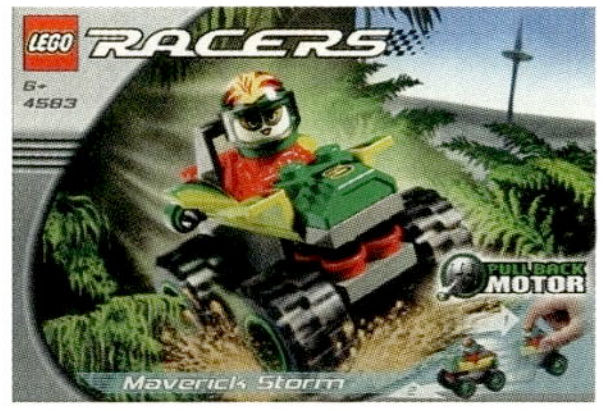

4583	EU NA AU AS	
Maverick Storm		
Maverick Storm		
Pcs: 38	2002	

4584	EU NA AU AS	
Hot Scorcher		
Hot Scorcher		
Pcs: 57	2002–2003	

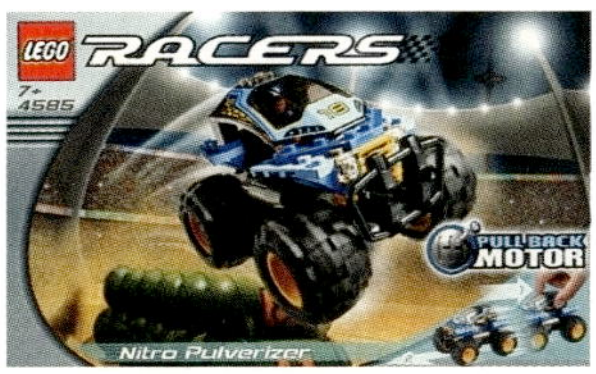

4585	EU NA AU AS	
Nitro Pulverizer		
Nitro Pulverizer		
Pcs: 66	2002–2003	

4586	EU NA AU AS	
Stunt Race Track		
Stunt Race Track		
Pcs: 168	2002–2003	

4587	EU NA AU AS	
Duel Racers		
Duel Racers		
Pcs: 195	2002–2003	

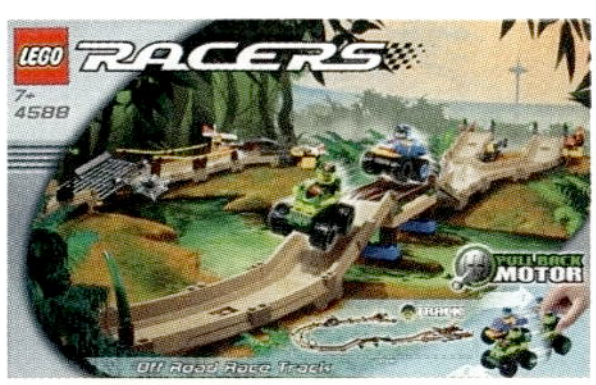

4588	EU NA AU AS	
Off Road Race Track		
Off-Road Race Track		
Pcs: 359	2002–2003	

4589	EU NA AU AS	
RC Nitro Flash		
RC Nitro Flash		
Pcs: 133	2002–2003	

4590	EU NA AU AS	
Flash Turbo		
Flash Turbo		
Pcs: 26	2002	Special

4591	EU NA AU AS	
Star Strike		
Star Strike		
Pcs: 29	2002–2003	Special

4592	EU NA AU AS	
Red Monster		
Red Monster		
Pcs: 25	2002–2003	Special

4593	EU NA AU AS	
Zero Hurricane & Red Blizzard		
Zero Hurricane & Red Blizzard		
Pcs: 77	2002–2003	

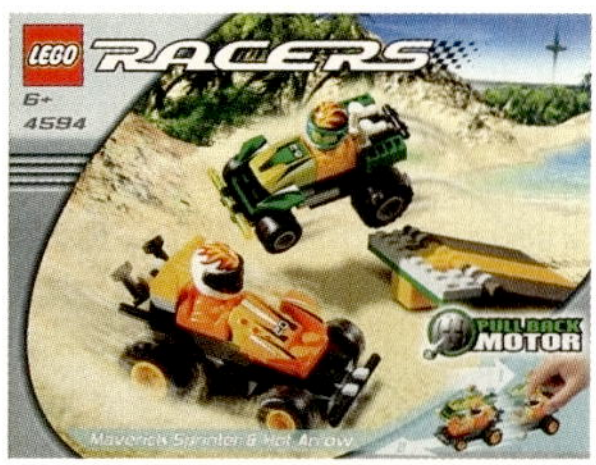

4594	EU NA AU AS	
Maverick Sprinter & Hot Arrow		
Maverick Sprinter & Hot Arrow		
Pcs: 68	2002–2003	

4595	EU NA AU AS	
Zero Tornado & Hot Rock		
Zero Tornado & Hot Rock		
Pcs: 71	2002–2003	

4596	EU NA AU AS	
Storming Cobra		
Storming Cobra		
Pcs: 90	2002–2003	

4612	EU NA AU AS	
Super Glider		
Drachenflieger		
Pcs: 7	2002	Special

4613	EU NA AU AS	
Turbo Chopper		
Turbo-Hubschrauber		
Pcs: 13	2002	Special

4612	Similar to: 1435 (2002)	Ähnlich zu: 1435 (2002)
4613	Similar to: 1437 (2002)	Ähnlich zu: 1437 (2002)

4614	EU NA AU AS	
Ultralight Flyer		
Ultraleichtflugzeug		
Pcs: 12	2002	Special

4615	EU NA AU AS	
Red Recon Flyer		
Rotes Propellerflugzeug		
Pcs: 21	2002–2003	

4616	EU NA AU AS	
Rapid Response Tanker		
Bereitschafts-Tankwagen		
Pcs: 35	2002–2003	

4617	EU NA AU AS	
Dual Prop Turbo		
Turbo-Propeller		
Pcs: 32	2002–2003	

4618	EU NA AU AS	
Twin Rotor Cargo		
Großer Transport-Hubschrauber		
Pcs: 45	2002–2003	

4619	EU NA AU AS	
A.I.R. Patrol Jet		
Forschungs-Flugzeug		
Pcs: 66	2002–2003	

4620	EU NA AU AS	
A.I.R. Operations HQ		
Wetterforschungszentrale		
Pcs: 173	2002–2003	

4621	EU NA AU AS	
Red Flash Station		
Feuerwehr-Einsatzwagen		
Pcs: 30	2002	

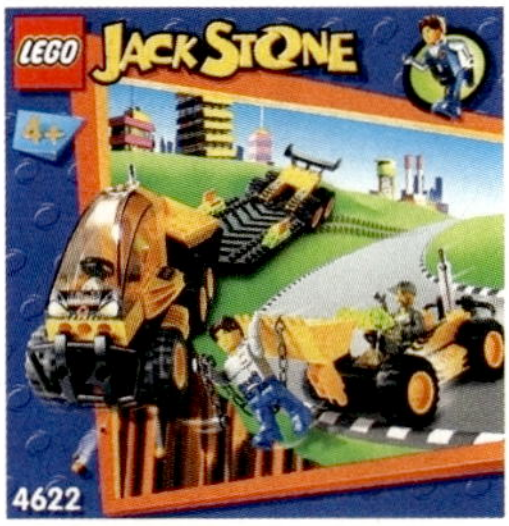

4622	EU NA AU AS	
ResQ Digger		
Transporter & Frontschaufellader		
Pcs: 67	2002	

i	4614	Similar to: 1436 (2002)	Ähnlich zu: 1436 (2002)

4711	EU NA AU AS
Flying Lesson	
Flugstunde	
Pcs: 24	2002–2003

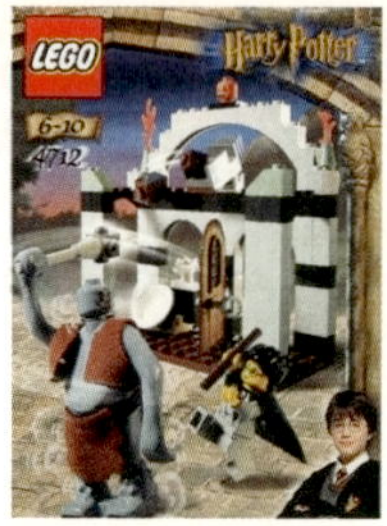

4712	EU NA AU AS
Troll on the Loose	
Der Troll ist los	
Pcs: 76	2002–2003

4714	EU NA AU AS
Gringotts Bank	
Gringotts Bank	
Pcs: 250	2002–2003

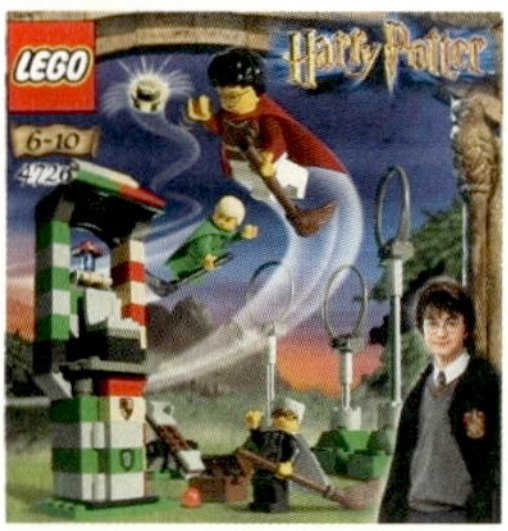

4726	EU NA AU AS
Quidditch Practice	
Quidditch Training	
Pcs: 128	2002–2005

4727	EU NA AU AS
Aragog in the Dark Forest	
Aragog im Verbotenen Wald	
Pcs: 178	2002–2003

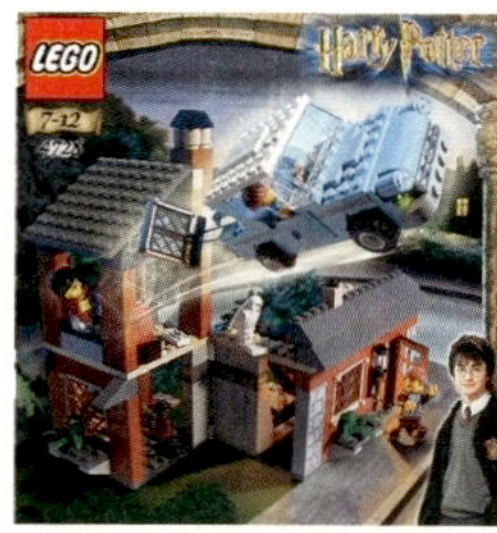

4728	EU NA AU AS
Escape from Privet Drive	
Flucht vom Ligusterweg	
Pcs: 278	2002–2005

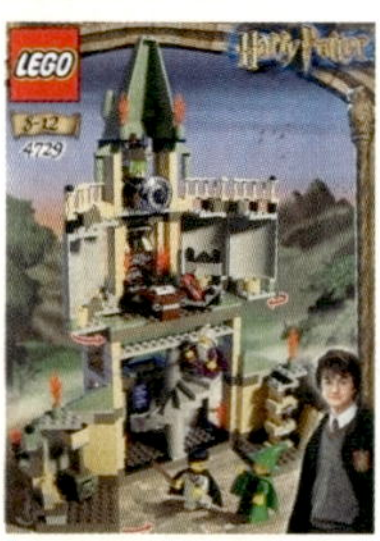

4729	EU
Dumbledore's Office	
Dumbledores Büro	
Pcs: 446	2002–2005

4730	EU NA AU AS
The Chamber of Secrets	
Die Kammer des Schreckens	
Pcs: 591	2002–2003

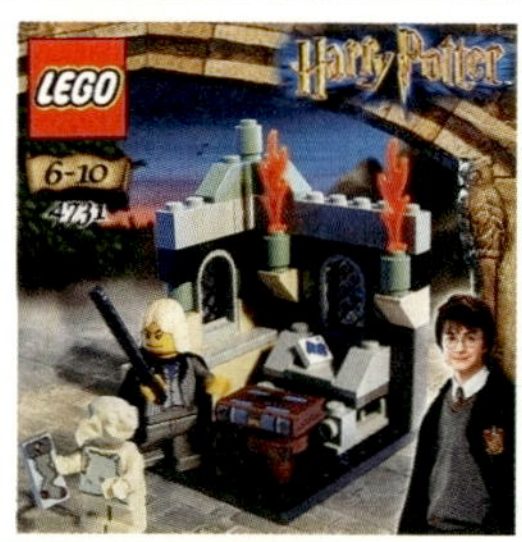

4731	EU NA
Dobby's Release	
Dobbys Befreiung	
Pcs: 70	2002–2003

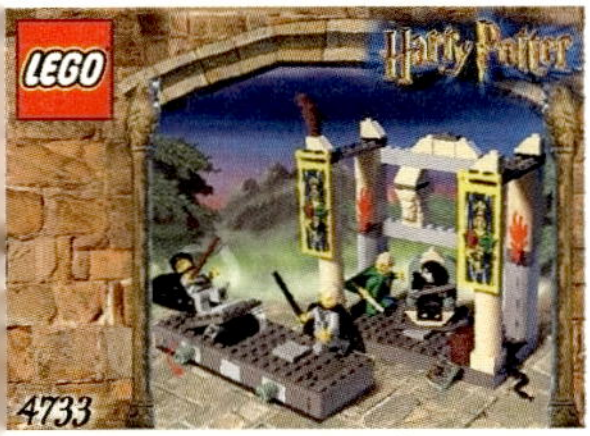

4733 EU NA AU AS

The Dueling Club	
Der Duellierclub	
Pcs: 129	2002–2003

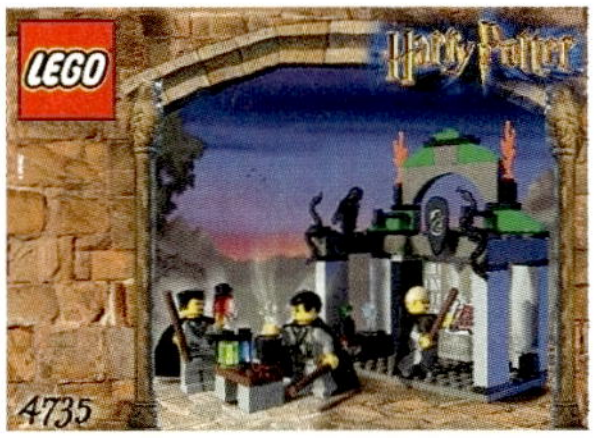

4735 EU NA AU AS

Slytherin	
Slytherin	
Pcs: 90	2002–2003

4788 EU NA AU AS

Ogel Mutant Ray		
Ogels Mutantenrochen		
Pcs: 70	2002	Special

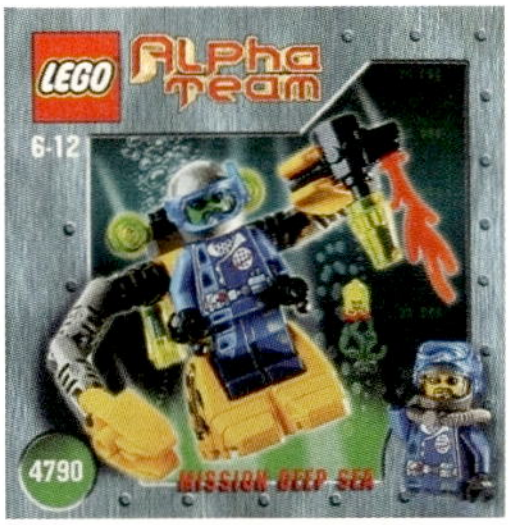

4790 EU NA AU AS

Alpha Team Robot Diver	
Alpha Team Tauchroboter	
Pcs: 38	2002–2003

4791 EU NA AU AS

Alpha Team Sub-Surface Scooter	
Unterwasser-Scooter	
Pcs: 49	2002–2003

4792 EU NA AU AS

Alpha Team Navigator and ROV	
U-Boot	
Pcs: 97	2002–2003

4793 EU NA AU AS

Ogel Shark Sub	
Ogels Hai-Cruiser	
Pcs: 116	2002–2003

4794 EU NA AU AS

Alpha Team Command Patrol	
Kommando U-Boot	
Pcs: 199	2002–2003

4795 EU NA AU AS

Ogel Underwater Base & AT Sub	
Ogels Unterwasserzentrale	
Pcs: 487	2002–2003

4796	EU NA AU AS
Ogel Mutant Squid	
Ogels Tintenfisch-Mutant	
Pcs: 61	2002–2003

4797	EU NA AU AS
Ogel Mutant Killer Whale	
Ogels Wal-Mutant	
Pcs: 62	2002–2003

4798	EU NA AU AS	
Evil Ogel Attack		
Ogels Angriff		
Pcs: 20	2002	Special

4799	EU NA AU AS	
Ogel Drone Octopus		
Ogels Tintenfisch		
Pcs: 17	2002	Special

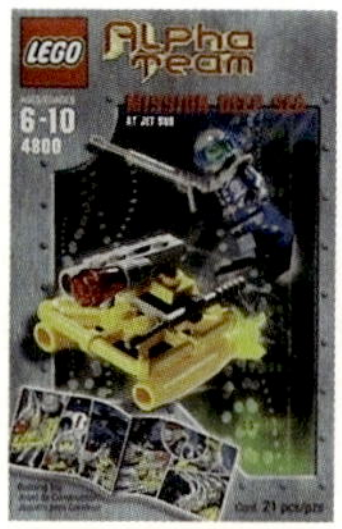

4800	EU NA AU AS	
AT Jet Sub		
Unterwassergleiter		
Pcs: 21	2002	Special

5420	EU NA AU AS
Soft Frog Rattle	
Klett-Frosch	
Pcs: 1	2002–2003

5421	EU NA AU AS
Star Teether	
Seestern	
Pcs: 1	2002–2003

5422	EU NA AU AS
Caterpillar Teether	
Raupen-Beißring	
Pcs: 1	2002–2003

5423	EU NA AU AS
Crib and Mirror Adventure	
Entdecken und Lernen	
Pcs: 1	2002–2003

i	Set	English	Deutsch
i	4798	Similar to: 1427 (2002)	Ähnlich zu: 1427 (2002)
i	4800	Similar to: 1425 (2002)	Ähnlich zu: 1425 (2002)
i	5420	Similar to: 3172 (2001)	Ähnlich zu: 3172 (2001)
i	5421	Similar to: 3212 (2001)	Ähnlich zu: 3212 (2001)
i	5422	Similar to: 3173 (2001)	Ähnlich zu: 3173 (2001)
i	5423	Similar to: 3169 (2001)	Ähnlich zu: 3169 (2001)

ⓘ 5424	EU NA AU AS
Take Along Friend	
Blumenmädchen und Freunde	
Pcs: 2	2002–2003

ⓘ 5425	EU NA AU AS
Soft Stacking Hen	
Überraschungshenne	
Pcs: 5	2002–2003

ⓘ 5426	EU NA AU AS
Shape and Color Sorter	
Form- und Farben-Sortierer	
Pcs: 9	2002–2003

ⓘ 5427	EU NA AU AS
Blinking and Playing Butterfly	
Schmetterling, Rassel & Co.	
Pcs: 11	2002–2003

ⓘ 5429	EU NA AU AS
Play Plane	
Propellerflugzeug	
Pcs: 2	2002–2005

ⓘ 5430	EU NA AU AS
Squirt Frog	
Zwinker-Frosch	
Pcs: 1	2002–2003

ⓘ 5431	EU NA AU AS
Roll-n-Play	
Figurenball	
Pcs: 3	2002–2003

ⓘ 5432	EU NA AU AS
Bendy Caterpillar	
Raupe „Löwenzahn“	
Pcs: 3	2002–2005

ⓘ 5433	EU NA AU AS
Stacking Tower	
Stapelbär	
Pcs: 5	2002–2003

ⓘ	5424	Similar to: 3162 (2001)	Ähnlich zu: 3162 (2001)
ⓘ	5425	Similar to: 3161 (2001)	Ähnlich zu: 3161 (2001)
ⓘ	5426	Similar to: 3238 (2001)	Ähnlich zu: 3238 (2001)
ⓘ	5429	Similar to: 3160 (2001)	Ähnlich zu: 3160 (2001)
ⓘ	5430	Similar to: 1456 (2001)	Ähnlich zu: 1456 (2001)
ⓘ	5431	Similar to: 3236 (2001)	Ähnlich zu: 3236 (2001)

ⓘ 5434	EU NA AU AS	
Stack-n-Learn		
Großer Bauspaß		
Pcs: 40	2002–2003	

ⓘ 5435	EU	
Flower		
Blume		
Pcs: 2	2002–2003	Special

ⓘ 5436	EU	
Stack N' Learn		
Stack N' Learn		
Pcs: 2	2002–2005	Special

ⓘ 5437	EU NA	
Parrot		
Papagei		
Pcs: 6	2002–2005	Special

ⓘ 5438	EU NA	
Ladybug Rattle		
Marienkäfer-Rassel		
Pcs: 1	2002–2004	Special

ⓘ 5494	EU NA	
Rolling Duck		
Ente auf Rädern		
Pcs: 4	2002–2004	Special

ⓘ 5836	EU	
Beautiful Baby Princess		
Reizende kleine Prinzessin		
Pcs: 23	2002–2003	

ⓘ 5837	EU NA AU AS	
Flora's Bubbling Bath		
Floras Badeparadies		
Pcs: 30	2002–2003	

ⓘ 5838	EU	
Wicked Madam Frost		
Die Hexe Madam Frost		
Pcs: 36	2002–2003	

ⓘ	5432	Similar to: 1457 (2001)	Ähnlich zu: 1457 (2001)
ⓘ	5433	Similar to: 3237 (2001)	Ähnlich zu: 3237 (2001)
ⓘ	5437	Similar to: 1201 (2001)	Ähnlich zu: 1201 (2001)

5842 EU NA AU AS

Vanilla's Frosty Sleighride		
Vanillas frostige Schlittenfahrt		
Pcs: 34	2002–2003	

5843 EU NA AU AS

Queen & the Little Prince		
Die Königin und der kleine Prinz		
Pcs: 4	2002–2003	

5850 EU NA AU AS

The Royal Crystal Palace		
Der königliche Kristallpalast		
Pcs: 150	2002–2003	

5871 EU NA AU AS

Riding Stables		
Reitschule		
Pcs: 14	2002	

5923 EU NA AU AS

Western Photo Frame		
Western Bilderrahmen		
Pcs: 138	2002–2003	Special

5924 EU NA AU AS

Knights' Kingdom Photo Frame		
Knights' Kingdom Bilderrahmen		
Pcs: 105	2002–2003	Special

5927 EU NA AU AS

Racers Photo Frame		
Racers Bilderrahmen		
Pcs: -	2002–2003	Special

5991 EU NA AU AS

Snowscooter Boy		
Schneemobil		
Pcs: -	2002–2004	Special

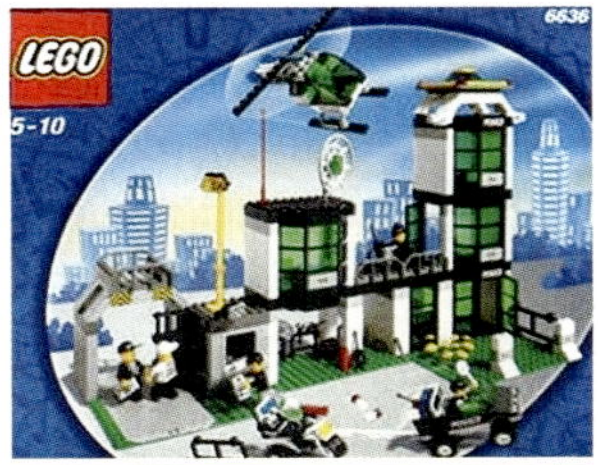

6636 EU NA AU AS

Police Headquarters		
Polizei-Hauptquartier		
Pcs: 311	2002	

i	Set	English	Deutsch
i	5871	Similar to: 5855 (1997)	Ähnlich zu: 5855 (1997)
i	5923	Available in LEGOLAND® Billund	Erhältlich im LEGOLAND® Billund
i	5924	Available in LEGOLAND® Billund	Erhältlich im LEGOLAND® Billund
i	5927	Available in LEGOLAND® Billund	Erhältlich im LEGOLAND® Billund
i	6636	Similar to: 6332 (1998)	Ähnlich zu: 6332 (1998)

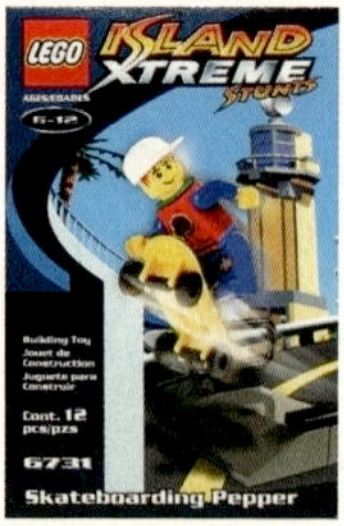

6731 EU NA AU AS
Skateboarding Pepper
Pepper auf dem Skateboard
Pcs: 12 | 2002

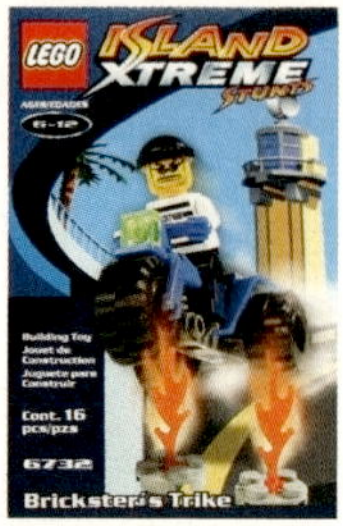

6732 EU NA AU AS
Brickster's Trike
Steinbrechers Trike
Pcs: 16 | 2002

6733 EU NA AU AS
Snap's Cruiser
Snaps Cruiser
Pcs: 18 | 2002

6734 EU NA AU AS
Beach Cruisers
Strand-Cruiser
Pcs: 53 | 2002–2003

6735 EU NA AU AS
Air Chase
Abenteuer in der Luft
Pcs: 83 | 2002–2003

6736 EU NA AU AS
Beach Lookout
Strandwache
Pcs: 90 | 2002–2003

6737 EU NA AU AS
Wake Rider
Motorboot mit Wakeboard
Pcs: 91 | 2002–2003

6738 EU NA AU AS
Skateboard Challenge
Skateboard-Funpark
Pcs: 114 | 2002–2003

6739 EU NA AU AS
Truck & Stunt Trikes
Großer Truck mit Stunt-Trikes
Pcs: 218 | 2002–2003

ⓘ 6740	EU NA AU AS
Xtreme Tower	
Extrem-Sport-Anlage	
Pcs: 342	2002–2003

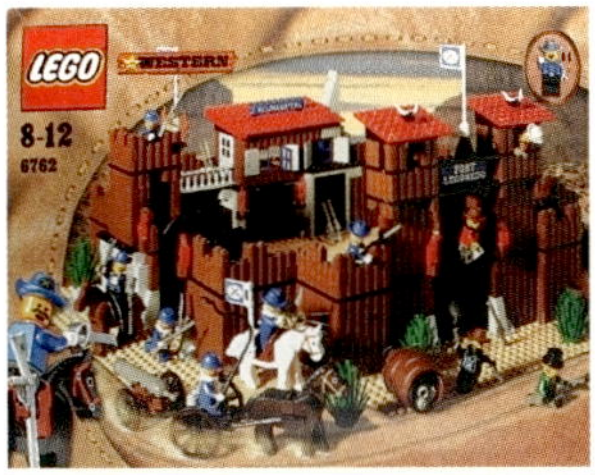

ⓘ 6762	EU NA AU AS
Fort LEGOREDO	
Fort LEGOREDO	
Pcs: 673	2002

ⓘ 6763	EU NA AU AS
Rapid River Village	
Großes Indianerlager	
Pcs: 343	2002–2003

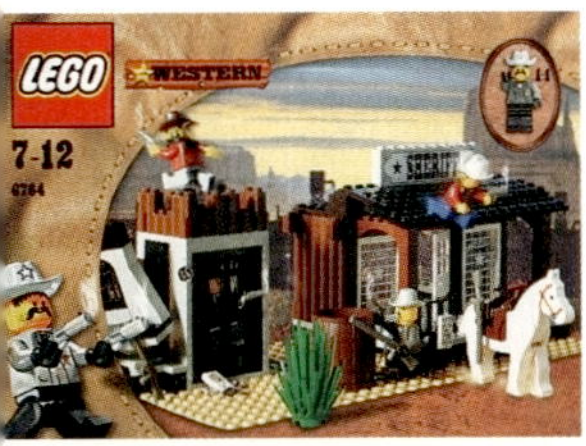

ⓘ 6764	EU NA AU AS
Sheriff's Lock-Up	
Sheriffs Büro und Gefängnis	
Pcs: 171	2002–2003

ⓘ 7103	EU NA AU AS
Jedi™ Duel	
Jedi™ Duel	
Pcs: 81	2002–2003

ⓘ 7113	EU NA AU AS
Tusken Raider™ Encounter	
Tusken Raider™ Encounter	
Pcs: 90	2002–2003

ⓘ 7119	EU NA AU AS
Twin-Pod Cloud Car™	
Twin-Pod Cloud Car™	
Pcs: 117	2002–2003

ⓘ 7133	EU NA AU AS
Bounty Hunter™ Pursuit	
Bounty Hunter™ Pursuit	
Pcs: 253	2002–2003

ⓘ 7139	EU NA AU AS
Ewok™ Attack	
Ewok™ Attack	
Pcs: 119	2002–2003

ⓘ	6762	Similar to: 6769 (1996)	Ähnlich zu: 6769 (1996)
ⓘ	6763	Similar to: 6766 (1997)	Ähnlich zu: 6766 (1997)
ⓘ	6764	Similar to: 6755 (1996)	Ähnlich zu: 6755 (1996)

7142	EU NA AU AS	
X-wing Fighter™		
X-wing Fighter™		
Pcs: 274	2002	Special

7143	EU NA AU AS	
Jedi Starfighter™		
Jedi Starfighter™		
Pcs: 138	2002–2003	

7152	EU NA AU AS	
TIE Fighter™ & Y-wing™		
TIE Fighter™ & Y-wing™		
Pcs: 413	2002	Special

7153	EU NA AU AS	
Jango Fett's Slave I™		
Jango Fett's Slave I™		
Pcs: 358	2002–2003	

7163	EU NA AU AS	
Republic Gunship™		
Republic Gunship™		
Pcs: 688	2002–2003	

7194	EU NA AU AS	
Yoda™		
Yoda™		
Pcs: 1075	2002–2003	

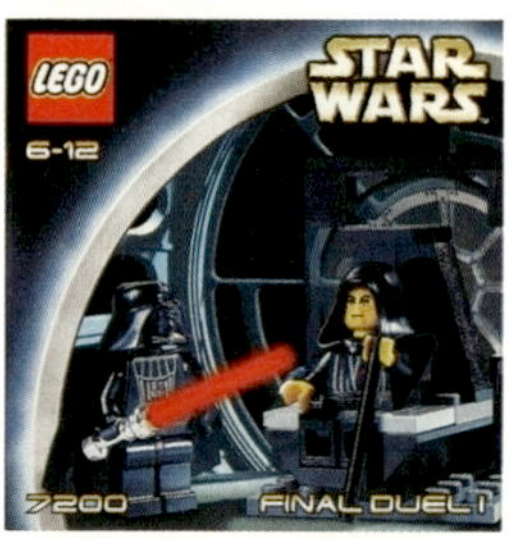

7200	EU NA AU AS	
Final Duel I		
Final Duel I		
Pcs: 29	2002–2003	

7201	EU NA AU AS	
Final Duel II		
Final Duel II		
Pcs: 28	2002	

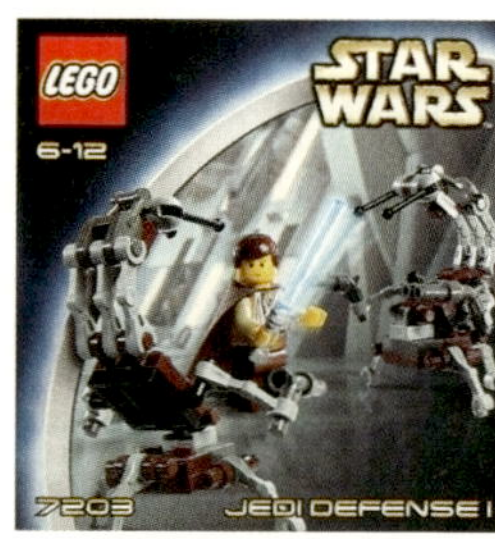

7203	EU NA AU AS	
Jedi™ Defense I		
Jedi™ Defense I		
Pcs: 63	2002–2003	

i	7142	Similar to: 7140 (1999); included in: 65145 (2002)	Ähnlich zu: 7140 (1999), enthalten in: 65145 (2002)
i	7152	Similar to: 7150 (1999); included in: 65145 (2002)	Ähnlich zu: 7150 (1999); enthalten in: 65145 (2002)

7204	EU NA AU AS	
Jedi™ Defense II		
Jedi™ Defense II		
Pcs: 57	2002	

7825	EU NA AU AS	
Bucket		
Eimer		
Pcs: 500	2002–2003	Special

7830	EU NA AU AS	
Small Bucket		
Kleiner Eimer		
Pcs: 200	2002–2006	

7831	EU NA AU AS	
Make-believe Bucket		
Fantasie-Eimer		
Pcs: 200	2002–2003	Special

7832	EU NA AU AS	
Small Bucket		
Kleiner Eimer		
Pcs: 200	2002–2003	Special

7837	EU NA AU AS	
Build and Create		
Bauen und Gestalten		
Pcs: 600	2002–2003	Special

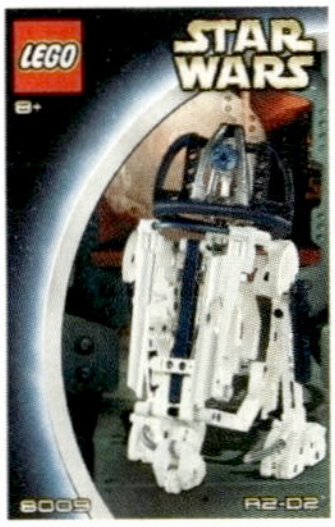

8009	EU NA AU AS	
R2-D2™		
R2-D2™		
Pcs: 248	2002–2003	

8010	EU NA AU AS	
Darth Vader™		
Darth Vader™		
Pcs: 412	2002–2003	

8011	EU NA AU AS	
Jango Fett™		
Jango Fett™		
Pcs: 429	2002–2003	

i	7825	Similar to: 4014 (2003), 4179 (2002), 4106 (2002)	Ähnlich zu: 4014 (2003), 4179 (2002), 4106 (2002)
i	8009	Included in: 65081 (2002)	Enthalten in: 65081 (2002)

8012	EU NA AU AS	
Super Battle Droid™		
Super Battle Droid™		
Pcs: 381	2002–2003	

8310	EU NA AU AS	
Nick		
Nick		
Pcs: 12	2002–2003	Special

8311	EU NA AU AS	
Gorm		
Gorm		
Pcs: 12	2002–2003	Special

8312	EU NA AU AS	
Jens		
Jens		
Pcs: 13	2002–2003	Special

8313	EU NA AU AS	
Nick Deluxe		
Nick Deluxe		
Pcs: 15	2002–2003	Special

8314	EU NA AU AS	
Gorm Deluxe		
Gorm Deluxe		
Pcs: 15	2002–2003	Special

8315	EU NA AU AS	
TDN Module		
TDN Module		
Pcs: 9	2002–2003	Special

8316	EU NA AU AS	
Kek Powerizer		
Kek Powerizer		
Pcs: 9	2002–2003	Special

8317	EU NA AU AS	
Allegra		
Allegra		
Pcs: 11	2002–2003	Special

8318	EU NA AU AS	
Ooni		
Ooni		
Pcs: 29	2002–2003	Special

8320	EU NA AU AS	
Nepol Basic Figure		
Nepol		
Pcs: 10	2002–2003	Special

8321	EU NA AU AS	
Nepol & Shimmel Super Deluxe		
Nepol & Shimmel Super Deluxe		
Pcs: 27	2002–2003	Special

8324	EU NA AU AS	
Euripides		
Euripides		
Pcs: 10	2002–2003	Special

8325	EU NA AU AS	
Tager		
Tager		
Pcs: 18	2002–2003	Special

8429	EU NA AU AS	
Aero Hawk II		
High Speed Helikopter		
Pcs: 138	2002	

8430	EU NA AU AS	
Motorbike		
Rennbike		
Pcs: 315	2002–2003	

8431	EU NA AU AS	
Crane Truck		
3-Achs-Kranwagen		
Pcs: 841	2002	

8461	EU NA AU AS	
Williams F1 Racer		
Williams F1 Team Racer		
Pcs: 1483	2002–2003	

Set	English	Deutsch
8429	Similar to: 8812 (1994)	Ähnlich zu: 8812 (1994)
8430	Similar to: 8417 (1998)	Ähnlich zu: 8417 (1998)
8431	Similar to: 8460 (1995), 8438 (2003)	Ähnlich zu: 8460 (1995), 8438 (2003)

8468	EU NA AU AS
Power Crusher	
Power Crusher	
Pcs: 92	2002–2003

8469	EU NA AU AS
Slammer Raptor	
Slammer Raptor	
Pcs: 144	2002–2003

8470	EU NA AU AS
Slammer G-Force	
Slammer G-Force	
Pcs: 153	2002

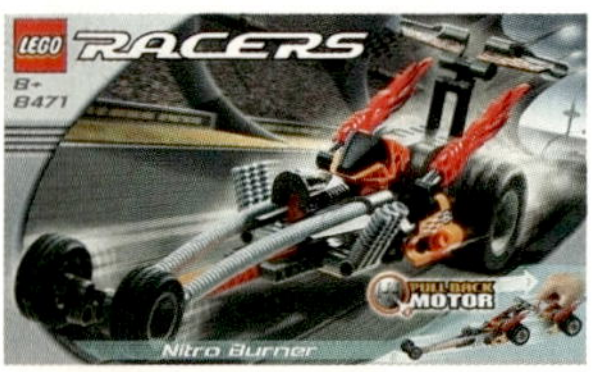

8471	EU NA AU AS
Nitro Burner	
Nitro Burner	
Pcs: 121	2002–2003

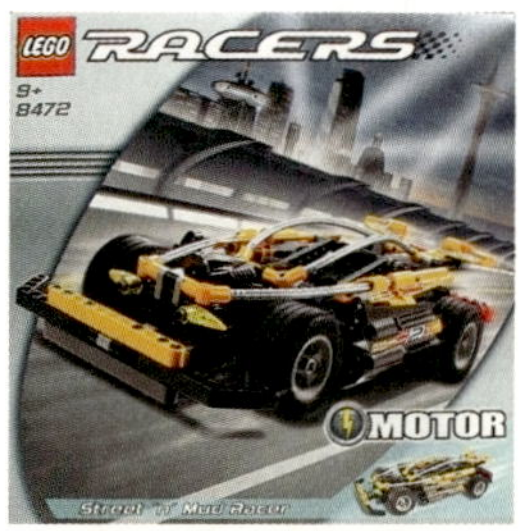

8472	EU NA AU AS
Street-n-Mud Racer	
Street-n-Mud Racer	
Pcs: 347	2002–2003

8473	EU NA AU AS
Nitro Race Team	
Nitro Race Team	
Pcs: 500	2002–2003

8475	EU NA AU AS
RC Race Buggy	
RC Race Buggy	
Pcs: 290	2002–2003

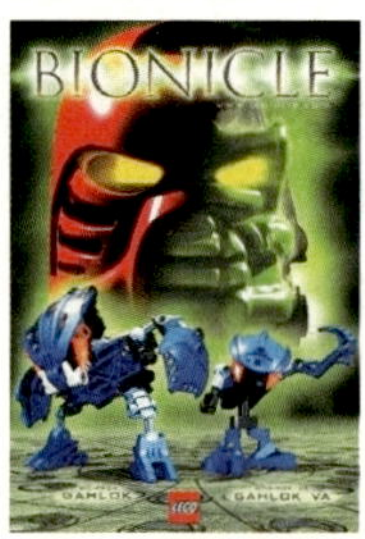

8550	EU NA AU AS
Gahlok Va	
Gahlok Va	
Pcs: 27	2002

8551	EU NA AU AS
Kohrak Va	
Kohrak Va	
Pcs: 29	2002

i	8550	Similar to: 1433 (2002)	Ähnlich zu: 1433 (2002)

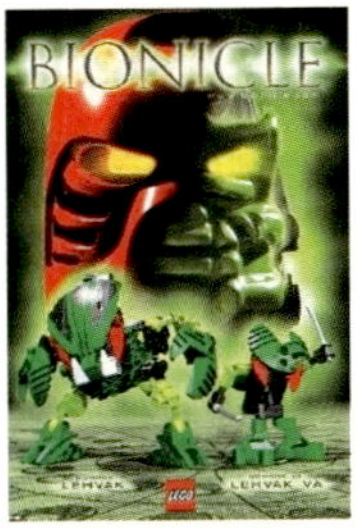

8552 EU NA AU AS

Lehvak Va	
Lehvak Va	
Pcs: 29	2002

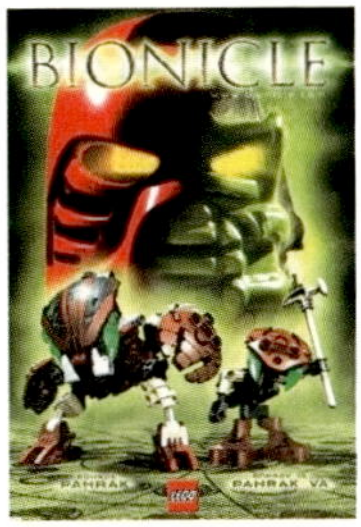

8553 EU NA AU AS

Pahrak Va	
Pahrak Va	
Pcs: 28	2002

8554 EU NA AU AS

Tahnok Va	
Tahnok Va	
Pcs: 27	2002

8555 EU NA AU AS

Nuhvok Va	
Nuhvok Va	
Pcs: 27	2002

8556 EU NA AU AS

Boxor Vehicle	
Boxor	
Pcs: 157	2002–2003

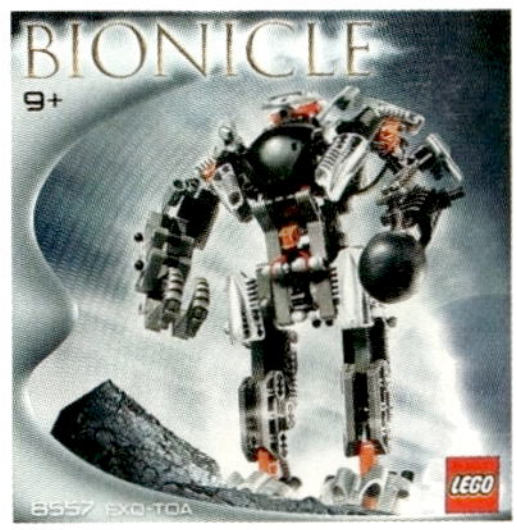

8557 EU NA AU AS

Exo-Toa	
Exo-Toa	
Pcs: 378	2002–2003

8558 EU NA AU AS

Cahdok and Gahdok	
Cahdok und Gahdok	
Pcs: 636	2002–2003

8559 EU NA AU AS

Krana		
Krana		
Pcs: 5	2002	Special

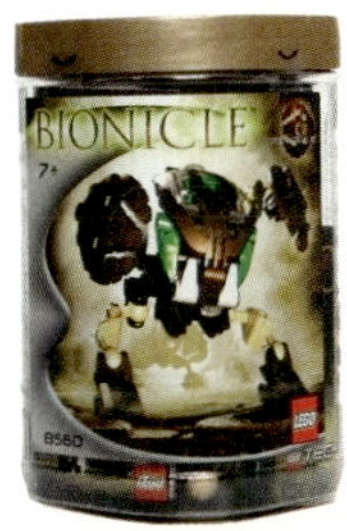

8560 EU NA AU AS

Pahrak	
Pahrak	
Pcs: 43	2002

i	8552	Similar to: 1434 (2002)	Ähnlich zu: 1434 (2002)
i	8554	Similar to: 1431 (2002)	Ähnlich zu: 1431 (2002)
i	8555	Similar to: 1432 (2002)	Ähnlich zu: 1432 (2002)
i	8559	Similar to: 8569 (2002)	Ähnlich zu: 8569 (2002)

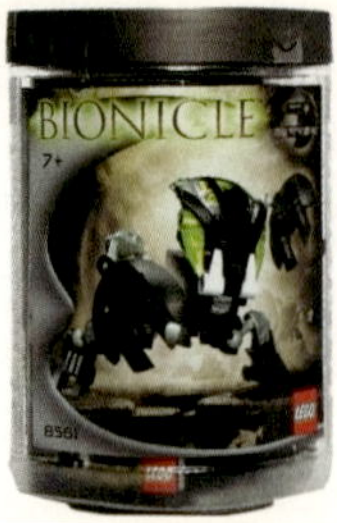

8561	EU NA AU AS	
Nuhvok		
Nuhvok		
Pcs: 43	2002	

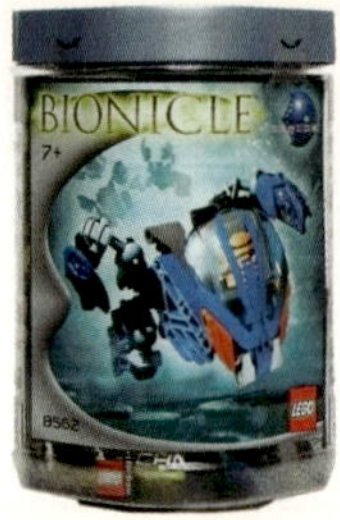

8562	EU NA AU AS	
Gahlok		
Gahlok		
Pcs: 43	2002	

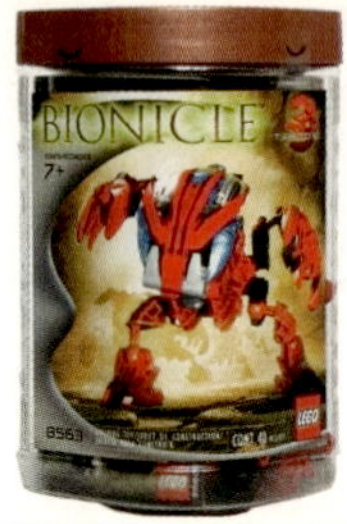

8563	EU NA AU AS	
Tahnok		
Tahnok		
Pcs: 43	2002	

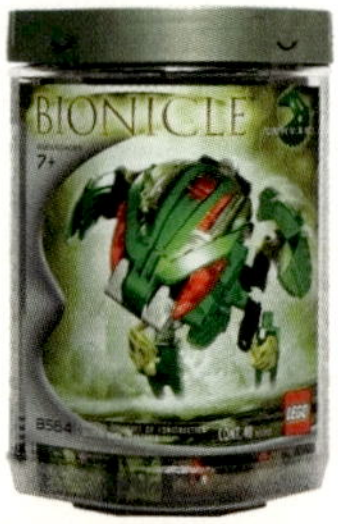

8564	EU NA AU AS	
Lehvak		
Lehvak		
Pcs: 43	2002	

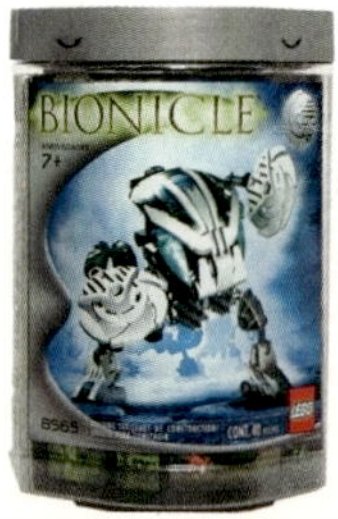

8565	EU NA AU AS	
Kohrak		
Kohrak		
Pcs: 43	2002	

8566	EU NA AU AS	
Onua Nuva		
Onua Nuva		
Pcs: 41	2002–2003	

8567	EU NA AU AS	
Lewa Nuva		
Lewa Nuva		
Pcs: 36	2002–2003	

8568	EU NA AU AS	
Pohatu Nuva		
Pohatu Nuva		
Pcs: 44	2002–2003	

8569	EU NA AU AS	
Krana		
Krana		
Pcs: 5	2002	Special

8569	Similar to: 8559 (2002)	Ähnlich zu: 8559 (2002)

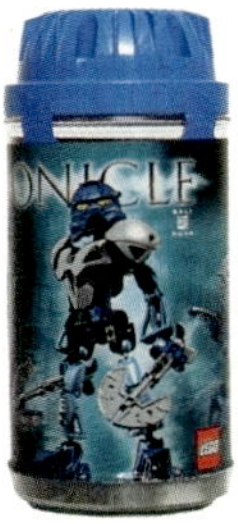

8570	EU NA AU AS
Gali Nuva	
Gali Nuva	
Pcs: 44	2002–2003

8571	EU NA AU AS
Kopaka Nuva	
Kopaka Nuva	
Pcs: 43	2002–2003

8572	EU NA AU AS
Tahu Nuva	
Tahu Nuva	
Pcs: 36	2002–2003

8597	EU NA AU AS	
Kanohi Nuva and Krana		
Kanohi Nuva Masken		
Pcs: 2	2002	Special

8598	EU NA AU AS	
Kanohi Nuva & Krana Pack		
Kanohi Nuva & Krana Set		
Pcs: 5	2002	Special

10020	EU NA AU AS	
Santa Fe Super Chief		
Santa Fe Super Chief		
Pcs: 436	2002–2006	Special

10022	EU NA AU AS	
Santa Fe Cars Set II		
Santa Fe Waggonbausatz II		
Pcs: 411	2002–2006	Special

10023	EU NA AU AS	
Master Builder Set		
Master Builder Set		
Pcs: 113	2002–2003	Special

10024	EU NA AU AS	
Red Baron		
Roter Baron		
Pcs: 670	2002–2005	Special

i	8597	Similar to: 8598 (2002)	Ähnlich zu: 8598 (2002)
i	8598	Similar to: 8597 (2002)	Ähnlich zu: 8597 (2002)
i	10020	Was also available as a limited Edition (10000 sets) via Shop at Home	Gab es auch als limitierte Version mit Auflage 10000; erhältlich bei Shop at Home
i	10022-10025	Was distributed via Shop at Home	Wurde über Shop at Home vertrieben

ⓘ 10025	EU NA AU AS	
Santa Fe Cars Set I		
Santa Fe Waggonbausatz I		
Pcs: 326	2002–2006	Special

ⓘ 10026	EU NA AU AS	
SE Naboo™ Starfighter		
Naboo Starfighter™ Sonderausgabe		
Pcs: 187	2002	Special

ⓘ 10030	EU NA AU AS	
Imperial Star Destroyer™		
Imperial Star Destroyer™		
Pcs: 3104	2002–2005	Special

ⓘ 10036	EU NA AU AS	
Pizza To Go		
Pizza To Go		
Pcs: 144	2002–2003	

ⓘ 10037	EU NA AU AS	
Breezeway Café		
Breezeway Café		
Pcs: 178	2002–2003	Special

ⓘ 10039	EU NA AU AS	
Black Falcon's Fortress		
Die Burg des schwarzen Falken		
Pcs: 424	2002–2003	

ⓘ 10040	EU NA AU AS	
Black Seas Barracuda		
Black Seas Barracuda		
Pcs: 896	2002–2003	

ⓘ 10052	EU NA AU AS	
Intelligent Locomotive		
Interaktive, intelligente Lokomotive		
Pcs: 6	2002–2005	

ⓘ 10068	EU NA AU AS	
Santa		
Weihnachtsmann		
Pcs: 39	2002–2005	Special

ⓘ	10026	Was distributed via Shop at Home	Wurde über Shop at Home vertrieben
ⓘ	10036	Re-release of: 6350 (1994)	Neuauflage von: 6350 (1994)
ⓘ	10037	Similar to: 6376 (1990)	Ähnlich zu: 6376 (1990)
ⓘ	10039	Re-release ofio: 6074 (1986)	Neuauflage von: 6074 (1986)
ⓘ	10040	Re-release of: 6285 (1989)	Neuauflage von: 6285 (1989)
ⓘ	10068	Similar to: 1978 (1991), 1127 (1999)	Ähnlich zu: 1978 (1991), 1127 (1999)

10069	EU NA AU AS	
Tree		
Christbaum		
Pcs: 33	2002–2005	Special

10070	EU NA AU AS	
Reindeer		
Rentier		
Pcs: 26	2002–2005	Special

10075	EU NA AU AS	
Action Pack		
Zubehör		
Pcs: 25	2002–2003	Special

10205	EU NA AU AS	
My Own Train		
Große Lokomotive mit Tender		
Pcs: 237	2002–2003	Special

65062	EU NA AU AS	
Racers Turbo Pack		
Racers Turbo Pack		
Pcs: 92	2002	Special

65081	EU NA AU AS	
Droid Collectors Set		
Droid Collectorsset		
Pcs: 602	2002	Special

65118	EU NA AU AS	
Secret Mission Collector's Pack		
Secret Mission Collector's Pack		
Pcs: 238	2002	Special

65145	EU NA AU AS	
Star Wars™ Fighter Value Pack		
Star Wars™ Fighter Kombiset		
Sets: 2	2002	Special

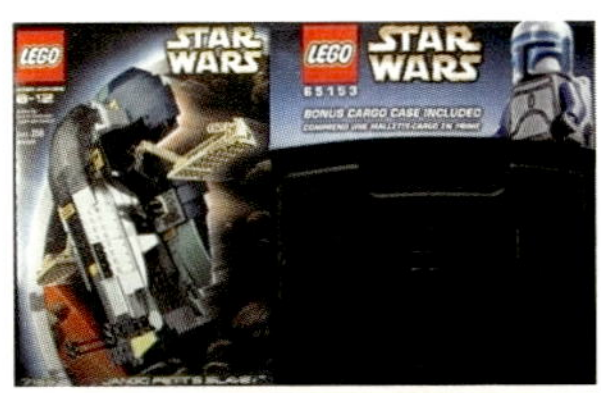

65153	EU NA AU AS	
Jango Fett's Slave I™ with Case		
Jango Fett's Slave I™ mit Koffer		
Pcs: 367	2002–2003	Special

65081	Includes: 8007 (2001), 8009 (2002)	Enthält: 8007 (2001), 8009 (2002)
65145	Included in: 7142 (2002), 7152 (2002)	Enthalten in: 7142 (2002), 7152 (2002)

65295		EU NA AU AS
Twin Pack with Gold Avohkii		
2er-Pack mit goldener Avohkii		
Sets: 2	2002–2003	Special

2003

1385	EU NA
Bracelet	
Armreif	
Pcs: 13	2003–2004	Special

3223	EU
Orange Fish	
Oranger Fisch	
Pcs: 48	2003–2004	Special

3284	EU NA AU
Bob's Busy Day	
Bob's anstrengender Tag	
Pcs: 10	2003	

3285	EU
Wendy in the Office	
Wendy im Büro	
Pcs: 10	2003	

3286	EU
Spud & Bird	
Knolle und Vogel Feder	
Pcs: 10	2003	

3380	EU
Johnny Thunder	
Johnny Thunder	
Pcs: 8	2003	Special

i	3380	Chupa Chups Promo	Chupa Chups Promo

3381	EU NA AU AS	
Sam Sinister		
Sam Sinister		
Pcs: 8	2003	Special

3382	EU NA AU AS	
Jing Lee		
Jing Lee		
Pcs: 6	2003	Special

3383	EU NA AU AS	
Chef		
Chefkoch		
Pcs: 8	2003	Special

3384	EU NA AU AS	
Train Worker		
Bahnarbeiter		
Pcs: -	2003	Special

3385	EU NA AU AS	
Conductor Charlie		
Schaffner Charlie		
Pcs: 9	2003	Special

3386	EU NA AU AS	
Pepper Roni		
Pepper Roni		
Pcs: 4	2003	Special

3387	EU NA AU AS	
Brickster		
Brickster		
Pcs: 4	2003	Special

3388	EU NA AU AS	
Snap Lockitt		
Snap Lockitt		
Pcs: 6	2003	Special

3389	EU NA AU AS	
Skateboarder		
Skateboarder		
Pcs: 6	2003	Special

3381-3389	Chupa Chups Promo	Chupa Chups Promo

3390	EU NA AU AS	
Streetball Player		
Streetball-Spieler		
Pcs: 2	2003	Special

3391	EU NA AU AS	
Dash		
Dash		
Pcs: 11	2003	Special

3427	EU NA AU AS	
NBA Slam Dunk		
NBA Slam Dunk		
Pcs: 54	2003–2004	

3428	EU NA AU AS	
One vs. One Action		
Eins gegen eins		
Pcs: 37	2003–2004	

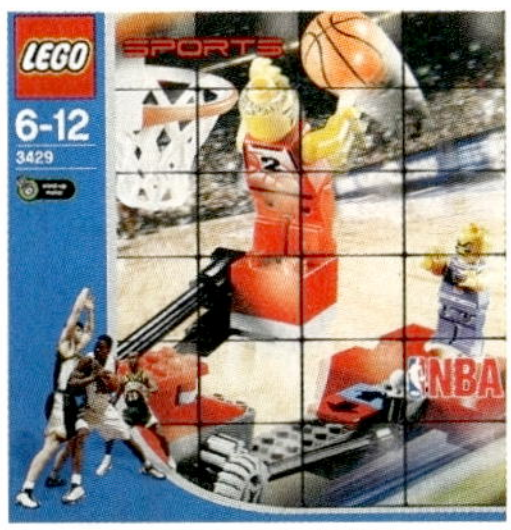

3429	EU NA AU AS	
Ultimate Defense		
Korbtraining		
Pcs: 80	2003	

3430	EU NA AU AS	
NBA Spin and Shoot		
Präzisionswerfen		
Pcs: 69	2003	

3431	EU NA AU AS	
Street Ball 2 vs. 2		
Streetbasketball		
Pcs: 182	2003–2005	

3432	EU NA AU AS	
NBA Challenge		
Basketballstadion		
Pcs: 441	2003–2005	

3433	EU NA AU AS	
Ultimate NBA Arena		
Die große NBA-Arena		
Pcs: 492	2003–2004	

3390	Chupa Chups Promo	Chupa Chups Promo
3391	Chupa Chups Promo	Chupa Chups Promo
3430	Similar to: 3440 (2003)	Ähnlich zu: 3440 (2003)

3440	EU NA AU AS	
NBA Jam Session Co-Pack		
NBA Jam Session Co-Pack		
Pcs: 71	2003	Special

3500	EU NA AU AS	
Kobe Bryant		
Kobe Bryant		
Pcs: 1	2003	Special

3511	EU NA AU AS	
Funny Crocodile		
Lustiges Krokodil		
Pcs: 16	2003–2004	

3512	EU NA AU AS	
Funny Giraffe		
Lustige Giraffe		
Pcs: 21	2003–2004	

3513	EU NA AU AS	
Funny Lion		
Lustiger Löwe		
Pcs: 23	2003	

3515	EU NA AU AS	
African Adventures		
Abenteuer Afrika		
Pcs: 56	2003–2005	

3517	EU NA AU AS	
Blue Deer		
Blauer Hirsch		
Pcs: 10	2003	

3518	EU NA AU AS	
Yellow Bird		
Gelber Vogel		
Pcs: 13	2003	

3519	EU NA AU AS	
Green Parrot		
Grüner Papagei		
Pcs: 10	2003	

i	3440	Similar to: 3430(2003)	Ähnlich zu: 3430(2003)

3529	EU NA AU AS
Pau Gasol	
Pau Gasol	
Pcs: 2	2003	Special

3530	EU NA AU AS
Tony Parker	
Tony Parker	
Pcs: 2	2003	Special

3535	EU NA AU AS
Skateboard Street Park	
Skate Trick Park	
Pcs: 68	2003–2004	

3536	EU NA AU AS
Snowboard Big Air Comp	
Snowboard Jump-Training	
Pcs: 82	2003–2005	

3537	EU NA AU AS
Skateboard Vert Park Challenge	
Große Skateboard Half-Pipe	
Pcs: 90	2003–2005	

3538	EU NA AU AS
Snowboard Boarder Cross Race	
Boarder Cross Rennen	
Pcs: 195	2003–2005	

3540	EU NA AU AS
Puck Passer	
Dribbler	
Pcs: 44	2003–2005	

3541	EU NA AU AS
Slap Shot	
Schlagschuß	
Pcs: 45	2003–2005	

3542	EU NA AU AS
Flip Shot	
Chipping	
Pcs: 46	2003–2005	

3543 — EU, NA

Slammer Goalie	
Torhüter	
Pcs: 43	2003–2005

3544 — EU, NA

Game Set	
Hockey Match	
Pcs: 146	2003–2005

3545 — EU, NA

Puck Feeder	
Trainingsset	
Pcs: 151	2003

3548 — EU, NA

Slam Dunk Trainer	
Slam Dunk Trainer	
Pcs: 16	2003

3549 — EU, NA

Practice Shooting	
Wurftechniktrainer	
Pcs: 18	2003

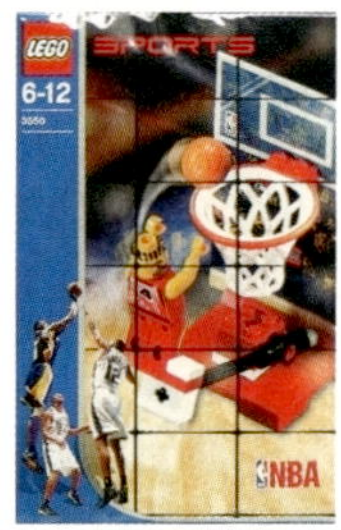

3550 — EU, NA

Jump and Shoot	
Spring und wirf	
Pcs: 16	2003

3557 — EU, NA

Blue Player and Goal	
Blauer Spieler und Tor	
Pcs: 34	2003

3558 — EU, NA

Red Player and Goal	
Roter Spieler und Tor	
Pcs: 34	2003

3559 — EU, NA

Red and Blue Player	
Roter und Blauer Spieler	
Pcs: 41	2003

i	3548	Also as Kabaya Promo	Auch als Kabaya Promo
i	3549	Also as Kabaya Promo	Auch als Kabaya Promo
i	3550	Also as Kabaya Promo	Auch als Kabaya Promo
i	3557	Also as Kabaya Promo	Auch als Kabaya Promo
i	3558	Also as Kabaya Promo	Auch als Kabaya Promo
i	3559	Also as Kabaya Promo	Auch als Kabaya Promo

3560
EU NA AU AS

NBA Collectors #1

NBA Minifig Sammelset 1

Pcs: 12 | 2003

3561
EU NA AU AS

NBA Collectors #2

NBA Minifig Sammelset 2

Pcs: 12 | 2003

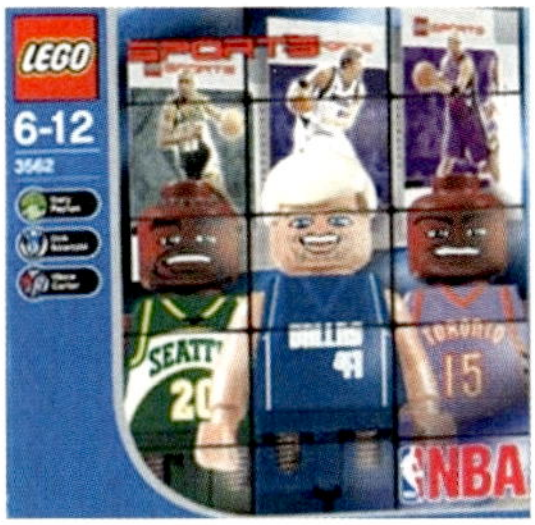

3562
EU NA AU AS

NBA Collectors #3

NBA Minifig Sammelset 3

Pcs: 13 | 2003

3563
EU NA AU AS

NBA Collectors #4

NBA Minifig Sammelset 4

Pcs: 12 | 2003

3564
EU NA AU AS

NBA Collectors #5

NBA Minifig Sammelset 5

Pcs: 12 | 2003

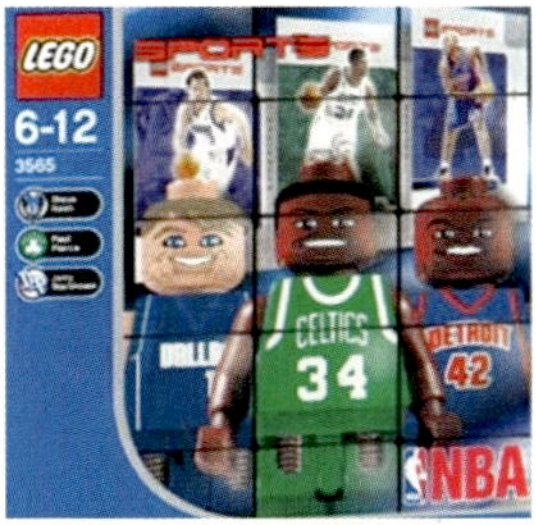

3565
EU NA AU AS

NBA Collectors #6

NBA Minifig Sammelset 6

Pcs: 12 | 2003

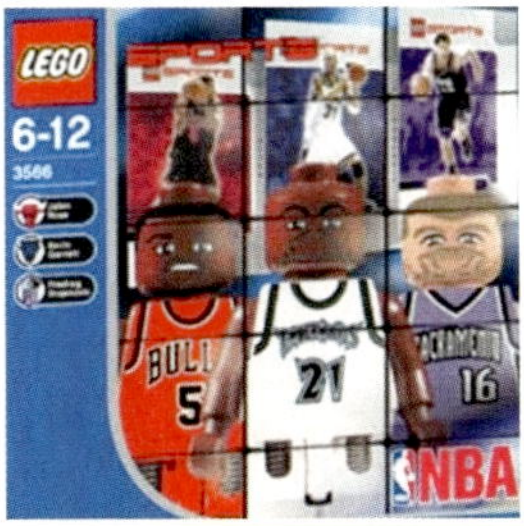

3566
EU NA AU AS

NBA Collectors #7

NBA Minifig Sammelset 7

Pcs: 12 | 2003

3567
EU NA AU AS

NBA Collectors #8

NBA Minifig Sammelset 8

Pcs: 10 | 2003

3584
EU NA AU AS

Rapid Return

Freiwurftraining

Pcs: 47 | 2003

3585	EU NA AU AS
Snowboard Super Pipe	
Snowboard Super Pipe	
Pcs: 225	2003–2004

3586	EU NA AU AS
Small Plane	
Kleines Flugzeug	
Pcs: 10	2003–2004

3587	EU NA AU AS
Mini Dozer	
Kleiner Schaufelbagger	
Pcs: 16	2003–2004

3588	EU NA AU AS
Heavy Truck	
Großer Laster	
Pcs: 19	2003–2004

3589	EU NA AU AS
Chopper	
Chopper	
Pcs: 22	2003–2004

3590	EU NA AU AS
Drill	
Interaktives Bohrfahrzeug	
Pcs: 25	2003–2004

3620	EU NA AU AS
Playhouse	
Spielhaus	
Pcs: 90	2003

3655	EU NA AU AS
Fire Action	
Kleine Feuerwehr	
Pcs: 14	2003

3656	EU NA AU AS
Police Action	
Mobile Polizei	
Pcs: 41	2003–2004

3657	EU NA AU AS	
Fire Fighters Deluxe Set		
Große Feuerwehr		
Pcs: 47	2003–2004	

3696	EU NA AU AS	
Tow-Me Truck		
Abschleppwagen		
Pcs: 6	2003	

3697	EU NA AU AS	
Fearless Fire Fighter		
Feuerwehrwagen		
Pcs: 6	2003–2004	

3698	EU NA AU AS	
Friendly Police Car		
Polizeiwagen		
Pcs: 5	2003–2004	

3699	EU NA AU AS	
Happy Constructor		
Lustiger Bauarbeiter		
Pcs: 9	2003–2004	

3700	EU NA AU AS	
Emergency Vehicles Set		
Notfallfahrzeuge		
Pcs: 17	2003	

4013	EU NA AU AS	
Create and Imagine		
Fantasievoller Baumeister		
Pcs: 1000	2003	Special

4014	EU NA AU AS	
Creator Exclusive		
Creator Exclusive		
Pcs: 500	2003	Special

4023	EU NA AU AS	
Fun and Adventure		
Spaß am Bauen		
Pcs: 55	2003	

i	4013	Similar to: 4107(2002)	Ähnlich zu: 4107(2002)
i	4014	Similar to: 4179 (2002), 4106 (2002), 7825 (2002)	Ähnlich zu: 4179 (2002), 4106 (2002), 7825 (2002)

4024	EU NA
Advent Calendar	
Adventskalender	
Pcs: 318	2003

4026	NA
Create Your Dreams	
Bau frei nach Verstand	
Pcs: 101	2003–2005	Special

4027	NA
Build and Imagine	
Bau frei nach Verstand	
Pcs: 101	2003–2005	Special

4028	EU NA AU AS
World of Bricks	
Eine ganze Welt mit Bausteinen	
Pcs: 500	2003–2006

4029	EU NA
Build with Bricks Bucket	
Riesen Eimer	
Pcs: 500	2003–2006

4032	EU NA AU AS
Passenger Plane	
Passagierflugzeug	
Pcs: 173	2003–2004	Special

4047	NA
Ultimate Wheels	
Ultimatives Fahrzeugset	
Pcs: 521	2003	Special

4048	NA
Mech Lab	
Mech Labor	
Pcs: 573	2003	Special

4090	EU NA AU AS
Motion Madness	
Zahnrad-Wunder	
Pcs: 243	2003–2004

4026	Similar to: 4027 (2003)	Ähnlich zu: 4027 (2003)
4027	Similar to: 4026 (2003)	Ähnlich zu: 4026 (2003)
4028	Similar to: 4029 (2003)	Ähnlich zu: 4029 (2003)
4029	Similar to: 4028 (2003)	Ähnlich zu: 4028 (2003)
4032	Promo of 13 several airlines	Promoset von 13 verschiedenen Airlines
4047	Includes: 4096 (2003), 4100 (2003)	Enthält: 4096 (2003), 4100 (2003)

4093	EU NA AU AS
Wild Wind Ups	
Mechanik-Wunder	
Pcs: 314	2003–2004

4094	EU NA AU AS
Motor Movers	
Motor-Wunder	
Pcs: 254	2003–2004

4095	EU NA AU AS
Record and Play	
Erinnerungs-Wunder	
Pcs: 342	2003–2004

4096	EU NA AU AS
Micro Wheels	
Mini-Fahrzeug-Set	
Pcs: 207	2003–2005

4097	EU NA AU AS
Mini Robots	
Mini-Roboter-Set	
Pcs: 219	2003–2005

4098	EU NA AU AS
High Flyers	
Flugzeug-Set	
Pcs: 197	2003–2005

4099	EU NA AU AS
Robobots	
Roboter-Set	
Pcs: 324	2003–2005

4100	EU NA AU AS
Maximum Wheels	
Fahrzeug-Set	
Pcs: 290	2003–2005

4101	EU NA AU AS
Wild Collection	
Buntes Tier-Set	
Pcs: 487	2003–2005

i	4048	Includes: 4097 (2003), 4099 (2003)	Enthält: 4097 (2003), 4099 (2003)
i	4096	Also included in: 4047 (2003)	Auch enthalten in: 4047 (2003)
i	4097	Also included in: 4048 (2003)	Auch enthalten in: 4048 (2003)
i	4099	Also included in: 4048 (2003)	Auch enthalten in: 4048 (2003)
i	4100	Also included in: 4047 (2003)	Auch enthalten in: 4047 (2003)

4278	EU NA AU AS	
Blue Tub		
Blauer Behälter		
Pcs: 1000	2003–2004	Special

4279	EU NA AU AS	
Red Creator Tub		
Roter Creator Eimer		
Pcs: 1000	2003–2004	Special

4300	EU NA AU AS	
Green Racer		
Grünes Rennauto		
Pcs: 22	2003–2004	Special

4301	EU NA AU AS	
Blue Racer		
Blauer Rennwagen		
Pcs: 24	2003–2004	Special

4343	EU NA AU AS	
Storybuilder Pink Palace Magic		
Erweiterungsset - Aschenputtel		
Pcs: 9	2003	

4344	EU NA AU AS	
Storybuilder Meet the Dinosaurs		
Erweiterungsset - Dinosaurier		
Pcs: 9	2003	

4345	EU NA AU AS	
Storybuilder Happy Home		
Erweiterungsset - Meine Familie		
Pcs: 9	2003	Special

4400	EU NA AU AS	
Creations & Bricks		
Bauten & Steine		
Pcs: 700	2003–2004	Special

4401	EU NA AU AS	
Little Creations		
Mini Tier-Set		
Pcs: 110	2003	

i	4301	C1000 Supermarkets Promo	C1000 Supermarkt Promo

4402	EU NA AU AS	
Sea Riders		
Speedboot		
Pcs: 547	2003–2005	

4403	EU NA AU AS	
Air Blazers		
Helikopter		
Pcs: 698	2003–2005	

4404	EU NA AU AS	
Land Busters		
Gelände-Pick-Up		
Pcs: 772	2003–2005	

4405	EU NA AU AS	
Large Bucket		
Großer Eimer		
Pcs: 1305	2003	Special

4475	EU NA AU AS	
Jabba's™ Message		
Jabba's™ Message		
Pcs: 44	2003	

4476	EU NA AU AS	
Jabba's™ Prize		
Jabba's™ Prize		
Pcs: 39	2003	

4477	EU NA AU AS	
T-16 Skyhopper™		
T-16 Skyhopper™		
Pcs: 96	2003	

4478	EU NA AU AS	
Geonosian™ Fighter		
Geonosian™ Fighter		
Pcs: 169	2003–2005	

4479	EU NA AU AS	
TIE Bomber™		
TIE Bomber™		
Pcs: 229	2003–2005	

i	4478	2004: Re-released with blue Box	2004: Neu aufgelegt mit blauer Box

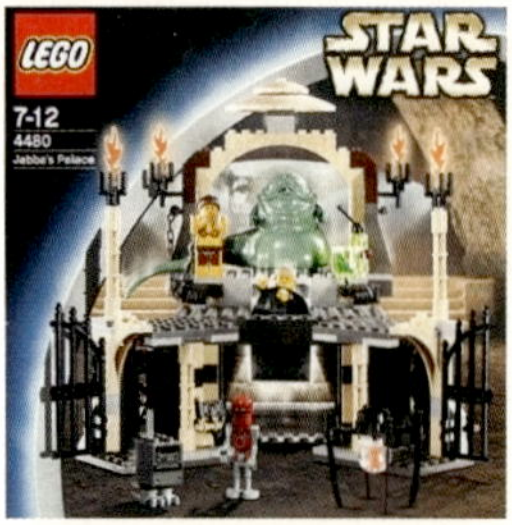

4480	EU NA AU AS
Jabba's™ Palace	
Jabba's™ Palace	
Pcs: 234	2003–2005

4481	EU NA AU AS
Hailfire Droid™	
Hailfire Droid™	
Pcs: 681	2003

4482	EU NA AU AS
AT-TE™	
AT-TE™	
Pcs: 658	2003–2005

4483	EU NA AU AS
AT-AT™	
AT-AT™	
Pcs: 1064	2003–2005

4484	EU NA AU AS
Mini X-wing™ & TIE Advanced™	
Mini X-wing™ & TIE Advanced™	
Pcs: 76	2003

4485	EU NA AU AS
Mini Sebulba's™ & Anakin's Podr.™	
Mini Sebulba's™ & Anakin's Podr.™	
Pcs: 72	2003

4486	EU NA AU AS
Mini AT-ST™ & Snowspeeder™	
Mini AT-ST™ & Snowspeeder™	
Pcs: 76	2003

4487	EU NA AU AS
Mini Jedi Starfighter™ & Slave I™	
Mini Jedi Starfighter™ & Slave I™	
Pcs: 53	2003

4488	EU NA AU AS
Mini Millennium Falcon™	
Mini Millennium Falcon™	
Pcs: 87	2003–2004

i	Set	English	Deutsch
i	4483	Also released as blue Box (2004)	Auch als blaue Box (2004)
i	4484	Also included in: 4207901 (2003)	Auch enthalten in: 4207901 (2003)
i	4485	Also included in: 4207901 (2003)	Auch enthalten in: 4207901 (2003)
i	4486	Also included in: 4207901 (2003)	Auch enthalten in: 4207901 (2003)
i	4487	Also included in: 4207901 (2003)	Auch enthalten in: 4207901 (2003)

4489	EU NA AU AS
Mini AT-AT™	
Mini AT-AT™	
Pcs: 98	2003–2004

4490	EU NA AU AS
Mini Republic Gunship™	
Mini Republic Gunship™	
Pcs: 102	2003–2004

4491	EU NA AU AS
Mini MTT™	
Mini MTT™	
Pcs: 99	2003–2004

4500	EU NA AU AS
Rebel Snowspeeder™	
Rebel Snowspeeder™	
Pcs: 219	2003–2006

4501	EU NA AU AS
Mos Eisley Cantina™	
Mos Eisley Cantina™	
Pcs: 192	2003–2005

4502	EU NA AU AS
X-Wing Fighter™	
X-Wing Fighter™	
Pcs: 563	2003–2006

4511	EU NA AU AS
High Speed Train	
Schnellzug mit Trafo	
Pcs: 333	2003–2006

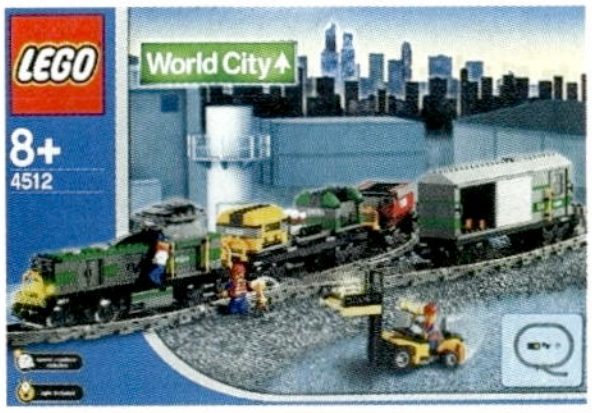

4512	EU NA AU AS
Cargo Train	
Güterzug mit Trafo	
Pcs: 544	2003–2006

4513	EU NA AU AS
Grand Central Station	
City-Bahnhof	
Pcs: 344	2003–2006

i	4500	2004: Original Trilogy Edition box, black layout	2004: Original Trilogy Edition Box, schwarzes Layout
i	4501	2004: Original Trilogy Edition box, black layout	2004: Original Trilogy Edition Box, schwarzes Layout
i	4502	2004: Original Trilogy Edition box, black layout	2004: Original Trilogy Edition Box, schwarzes Layout

4514	EU NA AU AS
Cargo Crane	
Verladekran	
Pcs: 175	2003–2006

4651	EU NA AU AS
Police Motorcycle	
Polizei-Motorrad	
Pcs: 12	2003

4652	EU NA AU AS
Tow Truck	
Abschleppwagen	
Pcs: 26	2003–2004

4653	EU NA AU AS
Dump Truck	
Kipplaster	
Pcs: 28	2003–2004

4654	EU NA AU AS
Tanker Truck	
Tankwagen	
Pcs: 44	2003–2004

4655	EU NA AU AS
Quick Fix Station	
Tankstelle	
Pcs: 101	2003–2004

4657	EU NA AU AS
Fire Squad HQ	
Feuerwehrstation	
Pcs: 144	2003–2004

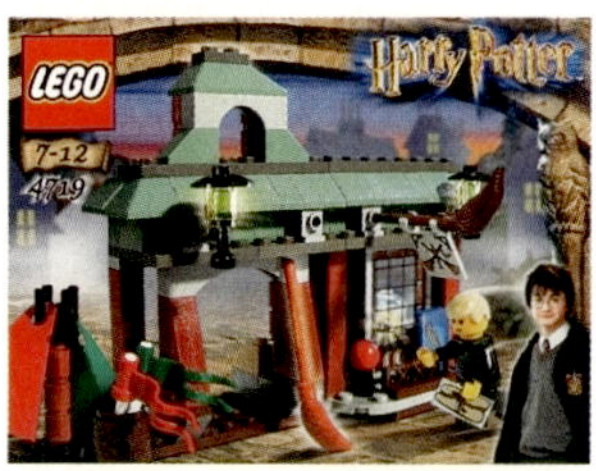

4719	EU NA AU AS
Quality Quidditch Supplies	
Fachhandlung für Quidditch	
Pcs: 120	2003–2005

4720	EU NA AU AS
Knockturn Alley	
Nokturngasse	
Pcs: 209	2003–2005

4850	EU NA AU AS	
First Chase		
First Chase		
Pcs: 188	2003–2004	

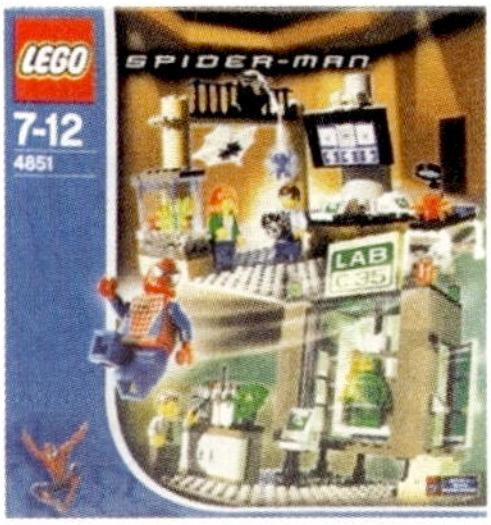

4851	EU NA AU AS	
The Origins		
Die Verwandlung		
Pcs: 212	2003–2004	

4852	EU NA AU AS	
The Final Showdown		
Das Kräftemessen		
Pcs: 355	2003–2004	

5012	EU NA AU AS	
Soccer Player with Goal		
Fußballspieler mit Tor		
Pcs: 12	2003–2004	Special

5013	EU NA AU AS	
Free Throw		
Freiwurf		
Pcs: 25	2003–2004	Special

5014	EU NA AU AS	
2 Players		
2 Hockeyspieler		
Pcs: 34	2003–2004	Special

5015	EU NA AU AS	
Skateboarder		
Skateboarder		
Pcs: 16	2003–2004	Special

5016	EU NA AU AS	
Player and Basket		
Spieler mit Basketballkorb		
Pcs: 17	2003	Special

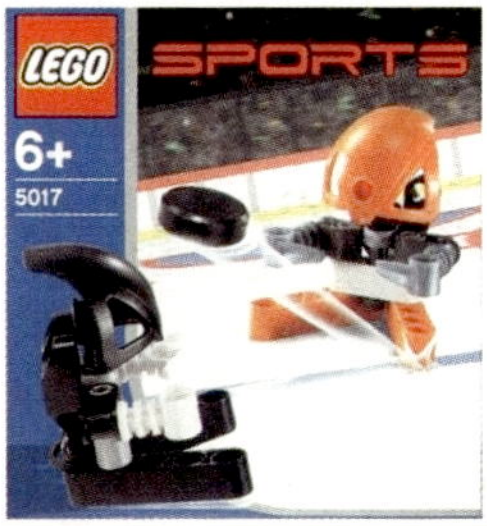

5017	EU NA AU AS	
2 Players		
2 Hockeyspieler		
Pcs: 36	2003	Special

i	5012	C1000 Supermarkets Promo	C1000 Supermarkt Promo
i	5013	C1000 Supermarkets Promo	C1000 Supermarkt Promo
i	5014	C1000 Supermarkets Promo	C1000 Supermarkt Promo
i	5015	C1000 Supermarkets Promo	C1000 Supermarkt Promo
i	5016	Duracell Promo	Duracell Promo
i	5017	Duracell Promo	Duracell Promo

5018	EU
Snowboarder	
Snowboarder	
Pcs: 17	2003	Special

5211	EU
Green Explore Tub	
Grüner Explore Eimer	
Pcs: 110	2003–2005	Special

5212	EU
Yellow Explore Tub	
Gelber Explore Eimer	
Pcs: 139	2003–2004	Special

5213	
Big Bricks Box	
Große Steinebox	
Pcs: 140	2003–2007	Special

5230	NA
Yellow Tub	
Gelber Eimer	
Pcs: 100	2003–2004	Special

5441	EU NA AU AS
Smiling Rattle	
Rasselstern	
Pcs: 1	2003	

5443	EU NA AU AS
Hanging Rattle	
Hängerassel	
Pcs: 1	2003–2004	

5446	EU
Dog on Wheels	
Der Wau-Wau	
Pcs: 1	2003–2004	

5449	EU NA AU AS
Stack-n-Learn Sorter	
Bunter Sortier-Eimer	
Pcs: 19	2003–2005	

i	5018	Duracell Promo	Duracell Promo
i	5212	Similar to: 5353 (2004), 5352 (2004)	Ähnlich zu: 5353 (2004), 5352 (2004)

5450	EU NA AU AS	
Discovery Bird		
Überraschungshaus		
Pcs: 2	2003	

5495	EU NA AU AS	
Ring & Rattle		
Klingel & Rassel		
Pcs: 1	2003–2004	Special

5856	EU NA AU AS	
Paprika and the bold Monkey		
Paprika und der freche Affe		
Pcs: 47	2003–2005	

5857	EU NA AU AS	
Safran's Amazing Bazaar		
Safrans funkelnder Basar		
Pcs: 92	2003–2005	

5858	EU NA AU AS	
The Golden Palace		
Orientalischer Palast		
Pcs: 172	2003–2005	

5859	EU NA AU AS	
Little Garden Fairy		
Kleine Gartenfee		
Pcs: 48	2003–2005	

5861	EU NA AU AS	
Fairy Island		
Märcheninsel		
Pcs: 105	2003–2005	

5862	EU NA AU AS	
Flower Fairy Party		
Blumenfest im Zaubergarten		
Pcs: 155	2003–2005	

5872	EU NA AU AS	
Golden Land		
Goldenes Land		
Pcs: 35	2003–2004	Special

i	Set	English	Deutsch
i	5858	2004: Re-released as purple/silver Box	2004: Als Lila/Silber Box neu aufgelegt
i	5862	2004: Released as purple/silver box	2004: als Lila/Silber Box erschienen
i	5872	C1000 Supermarkets Promo	C1000 Supermarkt Promo

5873	EU NA AU AS	
Fairy Land		
Feenland		
Pcs: 20	2003–2004	Special

7030	EU NA AU AS	
Squad Car		
Streifenwagen		
Pcs: 51	2003–2004	

7031	EU NA AU AS	
Helicopter		
Spionage-Hubschrauber		
Pcs: 87	2003–2005	

7032	EU NA AU AS	
Highway Patrol & Undercover Van		
Agenten-Jeep und Panzerwagen		
Pcs: 151	2003–2005	

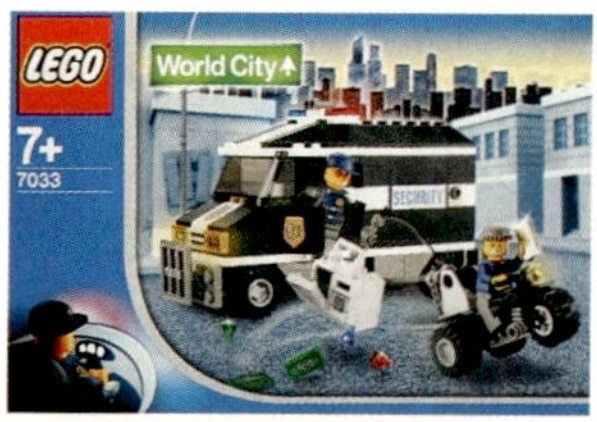

7033	EU NA AU AS	
Armored Car Action		
Geldtransporter und Trike		
Pcs: 186	2003–2005	

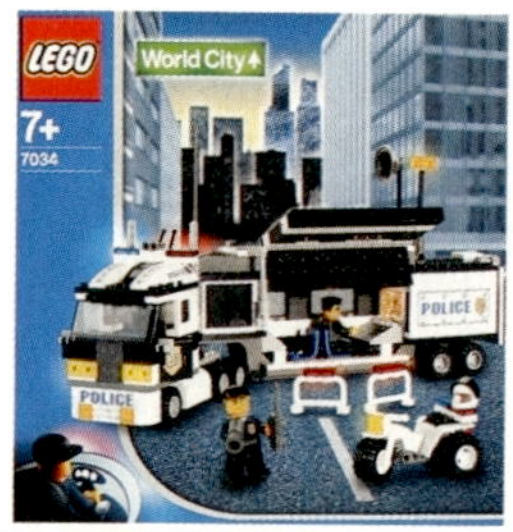

7034	EU NA AU AS	
Surveillance Truck		
Überwachungs- u. Abhörtruck		
Pcs: 266	2003–2005	

7035	EU NA AU AS	
Police HQ		
Geheimdienst-Hauptquartier		
Pcs: 418	2003–2005	

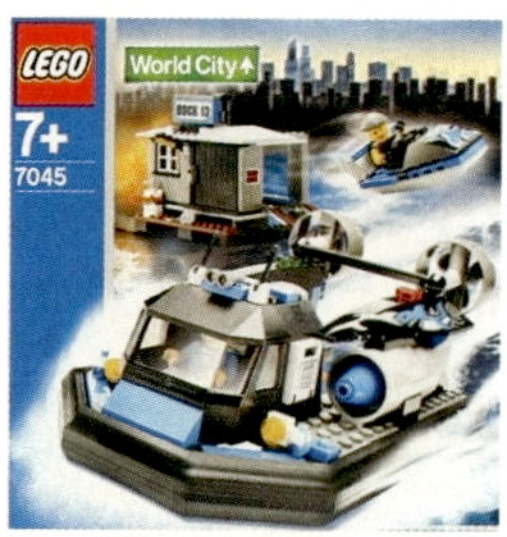

7045	EU NA AU AS	
Hovercraft Hideout		
Luftkissenboot mit Dock		
Pcs: 268	2003–2005	

7047	EU NA AU AS	
Coast Watch HQ		
Einsatzzentrale der Küstenwache		
Pcs: 373	2003–2005	

5873	C1000 Supermarkets Promo	C1000 Supermarkt Promo

7212	EU NA AU AS	
Sky Squad		
Sky Squad		
Pcs: 132	2003–2004	Special

7221	EU NA AU AS	
Robots		
Roboter		
Pcs: 31	2003–2004	Special

7222	EU AS	
Red Helicopter		
Roter Hubschrauber		
Pcs: 28	2003–2004	Special

7223	EU AS	
Yellow Truck		
Gelber Lastwagen		
Pcs: 38	2003–2004	Special

7224	EU AS	
Santa, Tree and Present		
Weihnachtsmann mit Geschenk		
Pcs: 36	2003–2005	Special

7409	EU NA AU AS	
Secret of the Tomb		
Geheimnisvolles Grab		
Pcs: 41	2003	

7410	EU NA AU AS	
Jungle River		
Abenteuer Dschungelfluss		
Pcs: 65	2003	

7411	EU NA AU AS	
Tygurah's Roar		
Sitz des Tygurah		
Pcs: 94	2003–2005	

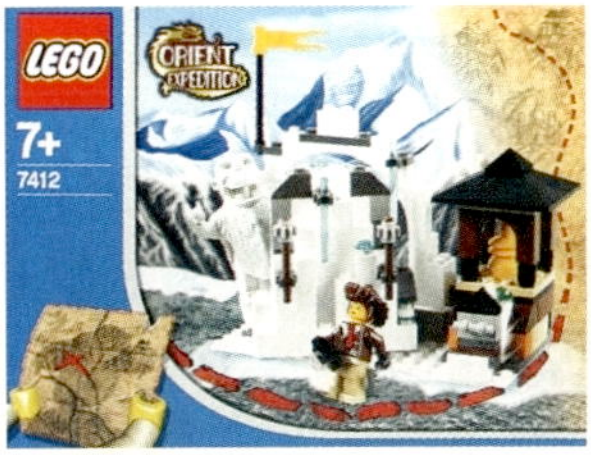

7412	EU NA AU AS	
Yeti's Hideout		
Versteck des Yeti		
Pcs: 114	2003–2005	

7212	Airline Promo	Airline Promo
7221	Promo set from various companies	Promo-set diverser Unternehmen
7222	C1000 Supermarkets (polybag), ANA (box)	C1000 Supermärkte (Tütchen), ANA (Box)
7223	C1000 Supermarkets (polybag), ANA (box)	C1000 Supermärkte (Tütchen), ANA (Box)

7413	EU NA AU AS
Passage of Jun-Chi	
Tor des Jun-Chi	
Pcs: 100	2003–2005

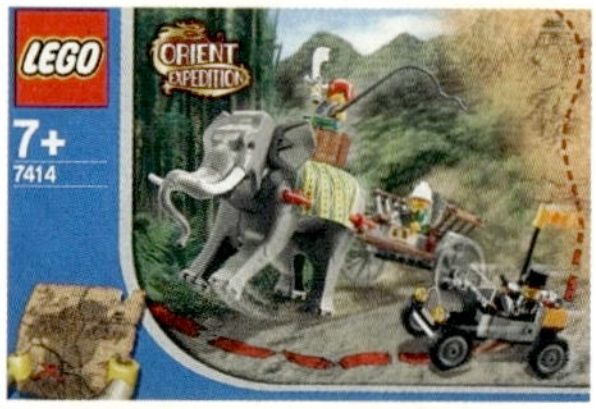

7414	EU NA AU AS
Elephant Caravan	
Elefanten-Treck	
Pcs: 102	2003–2005

7415	EU NA AU AS
Aero Nomad	
Fesselballon	
Pcs: 118	2003–2005

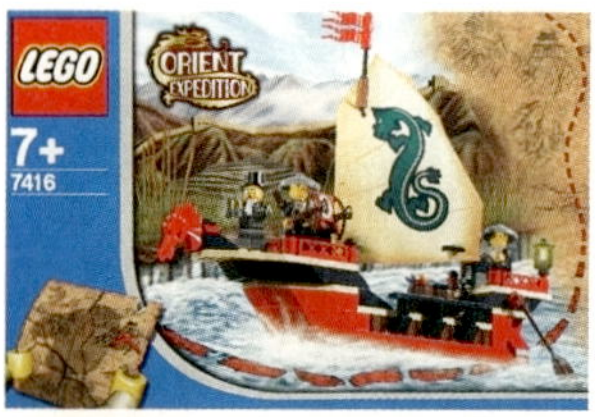

7416	EU NA AU AS
Emperor's Ship	
Kaiserliches Segelschiff	
Pcs: 175	2003–2005

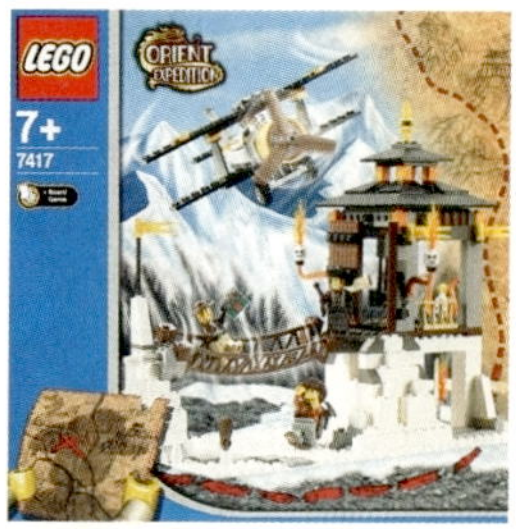

7417	EU NA AU AS
Temple of Mount Everest	
Mount-Everest-Tempel	
Pcs: 288	2003–2005

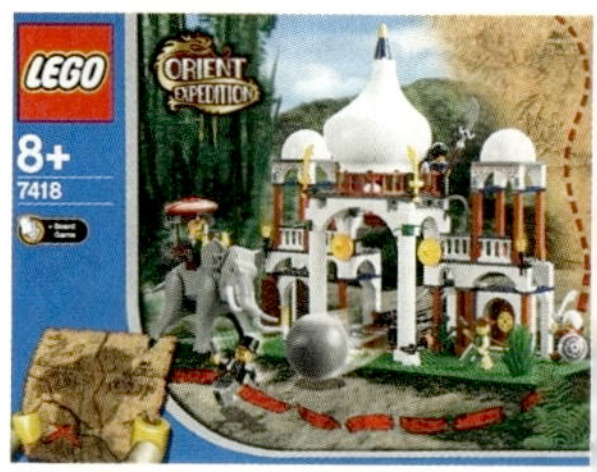

7418	EU NA AU AS
Scorpion Palace	
Maharadscha-Palast	
Pcs: 355	2003–2005

7419	EU NA AU AS
Dragon Fortress	
Drachen-Festung	
Pcs: 732	2003–2005

7420	EU NA AU AS
Thunder Blazer	
Donner-Kiste	
Pcs: 68	2003

7422	EU NA AU AS	
Red Eagle		
Roter Adler		
Pcs: 34	2003	Special

7422	Also released from Kabaya	Auch als Kabaya Set erschienen

ⓘ 7423	EU NA AU AS	
Mountain Sleigh		
Bergschlitten		
Pcs: 29	2003	Special

ⓘ 7424	EU NA AU AS	
Black Cruiser		
Schwarze Limousine		
Pcs: 27	2003	Special

ⓘ 7435	EU AU	
Tiny's Day and Night Lever		
Tiny's Day and Night Lever		
Pcs: 13	2003–2006	Special

ⓘ 7436	NA	
Sporty's Jumping Gym		
Sporty's Jumping Gym		
Pcs: 12	2003–2006	Special

ⓘ 7437	EU AU	
Gardening with Stripy		
Gartenarbeit mit Stripy		
Pcs: 24	2003–2006	Special

ⓘ 7439	EU AU	
Stretchy's Junk Yard		
Stretchy's Junk Yard		
Pcs: 40	2003–2006	Special

ⓘ 7441	EU AU	
Tiny & Friends		
Tiny mit Freunden		
Pcs: 58	2003–2006	Special

ⓘ 7446	EU AU	
Tiny		
Tiny		
Pcs: 3	2003–2006	Special

ⓘ 7449	EU AU	
Sporty		
Sporty		
Pcs: 3	2003–2006	Special

ⓘ	Sets	English	Deutsch
ⓘ	7423-7424	Also released from Kabaya	Auch als Kabaya Set erschienen
ⓘ	7435-7449	Was only available in the UK and Australia	Nur in UK und Australien erhältlich gewesen

7450	EU NA AU AS	
Stretchy		
Stretchy		
Pcs: 2	2003–2006	Special

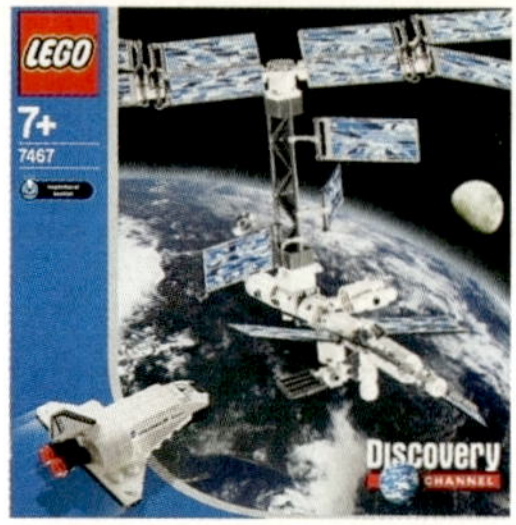

7467	EU NA AU AS
International Space Station	
ISS Raumstation	
Pcs: 162	2003–2004

7468	EU NA AU AS
Saturn V Moon Mission	
Saturn V Mondmission	
Pcs: 178	2003–2004

7469	EU NA AU AS
Mission to Mars	
Exkursion zum Mars	
Pcs: 417	2003–2004

7470	EU NA AU AS
Space Shuttle Discovery	
Space Shuttle Discovery	
Pcs: 826	2003–2004

7471	EU NA AU AS
Mars Exploration Rover	
Mars Erkundungs-Rover	
Pcs: 858	2003–2004

7501	EU NA AU AS
Bangle Minis	
Armbänder	
Pcs: 32	2003–2005

7502	EU NA AU AS
Photo Minis	
Bilderrahmen	
Pcs: 30	2003–2004

7503	EU NA AU AS
Memo Minis	
Deko- und Halskette	
Pcs: 24	2003–2004

7450	Was only available in the UK and Australia	Nur in UK und Australien erhältlich gewesen
7502	Included in: 65305 (2003)	Enthalten in: 65305 (2003)

7507 EU NA AU AS

Jewels-n-Rings

Glitzerschmuck und Fingerring

Pcs: 78 | 2003–2004

Rating: 3/6

7508 EU NA AU AS

Jewels-n-Bands

Glitzerschmuck und Haargummis

Pcs: 78 | 2003–2004

Rating: 3/6

7509 EU NA AU AS

Jewels-n-Clips

Glitzerschmuck und Haarclips

Pcs: 70 | 2003–2004

Rating: 3/6

7510 EU (NA AU AS greyed)

Trendy Tote Hot Pink

Trendtasche Pink

Pcs: 89 | 2003–2005

Rating: 3/6

7511 EU (NA AU AS greyed)

Trendy Tote Tangerine

Trendtasche Orange

Pcs: 94 | 2003–2005

Rating: 3/6

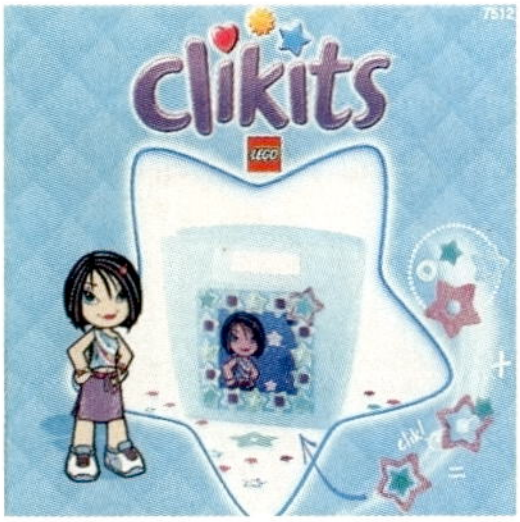

7512 EU (NA AU AS greyed)

Trendy Tote Sky Blue

Trendtasche Türkis

Pcs: 94 | 2003–2005

Rating: 3/6

7513 EU NA AU AS

Ultimate Design Studio

Designer-Studio

Pcs: 281 | 2003–2004

Rating: 3/6

7517 EU NA AU AS

Cool Room Decor

Beauty-Set

Pcs: 131 | 2003–2006

Rating: 3/6

7518 EU NA AU AS

Cool Room Catchers

Blumen-Mobile

Pcs: 129 | 2003–2005

Rating: 3/6

i	7508	Included in: 65305 (2003), 65363 (2003)	Enthalten in: 65305 (2003), 65363 (2003)
i	7509	Included in: 65364 (2003)	Enthalten in: 65364 (2003)
i	7511	Included in: 65305 (2003)	Enthalten in: 65305 (2003)

7519	EU NA AU AS	
Cool Room Frames		
Bilderrahmen-Sammelset		
Pcs: 111	2003–2006	

7520	EU NA AU AS	
Pillow Decor 'n More		
Kissen, Tasche und vieles mehr		
Pcs: 104	2003–2005	

7521	EU NA AU AS	
Pretty Punch Activity Set		
Lustiger Locher		
Pcs: 30	2003–2005	

7522	EU NA AU AS	
Let's Party		
Partyset		
Pcs: 210	2003–2005	

7836	EU NA AU AS	
Small Halloween Bucket		
Kleiner Halloween-Eimer		
Pcs: 200	2003	Special

8319	EU NA AU AS	
Aquart		
Aquart		
Pcs: 11	2003–2003	

8350	EU NA AU AS	
Pro Stunt		
Pro Stunt		
Pcs: 32	2003	Special

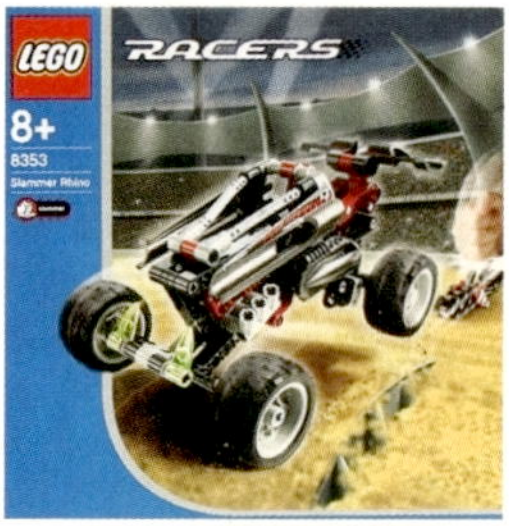

8353	EU NA AU AS	
Slammer Rhino		
Slammer Rhino		
Pcs: 218	2003	

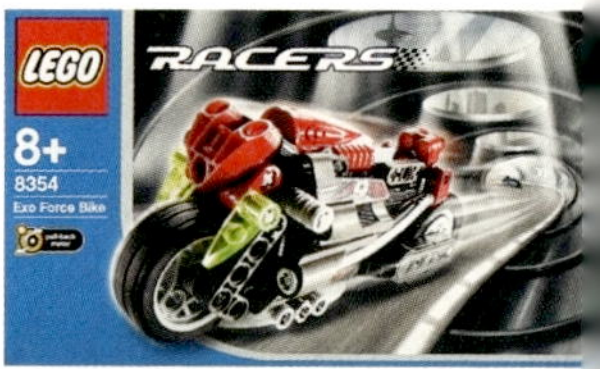

8354	EU NA AU AS	
Exo Force Bike		
Exo Force Bike		
Pcs: 100	2003–2005	

ⓘ 7836	Similar to: 7831 (2002), 7832 (2002)	Ähnlich zu: 7831 (2002), 7832 (2002)

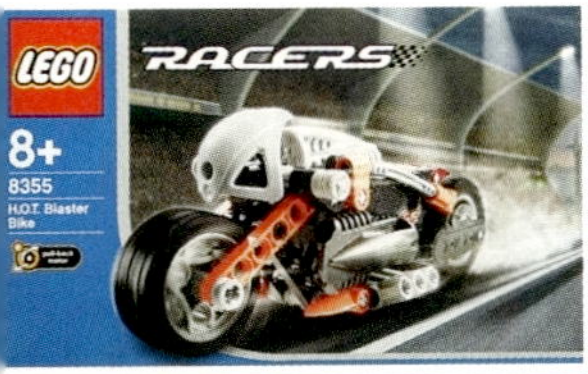

ⓘ 8355		EU NA AU AS
H.O.T. Blaster Bike		
Hot Blaster Bike		
Pcs: 91	2003–2005	

ⓘ 8356		EU NA AU AS
Jungle Monster		
Jungle Monster		
Pcs: 115	2003	

ⓘ 8357		EU NA AU AS
Zonic Strike		
Zonic Strike		
Pcs: 106	2003–2005	

ⓘ 8358		EU NA AU AS
Off-Roader		
Off Roader		
Pcs: 26	2003–2004	Special

ⓘ 8359		EU NA AU AS
Desert Racer		
Desert Racer		
Pcs: 27	2003–2004	Special

ⓘ 8360		EU NA AU AS
Track Racer		
Track Racer		
Pcs: 24	2003–2004	Special

ⓘ 8363		EU NA AU AS
Baja Desert Racers		
Baja Desert Racers		
Pcs: 326	2003	Special

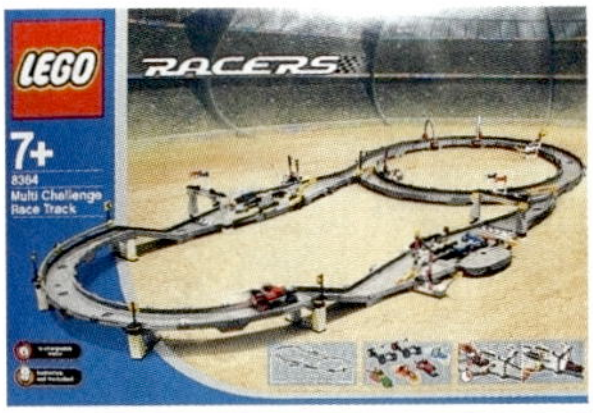

ⓘ 8364		EU NA AU AS
Multi-Challenge Race Track		
Multi Challenge Race Track		
Pcs: 623	2003–2005	

ⓘ 8365		EU NA AU AS
Tuneable Racer		
Tuneable Racer		
Pcs: 200	2003–2004	

ⓘ	Set	English	Deutsch
ⓘ	8358	Also released from Kabaya	Auch als Kabaya Set erschienen
ⓘ	8359	Also released from Kabaya	Auch als Kabaya Set erschienen
ⓘ	8360	Also released from Kabaya	Auch als Kabaya Set erschienen

8366	EU NA AU AS	
Supersonic RC		
Supersonic RC		
Pcs: 423	2003–2005	

8370	EU NA AU AS	
Nitro Stunt Bike		
Nitro Stunt Bike		
Pcs: 92	2003–2005	

8371	EU NA AU AS	
Extreme Power Bike		
Extreme Power Bike		
Pcs: 98	2003–2005	

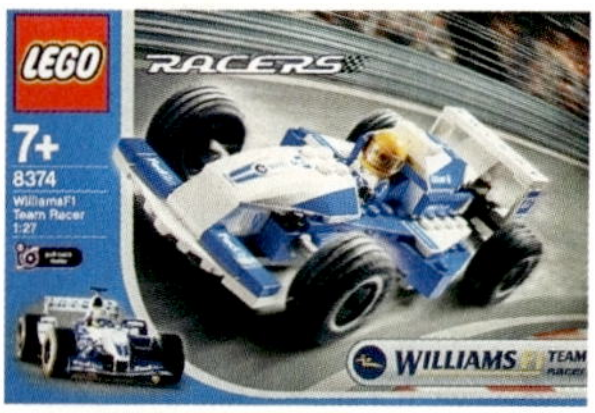

8374	EU NA AU AS	
Williams F1 Team Racer 1:27		
Williams F1 Team Racer 1:27		
Pcs: 92	2003–2004	

8376	EU NA AU AS	
Hot Flame RC Car		
Hot Flame RC Car		
Pcs: 244	2003–2004	Special

8380	EU NA AU AS	
Red Maniac		
Red Maniac		
Pcs: 87	2003–2006	Special

8381	EU NA AU AS	
Exo Raider		
Exo Raider		
Pcs: 98	2003–2006	

8382	EU NA AU AS	
Hot Buster		
Hot Buster		
Pcs: 68	2003–2006	

8383	EU NA AU AS	
Nitro Terminator		
Nitro Terminator		
Pcs: 75	2003–2006	

8380	Included in: 65573 (2003)	Enthalten in: 65573 (2003)
8383	Included in: 65573 (2003)	Enthalten in: 65573 (2003)

i 8384	EU NA AU AS
Jungle Crasher	
Jungle Crasher	
Pcs: 79	2003–2006

i 8385	EU NA AU AS
Exo Stealth	
Exo Stealth	
Pcs: 85	2003–2006

i 8438	EU NA AU AS
Pneumatic Crane Truck	
Pneumatik Kran-Lkw	
Pcs: 852	2003

i 8441	EU NA AU AS
Fork Lift Truck	
Gabelstapler	
Pcs: 72	2003–2005

i 8451	EU NA AU AS
Dumper	
Kipper	
Pcs: 183	2003–2004

i 8453	EU NA AU AS
Front End Loader	
Frontlader	
Pcs: 214	2003–2006

i 8454	EU NA AU AS
Rescue Truck	
Sondereinsatz-Truck	
Pcs: 634	2003–2004

i 8455	EU NA AU AS
Backhoe Loader	
Pneumatik Bagger	
Pcs: 703	2003–2005

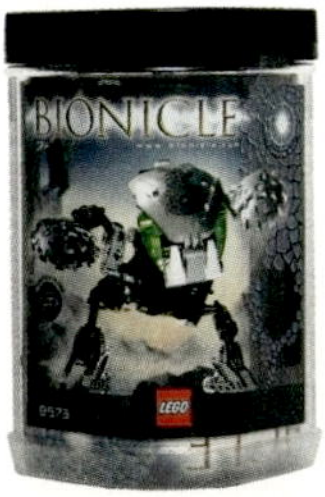

i 8573	EU NA AU AS
Nuhvok-Kal	
Nuhvok-Kal	
Pcs: 40	2003

i	8384	Included in: 65573 (2003)	Enthalten in: 65573 (2003)
i	8385	Included in: 65573 (2003)	Enthalten in: 65573 (2003)
i	8438	Similar to: 8460 (1995), 8431 (2002)	Ähnlich zu: 8460 (1995), 8431 (2002)
i	8453	2004: released as block box	2004: als schwarze Box veröffentlicht

8574 EU NA AU AS

Tahnok-Kal		
Tahnok-Kal		
Pcs: 40	2003	

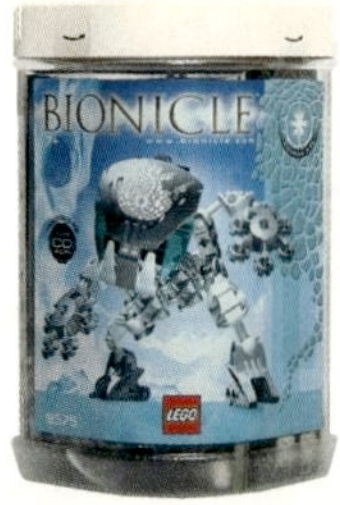

8575 EU NA AU AS

Kohrak-Kal		
Kohrak-Kal		
Pcs: 40	2003	

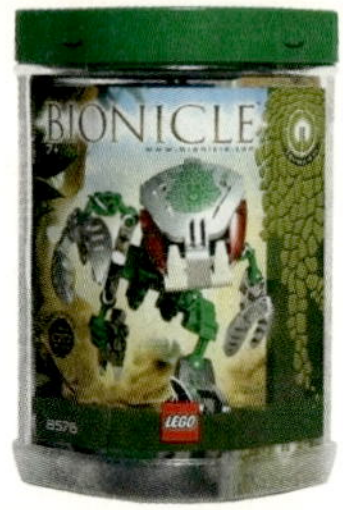

8576 EU NA AU AS

Lehvak-Kal		
Lehvak-Kal		
Pcs: 40	2003	

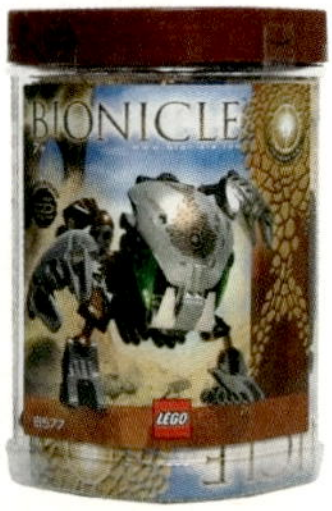

8577 EU NA AU AS

Pahrak-Kal		
Pahrak-Kal		
Pcs: 40	2003	

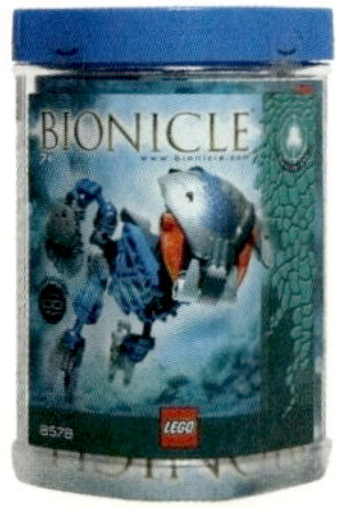

8578 EU NA AU AS

Gahlok-Kal		
Gahlok-Kal		
Pcs: 40	2003	

8580 EU NA AU AS

Kraata		
Kraata		
Pcs: 3	2003	

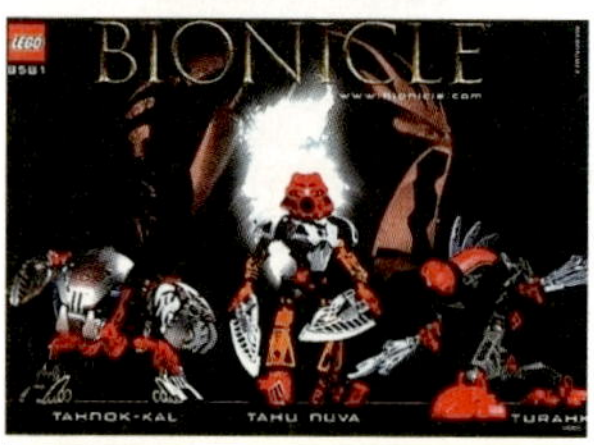

8581 EU NA AU AS

Kopeke		
Kopeke		
Pcs: 25	2003	Special

8582 EU NA AU AS

Matoro		
Matoro		
Pcs: 25	2003	Special

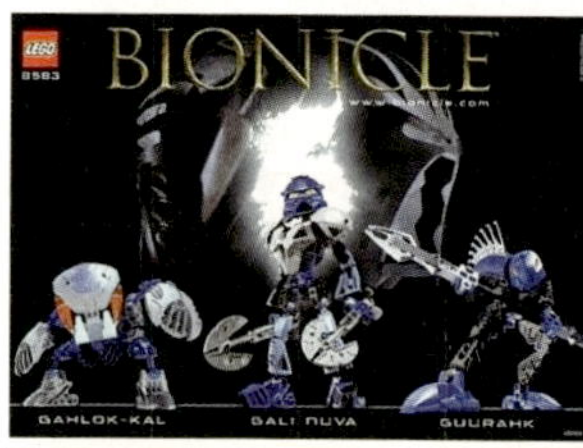

8583 EU NA AU AS

Hahli		
Hahli		
Pcs: 25	2003	Special

8584	EU NA AU AS	
Hewkii		
Hewkii		
Pcs: 25	2003	Special

8585	EU NA AU AS	
Hafu		
Hafu		
Pcs: 25	2003	Special

8586	EU NA AU AS	
Macku		
Macku		
Pcs: 25	2003	Special

8587	EU NA AU AS	
Panrahk		
Panrahk		
Pcs: 45	2003–2004	

8588	EU NA AU AS	
Kurahk		
Kurahk		
Pcs: 45	2003–2004	

8589	EU NA AU AS	
Lerahk		
Lerahk		
Pcs: 45	2003–2004	

8590	EU NA AU AS	
Guurahk		
Guurahk		
Pcs: 45	2003–2004	

8591	EU NA AU AS	
Vorahk		
Vorahk		
Pcs: 45	2003–2004	

8592	EU NA AU AS	
Turahk		
Turahk		
Pcs: 45	2003–2004	

8587	Released also as promo	Auch als Promo erschienen
8588	Released also as promo	Auch als Promo erschienen
8589	Released also as promo	Auch als Promo erschienen
8590	Released also as promo	Auch als Promo erschienen

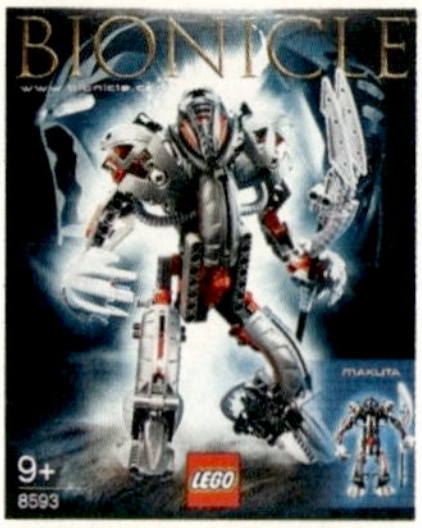

8593	EU NA AU AS	
Makuta		
Makuta		
Pcs: 199	2003–2004	

8594	EU NA AU AS	
Jaller and Gukko		
Jaller und Gukko		
Pcs: 165	2003–2004	

8595	EU NA AU AS	
Takua and Pewku		
Takua und Pewku		
Pcs: 221	2003–2004	

8596	EU NA AU AS	
Takanuva		
Takanuva		
Pcs: 199	2003–2004	

8599	EU NA AU AS	
Krana-Kal		
Krana-Kal		
Pcs: 5	2003	

8600	EU NA AU AS	
Krana-Kal		
Krana-Kal		
Pcs: 5	2003	

8607	EU NA AU AS	
Nuhrii		
Nuhrii		
Pcs: 30	2003–2005	

8608	EU NA AU AS	
Vhisola		
Vhisola		
Pcs: 30	2003–2005	

8609	EU NA AU AS	
Tehutti		
Tehutti		
Pcs: 30	2003–2005	

i	8593	Includes in: 3287 (2004), 10201 (2003)	Enthalten in: 3287 (2004), 10201 (2003)
i	8596	Included in: 3287 (2004), 10201 (2003)	Enthalten in: 3287 (2004), 10201 (2003)
i	8599	Similar to: 8600 (2003)	Ähnlich zu: 8600 (2003)
i	8600	Similar to: 8599 (2003)	Ähnlich zu: 8599 (2003)

8610 — **EU** NA AU AS

Ahkmou	
Ahkmou	
Pcs: 30	2003–2005

8611 — **EU** NA AU AS

Orkahm	
Orkahm	
Pcs: 30	2003–2005

8612 — **EU** NA AU AS

Ehrye	
Ehrye	
Pcs: 30	2003–2005

10021 — **EU** **NA** AU AS

U.S.S. Constellation	
U.S.S. Constellation	
Pcs: 973	2003–2004

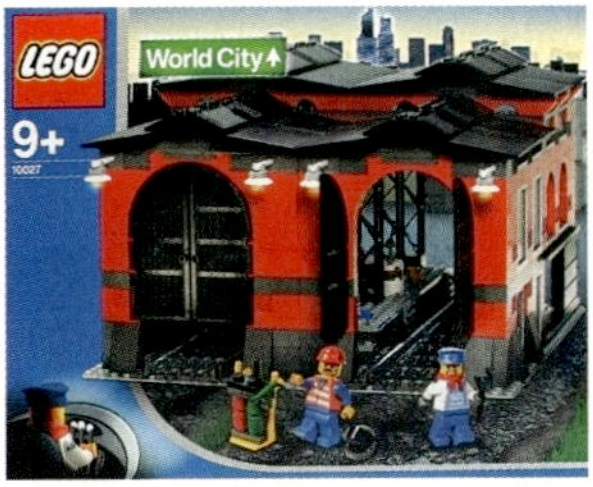

10027 — EU NA AU AS

Train Engine Shed		
Lokschuppen		
Pcs: 663	2003–2006	Special

10029 — EU **NA** AU AS

Lunar Lander		
Mondlander		
Pcs: 467	2003–2004	Special

10041 — **EU** **NA** AU AS

Main Street	
Hauptstraße	
Pcs: 616	2003–2004

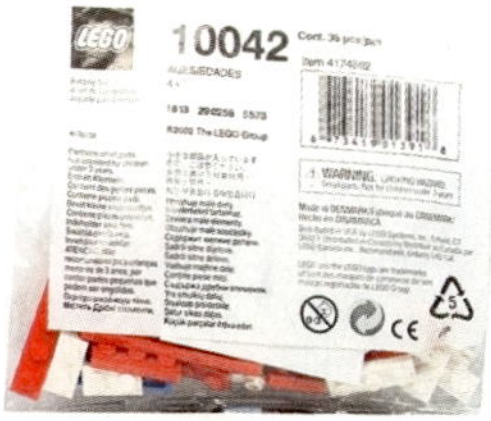

10042 — EU **NA** AU AS

U.S. Flag		
US-Flagge		
Pcs: 35	2003–2005	Special

10071 — EU **NA** AU AS

Mr. Bunny		
Herr Hase		
Pcs: 26	2003–2005	Special

10021	Re-release of: 398 (1978)	Neuauflage von: 398 (1978)
10027	Was distributed by Shop at Home	Wurde über Shop at Home vertrieben
10041	Re-release of: 6390 (1980)	Neuauflage von: 6390 (1980)
10042	Was produced to 4. July, Independence Day - USA	Erschienen zum 4. Juli, Unabhängigkeitstag in USA
10071	Similar to: 1677 (1990)	Ähnlich zu: 1677 (1990)

10079	EU NA AU AS	
Snowman		
Schneemann		
Pcs: 42	2003–2006	Special

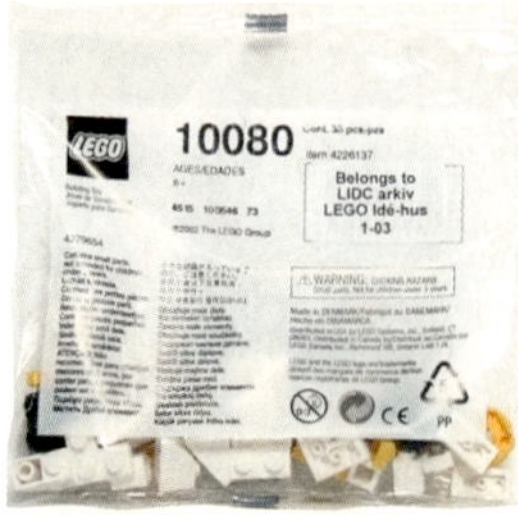

10080	EU NA AU AS	
Angel		
Engel		
Pcs: 33	2003–2006	Special

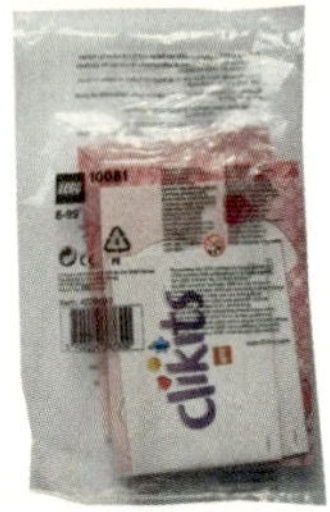

10081	EU NA AU AS	
"Heart" Birthday Pack		
Geburtstagspaket „Heart“		
Pcs: 70	2003–2004	Special

10082	EU NA AU AS	
"Daisy" Birthday Pack		
Geburtstagspaket „Daisy“		
Pcs: 70	2003–2004	Special

10083	EU NA AU AS	
"Star" Birthday Pack		
Geburtstagspaket „Star“		
Pcs: 70	2003–2004	Special

10090	EU NA AU AS	
Turkey		
Truthahn		
Pcs: 54	2003–2005	Special

10121	EU NA AU AS	
NBA Basketball Teams		
NBA Basketballteam		
Pcs: 15	2003–2005	Special

10123	EU NA AU AS	
Cloud City		
Cloud City		
Pcs: 719	2003–2005	Special

10124	EU NA AU AS	
Wright Flyer		
Flugzeug der Wright-Brüder		
Pcs: 664	2003–2005	Special

i		
10079	Similar to: 1979 (1991)	Ähnlich zu: 1979 (1991)
10080	Similar to: 1626 (1989)	Ähnlich zu: 1626 (1989)

10127 EU NA AU AS

NHL Action Set with Stickers		
NHL Action Set mit Aufklebern		
Pcs: 67	2003–2005	Special

10128 EU NA AU AS

Train Level Crossing		
Bahnübergang		
Pcs: 323	2003–2006	Special

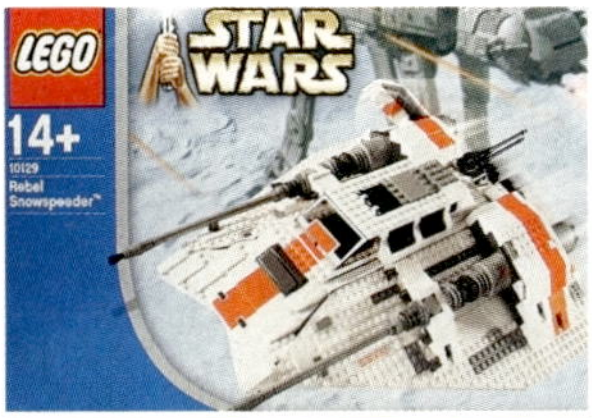

10129 EU NA AU AS

Rebel Snowspeeder™		
Rebel Snowspeeder™		
Pcs: 1457	2003–2005	Special

10201 EU NA AU AS

Takutanuva		
Takutanuva		
Pcs: 407	2003	Special

65182 EU NA AU AS

Slammer Stadium		
Eishockey-Stadion		
Pcs: 299	2003	Special

65258 EU NA AU AS

Power Chamber		
Power Kammer		
Sets: 4	2003	Special

65296 EU NA AU AS

Twin Pack with Gold Avohkii		
2er-Pack mit goldener Avohkii		
Sets: 2	2003	Special

65297 EU NA AU AS

Twin Pack with Gold Avohkii		
2er-Pack mit goldener Avohkii		
Sets: 2	2003	Special

65362 EU NA AU AS

Click-N-Store Jewellery Set		
Click-N-Store Juwelenset		
Sets:2	2003–2004	Special

10201	Includes: 8593 (203), 8596 (2003)	Enthält: 8593 (2003), 8596 (2003)
65258	Includes: 8550 (2002), 8553 (2002), 8554 (2002), 8562 (2002)	Enthält: 8550 (2002), 8553 (2002), 8554 (2002), 8562 (2002)
65362	Includes: 7505 (2003)	Enhält: 7505 (2003)

ⓘ 65363	EU NA AU AS	
Click-n-Store Jewellery Set		
Click-n-Store Schmuckset		
Pcs: 2	2003–2004	Special

ⓘ 65364	EU NA AU AS	
Click-n-Store Jewellery		
Click-n-Store Schmuckset		
Pcs: 2	2003–2004	Special

ⓘ 4207901	EU NA AU AS	
Star Wars™ Mini Bonus Pack		
Star Wars™ Mini Kombiset		
Sets: 4	2003	Special

ⓘ	EU NA AU AS	
Promo Set		
Promoset		
Pcs: -	2003	Special

ⓘ	Set	Includes	Enthält
ⓘ	65363	Includes: 7508 (2003)	Enthält: 7508 (2003)
ⓘ	65364	Includes: 7509 (2003)	Enthält: 7509 (2003)
ⓘ	4207901	Includes: 4484, 4485, 4486, 4487 (2003)	Enthält: 4484, 4485, 4486, 4487 (2003)

2004

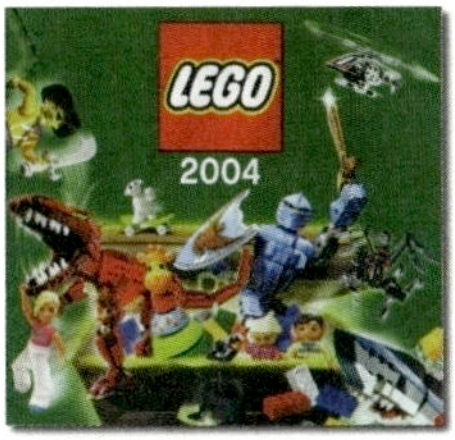

1386	EU NA AU AS	
Jewellery Sample		
Schnupperpackung		
Pcs: 13	2004–2006	Special

3194	EU NA AU AS	
Heart Bracelet		
Heart Bracelet		
Pcs: 9	2004–2006	Special

3195	EU NA AU AS	
Daisy Bracelet		
Daisy Bracelet		
Pcs: 9	2004–2006	Special

3196	EU NA AU AS	
Star Bracelet		
Star Bracelet		
Pcs: 9	2004–2006	Special

3259	EU NA AU AS	
Kanoka Disc Launcher		
Kanoka Disc Launcher		
Pcs: 2	2004	Special

3287	EU NA AU AS	
Takutanuva		
Takutanuva		
Sets: 2	2004–2005	Special

i	3259	Promotional release in France with Bionicle comic	Als Promo in Frankreich mit einem Comic erschienen
i	3287	Includes: 8593 (2003), 8596 (2003)	Enhält: 8593 (2003), 8596 (2003)

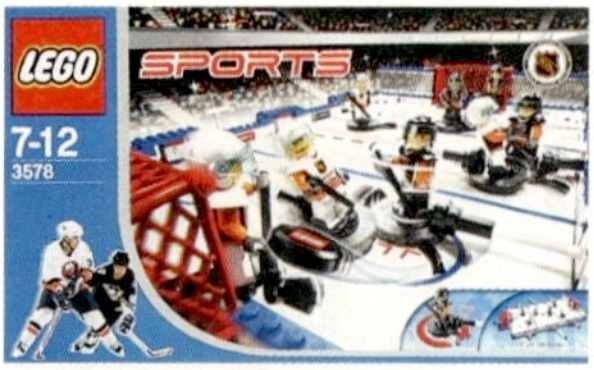

3578 — EU NA AU AS

NHL Championship Challenge

NHL Hockeystadion

Pcs: 382 | 2004–2006

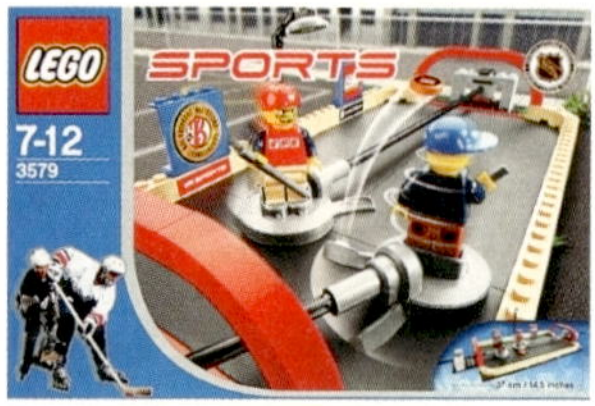

3579 — EU NA AU AS

NHL Street Hockey

NHL Straßenhockey

Pcs: 118 | 2004–2005

4296 — EU NA AU AS

Super Value Box

Vorteilseimer

Pcs: 180 | 2004 | Special

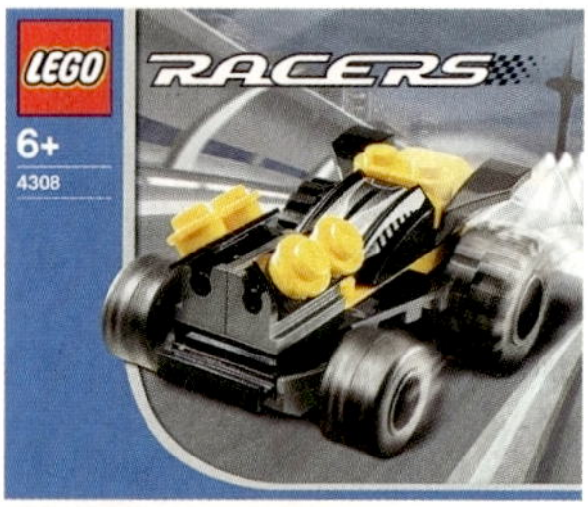

4308 — EU NA AU AS

Yellow Racer

Gelber Rennwagen

Pcs: 28 | 2004–2005 | Special

4309 — EU NA AU AS

Blue Racer

Blauer Rennwagen

Pcs: 30 | 2004–2005 | Special

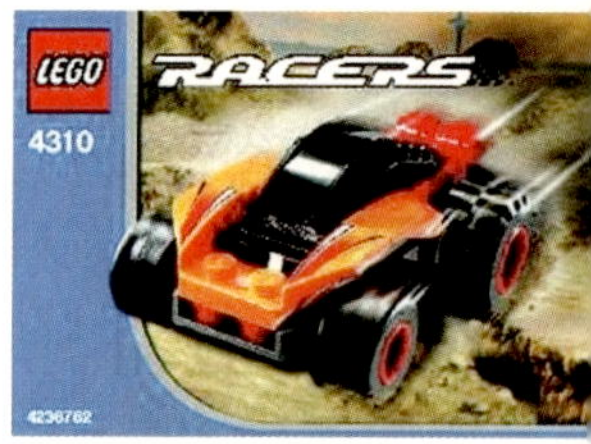

4310 — EU NA AU AS

Orange Racer

Oranger Rennwagen

Pcs: 25 | 2004–2005 | Special

4335 — EU NA AU AS

Black Robot Pod

X-Pod Schwarzer Roboter

Pcs: 50 | 2004–2005 | Special

4346 — EU NA AU AS

Robo Pod

X-Pod Robos

Pcs: 50 | 2004–2005

4347 — EU NA AU AS

Auto Pod

X-Pod Flitzer

Pcs: 39 | 2004–2005

i	4308	LEGOLAND Promo Set	LEGOLAND Promoset
i	4309	LEGOLAND Promo Set	LEGOLAND Promoset
i	4310	LEGOLAND Promo Set	LEGOLAND Promoset
i	4335	Also included in: 65535 (2004)	Auch enthalten in: 65535 (2004)
i	4346	Also included in: 65535 (2004)	Auch enthalten in: 65535 (2004)
i	4347	Also included in: 65535 (2004)	Auch enthalten in: 65535 (2004)

4348	EU NA AU AS	
Aero Pod		
X-Pod Flieger		
Pcs: 36	2004–2005	

4349	EU NA AU AS	
Wild Pod		
X-Pod Tiere		
Pcs: 44	2004–2005	

4406	EU NA AU AS	
Buildings		
Bauspaß Häuser		
Pcs: 506	2004–2007	

4407	EU NA AU AS	
Transportation		
Bauspaß Fahrzeuge		
Pcs: 301	2004–2007	

4408	EU NA AU AS	
Animals		
Bauspaß Tiere		
Pcs: 202	2004–2007	

4410	EU NA AU AS	
Build and Create		
Bunte Steinebox		
Pcs: 500	2004–2007	

4411	EU NA AU AS	
Blue Strata XXL		
Blue Strata XXL		
Pcs: 1205	2004	Special

4412	EU NA AU AS	
Olympia Bucket		
Einfallsreiches Bauen		
Pcs: 200	2004–2005	Special

4414	EU NA AU AS	
Creator Bucket		
Creator Eimer		
Pcs: 500	2004–2005	Special

4348	Also included in: 65535 (2004)	Auch enthalten in: 65535 (2004)
4349	Also included in: 65535 (2004)	Auch enthalten in: 65535 (2004)

4425	EU NA AU AS	
Better Building More Fun		
Besser bauen mit mehr Spaß		
Pcs: 2004	2004–2005	Special

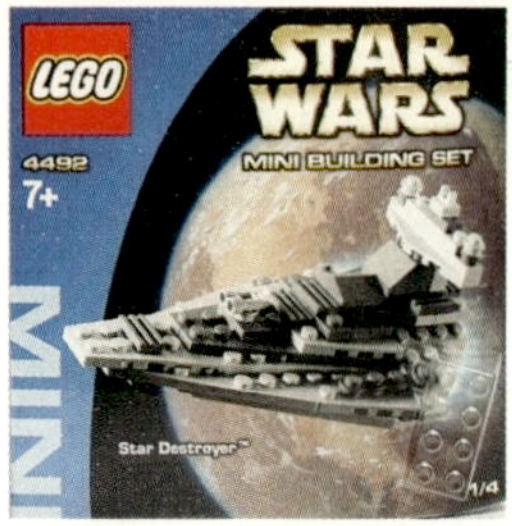

4492	EU NA AU AS
Mini Star Destroyer™	
Mini Star Destroyer™	
Pcs: 92	2004

4493	EU NA AU AS
Mini Sith Infiltrator™	
Mini Sith Infiltrator™	
Pcs: 55	2004

4494	EU NA AU AS
Mini Imperial Shuttle™	
Mini Imperial Shuttle™	
Pcs: 89	2004

4495	EU NA AU AS
Mini AT-TE™	
Mini AT-TE™	
Pcs: 63	2004

4496	EU NA AU AS
Fun with Building Tub	
Bauspaß ohne Grenzen	
Pcs: 1000	2004–2007

4497	EU NA AU AS	
Pretend and Create		
Pretend and Create		
Pcs: 1010	2004–2007	Special

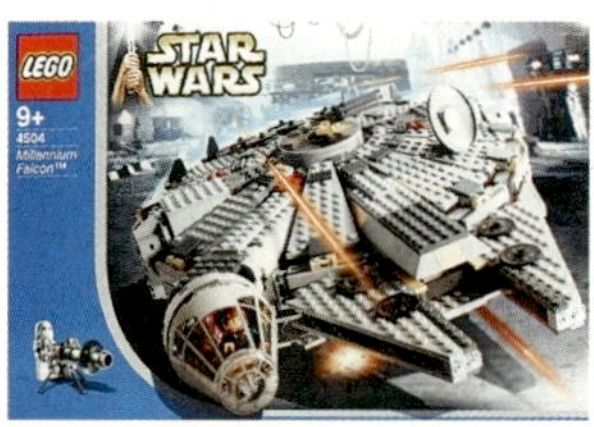

4504	EU NA AU AS
Millennium Falcon™	
Millennium Falcon™	
Pcs: 985	2004–2006

4505	EU NA AU AS
Sea Machines	
Hochseeschiffe	
Pcs: 169	2004–2006

i	4425	Was only released in Canada	Wurde nur in Kanada veröffentlicht
i	4496	Similar to: 4497 (2004)	Ähnlich zu: 4497 (2004)
i	4497	Similar to: 4496 (2004)	Ähnlich zu: 4496 (2004)
i	4504	2004: Original Trilogy Edition box	2004: Original Trilogy Edition box

4506	EU NA AU AS
Deep Sea Predators	
Meeresungeheuer	
Pcs: 360	2004–2006

4507	EU NA AU AS
Prehistoric Creatures	
Dino-Welt	
Pcs: 719	2004–2006

4508	EU NA AU AS
Titan XP	
Riesenroboter	
Pcs: 791	2004–2006

4518	EU NA AU AS	
Creator Set		
Creator Set		
Pcs: 805	2004	Special

4538	EU NA AU AS	
Special Edition		
Special Edition		
Pcs: 200	2004	Special

4562	EU NA AU AS	
Creator Box		
Creator Box		
Pcs: 778	2004	Special

4665	EU NA AU AS
Big Farm	
Großer Bauernhof	
Pcs: 72	2004–2007

4666	EU NA AU AS
Speedy Police Car	
Polizei-Streifenwagen	
Pcs: 25	2004

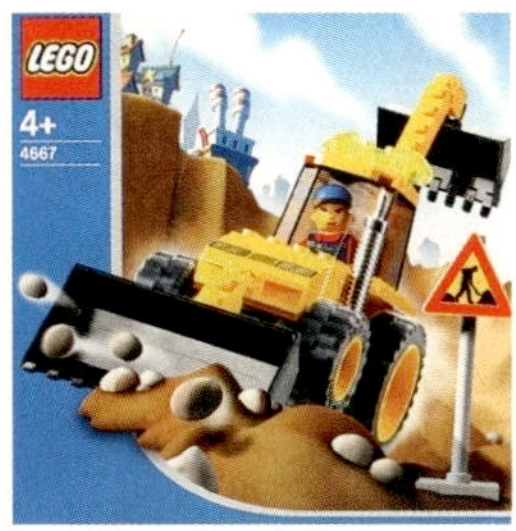

4667	EU NA AU AS
Loadin' Digger	
Kombi-Radlader	
Pcs: 30	2004–2005

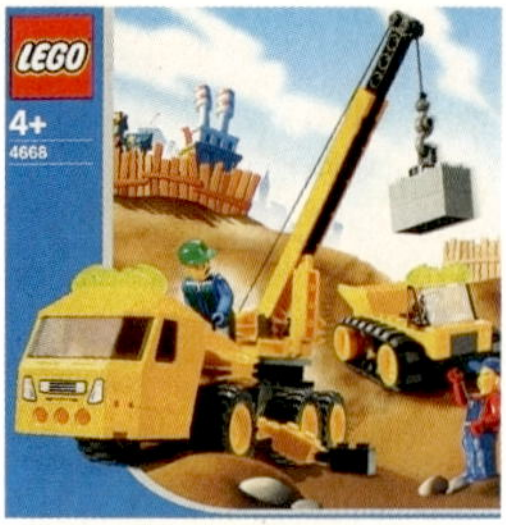

4668	**EU** NA AU AS	
Outrigger Construction Crane		
Kranwagen mit Raupe		
Pcs: 65	2004–2005	

4669	**EU** NA AU AS	
Turbo-Charged Police Boat		
Polizei-Schnellboot mit Motor		
Pcs: 57	2004	

4677	**EU NA** AU AS	
Name Letter Pack		
Buchstabenfliesen		
Pcs: 60	2004–2006	Special

4679	**EU NA AU AS**	
Bricks and Creations		
Bausteine		
Pcs: 1500	2004	Special

4680	**EU NA** AU AS	
Traffic Patrol		
Polizeimotorrad		
Pcs: 3	2004–2007	Special

4681	**EU** NA AU AS	
Fire Truck		
Feuerwehrlöschzug		
Pcs: 22	2004–2007	

4683	**EU NA** AU AS	
Pony and Cart		
Ponykutsche		
Pcs: 6	2004–2007	

4684	**EU** NA AU AS	
Pick Up Truck		
Transporter		
Pcs: 5	2004–2007	

4685	**EU** NA AU AS	
Fork Lift		
Gabelstapler		
Pcs: 11	2004–2007	

i	4677	Can be combined with keychain 4676	Mit Schlüsselanhänger 4676 kombinierbar
i	4679	Was re-released in 2005; was then available at Toys'R'Us in USA	Wurde 2005 neu aufgelegt; erhältlich von Toys'R'Us USA

4686	EU NA AU AS
Little Farm	
Kleiner Bauernhof	
Pcs: 52	2004–2007

4687	EU NA AU AS
Tractor Trailer	
Traktor mit Anhänger	
Pcs: 9	2004–2007

4688	EU NA AU AS
Team Construction	
Große Baustelle	
Pcs: 24	2004–2007

4689	EU NA AU AS
Playhouse	
Spielhaus	
Pcs: 62	2004–2007

4690	EU NA AU AS
Horse Stable	
Pferdestall	
Pcs: 31	2004–2007

4691	EU NA AU AS
Police Station	
Polizeiwache	
Pcs: 64	2004–2007

4692	EU NA AU AS
Fire Car	
Feuerwehrauto	
Pcs: 2	2004

4693	EU NA AU AS
Ferrari F1 Race Car	
Ferrari Rennwagen	
Pcs: 7	2004–2007

4694	EU NA AU AS
Ferrari F1 Racing Team	
Großer Ferrari Pit-Stop	
Pcs: 39	2004–2007

4695	EU NA AU AS	
Mini Knight Bus		
Mini Knight Bus		
Pcs: 54	2004	Special

4696	EU NA AU AS	
Value Bucket		
Kombieimer		
Pcs: 404	2004	Special

4742	EU NA AU AS	
Chill Speeder		
Motorschlitten		
Pcs: 57	2004–2007	

4743	EU NA AU AS	
Ice Blade		
Ice Blader		
Pcs: 108	2004–2007	

4744	EU NA AU AS	
Tundra Tracker		
Tundra Tracker		
Pcs: 144	2004–2007	

4745	EU NA AU AS	
Blue Eagle vs. Snow Crawler		
Blauer Adler gegen Schneeraupe		
Pcs: 272	2004–2007	

4746	EU NA AU AS	
Mobile Command Center		
Mobile Kommandozentrale		
Pcs: 430	2004–2007	

4748	EU NA AU AS	
Ogel's Mountain Fortress		
Ogels Basisstation		
Pcs: 446	2004–2007	

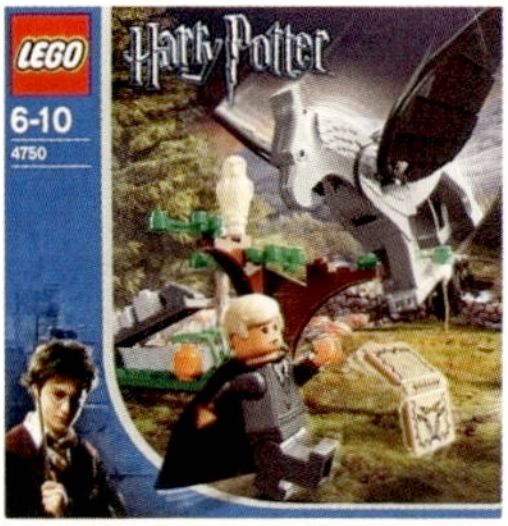

4750	EU NA AU AS	
Draco's Encounter with Buckbeak		
Draco und Seidenschnabel		
Pcs: 39	2004–2005	

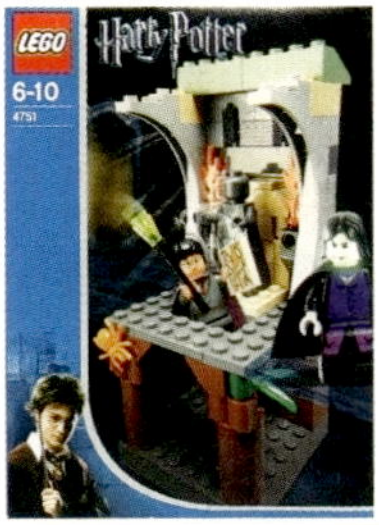

4751	EU NA AU AS
Harry and the Marauder's Map	
Harry & die Karte des Rumtreibers	
Pcs: 109	2004–2005

4752	EU NA AU AS
Professor Lupin's Classroom	
Schulstunde bei Professor Lupin	
Pcs: 164	2004–2005

4753	EU NA AU AS
Sirius Black's Escape	
Rettung von Sirius Black	
Pcs: 193	2004–2005

4754	EU NA AU AS
Hagrid's Hut	
Hagrids Hütte	
Pcs: 309	2004–2007

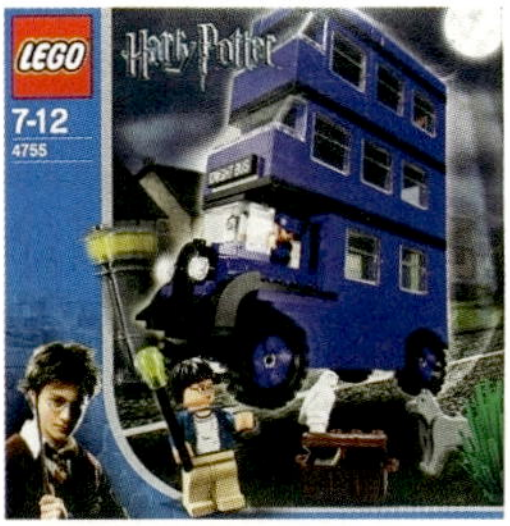

4755	EU NA AU AS
Knight Bus	
Der Fahrende Ritter	
Pcs: 249	2004–2006

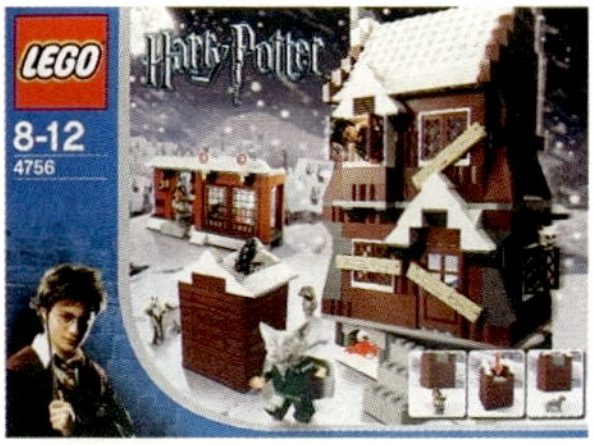

4756	EU NA AU AS
Shrieking Shack	
Heulende Hütte	
Pcs: 459	2004–2006

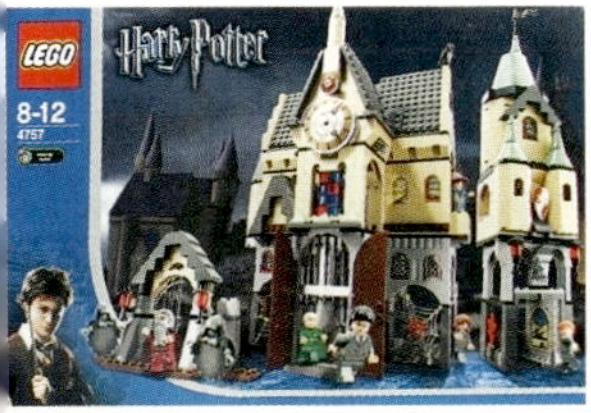

4757	EU NA AU AS
Hogwarts Castle	
Hogwarts	
Pcs: 936	2004–2007

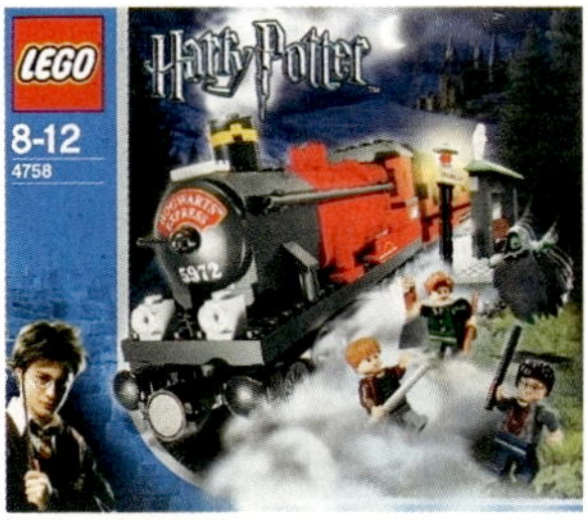

4758	EU NA AU AS
Hogwarts Express	
Hogwarts Express	
Pcs: 386	2004–2007

4759	EU NA AU AS	
Christmas Decorations		
Weihnachtsbaumschmuck		
Pcs: 133	2004–2006	Special

4775		EU NA AU AS
Knight and Squire		
Ritter und Knappe		
Pcs: 21	2004–2007	

4776		EU NA AU AS
Dragon Tower		
Drachenturm		
Pcs: 65	2004–2007	

4777		EU NA AU AS
Knight's Castle		
Große Burg		
Pcs: 169	2004–2007	

4853		EU NA AU AS
Street Chase		
Die Verfolgungsjagd		
Pcs: 79	2004–2005	

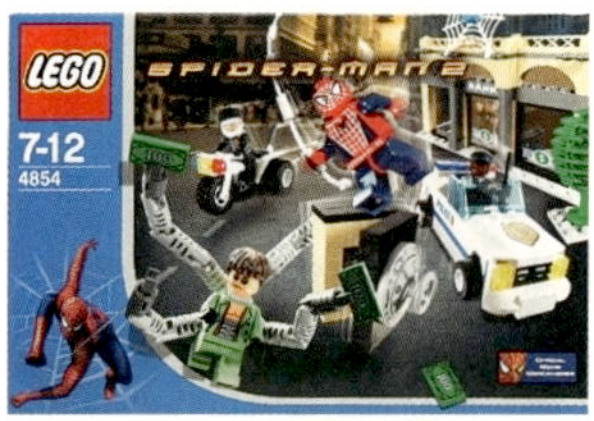

4854		EU NA AU AS
Doc Ock's Bank Robbery		
Doc Ocks Banküberfall		
Pcs: 189	2004–2005	Special

4855		EU NA AU AS
Train Rescue		
Zugrettung		
Pcs: 305	2004–2005	

4856		EU NA AU AS
Doc Ock's Hideout		
Doc Ocks Versteck		
Pcs: 489	2004–2005	

4857		EU NA AU AS
Doc Ock's Fusion Lab		
Doc Ocks Fusion-Lab		
Pcs: 243	2004–2005	

4858		EU NA AU AS
Doc Ock's Crime Spree		
Doc Ocks Amoklauf		
Pcs: 57	2004–2005	Special

4860	EU NA AU AS
Doc Ock's Café Attack	
Doc Ocks Café-Attacke	
Pcs: 132	2004–2005

4868	EU NA AU AS
Rahaga Gaaki	
Rahaga Gaaki	
Pcs: 30	2004–2005

4869	EU NA AU AS
Rahaga Pouks	
Rahaga Pouks	
Pcs: 30	2004–2005

4870	EU NA AU AS
Rahaga Kualus	
Rahaga Kualus	
Pcs: 30	2004–2005

4877	EU NA AU AS
Rahaga Norik	
Rahaga Norik	
Pcs: 30	2004–2005

4878	EU NA AU AS
Rahaga Bomonga	
Rahaga Bomonga	
Pcs: 30	2004–2005

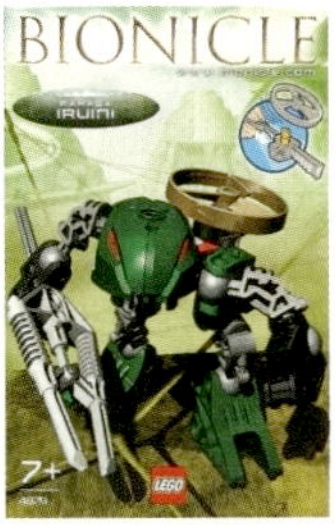

4879	EU NA AU AS
Rahaga Iruini	
Rahaga Iruini	
Pcs: 30	2004–2005

4881	EU NA AU AS
Robo Platoon	
Roboter-Set	
Pcs: 233	2004–2007

4882	EU NA AU AS
Speed Wings	
Flieger-Set	
Pcs: 164	2004–2007

4882	Airline Promo	Airline Promo

4886	EU NA AU AS	
Building Bonanza		
Häuser-Set		
Pcs: 667	2004–2007	

4908	EU NA AU AS	
Brick Box		
Steinebox		
Pcs: 100	2004	Special

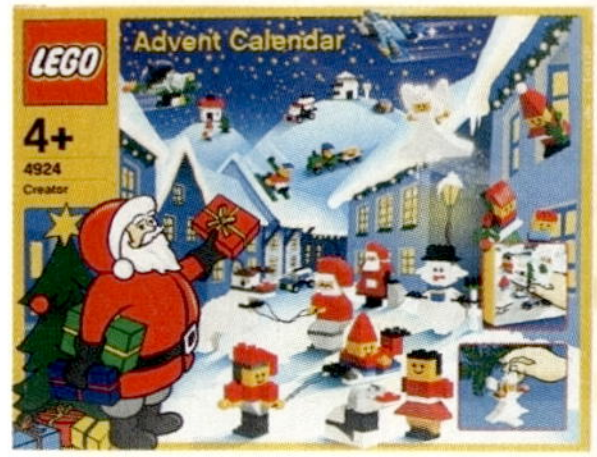

4924	EU NA AU AS	
Advent Calendar		
Adventskalender		
Pcs: 335	2004–2005	Special

5349	EU NA AU AS	
Brick Box		
Steinebox		
Pcs: 100	2004–2006	

5350	EU NA AU AS	
Large Bucket		
Großer Eimer		
Pcs: 90	2004–2008	Special

5351	EU NA AU AS	
Large Bucket		
Großer Eimer		
Pcs: 90	2004–2005	Special

5352	EU NA AU AS	
Bucket		
Eimer		
Pcs: 140	2004–2007	

5353	EU NA AU AS	
Bucket		
Eimer		
Pcs: 139	2004–2007	Special

5354	EU NA AU AS	
Tube		
Röhre		
Pcs: 82	2004–2007	

i	5350	Similar to: 3336 (2000)	Ähnlich zu: 3336 (2000)
i	5352	Similar to: 5353 (2004), 5212 (2003)	Ähnlich zu: 5353 (2004), 5212 (2003)
i	5353	Similar to: 5352 (2004), 5212 (2003)	Ähnlich zu: 5352 (2004), 5212 (2003)

5355 — EU NA AU AS

Small Bucket		
Kleiner Eimer		
Pcs: 22	2004–2007	

5356 — EU NA AU AS

Medium Bucket		
Mittlerer Eimer		
Pcs: 50	2004–2007	

5357 — EU NA AU AS

Large Bucket		
Großer Eimer		
Pcs: 75	2004–2006	

5358 — EU NA AU AS

XL Bucket		
Riesen Eimer		
Pcs: 100	2004–2006	Special

5359 — EU NA AU AS

Block-O-Dile		
Block-O-Dil		
Pcs: 27	2004–2007	

5361 — EU NA AU AS

Bulk Box		
Steinebox		
Pcs: 50	2004–2006	

5385 — EU NA AU AS

Special Edition Bucket		
Spezialeimer		
Pcs: 40	2004	Special

5453 — EU NA AU AS

Baby Elephant Stacker		
Steck-Elefant		
Pcs: 6	2004–2005	

5454 — EU NA AU AS

Stack & Learn Giraffe		
Stapelgiraffe		
Pcs: 5	2004–2005	

i 5455	EU NA AU AS	
Stacking Jungle Set		
Großes Dschungel-Set		
Pcs: 9	2004–2005	

i 5458	EU NA AU AS	
Pull Along Duck and Duckling		
Ziehente mit Küken		
Pcs: 7	2004–2005	

i 5513	EU NA AU AS	
Tubular Chest		
Eimer mit Röhren		
Pcs: 115	2004–2006	Special

i 5877	EU NA AU AS	
Wedding Coach		
Hochzeitskutsche		
Pcs: 74	2004	Special

i 5940	EU NA AU AS	
Doll House		
Puppenhaus		
Pcs: 213	2004–2006	

i 5941	EU NA AU AS	
Riding School		
Reitschule		
Pcs: 7	2004–2006	

i 5942	EU NA AU AS	
Pop Studio		
Popstudio		
Pcs: 112	2004–2006	

i 5943	EU NA AU AS	
Interior Designer		
Designer-Studio		
Pcs: 100	2004–2006	Special

i 5944	EU NA AU AS	
Cat Show		
Katzenfamilie		
Pcs: 31	2004–2006	

i	5877	On the occation of the marriage of crown prince Frederik and crown princess Mary	Anlässlich der Hochzeit von Kronprinz Frederik und Kronprinzessin Mary

5998	EU NA AU AS	
Vladek		
Vladek		
Pcs: 6	2004–2005	Special

5999	EU NA AU AS	
Jayko		
Jayko		
Pcs: 6	2004–2005	Special

6963	EU NA AU AS	
Mini X-wing Fighter™		
Mini X-wing Fighter™		
Pcs: 41	2004–2005	Special

6964	EU NA AU AS	
Mini Boba Fett's Slave I™		
Mini Boba Fett's Slave I™		
Pcs: 25	2004–2005	Special

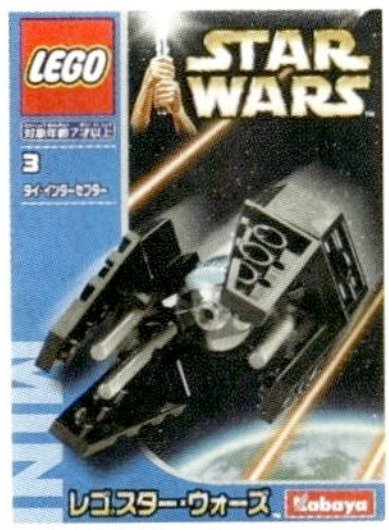

6965	EU NA AU AS	
Mini TIE Interceptor™		
Mini TIE Interceptor™		
Pcs: 32	2004–2005	Special

7042	EU NA AU AS	
Dune Patrol		
Strandstreife		
Pcs: 39	2004–2006	

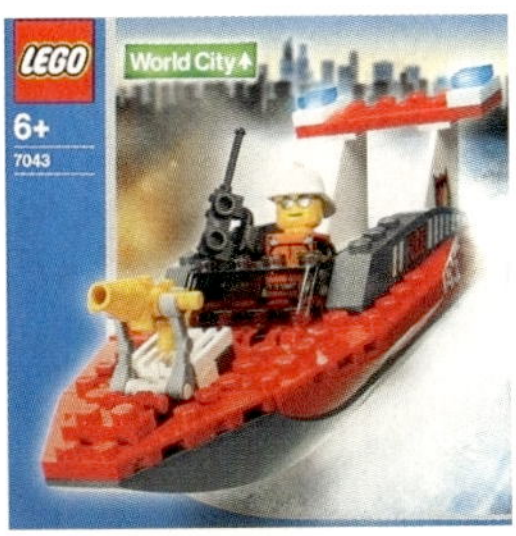

7043	EU NA AU AS	
Firefighter		
Kleines Löschboot		
Pcs: 69	2004–2005	

7044	EU NA AU AS	
Rescue Chopper		
Rettungshubschrauber		
Pcs: 211	2004–2007	

7046	EU NA AU AS	
Fire Command Craft		
Feuerwehrschiff		
Pcs: 277	2004–2007	

6963	Kabaya Promo	Kabaya Promo
6964	Kabaya Promo	Kabaya Promo
6965	Released as Polybag in 2005; Kabaya Promo	2005 als Tütchen erschienen; Kabaya Promo

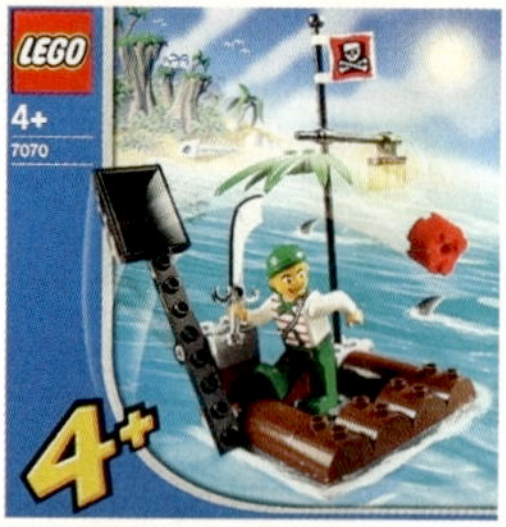

7070	EU NA AU AS
Catapult Raft	
Piratenfloß	
Pcs: 23	2004–2007

7071	EU NA AU AS
Treasure Island	
Schatzinsel	
Pcs: 30	2004–2005

7072	EU NA AU AS
Captain Kragg's Pirate Boat	
Blaues Piratenboot	
Pcs: 41	2004–2007

7073	EU NA AU AS
Pirate Dock	
Kaianlage	
Pcs: 68	2004–2005

7074	EU NA AU AS
Skull Island	
Pirateninsel	
Pcs: 81	2004–2006

7075	EU NA AU AS
Captain Redbeard's Pirate Ship	
Großes Piratenschiff	
Pcs: 134	2004–2007

7080	EU NA AU AS	
Scurvy Dog and Crocodile		
Skorbut-Piet und Krokodil		
Pcs: 7	2004	Special

7081	EU NA AU AS	
Harry Hardtack and Monkey		
Zwieback-Harry und der Affe		
Pcs: 10	2004	Special

7082	EU NA AU AS	
Cannonball Jimmy and Shark		
Kanonen-Jimmy und der Hai		
Pcs: 7	2004	Special

7209	EU NA AU AS	
Pteranodon		
Pteranodon		
Pcs: 30	2004–2005	Special

7210	EU NA AU AS	
Apatosaurus		
Apatosaurus		
Pcs: 33	2004–2005	Special

7214	EU NA AU AS	
Sea Plane		
Wasserflugzeug		
Pcs: 125	2004–2005	Special

7218	EU NA AU AS	
Orange Speedboat		
Orangenes Schnellboot		
Pcs: 26	2004–2005	Special

7219	EU NA AU AS	
Tyrannosaurus Rex		
Tyrannosaurus Rex		
Pcs: 36	2004–2005	Special

7220	EU NA AU AS	
Snowman		
Schneemann		
Pcs: 19	2004–2005	Special

7239	EU NA AU AS	
Fire Truck		
Feuerwehrlöschzug		
Pcs: 216	2004–2008	

7240	EU NA AU AS	
Fire Station		
Feuerwehr-Hauptquartier		
Pcs: 262	2004–2008	

7244	EU NA AU AS	
Speedboat		
Schnellboot		
Pcs: 107	2004–2006	Special

7209	Kabaya Promo	Kabaya Promo
7210	Kabaya Promo	Kabaya Promo
7214	Airline Promo	Airline Promo
7220	Nestlé Promo	Nestlé Promo
7239	Included in: 66195 (2007)	Enthalten in: 66195 (2007)

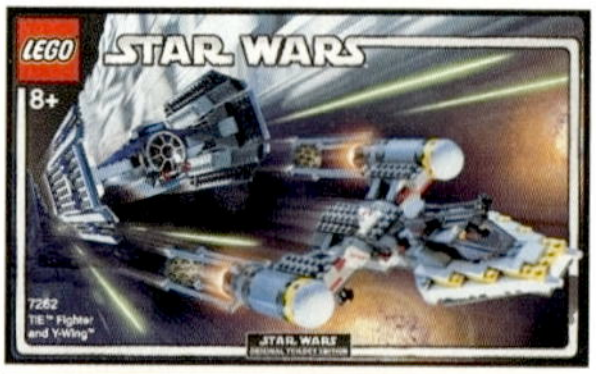

7262	EU NA
TIE Fighter™ & Y-wing™	
TIE Fighter™ & Y-wing™	
Pcs: 421	2004–2005	Special

7290	EU
Pirates Polybag	
Pirat im Fass	
Pcs: 5	2004	Special

7330	NA
Dora's Treasure Island	
Doras Schatzinsel	
Pcs: 22	2004–2007	

7331	NA
Diego's Rescue Truck	
Diegos Rettungswagen	
Pcs: 11	2004–2007	

7332	NA
Dora and Boots at Play Park	
Dora und Boots auf dem Spielplatz	
Pcs: 31	2004–2007	

7333	NA
Dora and Diego's Animal Adventure	
Dora und Diegos Tierabenteuer	
Pcs: 40	2004–2007	

7348	EU
Figure Set, female	
Figuren Set, weiblich	
Pcs: -	2004	Special

7349	EU
Skater Boy	
Skaterboy	
Pcs: 1	2004–2005	Special

7442	EU AU
Tiny's Lift Cart	
Tinys Hebewagen	
Pcs: 4	2004–2006	Special

7442	Was only available in the UK and Australia	Nur in UK und Australien erhältlich gewesen

ⓘ 7443		EU NA AU AS
Stretchy's Junk Cart		
Stretchys Schrottkarre		
Pcs: 4	2004–2006	Special

ⓘ 7444		EU NA AU AS
Sporty's Gym Cart		
Sportys Gymnastikwagen		
Pcs: 3	2004–2006	Special

ⓘ 7445		EU NA AU AS
Stripy's Flower Cart		
Stripy's Blumenwagen		
Pcs: 12	2004–2006	Special

ⓘ 7495		EU NA AU AS
Sporty's Skate Park		
Sporty's Skate Park		
Pcs: 12	2004–2007	Special

ⓘ 7496		EU NA AU AS
Stretchy at Work		
Stretchy bei der Arbeit		
Pcs: 12	2004–2007	Special

ⓘ 7504		EU NA AU AS
Friendship Frame or Mirror		
Bilderrahmen und Spiegel		
Pcs: 15	2004–2005	

ⓘ 7505		EU NA AU AS
Flowered Hair Bands		
Haarbänder mit Blumen		
Pcs: 16	2004–2005	

ⓘ 7506		EU NA AU AS
Starry Bangles and Rings		
Ringe u. Armbänder mit Sternen		
Pcs: 9	2004–2005	

ⓘ 7514		EU NA AU AS
Sweet Dreamy Jewels		
Glitzerschmuck Pink		
Pcs: 48	2004–2005	

ⓘ	7445-7496	Was only available in the Uk and Australia	Nur in UK und Australien erhältlich gewesen

7515	EU NA AU AS
Striped Sunny Jewels	
Glitzerschmuck Orange	
Pcs: 48	2004–2005

7516	EU NA AU AS
Cool Starry Jewels	
Glitzerschmuck Türkis	
Pcs: 52	2004–2005

7524	EU NA AU AS
Glamour Girl Purse	
Glitzergeldbörse	
Pcs: 18	2004–2006

7525	EU NA AU AS
Sunshine Picture Clips	
Bunte Bilderständer	
Pcs: 24	2004–2006

7526	EU NA AU AS
My Starry Notes	
Sternschnuppen-Notizblock	
Pcs: 28	2004–2006

7528	EU NA AU AS
Designer Desk Set	
Pinkes Schreibset	
Pcs: 71	2004–2006

7529	EU NA AU AS
Stylin' Stationery Set	
Briefpapierset Blume	
Pcs: 75	2004–2006

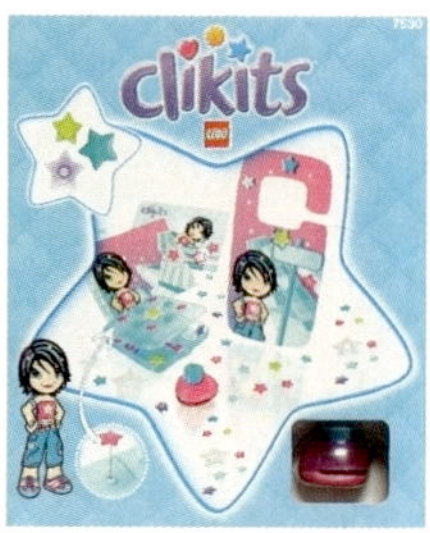

7530	EU NA AU AS
Starry Decoration Set	
Minilocher-Dekoset	
Pcs: 72	2004–2006

7531	EU NA AU AS
Ultimate Jewellery Collection	
Ultimative Schmuck-Sammlung	
Pcs: 148	2004–2006

7532	EU NA AU AS	
My Special Storage Space		
Großes Schreibtischset		
Pcs: 115	2004–2006	

7575	EU NA AU AS	
Clikits Holiday Gift Calendar		
Clikits Adventskalender		
Pcs: 1	2004–2005	

7910	EU NA AU AS	
Robot		
Roboter		
Pcs: 30	2004–2005	Special

7911	EU NA AU AS	
Ship		
Schiff		
Pcs: 34	2004–2005	Special

7912	EU NA AU AS	
Helicopter		
Hubschrauber		
Pcs: 25	2004–2005	Special

7917	EU NA AU AS	
Blue Basketball Player		
Blauer Basketballspieler		
Pcs: 5	2004–2005	Special

7918	EU NA AU AS	
Green Basketball Player		
Grüner Basketballspieler		
Pcs: 5	2004–2005	Special

7919	EU NA AU AS	
White Hockey Player		
Weißer Hockeyspieler		
Pcs: 6	2004–2005	Special

7920	EU NA AU AS	
Blue Hockey Player		
Blauer Hockeyspieler		
Pcs: 6	2004–2005	Special

7910-7912	Duracell Promo	Duracell Promo
7917-7920	McDonald's Promo	McDonald's Promo

ⓘ 7921	EU NA AU AS	
Skateboarder		
Skateboarder		
Pcs: 6	2004–2005	Special

ⓘ 7922	EU NA AU AS	
Snowboarder		
Snowboarder		
Pcs: 5	2004–2005	Special

ⓘ 7923	EU NA AU AS	
White Football Player		
Weißer Fußballspieler		
Pcs: 6	2004–2005	Special

ⓘ 7924	EU NA AU AS	
Red Football Player		
Roter Fußballspieler		
Pcs: 6	2004–2005	Special

ⓘ 7925	EU NA AU AS	
Hearts Stand-up Picture Holder		
Herzchen-Bilderhalter		
Pcs: 5	2004–2006	Special

ⓘ 7926	EU NA AU AS	
Hearts Hair Ribbons		
Herzchen-Haarschleifen		
Pcs: 4	2004–2006	Special

ⓘ 7927	EU NA AU AS	
Flower Hair Elastic		
Blümchen-Haargummi		
Pcs: 4	2004–2006	Special

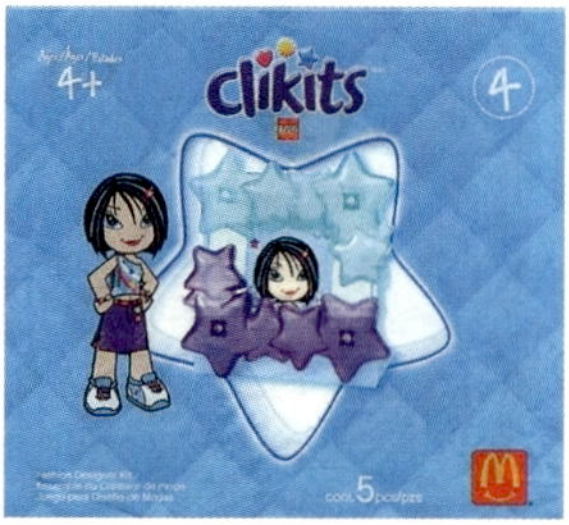

ⓘ 7928	EU NA AU AS	
Stars Photo Frame		
Sternchen-Bilderrahmen		
Pcs: 5	2004–2006	Special

ⓘ 7929	EU NA AU AS	
Hearts Jewlery Box		
Herzchen-Schmuckschatulle		
Pcs: 1	2004–2006	Special

ⓘ	7921-7929	McDonald's Promo	McDonald's Promo

ⓘ 7930	EU **NA** AU AS	
Hearts Lock		
Herzchen-Schmuckschatulle		
Pcs: 1	2004–2006	Special
5/6		

ⓘ 7931	EU **NA** AU AS	
Hearts Bag		
Herzchen-Tasche		
Pcs: 1	2004–2006	Special
5/6		

8026	EU NA AU AS	
Kraatu		
Kraatu		
Pcs: 20	2004–2005	Special
3/6		

8362	**EU** NA AU AS	
Ferrari F1 Racer 1:24		
Ferrari F1 Racer 1:24		
Pcs: 112	2004–2006	
2/6		

ⓘ 8369	**EU** NA AU AS	
Dirt Crusher RC		
Dirt Crusher RC		
Pcs: 90	2004–2007	
2/6		

8375	**EU** **NA** AU AS	
Ferrari F1 Pit Set		
Ferrari F1 Pit Set		
Pcs: 206	2004–2006	
2/6		

8378	**EU** NA AU AS	
Red Beast RC		
Red Beast RC		
Pcs: 71	2004–2006	
2/6		

8386	**EU** NA AU AS	
Ferrari F1 Racer 1:10		
Ferrari F1 Racer 1:10		
Pcs: 719	2004–2006	
2/6		

8389	**EU** NA AU AS	
M. Schumacher & R. Barrichello		
M. Schumacher & R. Barrichello		
Pcs: 22	2004–2006	
2/6		

ⓘ	7930	McDonald's Promo	McDonald's Promo
ⓘ	7931	McDonald's Promo	McDonald's Promo
ⓘ	8369	Available in: blue/yellow box version	Erhältlich in: blaue/gelbe Box-Version

ⓘ 8433	EU NA AU AS
Cool Movers	
Heli-Tieflader	
Pcs: 219	2004–2007

ⓘ 8434	EU NA AU AS
Aircraft	
Propellerflugzeug	
Pcs: 445	2004–2007

ⓘ 8435	EU NA AU AS
4WD	
Allrad-Geländewagen	
Pcs: 773	2004–2007

ⓘ 8436	EU NA AU AS
Truck	
Truck mit Pneumatik-Kran	
Pcs: 1051	2004–2007

ⓘ 8439	EU NA AU AS
Front End Loader	
Schaufelradlader	
Pcs: 582	2004

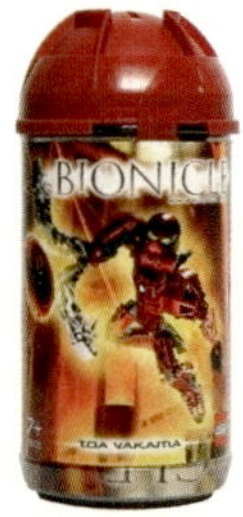

ⓘ 8601	EU NA AU AS
Toa Vakama	
Toa Vakama	
Pcs: 51	2004–2005

ⓘ 8602	EU NA AU AS
Toa Nokama	
Toa Nokama	
Pcs: 49	2004–2005

ⓘ 8603	EU NA AU AS
Toa Whenua	
Toa Whenua	
Pcs: 52	2004–2005

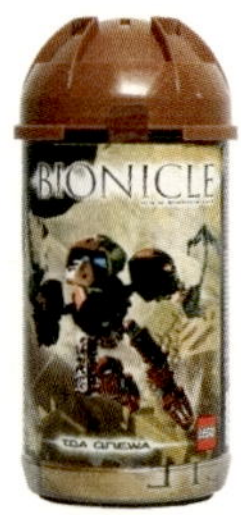

ⓘ 8604	EU NA AU AS
Toa Onewa	
Toa Onewa	
Pcs: 47	2004–2005

ⓘ	Set	English	Deutsch
ⓘ	8439	Similar to: 8464 (2001), 8459 (1997)	Ähnlich zu: 8464 (2001), 8459 (1997)
ⓘ	8601	Released also as promo	Auch als Promo erschienen

8605	EU NA AU AS	
Toa Matau		
Toa Matau		
Pcs: 49	2004–2005	

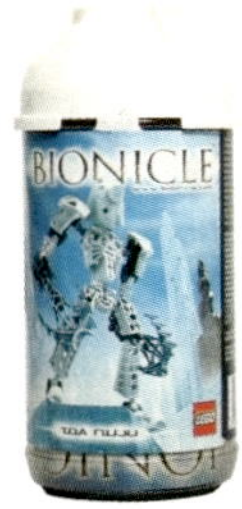

8606	EU NA AU AS	
Toa Nuju		
Toa Nuju		
Pcs: 51	2004–2005	

8613	EU NA AU AS	
Kanoka Disk Launcher Pack		
Kanoka Disk-Werfer		
Pcs: 4	2004–2005	

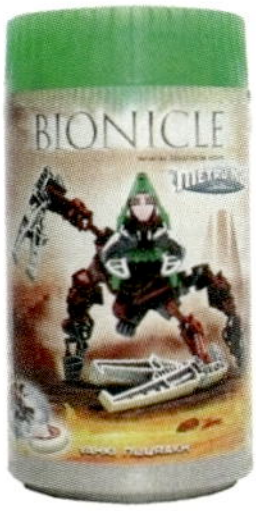

8614	EU NA AU AS	
Vahki Nuurakh		
Vahki Nuurakh		
Pcs: 32	2004–2005	

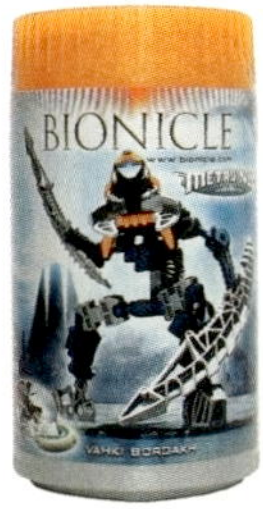

8615	EU NA AU AS	
Vahki Bordakh		
Vahki Bordakh		
Pcs: 33	2004–2005	Special

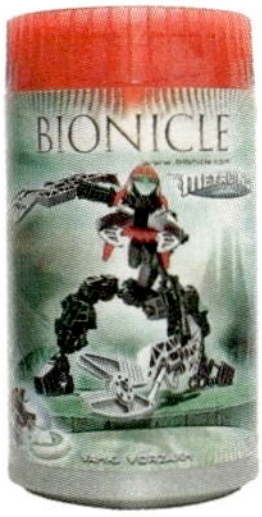

8616	EU NA AU AS	
Vahki Vorzahk		
Vahki Vorzahk		
Pcs: 32	2004–2005	

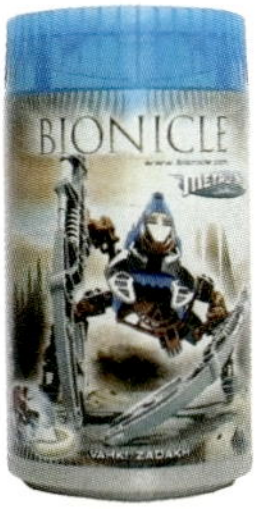

8617	EU NA AU AS	
Vahki Zadakh		
Vahki Zadakh		
Pcs: 32	2004–2005	

8618	EU NA AU AS	
Vahki Rorzakh		
Vahki Rorzakh		
Pcs: 32	2004–2005	

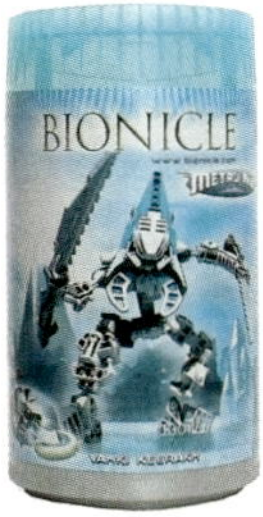

8619	EU NA AU AS	
Vahki Keerakh		
Vahki Keerakh		
Pcs: 32	2004–2005	

i	8615	Released also as promo	Auch als Promo erschienen

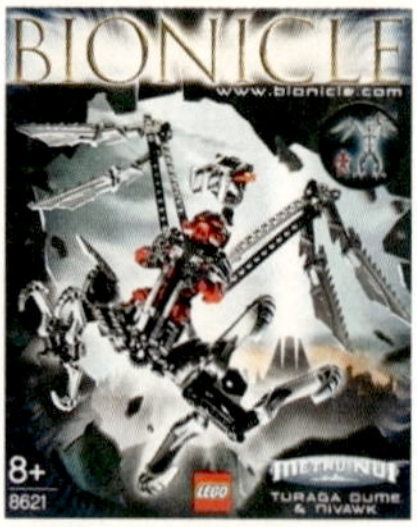

8621	**EU** **NA** AU AS
Turaga Dume and Nivawk	
Turaga Dume und Nivawk	
Pcs: 179	2004–2005

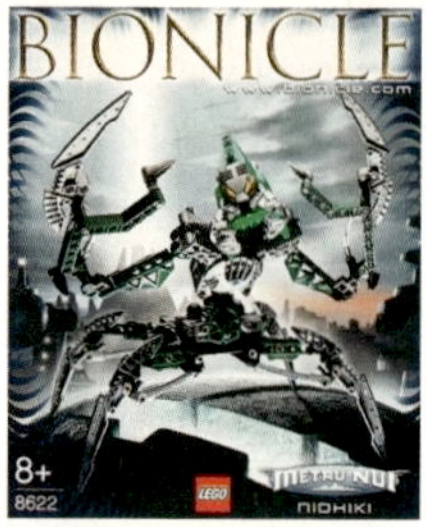

8622	**EU** **NA** AU AS
Nidhiki	
Nidhiki	
Pcs: 173	2004–2005

8623	**EU** NA AU AS
Krekka	
Krekka	
Pcs: 206	2004–2005

8641	**EU** **NA** **AU** **AS**
Flame Glider	
Flame Glider	
Pcs: 52	2004–2007

8642	**EU** **NA** **AU** **AS**
Monster Crusher	
Monster Crusher	
Pcs: 43	2004–2007

8643	**EU** **NA** **AU** **AS**
Power Cruiser	
Power Cruiser	
Pcs: 46	2004–2007

8644	**EU** **NA** **AU** **AS**
Street Maniac	
Street Maniac	
Pcs: 36	2004–2007

8711	EU **NA** AU AS
Bionicle Master Accessory Kit	
Bionicle Zubehör	
Pcs: 702	2004	Special

8770	**EU** NA AU AS
Danju	
Ritter Danju	
Pcs: 42	2004–2005

i	8621-8623	Also included in: 10202 (2004)	Auch enthalten in: 10202 (2004)
i	8711	Was sold from Toys'R'Us only	Wurde nur von Toys'R'Us verkauft
i	8770	Similar to: 8782 (2004)	Ähnlich zu: 8782 (2004)

8771	EU NA AU AS
Jayko - The Rookie	
Ritter Jayko - der Schnelle	
Pcs: 45	2004–2005

8772	EU NA AU AS
Rascus - The Joker	
Ritter Rascus - der Lustige	
Pcs: 46	2004–2005

8773	EU NA AU AS
Santis - The Strong	
Ritter Santis - der Starke	
Pcs: 46	2004–2005

8774	EU NA AU AS
Vladek - The Dark Knight	
Vladek - der Schwarze Ritter	
Pcs: 48	2004–2005

8777	EU NA AU AS
Vladek Encounter	
Angriff des schwarzen Ritters	
Pcs: 43	2004–2006

8778	EU NA AU AS
Border Ambush	
Der Hinterhalt	
Pcs: 181	2004–2006

8779	EU NA AU AS
The Grand Tournament	
Königliches Ritterturnier	
Pcs: 312	2004–2006

8780	EU NA AU AS
Citadel of Orlan	
Ritterfestung von Orlan	
Pcs: 452	2004–2006

8781	EU NA AU AS
The Castle of Morcia	
Große Ritterburg von Morcia	
Pcs: 645	2004–2006

8771	Similar to: 8783 (2004)	Ähnlich zu: 8783 (2004)
8772	Similar to: 8784 (2004)	Ähnlich zu: 8784 (2004)
8773	Similar to: 8785 (2004)	Ähnlich zu: 8785 (2004)
8774	Similar to: 8786 (2004)	Ähnlich zu: 8786 (2004)

8782	EU **NA** AU AS
Danju	
Danju	
Pcs: 43	2004–2005

8783	EU **NA** AU AS
Jayko	
Jayko	
Pcs: 46	2004–2005

8784	EU **NA** AU AS
Rascus	
Rascus	
Pcs: 47	2004–2005

8785	EU **NA** AU AS
Santis	
Santis	
Pcs: 47	2004–2005

8786	EU **NA** AU AS
Vladek	
Vladek	
Pcs: 48	2004–2005

8790	**EU** NA AU AS
King Mathias	
König Mathias	
Pcs: 44	2004–2006

8799	**EU** **NA** AU AS
Knights' Castle Wall	
Vladeks Angriff I	
Pcs: 178	2004–2006

8800	**EU** **NA** AU AS
Vladek's Siege Engine	
Vladeks Angriff II	
Pcs: 365	2004–2006

8809	EU **NA** AU AS	
King Mathias		
König Mathias		
Pcs: 45	2004–2006	Special

i	Set	English	Deutsch
i	8782-8786	Includes Trading Cards; similar to: 8770-8774 (2004); also as Target Promo	Mit Sammelkarten; ähnlich zu: 8770-8774 (2004); auch als Target Promo
i	8809	Includes Trading Cards	Mit Sammelkarten

8811	EU
Toa Lhikan & Kikanalo	
Toa Lhikan & Kikanalo	
Pcs: 216	2004–2005

10116	EU NA	
Accessories, Heart		
Zubehörteile, Heart		
Pcs: 50	2004–2005	Special

10117	EU NA	
Accessories, Daisy		
Zubehörteile, Daisy		
Pcs: 50	2004–2005	Special

10118	EU NA	
Accessories, Star		
Zubehörteile, Star		
Pcs: 50	2004–2005	Special

10131	EU NA AU AS	
TIE Fighter™ Collection		
TIE Fighter™ Collection		
Pcs: 687	2004–2006	Special

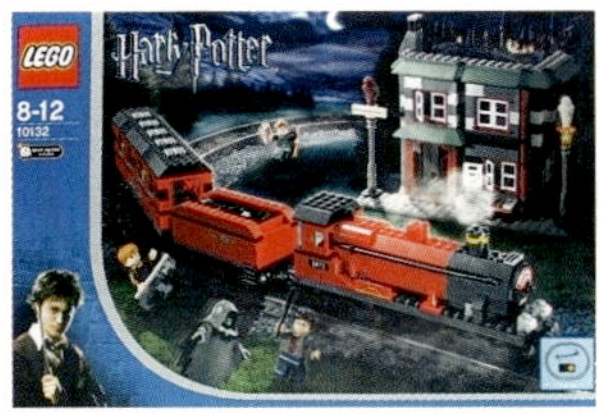

10132	EU NA AU AS
Motorized Hogwarts Express	
Motorisierter Hogwarts Express	
Pcs: 722	2004–2007

10134	EU NA AU AS	
Y-wing Attack Starfighter™		
Y-wing Attack Starfighter™		
Pcs: 1473	2004–2006	Special

10135	EU NA	
Holiday Decoration Kit		
Weihnachtsdekoration		
Pcs: 283	2004–2005	Special

10151	EU NA AU AS	
Hot Rod "Blue Fury"		
Hot Rod Speedster		
Pcs: 436	2004–2006	Special

i 10151	Similar to: 5541 (1995)	Ähnlich zu: 5541 (1995)

10152	EU NA AU AS	
Maersk Sealand		
Maersk-Sealand		
Pcs: 988	2004–2005	Special

10156	EU NA AU AS	
Show Truck		
Show-Truck		
Pcs: 104	2004–2005	Special

10157	EU NA AU AS	
High Speed Train Locomotive		
Hochgeschwindigkeitslokomotive		
Pcs: 141	2004–2006	

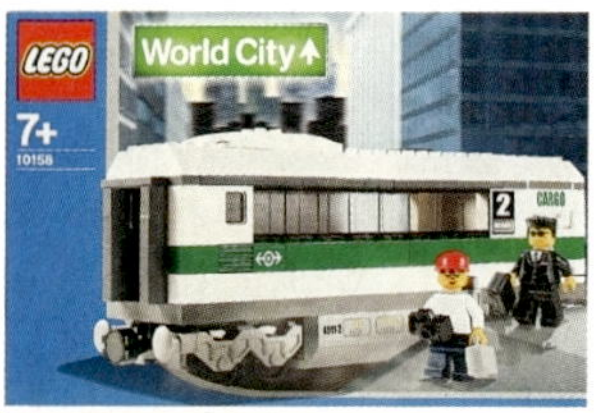

10158	EU NA AU AS	
High Speed Train Car		
Hochgeschwindigkeitswaggon		
Pcs: 159	2004–2006	Special

10159	EU NA AU AS	
City Airport		
Stadtflughafen		
Pcs: 929	2004–2006	Special

10165	EU NA AU AS	
Elf Boy		
Elf		
Pcs: 29	2004–2005	Special

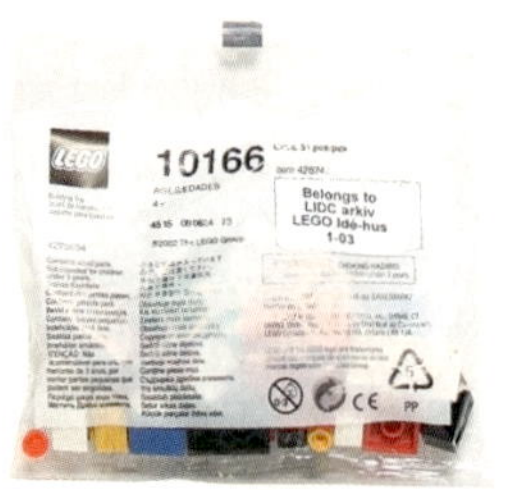

10166	EU NA AU AS	
Elf Girl		
Elfe		
Pcs: 34	2004–2005	Special

10167	EU NA AU AS	
BrickMaster		
BrickMaster		
Pcs: 195	2004–2005	Special

10202	EU NA AU AS	
Ultimate Dume		
Ultimate Dume		
Sets: 3	2004	Special

i	10152	Limited Editon, re-released twice in 2005 as "2005 Edition" and 2006 as "Marsk Line" Set	Limitierte Auflage, zweimal neu aufgelegt als „2005 Edition" und 2006 als „Maersk Line" Set
i	10156	Similar to: 2148 (1997); LEGO Truck Tour 2004 Promo	Ähnlich zu: 2148 (1997); LEGO Truck Tour 2004 Promo
i	10159	Similar to: 6597 (1994)	Ähnlich zu: 6597 (1994)
i	10202	Includes: 8621, 8622, 8623 (2004)	Enthält: 8621, 8622, 8623 (2004)

ⓘ 65535	EU NA AU AS	
X-Pod Play Off Game Pack		
X-Pod Brettspiel-Set		
Pcs: 240	2004	Special

ⓘ 65537	EU NA AU AS	
Classic Freight Train		
Klassischer Güterzug		
Pcs: 613	2004	Special

ⓘ 65542	EU NA AU AS	
Click-n-Store Jewelry Set		
Schmuckset mit Schatulle		
Pcs: 49	2004	Special

ⓘ 65545	EU NA AU AS	
Ta-Metru Collector's Pack		
Ta-Metru Sammleredition		
Pcs: 75	2004	Special

ⓘ 65573	EU NA AU AS	
Rumble Racers Value Pack		
Rumble Racers Kombiset		
Sets: 4	2004	Special

ⓘ 65642	EU NA AU AS	
Grand Tournament Value Pack		
Ritterturnier-Zusatzpack		
Pcs: 314	2004	Special

ⓘ	65535	Includes: 4335, 4346, 4347, 4348, 4349 (2004), Toys'R'Us	Enthält: 4335, 4346, 4347, 4348, 4349 (2004), Toys'R'Us
ⓘ	65573	Includes: 8380 (2003), 8383 (2003), 8384 (2003), 8385 (2003)	Enthält: 8380 (2003), 8383 (2003), 8384 (2003), 8385 (2003)

2005

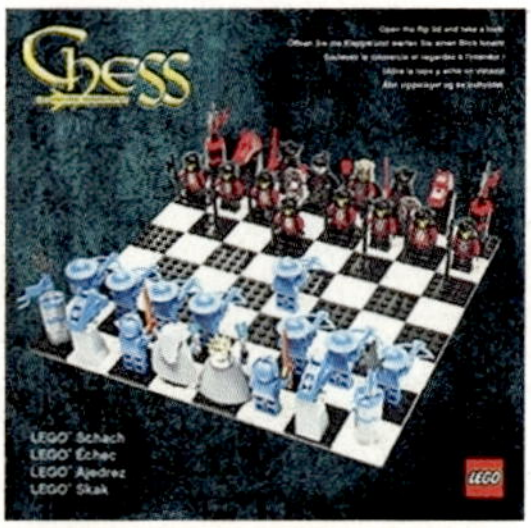

678	EU NA AU AS	
Chess Set		
Schachspiel		
Pcs: 255	2005	Special

1270	EU NA AU AS	
Trial Size Bag - Chromika		
Probepackung - Chromika		
Pcs: 15	2005	Special

3193	EU NA AU AS	
Fashion Designer Kit		
Fashion Designer Kit		
Pcs: 14	2005–2006	Special

3292	EU NA AU AS	
Dizzys Bridge Set		
Bob und Mixi bauen eine Brücke		
Pcs: 20	2005–2007	

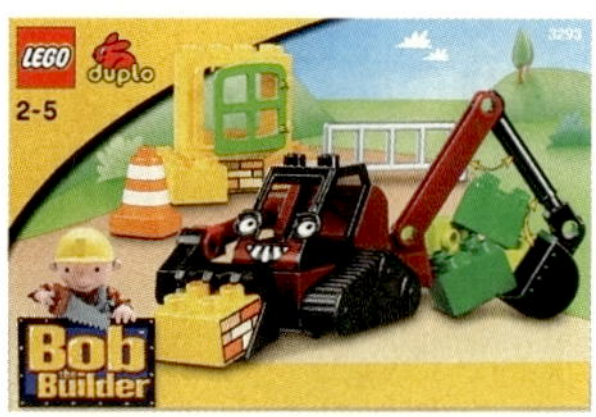

3293	EU NA AU AS	
Bennys Dig Set		
Benny der Kettenbagger		
Pcs: 20	2005–2007	

3294	EU NA AU AS	
Mucks Recycling Set		
Bob und Buddel sortieren den Müll		
Pcs: 33	2005–2007	

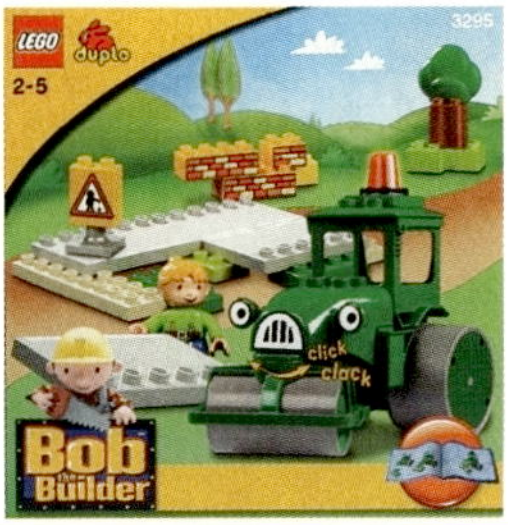

3295 — EU NA AU AS

Roleys Road Set		
Rollo & Wendy bauen eine Straße		
Pcs: 26	2005–2007	

3296 — EU NA AU AS

Travis and the Mobile Caravan		
Bob, Rumpel und der Wohnwagen		
Pcs: 26	2005–2007	

3297 — EU NA AU AS

Scoop & Lofty at the Building Yard		
Baggi & Heppo auf der Baustelle		
Pcs: 61	2005–2007	

3598 — EU NA AU AS

XXL 2000 Tube		
XXL 2000 Tonne		
Pcs: 2000	2005	Special

3599 — EU NA AU AS

XXL 250 Tube		
XXL 250 Tonne		
Pcs: 250	2005	Special

3600 — EU NA AU AS

Build Your Own House		
Bau dein eigenes Haus		
Pcs: 1200	2005–2006	Special

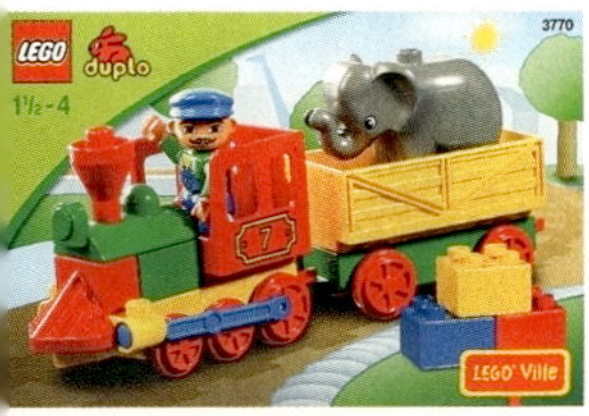

3770 — EU NA AU AS

My First Train		
Mein erster Zug		
Pcs: 12	2005–2008	

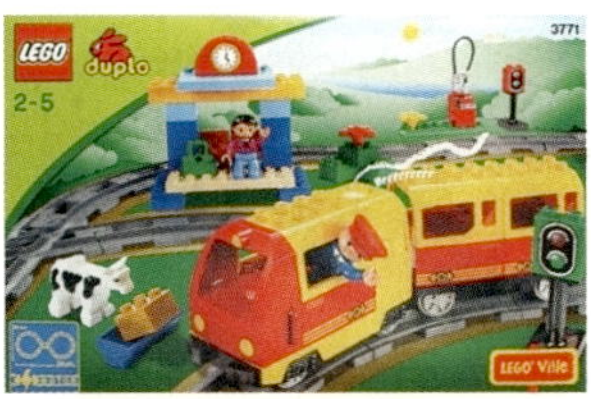

3771 — EU NA AU AS

Train Starter Set		
Eisenbahn Starterset		
Pcs: 67	2005–2008	

3772 — EU NA AU AS

Deluxe Train Set		
Eisenbahn Superset		
Pcs: 112	2005–2008	

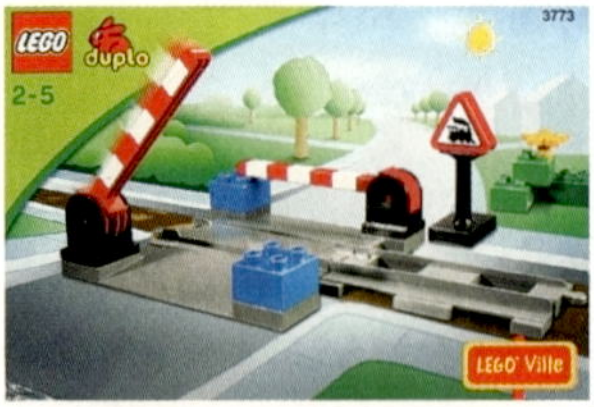

3773	EU NA AU AS	
Level Crossing		
Bahnübergang		
Pcs: 14	2005–2007	

3774	EU NA AU AS	
Bridge		
Eisenbahnbrücke		
Pcs: 26	2005–	

3775	EU NA AU AS	
Points		
Weiche		
Pcs: 2	2005–	

3778	EU NA AU AS	
Station		
Bahnhof		
Pcs: 48	2005–2006	

4085	EU NA AU AS	
50th Anniversary Bucket		
50-Jahre-Jubiläumseimer		
Pcs: 90	2005–2007	

4105	EU NA AU AS	
50th Anniversary Bucket		
50-Jahre-Jubiläumseimer		
Pcs: 500	2005	Special

4337	EU NA AU AS	
Dragon Pod		
X-Pod Drache		
Pcs: 53	2005–2006	Special

4338	EU NA AU AS	
Monster Pod		
X-Pod Monster		
Pcs: 51	2005–2006	Special

4339	EU NA AU AS	
Aqua Pod		
X-Pod Haie		
Pcs: 59	2005–2006	Special

4413	EU NA AU AS	
Arachno Pod		
X-Pod Spinne		
Pcs: 63	2005–2006	Special

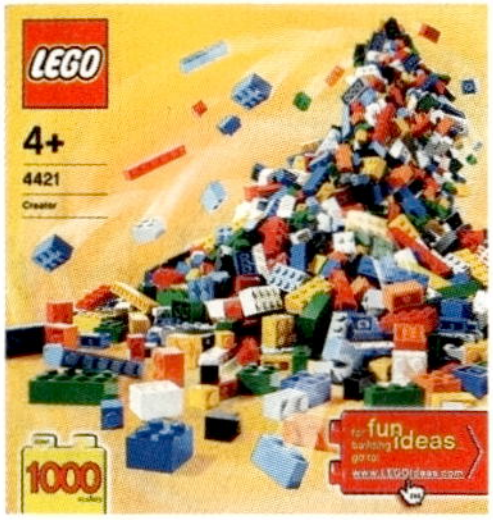

4421	EU NA AU AS	
Box of Bricks		
Box mit Bausteinen		
Pcs: 1000	2005	Special

4422	EU NA AU AS	
Handy Box		
Bunte Steinebox		
Pcs: 120	2005–2006	

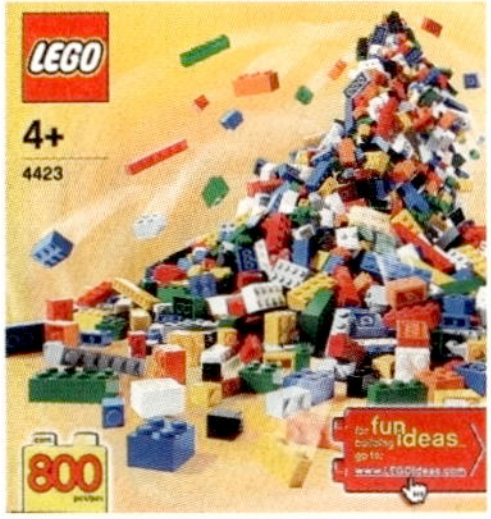

4423	EU NA AU AS	
Creator Handy Box		
Bunte Steinebox		
Pcs: 800	2005–2006	

4496	EU NA AU AS	
50th Anniversary Tub		
50-Jahre-Jubiläumseimer		
Pcs: 1000	2005	Special

4658	EU NA AU AS	
Farm Animals		
Bauernhoftiere		
Pcs: 5	2005–2006	

4659	EU NA AU AS	
Garbage Truck		
Müllabfuhr		
Pcs: 14	2005–2008	

4661	EU NA AU AS	
Construction Worker		
Bauarbeiter		
Pcs: 4	2005–2007	

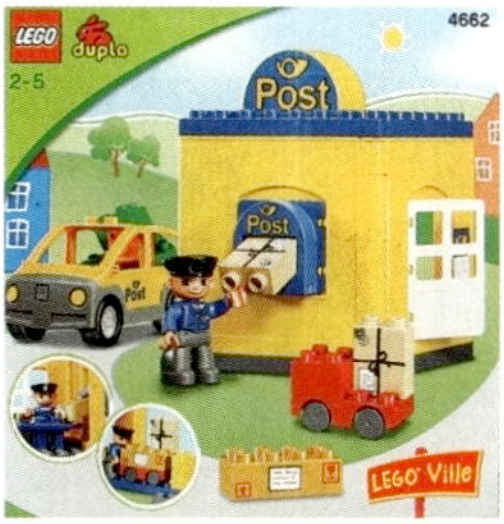

4662	EU NA AU AS	
Post Office		
Postamt		
Pcs: 23	2005–2007	

4663	EU NA
Zoo	
Zoo	
Pcs: 50	2005–2007

4664	EU
Fire Station	
Feuerwehr-Hauptquartier	
Pcs: 60	2005–2007

4762	EU
Rescue from the Merpeople	
Rettung unter Wasser	
Pcs: 175	2005–2006

4766	EU
Graveyard Duel	
Duell auf dem Friedhof	
Pcs: 562	2005–2006

4767	EU
Harry & the Hungarian Horntail	
Der ungarische Hornschwanz	
Pcs: 267	2005–2006

4768	EU
The Durmstrang Ship	
Durmstrang Schiff	
Pcs: 575	2005–2006

4770	EU NA	
Blizzard Blaster		
Blizzard Blaster		
Pcs: 310	2005–2007	Special

4774	NA	
Scorpion Orb Launcher		
Scorpion Orb Launcher		
Pcs: 233	2005–2007	Special

4778		
Biplane		
Doppeldecker		
Pcs: 108	2005	Special

4768	Also as Target Promo with exclusive figures	Auch als Target Promo mit exklusiven Figuren
4778	Airline Promo	Airline Promo

4779 EU NA AU AS

Defense Tower		
Verteidigungsturm		
Pcs: 64	2005–2007	

4780 EU NA AU AS

Box of Bricks		
500-Steine-Packung		
Pcs: 500	2005–2007	

4781 EU NA AU AS

Box of Bricks		
300-Steine-Packung		
Pcs: 300	2005–2007	Special

4782 EU NA AU AS

Box of Bricks		
200-Steine-Packung		
Pcs: 200	2005	Special

4783 EU NA AU AS

30 Pieces Free!		
30 Teile frei!		
Pcs: 30	2005	Special

4784 EU NA AU AS

Black Dragon		
Schwarzer Drache		
Pcs: 8	2005–2007	

4785 EU NA AU AS

Black Castle		
Schwarze Ritterfestung		
Pcs: 386	2005–2006	

4820 EU NA AU AS

Princess' Palace		
Prinzessinnen-Palast		
Pcs: 81	2005–2008	

4821 EU NA AU AS

Princess' Horse and Carriage		
Königliche Kutsche mit Pferd		
Pcs: 18	2005–2008	

4822	EU	NA	AU	AS
Princess' Bedroom				
Königliches Schlafgemach				
Pcs: 13	2005–2008			

4874	EU	NA	AU	AS
Cool Friend Notes				
Freundschafts-Notizen				
Pcs: 11	2005–2006			

4875	EU	NA	AU	AS
Groovy Friends Gems				
Freundschafts-Armreifen & -Ringe				
Pcs: 13	2005–2006			

4876	EU	NA	AU	AS
Fun Friends Hair Bands				
Freundschafts-Haargummis				
Pcs: 22	2005–2006			

4883	EU	NA	AU	AS
Gear Grinders				
Fahrzeugset				
Pcs: 277	2005–2007			

4884	EU	NA	AU	AS
Wild Hunters				
Wilde Tiere				
Pcs: 637	2005–2007			

4888	EU	NA	AU	AS
Ocean Odyssey				
Tiefsee-Expedition				
Pcs: 639	2005–2006			

4903	EU	NA	AU	AS
Lion				
Löwe				
Pcs: 42	2005–2006	Special		

4904	EU	NA	AU	AS
Elephant				
Elefant				
Pcs: 35	2005	Special		

i	4903	Quaker Cereal Promo	Quaker Cereal Promo
i	4904	Quaker Cereal Promo	Quaker Cereal Promo

ⓘ 4905	EU NA AU AS	
Giraffe		
Giraffe		
Pcs: 37	2005–2006	Special

ⓘ 4906	EU NA AU AS	
Helicopter		
Hubschrauber		
Pcs: 16	2005–2006	Special

ⓘ 4911	EU NA AU AS	
Blue Truck		
Sattelschlepper		
Pcs: 38	2005	Special

ⓘ 4912	EU NA AU AS	
Police Jet Ski		
Polizei Jet-Ski		
Pcs: 24	2005	Special

ⓘ 4914	EU NA AU AS	
Fire Chief's Car		
Jeep der Einsatzleitung		
Pcs: 33	2005	Special

ⓘ 4919	EU NA AU AS	
Blue Tub		
Blauer Eimer		
Pcs: 1500	2005–2006	Special

ⓘ 4941	EU NA AU AS	
Rascus		
Rascus		
Pcs: 4	2005–2006	Special

ⓘ 4942	EU NA AU AS	
Shadow Knight		
Schattenritter		
Pcs: 4	2005–2006	Special

ⓘ 4943	EU NA AU AS	
Vladek		
Vladek		
Pcs: 4	2005–2006	Special

ⓘ	4905	Quaker Cereal Promo	Quaker Cereal Promo
ⓘ	4941	Nestlé Promo	Nestlé Promo
ⓘ	4942	Nestlé Promo	Nestlé Promo
ⓘ	4943	Nestlé Promo	Nestlé Promo

4944	EU NA AU AS
Jayko	
Jayko	
Pcs: 4	2005–2006 · Special

4945	EU NA AU AS
Santis	
Santis	
Pcs: 4	2005–2006 · Special

4946	EU NA AU AS
Danju	
Danju	
Pcs: 4	2005–2006 · Special

5352	EU NA AU AS
50th Anniversary Tub	
50-Jahre-Jubiläumseimer	
Pcs: 139	2005 · Special

5363	EU NA AU AS
Mountain Climber	
Mountain Climber	
Pcs: 16	2005–2006

5367	EU NA AU AS
Yellow Tub	
Gelbe Box	
Pcs: 102	2005 · Special

5369	EU NA AU AS
Red Tub	
Rote Box	
Pcs: 703	2005 · Special

5370	EU NA AU AS
Bucket with Bonus Pack	
Eimer mit Bonuspaket	
Pcs: 700	2005 · Special

5371	EU NA AU AS
Bucket with Bonus Pack	
Eimer mit Bonuspaket	
Pcs: 120	2005 · Special

4944	Nestlé Promo	Nestlé Promo
4945	Nestlé Promo	Nestlé Promo
4946	Nestlé Promo	Nestlé Promo

5460 EU NA AU AS

Happy Flower Rattle and Teether		
Blumenrassel und Beißring		
Pcs: 2	2005–	

5461 EU NA AU AS

Shape Sorter House		
Formensortier-Haus		
Pcs: 12	2005–	

5462 EU NA AU AS

Bathtime Boat		
Boot zum Baden		
Pcs: 4	2005–	

5463 EU NA AU AS

Play Train		
Baby-Zug		
Pcs: 6	2005–	

5464 EU NA AU AS

Play Plane		
Propellerflugzeug		
Pcs: 2	2005–	

5465 EU NA AU AS

Bendy Caterpillar		
Raupe „Löwenzahn“		
Pcs: 3	2005–	

5467 EU NA AU AS

Yellow Baby Brick Rattle		
Gelbe Baby Rassel		
Pcs: 1	2005	Special

5468 EU NA AU AS

Baby Rattle		
Rassel		
Pcs: 2	2005–2006	Special

5503 EU NA AU AS

Dog		
Hund		
Pcs: 32	2005–2007	Special

5504	Regions: EU, NA	
Airplane		
Flugzeug		
Pcs: 34	2005–2007	Special
Rating: 1		

5524		
Airport		
Flughafen		
Pcs: 616	2005–2006	Special
Rating: 2		

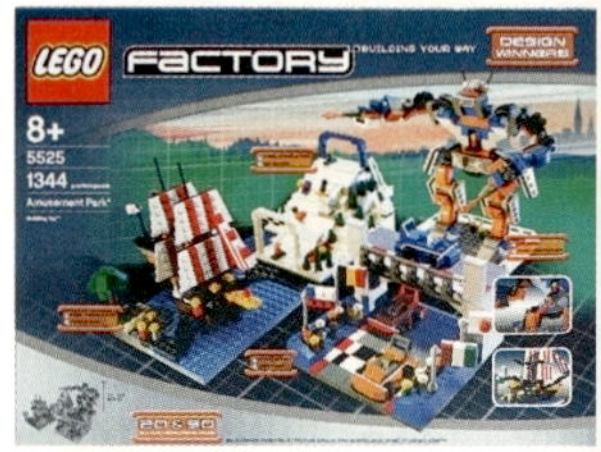

5525	Regions: EU	
Amusement Park		
Vergnügungspark		
Pcs: 1370	2005–2006	Special
Rating: 2		

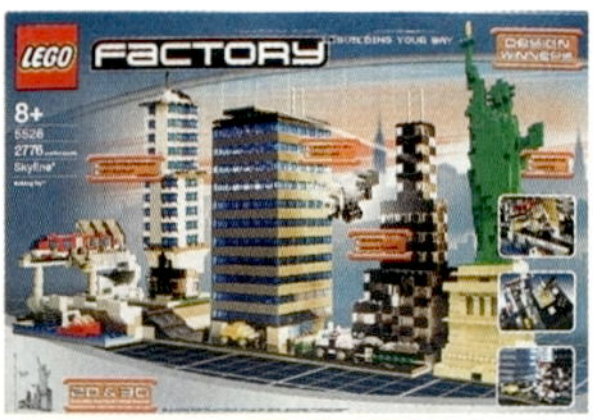

5526		
Skyline		
Skyline		
Pcs: 2793	2005–2006	Special
Rating: 2		

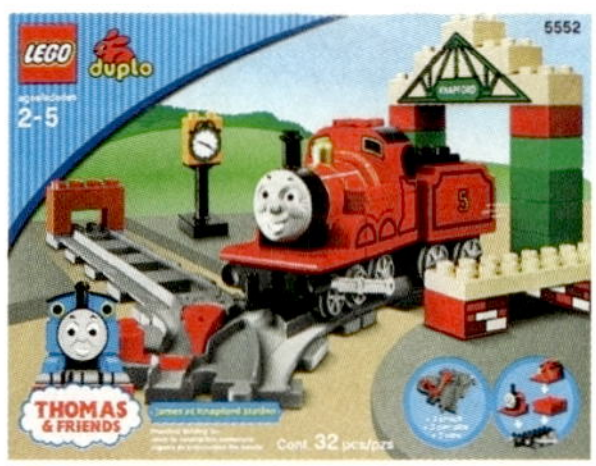

5552	Regions: EU	
James at Knapford Station		
James auf dem Bahnhof Knapford		
Pcs: 32	2005–2008	
Rating: 1		

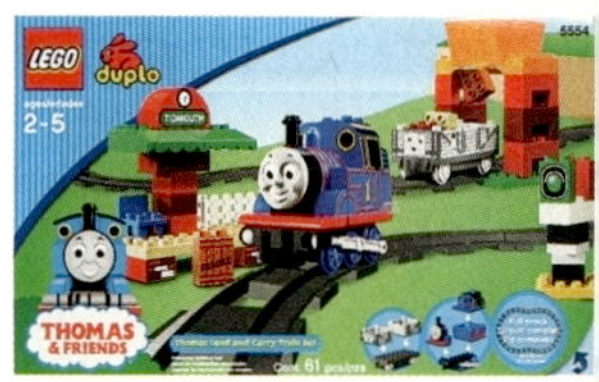

5554	Regions: EU	
Thomas Load and Carry Train Set		
Thomas Verladestation & Zugset		
Pcs: 61	2005–2008	
Rating: 1		

5555	Regions: EU	
Toby at Wellsworth Station		
Toby auf dem Bahnhof Wellsworth		
Pcs: 19	2005–2008	
Rating: 1		

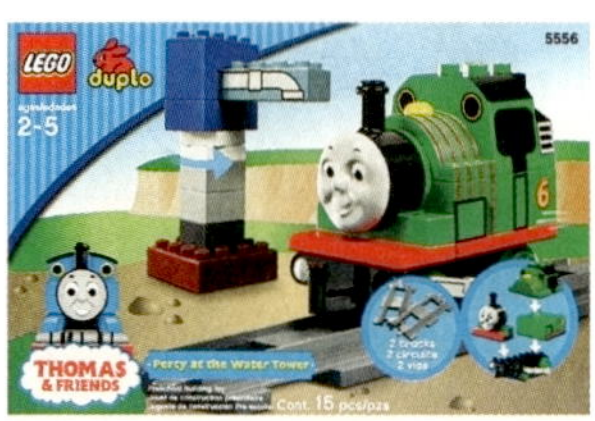

5556	Regions: EU	
Percy at the Water Tower		
Percy am Wasserturm		
Pcs: 15	2005–2008	
Rating: 1		

5960	Regions: EU	
The Mermaid Castle		
Schloss der kleinen Meerjungfrau		
Pcs: 236	2005–2007	
Rating: 1		

Set	English	Deutsch
5524	Only available via Shop at Home	Nur über Shop at Home zu beziehen
5525	Only available via Shop at Home	Nur über Shop at Home zu beziehen
5526	Only available via Shop at Home	Nur über Shop at Home zu beziehen

5961	EU
Snow Queen	
Die Schneekönigin	
Pcs: 58	2005–2007

5962	EU
The Tinderbox	
Das Feuerzeug	
Pcs: 86	2005–2007

5963	EU
The Princess and the Pea	
Die Prinzessin auf der Erbse	
Pcs: 55	2005–2007

5964	EU
Thumbelina	
Däumelinchen	
Pcs: 47	2005–2007

5994	NA	
Catapult		
Katapult		
Pcs: 29	2005–2006	Special

6637	EU	
Ultimate Battle Set		
Ultimate Battle Set		
Pcs: 195	2005	Special

6966	EU NA AS	
Mini Jedi Starfighter™		
Mini Jedi Starfighter™		
Pcs: 40	2005	Special

6967	EU NA AS	
Mini ARC-170 Starfighter™		
Mini ARC-170 Starfighter™		
Pcs: 42	2005	Special

7015	EU NA
Viking Warrior & the Fenris Wolf	
Wikinger und Wolf	
Pcs: 76	2005–2006

i	Nr.	English	Deutsch
i	5994	Was a Give Away	War ein Give Away
i	6637	German Toys'R'Us exclusive set	Deutsches Toys'R'Us Exklusivset
i	6966	Also as Duracell Promo (boxed Version with batteries)	Auch als Duracell Promo (Box mit Batterien)
i	6967	Also as Korean Duracell Promo with 8 batteries	Auch als Korea Duracell Promo mit 8 Batterien

7016 EU NA AU AS
Viking Boat vs. Wyvern Dragon
Wikinger-Boot und Flugdrache
Pcs: 116 | 2005–2006

7017 EU NA AU AS
Viking Catapult vs. Dragon
Wikiniger-Katapult und Drache
Pcs: 225 | 2005–2006

7018 EU NA AU AS
Viking Ship vs. Midgard Serpent
Wikinger-Schiff und Schlange
Pcs: 585 | 2005–2007

7019 EU NA AU AS
Viking Fortress vs. the Fafnir Dragon
Wikinger-Festung und Drache
Pcs: 1040 | 2005–2006

7235 EU NA AU AS
Police Motorcycle
Polizeimotorrad
Pcs: 34 | 2005–2008

7236 EU NA AU AS
Police Car
Streifenwagen
Pcs: 64 | 2005–2008

7237 EU NA AU AS
Police Station
Polizeirevier
Pcs: 582 | 2005–2007

7238 EU NA AU AS
Fire Helicopter
Feuerwehrhubschrauber
Pcs: 78 | 2005–2008

7241 EU NA AU AS
Fire Car
Feuerwehrauto
Pcs: 47 | 2005–2008

i	7235	Included in: 66116 (2006), 66246 (2008)	Enthalten in 66116 (2006), 66246 (2008)
i	7236	Included in: 66116 (2006), 66175 (2007)	Enthalten in 66116 (2006), 66175 (2007)
i	7237	With illuminated figure	Mit leuchtender Figur
i	7238	Included in: 66177 (2007), 66195 (2007), 66175 (2007)	Enthalten in: 66177 (2007), 66195 (2007), 66175 (2007)
i	7241	Included in: 66195 (2007)	Enthalten in: 66195 (2007)

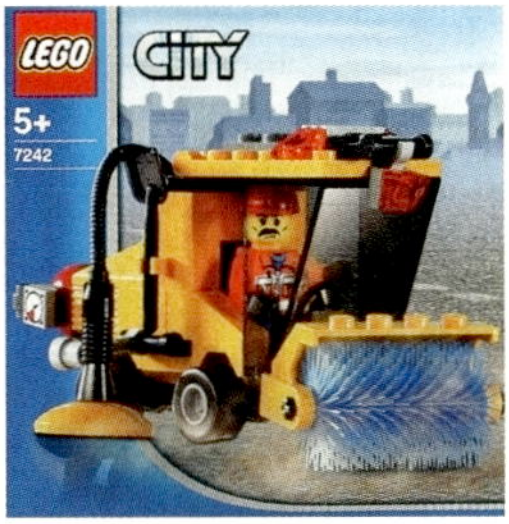

7242	EU NA AU AS
Street Sweeper	
Straßenkehrmaschine	
Pcs: 66	2005–2008

7243	EU NA AU AS
Construction Site	
Baustellen-Set	
Pcs: 307	2005–2008

7245	EU NA AU AS
Prisoner Transport	
Gefangenentransporter	
Pcs: 100	2005–2008

7246	EU NA AU AS
Mini Digger	
Mini-Bagger	
Pcs: 47	2005–2008

7248	EU NA AU AS
Digger	
Raupenbagger	
Pcs: 129	2005–2008

7249	EU NA AU AS
XXL Mobile Crane	
Mobiler Baukran	
Pcs: 524	2005–2008

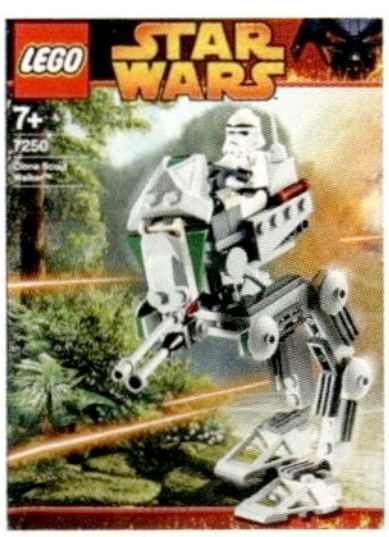

7250	EU NA AU AS
Clone Scout Walker™	
Clone Scout Walker™	
Pcs: 108	2005–2007

7251	EU NA AU AS
Darth Vader™ Transformation	
Darth Vader™ Transformation	
Pcs: 61	2005–2007

7252	EU NA AU AS
Droid Tri-Fighter™	
Droid Tri-Fighter™	
Pcs: 151	2005–2007

7242	Also included in: 65800 (2005)	Auch enthalten in: 65800 (2005)
7243	Also included in: 65800 (2005)	Auch enthalten in: 65800 (2005)
7245	Included in: 66116 (2006), 66246 (2008)	Enthalten in 66116 (2006), 66246 (2008)
7248	Also included in: 65800 (2005)	Auch enthalten in: 65800 (2005)
7249	Also included in: 65800 (2005)	Auch enthalten in: 65800 (2005)

7255	EU
General Grievous™ Chase	
General Grievous™ Chase	
Pcs: 117	2005–2007

7256	EU
Jedi Starfighter™ & Vulture Droid™	
Jedi Starfighter™ & Vulture Droid™	
Pcs: 206	2005–2007

7257	EU
Ultimate Lightsaber™ Duel	
Ultimate Lightsaber™ Duel	
Pcs: 293	2005–2007

7258	EU
Wookiee™ Attack	
Wookiee™ Attack	
Pcs: 383	2005–2007

7259	EU
ARC-170 Starfighter™	
ARC-170 Starfighter™	
Pcs: 406	2005–2007

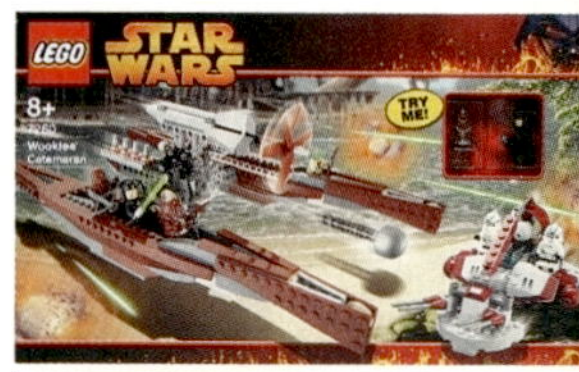

7260	EU
Wookiee™ Catamaran	
Wookiee™ Catamaran	
Pcs: 386	2005–2007

7261	EU
Clone Turbo Tank™	
Clone Turbo Tank™	
Pcs: 825	2005–2007

7263	EU
TIE Fighter™	
TIE Fighter™	
Pcs: 166	2005–2007

7264	NA	
Imperial Inspection		
Imperial Inspection		
Pcs: 391	2005	Special

7261	With or without battery operated light sabre	Mit oder ohne batteriebetriebenes Lichtschwert

7266	**EU** NA AU AS	
Fireman		
Feuerwehrmann		
Pcs: 19	2005–2007	Special

7267	**EU** NA AU AS	
Paramedic		
Sanitäter		
Pcs: 15	2005–2007	Special

7268	**EU** NA AU AS	
Crab		
Krabbe		
Pcs: 36	2005	Special

7269	**EU** NA AU AS	
Scorpion		
Skorpion		
Pcs: 37	2005	Special

7270	**EU** NA AU AS	
Bird		
Vogel		
Pcs: 30	2005	Special

7271	EU NA AU **AS**	
Apple		
Apfel		
Pcs: 15	2005	Special

7272	EU NA AU **AS**	
Pear		
Birne		
Pcs: 15	2005	Special

7274	EU NA AU **AS**	
Orange		
Orange		
Pcs: 13	2005	Special

7275	EU NA AU **AS**	
Cherry		
Kirsche		
Pcs: 12	2005	Special

7267	Dr. Oetker's (Czech Republic) Promo	Dr. Oetker's (Tschechische Republik) Promo
7268	Duracell Promo Set	Duracell Promo Set
7269	Duracell Promo Set	Duracell Promo Set
7270	Duracell Promo Set	Duracell Promo Set
7271-7275	Suntory Promo Set (Japan)	Suntory Promo Set (Japan)

7276		EU NA AU AS
Mango		
Mango		
Pcs: 8	2005	Special

7278		EU NA AU AS
Melon		
Melone		
Pcs: 13	2005	Special

7280		EU NA AU AS
Straight & Crossroad Plates		
Gerade Straße/Kreuzung		
Pcs: 2	2005–	

7281		EU NA AU AS
T-Junction & Curved Road Plates		
Kurve/T-Kreuzung		
Pcs: 2	2005–	

7283		EU NA AU AS
Ultimate Space Battle		
Die ultimative Weltraumschlacht		
Pcs: 575	2005	Special

7294		EU NA AU AS
Dino Quad		
Dino Offroader		
Pcs: 38	2005–2006	

7295		EU NA AU AS
Dino Buggy Chaser		
Dino Geländebuggy		
Pcs: 85	2005–2006	

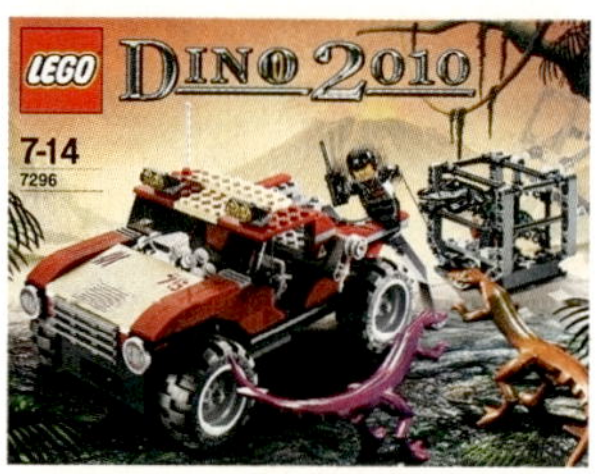

7296		EU NA AU AS
Dino 4WD Trapper		
Allrad-Dinojäger		
Pcs: 286	2005–2006	

7297		EU NA AU AS
Dino Track Transport		
Dinotransporter		
Pcs: 363	2005–2006	

	Set	English	Deutsch
i	7276-7278	Suntory Promo Set (Japan)	Suntory Promo Set (Japan)
i	7283	Target Promo	Target Promo
i	7294	Similar to: 7473 (2005)	Ähnlich zu: 7473 (2005)
i	7295	Similar to: 7474 (2005)	Ähnlich zu: 7474 (2005)
i	7296	Similar to: 7475 (2005)	Ähnlich zu: 7475 (2005)
i	7297	Similar to: 7476 (2005)	Ähnlich zu: 7476 (2005)

7298	EU NA AU AS	
Dino Air Tracker		
Dino Team Helikopter		
Pcs: 728	2005–2006	

7324	EU NA AU AS	
City Advent Calendar		
City Adventskalender		
Pcs: 203	2005	Special

7344	EU NA AU AS	
Dump Truck		
Kipplaster		
Pcs: 187	2005–2006	

7473	EU NA AU AS	
Steel Sprinter vs. Mutant Lizard		
Straßenflitzer vs. Mutantendino		
Pcs: 42	2005–2006	Special

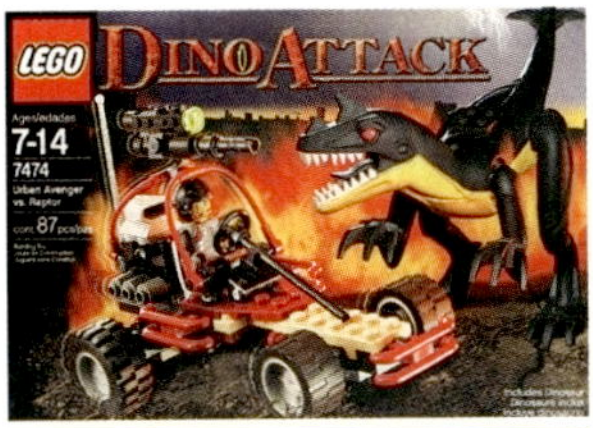

7474	EU NA AU AS	
Urban Avenger vs. Raptor		
Urban Avenger vs. Raptor		
Pcs: 89	2005–2006	

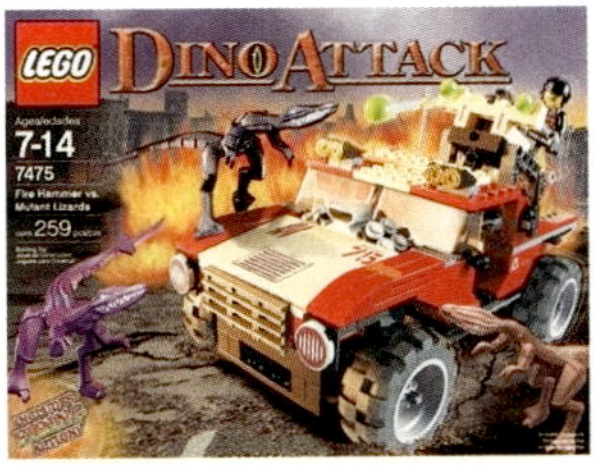

7475	EU NA AU AS	
Fire Hummer vs. Mutant Lizards		
Feuer Hummer vs. Mutantendino		
Pcs: 259	2005–2006	Special

7476	EU NA AU AS	
Iron Predator vs. T-Rex		
Iron Predator vs. T-Rex		
Pcs: 284	2005–2006	

7477	EU NA AU AS	
T1 Typhoon vs. T-Rex		
T1 Typhoon vs. T-Rex		
Pcs: 622	2005–2006	

7523	EU NA AU AS	
Hip Hair Set		
Cooles Haarset		
Pcs: 16	2005	

7298	Similar to: 7477 (2005)	Ähnlich zu: 7477 (2005)
7473	Similar to: 7294 (2005)	Ähnlich zu: 7294 (2005)
7474	Similar to: 7295 (2005)	Ähnlich zu: 7295 (2005)
7475	Similar to: 7296 (2005)	Ähnlich zu: 7296 (2005)
7476	Similar to: 7297 (2005)	Ähnlich zu: 7297 (2005)
7477	Similar to: 7298 (2005)	Ähnlich zu: 7298 (2005)

7527	EU NA AU AS
Pretty in Pink Beauty Set	
Pink Beauty Set	
Pcs: 134	2005–2006

7533	EU NA AU AS
Pretty in Pink Jewels-n-More	
Herz und Glitzersteine Schmuckset	
Pcs: 67	2005

7534	EU NA AU AS
Stylin' Citrus Jewels-n-More	
Blume Glitzersteine Schmuckset	
Pcs: 67	2005

7535	EU NA AU AS
Groovy Grape Jewels-n-More	
Lila Glitzersteine Schmuckset	
Pcs: 67	2005

7536	EU NA AU AS
Modern Magnetic Room Decor	
Zauberhaftes Magnet-Set	
Pcs: 72	2005

7537	EU NA AU AS
Cool Carry-All Set	
Coole Kosmetiktasche	
Pcs: 74	2005–2006

7538	EU NA AU AS
Fashion Bag and Accessories	
Modische Tasche mit Zubehör	
Pcs: 125	2005–2006

7540	EU NA AU AS
Friends 4-Ever Jewels & More	
Freundschafts-Schmuck für Zwei	
Pcs: 66	2005–2006

7541	EU NA AU AS
Friendship Frames & Notes	
Freundschafts-Briefchen	
Pcs: 70	2005

7542	EU NA AU AS
Flashin' Fashion Frame	
Blinkender Popstar Rahmen	
Pcs: 50	2005

7557	EU NA AU AS
Blooms and Butterflies	
Blüten und Schmetterlinge	
Pcs: 14	2005

7558	EU NA AU AS
Shells and Starfish	
Muscheln und Seesterne	
Pcs: 14	2005

7559	EU NA AU AS
Sports and Stars	
Sport und Sternchen	
Pcs: 14	2005

7574	EU NA AU AS	
Holiday Gift Calendar 2005		
Adventskalender 2005		
Pcs: 1	2005	Special

7840	EU NA AU AS
Airport Action	
Flughafen Superset	
Pcs: 105	2005–2008

7841	EU NA AU AS
Helicopter Rescue Unit	
Flughafen Rettungsteam	
Pcs: 36	2005–2008

7842	EU NA AU AS
Jet Fuel Truck	
Flughafen Tankwagen	
Pcs: 11	2005–2008

7843	EU NA AU AS	
Plane		
Flugzeug		
Pcs: 34	2005–	Special

7870	EU NA AU AS	
Hans Christian Andersen Bucket		
Hans Christian Andersen Eimer		
Pcs: 510	2005	Special

8415	EU NA AU AS	
Dump Truck		
Kipplaster		
Pcs: 290	2005–2008	

8416	EU NA AU AS	
Forklift		
Großer Gabelstapler		
Pcs: 723	2005–2008	

8418	EU NA AU AS	
Mini Loader		
Mini-Radlader		
Pcs: 68	2005–2008	

8419	EU NA AU AS	
Excavator		
Kettenbagger		
Pcs: 292	2005–2008	

8420	EU NA AU AS	
Street Bike		
Rennmaschine		
Pcs: 515	2005–2008	

8421	EU NA AU AS	
Mobile Crane / Crane Truck		
Pneumatik Kranwagen XXL		
Pcs: 1914	2005–2008	

8645	EU NA AU AS	
Muscle Slammer Bike		
Muscle Slammer Bike		
Pcs: 129	2005–2007	

8646	EU NA AU AS	
Speed Slammer Bike		
Speed Slammer Bike		
Pcs: 126	2005–2007	

8647 EU NA AU AS
Night Racer
Night Racer
Pcs: 78 | 2005–2007

8648 EU NA AU AS
Buzz Saw
Buzz Saw
Pcs: 67 | 2005–2007

8649 EU NA AU AS
Nitro Menace
Nitro Menace
Pcs: 625 | 2005–2007

8650 EU NA AU AS
Furious Slammer Racer
Furious Slammer Racer
Pcs: 257 | 2005–2007

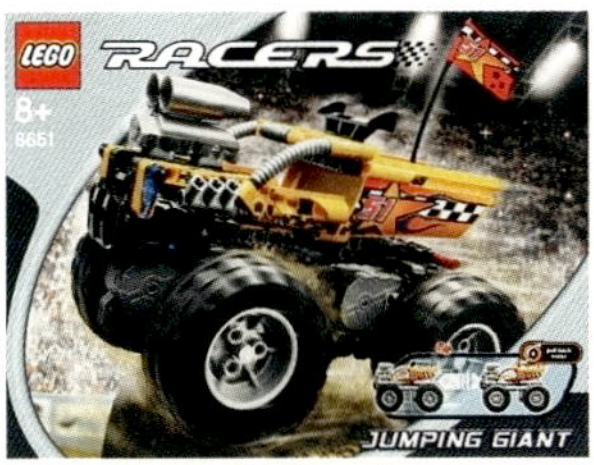

8651 EU NA AU AS
Jumping Giant
Jumping Giant
Pcs: 246 | 2005–2007

8652 EU NA AU AS
Enzo Ferrari 1:17
Enzo Ferrari 1:17
Pcs: 488 | 2005–2007

8653 EU NA AU AS
Enzo Ferrari 1:10
Enzo Ferrari 1:10
Pcs: 1360 | 2005–2007

8654 EU NA AU AS
Scuderia Ferrari Truck
Scuderia Ferrari Truck
Pcs: 825 | 2005–2007

8655 EU NA AU AS
RX-Sprinter
RX-Sprinter
Pcs: 61 | 2005–2007

8656	EU NA AU AS	
F6 Truck		
F6 Truck		
Pcs: 49	2005–2007	

8657	EU NA AU AS	
ATR 4		
ATR 4		
Pcs: 41	2005–2007	

8658	EU NA AU AS	
Big Bling Wheelie		
Big Bling Wheelie		
Pcs: 35	2005–2007	

8713	EU NA AU AS	
500 Piece Kit		
500 Einzelteile		
Pcs: 500	2005	Special

8715	EU NA AU AS	
Ultimate Creatures Accessory Set		
Ultimate Creatures Accessoryset		
Pcs: 409	2005	Special

8721	EU NA AU AS	
Velika		
Velika		
Pcs: 22	2005–2006	

8722	EU NA AU AS	
Kazi		
Kazi		
Pcs: 29	2005–2006	

8723	EU NA AU AS	
Piruk		
Piruk		
Pcs: 30	2005–2006	

8724	EU NA AU AS	
Garan		
Garan		
Pcs: 22	2005–2006	

i	8713	Toys'R'Us exklusive Set	Toys'R'Us exklusiv Set

8725 EU NA AU AS

Balta
Balta
Pcs: 25 | 2005–2006

8736 EU NA AU AS

Toa Hordika Vakama
Toa Vakama Hordika
Pcs: 50 | 2005–2006

8737 EU NA AU AS

Toa Hordika Nokama
Toa Nokama Hordika
Pcs: 50 | 2005–2006

8738 EU NA AU AS

Toa Hordika Whenua
Toa Whenua Hordika
Pcs: 50 | 2005–2006

8739 EU NA AU AS

Toa Hordika Onewa
Toa Onewa Hordika
Pcs: 50 | 2005–2006

8740 EU NA AU AS

Toa Hordika Matau
Toa Matau Hordika
Pcs: 50 | 2005–2006

8741 EU NA AU AS

Toa Hordika Nuju
Toa Nuju Hordika
Pcs: 50 | 2005–2006

8742 EU NA AU AS

Vohtarak
Visorak Vohtarak
Pcs: 48 | 2005–2006

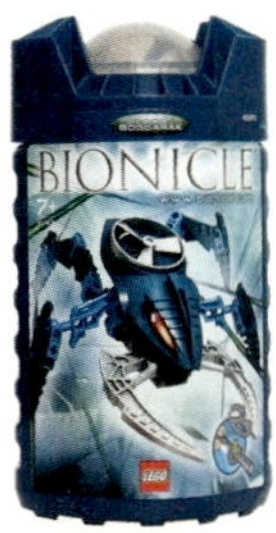

8743 EU NA AU AS

Boggarak
Visorak Boggarak
Pcs: 50 | 2005–2006

8744 EU NA AU AS

Oohnorak

Visorak Oohnorak

Pcs: 51	2005–2006	

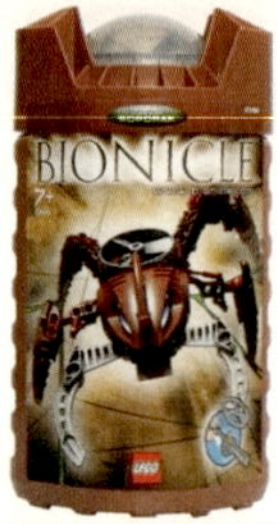

8745 EU NA AU AS

Roporak

Visorak Roporak

Pcs: 49	2005–2006	

8746 EU NA AU AS

Keelerak

Visorak Keelerak

Pcs: 51	2005–2006	

8747 EU NA AU AS

Suukorak

Visorak Suukorak

Pcs: 50	2005–2006	

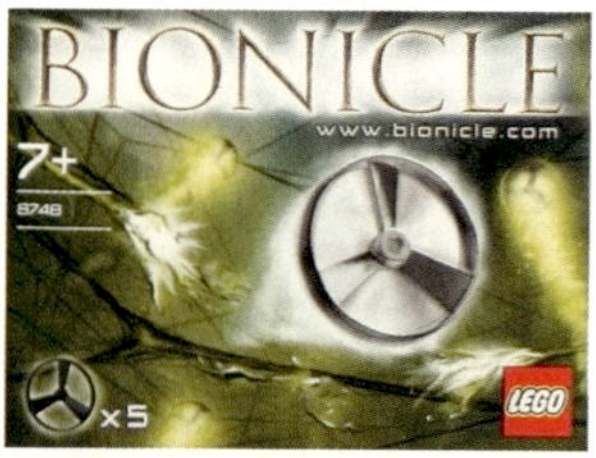

8748 EU NA AU AS

Rhotuka Spinners

Rhotuka Rotoren

Pcs: 5	2005	

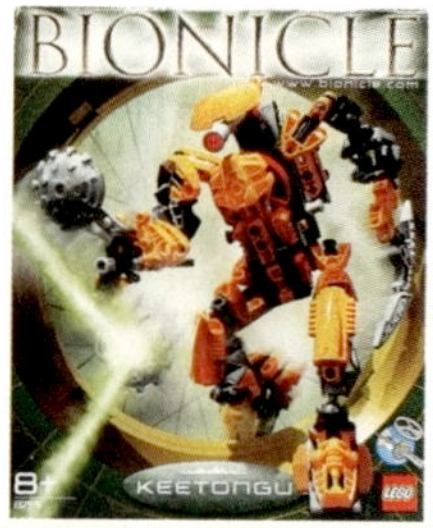

8755 EU NA AU AS

Keetongu

Keetongu

Pcs: 210	2005–2006	

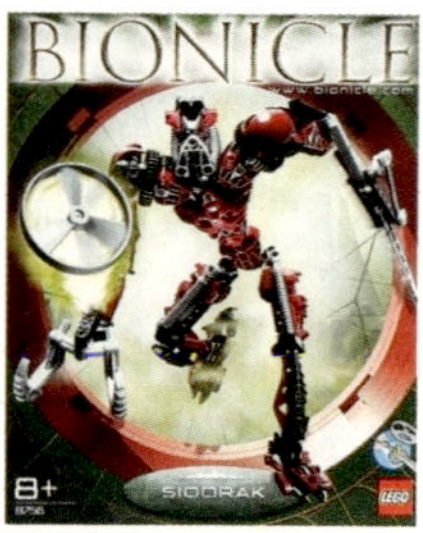

8756 EU NA AU AS

Sidorak

Sidorak

Pcs: 197	2005–2006	

8757 EU NA AU AS

Visorak Battle Ram

Visorak Rammbock

Pcs: 194	2005–2007	

8758 EU NA AU AS

Tower of Toa

Turm der Toa

Pcs: 415	2005–2007	

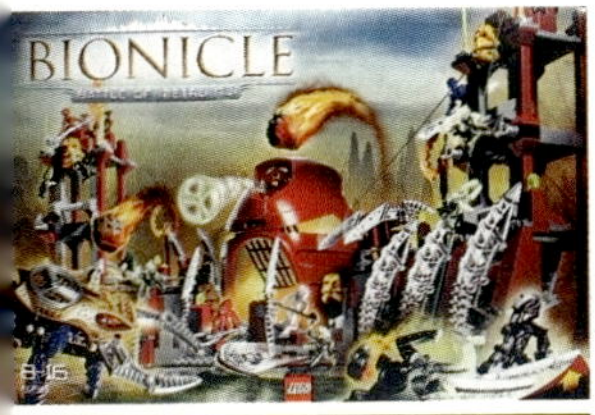

8759	EU NA AU AS	
Battle of Metru Nui		
Entscheidung um Metru Nui		
Pcs: 883	2005–2007	

8761	EU NA AU AS	
Roodaka		
Roodaka		
Pcs: 241	2005–2006	

8762	EU NA AU AS	
Toa Iruini		
Toa Iruini		
Pcs: 55	2005	

8763	EU NA AU AS	
Toa Norik		
Toa Norik		
Pcs: 56	2005	

8769	EU NA AU AS	
Visorak's Gate		
Visorak's Gate		
Pcs: 332	2005–2006	Special

8791	EU NA AU AS	
Sir Danju		
Sir Danju		
Pcs: 44	2005–2006	

8792	EU NA AU AS	
Sir Jayko		
Sir Jayko		
Pcs: 49	2005–2006	

8793	EU NA AU AS	
Sir Rascus		
Sir Rascus		
Pcs: 51	2005–2006	

8794	EU NA AU AS	
Sir Santis		
Sir Santis		
Pcs: 51	2005–2006	

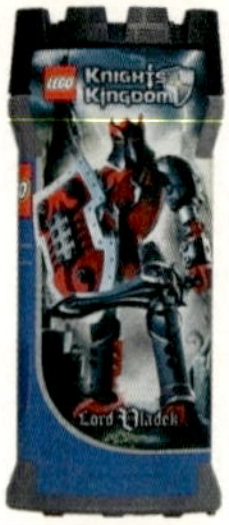

8795 EU NA AU AS

Lord Vladek

Lord Vladek

Pcs: 46	2005–2006	

8796 EU NA AU AS

King Mathias

König Mathias

Pcs: 43	2005–2006	

8801 EU NA AU AS

Knights' Attack Barge

Landungsboot

Pcs: 168	2005	Special

8802 EU NA AU AS

Dark Fortress Landing

Vladeks Hafenmauer

Pcs: 146	2005	Special

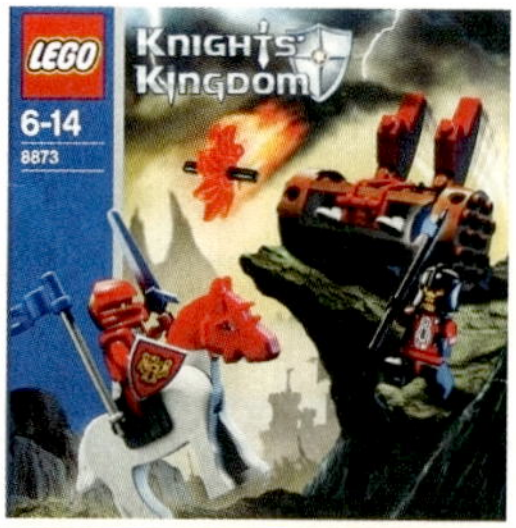

8873 EU NA AU AS

Fireball Catapult

Feuerball-Katapult

Pcs: 50	2005–2007	

8874 EU NA AU AS

Battle Wagon

Vladeks Angriffwagen

Pcs: 130	2005–2007	

8875 EU NA AU AS

King's Siege Tower

Königlicher Belagerungsturm

Pcs: 131	2005–2007	

8876 EU NA AU AS

Scorpion Prison Cave

Skorpiongefängnis

Pcs: 285	2005–2007	

8877 EU NA AU AS

Vladek's Dark Fortress

Vladeks schwarze Burg

Pcs: 1027	2005–2007	

10133	EU NA AU AS	
BNSF GP-38 Locomotive		
BNSF GP-38 Lokomotive		
Pcs: 412	2005–2006	

10143	EU NA AU AS	
Death Star II™		
Death Star II™		
Pcs: 3479	2005–2007	Special

10144	EU NA AU AS	
Sandcrawler™		
Sandcrawler™		
Pcs: 1703	2005–2007	Special

10152	EU NA AU AS	
Maersk-Sealand		
Maersk-Sealand		
Pcs: 988	2005	Special

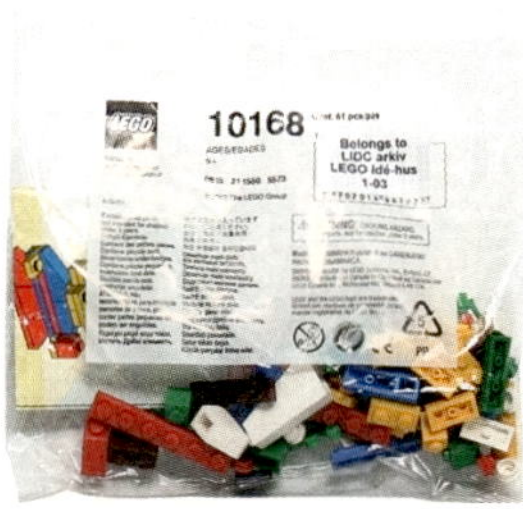

10168	EU NA AU AS	
Mrs. Bunny		
Frau Hase		
Pcs: 68	2005–2007	Special

10169	EU NA AU AS	
Chicken and Chicks		
Henne und Küken		
Pcs: 64	2005–2007	Special

10170	EU NA AU AS	
TTX Intermodal Double-Stack Car		
TTX Eisenbahngüterwagen		
Pcs: 366	2005–2006	Special

10203	EU NA AU AS	
Voporak		
Voporak		
Pcs: 647	2005	Special

65716	EU NA AU AS	
Limited Edition Collector Pack		
Sammler Set, limitierte Ausgabe		
Sets: 2	2005–2006	Special

10152	Re-released in 2006 as Maersk Line set	2006 als Maersk Line Set erneut aufgelegt

65743 (EU) (NA) AU AS

Limited Edition Value Pack

Limitierte Edition, Paket

Sets: 3 | 2005–2006 | Special

65757 EU (NA) AU AS

Special Edition Guardian Toa

Sonderedition: Wächter Toa

Sets: 2 | 2005 | Special

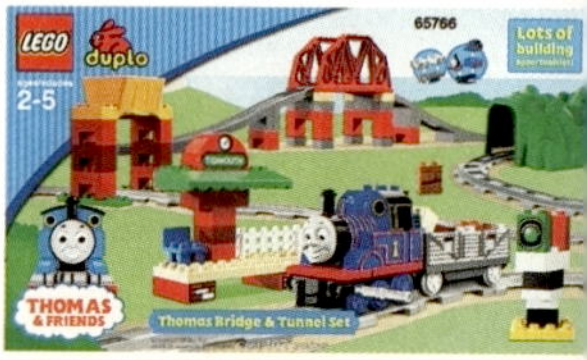

65766 EU (NA) AU AS

Thomas Bridge and Tunnel Set

Thomas, Brücken und Tunnelset

Pcs: 102 | 2005 | Special

65767 EU (NA) AU AS

Attack from the Sea

Angriff vom Meer

Sets: 2 | 2005 | Special

65769 (EU) NA AU AS

Value Pack Vladek

Vladek Zusatzset

Sets: 2 | 2005–2006 | Special

65771 EU (NA) AU AS

Episode III Collectors' Set

Sammler-Set zur Episode III

Pcs: 586 | 2005 | Special

65773 EU (NA) AU AS

James and Percy Tunnel Set

James und Percy, Tunnelset

Pcs: 66 | 2005 | Special

65799 (EU) NA AU AS

City Fire Value Pack

Stadt Feuerwehr, Paket

Sets: 5 | 2005 | Special

65800 (EU) NA AU AS

City Construction Value Pack

City 4er Pack

Sets: 4 | 2005 | Special

i	65771	Toys'R'Us Promo	Toys'R'Us Promo
i	65800	Includes: 7243 (2005), 7248 (2005), 7242 (2005), 7249 (2005)	Enthält: 7243 (2005), 7248 (2005), 7242 (2005), 7249 (2005)

65801 — EU

Trains Value Pack		
Zug-Kombiset		
Sets: 4	2005	Special

4287744 — AU

City Value Pack		
Stadt Kombiset		
Sets: 24	2005	Special

i	65801	Includes: 4512 (2003), 4514 (2003), 4515 (1991), 4520 (1991); Fedes Promo	Enthält: 4512 (2003), 4514 (2003), 4515 (1991), 4520 (1991); Fedes Promo
i	4287744	Target Country Promo; includes: 7241 (2005), 7246 (2005)	Target Country Promo; enthält: 7241 (2005), 7246 (2005)

2006

572	**EU** **NA** AU AS	
Parcheesi - Board Game		
Parcheesi - Brettspiel		
Pcs: 79	2006–2007	Special

574	**EU** **NA** AU AS	
Tic Tac Toe - Board Game		
Drei gewinnt - Brettspiel		
Pcs: 71	2006	Special

577	**EU** NA AU AS	
Vikings Chess Set		
Wikinger Schachspiel		
Pcs: 339	2006–2007	Special

1926	**EU** **NA** AU AS	
Limited Edition Green Container		
Limitierter grüner Eimer		
Pcs: 116	2006	Special

2598	**EU** NA AU AS	
Large Red Building Plate		
Große rote Bauplatte		
Pcs: 1	2006–	

2928	EU NA AU AS	
Airline Promotional Set		
Airline Promotional Set		
Pcs: 141	2006–2007	Special

2598	Similar to: 2302 (1982), 2305 (1984), 2306 (1991)	Ähnlich zu: 2302 (1982), 2305 (1984), 2306 (1991)
2928	Similar to: 2928 (2008)	Ähnlich zu: 2928 (2008)

3191	EU NA AU AS	
50 Jahre Anniversary DUPLO® Bucket		
Jubiläumseimer DUPLO® - 50 Jahre		
Pcs: 100	2006	Special

3298	EU NA AU AS	
Lift and Load Sumsy		
Lifti stapelt Sonnenblumenöl		
Pcs: 12	2006–2007	

3299	EU NA AU AS	
Bob's Workshop		
Sprinti und Mixi in Bobs Werkstatt		
Pcs: 50	2006–2008	

3300	EU NA AU AS	
Harold the Helicopter		
Harold der Hubschrauber		
Pcs: 7	2006–2007	Special

3301	EU NA AU AS	
Cargo-Loading Cranky		
Cranky der Kran		
Pcs: 34	2006–2007	Special

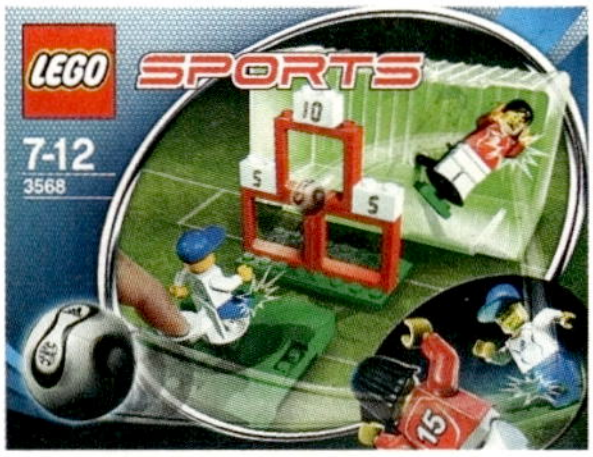

3568	EU NA AU AS	
Soccer Target Practice		
Fußball World Training		
Pcs: 26	2006	

3569	EU NA AU AS	
Grand Soccer Stadium		
Große Fußball Arena		
Pcs: 389	2006–2007	

3570	EU NA AU AS	
Street Soccer		
Straßenfußball-Set		
Pcs: 202	2006	

3573	EU NA AU AS	
Adidas Soccer Player #3 Goalie		
Adidas Fußballspieler #3 Torwart		
Pcs:	2006	Special

3825	EU NA	
The Krusty Krab		
Krosse Krabbe		
Pcs: 293	2006–2007	Special

3826	EU NA	
Build-A-Bob		
SpongeBob & Planktons Abenteuer		
Pcs: 464	2006–2007	

3827	EU NA	
Adventures in Bikini Bottom		
Abenteuer in Bikini Bottom		
Pcs: 579	2006–2007	Special

3828	NA	
Air Temple		
Lufttempel		
Pcs: 400	2006–2007	Special

3829	NA	
Fire Nation Ship		
Schiff der Feuernation		
Pcs: 725	2006–2007	Special

4085	NA	
Green Bucket		
Grüner Eimer		
Pcs: 75	2006	Special

4105	NA	
Large Bucket		
Großer Eimer		
Pcs: 487	2006	Special

4415	EU	
Auto Pod		
Auto-Pod		
Pcs: 61	2006	

4416	EU	
Robo Pod		
Robo-Pod		
Pcs: 71	2006	

i	4085	Similar to: 7790 (2006)	Ähnlich zu: 7790 (2006)

4417	EU NA AU AS	
Aero Pod		
Flieger-Pod		
Pcs: 63	2006	

4418	EU NA AU AS	
Dino Pod		
Dino-Pod		
Pcs: 55	2006	

4891	EU NA AU AS	
Highway Haulers		
Stars der Straße		
Pcs: 212	2006–2007	

4892	EU NA AU AS	
Prehistoric Power		
Dinosaurier		
Pcs: 380	2006–2008	

4893	EU NA AU AS	
Revvin' Riders		
Gelbe Flitzer		
Pcs: 370	2006–2007	

4894	EU NA AU AS	
Mythical Creatures		
Drachen		
Pcs: 596	2006–2007	

4895	EU NA AU AS	
Motion Power		
Helikopter mit Motor		
Pcs: 588	2006–2007	

4896	EU NA AU AS	
Roaring Roadsters		
Classic Car		
Pcs: 950	2006–2007	

4936	EU NA AU AS	
Doctor and Patient		
Doktor und Patient		
Pcs: 12	2006–2007	Special

4947	EU NA AU AS	
Yellow Sports Car		
Gelber Sportwagen		
Pcs: 28	2006	Special

4949	EU NA AU AS	
Blue and Yellow Racer		
Blauer und gelber Rennwagen		
Pcs: -	2006	Special

4960	EU NA AU AS	
Giant Zoo		
Zoo Superset		
Pcs: 126	2006–2008	

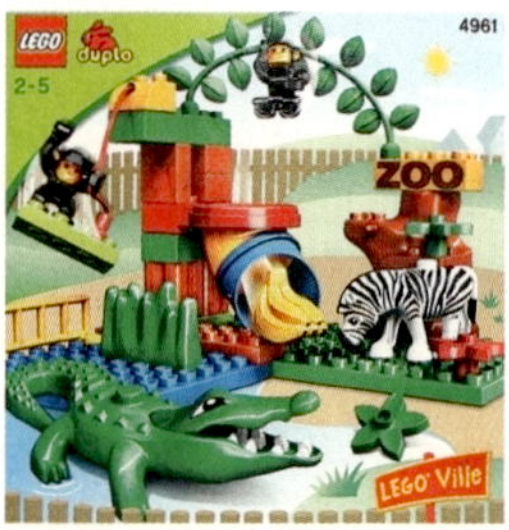

4961	EU NA AU AS	
Fun Zoo		
Exotische Tiere		
Pcs: 32	2006–2008	

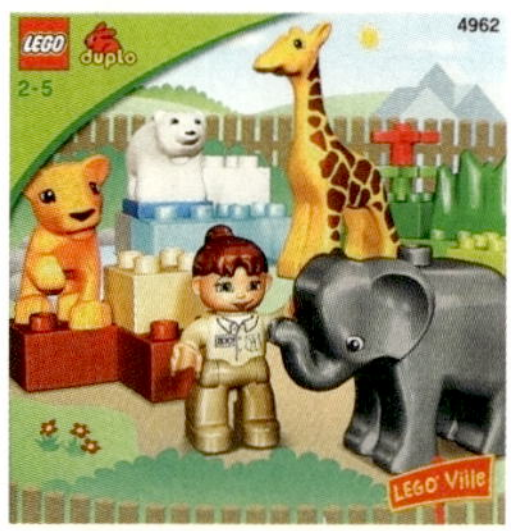

4962	EU NA AU AS	
Baby Zoo		
Tierbabys		
Pcs: 18	2006–	

4963	EU NA AU AS	
Police Patrol		
Polizeistreife		
Pcs: 8	2006–	

4964	EU NA AU AS	
Highway Help		
Pannenhilfe		
Pcs: 26	2006–2008	

4965	EU NA AU AS	
Police Action		
Polizeistation		
Pcs: 65	2006–2007	

4966	EU NA AU AS	
Doll's House		
Spielhaus		
Pcs: 95	2006–2008	

4967	EU NA AU AS	
Fire Helicopter		
Feuerwehr-Hubschrauber		
Pcs: 15	2006–2008	

4968	EU NA AU AS	
Friendly Zoo		
Zoo		
Pcs: 84	2006–2008	

4969	EU NA AU AS	
Tractor Fun		
Traktor		
Pcs: 4	2006–	

4971	EU NA AU AS	
Zoo Vehicles		
Tierpflegerset		
Pcs: 37	2006–2008	

5470	EU NA AU AS	
My First QUATRO™ Figure Set		
Mein erstes QUATRO™ Figurenset		
Pcs: 18	2006	

5475	EU NA AU AS	
Girls Fantasy Bucket		
Girls Fantasie-Eimer		
Pcs: 192	2006	

5476	EU NA AU AS	
My First QUATRO™ Set		
Mein erstes QUATRO™ Set		
Pcs: 20	2006	Special

5477	EU NA AU AS	
Classic House Building		
Classic Hausbau		
Pcs: 233	2006–2007	Special

5480	EU NA AU AS	
Town Building		
Hausbauset		
Pcs: 87	2006–2007	

5481	EU NA	
Zoo		
Zoo		
Pcs: 133	2006–2007	Special

5482	EU NA	
Town Building		
Stadtbau-Set		
Pcs: 664	2006–2007	Special

5483	EU NA	
Ready, Steady Build and Race		
Fahrzeuge-Set		
Pcs: 696	2006	Special

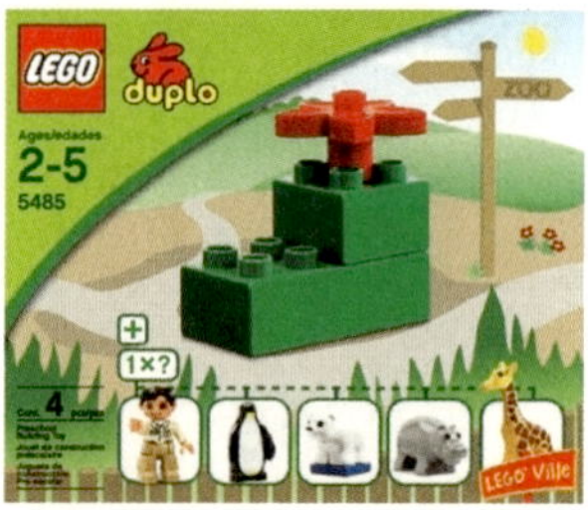

5485	NA	
Zoo Animals		
Zootiere		
Pcs: 4	2006–2007	Special

5490	EU	
XXL 250 Canister		
XXL 250 Tonne		
Pcs: 250	2006	Special

5491	EU NA AU	
XXL 2000 Canister		
XXL 2000 Tonne		
Pcs: 2000	2006	Special

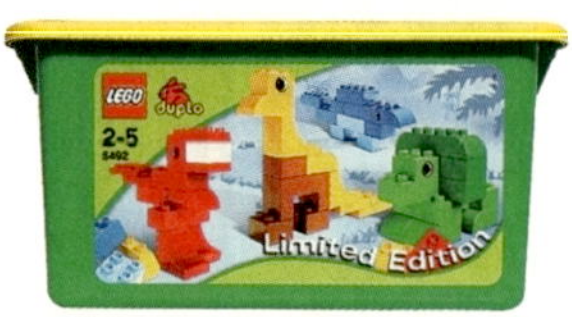

5492	EU NA	
Limited Edition Green Container		
Limitierter grüner Eimer		
Pcs: 116	2006	Special

5493	NA	
Emergency Rescue Box		
Rettungsbox		
Pcs: 705	2006	Special

5966	EU	
Glider		
Glider		
Pcs: 19	2006	Special

5492	Included in: 66151 (2006)	Enthalten in: 66151 (2006)
5966	Was in swedish Donald Duck Magazin	War im schwedischen Donald Duck Heft

5967	EU	NA	AU	AS
Exosuit				
Exosuit				
Pcs: 24	2006	Special		

6092	EU	NA	AU	AS
Special Edition Creative Building Tub				
50-Jahre-Jubiläumseimer				
Pcs: 711	2006	Special		

6111	EU	NA	AU	AS
Street Chase				
Street Chase				
Pcs: 197	2006	Special		

6112	EU	NA	AU	AS
World of Bricks				
Eine Welt aus Bausteinen				
Pcs: 1000	2006–2007	Special		

6114	EU	NA	AU	AS
200 Bricks + 40 Special Elements				
200 Steine + 40 Spezialelemente				
Pcs: 242	2006	Special		

6116	EU	NA	AU	AS
Box of Bricks				
Eine Box mit Bausteinen				
Pcs: 600	2006–2007	Special		

6205	EU	NA	AU	AS
V-wing Fighter™				
V-wing Fighter™				
Pcs: 121	2006–2007			

6206	EU	NA	AU	AS
TIE Interceptor™				
TIE Interceptor™				
Pcs: 215	2006–2007			

6207	EU	NA	AU	AS
A-wing Fighter™				
A-wing Fighter™				
Pcs: 202	2006	Special		

6208	EU NA AU AS	
B-wing Fighter™		
B-wing Fighter™		
Pcs: 447	2006–2007	

6209	EU NA AU AS	
Slave I™		
Slave I™		
Pcs: 544	2006–2007	

6210	EU NA AU AS	
Jabba's Sail Barge™		
Jabba's Sail Barge™		
Pcs: 790	2006–2007	

6211	EU NA AU AS	
Imperial Star Destroyer™		
Imperial Star Destroyer™		
Pcs: 1416	2006–2008	

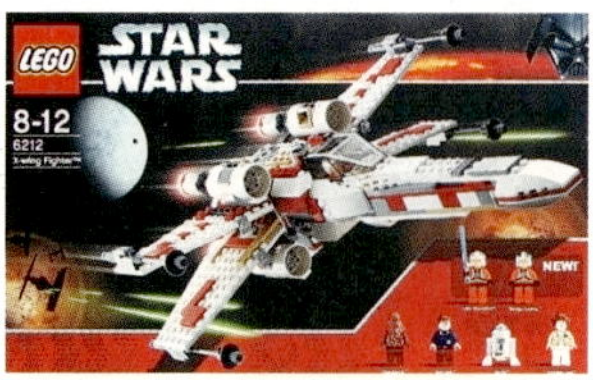

6212	EU NA AU AS	
X-wing Fighter™		
X-wing Fighter™		
Pcs: 435	2006–2008	Special

6620	EU NA AU AS	
Ultimate Accessory Set		
Ultimatives Zubehörset		
Pcs: 500	2006	Special

6638	EU NA AU AS	
Ultimate Creatures Accessory Set		
Ultimate Creatures Zubehör-Set		
Pcs: 300	2006	Special

6934	EU NA AU AS	
BIONICLE® Polybag		
BIONICLE® Polybag		
Pcs: 18	2006–2007	Special

6935	EU NA AU AS	
BIONICLE® Polybag		
BIONICLE® Polybag		
Pcs: 18	2006–2007	Special

6934	Was in swedish Donald Duck Magazine	War im schwedischen Donald Duck Heft
6935	Was in swedish Donald Duck Magazine	War im schwedischen Donald Duck Heft

ⓘ 6992	EU NA AU AS	
Inika Toa Jaller Nestle #6		
Inika Toa Jaller Nestle #6		
Pcs: -	2006	Special

ⓘ 6993	EU NA AU AS	
Inika Toa Kongu Nestle #5		
Inika Toa Kongu Nestle #5		
Pcs: -	2006	Special

ⓘ 6994	EU NA AU AS	
Inika Toa Hahli Nestle #4		
Inika Toa Hahli Nestle #4		
Pcs: -	2006	Special

ⓘ 6995	EU NA AU AS	
Piraka Thok Nestle #3		
Piraka Thok Nestle #3		
Pcs: -	2006	Special

ⓘ 6996	EU NA AU AS	
Piraka Reidak Nestle #1		
Piraka Reidak Nestle #1		
Pcs: -	2006	Special

ⓘ 6997	EU NA AU AS	
Piraka Avak Nestle #2		
Piraka Avak Nestle #2		
Pcs: -	2006	Special

ⓘ 7020	EU NA AU AS	
Army of Vikings with Heavy Artillery		
Wikinger-Armee mit Artilleriewagen		
Pcs: 317	2006–2007	

ⓘ 7021	EU NA AU AS	
Viking Double Catapult vs. Dragon		
Drache Ofnir gegen Doppelkatapult		
Pcs: 513	2006–2007	

ⓘ 7215	EU NA AU AS	
Mini Picture Frame		
Kleiner Bilderrahmen		
Pcs: -	2006	Special

ⓘ	6992-6993	Nestlé Promo	Nestlé Promo
ⓘ	6994-6997	Nestlé Promo	Nestlé Promo
ⓘ	7215	Duracell Promo Set	Duracell Promo Set

7216	EU NA AU AS	
Brutaka		
Turaga Lhikan		
Pcs: 22	2006	Special

7217	EU NA AU AS	
Braca		
Braca		
Pcs: 16	2006	Special

7237	EU NA AU AS	
Police Station		
Polizeirevier		
Pcs: 624	2006–2007	

7261	EU NA AU AS	
Clone Turbo Tank™		
Clone Turbo Tank™		
Pcs: 801	2006–2007	

7335	EU NA AU AS	
Foundation Set - Bucket		
Grundset - Eimer		
Pcs: 466	2006–2008	Special

7336	EU NA AU AS	
Foundation Set - Bucket		
Grundset - Eimer		
Pcs: 427	2006–2008	Special

7337	EU NA AU AS	
Foundation Set - Green Bucket		
Grundset - Grüner Eimer		
Pcs: 50	2006–2008	Special

7338	EU NA AU AS	
Pleasant Zoo		
Freundlicher Zoo		
Pcs: 116	2006–2008	Special

7339	EU NA AU AS	
Friendly Animal Bus		
Freundliche Tiere - Bus		
Pcs: 98	2006–2008	Special

7216	Duracell Promo Set	Duracell Promo Set
7217	Duracell Promo Set	Duracell Promo Set
7237	Without illuminated figure	Ohne leuchtende Figur
7261	With or without battery operated light sabre	Mit oder ohne batteriebetriebenes Lichtschwert

7545	EU NA AU AS
Pink & Pearls Jewels & More	
Schmuckset Pink & Perlmutt	
Pcs: 67	2006

7546	EU NA AU AS
Tropical Breeze Jewels & More	
Schmuckset Karibik	
Pcs: 71	2006

7548	EU NA AU AS
Fun Flamingo Frames & More	
Rahmenset Karibik	
Pcs: 79	2006

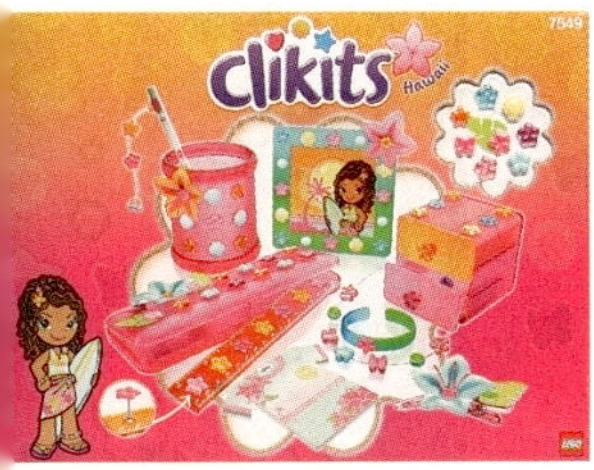

7549	EU NA AU AS
Totally Tropical Decor Set	
Großes Dekoset Tropenparadies	
Pcs: 135	2006

7554	EU NA AU AS
Pearly Pink Bracelet & Bands	
Beautyset Pink & Perlmutt	
Pcs: 63	2006

7555	EU NA AU AS
Glitter & Sparkle Beauty Set	
Beautyset Glitzer	
Pcs: 57	2006

7577	EU NA AU AS
Winter Wonder Palace	
Winterpalast	
Pcs: 168	2006–2007

7578	EU NA AU AS
Ultimate Princesses	
Ausfahrt in der Kutsche	
Pcs: 149	2006–2007

7579	EU NA AU AS
Blossom Fairy	
Die Blütenfee	
Pcs: 52	2006–2008

7602	EU NA AU AS	
Jeep		
Jeep		
Pcs: 46	2006–2007	Special

7604	EU NA AU AS	
Dinosaur		
Dinosaurier		
Pcs: 35	2006–2008	Special

7606	EU NA AU AS	
Frog		
Frosch		
Pcs: 33	2006–2007	Special

7609	EU NA AU AS	
Helicopter		
Hubschrauber		
Pcs: 30	2006–2007	Special

7610	EU NA AU AS	
Speedboat		
Schnellboot		
Pcs: 23	2006–2008	Special

7700	EU NA AU AS	
Stealth Hunter		
Stealth Hunter		
Pcs: 169	2006	

7701	EU NA AU AS	
Grand Titan		
Grand Titan		
Pcs: 196	2006	

7702	EU NA AU AS	
Thunder Fury		
Thunder Fury		
Pcs: 201	2006–2007	

7703	EU NA AU AS	
Fire Vulture		
Fire Vulture		
Pcs: 182	2006	

7602	Included in: 66208 (2007)	Enthalten in: 66208 (2007)
7604	Included in: 66208 (2007)	Enthalten in: 66208 (2007)
7606	Included in: 66208 (2007)	Enthalten in: 66208 (2007)
7609	Included in: 66208 (2007)	Enthalten in: 66208 (2007)
7610	Included in: 66208 (2007)	Enthalten in: 66208 (2007)

7704	**EU** NA AU AS	
Sonic Phantom		
Sonic Phantom		
Pcs: 223	2006–2007	

7705	**EU** NA AU AS	
Gate Assault		
Gate Assault		
Pcs: 406	2006	

7706	**EU** **NA** **AU** **AS**	
Mobile Defense Tank		
Hero Tank		
Pcs: 365	2006–2007	

7707	**EU** **NA** **AU** **AS**	
Striking Venom		
Striking Venom		
Pcs: 646	2006–2007	

7708	**EU** NA AU AS	
Uplink		
Uplink		
Pcs: 76	2006	

7709	**EU** NA AU AS	
Sentai Fortress		
Sentai Hauptquartier		
Pcs: 1499	2006–2007	

7711	**EU** **NA** AU AS	
Sentry		
Sentry		
Pcs: 84	2006	

7712	**EU** **NA** **AU** AS	
Supernova		
Supernova		
Pcs: 291	2006	Special

7713	EU **NA** AU AS	
Bridge Walker and White Lightning		
Bridge Walker und White Lightning		
Pcs: 669	2006	Special

7716	EU NA AU AS	
Good Guy White		
Good Guy White		
Pcs: 24	2006	Special

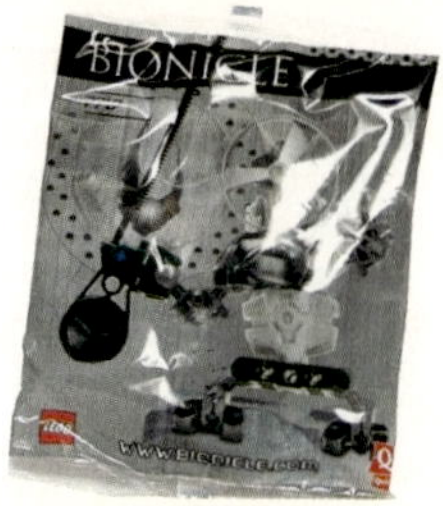

7717	EU NA AU AS	
Bad Guy Green		
Bad Guy Green		
Pcs: 26	2006	Special

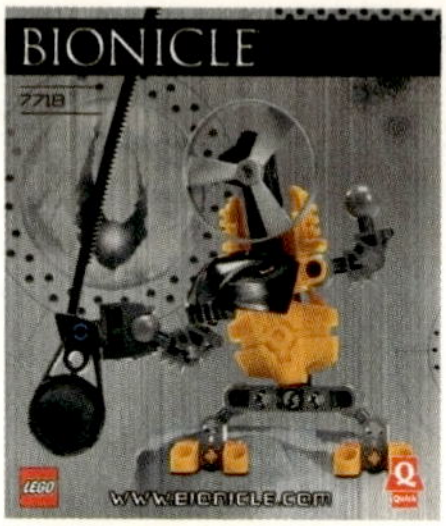

7718	EU NA AU AS	
Bad Guy Yellow		
Bad Guy Yellow		
Pcs: 26	2006	Special

7719	EU NA AU AS	
Good Guy Red		
Good Guy Red		
Pcs: 24	2006	Special

7779	EU NA AU AS	
The Batman Dragster		
Batman Dragster		
Pcs: 92	2006	

7780	EU NA AU AS	
The Batboat		
Batboat		
Pcs: 198	2006–2007	

7781	EU NA AU AS	
The Batmobile		
Batmobil		
Pcs: 404	2006–2007	

7782	EU NA AU AS	
The Batwing		
Batwing		
Pcs: 537	2006–2007	

7783	EU NA AU AS	
The Batcave		
Batcave		
Pcs: 1093	2006–2007	

ⓘ **7784** — **EU** NA AU AS

The Batmobile Collectors' Edition		
Batmobil: Ultimative Sammlerausgabe		
Pcs: 1052	2006–2007	

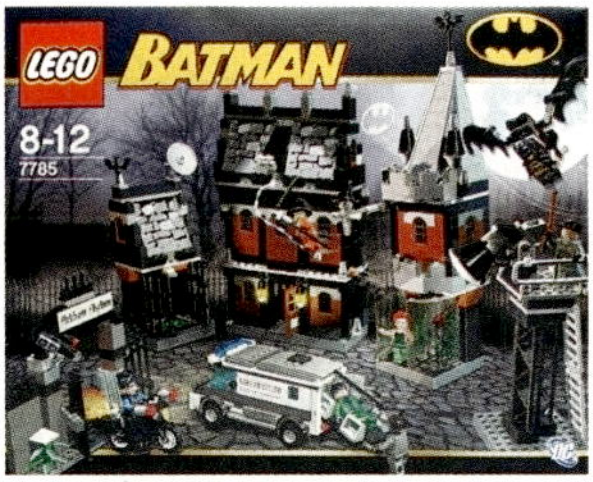

ⓘ **7785** — **EU** **NA** AU AS

Arkham Asylum		
Arkham Asylum		
Pcs: 869	2006–2007	Special

ⓘ **7790** — **EU** NA AU AS

Standard Starter Set		
Standard Starterset		
Pcs: 75	2006	

ⓘ **7792** — **EU** NA AU AS

Deluxe Starter Set		
Luxus Starterset		
Pcs: 120	2006	Special

ⓘ **7793** — **EU** **NA** **AU** **AS**

Standard Starter Set		
Mein erstes Starterset		
Pcs: 487	2006	

ⓘ **7795** — EU **NA** AU AS

Deluxe Starter Set		
Luxus Starterset		
Pcs: 1094	2006	

ⓘ **7844** — **EU** **NA** AU AS

Airport Rescue Truck		
Flughafen Löschzug		
Pcs: 30	2006	

ⓘ **7846** — **EU** NA AU AS

Dragon Tournament		
Drachenturnier		
Pcs: 44	2006	

ⓘ **7880** — **EU** NA AU AS

Big Pirate Ship		
Großes Piratenschiff		
Pcs: 60	2006–2007	

ⓘ 7790	Similar to: 4085 (2006)	Ähnlich zu: 4085 (2006)

7881	EU NA AU AS
Pirate Ship	
Piratenschiff	
Pcs: 33	2006–2007

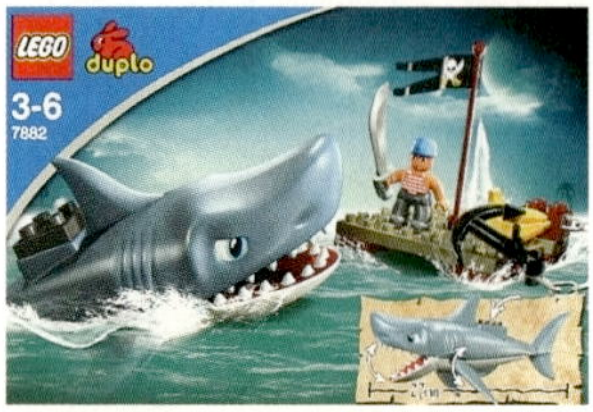

7882	EU NA AU AS
Shark Attack	
Haiangriff	
Pcs: 10	2006–2007

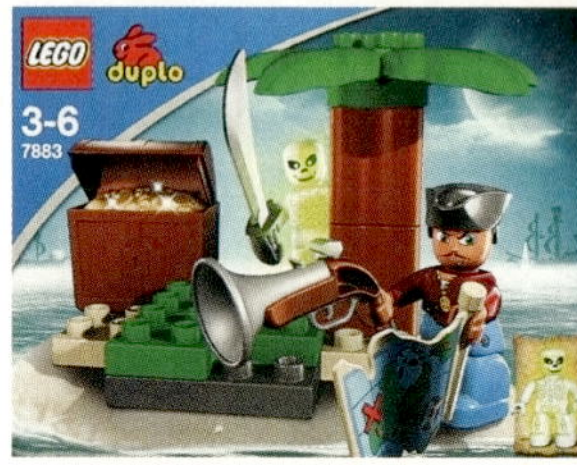

7883	EU NA AU AS
Treasure Hunt	
Schatzsuche	
Pcs: 14	2006–2007

7890	EU NA AU AS
Ambulance	
Krankenwagen	
Pcs: 126	2006–2008

7891	EU NA AU AS
Airport Firetruck	
Flughafen-Feuerwehrwagen	
Pcs: 155	2006–2007

7892	EU NA AU AS
Hospital	
Krankenhaus	
Pcs: 385	2006–2008

7893	EU NA AU AS
Passenger Plane	
Passagierflugzeug	
Pcs: 412	2006–2007

7894	EU NA AU AS
Airport	
Flughafen	
Pcs: 723	2006–2008

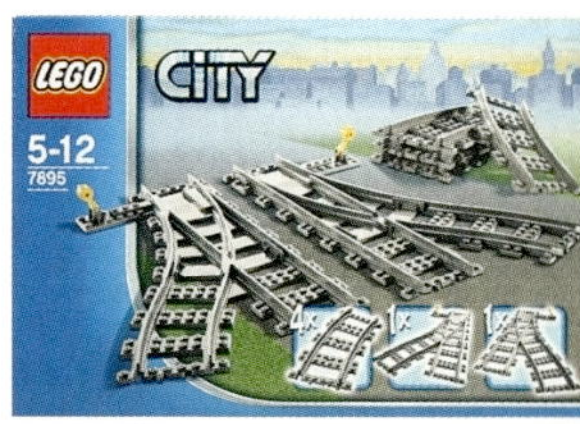

7895	EU NA AU AS
Switch Tracks	
Weichen	
Pcs: 8	2006–

i	7890	Included in: 66177 (2007), 66116 (2006), 66193 (2007), 66175 (2007)	Enthalten in: 66177 (2007), 66116 (2006), 66193 (2007), 66175 (2007)
i	7891	Included in: 66156 (2006)	Enthalten in: 66156 (2006)
i	7892	Included in: 66193 (2007)	Enthalten in: 66193 (2007)
i	7893	Also as Airline Promo	Auch als Airline Promo

7896 EU NA AU AS

Straight & Curved Rails

Gerade und gebogene Schienen

Pcs: 16	2006–	

7897 EU NA AU AS

Passenger Train

Passsagierzugset

Pcs: 503	2006–	

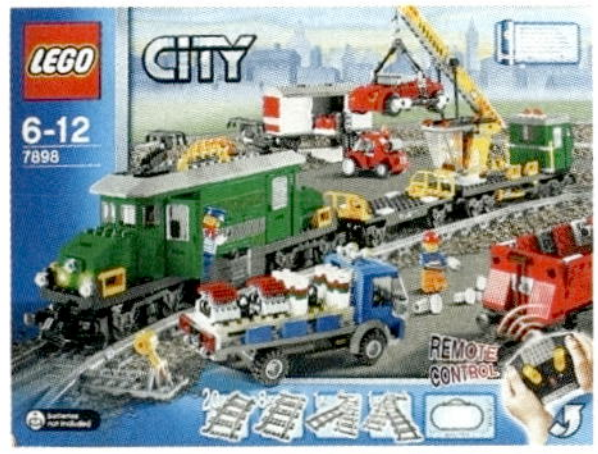

7898 EU NA AU AS

Cargo Train Deluxe

Großes Güterzugset

Pcs: 856	2006–	

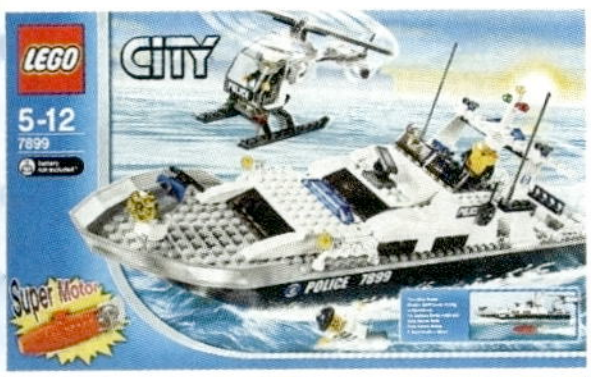

7899 EU NA AU AS

Police Boat

Polizeiboot

Pcs: 215	2006	

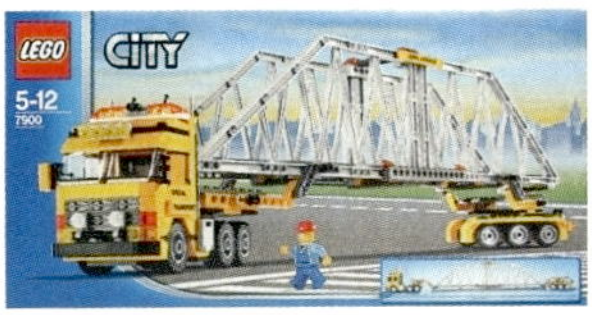

7900 EU NA AU AS

Heavy Loader

Schwertransporter

Pcs: 368	2006	

7901 EU NA AU AS

Airplane Mechanic

Flugzeugmechaniker

Pcs: 29	2006	

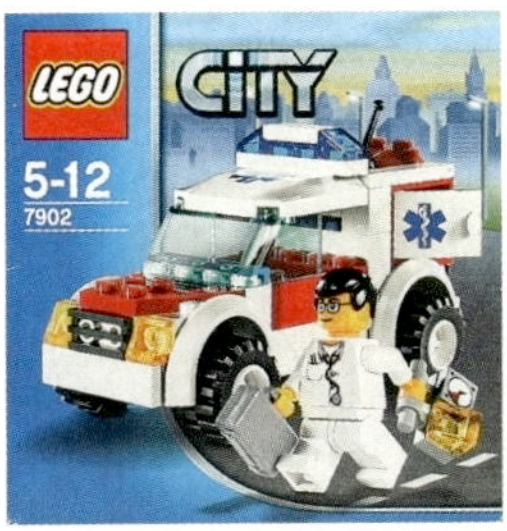

7902 EU NA AU AS

Doctor's Car

Notarztwagen

Pcs: 70	2006–2008	

7903 EU NA AU AS

Rescue Helicopter

Rettungshubschrauber

Pcs: 256	2006–2008	

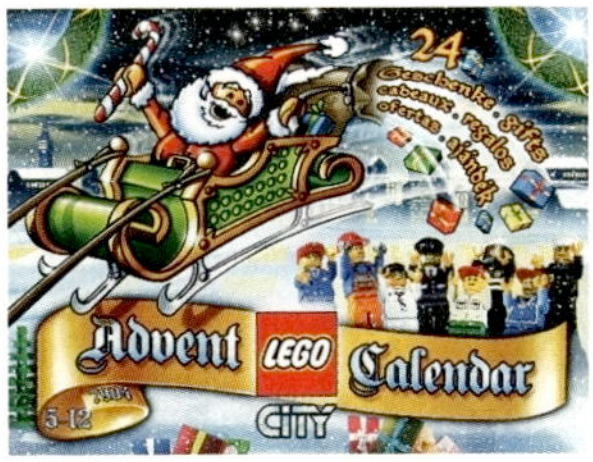

7904 EU NA AU AS

City Advent Calendar 2006

City Adventskalender 2006

Pcs: 297	2006	

i	7894	2007: released as ANA Promo (All Nippon Airlines); included in: 66156 (2006)	2007: als ANA Version erschienen (All Nippon Airlines); enthalten in: 66156 (2006)
i	7902	Included in: 66193 (2007)	Enthalten in: 66193 (2007)
i	7903	Also included in: 66156 (2006), 66116 (2006), 66193 (2007)	Auch enthalten in: 66156 (2006), 66116 (2006), 66193 (2007)

ⓘ 7905 EU NA AU AS

Building Crane

Großer Baukran

Pcs: 736 | 2006–2007

ⓘ 8281 EU NA AU AS

Mini Tractor

Minitraktor

Pcs: 121 | 2006–2007

ⓘ 8282 EU NA AU AS

Quad Bike

Quad-Bike

Pcs: 209 | 2006–2007

ⓘ 8283 EU NA AU AS

Telehandler

Teleskoplader

Pcs: 336 | 2006–2007

ⓘ 8284 EU NA AU AS

Dune Buggy

Großer Traktor

Pcs: 870 | 2006–2008

ⓘ 8285 EU NA AU AS

Tow Truck

Abschlepptruck

Pcs: 1877 | 2006–2008

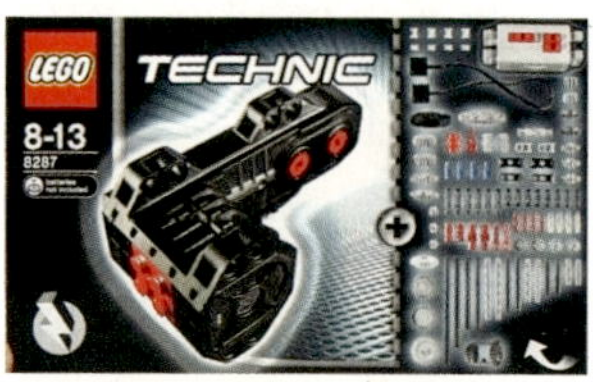

ⓘ 8287 EU NA AU AS

Motor Box

Motor

Pcs: 93 | 2006–2008

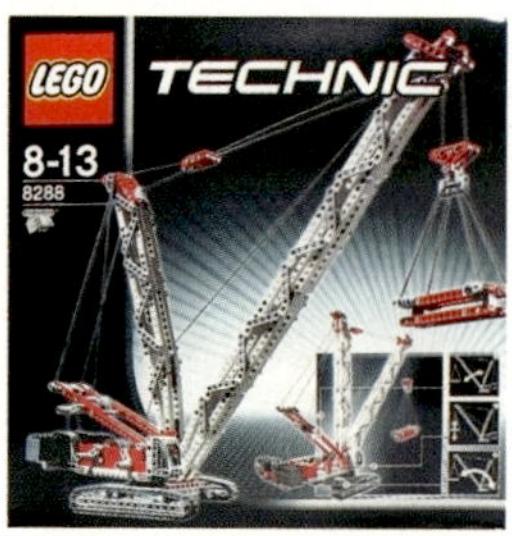

ⓘ 8288 EU NA AU AS

Crawler Crane

Raupenkran

Pcs: 800 | 2006–2007

ⓘ 8289 EU NA AU AS

Fire Truck

Roter Feuerwehr Truck

Pcs: 1066 | 2006–2007

8527	EU NA AU AS	
LEGO® MINDSTORMS™ NXT		
LEGO® MINDSTORMS™ NXT		
Pcs: 587	2006–	

8624	EU NA AU AS	
Race for the Mask of Life		
Wettlauf um die Maske des Lebens		
Pcs: 517	2006	Special

8625	EU NA AU AS	
Umbra		
Umbra		
Pcs: 179	2006	Special

8626	EU NA AU AS	
Irnakk		
Irnakk		
Pcs: 132	2006	Special

8661	EU NA AU AS	
Carbon Star		
Carbon Star		
Pcs: 48	2006	

8662	EU NA AU AS	
Blue Renegade		
Blue Renegade		
Pcs: 52	2006	

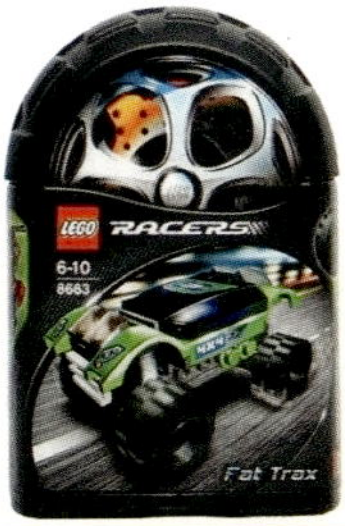

8663	EU NA AU AS	
Fat Trax		
Fat Trax		
Pcs: 45	2006	

8664	EU NA AU AS	
Road Hero		
Road Hero		
Pcs: 57	2006	

8665	EU NA AU AS	
Highway Enforcer		
Highway Enforcer		
Pcs: 58	2006	

8666 EU NA AU AS
TunerX
TunerX
Pcs: 61 | 2006

8667 EU NA AU AS
Action Wheelie
Action Wheelie
Pcs: 83 | 2006

8668 EU NA AU AS
Side Rider 55
Side Rider 55
Pcs: 113 | 2006

8669 EU NA AU AS
Fire Spinner 360
Fire Spinner 360
Pcs: 117 | 2006

8670 EU NA AU AS
Jump Master
Jump Master
Pcs: 110 | 2006

8671 EU NA AU AS
Ferrari 430 Spider 1:17
Ferrari 430 Spider 1:17
Pcs: 577 | 2006–2007

8672 EU NA AU AS
Ferrari Finish Line
Ferrari Zieleinfahrt
Pcs: 618 | 2006

8673 EU NA AU AS
Ferrari F1 Fuel Stop
Ferrari F1 Tankstopp
Pcs: 196 | 2006–2007

8674 EU NA AU AS
Ferrari F1 Racer 1:8
Ferrari F1 Racer 1:8
Pcs: 1253 | 2006–2007

8675	EU NA AU AS
Outdoor Challenger	
Outdoor Challenger	
Pcs: 104	2006–2007

8676	EU NA AU AS
Sunset Cruiser	
Sunset Cruiser	
Pcs: 58	2006–2007

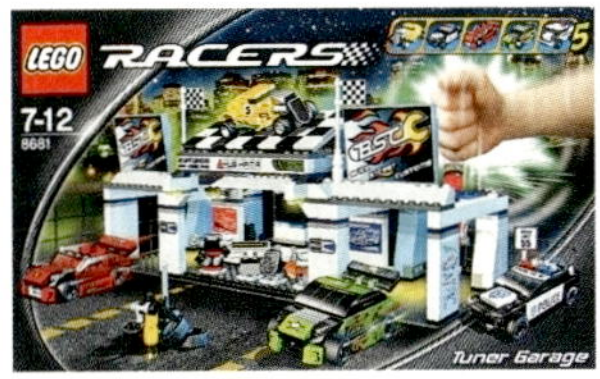

8681	EU NA AU AS
Tuner Garage	
Tiny Turbo Tuning-Werkstatt	
Pcs: 664	2006–2007

8682	EU NA AU AS
Nitro Intimidator	
Nitro Intimidator	
Pcs: 732	2006–2007

8701	EU NA AU AS
King Jayko	
König Jayko mit Katapult	
Pcs: 132	2006–2007

8702	EU NA AU AS
Lord Vladek	
Lord Vladek mit Katapult	
Pcs: 112	2006–2007

8703	EU NA AU AS
Sir Kentis	
Sir Kentis	
Pcs: 43	2006–2007

8704	EU NA AU AS
Sir Adric	
Sir Adric	
Pcs: 40	2006–2007

8705	EU NA AU AS
Dracus	
Dracus	
Pcs: 39	2006–2007

8706	EU NA AU AS
Karzon	
Karzon	
Pcs: 44	2006–2007

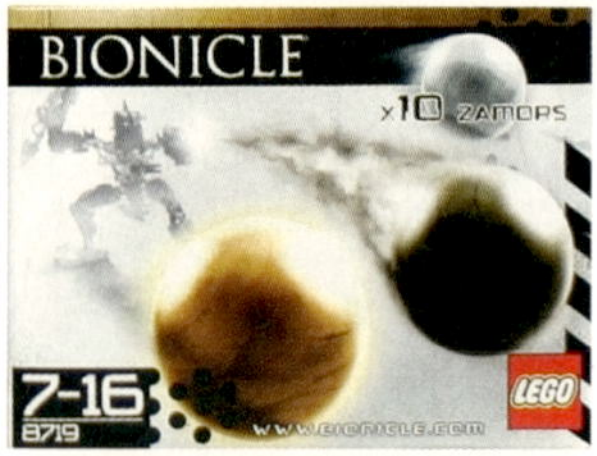

8719	EU NA AU AS
Zamor Spheres	
Zamor-Kugeln	
Pcs: 10	2006

8726	EU NA AU AS
Dalu	
Dalu	
Pcs: 28	2006–2007

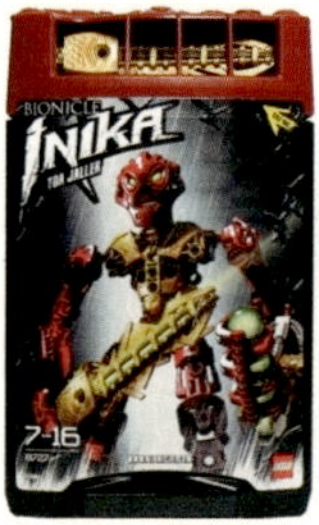

8727	EU NA AU AS
Toa Jaller	
Toa Jaller	
Pcs: 49	2006–2007

8728	EU NA AU AS
Toa Hahli	
Toa Hahli	
Pcs: 46	2006–2007

8729	EU NA AU AS
Toa Nuparu	
Toa Nuparu	
Pcs: 54	2006–2007

8730	EU NA AU AS
Toa Hewkii	
Toa Hewkii	
Pcs: 65	2006–2007

8731	EU NA AU AS
Toa Kongu	
Toa Kongu	
Pcs: 46	2006–2007

8732	EU NA AU AS
Toa Matoro	
Toa Matoro	
Pcs: 46	2006–2007

8733 EU NA AU AS

Axonn

Axonn

Pcs: 196 | 2006–2007

8734 EU NA AU AS

Brutaka

Brutaka

Pcs: 193 | 2006–2007

8764 EU NA AU AS

Vezon and Fenrakk

Vezon und Fenrakk

Pcs: 281 | 2006–2007

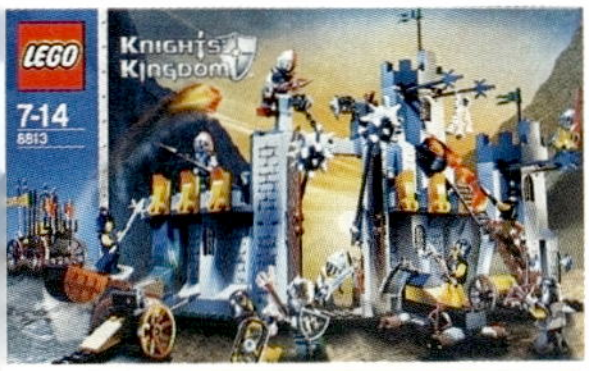

8813 EU NA AU AS

Battle at the Pass

Das Tor zum Bergpass

Pcs: 385 | 2006

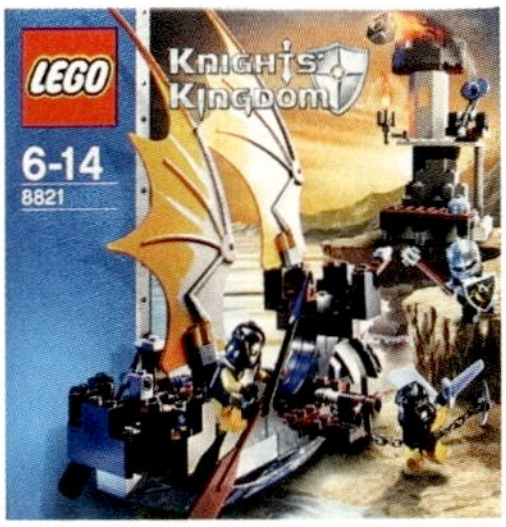

8821 EU NA AU AS

Rogue Knight Battleship

Schiff der Schattenritter

Pcs: 158 | 2006–2007

8822 EU NA AU AS

Gargoyle Bridge

Gargoyl Brücke

Pcs: 249 | 2006–2007

8823 EU NA AU AS

Mistlands Tower

Turm des Lichts

Pcs: 437 | 2006–2007

8892 EU NA AU AS

Piraka Outpost

Piraka-Außenposten

Pcs: 211 | 2006–2007

8893 EU NA AU AS

Lava Chamber Gate

Lavakammer-Tor

Pcs: 373 | 2006–2007

8894	EU NA AU AS
Piraka Stronghold	
Piraka-Festung	
Pcs: 648	2006–2007

8900	EU NA AU AS
Reidak	
Reidak „Der Verfolger“	
Pcs: 43	2006

8901	EU NA AU AS
Hakann	
Hakann „Der Tyrann“	
Pcs: 44	2006

8902	EU NA AU AS
Vezok	
Vezok „Das Biest“	
Pcs: 43	2006

8903	EU NA AU AS
Zaktan	
Zaktan „Die Schlange“	
Pcs: 43	2006

8904	EU NA AU AS
Avak	
Avak „Die Zange“	
Pcs: 43	2006

8905	EU NA AU AS
Thok	
Thok „Der Eisige“	
Pcs: 44	2006

10106	EU NA AU AS	
Snowflake		
Schneeflocke		
Pcs: 107	2006	Special

10152	EU NA AU AS	
Maersk Line		
Maersk Line		
Pcs: 988	2006	Special

i	10106	Was available via Shop at Home	War über Shop at Home verfügbar

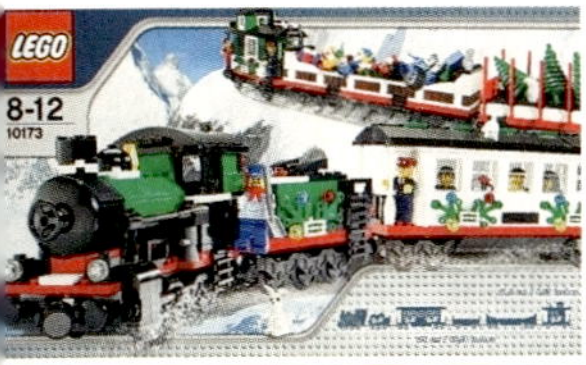

10173	EU NA AU AS
Holiday Train	
Winterzug	
Pcs: 965	2006–2007

10174	EU NA AU AS	
Imperial AT-ST™		
Imperial AT-ST™		
Pcs: 1081	2006–2008	Special

10175	EU NA AU AS	
Vader's TIE Advanced™		
Vader's TIE Advanced™		
Pcs: 1224	2006–2008	Special

10176	EU NA AU AS
King's Castle	
Die Burg des Königs	
Pcs: 876	2006–2007

10177	EU NA AU AS	
Boeing 787 Dreamliner		
Boeing 787 Dreamliner		
Pcs: 1197	2006–2007	Special

10204	EU NA AU AS	
Vezon & Kardas		
Vezon & Kardas		
Pcs: 670	2006	Special

66116	EU NA AU AS	
City Emergency Services Vehicles		
Rettungskräfteset		
Sets: 6	2006	Special

66151	EU NA AU AS	
Green Container + Bonus Pack		
Grüner Eimer mit Bonuspaket		
Pcs: 161	2006	Special

66156	EU NA AU AS	
Airport Exclusive Set Toys'R'Us		
Flughafen Exklusivset Toys'R'Us		
Sets: 4	2006	Special

i	10204	Target Promo	Target Promo
i	66116	Includes: 7890 (2006), 7902 (2006), 7903 (2006), 7236 (2005), 7235 (2005), 7245 (2005)	Enthält: 7890 (2006), 7902 (2006), 7903 (2006), 7236 (2005), 7235 (2005), 7245 (2005)
i	66151	Includes: 2242 (1997), 5492 (2006)	Enthält: 2242 (1997), 5492 (2006)
i	66156	Includes: 7901 (2006), 7894 (2006), 7891 (2006), 7903 (2006)	Enthält: 7901 (2006), 7894 (2006), 7891 (2006), 7903 (2006)

2007

2064	EU NA AU AS	
Air Ambulance Plane		
Rettungsflugzeug		
Pcs: 116	2007	Special

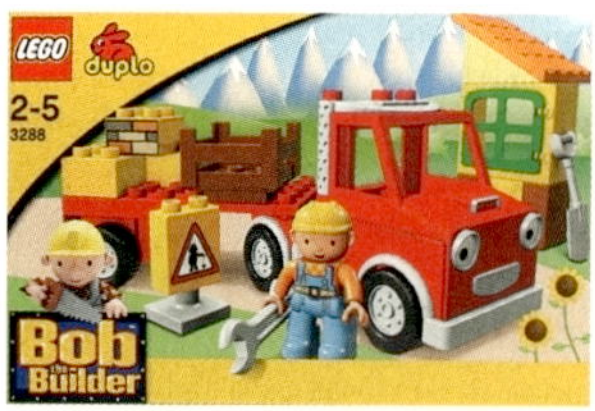

3288	EU NA AU AS	
Packer		
Packer, der Lastwagen		
Pcs: 22	2007	

3289	EU NA AU AS	
Muck & Roley in Sunflower Factory		
Muck & Roley in der Blumenfabrik		
Pcs: 38	2007	

3352	EU NA AU AS	
Salty the Dockyard Diesel		
Salty mit Anhänger		
Pcs: 8	2007	

3353	EU NA AU AS	
Spencer and Sir Topham Hat		
Spencer und der dicke Kontrolleur		
Pcs: 45	2007	

3354	EU NA AU AS	
Gordon's Express		
Gordon, der Passagierzug		
Pcs: 11	2007	

3870	EU NA AU AS	
Takeshi Walker 1		
Takeshi Walker 1		
Pcs: 26	2007	Special

3871	EU NA AU AS	
Ha-Ya-To Walker		
Ha-Ya-To Walker		
Pcs: 18	2007	Special

3872	EU NA AU AS	
Robo Chopper		
Roboter Hubschrauber		
Pcs: -	2007	Special

3885	EU NA AU AS	
Hikaru Little Flyer		
Hikaru Little Flyer		
Pcs: 22	2007	Special

3886	EU NA AU AS	
Ryo Walker		
Ryo Walker		
Pcs: -	2007	Special

4825	EU NA AU AS	
Princess and Horse		
Ausritt mit Pony		
Pcs: 8	2007	

4826	EU NA AU AS	
Princess and Pony Picnic		
Prinzessinnen-Pavillon		
Pcs: 19	2007	

4828	EU NA AU AS	
Princess Royal Stables		
Königlicher Pferdestall		
Pcs: 49	2007	

4861	EU NA AU AS	
Police Boat		
Polizeiboot		
Pcs: 28	2007	

3885	Also available without batteries and as polybag; also as Promo	Auch ohne Batterien und als PolyBag verfügbar; auch als Promo
3886	Also as Duracell Promo (boxed Version with batteries)	Auch als Duracell Promo (Box mit Batterien)

4915	EU NA AU AS	
Mini Construction		
Baufahrzeug-Set		
Pcs: 68	2007	

4916	EU NA AU AS	
Mini Animals		
Tier-Set		
Pcs: 77	2007	

4917	EU NA AU AS	
Mini Robots		
Roboter-Set		
Pcs: 79	2007	

4918	EU NA AU AS	
Mini Flyers		
Flieger-Set		
Pcs: 78	2007	

4937	EU NA AU AS	
Life Guard Tower		
Rettungsschwimmerturm		
Pcs: 35	2007	Special

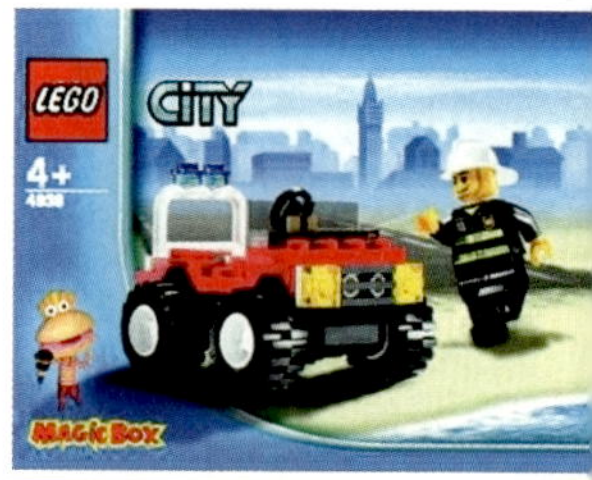

4938	EU NA AU AS	
Fire Car		
Feuerwehrauto		
Pcs: 25	2007	Special

4939	EU NA AU AS	
Cool Cars		
Coole Autos		
Pcs: 206	2007	

4948	EU NA AU AS	
Black and Red Racer		
Schwarz-roter Rennwagen		
Pcs: 25	2007	Special

4953	EU NA AU AS	
Fast Flyers		
Flinke Flieger		
Pcs: 312	2007	

4954 EU NA AU AS

Model Town House

Model Stadthaus

Pcs: 1185	2007	

4955 EU NA AU AS

Big Rig

Big Rig

Pcs: 560	2007	

4956 EU NA AU AS

House

Haus

Pcs: 750	2007	

4957 EU NA AU AS

Ferris Wheel

Riesenrad

Pcs: 1147	2007	

4958 EU NA AU AS

Monster Dino

Monster Dino

Pcs: 801	2007	

4972 EU NA AU AS

Animals

Bauernhoftiere

Pcs: 13	2007	

4973 EU NA AU AS

Harvester

Mähdrescher

Pcs: 14	2007	

4974 EU NA AU AS

Horse Stables

Pferdestall

Pcs: 36	2007	

4975 EU NA AU AS

Farm

Kleiner Bauernhof

Pcs: 42	2007	

4976	EU NA AU AS	
Cement Mixer		
Betonmischer		
Pcs: 12	2007	

4977	EU NA AU AS	
Fire Truck		
Feuerwehrlöschzug		
Pcs: 26	2007	

4978	EU NA AU AS	
Road Sweeper		
Straßenkehrmaschine		
Pcs: 11	2007	

4979	EU NA AU AS	
Ambulance		
Krankenwagen		
Pcs: 6	2007	

4981	EU NA AU AS	
Chum Bucket		
Chum Bucket		
Pcs: 351	2007	Special

4982	EU NA AU AS	
Mrs. Puff's Boating School		
Mrs. Puffs Bootsfahrschule		
Pcs: 393	2007	Special

4986	EU NA AU AS	
Digger		
Raupenbagger		
Pcs: 19	2007	

4987	EU NA AU AS	
Gravel Pit		
Kleine Baustelle		
Pcs: 40	2007	

4988	EU NA AU AS	
Construction Site		
Großbaustelle		
Pcs: 86	2007	

4991 EU NA AU AS

Police Helicopter
Polizei-Hubschrauber

Pcs: 34	2007–2008	Special

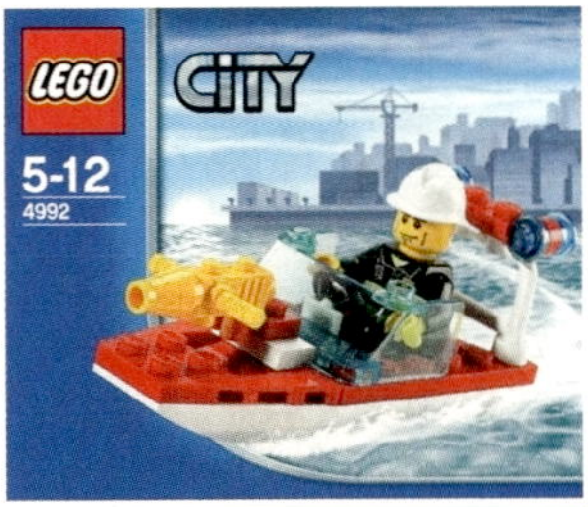

4992 EU NA AU AS

Small Fire Boat
Kleines Feuerwehrboot

Pcs: 24	2007–2008	Special

5378 EU NA AU AS

Hogwarts Castle
Schloß Hogwarts

Pcs: 954	2007	Special

5380 EU NA AU AS

Large Brick Box
Große Baustein Box

Pcs: 71	2007	

5416 EU NA AU AS

Brick Box
Baustein Box

Pcs: 33	2007	

5417 EU NA AU AS

Deluxe Brick Box
Luxus Baustein Box

Pcs: 95	2007	Special

5419 EU NA AU AS

Build a Farm
Bau deinen Bauernhof

Pcs: 107	2007	

5514 EU NA AU AS

Bricks
Bausteine

Pcs: 42	2007	Special

5515 EU NA AU AS

Fun Building with LEGO Bricks
Bausteine

Pcs: 240	2007	Special

4991	Promo from Quick, a restaurant chain	Promo der Restaurant-Kette Quick
4992	Promo from Quick, a restaurant chain	Promo der Restaurant-Kette Quick

5516	**EU** NA AU AS	
Canister		
Tonne		
Pcs: 250	2007	Special

5517	**EU** **NA** **AU** AS	
XXL 1800 Canister		
XXL 1800 Tonne		
Pcs: 1800	2007–2008	Special

5518	**EU** NA AU AS	
Creative Building		
Kreativ Eimer		
Pcs: 74	2007	Special

5519	**EU** NA AU AS	
Creative Building		
Kreativ Eimer		
Pcs: 481	2007	Special

5527	**EU** **NA** AU AS	
Canister		
Tonne		
Pcs: 80	2007	Special

5528	**EU** **NA** AU AS	
Canister		
Tonne		
Pcs: 700	2007	Special

5536	**EU** **NA** **AU** **AS**	
TUB (without Bonus Box)		
Eimer (ohne Bonus Box)		
Pcs: 106	2007	Special

5537	**EU** NA **AU** **AS**	
Blue Tub		
Blaue Steinebox		
Pcs: 683	2007	Special

6161	**EU** **NA** **AU** **AS**	
Brick Box		
Steinebox		
Pcs: 221	2007	

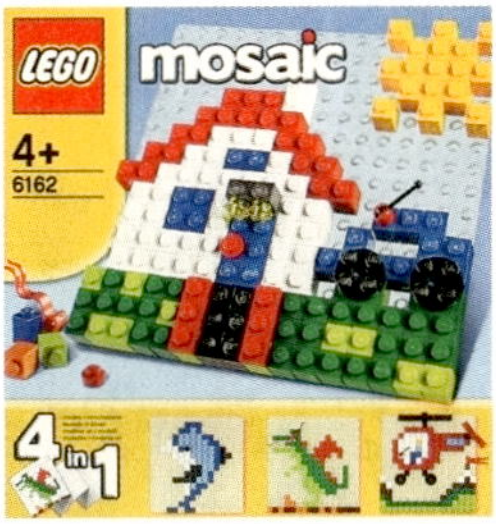

6162	EU NA AU AS	
Building Fun with Mosaic		
Mosaicset		
Pcs: 287	2007	

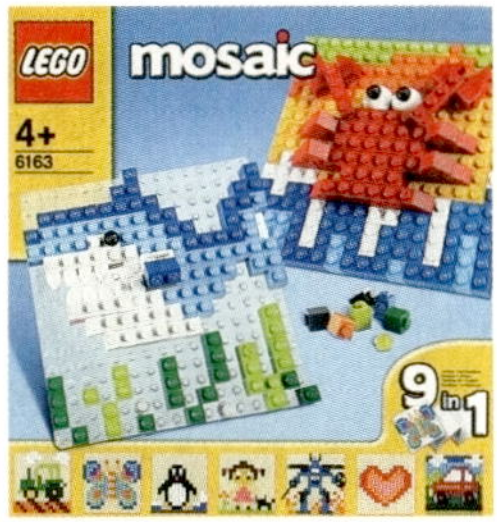

6163	EU NA AU AS	
A World of Mosaic		
Großes Mosaicset.		
Pcs: 604	2007	Special

6164	EU NA AU AS	
Rescue Building Set		
Rette die Stadt!		
Pcs: 520	2007	Special

6166	EU NA AU AS	
Large Brick Box		
Große Steinebox		
Pcs: 405	2007	

6167	EU NA AU AS	
Deluxe Brick Box		
Luxus Steineimer		
Pcs: 703	2007	Special

6944	EU NA AU AS	
Good Guy 07		
Good Guy 07		
Pcs:	2007	Special

6945	EU NA AU AS	
Bad Guy		
Bad Guy		
Pcs: 26	2007	Special

6946	EU NA AU AS	
Squid Launcher Function		
Squid Launcher Function		
Pcs: -	2007	Special

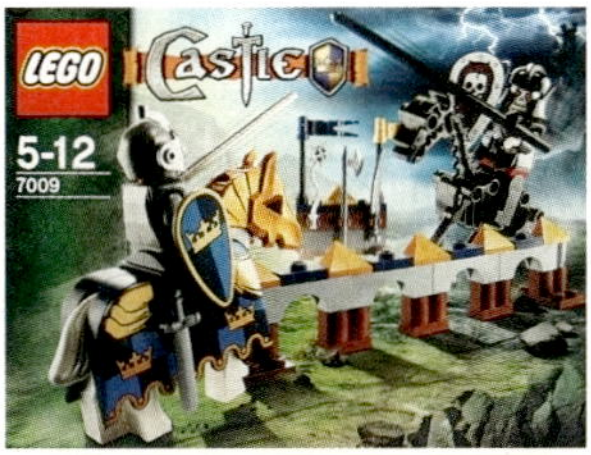

7009	EU NA AU AS	
The Final Joust		
Das Turnier		
Pcs: 63	2007	

ⓘ 7029 EU NA AU AS

Skeleton Ship Attack		
Geisterschiff und Hafen		
Pcs: 628	2007	Special

ⓘ 7090 EU NA AU AS

Crossbow Attack		
Armbrustwagen		
Pcs: 56	2007	

ⓘ 7091 EU NA AU AS

Knights' Catapult Defense		
Katapultverteidigung		
Pcs: 123	2007	

ⓘ 7092 EU NA AU AS

Skeletons' Prison Carriage		
Gefängniskutsche der Skelettritter		
Pcs: 198	2007	

ⓘ 7093 EU NA AU AS

Skeleton Tower		
Turm des bösen Magiers		
Pcs: 398	2007	

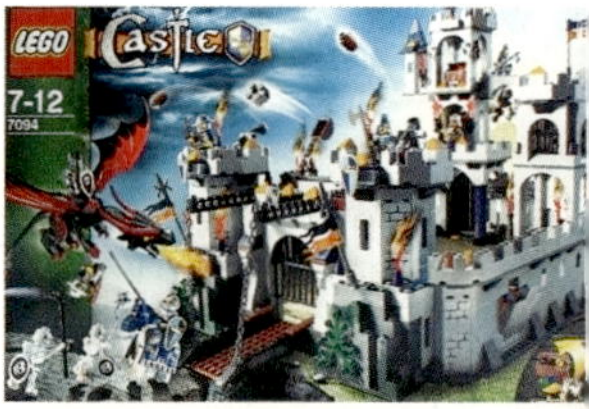

ⓘ 7094 EU NA AU AS

King's Castle Siege		
Große Königsburg		
Pcs: 974	2007	

ⓘ 7172 EU NA AU AS

Banana		
Bananen		
Pcs: 8	2007	Special

ⓘ 7173 EU NA AU AS

Pear		
Birne		
Pcs: 11	2007	Special

ⓘ 7174 EU NA AU AS

Apple		
Apfel		
Pcs: 10	2007	Special

ⓘ	Set	English	Deutsch
ⓘ	7029	Toys ‚R' Us Promo	Toys ‚R' Us Promo
ⓘ	7172-7174	Capespan (Switzerland) Promo	Capespan (Schweiz) Promo

ⓘ 7175	EU NA AU AS	
Grapes		
Weintrauben		
Pcs: 10	2007	Special

ⓘ 7176	EU NA AU AS	
Watermelon		
Wassermelone		
Pcs: -	2007	Special

ⓘ 7177	EU NA AU AS	
Orange		
Orange		
Pcs: 12	2007	Special

ⓘ 7178	EU NA AU AS	
Chef		
Koch		
Pcs: 5	2007	Special

ⓘ 7452	EU NA AU AS	
Black Racer		
Schwarzer Rennwagen		
Pcs: 36	2007–2008	Special

ⓘ 7453	EU NA AU AS	
Off Road Jeep		
Off Road Jeep		
Pcs: -	2007–2008	Special

ⓘ 7580	EU NA AU AS	
The Skating Princess		
Eislaufprinzessin		
Pcs: 26	2007	

ⓘ 7581	EU NA AU AS	
Winter Royal Stables		
Winter Stallungen		
Pcs: 86	2007	

ⓘ 7582	EU NA AU AS	
Royal Summer Palace		
Sommer Palast		
Pcs: 167	2007	

ⓘ	7175-7178	Capespan (Switzerland) Promo	Capespan (Schweiz) Promo
ⓘ	7452-7453	Was added to the Brickmaster magazine	Wurde dem Brickmaster Magazin beigelegt

7600	EU NA AU AS	
Advent Calendar		
Adventskalender		
Pcs: 215	2007	

7654	EU NA AU AS	
Droids™ Battle Pack		
Droids™ Battle Pack		
Pcs: 105	2007	

7655	EU NA AU AS	
Clone Troopers™ Battle Pack		
Clone Troopers™ Battle Pack		
Pcs: 58	2007	

7656	EU NA AU AS	
General Grievous Starfighter™		
General Grievous Starfighter™		
Pcs: 246	2007	

7657	EU NA AU AS	
AT-ST™		
AT-ST™		
Pcs: 245	2007	

7658	EU NA AU AS	
Y-Wing Fighter™		
Y-Wing Fighter™		
Pcs: 454	2007	

7659	EU NA AU AS	
Imperial Landing Craft™		
Imperial Landing Craft™		
Pcs: 478	2007	

7660	EU NA AU AS	
Naboo N-1 Starf.™ & Vulture Droid™		
Naboo N-1 Starf.™ & Vulture Droid™		
Pcs: 287	2007	

7661	EU NA AU AS	
Jedi Starfighter™ with Booster Ring		
Jedi Starfighter™ mit Booster Ring		
Pcs: 592	2007	

7662	EU NA AU AS	
Trade Federation MTT™		
Trade Federation MTT™		
Pcs: 1358	2007	

7663	EU NA AU AS	
Sith Infiltrator™		
Sith Infiltrator™		
Pcs: 310	2007	Special

7664	EU NA AU AS	
TIE Crawler™		
TIE Crawler™		
Pcs: 548	2007	Special

7665	EU NA AU AS	
Republic Cruiser™		
Republic Cruiser™		
Pcs: 924	2007	Special

7666	EU NA AU AS	
Hoth Rebel Base™		
Hoth Rebel Base™		
Pcs: 548	2007	Special

7690	EU NA AU AS	
MB-01 Eagle Command Base		
MX Kommandozentrale		
Pcs: 760	2007	

7691	EU NA AU AS	
ETX Alien Mothership Assault		
ETX Alien-Raumschiff		
Pcs: 451	2007	

7692	EU NA AU AS	
MX-71 Recon Dropship		
MX Forschungs-Transporter		
Pcs: 435	2007	

7693	EU NA AU AS	
ETX Alien Strike		
ETX Alien-Angriff		
Pcs: 258	2007	

7694	EU NA AU AS	
MT-31 Trike		
MT Trike		
Pcs: 95	2007	

7695	EU NA AU AS	
MX-11 Astro Fighter		
MX Astro Fighter		
Pcs: 57	2007	

7697	EU NA AU AS	
MT-51 Claw-Tank Ambush		
MT Robo-Raupe		
Pcs: 374	2007	

7699	EU NA AU AS	
MT-101 Armored Drilling Unit		
MT-101 Gepanzerte Bohreinheit		
Pcs: 619	2007	Special

7714	EU NA AU AS	
Golden Guardian		
Golden Guardian		
Pcs: 269	2007	Special

7721	EU NA AU AS	
Combat Crawler X2		
Combat Crawler X2		
Pcs: 581	2007	Special

7770	EU NA AU AS	
Deep Sea Treasure Hunter		
Tiefsee-Schatzsuche		
Pcs: 76	2007	

7771	EU NA AU AS	
Angler Ambush		
Leuchtfisch		
Pcs: 135	2007	

7772	EU NA AU AS	
Lobster Strike		
Riesenhummer		
Pcs: 223	2007	

i	7699	Toys ‚R‘ Us Promo	Toys ‚R‘ Us Promo

7773	EU NA AU AS
Tiger Shark Attack	
Tigerhai	
Pcs: 343	2007

7774	EU NA AU AS
Crab Crusher	
U-Boot und Riesenkrebs	
Pcs: 618	2007

7775	EU NA AU AS
Aquabase Invasion	
Aqua Basisstation	
Pcs: 840	2007

7776	EU NA AU AS
The Shipwreck	
Schiffswrack	
Pcs: 246	2007

7786	EU NA AU AS
Batcopter: Chase for Scarecrow	
Batcopter: Jagd auf Scarecrow	
Pcs: 293	2007

7787	EU NA AU AS
Bat-Tank: Riddler & Bane's Hideout	
Bat-Tank: Riddler & Banes Versteck	
Pcs: 645	2007

7871	EU NA AU AS	
Whale		
Wal		
Pcs: 31	2007	Special

7872	EU NA AU AS	
Lion		
Löwe		
Pcs: 57	2007	Special

7873	EU NA AU AS	
Airplane		
Flugzeug		
Pcs: 39	2007–2008	Special

i	Included in	Enthalten in
7871-7873	Included in: 66208 (2007)	Enthalten in: 66208 (2007)

ⓘ 7875	EU NA AU	
Backhoe		
Grabenbagger		
Pcs: 41	2007	Special

7876	NA	
Cement Mixer		
Betonmischer		
Pcs: 45	2007	Special

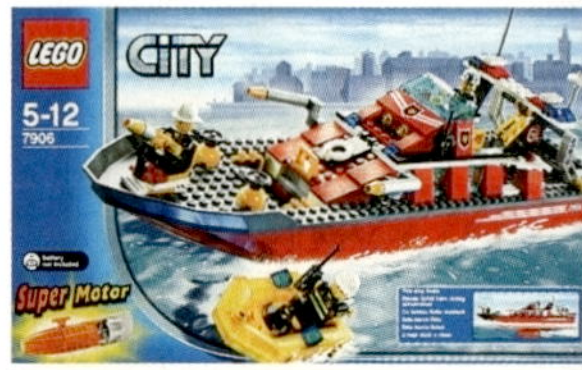

7906	EU NA AU AS	
Fireboat		
Feuerwehrboot		
Pcs: 191	2007	

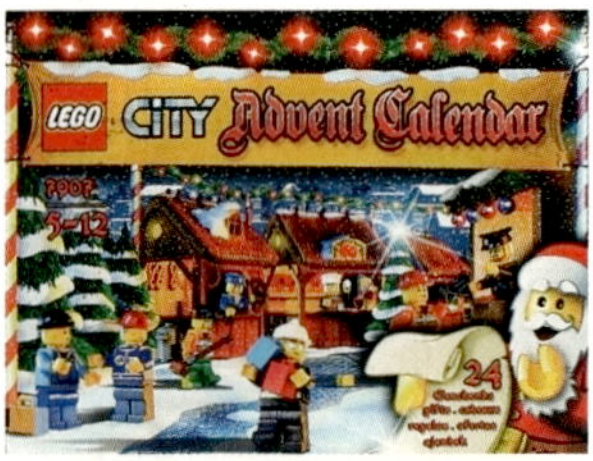

7907	EU NA AU AS	
City Advent Calendar 2007		
City Adventskalender 2007		
Pcs: 232	2007	

ⓘ 7942	EU NA AU AS	
Off-Road Fire Rescue		
Feuerwehr Pick-up		
Pcs: 132	2007	

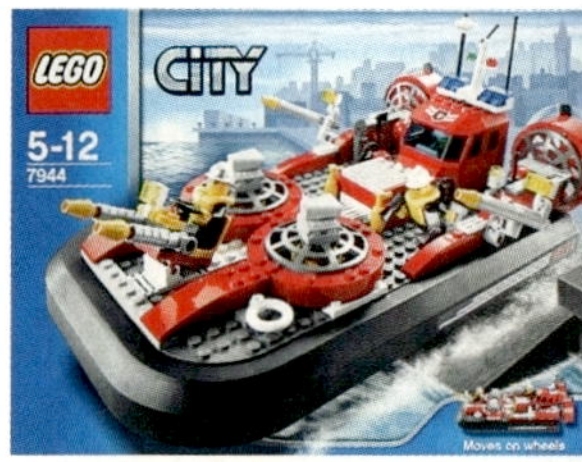

ⓘ 7944	EU NA AU AS	
Fire Hovercraft		
Feuerwehr Luftkissenboot		
Pcs: 274	2007	

ⓘ 7945	EU NA AU AS	
Fire Station		
Feuerwehr-Hauptquartier		
Pcs: 617	2007	

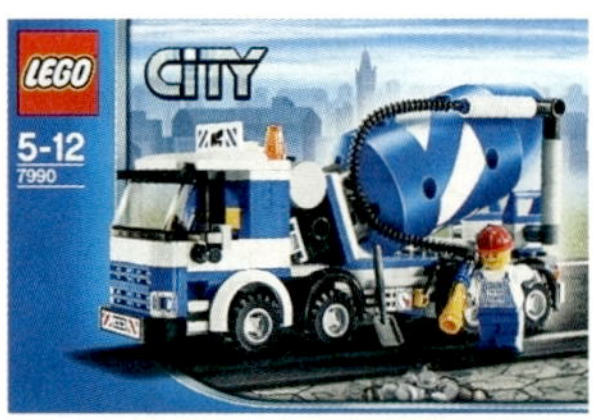

7990	EU NA AU AS	
Cement Mixer		
Betonmischer		
Pcs: 226	2007	

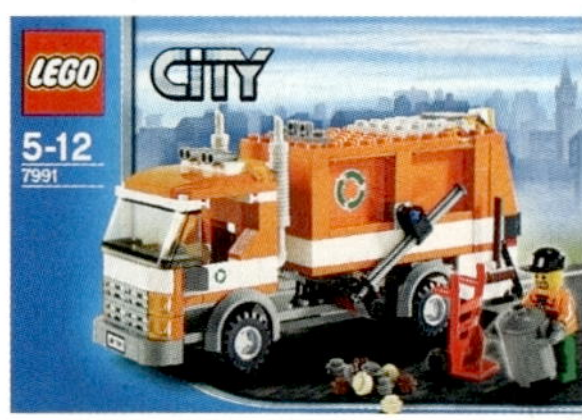

7991	EU NA AU AS	
Garbage Truck		
Müllabfuhr		
Pcs: 209	2007	

ⓘ 7875	Included in: 66208 (2007)	Enthalten in: 66208 (2007)
ⓘ 7942	Included in: 66195 (2007)	Enthalten in: 66195 (2007)
ⓘ 7944	Included in: 66177 (2007), 66175 (2007)	Enthalten in: 66177 (2007), 66175 (2007)
ⓘ 7945	Included in: 66195 (2007)	Enthalten in: 66195 (2007)

7992 EU NA AU AS

Container Stacker	
Containerstapler	
Pcs: 221	2007

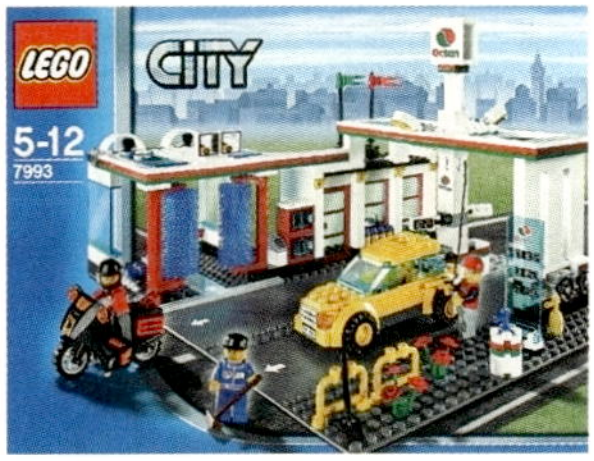

7993 EU NA AU AS

Service Station	
Tankstelle	
Pcs: 402	2007

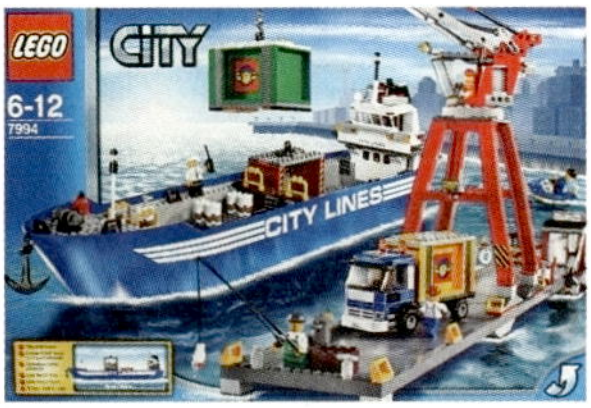

7994 EU NA AU AS

City Harbor	
City Hafen	
Pcs: 659	2007

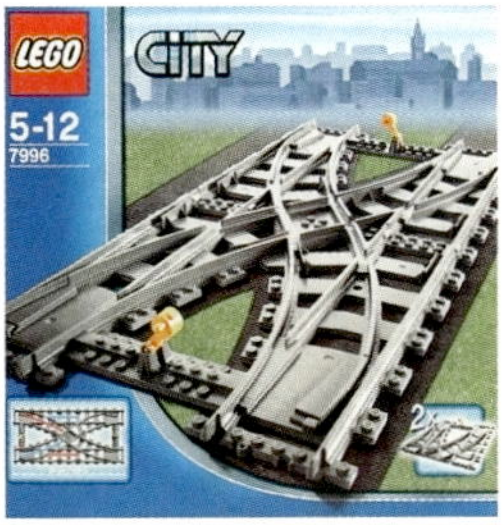

7996 EU NA AU AS

Train Rail Crossing for RC Trains	
Kreuzung	
Pcs: 4	2007

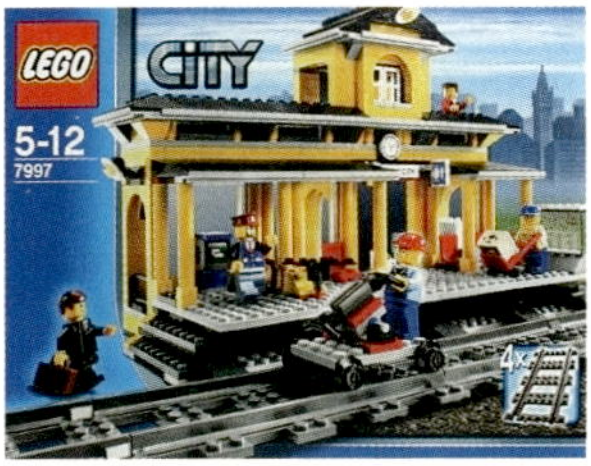

7997 EU NA AU AS

Train Station	
Bahnhof	
Pcs: 396	2007

7998 EU NA AU AS

Heavy Hauler	
Kippsattelzug	
Pcs: 340	2007

8100 EU NA AU AS

Cyclone Defender	
Cyclone Defender	
Pcs: 94	2007

8101 EU NA AU AS

Claw Crusher	
Claw Crusher	
Pcs: 100	2007

8102 EU NA AU AS

Blade Titan	
Blade Titan	
Pcs: 166	2007

8103	EU NA AU AS	
Sky Guardian		
Sky Guardian		
Pcs: 145	2007	

8104	EU NA AU AS	
Shadow Crawler		
Shadow Crawler		
Pcs: 159	2007	

8105	EU NA AU AS	
Iron Condor		
Iron Condor		
Pcs: 145	2007	

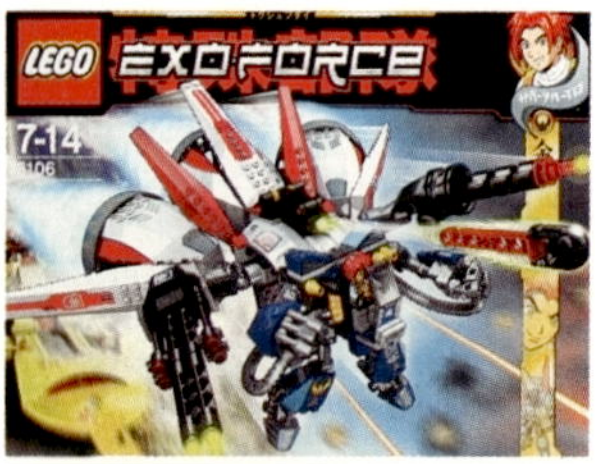

8106	EU NA AU AS	
Aero Booster		
Aero Booster		
Pcs: 312	2007	

8107	EU NA AU AS	
Fight for the Golden Tower		
Goldener Turm von Sentai		
Pcs: 571	2007	

8108	EU NA AU AS	
Mobile Devastator		
Robo-Mobil		
Pcs: 1009	2007	

8130	EU NA AU AS	
Terrain Crusher		
Terrain Crusher		
Pcs: 49	2007	

8131	EU NA AU AS	
Raceway Rider		
Raceway Rider		
Pcs: 51	2007	

8132	EU NA AU AS	
Night Driver		
Night Driver		
Pcs: 36	2007	

8133	EU NA AU AS
Rally Rider	
Rally Rider	
Pcs: 51	2007

8134	EU NA AU AS
Night Crusher	
Night Crusher	
Pcs: 268	2007

8135	EU NA AU AS
Bridge Chase	
Bridge Chase	
Pcs: 558	2007

8136	EU NA AU AS
Fire Crusher	
Fire Crusher	
Pcs: 67	2007

8137	EU NA AU AS
Booster Beast	
Booster Beast	
Pcs: 73	2007

8138	EU NA AU AS
Phantom Crasher	
Phantom Crasher	
Pcs: 90	2007

8139	EU NA AU AS
Night Blazer	
Night Blazer	
Pcs: 67	2007

8140	EU NA AU AS
Tow Trasher	
Tow Trasher	
Pcs: 189	2007

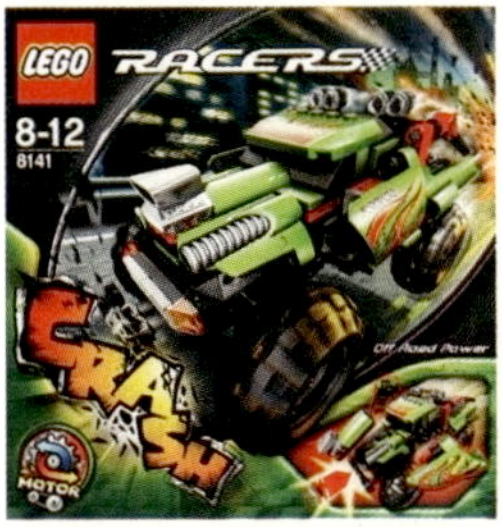

8141	EU NA AU AS
Off Road Power	
Off Road Power	
Pcs: 208	2007

8142	EU NA AU AS
Ferrari 248 F1 1:24	
Ferrari 248 F1 1:24	
Pcs: 169	2007

8143	EU NA AU AS
Ferrari F430 Challenge 1:17	
Ferrari F430 Challenge 1:17	
Pcs: 708	2007

8144	EU NA AU AS
Ferrari F1 Team	
Ferrari F1 Team	
Pcs: 726	2007

8145	EU NA AU AS
Ferrari 599 GTB Fiorano 1:40	
Ferrari 599 GTB Fiorano 1:40	
Pcs: 1340	2007

8146	EU NA AU AS
Nitro Muscle	
Nitro Muscle	
Pcs: 603	2007

8147	EU NA AU AS
Bullet Run	
Bullet Run	
Pcs: 811	2007

8270	EU NA AU AS
Rough Terrain Crane	
Mini Geländekran	
Pcs: 106	2007

8271	EU NA AU AS
Wheel Loader	
Radlader	
Pcs: 209	2007

8272	EU NA AU AS
Snowmobile	
Schneemobil	
Pcs: 337	2007

i	8144	Available as: Schumacher or Raikkonen Version	Verfügbar als: Schumacher oder Raikkonen Version

8273	EU NA AU AS	
Off Road Truck		
Truck		
Pcs: 830	2007	

8274	EU NA AU AS	
Combine Harvester		
Mähdrescher		
Pcs: 1032	2007	

8275	EU NA AU AS	
Motorized Bulldozer		
RC Bulldozer mit Motor		
Pcs: 1403	2007	

8910	EU NA AU AS	
Kongu		
Toa Mahri Kongu		
Pcs: 74	2007	

8911	EU NA AU AS	
Jaller		
Toa Mahri Jaller		
Pcs: 68	2007	

8912	EU NA AU AS	
Hewkii		
Toa Mahri Hewkii		
Pcs: 62	2007	

8913	EU NA AU AS	
Nuparu		
Toa Mahri Nuparu		
Pcs: 59	2007	

8914	EU NA AU AS	
Hahli		
Toa Mahri Hahli		
Pcs: 59	2007	

8915	EU NA AU AS	
Matoro		
Toa Mahri Matoro		
Pcs: 63	2007	

8916	EU NA AU AS
Takadox	
Takadox	
Pcs: 64	2007

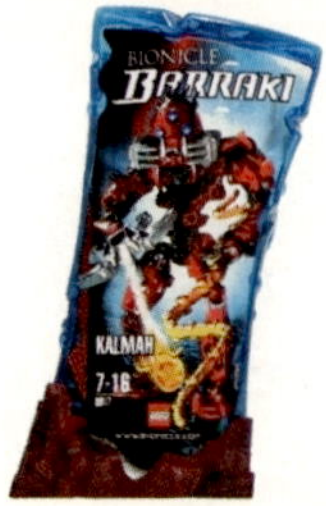

8917	EU NA AU AS
Kalmah	
Kalmah	
Pcs: 53	2007

8918	EU NA AU AS
Carapar	
Carapar	
Pcs: 49	2007

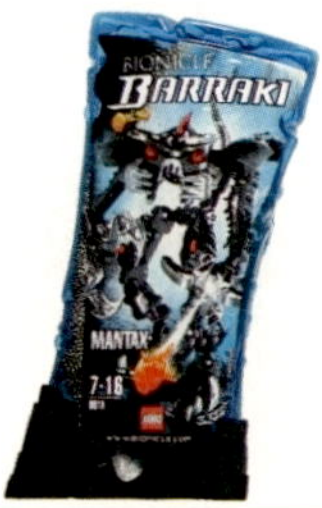

8919	EU NA AU AS
Mantax	
Mantax	
Pcs: 58	2007

8920	EU NA AU AS
Ehlek	
Ehlek	
Pcs: 54	2007

8921	EU NA AU AS
Pridak	
Pridak	
Pcs: 47	2007

8922	EU NA AU AS
Gadunka	
Gadunka	
Pcs: 176	2007

8923	EU NA AU AS
Hydraxon	
Hydraxon	
Pcs: 165	2007

8924	EU NA AU AS
Maxilos and Spinax	
Maxilos und Spinax	
Pcs: 256	2007

8925 EU NA AU AS

Barraki Deepsea Patrol		
Barraki Tiefseepatrouille		
Pcs: 228	2007	

8926 EU NA AU AS

Toa Undersea Attack		
Toa Unterwasserangriff		
Pcs: 401	2007	

8927 EU NA AU AS

Toa Terrain Crawler		
Toa Tiefseeraupe		
Pcs: 674	2007	

8929 EU NA AU AS

Defilak		
Defilak		
Pcs: 37	2007	

8930 EU NA AU AS

Dekar		
Dekar		
Pcs: 37	2007	

8931 EU NA AU AS

Thulox		
Thulox		
Pcs: 40	2007	

8932 EU NA AU AS

Morak		
Morak		
Pcs: 39	2007	

8934 EU NA AU AS

Squid Ammo		
Krakenmunition		
Pcs: 7	2007	

8935 EU NA AU AS

Nocturn		
Noctum		
Pcs: 116	2007	Special

8939	EU NA AU AS	
Lesovikk		
Lesovikk		
Pcs: 149	2007	Special

8940	EU NA AU AS	
Karzahni		
Karzahni		
Pcs: 373	2007	Special

10178	EU NA AU AS	
Motorized Walking AT-AT™		
Motorized Walking AT-AT™		
Pcs: 1145	2007	Special

10179	EU NA AU AS	
Ultimate Millennium Falcon™		
Ultimate Millennium Falcon™		
Pcs: 5195	2007	Special

10181	EU NA AU AS	
Eiffel Tower 1:300		
Eiffelturm 1:300		
Pcs: 3427	2007	Special

10182	EU NA AU AS	
Café Corner		
Eckcafé		
Pcs: 2056	2007	Special

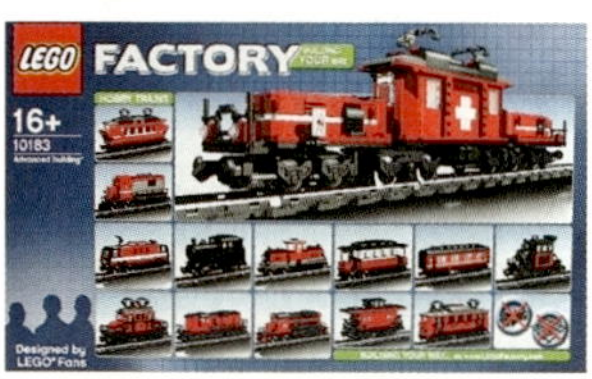

10183	EU NA AU AS	
Hobby Train Set		
Hobby-Zugset		
Pcs: 1062	2007	Special

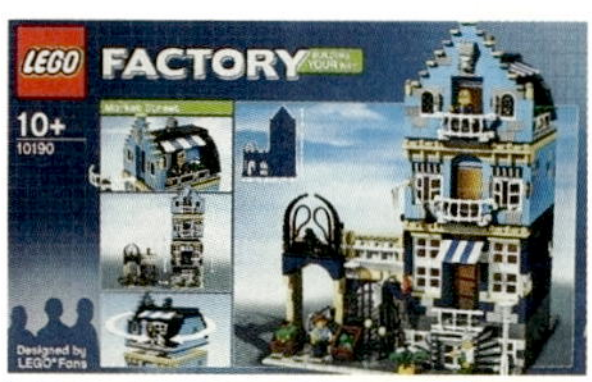

10190	EU NA AU AS	
Market Street		
Marktstraße		
Pcs: 1280	2007	Special

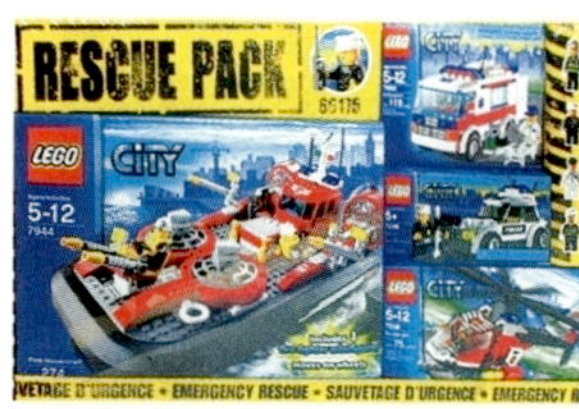

66175	EU NA AU AS	
Essential Vehicles Collection		
Essential Vehicles Collection		
Sets: 4	2007	Special

	66175	Includes: 7890 (2006), 7238 (2005), 7944 (2007), 7236 (2005)	Enthält: 7890 (2006), 7238 (2005), 7944 (2007), 7236 (2005)

66177 EU NA AU AS

Rescue Pack

Notfall-Set

Sets: 3	2007	Special

66193 EU

City Super Pack

City Superset

Sets: 4	2007	Special

66194 EU

City Super Pack

City Super Set

Sets: 4	2007	

66195 EU NA

City Super Pack

City Kombipack

Sets: 5	2007	Special

66208 EU NA AU

Mr. Magorium's Big Book

Mr. Magoriums Bauset

Sets: 9	2007	Special

66217 EU

Farm Value Pack

Farm Kombiset

Sets: 3	2007	Special

66221 NA

X-wing Fighter™ with Luke & Pilot

X-wing Fighter™ mit Luke & Pilot

Pcs: 437	2007	Special

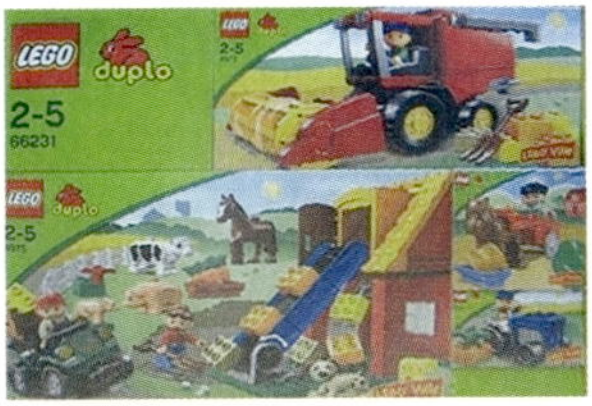

66231 EU

Farm Value Pack

Farm Kombiset

Sets: 4	2007	Special

66239 EU

Super Set

Superset

Sets: 4	2007	Special

i	66177	Includes: 7890 (2006), 7238 (2005), 7944 (2007)	Enthält: 7890 (2006), 7238 (2005), 7944 (2007)
i	66193	Includes: 7890 (2006), 7902 (2006), 7903 (2006), 7892 (2006)	Enthält: 7890 (2006), 7902 (2006), 7903 (2006), 7892 (2006)
i	66195	Includes: 7241 (2005), 7238 (2005), 7945 (2007), 7239 (2005), 7942 (2007)	Beinhaltet: 7241 (2005), 7238 (2005), 7945 (2007), 7239 (2005), 7942 (2007)

ⓘ 4521221	EU NA AU AS	
Star Wars™ C-3PO Metallic Gold		
Star Wars™ C-3PO Metallic Gold		
Pcs: 1	2007	Special

ⓘ	66208	Includes: 7873 (2007), 7875 (2007), 7872 (2007), 7604 (2006), 7606 (2006), 7609 (2006), 7602 (2006), 7610 (2006), 7871 (2007)	Enthält: 7873 (2007), 7875 (2007), 7872 (2007), 7604 (2006), 7606 (2006), 7609 (2006), 7602 (2006), 7610 (2006), 7871 (2007)
ⓘ	66217	Includes: 4665(2004), 4975(2007), 4687(2004)	Enthält: 4665(2004), 4975(2007), 4687(2004)
ⓘ	66231	Includes: 4969 (2006), 4683 (2004), 4973 (2007), 4975 (2007)	Enthält: 4969 (2006), 4683 (2004), 4973 (2007), 4975 (2007)
ⓘ	66239	Includes: 7895 (2006), 7896 (2006), 7898 (2006), 7997 (2007)	Enthält: 7895 (2006), 7896 (2006), 7898 (2006), 7997 (2007)
ⓘ	4521221	Randomly added to Star Wars Sets; Limited to 10.000	Figur wurde nach dem Zufallsprinzip Star Wars Sets beigefügt; Auflage: 10.000

2008

ⓘ 2230	EU NA AU AS	
Helicopter and Raft		
Hubschrauber und Floß		
Pcs: 115	2008–	Special

ⓘ 2928	EU NA AU AS	
ANA Airline Set		
ANA Fluglinienset		
Pcs: 141	2008–	Special

3830	EU NA AU AS	
Bikini Bottom Express		
Bikini Bottom Express		
Pcs: 202	2008–	

3831	EU NA AU AS	
Rocket Ride		
Raketenfahrt		
Pcs: 274	2008–	

4837	EU NA AU AS	
Minitrain		
Mini Züge		
Pcs: 73	2008–	

4838	EU NA AU AS	
Mini Vehicles		
Mini Fahrzeuge		
Pcs: 79	2008–	

ⓘ	2230	Airline Promo	Airline Promo
ⓘ	2928	Similar to: 2928 (2006), with additional stickers	Ähnlich zu: 2928 (2006), mit zusätzlichen Aufklebern

4994 EU NA AU AS

Fierce Creatures

Gruselige Tiere

Pcs: 193	2008–	

4995 EU NA AU AS

Cargo Copter

Frachthubschrauber

Pcs: 272	2008–	

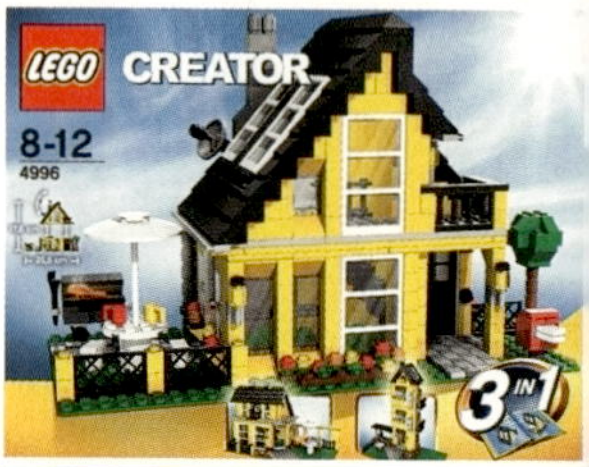

4996 EU NA AU AS

Beach House

Ferienhaus

Pcs: 522	2008–	

5574 EU NA AU AS

Basic Bricks

Grundbausteine

Pcs: 280	2008–	

5575 EU NA AU AS

Basic Bricks - Medium

Grundbausteine - Mittel

Pcs: 45	2008–	

5576 EU NA AU AS

Basic Bricks - Medium

Grundbausteine - Mittel

Pcs: 375	2008–	

5577 EU NA AU AS

Basic Bricks - Large

Grundbausteine - Groß

Pcs: 65	2008–	Special

5578 EU NA AU AS

Basic Bricks - Large

Grundbausteine - Groß

Pcs: 500	2008–	

5583 EU NA AU AS

Fun with Wheels

Bauspaß mit Bauplatte

Pcs: 78	2008–	Special

5584 EU NA AU AS

Fun with Wheels

Bauspaß mit Bauplatte

Pcs: 648	2008–	Special

5585 EU NA AU AS

Pink Brick Box

Bauspaß für Mädchen

Pcs: 216	2008–	

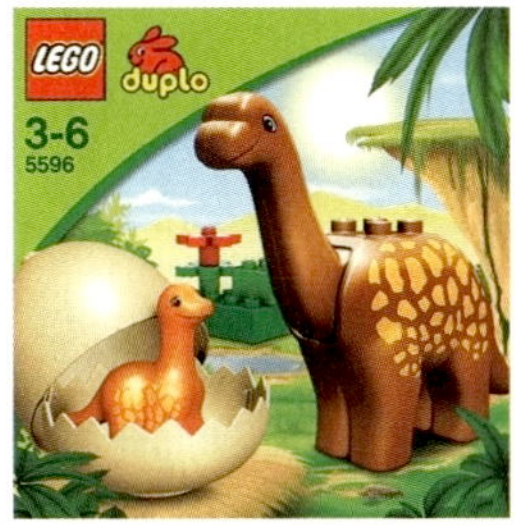

5596 EU NA AU AS

Dino Birthday

Dino Familie

Pcs: 9	2008–	

5597 EU NA AU AS

Dino Trap

Großer T-Rex

Pcs: 28	2008–	

5598 EU NA AU AS

Dino Valley

Die große Dino-Welt

Pcs: 52	2008–	

5601 EU NA AU AS

Fire Station

Feuerwehrstation

Pcs: 72	2008–	

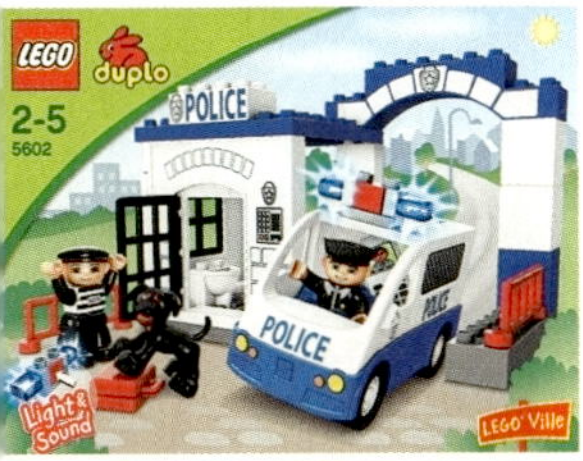

5602 EU NA AU AS

Police Station

Polizeiwache

Pcs: 28	2008–	

5603 EU NA AU AS

Fire Chief

Feuerwehr-Hauptmann

Pcs: 7	2008–	

5604 EU NA AU AS

Supermarket

Supermarkt

Pcs: 62	2008–	

5605 EU NA AU AS

Tanker Truck		
Tanklaster		
Pcs: 17	2008–	

5610 EU NA AU AS

Builder		
Bauarbeiter		
Pcs: 23	2008–	

5611 EU NA AU AS

Puplic Works		
Müllmann		
Pcs: 31	2008–	

5612 EU NA AU AS

Police Officer		
Polizist		
Pcs: 21	2008–	

5613 EU NA AU AS

Firefighter		
Feuerwehrman		
Pcs: 25	2008–	

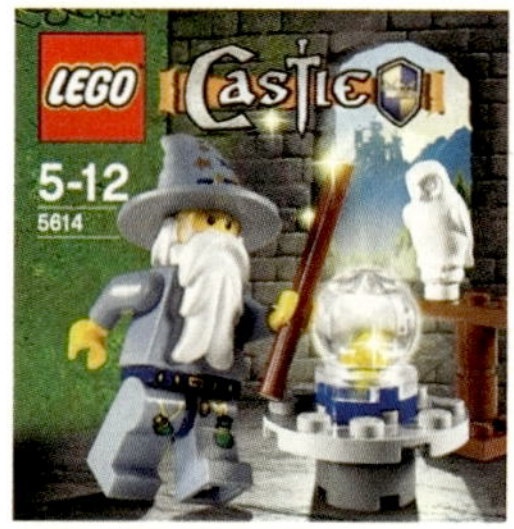

5614 EU NA AU AS

The Good Wizard		
Der gute Magier		
Pcs: 16	2008–	

5615 EU NA AU AS

The Knight		
Der Ritter		
Pcs: 21	2008–	

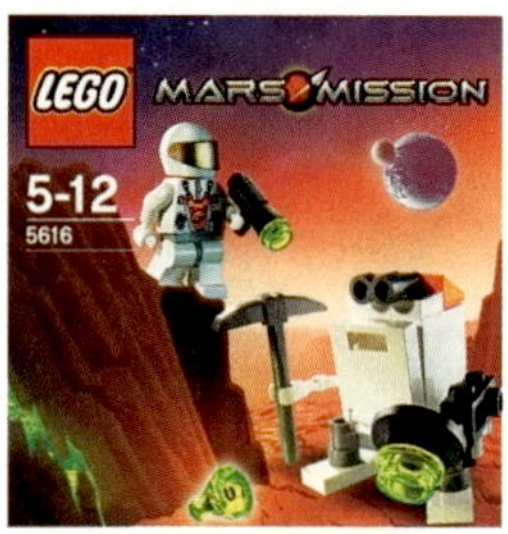

5616 EU NA AU AS

Mini-Robot		
Mini-Roboter		
Pcs: 24	2008–	

5617 EU NA AU AS

Alien Jet		
Alien-Jet		
Pcs: 21	2008–	

6117	EU NA AU AS
Doors and Windows	
Türen und Fenster	
Pcs: -	2008–

6118	EU NA AU AS
Wheels	
Räder	
Pcs: -	2008–

6176	EU NA AU AS
Basic Bricks - Deluxe	
Grundbausteine - Deluxe	
Pcs: 80	2008–

6177	EU NA AU AS
Basic Bricks Deluxe	
Grundbausteine - Deluxe	
Pcs: 650	2008–

6178	EU NA AU AS
My Town	
Hausbau-Set	
Pcs: -	2008–

6186	EU NA AU AS
Build Your Own Harbor	
Bausteine „Hafen"	
Pcs: 252	2008–

6187	EU NA AU AS
Road Construction Set	
Bausteine „Baustelle"	
Pcs: 300	2008–

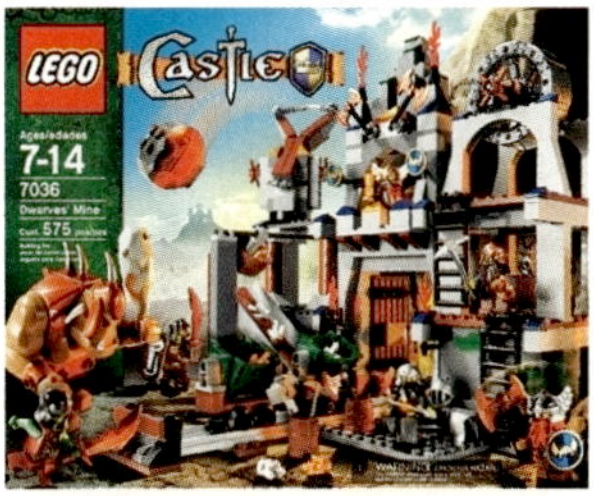

7036	EU NA AU AS	
Dwarves' Mine		
Zwergenmine		
Pcs: 575	2008–	Special

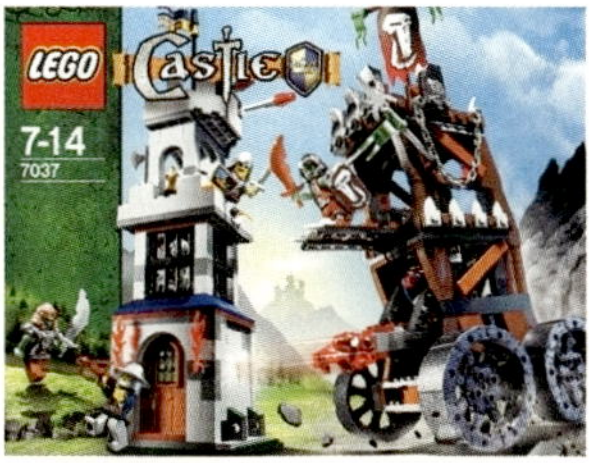

7037	EU NA AU AS
Tower Raid	
Turmangriff	
Pcs: 364	2008–

7038 EU NA AU AS

Troll Assault Wagon		
Troll-Angriffswagen		
Pcs: 161	2008–	

7040 EU NA AU AS

Dwarves' Mine Defender		
Verteidigung der Zwergenmine		
Pcs: 86	2008–	

7041 EU NA AU AS

Troll Battle Wagon		
Troll-Angriffsrad		
Pcs: 508	2008–	

7048 EU NA AU AS

Troll Warship		
Troll-Schiff		
Pcs: 493	2008–	

7583 EU NA AU AS

Playful Puppy		
Hundefamilie		
Pcs: 83	2008–	

7585 EU NA AU AS

Horse Stable		
Pferdestall		
Pcs: 209	2008–	

7586 EU NA AU AS

Sunshine Home		
Traumhaus		
Pcs: 450	2008–	

7587 EU NA AU AS

Horse Jumping		
Springreiten		
Pcs: 53	2008–	

7620 EU NA AU AS

Motorcycle Chase		
Motorradjagd		
Pcs: 79	2008–	

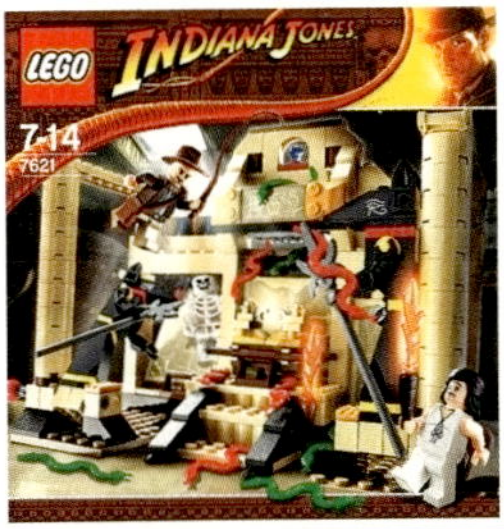

7621 EU NA AU AS

The Lost Tomb

Das verlorene Grab

Pcs: 277	2008–	

7622 EU NA AU AS

Race for the Stolen Treasure

Die Jagd nach dem gest. Schatz

Pcs: 272	2008–	

7623 EU NA AU AS

Temple Escape

Die Flucht aus dem Tempel

Pcs: 554	2008–	

7624 EU NA AU AS

Jungle Duel

Dschungelduell

Pcs: 77	2008–	

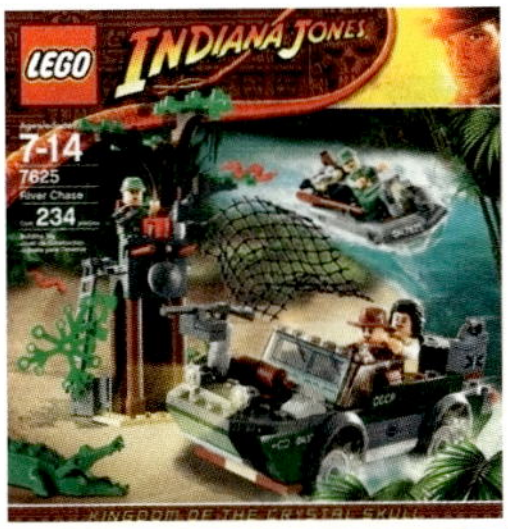

7625 EU NA AU AS

River Chase

Verfolgungsjagd am Fluss

Pcs: 234	2008–	

7626 EU NA AU AS

Jungle Cutter

Dschungelfräser

Pcs: 493	2008–	

7627 EU NA AU AS

Temple of the Crystal Skull

Der Tempel des Kristallschädels

Pcs: 874	2008–	

7644 EU NA AU AS

MX-81 Hypersonic Operations Aircraft

Mx-81 Überschall-Raumschiff

Pcs: 795	2008–	

7645 EU NA AU AS

MT-61 Crystal Reaper

MT-61 Einsatzfahrzeug

Pcs: 600	2008–	

7646	EU NA AU AS
ETX Alien Infiltrator	
ETX Alien-Transformer	
Pcs: 333	2008–

7647	EU NA AU AS
MX-41 Switch Fighter	
MX-41 Verwandlungsraumschiff	
Pcs: 217	2008–

7648	EU NA AU AS
MT-21 Mobile Mining Unit	
MT-21 Mobile Bohreinheit	
Pcs: 130	2008–

7667	EU NA AU AS
Imperial Dropship™	
Imperial Dropship™	
Pcs: 81	2008–

7668	EU NA AU AS
Rebel Scout Speeder™	
Rebel Scout Speeder™	
Pcs: 82	2008–

7669	EU NA AU AS
Anakin's Jedi Starfighter™	
Anakin's Jedi Starfighter™	
Pcs: 153	2008–

7670	EU NA AU AS
Hailfire Droid™ & Spider Droid™	
Hailfire Droid™ & Spider Droid™	
Pcs: 249	2008–

7671	EU NA AU AS
AT-AP Walker™	
AT-AP Walker™	
Pcs: 392	2008–

7672	EU NA AU AS
Rogue Shadow™	
Rogue Shadow™	
Pcs: 482	2008–

7723 EU NA AU AS

Police Pontoon Plane	
Polizei-Wasserflugzeug	
Pcs: 215	2008–

7731 EU NA AU AS

Mail Van	
Postauto	
Pcs: 66	2008–

7732 EU NA AU AS

Air Mail	
Postflugzeug	
Pcs: 88	2008–

7733 EU NA AU AS

Truck & Forklift	
Lkw mit Gabelstapler	
Pcs: 343	2008–

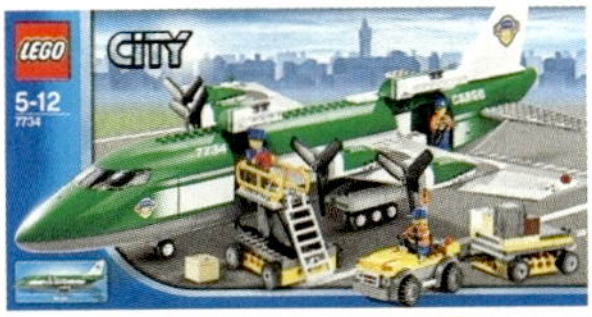

7734 EU NA AU AS

Cargo Plane	
Frachtflugzeug	
Pcs: 463	2008–

7736 EU NA AU AS

Coast Guard Quad Bike	
Quad-Bike der Küstenwache	
Pcs: 33	2008–

7737 EU NA AU AS

Coast Guard 4WD & Jet Scooter	
Geländewagen mit Wasserjet	
Pcs: 130	2008–

7738 EU NA AU AS

Coast Guard Helicopter & Life Raft	
Helikopter mit Rettungsinsel	
Pcs: 445	2008–

7739 EU NA AU AS

Coast Guard Patrol Boat & Tower	
Rettungsschiff und Turm	
Pcs: 444	2008–

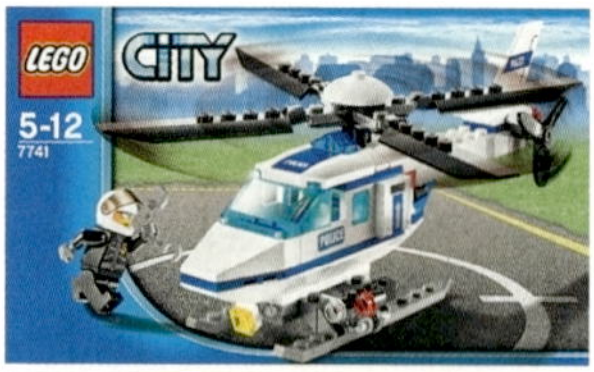

7741	EU NA AU AS
Police Helicopter	
Polizei-Hubschrauber	
Pcs: 94	2008–

7743	EU NA AU AS
Police Command Center	
Polizei-Überwachungswagen	
Pcs: 524	2008–

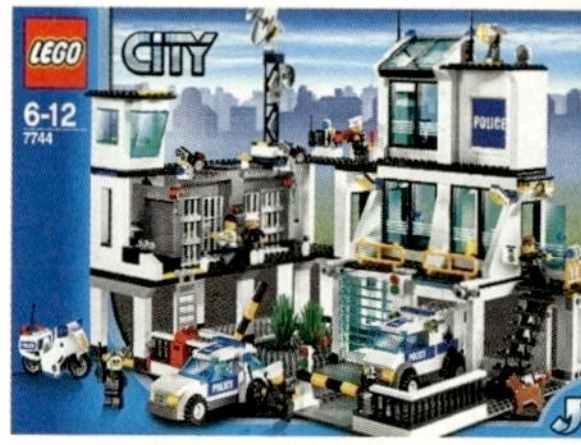

7744	EU NA AU AS
Police Headquarters	
Polizeistation	
Pcs: 953	2008–

8029	EU NA AU AS
Mini Snowspeeder™	
Mini Snowspeeder™	
Pcs: -	2008–

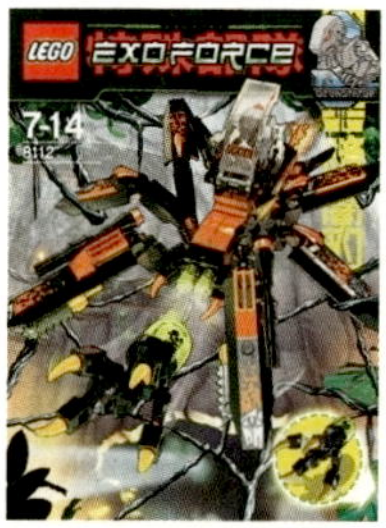

8112	EU NA AU AS
Battle Arachnoid	
Battle Arachnoid	
Pcs: 131	2008–

8113	EU NA AU AS
Assault Tiger	
Assault Tiger	
Pcs: 163	2008–

8114	EU NA AU AS
Chameleon Hunter	
Chameleon Hunter	
Pcs: 188	2008–

8115	EU NA AU AS
Dark Panther	
Dark Panther	
Pcs: 244	2008–

8117	EU NA AU AS
Storm Lasher	
Storm Lasher	
Pcs: 283	2008–

7743	Included in: 66246 (2008)	Enthalten in: 66246 (2008)

8118 EU NA AU AS
Hybrid Rescue Tank
Hybrid Rettungspanzer
Pcs: 339 | 2008–

8148 EU NA AU AS
EZ-Roadster
EZ-Roadster
Pcs: 45 | 2008–

8149 EU NA AU AS
Midnight Streak
Midnight Streak
Pcs: 43 | 2008–

8150 EU NA AU AS
ZX TURBO
ZX TURBO
Pcs: 55 | 2008–

8151 EU NA AU AS
Adrift Sport
Adrift Sport
Pcs: 52 | 2008–

8152 EU NA AU AS
Speed Chasing
Speed Chasing
Pcs: 142 | 2008–

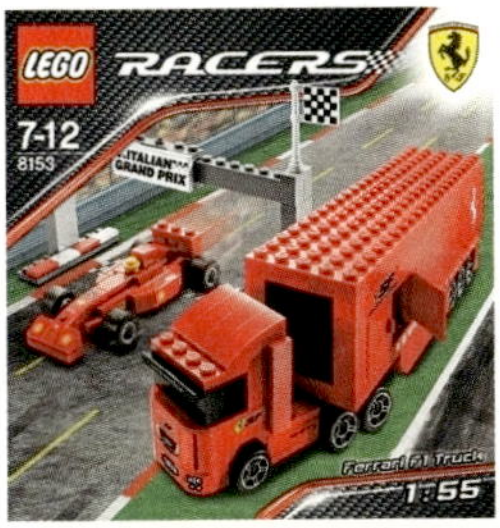

8153 EU NA AU AS
Ferrari F1 Truck
Tiny Turbo Ferrari Truck
Pcs: 270 | 2008–

8155 EU NA AU AS
Ferrari F1 Pit
Tiny Turbo Ferrari F1 Tankstopp
Pcs: 482 | 2008–

8156 EU NA AU AS
Ferrari FXX 1:17
Ferrari FXX 1:17
Pcs: 626 | 2008–

8158	EU NA AU AS
Speed Racer & Snake	
Speed Racer & Snake	
Pcs: 242	2008–

8159	EU NA AU AS
Racer X & Taejo Togokhan	
Racer X & Taejo Togokhan	
Pcs: 237	2008–

8160	EU NA AU AS
Cruncher Block & Racer X	
Cruncher Block & Racer X	
Pcs: 367	2008–

8161	EU NA AU AS
Grand Prix Race	
Grand Prix Race	
Pcs: 595	2008–

8290	EU NA AU AS
Mini Forklift	
Mini-Gabelstapler	
Pcs: 89	2008–

8291	EU NA AU AS
Dirt Bike	
Motocross Bike	
Pcs: 248	2008–

8292	EU NA AU AS
Cherry Picker	
Truck mit Hebebühne	
Pcs: 726	2008–

8296	EU NA AU AS
Dune Buggy	
Strand-Buggy	
Pcs: 199	2008–

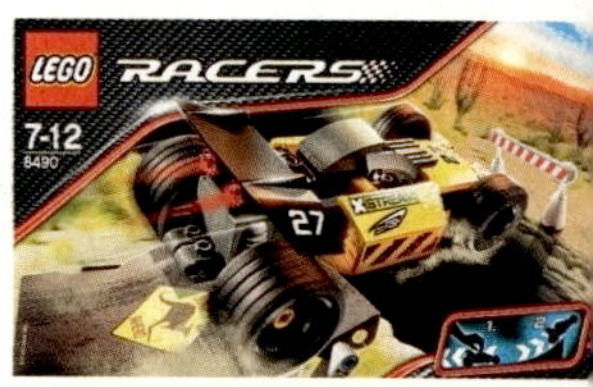

8490	EU NA AU AS
Desert Hopper	
Desert Hopper	
Pcs: 92	2008–

8491 EU NA AU AS

Ram Rod

Ram Rod

Pcs: 72	2008–	

8492 EU NA AU AS

Mud Hopper

Mud Hopper

Pcs: 59	2008–	

8493 EU NA AU AS

Red Ace

Red Ace

Pcs: 82	2008–	

8494 EU NA AU AS

Ring of Fire

Ring of Fire

Pcs: 268	2008–	

8685 EU NA AU AS

Toa Kopaka

Toa Kopaka

Pcs: 54	2008–	

8686 EU NA AU AS

Toa Lewa

Toa Lewa

Pcs: 52	2008–	

8687 EU NA AU AS

Toa Pohatu

Toa Pohatu

Pcs: 68	2008–	

8691 EU NA AU AS

Antroz

Antroz

Pcs: 53	2008–	

8692 EU NA AU AS

Vamprah

Vamprah

Pcs: 49	2008–	

8693 EU NA AU AS
Chirox
Chirox
Pcs: 49 | 2008–

8697 EU NA AU AS
Toa Ignika
Toa Ignika
Pcs: 140 | 2008–

8881 EU NA AU AS
Power Functions Batterybox
Power Functions Batteriebox
Pcs: 1 | 2008–

8882 EU NA AU AS
Power Functionis XL-Motor
Power Functions XL-Motor
Pcs: - | 2008–

8883 EU NA AU AS
Power Functions M-Motor
Power Functions M-Motor
Pcs: 1 | 2008–

8884 EU NA AU AS
Power Functions IR RX
Power Functions Infrarot Empfänger
Pcs: 1 | 2008–

8885 EU NA AU AS
Power Functions IR TX
Power Functions Infr. Fernbedienung
Pcs: 1 | 2008–

8944 EU NA AU AS
Tanma
Tanma
Pcs: 14 | 2008–

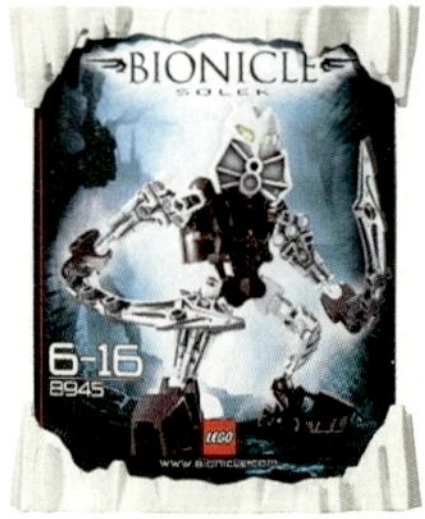

8945 EU NA AU AS
Solek
Solek
Pcs: 14 | 2008–

8946 EU NA AU AS

Photok		
Photok		
Pcs: 14	2008–	

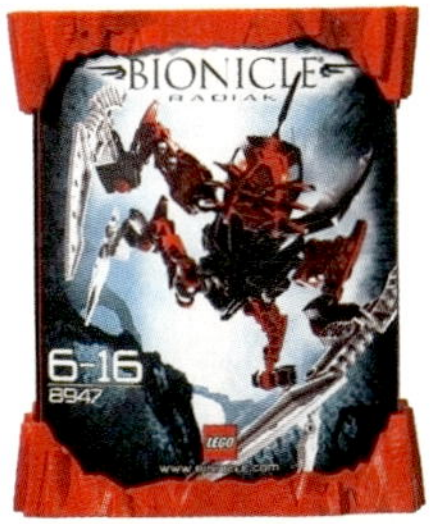

8947 EU NA AU AS

Radiak		
Radiak		
Pcs: 16	2008–	

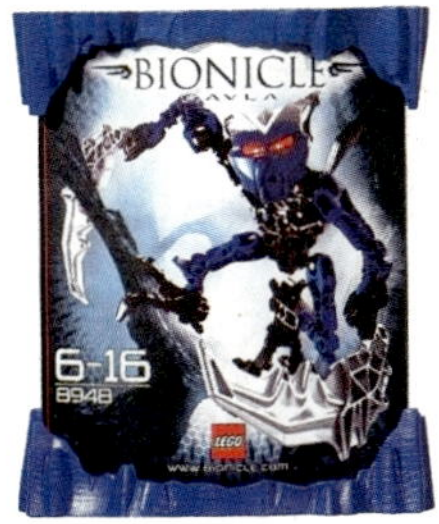

8948 EU NA AU AS

Gavla		
Gavla		
Pcs: 14	2008–	

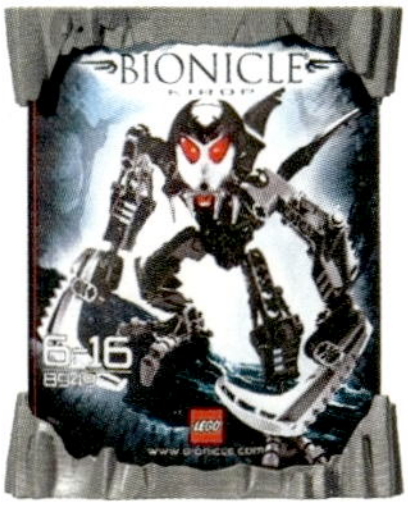

8949 EU NA AU AS

Kirop		
Kirop		
Pcs: 14	2008–	

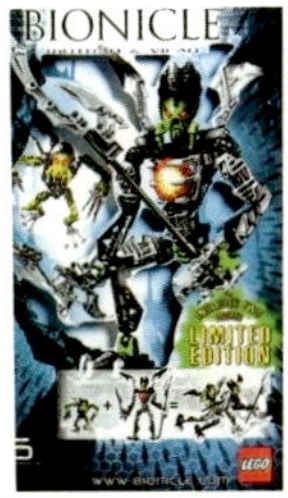

8952 EU NA AU AS

Mutran & Vican		
Mutran & Vican		
Pcs: 90	2008–	

8953 EU NA AU AS

Makuta Icarax		
Makuta Incarax		
Pcs: 159	2008–	

10184 EU NA AU AS

50 Years - Town Plan		
50 Jahre - Town Plan		
Pcs: 1947	2008–	

10185 EU NA AU AS

Green Grocer		
Green Grocer		
Pcs: 2328	2008–	Special

10186 EU NA AU AS

General Grievous™		
General Grievous™		
Pcs: 1085	2008–	Special

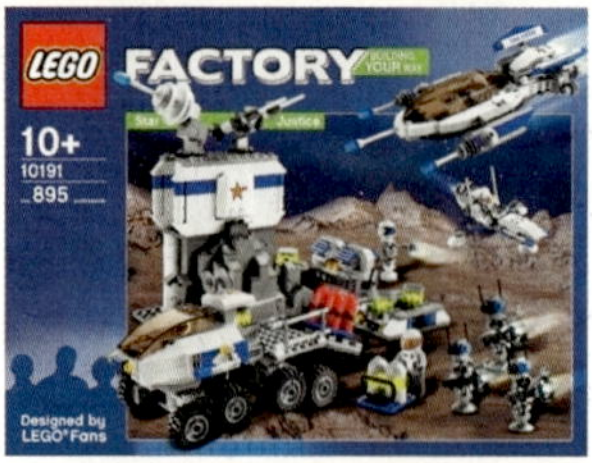

10191	EU NA AU AS	
Star Justice		
Star Justice		
Pcs: -	2008–	Special

10192	EU NA AU AS	
Space Skulls		
Space Skulls		
Pcs: 956	2008–	Special

20002	EU NA AU AS	
Fire Car		
Feuerwehrauto		
Pcs: 52	2008–	Special

20003	EU NA AU AS	
Creator Brickmaster™		
Creator Brickmaster™		
Pcs: 102	2008–	Special

66246	EU NA AU AS	
City Police Super Pack		
Stadt Polizei Kombipack		
Sets: 3	2008–	Special

i	20002	Only available with Brickmaster Magazine	Brickmaster Exklusiv-Set
i	20003	Only available with Brickmaster Magazine	Brickmaster Exklusiv-Set
i	66246	Includes: 7235 (2005), 7245 (2005), 7743 (2008)	Enthält: 7235 (2005), 7245 (2005), 7743 (2008)

Keyrings / Schlüsselanhänger

Legend for chains/ring-types

1	Metalchain, old:
1a-I	Ring 21 mm, five small chain links plus two rings, one attached to the wrist or foot
1a-II	Same as 1a-I, but chain is fixed with a metallic cramp on the head of the figure
1b	Ring 21 mm, four flat chain links plus two rings, chain is fixed with a metallic cramp on the head
1c	Ring 24 mm, four large, contorted chain links, chain ends with metallic cramp on the head
2	Plastic chain in black, plastic pin in the head
3	Metallic Chain, new: flat ring 27 mm and five flattened chain links, pin in the head
4	Other chain-/ or mounting type

LEGO® Logo

L0	No LEGO logo
L1	LEGO logo monochrome (plane black or only outline)
L2	LEGO logo four coloured (black, red, white, yellow)
L3	LEGO logo four coloured on white 2x2 tile
L4	LEGO logo four coloured on white 2x3 rounded tile
Lx	LEGO logo of another type

© in the leg (only Fabuland)

C0	no © printed on the leg (1979)
C1	© indented marking (1980-1982)
C2	© is embossed

Legende für Kette/Ring-Typen

1	Metallkette alt:
1a-I	Ring 21 mm, 5 kleine Kettenglieder + 2 Ringe, einer davon am Handgelenk oder Fuß
1a-II	Wie 1a-I, aber mit Befestigung an einer Metallkrampe im Kopf der Figur
1b	Ring 21 mm, 4 flache Kettenglieder + 2 Ringe, Kette an Metallkrampe im Kopf
1c	Ring 24 mm, vier große, gedrehte Kettenglieder, Kette an Metallkrampe im Kopf
2	Plastikkette schwarz, Plastikbolzen im Kopf
3	Metallkette neu: flacher Ring 27 mm und 5 abgeflachte Kettenglieder, Bolzen im Kopf
4	anderer Ketten-/Befestigungstyp

LEGO® Logo

L0	Kein LEGO Logo
L1	LEGO Logo monchrom (flächig schwarz oder nur Kontur)
L2	LEGO Logo vierfarbig (schwarz/rot/weiß/gelb)
L3	LEGO Logo vierfarbig auf weißer 2x2 Fliese
L4	LEGO Logo vierfarbig auf weißer 2x3 Fliese abgerundet
Lx	LEGO Logo anderer Art

© im Bein (nur Fabuland)

C0	kein © im Bein (1979)
C1	© in Tiefprägung (1980-1982)
C2	© im Hochprofil

Keyrings

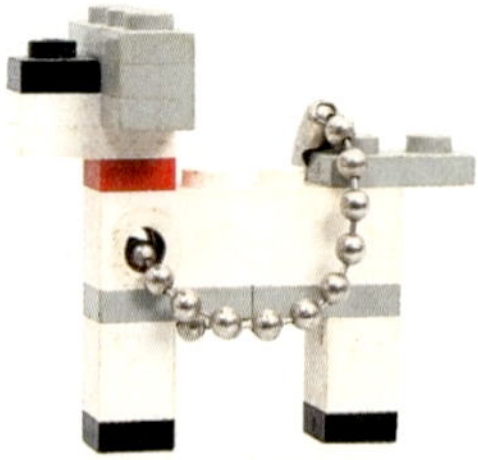

-	-	4L0
Dog made of Bricks		
Aus Steinen gebauter Hund		
-		
-		

-	-	4L0
H0 VW Pickup Muryar Bishara		
H0 VW Pickup Muryar Bishara		
Gift for scouts in a 1967 Danish/ Nigerian scout camp near Billund		
Geschenk für Teilnehmer eines Pfadfinderlagers bei Billund		

-	1974	1a-I/L0
Homemaker Girl		
Großkopf-Mädchen		
Probably given out with LEGO logo sticker		
Wahrscheinlich mit Logo-Aufkleber ausgegeben		

-	1974	1a-I/L2
Homemaker Boy		
Großkopf-Junge		
-		
-		

-	1977	1a-I/L1
Homemaker Firefighter, stickered		
Großkopf-Feuerwehrmann beklebt		
-		
-		

-	1977	1a-I/L2
Homemaker Firefighter, printed		
Großkopf-Feuerwehrmann bedruckt		
-		
-		

-	-	1b/L0
DUPLO® Dog		
DUPLO® Hund		
Figure appeared in set 2622 (1983)		
Figur erschien in Set 2622 (1983)		

-	-	1b/L0
DUPLO® Pilot		
DUPLO® Pilot		
Figure appeared in set 2622 (1983)		
Figur erschien in Set 2622 (1983)		

-	-	1b/L0
DUPLO® Sailor		
DUPLO® Matrose		
Figure appeared in set 2625 (1980)		
Figur erschien in Set 2625 (1980)		

-	1979	1a-I/L0/C0
Ricky Racoon		
Willie Waschbär		
Also 1a-II/L0/C1		
Auch 1a-II/L0/C1		

-	1979	1a-I/L0/C0
Mike Monkey		
Mike Affe		
Also 1a-II/L0/C2, 1c/L1/C2		
Auch 1a-II/L0/C2, 1c/L1/C2		

-	1979	1a-I/L0/C0
Charlie Cat		
Charly Kater		
-		
-		

-	1979	1a-I/L0/C1
Michael Mouse		
Moe Maus		
-		
-		

-	1979	1a-II/L0/C1
Leonard (Lion)		
Leo Löwe		
Also 1c/L0/C2		
Auch 1c/L0/C2		

-	1981	1a-II/L0/C1
Edward Elephant		
Edward Elefant		
-		
-		

-	1980	1a-II/L0/C1
Harry Horse		
Harry Pferd		
Black torso, red arms and legs		
Schwarzer Torso, rote Arme und Beine		

-	1979	1a-II/L0/C1
Mortimer Mouse		
Morty Maus		
Also 1b/L0/C1		
Auch 1b/L0/C1		

-	1979	1b/L0/C1
Billy Goat		
Olli Ziege		
Blue torso, yellow arms and legs		
Blauer Torso, gelbe Arme und Beine		

Keyrings

-	1982	1b/L0/C1
Ernie Elephant		
Ernie Elefant		
-		
-		

-	1982	1b/L0/C1
Charlie Cat		
Charlie Kater		
-		
-		

-	1981	1b/L0/C1
Bruno Bear		
Bruno Bär		
-		
-		

-	1981	1b/L0/C1
Monkey (green/black)		
Gabriel Affe		
-		
-		

-	1982	1b/L0/C1
Paul Parrot		
Paul Papagei		
Also 1c/L1/C2		
Auch 1c/L1/C2		

-	1982	1b/L0/C1
Majorie Mouse		
Moe Maus		
-		
-		

-	1979	1b/L0/C1
Lucy Lamb		
Louise Lamm		
Also 1b/L0/C2, 1c/L1/C2		
Auch 1b/L0/C2, 1c/L1/C2		

-	1981	1c/L1/C1
Bonnie Rabbit		
Bonnie Kaninchen		
Also 1b/L0/C2, 1c/L1/C2		
Auch 1b/L0/C2, 1c/L1/C2		

-	1979	1b/L0/C2
Catherine Cat		
Cathy Katze		
Also 1c/L0/C2, 1c/L1/C2		
Auch 1c/L0/C2, 1c/L1/C2		

-	1980	1b/L0/C2
Clara Cow		
Rosa/Clara Kuh		
-		
-		

-	1979	1b/L0/C2
Doctor Dog		
Doc David		
Also 1a/L0/C0, 1c/L1/C2		
Auch 1a/L0/C0, 1c/L1/C2		

-	1980	1b/L0/C2
Charlie/Joe Crow		
Joe Rabe		
Also 1c/L0/C2		
Auch 1c/L0/C2		

-	1982	1b/L0/C2
Bertie/Barty Bulldog		
Bully/Donny Dogge		
-		
-		

-	1981	1b/L0/C2
Peter Panda		
Percy Bär		
-		
-		

-	1984	1c/L0/C2
Mike Monkey		
Gabriel Affe		
Also 1c/L1/C2		
Auch 1c/L1/C2		

-	1984	1c/L0/C2
Percy Pilot		
Albert Albatros		
-		
-		

-	1984	1c/L0/C2
Tubby Pig		
Pierre Schwein		
-		
-		

-	1979	1c/L0/C2
Freddie Fox		
Freddy Fuchs		
Also 1a/L0/C0		
Auch 1a/L0/C0		

Keyrings

-	1984	1c/L0/C2
Wally Walrus		
Willem Walroß		
-		
-		

-	1984	1c/L0/C2
Croco (black/green)		
Kalle Krokodil		
Also 1c/L1/C2		
Auch 1c/L1/C2		

-	1984	1c/L0/C2
Crow Pilot (black/yellow)		
Joe Rabe		
-		
-		

-	-	1c/L0/C2
Elephant (yellow)		
Elefant (gelb)		
Never released in a LEGO set this way		
In der Art nie in einem LEGO Set erschienen		

-	1982	1c/L0/C2
Lisa Lamb		
Sofie Lamm		
-		
-		

-	1982	1c/L0/C2
The naughty Racoon		
Willie Waschbär		
-		
-		

-	1982	1c/L0/C2
Peter Pig		
Pierre Schwein		
White torso and arms, red legs		
Weißer Torso und Arme, rote Beine		

-	1984	1c/L1/C2
Bertie/Barty Bulldog		
Bully Dogge		
-		
-		

-	1985	1c/L2/C2
Elephant (yellow/black)		
Edward Elefant		
-		
-		

-	1986	1c/L0/C2
Lionel Lion		
Leo Löwe		
-		
-		

-	1986	1c/L0/C2
Ricky Racoon		
Wuschi Waschbär		
-		
-		

-	1986	1c/L0/C2
Bonnie Bunny		
Bonnie Kaninchen		
Also 2/L2/C2		
Auch 2/L2/C2		

-	1986	1c/L0/C2
Edward Elephant		
Edward Elefant		
Also 2/L2/C2		
Auch 2/L2/C2		

-	1986	1c/L2/C2
Max Mouse		
Morty Maus		
Also 2/L2/C2		
Auch 2/L2/C2		

-	1986	1c/L2/C2
Pig (white/grey)		
Henry Schwein		
-		
-		

-	1986	1c/L2/C2
Horse (white/grey)		
Ferdy Pferd		
-		
-		

-	1987	1c/L2/C2
Hannah Hippopotamus		
Nessy Nilpferd		
-		
-		

-	1987	2/L2/C2
Boris Bulldog		
Boris Bulldogge		
-		
-		

Keyrings

-	1987	2/L2/C2
Clive Crocodile		
Kalle Krokodil		
-		
-		

-	1988	2/L2/C2
Catherine Cat		
Cathy Katze		
-		
-		

-	-	1c/L0/C2
Crocodile		
Krokodil		
Backside print: BIRKENHEAD POINT SYDNEY		
Rückseitenaufdruck: BIRKENHEAD POINT SYDNEY		

-	-	1c/L0/C2
Crow pilot		
Rabe (Pilot)		
Backside print: BIRKENHEAD POINT SYDNEY		
Rückseitenaufdruck: BIRKENHEAD POINT SYDNEY		

-	-	1c/L0/C2
Lamb		
Schaf		
Backside print: BIRKENHEAD POINT SYDNEY		
Rückseitenaufdruck: BIRKENHEAD POINT SYDNEY		

-	-	1c/L0/C2
Elephant		
Elefant		
Backside print: BIRKENHEAD POINT SYDNEY		
Rückseitenaufdruck: BIRKENHEAD POINT SYDNEY		

-	-	1c/L0/C2
Horse		
Pferd		
Backside print: BIRKENHEAD POINT SYDNEY		
Rückseitenaufdruck: BIRKENHEAD POINT SYDNEY		

-	-	1c/L0/C2
Hippopotamus		
Nilpferd		
Backside print: BIRKENHEAD POINT SYDNEY		
Rückseitenaufdruck: BIRKENHEAD POINT SYDNEY		

-	-	1c/L0/C2
Rabbit		
Kaninchen		
Backside print: BIRKENHEAD POINT SYDNEY		
Rückseitenaufdruck: BIRKENHEAD POINT SYDNEY		

-	-	1bL0
Classic Space red with airtanks		
Roter Astronaut mit Lufttank		
-		
-		

-	-	1a-I/L1
Classic Space red w/o airtanks		
Roter Astronaut ohne Lufttank		
-		
-		

-	-	1bL0
Classic Space white with airtanks		
Weißer Astronaut mit Lufttank		
-		
-		

-	-	1cL2
Classic Space white w/o airtanks		
Weißer Astronaut ohne Lufttank		
-		
-		

-	-	1bL0
Classic Space yellow with airtanks		
Gelber Astronaut mit Lufttank		
-		
-		

-	1982	1cL2
Classic Space yellow w/o airtanks		
Gelber Astronaut ohne Lufttank		
-		
-		

-	-	1bL0
Classic Space black with airtanks		
Schwarzer Astronaut mit Lufttank		
-		
-		

-	-	1cL2
Classic Space black w/o airtanks		
Schwarzer Astronaut ohne Lufttank		
-		
-		

-	-	1cL2
Classic Space blue with airtanks		
Blauer Astronaut mit Lufttank		
-		
-		

Keyrings

-	1987	1cL2
Futuron Spaceman blue		
Futuron Astronaut blau		
-		
-		

-	1987	1cL2
Futuron Spaceman red		
Futuron Astronaut rot		
Also with plastic chain (2L2)		
Auch mit Plastikkette (2L2) -		

-	1988	1cL0
Blacktron I Spaceman		
Blacktron I Astronaut		
With and without LEGO logo (1cL0 + 1cL2)		
Mit und ohne LEGO Logo (1cL0 + 1cL2)		

-	1990	2L2
M-Tron Spaceman		
M-Tron Astronaut		
-		
-		

-	1991	2L2
Blacktron II Spaceman		
Blacktron II Astronaut		
-		
-		

9405	1993	3L2
Ice Planet Spaceman		
Ice Planet Astronaut		
-		
-		

-	1993	3L2
Ice Planet Spaceman (blue legs)		
Ice Planet Astronaut (blaue Beine)		
Irregular combination, never used in a LEGO set		
Diese Farbkombination erschien nie in einem Set		

3975	1994	3L2
Spyrius Droid		
Spyrius Droide		
Also known as 9408		
Auch unter Nummer 9408 bekannt		

9410	1996	3L2
Exploriens Spaceman		
Exploriens Astronaut		
-		
-		

3955	1997	3L2
UFO Droid		
UFO Droide		
-		
-		

-	1997	3L2
UFO Alien (grey helmet)		
UFO Alien (grauer Helm)		
-		
-		

-	1997	3L2
UFO Alien (black helmet)		
UFO Alien (schwarzer Helm)		
-		
-		

3950	1998	3L2
Insectoids Figure (green helmet)		
Insectoids Figur (grüner Helm)		
-		
-		

3951	1998	3L2
Insectoids Figure (yellow helmet)		
Insectoids Figur (gelber Helm)		
-		
-		

3926	2002	3L2
Martian in hypersled		
Marsianer im Hyperschlitten		
Figure “Arcturus” appeared in set 7317 (2001)		
Figur „Arcturus“ erschien in Set 7317 (2001)		

850759	2004	3L3
Classic Spaceman re-issue		
Blauer Astronaut (Neuauflage)		
Note the new helmet! (Also with 2x3 logo tile - 3L4)		
Beachte den neuen Helm! (Auch mit 2x3 Fliese - 3L4)		

Keyrings

-	-	1a-I/L0
Classic Knight blue		
Klassischer Ritter blau		
Unstickered version of 375/6075 knight (1978)		
Unbeklebte Version eines Ritters aus Set 375/6075 (1978)		

-	-	1c/L2
Crusader Axe Knight light grey		
Löwenritter mit Nasenschutz		
Irregular colour combination with light grey helmet		
Untypische Kombination mit hell-grauem Helm		

-	-	1c/L2
Crusader Axe Knight dark grey		
Löwenritter mit Nasenschutz		
First appeared in set 6022 (1984)		
Erstmals in Set 6022 erschienen (1984)		

-	-	1c/L2
Crusader Lion Knight		
Löwenritter mit Kinnschutz		
-		
-		

-	-	1c/L2
Black Falcon Knight 1		
Schwarzer Falke mit Nasenschutz		
Figure appeared in set 6035 (1987)		
Erstmals in Set 6035 erschienen (1987)		

-	-	2/L2
Black Falcon Knight 2		
Schwarzer Falke mit Kinnschutz		
Figure appeared in set 6102 (1985)		
Erschien in Set 6102 (1985)		

850076	2003	3/L3
Castle Robber / Wolfpack logo		
Räuber der Wolfsbande		
Similar to robber of set 6096 (2000)		
Ähnlich zum Räuber aus Set 6096 (2000)		

851495	2005	3L4
King Mathias		
König Mathias		
-		
-		

851734	2006	3L4
King Jayko (Knights Kingdom II)		
König Jayko (Knights Kingdom II)		
-		
-		

851735	2006	3L4
Dracus (Knights Kingdom II)		
Dracus (Knights Kingdom II)		
-		
-		

-	-	2/L2
Imperial Governor		
Imperialer Gouverneur		
Similar to governor of set 6276 (1989)		
Ähnlich zur Gouverneursfigur aus Set 6276 (1989)		

3983	-	2-3L2
Captain Red Beard		
Käpt'n Rotbart		
First appeared in set 6285 (1989); also known as 9403		
Erstmals in Set 6285 (1989) erschienen; auch als 9403 bekannt		

-	-	3/L2
Pirate with peg leg		
Pirat mit Holzbein		
-		
-		

850301	2004	3L3
Pirate with blue bandana		
Pirat mit blauem Kopftuch		
-		
-		

-	2003	3L3
Pirate with red bandana		
Pirat mit rotem Kopftuch		
-		
-		

3912	-	3/L2
Red Ninja		
Roter Ninja		
Figure first appeared in set 3050 (1999)		
Erstmals in Set 3050 (1999) erschienen		

-	-	3/L2
Black Ninja		
Schwarzer Ninja		
Figure first appeared in set 6045 (1999)		
Erstmals in Set 6045 (1999) erschienen		

852194	2008	3L0
Dwarf		
Zwerg		
-		
-		

-	-	1cL0
Male plain white		
Mann komplett weiß		
Backside print: BIRKENHEAD POINT SYDNEY		
Rückseitenaufdruck: BIRKENHEAD POINT SYDNEY		

-	-	1cL0
Male white/blue		
Mann weiß/blau		
Backside print: BIRKENHEAD POINT SYDNEY		
Rückseitenaufdruck: BIRKENHEAD POINT SYDNEY		

-	-	1cL0
Classic Spaceman white		
Weißer Astronaut ohne Lufttank		
Backside print: BIRKENHEAD POINT SYDNEY		
Rückseitenaufdruck: BIRKENHEAD POINT SYDNEY		

-	-	1cL0
Classic Spaceman yellow		
Gelber Astronaut ohne Lufttank		
Backside print: BIRKENHEAD POINT SYDNEY		
Rückseitenaufdruck: BIRKENHEAD POINT SYDNEY		

-	-	1cL2
DUPLO® Benefits Fair 1997		
DUPLO® Benefits Fair 1997		
-		
-		

-	-	1cL2
DUPLO® Safety Fest 1997		
DUPLO® Safety Fest 1997		
-		
-		

-	-	4L2
DUPLO® Distribution Center		
DUPLO® Distribution Center		
-		
-		

-	-	4L2
DUPLO® 1998 First Competition		
DUPLO® 1998 First Competition		
-		
-		

-	-	1a-I/LO
FALCK male		
FALCK Mann		
FALCK logo on both sides of the torso		
FALCK Logo auf beiden Seiten des Torsos		

-	-	1cL0
FALCK female		
FALCK Frau		
FALCK logo on both sides of the torso		
FALCK Logo auf beiden Seiten des Torsos		

-	-	1a-I/LO
Jester male		
Harlekin Mann		
-		
-		

-	-	1a-I/LO
Jester female		
Harlekin Frau		
-		
-		

-	-	1cL0
LEGOLAND® male		
LEGOLAND® Mann		
Also 1a-I/LO		
Auch 1a-I/LO		

-	-	1cL0
LEGOLAND® female		
LEGOLAND® Frau		
-		
-		

-	-	1a-I/LO
BRF female		
BRF Frau		
-		
-		

-	2005	3L2
Nvidia male		
Nvidia Mann		
Nvidia sticker on back, given out at the E3 in Los Angeles		
Nvidia Aufkleber auf Rückseite, ausgegeben auf der E3, L.A.		

-	2005	3L2
Nvidie female		
Nvidia Frau		
Nvidia sticker on back, given out at the E3 in Los Angeles		
Nvidia Aufkleber auf Rückseite, ausgegeben auf der E3, L.A.		

Keyrings

-	-	1a-I/LO
icopal worker		
icopal Arbeiter		
icopal logo on both sides of the torso		
icopal Logo auf beiden Seiten des Torsos		

-	-	1a-I/LO
WWF female		
WWF Frau		
World Wide Fund for Nature Promo		
World Wide Fund for Nature Promo		

-	-	1a-I/LO
Woman with SE OG HØR logo		
Frau mit SE OG HØR Logo		
Promo from a danish TV magazine		
Promo einer dänischen Fernsehzeitung		

-	-	
Sterling Silver skeleton		
Skelett aus Sterlingsilber		
-		
-		

-	-	4L1
Sterling Silver worker minifig		
Arbeiter aus Sterlingsilber		
-		
-		

-	-	4L0
Sterling Silver 2x4 brick		
2x4 Stein aus Sterlingsilber		
-		
-		

-	-	1a-I/LO
Town motorcyclist		
Motorradfahrer		
Figure appeared in set 603 (1978)		
Figur erschien in Set 603 (1978)		

-	-	1a-II/LO
Racing driver		
Rennfahrer		
Figure appeared in set 6609 (1980)		
Figur erschien in Set 6609 (1980)		

-	-	1a-II/LO
Town male with cowboy hat		
Mann mit Cowboyhut		
-		
-		

-	-	1a-II/L0
Town mailman		
Postbote		
-		
-		

-	-	1b/L0
Town female with red hair		
Frau mit roten Haaren		
-		
-		

-	-	1b/L0
Town chef		
Koch		
-		
-		

3977	-	2L0
LEGOLAND® Ambassador		
LEGOLAND® Soldat		
Also 1c/L0 and 3L2, L0 types with stripes on back		
Auch als 1c/L0 und 3L2, L0 jeweils mit Streifen auf Rücken		

-	-	1c/L2
Airport employee		
Flughafen-Mitarbeiter		
Figure appeared in set 6392 (1985)		
Figur erschien in Set 6392 (1985)		

-	-	1c/L2
Town male red torso		
Mann mit rotem Torso		
Exists with front or back logo and without logo (L0)		
Gibt es mit Logo vorne oder hinten und ohne Logo (L0)		

-	-	1c/L2
Town male dungarees		
Mann mit Latzhose		
-		
-		

-	-	1c/L2
Town female striped shirt		
Frau mit gestreiftem Torso		
-		
-		

-	-	1cL2
Truck Driver		
LKW-Fahrer		
-		
-		

Keyrings

-	-	1b/L1
Firefighter black helmet		
Feuerwehrmann schwarzer Helm		
Also exists with golden logo (also 1a-I/L1)		
Auch mit goldenem Logo bekannt (auch 1a-I/L1)		

-	-	2/L2
Firefighter white helmet		
Feuerwehrmann weißer Helm		
Also exists with white airtanks		
Auch mit weißen Lufttanks bekannt		

-	-	3L2
Town girl yellow legs		
Frau mit gelben Beinen		
-		
-		

-	-	3L2
Town girl green legs		
Frau mit grünen Beinen		
Appeared in set 6326 (1998)		
Figur erschien in Set 6326 (1998)		

-	-	3L2
Man with sunglasses		
Mann mit Sonnenbrille		
-		
-		

3911	-	3L2
Spaceport Astronaut		
Spaceport-Astronaut		
Also 3L3		
Auch 3L3		

3915	-	3L2
Red Racer		
Roter Rennfahrer		
-		
-		

3916	2000	3L2
Rock Raider		
Rock-Raiders Figur		
-		
-		

3918	-	3L2
Coast-Guard girl		
Frau der Küstenwache		
-		
-		

3918	-	3L2
Paradisa girl		
Paradisa-Frau		
-		
-		

3923	-	3L2
King Leo		
König Leo		
Also 3L3		
Auch 3L3		

3924	-	3L2
Director		
Regisseur		
Inspired by Steven Spielberg		
Inspiriert durch Steven Spielberg		

3925	-	3L2
Brickster		
Brickster		
-		
-		

3945	-	3L2
Drome Racer		
Drome Racer		
-		
-		

3945b	-	3L3
Drome Racer		
Drome Racer		
Re-release of 3945 - with different minifig head!		
Neuveröffentlichung von 3945 mit anderem Gesicht		

3952	-	3L2
Policeman		
Polizist		
-		
-		

3953	-	3L2
Santa Claus		
Weihnachtsmann		
Also 3L3		
Auch 3L3		

3954	-	3L2
Policeman		
Polizist		
-		
-		

Keyrings

3959	-	3L2
Timmy		
Timmy		
Time-Cruisers theme		
Time-Cruisers Serie		

3960	-	3L2
Professor		
Professor		
Time-Cruisers theme		
Time-Cruisers Serie		

3961	2000	3L2
Johnny Thunder		
Johnny Thunder		
-		
-		

3962	-	3L2
Chief		
Indianerhäuptling		
Also 3L3		
Auch 3L3		

3974	-	3L2
Cowboy with white hat		
Cowboy mit weißem Hut		
Also 3L3		
Auch 3L3		

3974b	-	3L3
Cowboy with brown hat		
Cowboy mit braunem Hut		
Alternate version to 3974 with brown cowboy hat		
Variante zu 3974 mit braunem Cowboy-Hut		

3978	1998	3L2
Majisto the Wizard		
Majisto der Zauberer		
Also exists as 9404; 3L2 version has a printed torso, 3L3 a blank one		
Existiert auch als 9404; 3L2 hat bedruckten Torso, 3L3 ohne Druck		

9409	-	3L2
Islander		
Eingeborener		
-		
-		

-	-	3L2
Spaceport Scientist		
Spaceport Wissenschaftler		
-		
-		

-	2003	3L3
Dr. Kilroy		
Dr. Kilroy		
-		
-		

-	2003	3L3
Dragon Fortress Guard		
Dragon Fortress Guard		
-		
-		

-	2003	3L3
Lord Sam Sanister		
Lord Sam Sanister		
-		
-		

-	2003	3L3
Jing Lee the Wanderer		
Jing Lee the Wanderer		
-		
-		

-	2003	3L3
Pippin Read		
Pippin Read		
-		
-		

-	2003	3L3
Maharaja Lallu		
Maharaja Lallu		
-		
-		

-	2003	3L3
Sherpa Sangye Dorje		
Sherpa Sangye Dorje		
-		
-		

-	2003	3L3
Johnny Thunder II		
Johnny Thunder II		
-		
-		

-	-	3L3
Red Racer		
Roter Rennfahrer		
-		
-		

Keyrings

-	-	3L3
Princess		
Prinzessin		
-		
-		

-	-	3L2
Paradisawoman		
Paradisa-Frau		
-		
-		

-	-	3L3
4 Juniors Truck Driver		
4 Juniors LKW-Fahrer		
Appeared in sets 4652 & 4654 (2003)		
Erschien in Sets 4652 & 4654 (2003)		

-	-	3L3
4 Juniors Fireman		
4 Juniors Feuerwehrmann		
First appeared in set 4601 (2001)		
Erschien zuerst in Set 4601 (2001)		

-	-	3L3
4 Juniors Jack Stone		
4 Juniors Jack Stone		
First appeared in set 4606 (2001)		
Erschien zuerst in Set 4606 (2001)		

-	-	3L3
4 Juniors Policeman		
4 Juniors Polizist		
Appeared in set 4651 (2003)		
Erschien in Set 4651 (2003)		

-	-	4L0
CLIKITS™ girl "Heart"		
CLIKITS™ Figur „Heart“		
Part of set 7533; also available as toy fair promo 2005		
Aus Set 7533; auch als Messepromo 2005 erhältlich		

-	-	4L0
CLIKITS™ girl "Daisy"		
CLIKITS™ Figur „Daisy“		
Part of set 7534, also available as toy fair promo 2005		
Aus Set 7534; auch als Messepromo 2005 erhältlich		

-	-	4L0
CLIKITS™ girl "Star"		
CLIKITS™ Figur „Star“		
Part of set 7535; also available as toy fair promo 2005		
Aus Set 7535; auch als Messepromo 2005 erhältlich		

851584	2006	3L4
Viking		
Wikinger		
-		
-		

851945	2007	3L4
Viking 2		
Wikinger 2		
-		
-		

851035	2004	3L3
Vampire		
Vampir		
-		
-		

850149	2003	3L3
Policeman		
Polizist		
Also known as 3981		
Auch als 3981 bekannt		

851626	2006	3L4
Policeman		
Polizist		
-		
-		

851538	2005	3L4
Agent		
Agent		
-		
-		

851042	2004	3L3
Fireman white helmet		
Feuerwehrmann weißer Helm		
-		
-		

851537	2005	3L4
Fireman silver helmet		
Feuerwehrmann silberner Helm		
The shown tag 850150 might be a labelling error		
Das gezeigte Etikett 850150 könnte ein Auszeichnungsfehler sein		

851746	2006	3L4
Pilot		
Pilot		
-		
-		

Keyrings

850495	2004	3L3
Snowboarder		
Snowboarder		
-		
-		

851658	2006	3L4
Racing driver		
Rennfahrer		
-		
-		

851038	2004	3L3
Snap Lockitt		
Snap Lockitt		
-		
-		

851036	2004	3L4
Ghost		
Gespenst		
-		
-		

850744	2004	3L3
Princess		
Prinzessin		
Also 3L4		
Auch 3L4		

851037	2004	3L3
Roadman		
Straßenarbeiter		
-		
-		

-	2003	3L3
Skateboarder		
Skateboarder		
-		
-		

-	-	3L3
Young Chef		
Junger Koch		
-		
-		

851039	2004	3L3
Chef		
Koch		
-		
-		

851747	2006	3L4
Doctor		
Arzt		
-		
-		

852145	2008	4L0
Indiana Jones		
Indiana Jones		
-		
-		

852146	2008	4L0
Professor Henry Jones		
Professor Henry Jones		
-		
-		

852147	2008	4L0
Pilot (Indiana Jones)		
Pilot (Indiana Jones)		
-		
-		

Keyrings

3913	2000	3L2
Darth Vader™		
Darth Vader™		
Re-released as 850353 in 2005 (3L4)		
Neuauflage 2005: 850353 (3L4)		

3914	2000	3L2
Luke Skywalker™		
Luke Skywalker™		
-		
-		

3922	2000	3L2
Darth Maul™		
Darth Maul™		
-		
-		

3947	2001	3L2
Yoda™		
Yoda™		
Re-released as 850354 in 2005 (3L4)		
Neuauflage 2005: 850354 (3L4)		

3948	2001	3L2
Stormtrooper™		
Stormtrooper™		
Re-released as 850355 in 2005 (still 3L2!)		
Neuauflage 2005: 850355 (immer noch 3L2!)		

-	2002	3L2
C-3PO™		
C-3PO™		
Re-released as 850356 in 2005 (3L4)		
Neuauflage 2005: 850356 (3L4)		

850352	2002	3L2
Snowtrooper™		
Snowtrooper™		
Item code belongs to the 2005 release only		
Nummer gehört nur zur Auflage von 2005		

851044	2004	3L4
R2-D2™		
R2-D2™		
-		
-		

851461	2005	3L4
Obi-Wan Kenobi™		
Obi-Wan Kenobi™		
-		
-		

851462	2005	3L4
Anakin Skywalker™		
Anakin Skywalker™		
-		
-		

851463	2005	3L4
Clone Trooper™		
Clone Trooper™		
-		
-		

851464	2005	3L4
Chewbacca™		
Chewbacca™		
-		
-		

851659	2006	3L4
Boba Fett™		
Boba Fett™		
-		
-		

851683	2006	3L4
Imperial Royal Guard™		
Imperial Royal Guard™		
-		
-		

851937	2007	3L4
Astromech Droid™		
Astromech Droid™		
-		
-		

851938	2007	3L4
Princess Leia™		
Princess Leia™		
-		
-		

852129	2007	3L4
Emperor Palpatine™		
Emperor Palpatine™		
-		
-		

Keyrings

-	2003	3L2
Tracy McGrady, Orlando Magic #1		
Tracy McGrady, Orlando Magic #1		
-		
-		

-	2003	3L2
Vince Carter, Toronto Raptors #15		
Vince Carter, Toronto Raptors #15		
-		
-		

-	2003	3L2
Steve Nash, Dallas Mavericks #13		
Steve Nash, Dallas Mavericks #13		
-		
-		

-	2003	3L2
Dirk Nowitzki, Dallas Mavericks #41		
Dirk Nowitzki, Dallas Mavericks #41		
-		
-		

-	2003	3L2
Antoine Walker, Boston Celtics #8		
Antoine Walker, Boston Celtics #8		
-		
-		

-	2003	3L2
Kobe Bryant, Los Angeles Lakers #8		
Kobe Bryant, Los Angeles Lakers #8		
-		
-		

-	2003	3L2
Allen Iverson, Philadelphia 76ers #3		
Allen Iverson, Philadelphia 76ers #3		
-		
-		

-	2003	3L2
Shaquille O'Neal, L.A. Lakers #34		
Shaquille O'Neal, L.A. Lakers #34		
-		
-		

850630	2004	3L2
Atlanta Hawks 04		
Atlanta Hawks 04		
-		
-		

850687	2004	3L2
Denver Nuggets 04		
Denver Nuggets 04		
-		
-		

850688	2004	3L2
Golden Star Warriors 04		
Golden Star Warriors 04		
-		
-		

850689	2004	3L2
Indiana Pacers 04		
Indiana Pacers 04		
-		
-		

850690	2004	3L2
Los Angeles Clippers 04		
Los Angeles Clippers 04		
-		
-		

850691	2004	3L2
Miami Heat 04		
Miami Heat 04		
-		
-		

850692	2004	3L2
Portland Trailblazers 04		
Portland Trailblazers 04		
-		
-		

850693	2004	3L2
Phoenix Suns 04		
Phoenix Suns 04		
-		
-		

850694	2004	3L2
Washington Wizards 04		
Washington Wizards 04		
-		
-		

850698	2004	3L2
New Orleans Hornets 04		
New Orleans Hornets 04		
-		
-		

Keyrings

850748	2004	3L2
Cleveland Cavaliers 04		
Cleveland Cavaliers 04		
-		
-		

3946	2002	3L2
Soccer Player		
Fußballer		
Re-released 2004 as 850343 (3l3); with football attached		
Neu aufgelegt 2004 als 850343 (3L3); mit Ball angehängt		

851826	2006	3L4
Soccer Player Brazil		
Fußballer Brasilien		
With football attached to third chain		
Mit Fußball an dritter Kette		

851825	2006	3L4
Soccer Player England		
Fußballer England		
With football attached to third chain		
Mit Fußball an dritter Kette		

851656	2006	3L4
Soccer Player Germany		
Fußballer Deutschland		
With football attached to third chain		
Mit Fußball an dritter Kette		

851026	2004	3L3
Mary Jane		
Mary Jane		
Spider-Man theme		
Spider-Man Serie		

851027	2004	3L3
Spider-Man™		
Spider-Man™		
Spider-Man theme - also available as 3L4		
Spider-Man Serie - auch als 3L4 verkauft		

851028	2004	3L3
Dr. Octopus		
Dr. Octopus		
Spider-Man theme		
Spider-Man Serie		

851029	2004	3L3
Mr. Jonah Jameson		
Mr. Jonah Jameson		
Spider-Man theme		
Spider-Man Serie		

851030	2004	3L2
Harry Potter™		
Harry Potter™		
-		
-		

851031	2004	3L2
Hermione Granger		
Hermine Granger		
-		
-		

851032	2004	3L3
Rubeus Hagrid		
Rubeus Hagrid		
Re-release 2007: 851999, two 2x3 rounded tiles (3L4)		
Neuauflage 2007: 851999, zwei Fliesen 2x3 (3L4)		

851033	2004	3L2
Prof. Albus Dumbledore		
Prof. Albus Dumbledore		
-		
-		

851034	2004	3L2
Prof. Severus Snape		
Prof. Severus Snape		
-		
-		

851730	2006	3L4
Wizard		
Zauberer		
-		
-		

851731	2006	3L4
Harry Potter™ II		
Harry Potter™ II		
-		
-		

852000	2007	3L4
Hermione Granger II		
Hermine Granger II		
-		
-		

852091	2007	3L4
Harry Potter™ III		
Harry Potter™ III		
-		
-		

851686	2006	3L4
Batman™		
Batman™		
Batman licensed product		
Batman Lizenzartikel		

851687	2006	3L4
Robin™		
Robin™		
Batman licensed product		
Batman Lizenzartikel		

851814	2006	3L4
Joker™		
Joker™		
Batman licensed product		
Batman Lizenzartikel		

851815	2006	3L4
Catwoman™		
Catwoman™		
Batman licensed product		
Batman Lizenzartikel		

852080	2007	3L4
Two-Face™		
Two-Face™		
Batman licensed product		
Batman Lizenzartikel		

852081	2007	3L4
Penguin™		
Penguin™		
Batman licensed product		
Batman Lizenzartikel		

852090	2007	3L4
Riddler™		
Riddler™		
Batman licensed product		
Batman Lizenzartikel		

852130	2007	3L4
Scarecrow™		
Scarecrow™		
Batman licensed product		
Batman Lizenzartikel		

852131	2007	3L4
Mr. Freeze™		
Mr. Freeze™		
Batman licensed product		
Batman Lizenzartikel		

851729	2006	3L4
Takeshi		
Takeshi		
-		
-		

851818	2006	3L4
Hikaru		
Hikaru		
-		
-		

851838	2006	3L4
SpongeBob™ 1		
SpongeBob™ Schwammkopf™ 1		
SpongeBob licensed product		
SpongeBob Lizenzartikel		

851839	2006	3L4
Patrick™		
Patrick Richard Star™		
SpongeBob licensed product		
SpongeBob Lizenzartikel		

851853	2006	3L4
Mr. Krabs™		
Mr. Eugene H. Krabs™		
SpongeBob licensed product		
SpongeBob Lizenzartikel		

852021	2007	3L4
Squidward Tentacles™		
Thaddäus Johannsen Tentakel™		
SpongeBob licensed product		
SpongeBob Lizenzartikel		

852238	2008	3L4
Mrs. Puff™		
Mrs. Puff™		
SpongeBob licensed product		
SpongeBob Lizenzartikel		

852239	2008	3L4
SpongeBob™ II Spacesuit		
SpongeBob™ Schwammkopf II		
SpongeBob licensed product		
SpongeBob Lizenzartikel		

852240	2008	3L4
Sandy Cheeks™ in Spacesuit		
Sandy Cheeks™ im Weltraumanzug		
SpongeBob licensed product		
SpongeBob Lizenzartikel		

Keyrings

3917	-	-
Red 2x4		
2x4 Stein rot		
One of the most popular key-chains, sold later as 850154 (L3/L4)		
Einer der bekanntesten Anhänger, zuletzt als 850154 (L3/L4) verkauft		

-	-	4L0
Blue 2x3 with black plate		
2x3 Stein blau mit schw. Platte		
-		
-		

-	-	4L0
Metal 2x4		
2x4 Stein aus Gußmetall		
Promotional giveaway to LEGO retailers		
Werbegeschenk an LEGO Einzelhändler		

850152	2003	3/L3 + 4/L0
Blue 2x4		
2x4 Stein blau		
-		
-		

852095	2007	3L3/L4
Yellow 2x4		
2x4 Stein gelb		
Re-release of 850156 (2003)		
Neuauflage von 850156 (2003)		

852096	2007	3L3/L4
Green 2x4		
2x4 Stein grün		
Re-release of 850153 (2003)		
Neuauflage von 850153 (2003)		

852098	2007	3L3/L4
Black 2x4		
2x4 Stein schwarz		
Re-release of 850151 (2003)		
Neuauflage von 850151 (2003)		

852100	2007	3L3/L4
White 2x4		
2x4 Stein weiß		
Re-release of 850155 (2003)		
Neuauflage von 850155 (2003)		

851024	2004	3L3/L4
Pink 2x4		
2x4 Stein pink		
2008 Re-release 852273 is 3L0		
Neue Version 852273 aus 2008 ist Typ 3L0		

851025	2004	3L3
Light purple 2x4		
2x4 Stein hellviolett		
-		
-		

852097	2007	3L4
Orange 2x4		
2x4 Stein orange		
-		
-		

852099	2007	3L4
Lime 2x4		
2x4 Stein hellgrün		
-		
-		

852095	2007	3L4
Yellow 2x4 LEGO®WORLD		
2x4 Stein gelb LEGO®WORLD		
De bouwsteen special LEGOWORLD 2007		
De Bouwsteen Version zur LEGOWORLD 2007		

852274	2008	3L0
Medium Blue 2x4		
2x4 Stein mittelblau		
-		
-		

852445	2008	3L0
Chrome gold 2x4		
2x4 Stein goldfarben		
Chrome gold brick with 50 years logo on tile		
Goldfarbener Stein mit 50 years Logo auf 2x3 Fliese		

852445p	2008	3L0
Chrome gold 2x4 with red plate		
2x4 Stein gold mit roter Platte		
Giveaway at the annual German toy fair 07.-12.02.2008 in Nürnberg		
Giveaway bei der jährlichen Spielwarenmesse in Nürnberg, 07.-12.02.2008		

3966	-	3L2
Tiger		
Tiger		
-		
-		

3965	-	3L2
Lion		
Löwe		
-		
-		

Keyrings

852113	2007	3L4
Millenium Falcon™		
Millenium Falcon™		
Sold as bag charm, too large to be a keychain		
Als Taschenanhänger verkauft, zu groß für einen Schlüsselanhänger		

852114	2007	3L4
Y-Wing Fighter™		
Y-Wing Fighter™		
Sold as bag charm, too large to be a keychain		
Als Taschenanhänger verkauft, zu groß für einen Schlüsselanhänger		

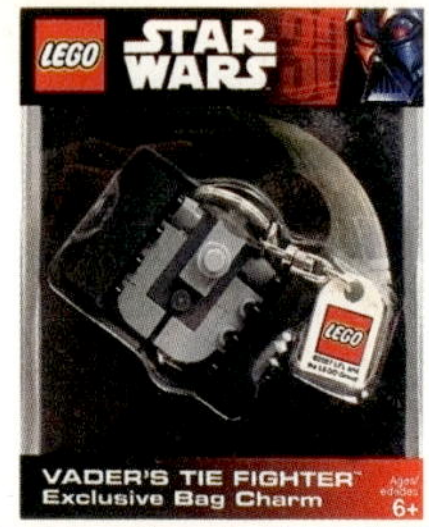

852115	2007	3L4
Vader's Tie Fighter™		
Vaders Tie Fighter™		
Sold as bag charm, too large to be a keychain		
Als Taschenanhänger verkauft, zu groß für einen Schlüsselanhänger		

4676	-	3L0
Police Keychain		
Polizist		
Includes name tag to be filled with printed letter tiles sold as pack 4677		
Mit Namensschild, zu bestücken mit Buchstabenfliesen aus Packung 4677		

-	-	4L0
Key Chain Name Kit		
Anhänger mit Namensbausatz		
Includes printed letter tiles to „write“ your name		
Enthält Buchstabenfliesen für das Namensschild		

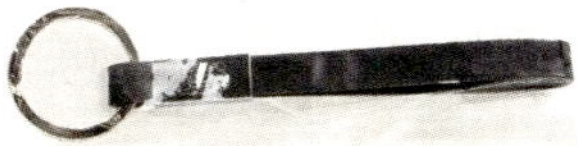

-	-	4L0
Leather strap		
Lederriemen		
Leather strap with an engraved block of solid metal		
Lederriemen mit graviertem Metallsegment		

-	-	4Lx
Japanese Duck		
Japanische Ente		
No real LEGO bricks. LEGO Japan only merchandise		
Keine echten LEGO Steine, Merchandise Artikel von LEGO Japan		

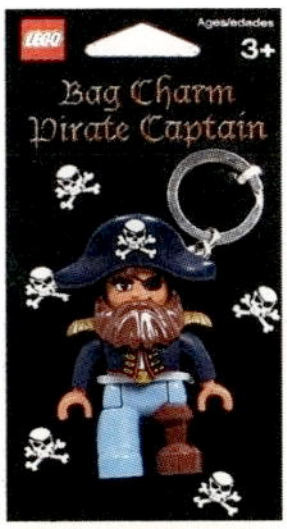

851991	2007	3L2
DUPLO® Pirate Captain Bag Charm		
DUPLO® Piratenkapitän		
-		
-		

851043	2004	3L3
Tiny (from Little Robots)		
Tiny (von Little Robots)		
Figure first appeared in set 7441 (2003)		
Figur erschien erstmals in Set 7441 (2003)		

852266	2008	4L0
Ollie the dragon		
Ollie der Drache		
-		
-		

-	-	4Lx
Solid Metal 2x4 brick		
2x4 Stein massiv Metall		
Engraving "LEGO toy of the century“, employee present		
Mitarbeitergeschenk mit Gravur „LEGO toy of the century“		

-	-	4L2
SCALA™ Cloth bag		
SCALA™ Stofftasche		
-		
-		

850558	2004	4L0
CLIKITS™ Heart Minibag		
CLIKITS™ Kleine Herztasche		
-		
-		

850651	2004	4L0
Rubber strap		
Gummistreifen		
Writing means "BIONICLE®"		
Schriftzug bedeutet „BIONICLE®“		

850652	2004	4L0
Rubber strap		
Gummistreifen		
BIONICLE® logo on pendant		
BIONICLE® Logo auf Anhänger		

-	-	3L0
Kanohi Hau		
Kanohi Hau		
Mask of Toa Onua of set 8532 (2001)		
Maske des Toa Onua aus Set 8532 (2001)		

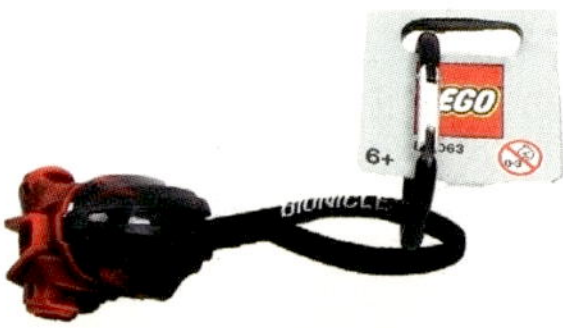

851063	2004	4L0
Mask Kiril		
Maske Kiril		
Appeared in set 8621 (2004)		
Erschien in Set 8621 (2004)		

851098	2004	4L0
Mask Toa Hordika		
Maske Toa Hordika		
Appeared in set 8736 (2005)		
Erschien in Set 8736 (2005)		

851592	2006	4L0
Piraka head with light		
Piraka Kopf mit Licht		
With glow-in-the-dark teeth and light-up eyes		
Mit in der Nacht leuchtenden Zähnen und leuchtenden Augen		

851167	2005	4L0
Toa Hordika Sword		
Toa Hordika Schwert		
First appeared in set 8736 (2005)		
Erschien zuerst in Set 8736 (2005)		

851883	2007	3L4
White CLIKITS™ cat		
Weiße CLIKITS™ Katze		
-		
-		

852182	2008	4L0
Black CLIKITS™ cat		
Schwarze CLIKITS™ Katze		
-		
-		

-	2007	4L0
NXT sound sensor		
NXT Geräuschsensor		
Giveaway from a 2007 NXT promo - sensor is an empty dummy!		
Giveaway für eine NXT Promo 2007. Der Sensor ist nicht funktionsfähig		

-	-	4Lx
Picture frame yellow/red		
Bilderrahmen gelb/rot		
-		
-		

-	-	4Lx
Picture frame green/blue		
Bilderrahmen grün/blau		
-		
-		

-	-	4Lx
Imagination Center souvenir		
Souvenir Imagination Center		
One example for a larger serie with various flat figures attached		
Nur ein Beispiel für eine ganze Serie mit diversen flachen Figuren		

-	-	4L0
Girl head with red cap		
Mädchenkopf mit roter Kappe		
Sold in LEGOLAND® California		
Im LEGOLAND® Kalifornien verkauft		

-	-	1b/L2
Mini pinball game		
Mini Flipperspiel		
Promotes the LEGO® adventures! Magazine		
Bewirbt das LEGO® Adventures! Magazin		

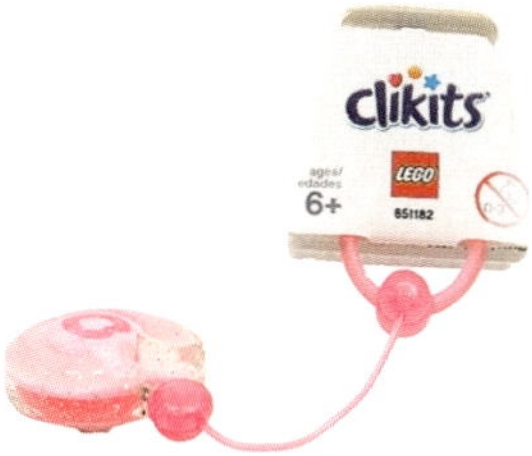

851182	2005	4L0
CLIKITS™ Heart		
CLIKITS™ Herz		
-		
-		

-	-	4L2
Metal LEGO® logo		
LEGO® Logo aus Metall		
Engraving "1 YEAR OF SERVICE"		
Gravur „1 YEAR OF SERVICE“		

-	-	4L2
LEGO® logo, acrylic		
LEGO® Logo, Acryl		
LEGO® logo on both sides		
LEGO® Logo auf beiden Seiten		

-	-	4L2
DUPLO® logo, acrylic		
DUPLO® Logo, Acryl		
LEGO® logo on both sides		
LEGO® Logo auf beiden Seiten		

-	-	4L0
DUPLO® triangle, acrylic		
DUPLO® Dreieck, Acryl		
Zipper from red DUPLO® plush rabbit bag - not intended to be a keychain		
Zipper d. roten DUPLO® Plüschhasen, nicht als Schlüsselanhänger gedacht		

-	-	4L0
LEGOLAND® souvenir, acrylic		
LEGOLAND® Souvenir, Acryl		
-		
-		

-	-	4L2
Professor Owl, acrylic		
Professor Eule, Acryl		
-		
-		

Service-Packs

Service-Packs

No.	Year	English Name	German Name
710	1964	Wooden Storage Box, Large with Bricks	Hölzerne Aufbewahrungsbox, groß mit Steinen
712	1964	Wooden Storage Box with Building Bricks	Hölzerne Aufbewahrungsbox mit Steinen
713	1964	Wooden Storage Box, empty	Hölzerne Aufbewahrungsbox, leer
44	1966	Trees and Bushes	Bäume und Büsche
051	1966	Red assorted Bricks	Rote Steine
052	1966	White assorted Bricks	Weiße Steine
053	1966	Blue assorted Bricks	Blaue Steine
054	1966	Yellow assorted Bricks	Gelbe Steine
055	1966	Trees and Bushes	Bäume und Büsche
056	1966	Assorted Windows and Doors	Fenster und Türen
057	1966	Large Wheels	Große Räder
058	1966	Small Wheels	Kleine Räder
059	1966	Bevelled Red Bricks	Schräge Steine
060	1966	Flat Plates	Flache Platten
061	1966	Green Base Plates	Grüne Bodenplatten
062	1966	White Base Plates	Weiße Bodenplatten
063	1966	Blue Base Plates	Blaue Grundplatten
451	1966	1x6x3 Window, red or white	1x6x3 Fenster, rot oder weiß
452	1966	1x6x2 Window, red or white	1x6x2 Fenster, rot oder weiß
453	1966	1x6x2 shuttered Windows, red or white	1x6x2 verschlossene Fenster, rot oder weiß
454	1966	1x4x2 Window, red or white	1x4x2 Fenster, rot oder weiß
455	1966	1x3x2 Window, red or white	1x3x2 Fenster, rot oder weiß
456	1966	1x2x2 Window, red or white	1x2x2 Fenster, rot oder weiß
457	1966	1x1x2 Window, red or white	1x1x2 Fenster, rot oder weiß
458	1966	1x2x1 Window, red or white	1x2x1 Fenster, rot oder weiß
459	1966	1x1x1 Window, red or white	1x1x1 Fenster, rot oder weiß
460	1966	1x2x3 Door, red or white	1x2x3 Tür, rot oder weiß
486	1966	Extra Bulb for 485	Zusatzlampe für 485
710	1966	Lockable Storage Case	Verschließbarer Aufbewahrungskasten
711	1966	LEGO wooden Storage Box, Empty	LEGO hölzerne Aufbewahrungsbox, leer
47	1967	Gates and fences	Tore und Zaunstücke
890	1967	Lockable Storagebox	Verschließbarer Aufbewahrungskasten
45	1969	Clear Assorted Bricks & red 10x10 Baseplates	Klare Steine & 10x10 Bodenplatten
46	1969	Assorted white bricks and flat plates	Weiße Steine und flache Platten
48	1969	Blue/yellow Assorted Bricks	Blaue/gelbe Steine
49	1969	Assorted Windows, Doors and Trees	Fenster, Türen und Bäume
50	1969	Lighting Device Set	Leuchtsteinset
64	1969	White/blue Base Plates	Weiße/blaue Grundplatten
65	1969	Garage Door	Garagentor
103	1969	4.5V Motor Set with Rubber Tracks	Batteriemotor, blau
441	1969	Wheel Accessories	Räderzubehör
444	1969	Truck Accessories	Truckzubehör
501	1969	Empty wooden Storage Box	Leere hölzerne Aufbewahrungsbox
702	1969	12V Electric Motor with Accessories	12V Elektromotor mit Rädern und Zubehör
104	1970	Replacement Motor	Austauschmotor
703	1970	Loose 12V Electric Motor	Austauschmotor
705	1970	Motor Bushings	Radbuchsen
707	1970	Tile parts Pack	Fliesenteile
708	1970	2m Extension Cord for Electric Points	2m Verlängerungskabel für Weichen
793	1972	Storage Box, blue	Tragebox, blau
785	1973	Red Box	Roter Aufbewahrungsbehälter
791	1973	Red Storage Box	Rote Aufbewahrungsbox
996	1973	Wire with Banana Plug	Kabel mit Bananenstecker
789	1974	Suitcase with Trays, red	Koffer mit Einsatz, rot
790	1974	Suitcase with Trays, blue	Koffer mit Einschubfächern, blau
1	1977	Wooden Storage Box	Hölzerne Aufbewahrungsbox

No.	Year	English Name	German Name
1	1977	Starter Set Italy	Anfängerset Italien
1	1977	4.5V Replacement Motor	4,5V Ersatzmotor
2	1977	Motor Bushings	Motorgehäuse
2	1977	Idea Book No. 2	Ideenbuch Nr. 2
3	1977	4.5V Motor Battery Box	4,5V Motor Batteriebox
4	1977	4.5V Motor Battery Cables	4,5V Motor Batteriekabel
5	1977	Treads	Laufflächen
6	1977	4.5V Battery Train Wagon	4,5V Batterie Zugwaggon
7	1977	Train Signal with Ties	Zugsignal mit Schwellen
8	1977	Magnetic Train Couplers with Plates	Magnetische Zugkupplungen mit Platten
9	1977	Magnetic Train Couplers	Magnetische Zugkupplungen
10	1977	Locomotive Wheels	Lokomotivräder
11	1977	Locomotive Traction Tires	Antriebsräder für Lokomotive
12	1977	Wheel Bearings for Locomotives	Radaufhängung für Lokomotiven
13	1977	Train Motor Plate with Buffers	Motorplatte mit Puffer für Züge
14	1977	Train Motor Plate with Coupler	Zugmotorplatte mit Kupplungen
15	1977	Lighting Brick (2 X 2)	Leuchtstein (2 x 2)
16	1977	Length of Chain Links	Kettenglieder
17	1977	Axles with Connectors	Achsen mit Verbindungsstücken
18	1977	Ship Keel	Schiffskiel
19	1977	Locomotive Piston Assemblies	Lokomotivkolben
20	1977	Cross Country 42mm Tires	42mm Reifen
21	1977	Propellers, Wheels and Rotors	Propeller, Reifen und Rotoren
22	1977	Horizontal Hinges	Horizontalscharniere
23	1977	Ball/Socket Coupling/Unit	Kugel-Kupplungen
24	1977	Digger Buckets	Baggerschaufeln
25	1977	Steam Shovel/Plates with Holes	Löffelbagger/Lochplatten
26	1977	12V Motor	12V Motor
27	1977	Train Contact Bricks	Zugverbindungssteine
28	1977	Train Contact Plate with Cables	Zugverbindungsplatten mit Kabel
29	1977	4.5V Motor	4,5V Motor
30	1977	Small Turntables / Gear Racks	Kleine Drehplatten/Zahnstangen
31	1977	Universal Joint/Connectors	Verbindungssteine
32	1977	Small Tire/Large Tire	Kleine/große Reifen
33	1977	Small/Large Red Spoked Wheel	Kleine/große rote Speichenräder
34	1977	Sloped convex Corner Bricks, Red (2 X 2)	Konvex geneigte Ecksteine, rot (2 x 2)
35	1977	Motor Case with Screws	Motorgehäuse mit Schrauben
36	1977	Small Tractor Tires	Kleine Traktorreifen
37	1977	Small Wheels	Kleine Reifen
38	1977	Open Stud Round Bricks (1 X 1)	Rundstein (1 x 1)
39	1977	Motor Gearbox	Motorgetriebebox
40	1977	Axle Brick with Small Wheels (2 X 2)	Achsenstein mit kleinen Rädern (2 x 2)
41	1977	Train Wagon Wheels in Red	Waggonräder, rot
42	1977	Motor Case/Lower Part	Motorgehäuse Unterseite
786	1977	Storage cloth	Aufbewahrungsbeutel
870	1977	4.5V Motor with Battery Box	4,5V Motor mit Batteriekasten
871	1977	Gears, Axes, Beams	Zahnräder, Achsen, Balken
1101	1977	Replacement 4.5V Motor	4,5V Austauschmotor
1102	1977	Motor Bushes	Motorbuchsen
1103	1977	Battery Box	Batteriekasten
1104	1977	Battery Cables (75cm)	Batteriekabel (75 cm)
1105	1977	Crawler Tracks	Gummiraupen
1106	1977	Battery Tender	Batterietender
1107	1977	Signal and Direction-Change Switch	Signal mit Umschaltstift
1108	1977	Magnetic Couplings	Magnetkupplungen
1109	1977	Magnetic Couplings for Railway Car	Magnetkupplungen für Waggons

No.	Year	English Name	German Name
1110	1977	Train Wheels	Zugräder
1111	1977	Rubber Rims for Locomotive Wheels	Haftreifen für Lokomotivräder
1112	1977	Train Sliding Wheel Blocks	Vor- oder Nachlaufachsen
1113	1977	Motor Frame and Couplers	Motorrahmenplatte und Koppler
1114	1977	Motor Frame	Motorrahmenplatte
1115	1977	4.5V Lighting Brick (2x2)	4,5V Leuchtstein (2x2)
1116	1977	Chain Links, small	Kettenglieder, klein
1117	1977	Axes and Bushes	Achsen und Buchsen
1118	1977	Boat Weight, red	Schiffsgewicht, rot
1119	1977	Locomotive Piston Assemblies	Dampfventile, Zugstangen, Kurbelglieder
1120	1977	Tires (42mm)	Reifen (42 mm)
1121	1977	Propellors, Wheels and Rotor Unit	Propeller, Flugzeugräder und Rotoreinheit
1122	1977	Hinges	Scharniere
1123	1977	Ball and Socket Couplings, articulated Joint	Kugelkupplungen, bewegliche Verbindung
1124	1977	Digger Bucket	Baggerschaufel
1125	1977	Crane Grab	Baggerklaue mit Aufhängung
1150	1977	Replacement Motor 12V	Austauschmotor 12V
1151	1977	Train Power Pick-up Blocks	Schleifer
1152	1977	Electric Wire	Elektrokabel
788	1978	Service Box, filled	Servicekasten, gefüllt
960	1978	Expert Builder Power Pack	Experten Bauset
961	1978	Expert Builder Parts Pack	Bauset für Experten
1175	1978	4.5V Motor	4,5V Motor
1176	1978	Gear Racks and Turntables	Zahnstangen und Drehscheiben
15	1979	Space Mini Figures	Astronauten
874	1979	Yellow Beams and Connector Bushes	Gelbe Lochbalken und Verbindungsbuchsen
875	1979	Red Beams and Connector Bushes	Rote Lochbalken und Verbindungsbuchsen
876	1979	Blue Beams and Connector Bushes	Blaue Lochbalken und Verbindungsbuchsen
877	1979	Steering-Accessoires	Elemente für Lenk-Konstruktionen
878	1979	Axes, Pistons and Connection Rod	Achsen, Kolben und Pleuelstangen
879	1979	Gears, Axes, Beams and Chain Links	Zahnrädern,Achsen und Kettengliedern
880	1979	12V Motor with Supplements	12V Motor mit Zubehör
1	1980	Bulldozer Chainlinks	Bulldozer Kettenglieder
6	1980	Motor Wires	Motorkabel
7	1980	Battery Box	Batteriebox
12	1980	Blue Space Elements	Blaue Weltraumelemente
13	1980	Grey Space Elements	Graue Weltraumelemente
1002	1980	Play Table - 2 Seats	Spieltisch - 2 Sitze
1130	1980	Storage Folder for Building Instructions	Sammelmappe für Bauanleitungen
2	1981	Digger Bucket Assembly	Verschiedene Baggerschaufeln
5	1981	Hinges	Scharniere
8	1981	Replacement 4.5V Motor	Austauschmotor 4,5V Motor
9	1981	Trees and Flowers	Bäume und Blumen
10	1981	Trees and Signs	Bäume und Schilder
11	1981	Police Pack	Polizei Set
14	1981	Expert Builder Parts	Expertenbauteile
1060	1981	Road Plates and Signs	Straßenplatten und Schilder
1132	1981	Hinges	Scharniere
1133	1981	Brick Hinges	Scharniere
1134	1981	Battery Wagon	Batteriewaggon
1135	1981	Battery Cable Kit	Einzelstecker mit Kabel
1136	1981	Buffers, Magnetic Couplers	Puffer, Magnetkupplungen
1137	1981	Train Couplings	Kupplungen für Eisenbahnwagen
1138	1981	Replacement Rubber Wheel Treads for Trains	Ersatzhaftreifen für Züge
1139	1981	Motor-Mount Plate with Magnetic Couplers	Motorrahmen mit Magnetkupplungen
1140	1981	12V Light Bricks	12V Leuchtsteine

No.	Year	English Name	German Name
1141	1981	Wheel Bricks with small red Train-Wheels	Achtersteine mit kleinen roten Rädern
1142	1981	Wheel Bricks with small black Train-Wheels	Achtersteine mit kleinen schwarzen Rädern
1143	1981	Wheel Bricks with large red Train-Wheels	Achtersteine mit großen roten Zugrädern
1144	1981	Train Baseplate	Zuggrundplatte
1145	1981	Bogie Plate	Zugdrehplatte
1146	1981	Pushrods, Cylinder Housings	Schubstangen, Zylindergehäuse
1147	1981	Light Prisms & Holder, red/yellow Light Covers	Lichtführungen, Scheinwerfereinsatz, rot/gelb
1148	1981	Differential	Achsgetriebe
1149	1981	Bulldozer Chainlinks	Bulldozer Kettenglieder
1197	1981	Crown Gears (Old Style)	Zahnkränze (Alte Variante)
1215	1981	Train Motor 4.5V Type II Lower Housing	Gehäuseunterteil für 4,5V Zugmotor Typ II
2	1982	X-Large Tires And Hubs	Extragroße Reifen und Felgen
3	1982	Doors und Fences	Türen und Zäune
4	1982	Propellers und Wheels	Propeller und Räder
781	1982	Storage Case	Aufbewahrungsbehälter
1003	1982	Supplementary Storage Trays	Ergänzungslagerbretter
1006	1982	Storage Stand	Aufbewahrungsgestell
1014	1982	Universal Joints	Universelle Verbindungen
1201	1982	Hooks	Abschlepphaken
1205	1982	Keys for Wind-Up Motor	Schlüssel für Aufziehmotor
1206	1982	Round Bricks (2x2), white	Rundsteine (2x2), weiß
1207	1982	Turntables (4x4), red	Drehscheiben (4x4), rot
1208	1982	Inverted Slope Bricks, assorted, red	Seitenverkehrte schräge Dachsteine, rot
1209	1982	Fences and Gates	Zäune und Türen
1210	1982	Winch Block and Hook Assembly	Ziehwinde und Halterung
1211	1982	Space Stands and Brackets	Landebeine und Winkelklammern
1212	1982	Rocket Tops, black	Raketenspitzen, schwarz
1213	1982	Radar Disks	Radarschüsseln
1216	1982	Semaphores wiht Feet	Signalmaste mit Füßen
1217	1982	Girder Beams and Plates, yellow	Lochbalken und -platten, gelb
1218	1982	Girder Beams and Plates, blue	Lochbalken und -platten, blau
1219	1982	Girder Beams and Plates, red	Lochbalken und -platten, rot
1220	1982	Girder Beams and Plates, black	Lochbalken und -platten, schwarz
1221	1982	Beams, yellow	Lochbalken, gelb
1222	1982	Beams, blue	Lochbalken, blau
1223	1982	Beams, black	Lochbalken, schwarz
1224	1982	Beams, red	Lochbalken, rot
1225	1982	Assortment of Axles	Verschiedene Achsen
1226	1982	Tractor Tires and Hubs	Traktorreifen und -felgen
1227	1982	Gear Wheel Assortment	Verschiedene Getrieberäder
1228	1982	Differential Gear Housing	Gehäuse für Differentialgetriebe
1229	1982	Small Technical Chainlinks	Kleine Kettenglieder
1230	1982	Bulldozer Chainlinks	Bulldozer Kettenglieder
1231	1982	X-Large Tires and Hubs	Extra große Reifen und Felgen
1232	1982	Toggle Joints and Connectors	Umschaltverbindungen und Anschlussbuchsen
15	1983	Castle Mini Figures	Ritterfiguren
1010	1983	Supplementary Bricks for 1001	Ergänzungsbausteine für 1001
1126	1983	Jack Complete Assembly, blue	Wagenheber, blau
1154	1983	Battery Control Unit	Batterie Kontrolleinheit
1231	1983	Replacement Gearbox for Electric Motor	Ersatzgetriebegehäuse für elektrischen Motor
16	1984	Transparent Bricks	Durchsichtige Steine
782	1984	Storage Case	Roter Aufbewahrungsbehälter
1204	1984	Fences, red and black	Zaunteile, rot und schwarz
1214	1984	Upper Part of Motorhome for 4.5V/12V Trainmotor	Gehäuseoberteil für 4,5V/12V Zugmotor
1233	1984	Axle Assortment	Verschiedene Achsen
1234	1984	Gear Wheel Assortment	Verschiedene Antriebsräder

No.	Year	English Name	German Name
1235	1984	Differential Gear Housing	Gehäuse für Differentialgetriebe
1236	1984	Wheels	Reifen
1267	1984	Shock Absorbers	Stoßdämpfer
17	1985	Hinges	Scharniere
18	1985	Trees and Signs	Bäume und Schilder
710	1985	Baseplate Assortment	Verschiedene Grundplatten
759	1985	Storage Cabinet	Aufbewahrungsbehälter
760	1985	Storage Cabinet	Aufbewahrungsbehälter
783	1985	Storage Case	Aufbewahrungsbehälter
1160	1985	Pneumatic Tubing, 50mm grey and 100mm black	Luftschlauch, 50mm grau und 100mm schwarz
1161	1985	Pneumatic Pump Cylinder (4,8cm)	Pneumatische Zylinderpumpe (4,8cm)
1162	1985	Pneumatic Pump Cylinder, yellow	Pneumatischer Zylinderkolben, gelb
1163	1985	Pneumatic Piston Cylinder (6cm)	Pneumatischer Kolbenzylinder (6 cm)
1164	1985	Pneumatic 2 Way Valve and Nonreturn Valve	Pneumatisches Zweiwege- und Einwegventil
1203	1985	Turntables (4x4), Turntables (2x2)	Drehscheiben (4x4), Drehscheiben (2x2)
1239	1985	Remote Control for Electric Points	Fernbedienung für automatische Weichen
1241	1985	Digger Bucket Assembly	Bagger Zubehör
1314	1985	Stop Bushes and Small Pulleys	Muffe und schmale Rolle
1315	1985	Piston Rods	Kolbenstangen
1316	1985	Connector Pegs	Verbindungsstöpsel
1317	1985	Small Chain Links	Kleine Kettenglieder
1318	1985	Small Gears and Crown Wheels	Kleine Zahn- und Kronräder
1319	1985	Large Gear Wheels	Große Zahnräder
1320	1985	Differential and Bevel Gears	Achs- und Kegelradgetriebe
1321	1985	Worm Gears and Gear Racks	Schneckengetriebe und Zahnstangen
1322	1985	Pulleys, Tires and Steering Wheels	Flaschenzüge, Reifen und Lenkräder
1323	1985	Hubs and Tyres	Felgen und Reifen
1324	1985	Rubber Bands and String	Gummiringe und Kordel
1325	1985	Small Cross Axles	Kleine Kreuzachsen
1326	1985	Large Cross Axles	Große Kreuzachsen
1327	1985	Red/black Plates	Rote/schwarze Platten
1328	1985	Red/black Plates	Rote/schwarze Platten
1329	1985	Red/black Plates	Rote/schwarze Platten
1330	1985	Red/black Plates	Rote/schwarze Platten
1331	1985	Red/blue Bricks	Rote/blaue Bausteine
1332	1985	Red/blue Beams	Rote/blaue Balken
1333	1985	Red/blue Beams	Rote/blaue Balken
1334	1985	Motors (4.5V)	Motoren (4,5V)
1335	1985	Battery Boxes (4.5V)	Batteriekasten (4,5V)
1336	1985	Pole Reverser Switches for Battery Box	Polumschalter für Batteriekästen
1337	1985	Connecting Leads	Anschlussadern
1338	1985	Angles, Swivels,Turntables	Winkelstücke, Drehpunkte, Drehscheiben
1339	1985	Joints, Pistons, round Plates	Anschlüsse, Kolben, runde Platten
1340	1985	Weight Elements and Bricks	Gewichte und Bausteine
1341	1985	Building Plates, green	Bauplatten, grün
6213	1985	Replacement Gearbox for Electric Motor	Ersatz Getriebebox für elektrischen Motor
70012	1985	Rubber Bands	Gummiringe
73129	1985	Shocks Absorbers	Stoßdämpfer
1168	1986	Battery Box	Batteriekasten
1169	1986	Bogie Plates	Drehplatten
1170	1986	Replacement Train Battery Tender	Austauschbatterietender
1171	1986	Lighting Brick with red and blue Globes	Leuchtstein mit roten und grünen Lichtern
1172	1986	Colored Globes	Farbige Leuchten
1174	1986	Motorhome for Basic Motor 4.5V/Train Motor 12V	Motorgehäuse für Basismotor 4,5V/Zugmotor 12V
1178	1986	Siren, black	Martinshorn, schwarz
1179	1986	Replacement Space Siren	Ersatzmartinshorn für die Raumfahrt

No.	Year	English Name	German Name
1240	1986	Hinges and Tilted Bearings, light grey	Scharniere und schräge Aufhängungen, hellgrau
1242	1986	Crane Grab and Winch	Kranschaufel und Winde
1243	1986	Hinges and Couplings	Scharniere und Kupplungen
1244	1986	Runway Plates	Straßenplatten
1245	1986	T- and Intersection Plates	T-Kreuzungen und Kreiselbodenplatten
1342	1986	Electric Switches and Tiles	Elektrische Schalter und Platten
1343	1986	Opto Sensores (4.5V) and Discs	Optosensoren (4,5V) und Scheiben
1344	1986	Light Bricks (4.5V)	Leuchtbausteine (4,5V)
1345	1986	Pinions, Pegs, Axles and Nuts	Zahnradgetriebe, Klammern, Achsen u. Muttern
356	1987	Basic Building Set with Storage Case	Basisbaukasten mit Aufbewahrungskoffer
757	1987	Red Storage Tray	Roter Sortiereinsatz
758	1987	Blue Storage Tray	Blauer Sortiereinsatz
1339	1987	Technic Parts	Technikteile
1346	1987	Touch Sensors (4.5V)	Berührungssensoren (4,5V)
1347	1987	Leads (4.5V), Spirals	Anschlusskabel (4,5V), Spiralen
1348	1987	Base Plates, grey	Bodenplatten, grau
5000	1987	Replacement 4.5V Motor	Austauschmotor 4,5V
5001	1987	Wheel Bushes for 4.5V Basic Motor	Motorbuchsen für 4,5V Basismotor
5002	1987	Rubber Chain Tracks	Fahrzeugketten aus Gummi
5003	1987	Light Bricks, 4.5V	Leuchtsteine, 4,5V
5004	1987	Keys for Windup Motor	Schlüssel für Aufziehmotor
5005	1987	Battery Box 4,5V, grey	Batteriekasten 4,5V, grau
5006	1987	Replacement 2-Piece Battery Motor Housing	Ersatzmotorgehäuse
5007	1987	Basic Motor 4.5V	Basismotor 4,5V
5031	1987	Propellers, Wheels, Rotor Unit	Propeller, Räder, Rotoreinheit
5032	1987	Jack	Wagenheber
5033	1987	1x4 Lighting Brick and 4 Colour Globes	Blinkelement 1x4, 4-farbige Hauben
5034	1987	1x2 Lighting Brick and 4 Colour Globes	Blinkelement 1x2, 4-farbige Hauben
5035	1987	Town Siren, 2x2	Stadtsirene, 2x2
5036	1987	Space Siren, 2x2	Weltraumsirene, 2x2
5039	1987	Monorail Stop/Reverse Switch	Umschalter mit Fahrtrichtungsanzeiger
5061	1987	Connector Leads, 75cm and 25cm	Verbindungskabel, 75cm und 25cm
5062	1987	Shunting Trip Posts and Signal	Haltesignal- und Umschaltbalken
5063	1987	Power Supply Rail	Anschlussschiene
5064	1987	Locomotive Wheels	Lokomotivräder
5065	1987	3m Wiring and 2 Two-Way Plug	3m Kabel und Doppelstecker
5066	1987	Magnetic Train Coupler	Magnetische Zugkupplung
5067	1987	Rubber Wheel Rims, grey	Gummihaftreifen, grau
5068	1987	Motor Frame and Coupling	Motorrahmenplatte und Kupplung
5069	1987	12V Lighting Bricks	12V Leuchtsteine
5070	1987	Wheel Sets, black	Zugradsets, schwarz
5071	1987	Wheel Sets, large, red	Zugradsets, groß, rot
5072	1987	Wagonplate, 6x28 Studs	Waggongrundplatte, 6x28 Knöpfe
5073	1987	Light Transmitting Elements for Train Sets	Lichtelemente für Zugbeleuchtung
5074	1987	Boogie Plates, black	Zuggrundplatte, schwarz
5075	1987	Battery Tender, red	Batterietender, rot
5077	1987	Sliding Gates and Rails	Schiebetore und Führungsschienen
5100	1987	Battery Rod 4.5V	4,5V Batteriestab
5101	1987	4.5V Motor with Technical Sets	4,5V Motor mit technischen Sets
5102	1987	Hose, Pneumatic	Pneumatische Schläuche
5103	1987	Pneumatic Spring Cylinder, 48 mm, red	Pneumatischer Zylinder mit Feder 48 mm, rot
5104	1987	Pneumatic Cylinder, 48mm, yellow	Pneumatischer Zylinder, 48mm, gelb
5105	1987	Pneumatic Cylinder, 64mm, yellow	Pneumatischer Zylinder, 64mm, gelb
5106	1987	Two-Way Valve and Non-Return Valve	Zwei-Weg- und Einweg-Ventil
5140	1987	Bricks, red	Steine, rot
5141	1987	Bricks, blue	Bausteine, blau

Service-Packs

No.	Year	English Name	German Name
5142	1987	Bricks, white	Bausteine, weiß
5143	1987	Bricks, yellow	Bausteine, gelb
5144	1987	Bricks, black	Bausteine, schwarz
5145	1987	Bricks, grey	Bausteine, grau
5146	1987	Plates, blue	Platten, blau
5147	1987	Plates, red	Platten, rot
5148	1987	Wheels	Räder
5149	1987	Doors and Windows	Türen und Fenster
5151	1987	Roof Bricks, red, 45 Degrees	Dachbausteine, rot, 45 Grad
5152	1987	Roof Bricks, 25 Degrees, red	Dachbausteine, 25 Grad, rot
5161	1987	Inverted Slope Bricks	Schrägsteine, negativ, 45 Grad
5162	1987	Fences and Hinges	Zaunelemente und Scharniere
5163	1987	Turntables, 4x4 and 2x2	Drehscheiben, 2x2 und 2x4
5167	1987	Hinges, Tilting Bearings	Schanieren und Kipplager
5168	1987	Digger Bucket Assembly	Baggerschaufelset
5169	1987	Crane Set Assembly	Kranzubehör
5171	1987	Decorated Elements	Verzierte Elemente
5172	1987	Rocket Stages	Racketenstufen
5173	1987	Space Jet and Wings	Weltraumjet und Tragflächen
5174	1987	Wheels and Bearings	Räder und Lager
5175	1987	Space Elements	Raumfahrtelemente
5176	1987	Bricks, transparent	Bausteine, durchsichtig
5177	1987	Town and Space Accessoires	Stadt- und Weltraum-Zubehör
5178	1987	Wheels, Motors, Propeller Motors	Räder, Motoren, Propellermotoren
5179	1987	Hinges and Couplings	Scharniere und Kupplungen
5180	1987	T-Junction, Circle (Airport)	T-Kreuzung, Kreisverkehr (Flughafen)
5181	1987	Runways, straight (Airport)	Runway Platten, gerade (Flughafen)
5200	1987	Signal Masts and Feet	Signalmast mit Füßen
5231	1987	Beams and Plates with Holes, yellow	Lochbalken u. -platten, gelb
5232	1987	Beams and Plates, blue	Balken und Platten, blau
5234	1987	Beams and Plates with Holes, black	Lochbalken u. -platten, schwarz
5236	1987	Beams, blue	Lochbalken, blau
5237	1987	Bricks with Holes, black	Lochbalken, schwarz
5238	1987	Bricks with Holes, red	Lochbalken, rot
5239	1987	Axles Assortment	Sortiment von Achsen
5240	1987	Wheel Hubs and Tire	Radnaben und Reifen
5241	1987	Gear Rack and Wheels	Zahnstangen und Räder
5242	1987	Differential Housing and Steering Elements	Differentialgehäuse und Steuerungselemente
5243	1987	Chain links, small	Kettenglieder, schmal
5244	1987	Bulldozer Chainlinks	Kettenglieder, für Bulldozer
5246	1987	Tires (81mm) with Hubs	Reifen (81mm) und Felgen
5247	1987	Toggle Joints and Connectors	Verbindungselemente
5248	1987	Tires (62 mm) with Hubs	Reifen (62 mm) und Felgen
5249	1987	Beams and Plates with Holes, red	Lochbalken u. -platten, rot
5250	1987	Beams with Holes, yellow	Lochbalken, gelb
5251	1987	Small Shock Absorbers	Kleine Stoßdämpfer
5270	1987	Tires (43 mm) with Hubs	Reifen (43 mm) mit Felgen
5289	1987	Toggle Joints and Connectors	Verbindungselemente
701	1988	Hinges	Scharniere
5037	1988	Current Carrying Plates	Stromleitplatten
5038	1988	9V Battery Box	9V Batteriekasten
5040	1988	Monorail 9V Motor	9V Motor für Monorail
5041	1988	Wire for 9V (9cm)	9V Verbindungskabel m. Anschlussplatten (9 cm)
5076	1989	Plates 2x8	Platten 2x8
5079	1989	Change-Over Unit	Wechseleinheit für E-Weichen
5080	1989	Remote Control for Switch	Fernbedienung für E-Weichen

No.	Year	English Name	German Name
5081	1989	Remote Control for Signal	Fernbedienung für Signal
5082	1989	Flash Light Unit	Blinklicht für Bahnübergang
5083	1989	Remote Control for Crossing	Fernbedienung für Bahnübergang
5084	1989	12V Light Brick	12V Lichtstein
5085	1989	Power Supply Rail with Socket	Anschlussschiene mit Fassung
5095	1989	Fence	Zaun
5096	1989	Brick 2x2, Milwing	Mühlenflügel mit Haltestein 2x2
5107	1989	Pneumatic Pump (New System)	Pneumatische Druckpumpe
5108	1989	Pneumatic Cylinder, 48mm	Pneumatischer Zylinder m. 2 Anschlüssen, 48mm
5109	1989	Pneumatic Tubes and Pieces	Pneumatische Schläuche und Teile
5182	1989	Hinges and Couplings	Scharniere und Kupplungen
5183	1989	Hinges and Couplings	Scharniere und Kupplungen
5184	1989	Castle Equipment	Ritter Zubehör
5185	1989	Dustbins with Lids	Mülltonnen mit Deckeln
5186	1989	Fence	Zaunelemente
5187	1989	Bricks with Groove and Garage Panels	Bausteine mit Nut und Garagenelemente
5188	1989	Seats, Steering Wheels and Windscreens	Sitze, Lenkräder und Windschutzscheiben
5189	1989	Ladder (black and grey)	Leitern (schwarz und grau)
5190	1989	Seats and Windscreens	Sitze und Windschutzscheiben
5191	1989	Balloone Tires	Ballonreifen
5192	1989	Cypress	Zypressen
5193	1989	Sloping Frames	Schrägständer
5194	1989	Hinge Plate, Fork-Lift	Scharniere und Gabel für Gabelstapler
5195	1989	Assorted Arches	Gemischte Bögen
5196	1989	Ladders, Crane, Crane Hook	Kranaufsatz, Kranhaken, Leitern
5197	1989	Lampholder, Plate with Holders	Lampenhalter, Platten mit Haltern
5198	1989	Small Plates, Disks and Cones	Kleine Platten, Drehscheiben und Düsen
5199	1989	Mini Antennas and Stick	Mini-Antennen und Schalthebel
5253	1989	Cross Axles	Kreuzachsen
5254	1989	Cross Axles	Kreuzachsen
5255	1989	Connector Pegs	Doppelverbinder
5256	1989	Suspension Pack	Aufhängungen
5257	1989	Connector Pegs, Toggle Joints, Wheels	Doppelverbinder, Verbindungselemente, Räder
5258	1989	Crown/Point Wheels, Gear Racks, Worm Gears	Kronräder, Zahnstangen, Schnecken, Zahnräder
5259	1989	Universal Joint, Rubber Bands and Wheels	Univ. Verbindungselem., Gummibänder, Räder
5260	1989	Connecting Rods and Stop Bushes	Verbindungspleul und Muffe
5261	1989	Plates and Gear Racks	Platten und Zahnstangen
5262	1989	Gear Wheels	Zahnräder
5263	1989	Universal Joint, Differential Housing, Point Wheels	Verbindungen, Differentialgehäuse, Zahnräder
5264	1989	Rotors and Bush/Cross Axles	Rotoren, Muffen mit Kreuzachsen
5265	1989	Tires (24-43 mm) with Spoked Hubs	Reifen (24-43 mm) mit Speichenfelgen
5266	1989	Gear Racks, Gear Wheels and Pulley Wheels	Zahnstangen und Zahnräder und Rillenscheiben
821	1990	Brick Sparator	Elementetrenner
5008	1990	Element Separator	Elementetrenner
5009	1990	Building Plate 16x32, yellow	Bauplatte 16x32, gelb
5010	1990	Building Plate 16x32, green	Bauplatte 16x32, grün
5110	1990	Cross Axles and Nuts	Gewindestangen, Muttern und Hebel
5110	1990	Pneumatic Value Pack	Pneumatisches Kombiset
5111	1990	9V Wire (128cm)	9V Verbindungskabel mit Platten (128cm)
5112	1990	Loading Grabs Crane Hook	Baggerschaufeln und Kranhaken
5113	1990	Airscrew	Propeller
5150	1990	Pirates Elements	Piraten Elemente
5158	1990	T-Junction, Circle Plates	T-Kreuzung, Landekreuz
5159	1990	Straight Runway	Landebahn gerade
5042	1991	Space Light and Radar Plates, Disks, Cones	Licht und Radarplatten, Haftscheiben, Kegel
5043	1991	Mini Antennas, Control Sticks and Antennas	Miniantennen, Greifarme und Antennen

Service-Packs

No.	Year	English Name	German Name
5044	1991	Plateau, Approach for Habour	Auffahrrampe, Hafenrampen
5045	1991	Magnets, Magnetholder	Magnete, Halterungen
5046	1991	Hub, Tire and Wheelsuspension	Reifen, Felgen und Radaufhängung
5099	1991	Pneumatic Valve	Pneumatisches Ventil
5114	1991	9V Motor	9V Motor
5115	1991	9V Battery Box	9V Batteriebox
5118	1991	Flex System	Flex-System
5153	1991	Propellers, Wheels, Rotor Unit	Propeller, Flugzeugräder, Rotor-Einheit
5154	1991	Decorated Elements	Verzierte Elemente
5155	1991	Sloping Frames, Space Wings, Motors, Seats	Tragflächen, Düsen, Motoren, Sitze
5156	1991	Bricks, transparent	Bausteine, durchsichtig
5157	1991	Town and Space Tools	Werkzeuge für Stadt und Raumfahrt
5164	1991	Hinges and Couplings	Scharniere und Kupplungen
5165	1991	Hinges	Scharniere und Wipplager
5166	1991	Lampholders, Plates with Holder	Leuchtenhalter, Platten mit Halter
5271	1991	Tires (50 mm) with Hubs	Reifen (50 mm) mit Felgen
5272	1991	Cylinder Motor	Zylindermotor
5300	1991	Electric Train Motor	Motor für elektrische Eisenbahn
846	1992	Lighting Bricks	Leuchtsteine
5011	1992	9V Basic Motor	9V Basismotor
5030	1992	Signs for use with Lighting Bricks 9V	Schilder für 9 V Leuchtsteine
5097	1992	3 Sleepingbacks	3 Schlafsäcke
5098	1992	Toolo Screwdriver	Toolo Schraubenzieher
5116	1992	Pneumatic Cylinder, 32mm	Pneumatischer Zylinder, 32mm
5273	1992	Tires (62 mm) with Hubs	Reifen (62 mm) mit Felgen
5274	1992	Tires with Hubs	Reifen mit Felgen
5301	1992	Waggonplate 6x28	Waggonplatten
5302	1992	Bogieplates, black	Drehgestellplatten, schwarz
5303	1992	Buffers, Magnets and Couplers	Puffer, Magneten und Kupplungen
5304	1992	Wheelsets	Zugräder
5305	1992	Connectionwire	Eisenbahn-Anschlusskabel
5306	1992	Plates (2x2) with Wire (26 cm)	Platten (2x2) mit Kabel (26 cm)
5307	1992	Head Light Brick	Zugspitzensignal
9851	1992	Assortment of Connectors	Verschiedene Verbindungselemente
9852	1992	Chain Link Pack	Verschiedene Kettenglieder
9853	1992	Assortment of Gears	Verschiedene Getriebe
9854	1992	Worm Gear Pack	Verschiedene Schneckengetriebe
9855	1992	Assortment of Tires/Wheels	Verschiedene Reifen und Räder
9856	1992	Assortment of Cross Axles	Verschiedene Kreuzachsen
9857	1992	Red and black Plates	Rote und schwarze Platten
9858	1992	Red and blue Beams	Rote und blaue Querbalken
9859	1992	Motor (4.5V)	Motor (4,5V)
9860	1992	Battery Box and Switch (4.5V)	Batteriebox mit Schalter (4,5V)
9861	1992	Connecting Leads (4.5V)	Verbindungskabel (4,5V)
9862	1992	Random Special Pieces	Verschiedene Sonderelemente
9863	1992	Weighted Brick Pack	Gewichtete Bausteine
9864	1992	Building Plates, green	Bauplatten, grün
9865	1992	Optosensor	Optosensor
9866	1992	Light and Transparent Bricks	Durchsichtige und Lichtbausteine
9867	1992	Touch Sensor(4.5V)	Berührungssensor (4,5V)
9868	1992	Plugholders and Leads	Anschlüsse und Halterungen
9870	1992	Pneumatic Rubber Bands, Pneumatic Tubing	Pneumatische Gummiringe, Röhren
9871	1992	Beams, yellow	Querbalken, gelb
9872	1992	Pneumatic Elements and Tubes	Pneumatische Elemente und Röhren
9876	1992	Large Turntables	Große Drehscheiben
5047	1993	Hinges, Couplings, Turntables	Gelenke, Kupplungen, Drehscheiben

No.	Year	English Name	German Name
5048	1993	Town Accessoires	Zubehör für die Stadt
5049	1993	Transparent Windows and Bricks	Transperente Fenster und Bausteine
5050	1993	Plane Accessoires	Zubehör für Flugzeug
5051	1993	Windows, Seats, Steering Wheel	Windschutzscheibe, Sitze und Lenker
5052	1993	Antenna, Control Sticks	Antennen, Steuerknüppel
5053	1993	Small Plates with Tool Holders, Disks, Cones	Kl. Platten m. Werkzeughaltern, Scheibe, Kegel
5054	1993	Decorated Elements	Verzierte Elemente
5055	1993	Magnet and Magnetholder	Magnete mit Magnetfassungen
5056	1993	Space Elements	Weltraumzubehör
5057	1993	Space Accessoires	Weltraumzubehör
5058	1993	Pirate Accessoires	Piratenzubehör
5059	1993	Castle Accessoires	Zubehör für Burgen
5060	1993	Cannons	Kanonen
5078	1993	Crane Accessoires	Kranzubehör
5086	1993	12V Motor (old)	12V Motor (alt)
5093	1993	Battery Train with Polarity Switch	Batterie Zug mit Polumschalter
5117	1993	Compressor Pump	Kompressor Pumpe und Riemenscheibe
5119	1993	9V Micromotor	9V Mikromotor
5120	1993	Polarity Switch	Polwechsler und Schalthebel
5225	1993	9V Motor with Gear Reduction	9V Motor mit Untersetzung
5233	1993	Small Beams and Plates with Holes	Kleine Lochplatten und -balken
5235	1993	Large Beams with Holes	Große Lochbalken
5252	1993	Large Shock Absorbers	Große Stoßdämpfer
5267	1993	Assorted Cross Axles	Gemischte Kreuzachsen
5275	1993	Toggle Joints and Connectors	Verbindungselemente
5276	1993	Gear Wheels, Worm Gears, Racks, Universal Joints	Getrieberäder, Schnecken, Träger, Verbindungen
5277	1993	Wedge-Belt Wheels and Rubber Bands	Keilriemen-Räder und Gummiringe
5279	1993	Steering Elements, Plates and Gear Racks	Lenkelemente, Platten und Zahnstangen
5280	1993	Liftarms and Triangles	Lastarme und Dreiecke
9203	1993	Deluxe Lighting Kit	Luxus Beleuchtungsset
9883	1993	Motor (9V)	Motor (9V)
9884	1993	Light Bricks	Lichtbausteine
9885	1993	Sound Element (9V)	Klangerzeuger (9V)
9889	1993	Temperature Sensor (9V)	Temperatur Sensor (9V)
9891	1993	Angle Sensor (9V)	Winkelsensor (9V)
9892	1993	Brick Separators	Bausteintrenner
5092	1994	Sleeping Bags	Schlafsäcke
5094	1994	Window and Shower Curtain	Fenster- und Duschvorhang
5121	1994	Decorated Elements	Verzierte Elemente
5122	1994	Pirate Accessoires	Piratenzubehör
5124	1994	Wheels and Bearings	Reifen und Radaufhängung
5137	1994	Town Accessoires	Stadt Zubehör
5138	1994	Castle Accessoires	Burg Zubehör
5139	1994	Cannons with Wheels	Kanonen mit Rädern
5245	1994	Differential Housing	Differentialgehäuse
5278	1994	Chain Links	Kettenglieder
5281	1994	Balloon Tires (49,6 mm)	Ballonreifen mit Felgen (49,6 mm)
5282	1994	Balloon Tires (68,8 mm)	Ballonreifen mit Felgen (68,8 mm)
5283	1994	Balloon Tires (43,2 mm)	Ballonreifen mit Felgen (43,2 mm)
5284	1994	Loading Grabs with Crane Hook	Baggerschaufeln und Kranhaken
5285	1994	Large Shock Absorbers	Große Stoßdämpfer
5286	1994	Toggle Joints and Connectors	Verbindungselemente
5308	1994	Head Light Brick	Zugspitzensignal
9820	1994	Special Elements for 1030	Zusatzelemente für Artikel 1030
9821	1994	Rubber Bands	Gummiringe
9822	1994	Red Beams with Holes	Rote Lochquerbalken

No.	Year	English Name	German Name
9823	1994	Blue Beams with Holes	Blaue Lochquerbalken
9824	1994	Yellow Beams with Holes	Gelbe Lochquerbalken
9825	1994	Pneumatic Elements	Pneumatische Elemente
9826	1994	Pneumatic Tubes and T-Pieces	Pneumantische Röhren und T-Stücke
9831	1994	Battery Box with Switch (9V)	Batteriebox mit Schalter (9V)
9960	1994	Crane Hook, Cams and Propellers	Kranhaken, Schaltnocken und Propeller
9961	1994	Belts, white	Gurte, weiß
9962	1994	Couloured Tiles	Farbige Bauplatten
9963	1994	Fittings for Cross Axles	Anschlussstücke für Kreuzachsen
9964	1994	Fittings for Beams with Holes	Anschlussstücke für Lochbalken mit Löcher
9965	1994	Small Gear Wheel	Kleine Getriebeäder
9966	1994	Large Gear Wheels	Große Getriebeäder
9967	1994	Differentials and Crown Wheels	Differentiale und Kronräder
9968	1994	Pulleys and Tires	Flaschenzüge und Reifen
9969	1994	Tires and Hubs	Felgen und Reifen
9970	1994	Short Cross Axles	Kurze Kreuzachsen
9971	1994	Long Cross Axles	Lange Kreuzachsen
9972	1994	Plates, red	Platten, rot
9973	1994	Plates, black	Platten, schwarz
9974	1994	Plates, yellow	Platten, gelb
5029	1995	Caucasian Family	Kaukasische Familie
5088	1995	Long Beams, 2x8 Studs	Lange Steine, 2x8 Knöpfe
5089	1995	Family Outing (Afro American)	Afroamerikanische Familie
5090	1995	Family Outing (Asian)	Asiatische Familie
5091	1995	Family Outing (Hispanic)	Lateinamerikanische Familie
5125	1995	Spaceport Accessoires	Space Port Zubehör
5126	1995	Crane and Digger Accessoires	Kran und Bagger Zubehör
5127	1995	Antenna Control Sticks	Antennen
5132	1995	Wheels, Bearings and Suspension	Reifen, Lager und Aufhängungen
5134	1995	Cannons with Wheels	Kanonen mit Rädern
5135	1995	Castle Accessoires	Burg Zubehör
5136	1995	Accessoires	Zubehör
5160	1995	Aquazone Accessoires	Aquazone Zubehör
5268	1995	Small low-profile Tires	Kleine Niederquerschnittsreifen
5269	1995	Liftarms and Triangles	Greifarme und Dreiecke
5287	1995	Plates and Gear Racks	Platten und Getriebeelemente
5288	1995	Gear Blocks, Housings and Axles	Getriebeblöcke, Gehäuse und Achsen
9921	1995	Large Storage Box	Großer Ablagebehälter
9922	1995	Medium Storage Box	Mittelgroßer Ablagebehälter
9923	1995	Small Set	Kleines Set
9924	1995	Mini Set	Mini Set
630	1996	Brick Separator	Elemententrenner
5027	1996	Start/Stop Rail, Straight Rail	Start/Stop-Schiene, gerade Schiene
5028	1996	Plate 4x4	Grundplatte 4x4
5087	1996	Toolo Wrench	Toolo Schraubenschlüssel
5128	1996	Transparent Plate, Bricks and Toolholders	Durchsichtige Platten, Steine, Werkzeughalter
5129	1996	Space Accessoires	Space-Zubehör
5130	1996	Windows, Seats, Stearing Wheels	Frontscheiben, Sitze und Lenkräder
5131	1996	Hinges, Couplings, Turntables	Gelenke, Verschraubungen, Drehscheiben
5133	1996	Town Accessoires	Stadt Zubehör
5290	1996	Plates and Gear Racks	Platten und Zahnstangen
5291	1996	Liftarms and Triangles	Hebearme und Dreiecke
5292	1996	Technic Suitcase	Koffer
5293	1996	9V Battery Box	9V Batteriebox
5309	1996	Wagon Plate, red (6x28)	Zugrundplatte, rot (6x28)
5310	1996	Lighting Brick	Leuchtstein mit Zubehör

No.	Year	English Name	German Name
5311	1996	Plates (2x2) with Wire	9V Verbindungskabel mit Anschlussplatten
5395	1996	Belville Hospital Accessoires	Belville Krankenhaus Zubehör
5396	1996	Transparent Windows and Bricks	Cockpit-Fenster und Steine
5397	1996	Magnets and Magnet Holders	Magnete und Halterungen
5398	1996	Decorated Elements	Verzierte Elemente
9898	1996	Long Connecting Leads (9V)	Lange Verbindungskabel (9V)
5024	1997	Start/Stop Rail, Single Rail, Direction Switch	Start/Stop Schiene, 1 Schiene, Polwechsler
5026	1997	Toolo Loader and Turntable Loader Hook	Toolo Baggerschaufel, Kranhaken, Drehfuß
5201	1997	Angle Bricks	Winkelbausteine
5202	1997	Angle Beams	Winkellochbalken
5210	1997	Elastic Bands	Elastische Bänder
5227	1997	Cables for Fibre Optic	Fiber Optic Kabel
5228	1997	Beams and Plates with Holes, black	Lochbalken und -platten, schwarz
5229	1997	Gears and Differentials	Getriebe und Differentiale
5391	1997	9V Battery Box	9V Batteriebox
5392	1997	Wild West Accessoires	Westernzubehör
5393	1997	Head Wear (Hair and Hats)	Kopfbedeckungen (Hüte und Frisuren)
5394	1997	Horses and Saddles	Pferde und Sättel
5400	1997	Bathroom Accessories	Zubehör fürs Badezimmer
5401	1997	Kitchen Accessoires	Küchenzubehör
5402	1997	Floor Plate 1/2	Kleine Bauplatte
5403	1997	Floor Plate 1/1	Große Bauplatte
5404	1997	House	Haus
9833	1997	Transformer (9V)	Transformer (9V)
9848	1997	9V Lamps	9V Lampen
5022	1998	Bricks with Studs	Adaptersteine
5023	1998	Fence	Zaunelemente
5226	1998	Assorted Cross Axles	Gemischte kleine Achsen
5294	1998	Toggle Joints and Connectors	Verbindungselemente
5295	1998	Steering Elements	Steuerungselemente
5381	1998	Adventurer's Accessoires	Abenteurer Zubehör
5382	1998	Aquazone Accessoires	Aquazone Zubehör
5383	1998	Castle Accessoires	Burg Zubehör
5384	1998	Space Accessoires	Raumfahrtzubehör
5386	1998	Antenna and Control Sticks	Antennen und Greifarme
5387	1998	Belville Beach Accessoires	Belville Strand Zubehör
5388	1998	Hinges, Couplings and Turntables	Scharniere, Kupplungen und Drehscheiben
5389	1998	Divers' Accessoires	Tauchzubehör
5390	1998	Crane and Digger Accessoires	Kran- und Baggerzubehör
5405	1998	Floor Plate	Kleine Grundplatte
9709	1998	RCX Programmable Brick	RCX programmierbarer Legostein
9738	1998	Remote Control	Fernbedienung
9776	1998	Pneumatic Circuit	Pneumatische Leitung
9834	1998	Belts for Primary Simple Machines	Ring für einfache Maschinen
9838	1998	Gears	Getriebe
9839	1998	Small Pulley and Handles	Kleine Flaschenzüge und Griffe
9897	1998	Connecting Leads (9V)	Verbindungskabel (9V)
9899	1998	Hubs and Tires	Felgen und Reifen
9900	1998	Small Gear Wheels	Kleine Getrieberäde
9912	1998	Solar Panel	Sonnenlichtkollektor
9925	1998	Small red Storage Bin	Kleiner roter Ablagebehälter
9926	1998	Extra small yellow Storage Bin	Exktra kleiner Ablagebehälter
9927	1998	Beams with Holes, red	Lochbalken, rot
9928	1998	Beams with Holes, blue	Lochbalken, blau
9929	1998	Plates, red	Platten, rot
9930	1998	Plates, blue	Platten, blau

Service-Packs

No.	Year	English Name	German Name
9931	1998	Plates, yellow	Platten, gelb
9932	1998	Plates, black	Platten, schwarz
9933	1998	Basic Bricks, red	Bausteine, rot
9934	1998	Basic Bricks, yellow	Bausteine, gelb
9935	1998	Basic Bricks, black	Bausteine, schwarz
9936	1998	Weight Elements	Gewichtselemente
9937	1998	Small Chain Links	Kleine Kettenglieder
9938	1998	Conveyor Belt Links	Verbindungselemente für Förderbänder
9939	1998	Assorted Pulleys	Verschiedene Flaschenzüge
9940	1998	Rubber Bands and String	Gummiringe und Kabel
9941	1998	Cams and Linkages	Schlatnocken und Verknüpfungen
9942	1998	Connectors and Bushings	Anschlüsse und Verbindungsglieder
9943	1998	Axles and Extenders	Achsen und Erweiterungen
9945	1998	Differentials	Differentiale
9958	1998	Special Elements for 9701	Bauelemente für Artikel 9701
5021	1999	Wagons	Waggons
5025	1999	Tubes with Ball	Röhrenelemente mit Ball
5203	1999	Alloy Wheels with Tires	Alufelgen mit Reifen
5204	1999	Competition Accessory	Competition Zubehör
5205	1999	Wheels and Rubber Bands	Räder und Riemenscheiben
5215	1999	Bricks Assorted, green	Gemischte Bausteine, grün
5216	1999	Roof Bricks Assorted, black	Gemischte Dachelemente, schwarz
5313	1999	Space Accessoires	Space Zubehör
5314	1999	RES-Q Equipment (Tools)	Rettungs-Zubehör
5315	1999	Connectors	Anschlussklemmen
5316	1999	Transparent Accessoires	Durchsichtiges Zubehör
5317	1999	Wild West Accessoires	Western Zubehör
5318	1999	Head Wear	Helme, Hüte und Frisuren
5319	1999	Decorated Elements	Verzierte Elemente
5320	1999	Plates, small	Platten, klein
5321	1999	Large Plates	Große Platten
5399	1999	Fairy Tale Accessories	Zubehör für Märchen
5413	1999	Beauty Set	Beauty Set mit Koffer
5414	1999	Kitchen Set	Küchen Set
5415	1999	Garden Set	Garten Set
9301	1999	Road Signs	Straßenschilder
9757	1999	Touch Sensor with Cable	Berührungssensor mit Kabel
9916	1999	Capacitor	Kondensator
9918	1999	Gear Block, yellow	Getriebeblock, gelb
3444	2000	Ridge Tile, black (2x4)	Dachfirste, schwarz (2x4)
3445	2000	Ridge Tile, red (2x4)	Dachfirste, rot (2x4)
3447	2000	Wallelement, transparent blue	Paneele, transparentes Blau
3448	2000	Windows, black	Fenster, schwarz
3453	2000	Bricks, black (2x2)	Steine, schwarz (2x2)
3455	2000	Bricks, white (2x2)	Steine, weiß (2x2)
3456	2000	Bricks, green (2x2)	Steine, grün (2x2)
3458	2000	Bricks, black (2x4)	Steine, schwarz (2x4)
3459	2000	Bricks, grey (2x4)	Steine, grau (2x4)
3460	2000	Bricks, white (2x4)	Steine, weiß (2x4)
3461	2000	Bricks, green (2x4)	Steine, grün (2x4)
3462	2000	Bricks, red (2x4)	Steine, rot (2x4)
3463	2000	Bricks, black (2x8)	Steine, schwarz (2x8)
3464	2000	Bricks, grey (2x8)	Steine, grau (2x8)
3465	2000	Bricks, white (2x8)	Steine, weiß (2x8)
3466	2000	Bricks, green (2x8)	Steine, grün (2x8)
3467	2000	Bricks, red (2x8)	Steine, rot (2x8)

No.	Year	English Name	German Name
3469	2000	Bricks, grey (1x4)	Steine, grau (1x4)
3470	2000	Bricks, white (1x4)	Steine, weiß (1x4)
3471	2000	Bricks, green (1x4)	Steine, grün (1x4)
3472	2000	Bricks, red (1x4)	Steine, rot (1x4)
3473	2000	Bricks, black (1x6)	Steine, schwarz (1x6)
3474	2000	Bricks, grey (1x6)	Steine, grau (1x6)
3475	2000	Bricks, white (1x6)	Steine, weiß (1x6)
3476	2000	Bricks,green (1x6)	Steine, grün (1x6)
3477	2000	Bricks, red (1x6)	Steine, rot (1x6)
3478	2000	Bricks, black (1x8)	Steine, schwarz (1x8)
3479	2000	Bricks, grey (1x8)	Steine, grau (1x8)
3480	2000	Bricks, white (1x8)	Steine, weiß (1x8)
3481	2000	Bricks, green (1x8)	Steine, grün (1x8)
3482	2000	Bricks, red (1x8)	Steine, rot (1x8)
3483	2000	Plates, black (2x4)	Platten, schwarz (2x4)
3484	2000	Plates, white (2x4)	Platten, weiß (2x4)
3485	2000	Plates, red (2x4)	Platten, rot (2x4)
3486	2000	Plates, black (1x6)	Platten, schwarz (1x6)
3487	2000	Plates,white (1x6)	Platten, weiß (1x6)
3488	2000	Plates, red (1x6)	Platten, rot (1x6)
3489	2000	Plates, black (2x8)	Platten, schwarz (2x8)
3490	2000	Plates, white (2x8)	Platten, weiß (2x8)
3491	2000	Plates, red (2x8)	Platten, rot (2x8)
3492	2000	Flat Tiles, black (2x2)	Fliesen, schwarz (2x2)
3493	2000	Flat Tiles, white (2x2)	Fliesen, weiß (2x2)
3494	2000	Flat Tile, red (2x2)	Fliesen, rot (2x2)
3495	2000	Roof Tiles, black (2x2)	Dachsteine, schwarz (2x2)
3496	2000	Roof Tiles, red (2x2)	Dachziegel, rot (2x2)
3497	2000	Roof Tiles, black (2x4)	Dachziegel, schwarz (2x4)
3498	2000	Roof Tiles, red (2x4)	Dachziegel, rot (2x4)
3725	2000	Bricks, grey (1x2)	Steine, grau (1x2)
3726	2000	Bricks, dark grey (1x2)	Steine, dunkelgrau (1x2)
3727	2000	Bricks, tan (1x2)	Steine, beige (1x2)
3729	2000	Bricks, dark grey (2x4)	Steine, dunkelgrau (2x4)
3730	2000	Bricks, tan (2x4)	Steine, beige (2x4)
3733	2000	Train Windows with Panes	Zugfenster mit Scheiben
3734	2000	Train Windows, blue, with Panes	Zugfenster, blau, mit Scheiben
3735	2000	Grey Traindoors l/r with Panes	Graue Zugtüren l/r mit Fenstern
3754	2000	Bricks, brown (2x4)	Steine, braun (2x4)
9926	2000	Extra small yellow Storage Bin	Extra kleiner gelber Ablagebehälter
3446	2001	Windows, white (2x2)	Fenster, weiß (2x2)
3449	2001	Black Door Frame with Transparent Blue Panes	Schwarzer Türrahmen m. transp. bl. Scheiben
3499	2001	Spruce Trees, small	Fichten, klein
3507	2001	Train Windows, clear	Zugfenster, durchsichtig
3508	2001	Windows, black with blue Panes	Fenster, schwarz mit blauen Scheiben
3732	2001	Castle Expander Set	Burg Erweiterungsset
3736	2001	Train Doors, blue	Zugtüren, blau
3737	2001	Train Accessories	Zugzubehör
3738	2001	Large Spruce Tree (H 64)	Große Tanne, 6 cm
3748	2001	Light Unit for Train	Lichteinheit für Züge
3750	2001	Life on Mars Accessoires	Life on Mars-Zubehör
3751	2001	Bricks, brown (1x2)	Steine, braun (1x2)
3752	2001	Bricks, brown (1x6)	Steine, braun (1x6)
3753	2001	Bricks, brown (2x2)	Steine, braun (2x2)
3755	2001	Roof Tiles, brown (2x4)	Dachziegel, braun (2x4)
3756	2001	Ridge Tiles, brown (2x4)	Dachfirste, braun (2x4)

No.	Year	English Name	German Name
9959	2001	Special Elements f. Intelligent House Building Set	Spezielle Elemente für den Hausbau
10003	2001	Bricks, sandred (1x2)	Steine, sandrot (1x2)
10004	2001	Bricks, sandred (2x2)	Steine, sandrot (2x2)
10005	2001	Bricks, sandred (2x4)	Steine, sandrot (2x4)
10006	2001	Bricks, sandred (1x6)	Steine, sandrot (1x6)
10007	2001	Ridge Tiles, sandred (2x4)	Dachfirste, sandrot (2x4)
10008	2001	Roof Tiles, sandred (2x4)	Dachsteine, sandrot (2x4)
10009	2001	Assorted Bricks, blue	Verschiedene Steine, blau
10112	2001	Bushes	Büsche
10113	2001	Cypress Trees	Zypressenbäume
10114	2001	Roof Tiles Sand, red (2x2)	Dachsteine, sandrot (2x2)
10010	2002	Assorted Bricks, yellow	Verschiedene Steine, gelb
10011	2002	Assorted Plates, blue	Verschiedene Platten, blau
10012	2002	Assorted Plates, yellow	Verschiedene Platten, gelb
10043	2002	9V Wires	9V Verbindungskabel
10044	2002	Windows and Doors	Fenster und Türen
10045	2002	Bridge Elements	Brückenelemente
10046	2002	Assorted Tiles, brown	Verschiedene Fliesen, braun
10047	2002	Arch, grey	Bögen, grau
10048	2002	Small Wheels and Axles	Kleine Räder und Achsen
10049	2002	Large Wheels and Axles	Große Räder und Achsen
10050	2002	Fences, grey	Zäune, grau
10051	2002	Bricks Clear (1x2)	Steine, transparent (1x2)
10053	2002	Roof Tiles, black	Dachziegel, schwarz
10054	2002	Roof Tiles, black	Dachziegel, schwarz, flach
10055	2002	Roof Tiles, black	Dachziegel, schwarz, flach
10056	2002	Assorted Plates, white	Verschiedene Platten, weiß
10057	2002	Assorted Plates, black	Verschiedene Platten, schwarz
10058	2002	Assorted Plates, red	Verschiedene Platten, rot
10059	2002	Aassorted Plates, green	Verschiedene Platten, grün
10060	2002	Assorted Plates, grey	Verschiedene Platte, grau
10061	2002	Assorted small Plates, black	Verschiedene kleine Platten, schwarz
10062	2002	Assorted small Plates,red	Verschiedene kleine Platten, rot
10063	2002	Assorted small Plates, green	Verschiedene kleine Platten, grün
10064	2002	Assorted small Plates, grey	Verschiedene kleine Platten, grau
10065	2002	Assorted small Plates, white	Verschiedenen kleine Platten, weiß
10066	2002	Castle Accessories	Burgzubehör
10067	2002	Mini-Fig Headgear	Hüte und Mützen
10076	2002	Gear Wheels	Zahnräder
10111	2002	Foliferous Trees	Laubbäume
10115	2002	Jumper Bricks	Aus-zwei-mach-eins-Plättchen
10153	2002	9V Train Motor	9 V Lokmotor
970687	2002	Team Challenge Upgrade Kit	Team Challenge Erweiterungsset
991118	2002	Connecting Lead (3 m)	Verbindungskabel (3 m)
3454	2003	Bricks, grey (2x2)	Steine, grau (2x2)
3457	2003	Bricks, red (2x2)	Steine, rot (2x2)
10072	2003	Beams	Balken
10073	2003	Bushes	Buchsen
10074	2003	Cross Axles	Kreuzachsen
10077	2003	Technic Motor	Technic Motor
10078	2003	Train Connection Wire	Zug Verbindungskabel
670	2004	Wheel Pack	Räder
671	2004	Antenna Pack	Antennen
673	2004	Gearbox Pack	Getriebe
7099	2004	Accessory Boat Motor	Zubehör-Bootsmotor
10145	2004	Assorted Bricks, grey	Verschiedene Bausteine, grau

No.	Year	English Name	German Name
10146	2004	Assorted Bricks, dark grey	Verschiedene Baustein, dunkelgrau
10147	2004	Assorted Bricks, brown	Verschiedene Bausteine, braun
10148	2004	Assorted Plates, light grey	Verschiedene Platten, hellgrau
10149	2004	Assorted Plates, dark grey	Verschiedene Platten, dunkelgrau
10150	2004	Assorted Plates, brown	Verschiedene Platten, braun
10160	2004	Assorted Ridge Tiles, black	Verschiedene Dachsondersteine, schwarz
10161	2004	Assorted Roof Tiles, black	Verschiedene Dachsteine, schwarz
10162	2004	Assorted Ridge Tiles, red	Verschiedene Dachsondersteine, rot
10163	2004	Assorted Roof Tiles, red	Dachsteine, rot
4285968	2005	Transformation Kit, Dirt Crusher, red	Verwandlungsset für Dirt Crusher, rot
4285969	2005	Transformation Kit, Dirt Crusher, blue	Verwandlungsset für Dirt Crusher, blau
4285970	2005	Transformation Kit, Dirt Crusher, green	Verwandlungsset für Dirt Crusher, grün
4286013	2005	Big Wheels Pack, Dirt Crusher, red	Große Reifen für Dirt Crusher, rot
4286024	2005	Big Wheels Pack, Dirt Crusher, blue	Große Reifen für Dirt Crusher, blau
4286025	2005	Big Wheels Pack, Dirt Crusher, green	Große Reifen für Dirt Crusher, grün
4286784	2005	Extra Motor (with light) kit for Dirt Crusher	Zusatzmotor (mit Licht) für Dirt Crusher
4287082	2005	Antenna Pack for Dirt Crusher	Antennen für Dirt Crhusher
4206	2006	9V Train Switching Track Collection	9V Schienenset
8528	2006	Converter Cables	Adapterkabel
8529	2006	Connector Cables	Verbindungskabel
9847	2006	NXT Bluetooth Dongle	NXT Bluetooth Dongle
2159	2007	9V Train Track Starter Collection	9V Zug Beginnerset
9241	2007	Wheels Set	Reifen Set
991327	2007	12-Tooth Black Double Conical Wheels	Zwölfzackige doppeltkonische Zahnräder
991328	2007	36-Tooth Double Conical Wheels	36-zahnige doppeltkonische Zahnräder
991329	2007	Axes, 7-stud	Achsen, 7 Knöpfe
991330	2007	New Turntables	Drehscheiben, neu
991331	2007	Small Wide Tires and Hubs	Kleine breite Reifen und Felgen
991332	2007	Triangle	Triangel
991333	2007	Cam Wheel (Pack of 25)	Hebnägelrad
991335	2007	Swivel Magnet	Magnet mit schwenkbarem Halter
991336	2007	2-Stud Axles with Grooves	2er Achse mit Einkerbungen
991337	2007	Connector Peg with Axle	Verbindungspin mit Achse
8886	2008	Power Functions Extension Wire	Power Functions Verlängerungskabel
991369	2008	Tracks and Sprockets	Schienen und Kettenräder
991402	2008	Studless Beams	Runde Lochstangen
991403	2008	Angle Beams	Lochstangen mit Winkel
991404	2008	Beams with Snaps	Lochstangen mit Pins
991405	2008	Technic Crossblocks	Technic Achsenblöcke

Index